8th Edition

Washington Real Estate Law

Kathryn Haupt
Jennifer Gotanda
Dawn Henry
Joe Reiner

Rockwell Publishing Company

Table of Contents

1 An Introduction to Law and the Legal System

Outline

Key Terms

- Substantive/procedural
- Affirm/modify/reverse/ remand
- Criminal/civil
- Prejudicial error
- Plaintiff/defendant
- Subject matter jurisdiction
- Damages
- Federal question
- Tort
- Diversity jurisdiction
- Unconstitutional
- Case or controversy requirement
- Due process
- Declaratory relief
- Equal protection

- Statute of limitations
- Discovery rule
- State action
- Res judicata
- Statute/ordinance
- Summons/complaint/answer
- Bill
- Garnishment
- Veto/override
- Personal jurisdiction
- Service of process
- Case law
- Pretrial discovery
- Stare decisis
- Deposition/interrogatories
- Precedent
- Settlement

- Summary judgment
- Equitable/common law remedies
- Opinion
- Injunction
- Judicial review
- Fact witness/expert witness
- Statutory construction
- Direct/cross examination
- Trial record
- Jury instructions
- Exhibit
- Burden of proof
- Question of fact/of law
- Standard of proof
- Trier of fact
- Appellant/appellee

Chapter Overview

This chapter is a broad survey of the legal system in the United States, with a particular focus on Washington's legal system. It begins with a discussion of the nature and purposes of our system of laws, and explains some fundamental legal categories and concepts. It goes on to discuss the sources of law: constitutions, legislatures, courts, and administrative agencies. Finally, it examines the judicial system in detail, and describes a typical lawsuit from its outset through enforcement of the judgment.

You should come away from this chapter with a better understanding of how laws are made, how legal rights are enforced, and how legal disputes are resolved. This information serves as a foundation for the material covered in the rest of the book.

Law and the Real Estate Profession

The law has a tremendous impact on the work of a real estate agent. Hundreds of federal, state, and local laws control the use and transfer of real property. These laws affect property values as well as the structure of various real estate transactions. In addition, the real estate profession itself is strictly regulated. Laws prescribe the agent's qualifications and his or her duties to clients, customers, and employees.

The law's impact on the real estate profession is steadily expanding. In some areas of law (environmental law, for example), regulations have multiplied dramatically. In other areas, legal standards of conduct are being raised by judges: a landlord or a designated broker might now be held liable for an oversight that would not have been the basis for a lawsuit 25 years ago.

Avoiding liability is one of the most compelling reasons to learn about the law. Even if you would never consider doing anything dishonest, an honest mistake could leave you threatened with a lawsuit. A firm grasp of your duties toward the buyer and seller minimizes the risk of a lawsuit.

Sometimes a well-informed agent can also prevent litigation between the buyer and seller. By recognizing issues that are common causes of lawsuits, you can help the buyer and seller clarify their agreement and avoid misunderstandings.

Learning about the law is not just a matter of memorizing rules. It's important to understand where the rules come from and what backs them up. It's one thing to memorize the phrase, "A real estate agent must disclose all material facts to his or her client." But who made that rule? What happens if that rule is ignored? How is it enforced? Can the rule be challenged or changed? Knowing how the legal system works gives the rule substance. In learning how laws are developed, you'll see that it is sometimes possible to influence the process to advance the interests of your clients or yourself.

Of course, learning about the law won't enable you to give clients legal advice, or to act without legal advice yourself. But it will give you a clearer sense of when legal advice is needed. And when it is needed, you'll be much better equipped to assist a client's lawyer or your own lawyer in analyzing the situation and preparing the case.

The Nature and Role of the Law

The law is a system of rights and duties established and enforced by a government. It takes the form of general rules that citizens and everyone else in the government's domain must obey.

Example: The law sets forth rights and duties connected with land ownership. As a landowner, Brown has a legal right to the exclusive possession of his property. This creates a corresponding legal duty for others to avoid entering the property without permission. If someone violates this rule, the government will enforce Brown's rights by ejecting the trespasser.

On the other hand, Brown has a legal duty to maintain the property so that a person entering it at his request will be reasonably safe. If Brown fails to live up to this duty and someone is injured as a result, the government will enforce Brown's duty by requiring him to pay compensation to the injured person.

Functions of the Law

The law serves a number of related functions. It:

- establishes order,
- resolves disputes,
- enforces promises,
- prevents exploitation, and
- promotes equality.

First and foremost, law establishes order. Without law, might makes right: the strong and ruthless use violence and the threat of violence to dominate anyone who is weaker. But a legal system establishes rules of conduct based on considerations other than brute force. A court or similar tribunal provides a forum for resolving disputes without violence. Thus, the law makes it easier for people to live together peacefully.

An important function of the law in any complex society is the enforcement of promises. Commerce depends on promises: a builder who agrees to construct a house must be able to rely on the owner's promise to pay for the house. Otherwise, the builder would have to demand payment in advance; but in that case, the owner would have to rely on the builder's promise to go through with the work. By enforcing certain promises called **contracts**, the law makes it possible to plan ahead and to deal with strangers.

In the United States today, the law reflects widely accepted ideas of fairness and equality. We have laws intended to protect people not merely from physical force, but also from many forms of exploitation. For example, a real estate agent is not allowed to take unfair advantage of a buyer by misrepresenting or concealing facts about a property. We also have laws that promote equal treatment: a real estate agent may not refuse to show a couple a house because of their race or religion.

Morality and Efficiency

The passage of laws preventing exploitation and promoting equality is an example of **sociological jurisprudence**: using the law as a tool for reforming society. But laws can also be used as a tool for oppression. For example, in the 1850s and 1860s, people in parts of the U.S. felt their jobs were threatened by a wave of Chinese immigrants who were willing to work for low wages. Some state and city governments responded to public pressure by issuing tax and licensing laws designed to create social and economic hardships for the Chinese.

It's clear that a society's laws are closely connected to its ideas of justice and morality. But although the law reflects and often changes with public morality, they are by no means the same thing. There are many moral issues that the law does not address, leaving them up to the individual's conscience, to the family, to religious groups, and to public opinion.

Morality is not the only force that shapes the law. Efficiency, rather than justice, is the goal of many rules. A law may arbitrarily require everyone to use a particular method simply because uniform procedures help society run more smoothly. For instance, there are many different standards a local government could set when enacting a building code. Some standards might emphasize safety but be expensive or cumbersome; others might be cost-effective but increase risks of harm. The lawmakers will typically seek to balance those competing interests, but it is also important to establish a rule that provides builders and inspectors a predictable and objective standard.

Historical Background

When English settlers colonized the New World, they brought English law with them. After gaining its independence, the United States retained many aspects of English law and legal institutions. These are still the foundation of the U.S. legal system.

For example, judges in the U.S. have played almost as great a role in establishing rules of law as our legislatures have (see the discussion of sources of law, below). This is based on the English model, and it contrasts with the European tradition. In France, Germany, Spain, and Italy, lawmaking has been more strictly reserved to the legislatures, and judicial decisions have not carried nearly as much weight.

In addition, many of our basic legal concepts and rules were inherited directly from England. This history accounts for much of the strange legal terminology that is especially common in real property law: "escheat," "emblements," and "appurtenance" were all part of English law centuries ago. Early English law based on court decisions was known as the **common law** of England. As a result, long-established rules based on English law are sometimes referred to as "common law rules."

Legal Categories and Concepts

In today's complicated society, the law covers a vast territory. Mapping out some fundamental categories and concepts will make it easier to explore.

Substantive Law and Procedural Law

One of the most basic divisions in the law is the distinction between substantive law and procedural law. **Substantive law** establishes and defines rights and duties. **Procedural law** sets forth the methods of enforcing substantive rights.

Example: The rule that a landowner has the exclusive right to possess his own land is substantive law: it gives a landowner a legal right. If the landowner is prevented from exclusive possession because another person has trespassed and refuses to leave, the landowner can start a lawsuit. There are rules prescribing how to sue someone: file a complaint with the court, send a summons to the other party within a certain number of days, and so forth. These rules setting forth the procedure for enforcing the right to possess one's own land are procedural law.

Criminal Law and Civil Law

Another fundamental distinction is the one between criminal law and civil law. A person who fails to live up to a legal duty, or fails to respect another's legal right, may cause harm to another person or to property. The failure may be accidental or deliberate. The injury may be slight or serious; it may be physical, emotional, or financial.

Someone who has been injured as a result of another's act generally has the right to sue that other person for compensation. The government offers a forum (the courts) for resolving the dispute. One individual suing another—or any lawsuit that doesn't involve a criminal prosecution by the government—is called a **civil suit**, a civil action, or civil litigation.

- **Plaintiff**—The person who starts the lawsuit.
- **Defendant**—The person being sued.
- **Litigant**—Both plaintiff and defendant may be called litigants.

Certain harmful or potentially harmful acts are classified as **crimes**. In general, crimes are those acts that are particularly dangerous to society.

> **Example:** Accidentally rear-ending another car causes harm, but it isn't a crime. Drunk driving is a crime (even if the driver has not caused an accident) because it has the potential to cause a great deal of harm.

Because crimes are so disruptive, the government takes a greater interest in them than it does in other harmful acts. Instead of simply offering the injured person an opportunity to sue for compensation, the government itself (represented by the public prosecutor) takes legal action against the person accused of a crime. In some cases the government may start a criminal action without the victim's cooperation, or even if there was no victim. A civil suit, on the other hand, will take place only if the injured person decides to start one.

Civil suits and criminal actions have different purposes, so they offer different remedies. The main goal of a civil suit is to compensate the injured person for the harm that was done. The remedy granted is usually a monetary award (called damages), paid by the person who caused the harm to the person who was harmed. A damages award is usually limited to the financial losses that the injured person incurred. These might include lost profits or wages, or money spent on repairs or hospital bills.

A criminal prosecution has broader goals: to punish the wrongdoer and prevent him or her from committing more crimes, and to deter others from committing similar crimes.

The penalties are not based on paying for the damage done. A person convicted of a crime might have to pay a heavy fine to the government, even if the criminal act (such as drunk driving) did not result in any actual damage. She might also have to serve a jail sentence.

It's important to note that the same harmful act might lead to both a criminal action and a civil action.

> **Example:** A drunk driver causes an accident, injuring several people. The government brings a criminal action against the driver, resulting in a fine and a jail sentence. However, the criminal action does not compensate the victims. They will have to sue in civil court to force the driver to pay for their medical expenses, lost wages, and car repairs.

Real estate lawsuits are nearly always civil, not criminal. The exceptions to this rule are cases involving fraud, conversion of funds, or a violation of a specific law. For example, the victim of a fraud can bring a civil suit for compensation. But if the fraud was serious enough, the government will also impose criminal penalties.

Since most real estate disputes do not involve crimes, the focus of this chapter (and of the book as a whole) will be on civil law.

Basic Civil Law Concepts

As our laws have grown more complex, it has become necessary for most lawyers to specialize in a particular area of law. Their specialties correspond to all the different areas in which disputes arise: real estate law, corporate law, family law, personal injury law, and so on. But there are three fundamental categories underlying all of these specialties:

- contracts,
- torts, and
- property.

Each of these categories represents a group of basic legal concepts, relationships, and principles.

Contracts. A **contract** is a legally binding promise. When two people enter into a contractual relationship, they voluntarily take on legal duties toward one another.

> **Example:** If Chin contracts to sell his bike to Martinez in exchange for $100, Chin has a legal duty to give Martinez the bike, and Martinez has a legal duty to pay Chin $100. Without the contract, Chin had no duty to give Martinez the bike, and Martinez had no duty to pay Chin $100. By entering into the contract, they voluntarily assumed these duties.

The legal relationships created by contracts are governed by a whole body of rules known as **contract law**. In Chapter 8, we'll discuss contract law as it applies to contracts concerning real property.

Torts. Other legal duties are not voluntarily assumed but are instead imposed by law. The law imposes the duty on everyone to take reasonable care to avoid injuring another person or damaging someone else's property. If someone breaches this imposed duty—by failing to behave as a reasonable person would and thereby causing an injury or damage—it's called a **tort**. Torts are sometimes referred to as "civil wrongs," to distinguish them from criminal wrongs, or crimes.

> **Example:** Running desperately through the depot to catch a train, Garner accidentally knocks Harrison down. Harrison's arm is broken in the fall. Garner has breached the legal duty to use reasonable care in passing through a public place. In other words, Garner has committed a tort against Harrison. (However, since he knocked Harrison down accidentally rather than deliberately or recklessly, Garner hasn't committed a crime.)

Tort law is the body of rules concerning legally imposed duties and standards of reasonable conduct. There are rules for intentional and unintentional acts; for public places and private homes; and for family members, business associates, and total strangers.

Property. The third fundamental category, **property law**, concerns ownership of or an interest in real or personal property. It includes rules for acquiring and losing property ownership, and rules about the rights and duties associated with property ownership.

> **Example:** Ortega deeds a property called Blackacre to Howell. The law gives Howell, as the property owner, the right to use, encumber, will, sell, or ignore Blackacre. The law also places some restrictions on Howell's use of the property: for instance, the zoning ordinance allows Howell to build a house on Blackacre, but not a shopping mall. And the law imposes a duty on Howell to pay taxes on the property. These rights and duties are automatic consequences of ownership.

- **Contract**—A legally binding promise.
- **Tort**—A civil wrong; a violation of the duty to use reasonable care.
- **Property Law**—Legal rules concerning ownership of real or personal property and the rights and duties related to property.

Nearly every specialized area of law involves contract, tort, and property issues to some degree. For example, a lawyer specializing in maritime law might have to deal with the legal problems arising from a contract to ship goods to Japan, an accident at sea in which crew members were injured, and the transfer of ownership of a vessel.

Contract, tort, and property issues can also be tangled up together in a single legal problem.

> **Example:** Jones and Bailey are neighbors. Jones has an easement over Bailey's property for a driveway leading to his own property. Jones and Bailey disagree about where the boundary between their lots is located.
>
> Jones leased his house to Collins. Jones believes the lease expired at the end of the summer, but Collins won't give up possession, claiming the lease was supposed to last until the end of the year. One day Collins slips in the driveway and breaks her collarbone. It's not clear whether she was on Jones's property or Bailey's property when she slipped, because of the boundary dispute.

Fig. 1.1 Sources of law

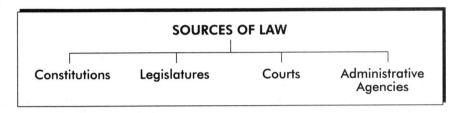

In order to determine whether either Jones or Bailey must compensate Collins for her injury, the lawyers will have to sort out contract issues (Had the lease expired? What evidence can be introduced to prove the contents of the agreement between Jones and Collins?); property issues (Who owned that part of the driveway? Did Jones have a responsibility to maintain the easement? Did Collins have a right to use the easement, or was she trespassing?); and tort issues (Did Collins slip because someone failed to make the driveway reasonably safe? Or was it because of her own carelessness?).

Sources of Law

Who makes the laws? The simple answer is that the government does. But in the United States, "the government" has numerous elements that play a role in lawmaking. Governmental power is divided between the federal government and the 50 independent state governments, and in each state there are regional and local governmental bodies. To complicate matters even more, there are different sources of law within the federal government and each of the state governments.

A single legal problem can involve both state and federal laws, and may be the subject of constitutional provisions, statutes, court decisions, and administrative regulations, all at the same time.

Constitutions

A constitution is a grant of power to a government. It sets forth the government's basic structure and defines the limits of the government's power.

A constitution is, in effect, the fundamental law with which all other laws must comply. In issuing a new law, a government sometimes exceeds its constitutional power. Then the new law is **unconstitutional**: it is an illegal law, and cannot be enforced. Even a constitutional law can be applied by a government official in a way that oversteps the limits of the government's power. In that case, the law still stands, but the official's action is unconstitutional and illegal.

Constitutions are intended to be long-lasting documents that provide government stability. They can be changed (**amended**), but the procedure for amending a constitution is more difficult than the procedure for changing an ordinary law.

In the United States, there is a federal Constitution that applies to the whole country, and each of the states has its own constitution as well.

The Federal Constitution

The United States Constitution was drawn up at the Constitutional Convention in 1787 and, after approval by the states, took effect in 1789. The Constitution declares itself to be the "supreme law of the land" (Article VI, Section 2).

Power of Federal and State Governments. The U.S. Constitution defines the relationship between the federal government and the state governments. Only the federal government may make laws concerning certain matters; these include interstate commerce, wars and the military, immigration, bankruptcy, copyrights and patents, and currency (Article I, Section 8).

In many other areas, both the federal government and the state governments can and do make laws. Discrimination and environmental protection are examples.

Certain matters are left up to the state governments, such as the ownership and transfer of real property. As a result, most of the laws affecting a parcel of land are the laws of whichever state the land is located in.

If there's a conflict between a federal law and a state law, the stricter rule generally prevails. If a federal air pollution law is tougher than a Washington air pollution law, a factory in Washington must comply with the federal standard. But if the federal law is looser than the Washington law, the factory must comply with the Washington standard.

Protection of Individual Rights. The first ten amendments to the U.S. Constitution are known as the **Bill of Rights**. They were adopted in 1791. The Thirteenth, Fourteenth, and Fifteenth Amendments were added soon after the Civil War. Together, these amendments protect the rights of individuals by limiting government power. The protections range from freedom of religion to the right to a jury trial.

Some of these amendments have a particular impact on property and the real estate profession. These include the following guarantees:

- due process,
- equal protection,
- just compensation, and
- no unreasonable searches or seizures.

Due process. According to the Fifth and Fourteenth Amendments, no one shall be "deprived of life, liberty, or property without due process of law." This is known as the due process requirement. Due process includes a fair hearing by an impartial judge.

Example: A real estate agent is accused of grossly misrepresenting the condition of a home. The Washington State Department of Licensing has the power to revoke an agent's license for this misconduct. But a real estate license is considered "property" for the purposes of the due process requirement. As a result, the Department of Licensing cannot deprive the agent of his license without first holding a hearing that gives the agent an opportunity to tell his side of the story.

Equal protection. The Fourteenth Amendment also provides that the government may not deny an individual the "equal protection of the laws." The equal protection requirement prohibits governments from adopting laws that unfairly discriminate between different groups of people.

Most laws involve some sort of discrimination. For example, a law that says a person must have a real estate license to negotiate the sale of land can be said to discriminate against people who don't have licenses. But that discrimination is not considered unfair, since people with licenses are usually better qualified to negotiate land sales than people without licenses. However, discrimination on the basis of race, ethnic background, or gender is considered unfair. That kind of discrimination violates the equal protection requirement.

Just compensation. Another provision of the Fifth Amendment prevents the government from taking private property for public use "without just compensation." The government has the power to turn your land into a public garden or parking lot, but the Constitution requires the government to pay you for it. (See the discussion of eminent domain and condemnation in Chapter 9.)

Unreasonable searches and seizures. The Fourth Amendment prevents the government from making "unreasonable searches and seizures" of an individual's person or property. A search warrant issued by a judge is required, and a warrant may be issued only if there is "probable cause" for a search.

The Fourth Amendment is primarily applied in criminal cases. In that context, probable cause means that the government must have reasonable grounds for believing that a search will uncover items used in the commission of a crime. But the Fourth Amendment also applies to "administrative searches," such as a routine inspection by the fire department or health department. A search warrant is required to inspect a residence or business, unless there is an emergency or the owner or occupant consents to the inspection.

It is not necessary to show that there is probable cause to believe the administrative search will uncover a code violation in a particular building. A legitimate government interest in conducting inspections in that neighborhood is a sufficient basis for the issuance of a search warrant. (*Camara v. Municipal Court*, 387 U.S. 523 (1967) and *See v. City of Seattle*, 387 U.S. 541 (1967).)

State action. To claim the rights guaranteed by the Constitution, there must be state action involved, which is action by a government or a government official. The federal Constitution's protection of individual rights is primarily protection against abuses by the government. It generally does not protect a person against actions taken by private individuals or entities.

Example: The First Amendment protects freedom of speech. A city cannot pass a law or take action to prevent groups of protesters from gathering on city sidewalks or in city parks for political rallies. That interference with their freedom of speech would violate the First Amendment.

On the other hand, as far as the federal Constitution is concerned, the owner of a shopping center may prevent the same groups from gathering in the center's mall or parking lot. Because the shopping center is private property, this policy does not involve state action, so it is not considered a violation of the First Amendment. (*Hudgens v. NLRB*, 424 U.S. 507 (1976).)

However, a city or state may pass a law requiring shopping center owners to allow peaceful protests on their property. Such a law would make it illegal for a shopping center owner to interfere with an orderly protest, even though preventing the orderly protest would not be a violation of the federal Constitution. (*PruneYard Shopping Center v. Robins*, 447 U.S. 74 (1980).)

- **Due Process**—The right to a fair hearing by an impartial judge.
- **Equal Protection**—Everyone has the right to equal protection of the laws. The government may not adopt laws that unfairly discriminate between different groups of people.
- **Just Compensation**—If the government takes private land, it must pay fair compensation.
- **Unreasonable Search and Seizure**—The government may not seize or search private property without probable cause. A search warrant is usually required.
- **State Action**—Action by a government or a government official.

Washington's State Constitution

The Washington state constitution was adopted in 1889. It begins with a Declaration of Rights. Among many other guarantees, it provides that everyone has a right to acquire, possess, and protect property.

Many of the state constitutional rights overlap those rights protected by the U.S. Constitution, such as freedom of speech and due process of law. But in some cases, the Washington constitution may offer greater protection than the U.S. Constitution.

Legislatures: Statutory Law

Legislative bodies are the dominant source of new laws in the United States. Representatives elected to the U.S. Congress, the 50 state legislatures, and county and city councils across the country make hundreds of new laws every year. The laws adopted by Congress and the state legislatures are called **statutes**. The laws adopted by county and city councils are generally called ordinances.

The Legislative Process

The members of a legislative body write and adopt laws through a process of argument and compromise. Each legislative body has its own procedures. As an example, here is a brief outline of the procedures used in Congress.

Congress is divided into two houses, the Senate and the House of Representatives. A **bill**—a proposal to amend a statute or create a new one—is introduced in either the Senate or the House. Members of Congress may introduce bills at the request of their constituents (voters), a government agency (such as the Department of Housing and Urban Development), or a lobbying group (such as the National Association of Realtors®).

After a bill is introduced, the appropriate legislative committee analyzes and redrafts the bill as necessary. For example, the House Committee on Energy and Commerce and the Senate Energy and Natural Resources Committee work on bills related to energy. If the house in which the bill was proposed passes the bill, it is sent to the other house for consideration. The other house may pass the bill as written, rewrite or amend it, vote it down, or let it die in committee.

If the second house passes an amended version of the bill, it must be **reconciled** with the original version passed by the first house. A **conference committee** made up of members from both houses works out a compromise version of the bill. If a majority in each house votes for this version, the bill is passed.

The final stage of the legislative process involves the president. The president can express approval of the bill by signing it, or can take no action on it. Either way, the bill becomes law from the effective date forward. But if the president **vetoes** the bill, it will not become law unless Congress votes to override the veto. To override a presidential veto, a two-thirds majority in each house must vote in favor of the bill. If the bill can't muster the required support in Congress, it dies. If the veto is overridden, however, the bill becomes law in spite of the president's disapproval.

The Washington legislature follows a similar procedure. It also is divided into two houses, the state senate and the state house of representatives. The state governor has the power to veto legislation.

A citizen can influence the legislative process. You can campaign and vote for representatives who seem likely to promote your interests. You can also join or organize a lobbying group that will propose new legislation or changes in the law to the representatives. And when the Congress, the legislature, or a local council is considering a proposal that you support or oppose, you can urge your representatives to vote for or against it.

Revised Code of Washington (RCW)

Related statutes are grouped together, numbered sequentially, and published in a set of indexed volumes called a **code**. The **Revised Code of Washington**, referred to as the **RCW**, is the compilation of state statutes currently in effect. The RCW can be located online at the Washington State Legislature's website: http://apps.leg.wa.gov/rcw/. You can view the statutes organized by title, or search the text of the RCWs for a particular keyword or phrase.

Courts: Case Law

Although legislative bodies are the main source of new law, the courts are also an important source. However, judges do not issue general rules in the same way that legislative bodies do. A legislative body can make laws on any subject it chooses (as long as it doesn't violate the federal or state constitution). But a judge can only address a point of law if it is at issue in a lawsuit. Because the rules of law developed by judges are extracted from decisions reached in court cases, they are referred to as **case law**.

Lawmaking and Dispute Resolution

A judge's primary task is resolving disputes. One person accuses another of committing a tort or breaching a contract; the other denies it. They can't work out their disagreement, so there is a lawsuit. The judge acts as a referee and settles the argument by applying the law to the facts of the particular dispute.

> **Example:** Sloan is selling his house to Baker. There's a valuable antique chandelier in the front hall; Baker assumes it's included in the sale but never asks. The purchase agreement doesn't mention the chandelier. After the sale closes and Sloan moves out, Baker discovers that Sloan has taken the chandelier with him. Sloan says he had a right to, because it's a family heirloom that he installed himself.
>
> Sloan is unwilling to return the chandelier or pay Baker any compensation, much less an amount that Baker considers adequate. So Baker sues Sloan.
>
> Applying established principles of contract law and property law, the judge rules that the chandelier was included in the sale. It was a fixture and therefore part of the real estate unless otherwise agreed in writing, which didn't happen in this case. The judge orders Sloan to return the chandelier to Baker or else pay her its market value, as determined by an independent appraiser.

In the course of resolving disputes, judges may have to engage in a form of lawmaking. Applying the law to the facts isn't a mechanical process. Nearly every case presents a new combination of circumstances which could raise issues that haven't been settled by existing law. A judge may need to extend or reshape established rules of law, or even forge new ones. For instance, the judge in our example might have decided that the established rules concerning fixtures should not apply in this case because the chandelier is an heirloom.

The decision a judge makes in a lawsuit will, of course, directly affect the parties involved (in our example, Sloan and Baker). But it may also affect everyone who's in a similar situation. In other words, the judge's decision may become a rule of law for everyone within the court's jurisdiction. We'll explain how that can happen next.

Stare Decisis and Precedent

A judge's decision in a specific case can become a rule of law applied to all cases because of the **doctrine of stare decisis**. The doctrine holds that once a judge has decided a particular point of law, other judges faced with the same issue must decide it the same way. ("Stare decisis" is a Latin phrase that means, roughly, "to abide by the decision.")

Since the judge in our previous example ruled that a chandelier is a fixture (and thus is included in the sale unless otherwise agreed), the doctrine of stare decisis would require another judge in a later case involving a similar situation to also rule that a chandelier is a fixture. The first judge's decision is called a **precedent**, and under certain circumstances it is considered binding on other judges.

- **Stare Decisis**—A doctrine requiring judges to abide by previous judicial decisions.
- **Precedent**—A previously decided case that serves as an example for a similar case arising later.
- **Jurisdiction**—An area under the authority of a particular court.

Stare decisis is not a law, but a policy that judges have followed for centuries (we inherited it from the English common law). It tries to ensure that two people who do the same thing will be treated the same way by the law. That fits with our sense of fairness; it also makes the law more predictable. If a binding precedent holds that a chandelier is a fixture, sellers are given warning that they cannot take a chandelier with them unless they expressly exclude it from the sale.

Not every court decision is a binding precedent for all other judges, however. It depends, for the most part, on three factors:

- jurisdiction,
- position in the court hierarchy, and
- a written opinion.

For a judge to be bound by the decision of another court, the other court must be in the same jurisdiction. A **jurisdiction** is the area under the authority of a particular court. For example, the jurisdiction of the Washington Supreme Court is the state of Washington. A decision of the Washington Supreme Court is not binding on a Nevada state court.

Within each jurisdiction, courts are arranged in a hierarchy, with numerous courts on the lowest level and a smaller number of courts on each higher level. (See the diagram of an imaginary court system shown in Figure 1.2 on the following page.) There may be just one judge or several judges on a given court, depending on its function and the population of the area it serves. A judge is required to follow the precedents decided by a higher court in the same jurisdiction.

For example, refer again to Figure 1.2. Suppose Intermediate Court A hears the appeal of a case involving a chandelier and rules that it is a fixture and included in the sale. All the judges on Lower Courts A1, A2, and A3 must follow that precedent if a similar case is brought before them.

But when a judge on Lower Court B2 decides a similar case, she is free to hold that a chandelier is not a fixture and can be removed by the seller. That's because Lower Court B2 is not in the same jurisdiction as Intermediate Court A.

Fig. 1.2 An imaginary, simplified court system

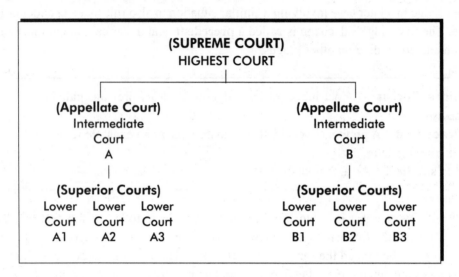

Intermediate Court B is also not bound by the precedents of Intermediate Court A, since Court A is not higher than Court B. Both intermediate courts are bound by the decisions of the Highest Court, however.

Judges are expected to follow the earlier decisions of their own court, but they have the power to depart from these precedents. Conditions may have changed significantly since the earlier case was decided, or the earlier decision may simply seem wrong. If so, a judge may modify the rule or overrule the precedent altogether.

> **Example:** Four years later, another chandelier case is appealed to Intermediate Court A. The judges on Intermediate Court A would ordinarily follow their own court's precedent, but this time they reconsider the earlier decision and decide to overrule it. They hold that a chandelier is not a fixture unless it is physically attached to the real estate in such a manner that it can't be removed without damaging either the chandelier itself or the real estate. (Note that if the earlier case had been decided by the Highest Court, rather than by Intermediate Court A, the precedent could not be overruled by Intermediate Court A. Judges can't overrule precedents decided by a higher court.)

No decision can be a binding precedent unless a written **opinion** is published. In addition to stating the court's decision, an opinion describes the facts of the case and the court's reasoning: why it concluded that a chandelier is a fixture. Some courts publish an opinion for every case decided; others publish opinions only for their most important cases.

By reading the higher court's opinion, a lower court judge can determine how similar the facts of the earlier case were to the case she is deciding, and whether the same reasoning

Fig. 1.3 How cases are cited

Case Law Citations

Judicial opinions are published in books called **case reporters**. Case citations—references to particular cases in the reporters—are given in a standardized form.

Example: *Alby v. Banc One Fin.*, 156 Wn.2d 367, 128 P.3d 81 (2006).

The citation includes the name of the case, followed by the volume (156) of the case reporter (Wn.2d) where the opinion can be found. Then it states the page number (367) the opinion begins on. Washington cases can also be found in the Pacific Reporter. The second cite tells you that this opinion is also found in volume 128 of the Pacific Reporter, third series (P.3d), beginning on page 81. The citation ends with the year that the case was decided, in parentheses (2006).

There are separate case reporters for most state appellate courts in the country, as well as federal case reporters. In addition, there are regional reporters that compile important cases from state courts in a given region (the Pacific Reporter and the Northeastern Reporter, for example). Each reporter's title has its own abbreviation for purposes of citation. Here are some of the abbreviations that someone in Washington State may encounter:

State Court Decisions
Decisions of the Washington Supreme Court:
Washington Reports   Wash., Wn. 2d, or Wn. 3d

Decisions of the Washington Court of Appeals:
Washington Appellate Reports   Wn. App.

Decisions from appellate courts in Washington and 14 other western states:
Pacific Reporter   P., P.2d, or P.3d

Federal Court Decisions
Decisions of the United States Supreme Court:
United States Reports   U.S.
Supreme Court Reporter   S. Ct.

Decisions of the United States Courts of Appeals (including the Ninth Circuit):
Federal Reporter   F., F.2d, or F.3d

Decisions of the United States District Courts:
Federal Supplement   F. Supp., F. Supp. 2d, or F. Supp. 3d

A citation to a case from a federal Court of Appeals includes the circuit number in parentheses, along with the year the case was decided. A Ninth Circuit decision would be cited like this: *Skranak v. Castenada*, 425 F.3d 1213 (9th Cir. 2005).

A citation to a case from a federal district court includes the name of the district in the parentheses. A decision from the Western District of Washington would be cited like this: *Corrie v. Caterpillar, Inc.*, 403 F. Supp. 2d 1019 (W.D. Wash. 2005).

applies. When the facts are significantly different, the current case is **distinguished** from the earlier case. If the current case can be distinguished, the lower court judge can reach a different result than was reached in the earlier case.

Even though judges are not bound by lower court decisions or decisions from other jurisdictions, they often take those decisions into consideration. When there's no existing precedent in a judge's own jurisdiction, a well-reasoned opinion from another jurisdiction— or simply a decision whose facts closely mirror those of the case under consideration—can have a great deal of persuasive influence.

> **Example:** A judge in Washington is deciding a case involving a very unusual type of easement. Although no other court in Washington has ever dealt with such an easement, courts in other states have. The Washington judge reads opinions from courts in New York, Florida, and Alabama. The Florida court decided the easement was valid, but the New York and Alabama courts decided it was invalid.
>
> The Florida court's reasoning makes much more sense to the Washington judge than the other courts' reasoning. He decides to rule that the easement in his case is valid, and writes an opinion that is based on the Florida court's arguments.

The process of deciding cases and the relationship of different courts are more complicated than this initial discussion might suggest. They will be examined in greater detail later in this chapter.

Administrative Agencies

Over the past few decades, another source of law has become increasingly important in the United States: federal, state, and local administrative agencies. Executives (the president, governors, and mayors) and legislative bodies do not have the time or the expertise to take care of all the details of a complex area of law, so they create administrative agencies to handle specific areas.

There are agencies concerned with nearly every aspect of society. Federal agencies range from the Department of Housing and Urban Development and the Environmental Protection Agency to the Internal Revenue Service. Washington state agencies include the Department of Licensing and the Department of Labor and Industries. Every county and city also has a zoning authority, a building department, a planning commission, and so forth.

Rulemaking

An administrative agency is usually given broad powers within its area of authority. This includes the power to issue regulations that have the force of law. For example, the Director of the Department of Licensing has issued regulations prohibiting the discriminatory sales practice called blockbusting (see Chapter 12). A real estate agent who violates these regulations may have his or her license revoked. The Director also has the power to fine agents for violations.

Before issuing a new regulation, an agency is generally required to publish a notice of its intention to do so. This gives interested parties (such as real estate agents or homeowners) the opportunity to express their ideas and concerns. The regulation must, of course, be constitutional. Furthermore, it must not exceed the authority granted to the agency by the legislative body or executive that created it. In Washington, a public hearing is required to be held on the proposed new rule. In some cases the agency may ask for additional written comments.

Adjudication and Enforcement

Detailed regulations give rise to many disagreements: licenses, permits, and benefits may be denied or revoked; rules may be violated. These disputes would overwhelm the court system, so most of them are decided by the agencies themselves.

Many of these disputes are handled through an informal negotiation process. But when a significant liberty or property interest (such as a real estate license) is at stake, the agency usually must hold a formal administrative hearing in order to comply with the Constitution's due process requirement. These cases are decided by administrative law judges.

An administrative law judge is part of the agency, and is an expert in the agency's area of authority. But he or she is supposed to consider disputes impartially, rather than taking the agency's point of view. If you're unhappy with an administrative law judge's decision, you can appeal to the superior court. However, a court is not very likely to overturn the agency's decision. If the agency's record of the case contains substantial evidence to support the decision, the court will simply consider whether the agency has exceeded its grant of power or incorrectly followed a required administrative procedure. If not, the court will affirm the agency's ruling.

How Laws Interact

Constitutional provisions, statutes, case law, and administrative regulations are not isolated from one another. They are often complementary, and a judge may apply all of them in resolving a lawsuit. There is also interaction between the different kinds of laws: a statute or a regulation can be held unconstitutional by a court, new case law can be developed to interpret a statute, or a new statute can replace case law.

Judicial Review

Earlier in the chapter, the concept of unconstitutionality was introduced. If a law exceeds the limits of government power as outlined in the U.S. Constitution (or the state constitution), it is unconstitutional.

Judges determine whether statutes, ordinances, or regulations are unconstitutional. The Constitution did not expressly assign that role to them, but in an early case the U.S. Supreme Court declared that the judiciary had that power. (*Marbury v. Madison*, 5 U.S. (1 Cranch) 137 (1803).) **Judicial review** of legislation and regulations is established and accepted today.

Judges do not routinely review all of the statutes adopted by a legislative body or all of an administrative agency's regulations. Someone who believes she has been harmed by an unconstitutional statute or regulation must file a lawsuit challenging the law's constitutionality before a court will review it.

Once a court decides that a law is unconstitutional, it cannot be enforced. At that point, the legislative body or administrative agency may try to revise the statute or regulation to bring it within constitutional limits.

Statutory Construction

The most common kind of interaction between different types of laws occurs when a judge applies a statute in a lawsuit. This is a straightforward task when the facts of the case clearly fall inside or outside of the statute's rule. But it often isn't clear whether the statute covers a particular situation or not, so the judge must decide. This process of interpretation is called **statutory construction**. Judges have to interpret administrative regulations in the same way.

In interpreting a statute or regulation, the judge's goal is to carry out the intention of the legislature or the administrative agency. As judges interpret a statute or a regulation, the case law clarifies the meaning of that statute or regulation. A whole series of cases may develop the meaning of a single statutory phrase or term such as "discrimination." For example, a judge in one case might rule that a statute prohibits discrimination against disabled people; a judge in another case might rule that although the statute prohibits discrimination against disabled people, someone who is HIV-positive is not disabled.

Fig. 1.4 How laws interact

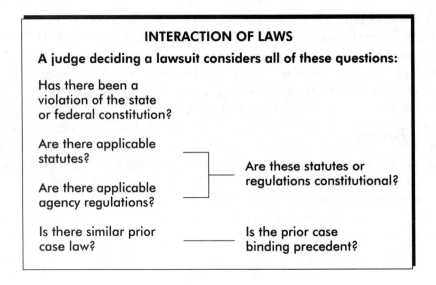

The legislature may disagree with some of the case law that develops through this process of interpretation. It can then rewrite the statute to make it clear that people who are HIV-positive are indeed considered to be disabled and cannot be discriminated against. The revised statute will cancel out any case law that conflicts with it. An administrative agency can revise its regulations in the same way.

But the process of judicial interpretation will begin all over again with the revised statute or regulation. There's no such thing as a perfectly clear rule that covers all possible cases and requires no interpretation. This interaction between statutes, regulations, and court decisions is a necessary part of the law.

The Judicial System

As you've seen, judges resolve disputes by interpreting and applying existing laws, and developing new ones if necessary. This section focuses on the structure of the judicial system. It explains the different functions of trial and appellate courts, and outlines the state and federal court systems. It also describes some rules that limit access to the courts.

Many court systems are overcrowded; sometimes there are too many cases and not enough judges to hear them, which can cause long delays. So procedures and limitations have been developed to help reserve the courts' resources for the cases where adjudication is most necessary and most likely to be effective.

Trial Courts and Appellate Courts

The fundamental court proceeding in a lawsuit is the **trial**. The general outlines of a trial are no doubt familiar to you: lawyers present arguments and evidence, witnesses testify and are cross-examined, and a jury or a judge decides the case. Trials take place in a jurisdiction's lower courts, so those are often referred to as **trial courts**.

If you're dissatisfied with the outcome of a trial, you generally have the opportunity to appeal at least once. On appeal, you are asking a higher court in the same jurisdiction to reconsider the trial court's decision. A court that has the power to review the decisions of lower courts is called an **appellate court**, and is said to have **appellate jurisdiction**. (Trial courts are said to have **original jurisdiction** because they hear cases for the first time.)

Many people expect an appeal to be just like another trial, but it is a very different proceeding. To try every appealed case all over again would be extremely expensive, both for the parties and for the court system. So the evidence is not presented again, the witnesses do not testify again, and there is no jury.

Instead, the appellate court reviews the **trial record**, which includes a word-for-word transcript of everything that the lawyers, witnesses, and trial judge said in the courtroom. The record also includes any exhibits that were admitted in the trial. An **exhibit** is documentary or physical evidence: a listing agreement, a deed, fingerprints, or an old tire.

In reviewing the record, the appellate court is looking for errors committed by the trial judge. Most appellate courts will only change a trial court's decision if:

- the judge committed an error,
- the error concerned a question of law, and
- the error was prejudicial.

Questions of Fact and Questions of Law. All the issues in a trial can be classified as either questions of fact or questions of law. A **question of fact** is any question about what actually took place: Did Abernathy tell Barlow she could lease the apartment for nine months or for a year and a half? A **question of law**, on the other hand, is any question about what the law is on a particular point: Is a lease for a year and a half valid if it isn't in writing?

Questions of fact are decided by the trier of fact. In a jury trial, the trier of fact is the jury. In a non-jury trial, the trier of fact is the judge. Questions of law are always decided by the judge, regardless of whether there is a jury.

An appellate court generally accepts the trier of fact's conclusions on questions of fact. The trier of fact had a better opportunity to assess the evidence than the appellate court. The trier of fact heard the testimony firsthand and could observe the witnesses as they were testifying, whereas the appellate judges only read a transcript of the testimony. So if the trier of fact concluded that Abernathy told Barlow she could lease the apartment for a year and a half, the appellate court will assume that conclusion is correct. An exception is made only if the trier of fact's findings are completely unsupported by the evidence.

An appellate court's main focus is on the questions of law, reviewing the record to see if the trial judge decided any of those incorrectly. The trial judge may have made a mistake about an established point of law (substantive or procedural). Or the trial judge may have ruled on an issue that had never been decided before, and the appellate court might disagree with the ruling. In either case, the trial court is said to have committed an error.

Prejudicial Error and Harmless Error. If the appellate court finds that the trial judge committed an error, it considers whether the error was prejudicial or harmless. A **prejudicial** error is one that adversely affects a substantial right of one of the litigants. This is generally interpreted to mean an error that may make a difference in the outcome of the trial. If the trier of fact would almost certainly have reached the same final decision if the error had not been made, the error is considered **harmless**.

Appellate Decision. If the appellate court does not find any error in the record, or decides that the error was harmless, it will **affirm** the trial court's decision. If it decides that there was prejudicial error, it will **modify** or **reverse** the decision.

When a trial court's decision is reversed, the appellate court may substitute its own ruling for the trial court's judgment, or it may **remand** the case back to the lower courts. If the case is remanded, the appellate court may order the original trial judge to conduct additional proceedings, or it may order a new trial.

Whereas a trial is presided over by a single judge, an appeal is usually heard by a panel of three or more judges. Sometimes not all of the judges on an appellate panel agree on how a case should be decided. Then the decision will be reached by majority vote.

Second Appeal. A litigant dissatisfied with the result of an appeal may appeal again, to an even higher court. But while a first appeal is generally an **appeal by right**, a second appeal is often **discretionary**. The litigant petitions the high court to hear the case, but the high court may refuse. In fact, because the courts are so crowded, the great majority of discretionary appeals are turned down.

State Courts and Federal Courts

Just as there is a federal legislature (Congress) and 50 state legislatures, there is a federal court system and 50 state court systems. But the federal court system isn't centralized in Washington, D.C.; there are federal courts in every state, along with the state courts. The jurisdictions of federal courts and state courts overlap.

Taking a closer look at the concept of jurisdiction will make it easier to understand the two systems and their relationship to one another. You have already seen how a court's jurisdiction can be limited to a particular geographical area: the Washington state courts don't have authority over what takes place in Nevada. But jurisdiction can be limited in other ways as well.

A court's jurisdiction may be limited to a certain type of lawsuit, such as tax cases or patent cases. The types of cases that a court has authority to hear are called its **subject matter jurisdiction**. A court that is not limited to a specific subject is called a court of **general jurisdiction**.

There may also be monetary limits on a court's jurisdiction. For example, some courts can only hear a case if the amount of money involved in the dispute (called the **amount in controversy**) is more than a certain amount, such as $10,000. In contrast, other courts can only hear a case if the money amount involved is less than a certain amount, such as $5,000.

Limitations like these define the jurisdiction of the various state and federal courts. We'll look at the Washington state court system, then at the federal system, and then at the relationship between the two.

District Courts and Municipal Courts

The trial courts at the lowest level of the hierarchy in Washington are courts of limited jurisdiction: district courts and municipal courts. District courts share jurisdiction with the higher-level superior courts over criminal matters such as misdemeanors, gross misdemeanors, and criminal traffic cases (for example, driving under the influence, hit-and-run, and driving with a suspended license), as well as civil cases involving personal injuries, damage to personal property, or contract disputes, with an amount in controversy of up to $100,000. With certain exceptions, such as convictions for driving while intoxicated and

Fig. 1.5 Washington's state court system

some game violations, those convicted of criminal offenses in district court may be fined no more than $5,000, sentenced to no more than one year in jail, or both.

District courts have exclusive jurisdiction over traffic infractions (such as speeding tickets) and small claims disputes.

Small Claims Departments. Each district court has a small claims department for resolving minor civil disputes quickly and inexpensively. The amount in controversy must be $5,000 or less.

To save time and expense, the small claims process is simplified in several respects. There is no jury. Neither the plaintiff nor the defendant can be represented by a lawyer in the courtroom, although they are allowed to consult a lawyer about the case. The plaintiff (the party who chose small claims court) gives up the right to an appeal unless the amount claimed is over $1,000. The defendant has the right to an appeal unless the amount of the claim is less than $250.

Municipal Courts. Violations of municipal or city ordinances are handled in municipal courts. Some cities contract with district courts to handle such cases. As in district courts, penalties in municipal courts are limited to a fine of up to $5,000, a year in jail, or both.

Judges. District court judges are elected to a four-year term. Municipal judges are either elected or appointed, depending on the particular statutory provisions under which the courts were established. It is not a requirement that a district or municipal court judge be an attorney.

Superior Courts

Superior courts have concurrent jurisdiction over the matters that can be filed in district courts, except for traffic infractions and small claims disputes. In addition, superior courts are the trial courts for all cases that exceed the limits of district and municipal court jurisdiction. Thus, superior courts try serious criminal cases (felonies). A civil case can be brought in superior court regardless of the amount in controversy; there's no minimum or maximum. But most superior court cases have an amount in controversy over $100,000, since that's the maximum limit for district court cases. Any case affecting title to real property must be brought in superior court, no matter what the amount in controversy is. Most civil cases in which the plaintiff is seeking a non-monetary remedy, such as an injunction, are also brought in superior court. In addition, superior courts can hear appeals in cases that were decided in the district or municipal court.

There are 30 judicial districts in the state, and one superior court in each district. The number of judges on each court depends on the district's population. Counties with large populations usually comprise one district, while in less populated areas there are several counties in one district. In very rural counties, judges rotate among the counties as needed.

Although not required to, a superior court judge will usually try to follow precedents decided by other judges on the same court. A King County superior court judge will follow another King County judge's lead. A judge on another superior court (the superior court in Spokane County, for example) may disregard the King County precedent altogether.

Juvenile Court. Juvenile court is a division of the superior court that deals with youths under the age of 18. It handles cases involving youths who commit offenses or who are abused or neglected.

Judges. Like district court judges, superior court judges are elected to four-year terms. Vacancies between elections are filled by the governor. Superior court judges must be attorneys admitted to practice in the state of Washington.

Some courts employ court commissioners to ease the judges' caseloads. Most commissioners are attorneys licensed to practice in Washington. Working under the direction of the presiding judge, the commissioner assumes many of the same powers as a superior court judge. However, a commissioner does not preside over criminal cases or jury trials.

Washington Court of Appeals

A litigant who is unhappy with a superior court's decision has a right to a review by a state court of appeals. These courts have appellate jurisdiction in all matters except criminal cases involving the death penalty. (Death penalty cases are appealed directly from superior court to the state supreme court.)

An opinion by a state court of appeals is published only if it involves a new and important issue, or changes an established rule. The state is divided into three appellate divisions, with Division One in Seattle, Division Two in Tacoma, and Division Three in Spokane. A published decision from one of the three appellate divisions is binding precedent within that division. However, the three divisions are semi-independent. A court of appeals in one division is not bound to follow precedents decided by another division.

The decision of any court of appeals is binding precedent for all the trial courts in the state (district, municipal, and superior courts). This is true even when the trial court is not in the same appellate district as the court that established the precedent.

> **Example:** A Spokane County superior court judge is hearing a case involving breach of contract. In resolving the questions of law that the case presents, the judge looks first for precedents decided by Division Three of the Court of Appeals, because Spokane is in Division Three. But the judge finds that the main point of law in the case has never been addressed by Division Three. That doesn't mean the judge gets to make up her own mind about the issue. She must do further research to determine whether either of the other two divisions has decided the question yet. It turns out that Division One has established a precedent on the issue. The Spokane superior court judge must follow the Division One precedent, even though Spokane is not in that division.

What if the judge had found two conflicting precedents, one from Division One and one from Division Two? She could choose between the two. That kind of conflict would eventually be cleared up by the highest court in the state system, the Washington Supreme Court.

Judges. The judges on the court of appeals serve six-year staggered terms. This ensures that not all judges will be up for re-election at the same time. To be elected to the state court of appeals, a prospective judge must have been an attorney admitted to practice law in the state of Washington for at least five years, and must have resided for at least one year in the district he or she will serve.

Washington Supreme Court

The Washington Supreme Court is the state's highest court. It consists of a chief justice and eight associate justices. A criminal defendant who has been sentenced to death has the right to appeal to the state supreme court directly from superior court. Most other cases must go from superior court to the court of appeals before they can be appealed to the supreme court.

An appeal to the Washington Supreme Court from a court of appeals decision is discretionary. The supreme court will generally hear an appeal only if the case presents a particularly important legal question, or if the divisions of the courts of appeals have developed conflicting precedents. The supreme court can resolve these conflicts because its decisions are binding on all other Washington state courts. One of the supreme court's most important functions is making the law uniform throughout the state. All supreme court opinions are published; they are the final word on Washington law.

Judges. Just like the court of appeals judges, the supreme court justices are elected to staggered six-year terms. The only requirement for office is that the prospective justice be an attorney admitted to practice law in the state of Washington. Any midterm vacancies are filled by the governor.

United States District Courts

The U.S. district courts are the main trial courts of the federal system. There are dozens of district courts across the country, with at least one in each state. Washington has two district courts, a Western District Court (located in Seattle and Tacoma) and an Eastern District Court (located in Spokane). A federal district court judge's decision is binding on other federal judges in the same district, but not on federal judges in other districts. So a judge in the Eastern District of Washington must follow Eastern District precedents, but doesn't have to follow Western District precedents. The U.S. district courts can hear cases that fall into one of three categories:

1. The United States government is a party.
2. A federal question is presented.
3. There is diversity of citizenship, and the amount in controversy is more than $75,000.

Cases in which the United States is a party include suits involving federal crimes: interstate car theft, racketeering, drug smuggling, and so forth. The U.S. can also be a party in a civil suit. For example, a defense contractor might sue the U.S. Army over a contract dispute. That case could be tried in a federal district court, since the army is a branch of the U.S. government.

The district courts also have jurisdiction over civil cases in which a **federal question** is presented. A federal question is any issue regarding the application or interpretation of the U.S. Constitution, a federal statute, or a U.S. treaty. If a group of political protesters sues a city for interfering with their First Amendment right to freedom of speech, the case could be heard in a federal district court.

The third category of federal district court jurisdiction covers civil cases in which there is **diversity of citizenship** and the amount in controversy is more than $75,000. Diversity of citizenship exists when the plaintiff and the defendant are not citizens of the same state. If a citizen of Alabama sues a citizen of Washington, or if a citizen of Washington sues a citizen of Brazil, the case can be heard in federal district court if more than $75,000 is at stake. This is called **diversity jurisdiction**.

Judges. All federal judges are appointed by the president and confirmed by the Senate. The Constitution provides that they will hold office "during good behavior," which generally means for life or until they retire.

United States Courts of Appeals

The result of a trial in a U.S. district court can be appealed (by right) to one of the U.S. Courts of Appeals. There is a federal court of appeals for each of eleven circuits. Each circuit covers several states (see Figure 1.7). There is an additional court of appeals in Washington, D.C., which is called the D.C. Circuit. Washington is in the Ninth Circuit, along with Oregon, California, Montana, Idaho, Nevada, Arizona, Alaska, Hawaii, Guam, and the Northern Mariana Islands. The decision of a U.S. district court sitting in any of those states (for instance, the District Court for the Eastern District of Washington, or the Idaho District Court), could be appealed to the Ninth Circuit Court of Appeals.

There are 29 seats on the Ninth Circuit, which is the largest federal appeals court. Most appeals are heard by panels made up of three of the circuit's judges. A Ninth Circuit decision is a binding precedent for all the U.S. district courts within the circuit.

> **Example:** A judge on the U.S. District Court for the Western District of Washington rules that a brokerage's hiring policies violated federal employment discrimination statutes. If a case involving similar hiring policies comes before the U.S. District Court for the Eastern District of California, the judge does not have to follow the Western District of Washington's decision. She may decide that the hiring policy did not violate the federal statute.
>
> However, it's a different matter if the Washington brokerage appeals to the Ninth Circuit, and a three-judge panel affirms the Washington district court's decision. Now a district court in California (or Hawaii, Arizona, or any Ninth Circuit state) is required to follow the precedent and hold that the hiring policy violated the statute.

Other circuit courts of appeals do not have to follow the Ninth Circuit's precedent. And district courts in other circuits—the District Court for the Western District of Kentucky, or for the Southern District of New York—are also free to ignore the Ninth Circuit's decision. But a decision by one of the U.S. Courts of Appeals usually has significant persuasive value for other courts.

Not every opinion of the U.S. Courts of Appeals is published, but all the opinions that decide new issues or change old rules are.

Fig. 1.6 The federal court system

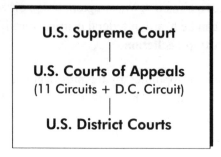

Fig. 1.7 The federal judicial circuits

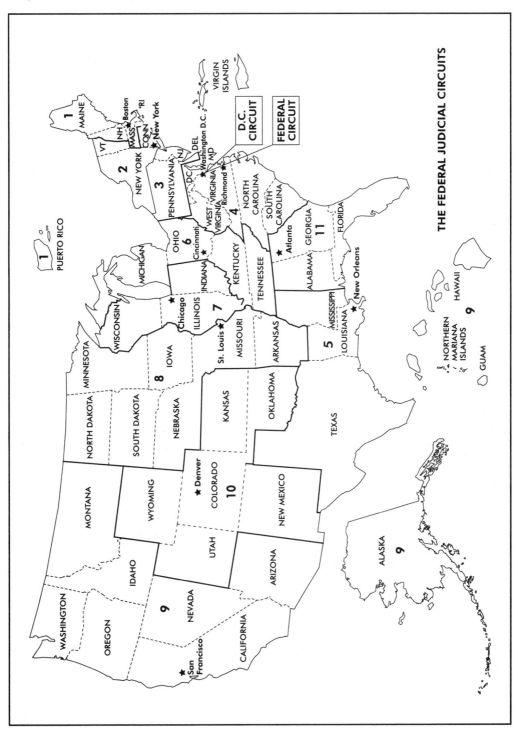

United States Supreme Court

The U.S. Supreme Court is made up of a chief justice and eight associate justices. Although it is the highest and most influential court in the country, its jurisdiction is limited just as the jurisdiction of the lower federal courts is limited.

The Supreme Court has original jurisdiction in a few special types of cases: for example, a lawsuit involving officials of a foreign government, or a lawsuit filed by a state against a citizen of a different state. However, even though the Court is empowered to conduct the trials in these cases, they will usually take place in a U.S. district court instead. The only trials that must take place in the Supreme Court are those for cases in which one state is suing another state.

The Supreme Court has appellate jurisdiction in all cases decided by the U.S. Courts of Appeals. Its decisions in these cases are binding precedents for all other courts. This gives the Supreme Court power to resolve conflicts between the decisions of U.S. Courts of Appeals in different circuits.

All appeals to the Supreme Court are discretionary. A litigant files a petition requesting a hearing, and the Supreme Court decides whether or not to grant the request. Petitions are filed for thousands of cases each year, but the Court hears less than five percent of them. Although "I'll take my case all the way to the Supreme Court!" is a standard threat, it can rarely be carried out. The U.S. Court of Appeals is the end of the line for the overwhelming majority of federal cases.

Specialized Courts

There are a few specialized federal courts with narrow subject matter jurisdiction. The U.S. Tax Court hears only cases involving the federal tax laws, the Federal Circuit Court hears only cases concerning patents, foreign trade, or tort claims against the federal government, and the U.S. Bankruptcy Court hears nothing but bankruptcy cases.

Federal and State Court Jurisdiction

Because federal jurisdiction and state jurisdiction overlap, the relationship between the two court systems is complicated. We'll start with the simpler cases—those that must be heard in federal court and those that must be heard in state court—before moving on to the cases that can be heard in either one.

Exclusive Jurisdiction

Federal Court. In some federal statutes, Congress has included a requirement that lawsuits based on the statute can be brought only in federal court. For example, cases

Fig. 1.8 Specialized federal courts

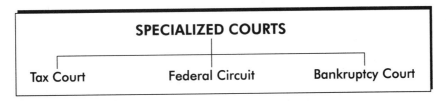

involving the Voting Rights Act of 1965 cannot be heard in state court. The same is true for suits regarding patents, copyrights, immigration, admiralty, and a number of other subjects that are controlled by federal statutes. Very few cases involving real property are in this category.

State Court. Any case that does not fall within the jurisdiction of the federal courts must be brought in state court. In other words, a case has to be heard in state court if:

- the U.S. government is not a party,
- no federal question is presented, and
- there is no diversity of citizenship (or there is diversity but the amount in controversy is $75,000 or less).

For example, most real estate cases must be brought in state court rather than federal court. In a typical real estate lawsuit, the plaintiff and the defendant are citizens of the same state, only questions of state law are involved, and the U.S. government is not a party.

Concurrent Jurisdiction

Either State or Federal Court. The reason state and federal jurisdiction overlap is that the cases that may be brought in federal court do not have to be. A state court can hear a diversity of citizenship case, even if the amount in controversy is over $75,000. A state court can also hear a federal question case, except if it concerns those subjects (like patents) that Congress has expressly reserved for the federal courts.

When a state trial court decides a federal question case, the decision can be appealed only in the state system. In other words, the case must be taken to the Washington Court of Appeals, rather than to the Ninth Circuit Court of Appeals. On a second appeal, it would go to the Washington Supreme Court.

From that point, there is the possibility of a third appeal, to the U.S. Supreme Court. The U.S. Supreme Court will review the decision of a state supreme court if (and only if) the case presents an important federal question. It will not interfere in cases that involve only questions of state law.

Choosing Between Federal and State Court. When a case could be filed in either state or federal court, why does the plaintiff choose one over the other? The reasons aren't clear-cut. Sometimes federal court is chosen just because the plaintiff's lawyer is accustomed to federal court and is more familiar with federal court procedures. Some lawyers believe that federal court judges tend to be better qualified or more sophisticated, since they are appointed rather than elected.

At times, the federal or state courts gain a reputation for favoring plaintiffs or defendants in a particular type of case. Civil rights cases are the most prominent example. In the 1960s (and later), state courts in southern states were seen as more likely to support racial segregation than the federal courts in those states. As a result, a southern plaintiff claiming that his civil rights had been violated would almost invariably choose to bring the case in federal court.

Limitations on Adjudication

Our judicial system has several rules that bar lawsuits in specific situations. It's important to understand these limitations, as they can prevent an aggrieved plaintiff from being able to sue.

Case or Controversy

As a general rule, a lawsuit must involve an active conflict, not just a theoretical or potential conflict. Based on Article III of the U.S. Constitution, this is known as the **case or controversy requirement**.

> **Example:** The landlord of a large new apartment building wonders if it is necessary to go to the expense of installing various security devices. If he doesn't install them, would he be liable if one of the apartments were burglarized? Could a tenant have them installed and then deduct the cost from the rent?

The landlord can consult a lawyer about these issues. The lawyer will give her opinion about what a court would probably decide if these cases arose. But a court would refuse to consider these hypothetical questions.

A judge won't issue a binding decision on what this landlord's duty is unless one of the apartments is actually burglarized and the tenant sues the landlord, or unless a tenant actually deducts the installation costs and the landlord sues for the deducted portion of the rent.

In some situations, however, a court has discretion to grant **declaratory relief**. This means that instead of requiring a problem to reach a crisis, the court will let the parties know in advance what their duties under a contract are, or what their property rights are. A **quiet title action** is an example of declaratory relief. If there is a possible claim against a property holder's title (a boundary dispute, for example), he can ask a court to decide whether or not the claim is valid. The title holder does not have to wait for the potential claimant to sue. Without a quiet title action, the title holder might be reluctant to develop the property, since it could turn out to belong to someone else.

Statute of Limitations

A statute of limitations precludes a court from hearing a case if too much time has passed since the conflict arose. The reason for these time limits is that it becomes more and more difficult to prove or disprove a claim as years go by. Evidence is often lost, and witnesses' memories fade.

The time limits vary depending on the type of case. In Washington, most contract suits must be filed within six years after the breach occurred if the contract was in writing, or within three years if the contract was oral. A suit to recover possession of real property must be filed within ten years.

It's important to note that in certain types of cases, the statute of limitations doesn't start running until the injury or loss is discovered, even if the wrongful act occurred much earlier. This is called the **discovery rule**.

> **Example:** Six months after she purchases a house, a buyer learns that the seller acted fraudulently in the transaction. The time limit for the buyer to bring an action against the seller doesn't begin until the buyer discovers the fraud.

The statute of limitations may offer special protection to a minor or incompetent person. In many cases, the statute of limitations does not begin to run until the minor reaches the age of majority, or the incompetent person regains competence.

Anyone thinking about starting a lawsuit should find out the limitations period for that type of action, and keep it in mind. Once the statutory period has run out, you've lost your legal remedy for good.

Res Judicata

"Res judicata" is a Latin phrase meaning "the thing has been decided." The doctrine of **res judicata** holds that once a dispute between two parties has been tried and appealed and a final judgment has been issued, the same dispute cannot be tried again. The dissatisfied party can't start a new lawsuit on the same question, hoping to find a more sympathetic judge or a more persuasive lawyer. The purpose of the doctrine is simple: finality. It puts the case to rest, at least as far as the court system is concerned. Without res judicata, some parties would go on suing each other over the same matter forever.

A Civil Lawsuit

Now we'll take a closer look at the litigation process. This section follows a simple civil lawsuit from its filing to the enforcement of the final judgment. The entire process would probably take at least several months; in many cases, it takes years.

The Dispute

Henry Palermo has lived near the Little Spokane River for many years. The lot to the west of his property had always been vacant, until Claire Mulligan bought it six months ago. Mulligan has had the lot cleared and regraded in preparation for the construction of a house.

Recently, very heavy rains occurred and Palermo's house was flooded. The water caused considerable damage to the house and yard and many of Palermo's belongings were ruined, including expensive stereo and recording equipment and a large collection of vinyl records. Palermo had let his homeowner's insurance lapse two months earlier.

Since his house was never flooded before, Palermo believes Mulligan's clearing and regrading next door changed the pattern of runoff and caused the flooding. He explains this to Mulligan and says she should help pay for the damage. Mulligan is furious. She tells Palermo his property flooded simply because it rained so hard, and that the changes she made in her property had nothing to do with it. In the course of a ten-minute conversation, the neighbors become enemies.

So Palermo consults a lawyer. The lawyer evaluates Palermo's claim by researching the law (looking up statutes and case law) about drainage onto adjoining property. He decides Palermo has a fairly strong case. Washington law holds that a landowner who disturbs the natural flow of surface waters may be liable for resulting damage to adjacent property.

Mulligan also hires a lawyer to look into the matter. Her lawyer concludes that it would be difficult for Palermo to prove that Mulligan's clearing caused his property to flood. Unless Palermo can prove that in court, Mulligan will not be held liable for the damage.

The two lawyers discuss their clients' positions. Palermo's lawyer says that unless Mulligan pays Palermo $110,000, Palermo will sue her. Mulligan's lawyer says that Mulligan won't pay Palermo a nickel, because the damage was not her fault.

Starting a Lawsuit

Palermo and his lawyer decide to proceed with a lawsuit. Palermo's lawyer starts the suit (*Palermo v. Mulligan*) by filing a **complaint** in the superior court of the county where Mulligan and Palermo live. The complaint outlines the dispute, explains how the plaintiff (Palermo) believes his legal rights have been violated by the defendant (Mulligan), and asks the court to grant judgment in the plaintiff's favor. Palermo asks the court to order Mulligan to prevent any future flooding and pay him $110,000.

Choosing a Court. What kind of court a lawsuit takes place in depends on the jurisdictional issues we discussed earlier. The case must come within the court's jurisdictional limits—geographical, subject matter, and monetary limits. This case had to be brought in state court, because Mulligan and Palermo are both citizens of Washington, and the case does not involve any federal laws (the laws concerning drainage and flooding are state laws). And since the amount in controversy is $110,000, the case had to be filed in superior court rather than in district court.

Personal Jurisdiction. Even when a case is within a particular court's jurisdictional limits (geographical, subject matter, and monetary limits), as a general rule that court can

Fig. 1.9 Steps in a civil lawsuit

> ## A CIVIL SUIT
>
> 1. Plaintiff files complaint
> 2. Defendant served with summons and complaint
> 3. Defendant files notice of appearance and answer
> 4. Pretrial discovery
> 5. Settlement negotiations
> 6. Trial

hear the case only if it has authority over the defendant. That authority is referred to as **personal jurisdiction.**

A court has personal jurisdiction over anyone who resides in the state where the court sits. It also has personal jurisdiction over a defendant who doesn't reside in that state if she has committed an act in the state that justifies the court's jurisdiction over her. (For example, Washington courts have personal jurisdiction over someone from Montana who comes to Washington and causes a car accident or enters into a contract with someone here.)

Every defendant in a lawsuit must receive **service of process**, which is the delivery of a summons and a copy of the complaint. The **summons** notifies the defendant that the complaint has been filed and that he must file a response with the court. In most cases, the plaintiff has a process server take the summons and complaint to the defendant's home or business and hand it directly to the defendant. If the defendant tries to evade the process server, service can be accomplished by publication, or through an agent of the defendant.

Jurisdiction Over Property. A court must also have jurisdiction over any property at issue in a lawsuit. Washington courts have jurisdiction over all real and personal property within the state's boundaries.

Defendant's Answer. A summons and complaint was served on Mulligan at her home. Now her lawyer has 20 days to prepare a **notice of appearance and answer** and file it with the court.

In the answer, a defendant may challenge the court's jurisdiction. The defendant may also deny the plaintiff's allegations, discuss facts that the plaintiff left out of the complaint, or make a **counterclaim** against the plaintiff. Mulligan's answer simply denies that the clearing and regrading on her property were the cause of Palermo's flood damage.

If a defendant fails to respond to the complaint, in some cases the plaintiff can win the case by default. A **default judgment** would then be entered against the defendant.

The complaint, the answer, and other additional documents filed with the court are called **pleadings**.

Summary Judgment. After the initial pleadings have been filed, one or both parties may submit a **pretrial motion** asking the court to grant **summary judgment**. A litigant who requests summary judgment wants the judge to decide the case (or an issue in the case) in his or her favor without a trial. The litigant argues that a trial is unnecessary because, based on the pleadings submitted, it's clear what the legal outcome should be. Generally, a judge may grant a motion for summary judgment only if there is no genuine issue of material fact—in other words, only if the essential facts of the case aren't in dispute. (Facts are in dispute in *Palermo v. Mulligan*—for example, the parties disagree about what caused the flooding of Palermo's property—so summary judgment isn't an option in this case.)

Pretrial Discovery

Once a lawsuit is under way, both the plaintiff and the defendant are given an opportunity to find out more about the disputed facts through the **discovery process**. The rules of discovery require each side to provide the other with information upon request. They also enable a litigant to obtain information from reluctant witnesses.

One method of acquiring information during discovery is a deposition. In a **deposition**, one party's lawyer questions the other party or a witness about the case. The **deponent** (the person responding to the lawyer's questions) is under oath, just as if he or she were testifying in court. A word-for-word transcript of the deposition can be used as evidence in the trial.

Interrogatories are another important discovery tool. They are like a deposition conducted by mail instead of in person. One party's lawyer sends a series of questions to the other party; the other party must send back answers. Interrogatories are also answered under oath.

Palermo's lawyer sends Mulligan interrogatories asking about the clearing and grading process, and about what measures were taken regarding runoff. Mulligan's lawyer sends Palermo interrogatories asking about the extent of the water damage, and about flooding in previous years. In addition, each side deposes the other party about the facts of the dispute. If Mulligan and Palermo fail to show up for their depositions or fail to answer the interrogatories, they may be fined for contempt of court.

Settlement Negotiations

Litigation is almost always expensive, time-consuming, and unpleasant. Both parties must weigh those costs against what they stand to gain, and how likely they are to win, if the case goes to trial.

Throughout the litigation process, Palermo's and Mulligan's lawyers negotiate to **settle** the case. In a settlement, the defendant pays the plaintiff a sum of money, or agrees to do or to refrain from doing something, so that the plaintiff will call off the lawsuit.

Soon after the action is filed, on the advice of her lawyer, Mulligan offers to install culverts on her property to rechannel runoff if Palermo will drop the suit. On the advice of his lawyer, Palermo refuses this offer; he will take the case to trial unless Mulligan pays him $50,000 and rechannels the runoff. As each lawyer learns more about the facts of the case through the discovery process, he re-evaluates his client's claim. Palermo's lawyer may realize that it will be much more difficult than he first thought to prove that it was Mulligan's clearing and grading that caused Palermo's property to be flooded. Or Mulligan's lawyer may realize that it may be much easier to prove that than he thought.

On the basis of these re-evaluations, the gap between the parties' settlement offers narrows. As the trial date approaches, Palermo is asking only $32,000 to settle, and Mulligan is offering $15,000. It is very likely that Palermo and Mulligan will come to an agreement. Over 95% of civil cases settle or are decided by arbitration rather than going through a trial. (The percentage may be even higher in some counties, especially where there is a backlog of cases and it might be quite some time before the case would ever get to trial.)

In some cases, however, the parties are unable to settle. It may be that the facts of the case are truly unclear, or that the case presents legal issues that courts in this jurisdiction haven't resolved yet. Or it may be that the litigants are unusually stubborn, or extremely angry with one another. We'll assume that for some combination of these reasons, Palermo and Mulligan do not settle, and the case proceeds to trial.

Jury or Judge

The U.S. Constitution and the Washington Constitution guarantee litigants the right to trial by jury. That right applies in most civil cases, but some cases (and certain issues within some cases) cannot be tried by a jury. It depends on the remedies requested by the plaintiff.

Common Law and Equitable Remedies. The remedies awarded in civil cases are classified either as common law remedies or as equitable remedies. A **common law remedy** is generally an award of money (damages). An **equitable remedy**, on the other hand, usually involves an **injunction**: an order to do something, or to refrain from doing something.

> **Example:** If the court ordered Mulligan to install culverts and plant protective vegetation, that would be an equitable remedy. If Mulligan were ordered to pay Palermo $65,000, that would be a common law remedy.

Equitable remedies can be awarded only when money would not adequately correct the problem. Specific performance, contract reformation, foreclosure, and quiet title are all equitable remedies.

For historical reasons, a jury is not allowed to decide equitable issues. If a plaintiff is asking only for an equitable remedy (such as foreclosure), the case cannot be heard by a jury. If a plaintiff is asking for both types of remedies (such as damages and an injunction), a jury may hear the case. The jury will decide on the common law remedy, but the judge will decide on the equitable remedy.

Choosing a Jury. Even when a lawsuit does not involve any equitable issues, a jury isn't automatically assigned to the case. One or both of the parties must request a jury. If neither party does, the judge will decide the questions of fact as well as the questions of law.

When should a litigant request a jury? It's an intuitive choice rather than a scientific one. Juries are supposed to be more sympathetic than judges in some cases. A jury hearing a personal injury suit may be more likely to feel compassion for the plaintiff than a judge, who might have heard dozens of similar cases. A jury may tend to side with the underdog, and favor an individual against a large corporation.

On the other hand, if a litigant's case is based on a complicated legal argument or on detailed technical or scientific evidence, a jury might have a hard time understanding it. And jury trials take longer and are more expensive than non-jury trials.

Although Palermo's lawyer thinks that a jury would feel sorry for his client because of the property damage, he decides not to request a jury. Palermo's case depends too much on technical proof that Mulligan's changes caused the flooding. Mulligan's lawyer decides to request a jury. He hopes the jury will feel that Mulligan did nothing unreasonable, and that it is unfair to hold her responsible for Palermo's misfortune.

Jurors are taken from a pool of citizens chosen at random. Both lawyers have an opportunity to question the potential jurors, to learn about their backgrounds and discover their personal prejudices. Those who seem biased against or in favor of one of the parties may be eliminated from the jury. A jury in district court consists of up to six people. A jury in superior court consists of six or twelve people.

Trial

Presentation of the Evidence. The plaintiff's case is presented first. The plaintiff's lawyer makes an **opening statement**, telling his or her client's version of the events that gave rise to the lawsuit. This explanation helps the judge and jurors understand the point of the evidence and testimony the lawyer is about to present. The defendant's lawyer can also make an opening statement at this point, or wait until after the plaintiff's case has been fully presented.

The plaintiff's lawyer examines witnesses whose testimony supports his client's version of the facts. There are two types of witnesses, fact witnesses and expert witnesses.

A **fact witness** is someone who had an opportunity to observe events connected with the dispute. For example, Palermo's lawyer has some of his client's neighbors testify that

Fig. 1.10 Stages of a civil trial

THE TRIAL

1. Opening statements
2. Presentation of evidence (plaintiff goes first)
   - fact witnesses
   - expert witnesses
   - physical or documentary evidence
3. Jury instructions
4. Closing arguments

there were even heavier rains three years earlier, yet Palermo's property did not flood. A fact witness is supposed to describe only those events that he personally observed, and is not allowed to offer opinions about the facts.

An **expert witness** is someone who has expert knowledge of a subject, either through experience or education. Litigants hire expert witnesses to evaluate their claims. If the expert's opinion supports the litigant's case, the expert is paid to testify at the trial. Palermo's lawyer calls two engineering consultants to testify about the effect of Mulligan's clearing and grading on her property's drainage. The lawyer also examines an appraiser, who testifies about how much it will cost to repair or replace the water-damaged property.

The initial questioning of witnesses by the lawyer who called them to testify is the **direct examination**. Immediately after the direct examination of a witness, the opposing lawyer has a chance to **cross-examine** that witness. In the cross-examination, the opposing lawyer tries to cast doubt on the witness's testimony and bring out any facts that are unfavorable to the other side. Then the first lawyer has a chance to repair any damage done on cross-examination by **redirect examination** of the witness. Sometimes the opposing lawyer will cross-examine the witness a second time.

Court rules provide that some testimony (or documentary or physical evidence) cannot be used in court because it is considered unreliable or unfair. Such testimony or evidence is inadmissible.

> **Example:** Testimony must be relevant to the issues involved in the dispute. If a neighbor testifying on behalf of Palermo says, "Mrs. Mulligan struck me as a troublemaker," Mulligan's lawyer can object. The witness's impression of Mulligan has no bearing on whether or not her activities caused Palermo's property to flood. The witness's comment is irrelevant and therefore inadmissible.

A lawyer can object to a witness's testimony, or to the other lawyer's questioning, on a variety of grounds: a fact witness is giving an opinion; a minister is being asked to divulge confidential information; the other lawyer is leading the witness (asking yes or no questions, instead of asking the witness to describe the events in her own words).

If the judge agrees with the objecting lawyer that the questioning is improper, the judge will tell the witness not to answer. If the judge agrees that testimony already given is inadmissible, he will tell the jury to disregard the witness's remarks, and may have them stricken from the trial record.

When the plaintiff's lawyer has finished presenting evidence, it is the defense lawyer's turn. The same procedure is repeated: direct and cross-examination of the defendant's witnesses, with objections from the lawyers and rulings on admissibility by the judge. The plaintiff's lawyer then has a chance to present additional evidence to rebut the defendant's case.

Jury Instructions. After all the evidence has been presented, the judge gives the jury instructions about the law that applies to the case.

> **Example:** The judge explains that Washington law does not hold a landowner responsible for damage caused by the natural flow of surface water from his or her property onto adjoining property. However, if the landowner changes the natural pattern of

drainage, he or she is liable for the resulting damage. The judge points out that this liability does not depend on whether the defendant intended to cause damage, nor on whether the defendant was careless.

The jury instructions include an explanation of the **burden of proof**. Here, as in most cases, the plaintiff has the burden of proof. That is, it is up to Palermo to prove that Mulligan's clearing and regrading were the cause of the damage. Mulligan is not required to prove that her changes did not cause the damage.

The judge will also explain that the plaintiff must prove his claim by a **preponderance of the evidence.** In other words, the jury doesn't have to be absolutely certain that Mulligan's changes caused the damage. It is enough if Palermo convinced the jury that it is more likely than not that Mulligan's changes were the cause. This is the **standard of proof** used in nearly all civil cases. (In criminal cases, where the defendant has so much at stake, a stricter standard of proof is applied: the prosecution must prove its case **beyond a reasonable doubt.**)

Finally, each lawyer makes a **closing argument**, explaining how all the evidence fits together.

Decision. In a civil case in Washington, 5 out of 6 or 10 out of 12 jurors must agree on the decision; a unanimous verdict is not necessary. However, in a criminal trial, the decision must be unanimous (all of the jurors must agree). If there is a **hung jury**—that is, the jury cannot agree on a verdict after deliberating for a long time—the case must be tried all over again before a new jury.

The jury in *Palermo v. Mulligan* votes 10 to 2 in favor of the plaintiff. Most of the jurors found Palermo's expert witnesses more convincing than Mulligan's expert witnesses. The jurors concluded that the flooding would not have occurred if Mulligan had not cleared and regraded her lot.

The jury awards Palermo $39,000 to repair and replace his water-damaged property, much less than the $110,000 he originally requested. The jury wasn't willing to believe that Palermo's stereo equipment and record collection were worth as much as the appraiser testified. The lower award may also reflect some sympathy for Mulligan.

In addition to the jury's damages award, the judge issues an injunction ordering Mulligan to install culverts that will rechannel runoff. Based on the experts' testimony, the judge specifies changes that will prevent future flooding of Palermo's property, without damaging Mulligan's property.

In hindsight, Mulligan and her lawyer appear to have miscalculated. Mulligan would have been better off accepting Palermo's $32,000 settlement offer, instead of going through with the trial in the hope of avoiding liability altogether.

Appeal

Both Mulligan and Palermo have the right to appeal the superior court decision to the Washington Court of Appeals. After the lower court's judgment has been entered, there is a limited period (usually 30 days) for filing a **notice of appeal**.

If Mulligan were to appeal, she would be the **appellant**, and Palermo would be the **appellee**. If Palermo were to appeal, he would be the appellant, and Mulligan would be the appellee. Both of them decide not to appeal, however. Since the jury's fact conclusions cannot be challenged on appeal, neither Palermo nor Mulligan could expect to gain much, and they are both very tired of the whole thing.

Collecting a Judgment

Just because the jury has awarded Palermo $39,000 doesn't mean that Mulligan will take out her checkbook and pay him on the spot. It can take a long time to collect a judgment; some are never collected.

Judgment Liens. Mulligan (the **judgment debtor**) doesn't pay the judgment immediately, so Palermo (the **judgment creditor**) secures his interest by claiming a lien against Mulligan's real property. If Mulligan still fails to pay the judgment, Palermo can **foreclose** on the lien, hoping to collect his $39,000 from the proceeds of a forced sale of the property. (Liens on real property are discussed in more detail in Chapter 4.)

Judgment liens can also attach to some personal property, such as business equipment and inventory. However, many types of personal property are exempt from judgment liens, including the debtor's household furnishings and clothing.

Garnishment. When a judgment debtor is a wage earner, the judgment creditor can use wage garnishment to collect the judgment in installments. An **earnings withholding order** is served on the debtor's employer, who must set aside the debtor's earnings for the creditor. The amount of money required to support the debtor and his or her family is exempt from garnishment.

A judgment debtor's bank account may also be garnished. For instance, money in a savings account could be garnished and collected to pay the judgment.

These collection devices are cumbersome, and they aren't always successful. Some defendants turn out to be "judgment-proof," which means they have no wages and no assets, or assets that are either exempt from judgment liens or already heavily encumbered with other liens. Inability to collect a judgment may be a real hardship for a judgment creditor who owes his own lawyer a substantial fee. That can make winning a lawsuit a hollow victory.

Conclusion

Lawsuits can be extremely time-consuming, frustrating, and expensive. However, you can reduce the risk of litigation if you are familiar with real estate law and understand your duties and obligations toward your clients and other parties.

Chapter Summary

- The law is a system of rights and duties established and enforced by a government. It maintains order, resolves disputes, enforces promises, and prevents exploitation. The law reflects a society's ideas of justice, but also serves other goals, such as efficiency.

- Substantive law defines rights and duties, while procedural law sets forth the methods for enforcing substantive rights.

- The government brings a criminal action to punish a wrongdoer and protect society. In a civil action, on the other hand, an injured party sues for compensation. Some wrongful acts can lead to both criminal and civil penalties.

- Contracts, torts, and property are the fundamental concepts of civil law. Contract law concerns voluntarily assumed duties; tort law concerns the duties of reasonable conduct imposed by law; property law concerns the duties inherent in ownership.

- Federal and state constitutions, legislative bodies, courts, and administrative agencies are the sources of law in the United States. Constitutions protect individual rights by limiting government power. Within those constitutional limits, legislative and administrative bodies issue general rules in the form of statutes, ordinances, and regulations.

- Courts apply those rules to resolve lawsuits. In the process of interpreting the rules, judges develop case law. The doctrine of stare decisis requires judges to follow established precedents, so that the law will be evenhanded and predictable.

- A court system is a hierarchy of trial courts and appellate courts. An appeal is not a second trial. The appellate court reviews the trial record for prejudicial errors, focusing primarily on questions of law rather than fact.

- The federal and state court systems are independent, with overlapping jurisdictions. Federal jurisdiction is limited to cases involving federal questions, diversity of citizenship, or the U.S. government. State courts can hear any cases except those that Congress has expressly reserved for the federal courts.

- The case or controversy requirement, statutes of limitation, and the doctrine of res judicata limit access to the courts. But the court systems are severely overcrowded in spite of these rules.

- A civil suit begins when the plaintiff files a complaint with the court and has a summons served on the defendant. The pretrial discovery process gives each side access to information the other might prefer to conceal. The parties' lawyers try to negotiate a settlement, to save the expense and trouble of a trial.

- Litigants have a right to trial by jury on any issue that does not involve an equitable remedy. In the trial, each side presents testimony and other evidence favorable to its case. Evidence is only admissible if it meets established standards of reliability and fairness.

- If the plaintiff wins, he may have to resort to using garnishment or a lien to collect the judgment from the defendant.

Chapter Quiz

1. The main historical influence on law in the United States was:

    a. Spanish law
    b. feudal law
    c. European law
    d. English law

2. When one individual sues another, the lawsuit is called:

    a. a civil action
    b. an equity suit
    c. declaratory relief
    d. criminal litigation

3. The primary purpose of most civil lawsuits is to:

    a. punish a wrongdoer
    b. compensate a person who has been harmed
    c. protect society
    d. deter crime

4. A person who commits a tort:

    a. will be prosecuted by the government
    b. will be held liable for breach of contract
    c. has violated the standards of reasonable conduct imposed by law
    d. must pay a fine or serve a jail term

5. An unconstitutional law:

    a. exceeds the powers granted to the government
    b. can only be enforced retroactively
    c. may be used to modify a Supreme Court decision
    d. violates the case or controversy requirement

6. The constitutional provision that guarantees a fair hearing by an impartial judge is known as the:

    a. equal protection clause
    b. stare decisis rule
    c. administrative law doctrine
    d. due process requirement

7. Which of the following would be most likely to issue an ordinance?

    a. Bellevue City Council
    b. Department of Licensing
    c. Washington State House of Representatives
    d. King County Superior Court

8. Litigants can gather more information about the disputed facts in their case through:

    a. statutory construction
    b. judicial review
    c. pretrial discovery
    d. jury instructions

9. The main purpose of the doctrine of stare decisis is to:

    a. limit access to the courts
    b. prevent courts from exceeding their subject matter jurisdiction
    c. clarify ambiguous statutes
    d. make court decisions more consistent and predictable

10. A binding precedent can be overruled:

    a. by a lower court within the same jurisdiction
    b. by the same court that established it
    c. only by a court that has original jurisdiction
    d. only by a court higher than the court that established it

11. A current case is distinguished from a precedent when:

    a. it was decided in a different jurisdiction
    b. it violates the doctrine of res judicata
    c. its facts are significantly different
    d. it overrules the precedent

12. When a precedent is not binding on a particular court:

    a. the judge may still consider it and follow it if it is persuasive
    b. it cannot be admitted into evidence during the trial
    c. the judge may not refer to it in his or her opinion
    d. the judge is not allowed to follow it

13. An administrative law judge:

    a. works in the small claims division of a municipal court
    b. is concerned only with procedural law
    c. resolves disputes involving an administrative agency's regulations
    d. All of the above

14. Which of these usually takes place during an appeal?

    a. Expert witnesses testify
    b. The trial transcript is reviewed
    c. New documentary evidence is introduced
    d. A new jury is chosen

15. Which of these is a question of law?

    a. Was the real estate agent required to put the earnest money in a trust account?
    b. Did the tenant inform the landlord that the railing was broken?
    c. Did the real estate agent inspect the attic?
    d. Was the buyer told that the agent was representing the seller?

16. A prejudicial error is one that:

    a. involves racial discrimination
    b. is committed during the discovery process
    c. involves administrative regulations
    d. may have affected the outcome of the trial

17. When an appellate court can choose whether or not to review a lower court's decision, the appeal is called a/an:

    a. appeal by favor
    b. appeal by right
    c. discretionary appeal
    d. grant review

18. Which of these can limit a court's jurisdiction?

    a. Geographical boundaries
    b. Subject matter of the case
    c. Amount of money at issue in a case
    d. All of the above

19. What's the difference between district and municipal courts?

    a. Municipal courts hear criminal cases and district courts don't
    b. Municipal courts handle violations of city ordinances
    c. Municipal courts have small claims divisions and district courts don't
    d. All of the above

20. Able is going to sue Beckett for breach of contract, claiming $105,000 in damages. Which kind of state court can Able file suit in?

    a. Municipal court
    b. District court of appeals
    c. Circuit court of appeals
    d. Superior court

21. To start a lawsuit, the plaintiff files a/an:

    a. deposition
    b. complaint
    c. answer
    d. interrogatory

22. A jury is not allowed to:

    a. grant an equitable remedy
    b. grant a damages award
    c. decide a criminal case
    d. decide a superior court case

23. Unlike an expert witness, a fact witness:

    a. testifies during the appeal
    b. should not state his or her opinions while testifying
    c. may not be cross-examined
    d. All of the above

24. In most civil lawsuits, the case must be proven by a preponderance of the evidence. This is known as the:

    a. burden of proof
    b. reasonable doubt rule
    c. standard of proof
    d. standard of doubt

25. If a judgment debtor refuses to pay a judgment:

    a. there is nothing the judgment creditor can do except wait and hope that he or she will eventually be paid
    b. the judgment creditor may have the debtor's wages and bank account garnished
    c. the judgment creditor can claim a lien against the debtor's property
    d. Both b) and c)

2 Real Estate License Law

Outline

Key Terms

- License law
- Real Estate Commission
- Real estate firm
- Managing broker
- Broker
- Affiliated licensee
- Designated broker
- Business opportunity
- Interim license
- Inactive license
- Blind ad
- Trust account
- Commingling
- Conversion
- Transaction folder
- Statement of charges
- Cease and desist order
- Antitrust
- Conspiracy
- Price fixing
- Group boycotts
- Tie-in arrangements
- Market allocation
- Unfair practices

Chapter Overview

This chapter explains the provisions of the state's real estate license law. As we explore these provisions, we'll explain who administers Washington's license law, when a real estate license is required, and the qualifications for licensure. Next, we'll discuss how the license law regulates the business practices of real estate professionals, controlling how firms form agency relationships, run their offices, supervise their sales agents, and handle client funds. Then we'll cover license law violations and disciplinary procedures. The final section of the chapter discusses how other laws—such as Washington's consumer protection law and federal antitrust laws—affect real estate agents.

Administration of the License Law

Becoming a successful agent takes more than an outgoing personality and good business skills. Successful real estate agents also take their legal and ethical responsibilities seriously. So with that in mind, let's turn our attention to the real estate license law and the duties and obligations it imposes on real estate agents.

The real estate license law is administered by Washington's Department of Licensing. The Director of the Department of Licensing is in charge of all of the divisions within the department, including the Real Estate Section. The Director and all Real Estate Section staff are employees of the state of Washington. They are not allowed to own any interest in a real estate firm.

The Director

The Director of the Department of Licensing is appointed by the Governor. The Director is charged with enforcing all laws, rules, and regulations relating to the licensing of real estate licensees. The Director has the authority to grant or deny licenses, and to hold disciplinary hearings and impose penalties for violations of the license law. And with the advice and approval of the Real Estate Commission, the Director also issues rules and regulations to govern the activities and practices of real estate licensees.

In fact, the term "real estate license law" is commonly used to refer not only to the statutory provisions adopted by the state legislature, but to the regulations issued by the Director as well. All real estate licensees are required to obtain a copy of the Director's regulations (available at the Department of Licensing website) and to keep informed of changes in the regulations.

The Real Estate Commission

The Real Estate Commission is made up of the Director and six commissioners. The commissioners are appointed by the Governor to advise the Director on the real estate industry and profession.

The commissioners are generally required to have at least five years of real estate experience; they are usually real estate managing brokers. Each commissioner serves on a part-time basis for a six-year term. At least two commissioners must be from west of the Cascade mountain range, and two must be from east of the Cascades.

The Commission prepares and conducts the real estate license examinations. It is also authorized to hold educational conferences for the benefit of the real estate industry.

The Attorney General

The state Attorney General is the Director's legal advisor on matters relating to the license law. The Attorney General also acts as the attorney for the Director in any legal proceedings involving the Real Estate Section.

Real Estate Licenses

By requiring real estate agents to be licensed, the state tries to ensure that they have at least a minimum level of competence in handling real estate transactions. Licenses also serve as a tool for enforcement of real estate regulations; if an agent fails to comply with the law, her license can be suspended or taken away altogether.

When a License is Required

It's unlawful to perform real estate brokerage services without first obtaining the appropriate license. The license law defines **real estate brokerage services** to include any of the following services offered or rendered directly or indirectly to another, or on behalf of another for compensation or the promise or expectation of compensation, or by a licensee on the licensee's own behalf:

1. Listing, selling, purchasing, exchanging, optioning, leasing, or renting of real estate, or any real property interest therein; or any interest in a cooperative; or any interest in a floating home or other floating on-water residence.
2. Negotiating or offering to negotiate, either directly or indirectly, the purchase, sale, exchange, lease, or rental of real estate, or any real property interest therein; or any interest in a cooperative; or any interest in a floating home or other floating on-water residence.
3. Listing, selling, purchasing, exchanging, optioning, leasing, renting, or negotiating the purchase, sale, lease, or exchange of a manufactured or mobile home in conjunction with the purchase, sale, lease, exchange, or rental of the land upon which the manufactured or mobile home is or will be located.
4. Advertising or holding oneself out to the public by any solicitation or representation that one is engaged in real estate brokerage services.
5. Advising, counseling, or consulting buyers, sellers, landlords, or tenants in connection with a real estate transaction.

6. Issuing a broker price opinion (an oral or written report of property value that is prepared by a real estate licensee and is not an appraisal).
7. Collecting, holding, or disbursing funds in connection with the negotiating, listing, selling, purchasing, exchanging, optioning, leasing, or renting of real estate or any real property interest.
8. Performing property management services, which include marketing, leasing, or renting of real property; the physical, administrative, or financial maintenance of real property; or the supervision of such actions.

The main thrust of this definition is that it applies to anyone engaged in any of the listed activities: 1) on behalf of another person, and 2) for compensation. However, the law states that the definition also applies to "a licensee [acting] on the licensee's own behalf." Thus, real estate agents are required to comply with the license law even when they are buying, selling, or leasing property for themselves, not just when they are representing others.

The license law covers **business opportunities** as well as more traditional real estate transactions. The term business opportunity refers to the sale or acquisition of a business (either an existing business or the equipment, supplies, and services needed to start a new one, as in a franchise arrangement). When a transfer of an interest in real property is included in the transaction, the agent or agents involved must be real estate licensees.

Also note that the definition of brokerage services may include a person who sells a manufactured home before it has become attached to real property, if it is sold or leased at the same time as the land where the home is located or will be placed.

Exemptions from Licensing Requirements

Some people are not required to have a real estate license, even when their activities fall within the definition of real estate brokerage services. The license law specifically exempts the following people from the licensing requirement:

1. Anyone buying or leasing property for herself or selling property she owns or co-owns; this exemption also covers employees acting on behalf of their employers or other persons acting on behalf of a group to which they belong.
2. An authorized attorney in fact acting without compensation.
3. An attorney at law, when practicing law.
4. A receiver, trustee in bankruptcy, executor, administrator, guardian, or personal representative, when acting in that capacity; any person acting under court order; or a trustee acting on behalf of a trust or selling under a deed of trust.
5. A secretary, assistant, bookkeeper, accountant, or other office personnel performing purely clerical duties.
6. Employees of a city, county, or other government, when involved in acquiring property for their employer.
7. The owner or manager of a self-storage facility renting units in the facility.
8. A person who provides referrals to real estate licensees but is not involved in negotiation or execution of documents, and whose compensation is not contingent on the licensee receiving compensation.

9. Certified public accountants, as long as they do not promote the purchase, listing, sale, exchange, optioning, leasing, or renting of a specific property interest. (This prohibition against promoting the transfer of a specific property interest also applies to exemptions 10, 11, and 12.)
10. Title companies, escrow companies, attorneys, financial institutions, or other persons or entities acting as escrow agents.
11. Investment counselors.
12. Community association managers.
13. A person who is employed or retained by a property owner or a designated or managing broker to perform only limited property management tasks, such as delivering or receiving lease applications or leases; receiving security deposits, rent payments, or related payments; showing rental units or executing leases under the direct instruction of the owner or the real estate firm; providing information about rental units, leases, applications, security deposits, and rents; or carrying out administrative, clerical, financial, or maintenance tasks.

As we said, the license law defining real estate brokerage services applies to those who act on behalf of another and for compensation. Thus, someone who acts on her own behalf in a real estate transaction is exempt from the licensing requirement; this is the first exemption on the list above.

> **Example:** Matilda Thorn owns several pieces of property: three single-family homes, a duplex, an apartment building, and two vacant lots. If she decides to sell one of these properties, she can do so without having to obtain a real estate license.

In addition, someone acting on behalf of another but without compensation is also exempt; this is the second exemption on the list, the one for an authorized attorney in fact. An attorney in fact is not necessarily a lawyer—it is anyone a principal appoints to act as her agent through a document called a power of attorney. As long as the attorney in fact is not compensated for services rendered, he is allowed to engage in the activities of a real estate agent without a license.

> **Example:** Suppose Matilda from the previous example is old and unwell. She gives her nephew, Truman, a power of attorney, which authorizes Truman to sell Matilda's property for her. As long as Truman is acting without compensation, he doesn't need a real estate license to sell the property.

Unlicensed Assistants. The Real Estate Commission has issued detailed guidelines (available at the Department of Licensing website) concerning the activities that an unlicensed assistant working for a real estate licensee is and is not allowed to engage in. Here are some of the types of tasks an unlicensed assistant is allowed to perform:

- providing information about a real estate listing or transaction, as written and approved by the licensee;
- writing and placing advertising;
- gathering market analysis information;
- driving people to properties;

- greeting people at an open house and distributing pre-printed material; and
- making keys, installing keyboxes, and placing signs on property.

Activities that an unlicensed assistant cannot perform include answering questions or interpreting information about a property or its condition (except by providing answers from pre-printed material prepared by a licensee); negotiating prices or other terms of sale; filling in legal forms; and handling trust funds. Furthermore, an unlicensed assistant may not perform any act with the intent to circumvent the license law, or that results in a circumvention of the law.

Out-of-State Licensees. A real estate licensee who is licensed in another state may handle transactions concerning commercial real estate in Washington without obtaining a Washington license. (For the purposes of this rule, commercial real estate is any property other than residential property with up to four dwelling units.) However, the out-of-state licensee must have a written agreement with and work in cooperation with a real estate firm that is licensed in Washington. The Washington firm's name must be included on all advertising, and the Washington firm must have custody of the records for the out-of-state licensee's Washington transactions. The records must be maintained for at least three years, just like an in-state firm's records.

The out-of-state licensee must provide the Washington firm's designated broker with a copy of a current, active license in good standing, and must consent to Washington jurisdiction for any legal disputes that may arise from the transaction.

Types of Licenses

There are two basic types of real estate licenses in Washington: broker and managing broker. Applicants for these real estate licenses must satisfy age and educational requirements and pass an examination. In addition, applicants for a managing broker's license are required to satisfy experience requirements. All education and experience requirements must be met before applying for the exam.

In addition to these real estate licenses for individuals, each real estate firm must also have a real estate license.

Broker's License. A broker's license can be issued only to an individual. The license authorizes the broker to work with and represent a real estate firm. A broker may represent only one firm at a time, must be supervised by the firm's designated broker or a managing broker, and is not authorized to manage a branch office. A broker with less than two years of experience is subject to a heightened level of supervision, including a supervisor's review of brokerage service contracts prepared by the broker within five business days after they are signed by all of the parties.

An applicant for a broker's license must:

1. be at least 18 years old;
2. have a high school diploma or the equivalent;

3. complete 90 clock hours of prelicense education: a 60 clock-hour course in real estate fundamentals and a 30 clock-hour course in real estate practices; and
4. pass the broker's examination.

Both prelicense courses must be completed within two years before applying for the broker's license examination.

The Director of the Department of Licensing may waive the 90 clock-hour requirement if the applicant has completed the equivalent educational course work at an institution of higher learning or a degree-granting institution.

Managing Broker's License. Like a broker's license, a managing broker's license may be issued only to an individual. A managing broker is authorized to work with and represent a real estate firm, to manage other licensees, and to manage a branch office of the firm. A managing broker may also be appointed as a firm's designated broker. A managing broker can be affiliated with only one firm at a time.

An applicant for a managing broker's license must:

1. be at least 18 years old;
2. have a high school diploma or the equivalent;
3. have at least three years of experience within the last five years as a full-time real estate broker in Washington or another state with similar licensing requirements;
4. complete 90 clock hours of approved real estate education courses within the previous three years, including one 30-hour course in advanced real estate law, one 30-hour course in brokerage management, and one 30-hour course in business management; and
5. pass the managing broker's examination.

An applicant who lacks three years of experience as a broker may be allowed to take the managing broker's exam if the Director determines that the applicant has other education or experience that is a satisfactory substitute.

The 90 clock hours of approved courses required for a managing broker's license are in addition to any courses the Department required the applicant to take for other reasons. For example, if the applicant had to take a 30-hour course to fulfill his continuing education requirement for license renewal, those 30 hours cannot be counted as part of the 90 hours required for a managing broker's license.

As with a broker's license, the Director may waive the 90 clock-hour requirement if the applicant is deemed to have completed equivalent course work at an institution of higher learning or a degree-granting institution.

Firm License. A real estate firm is a business entity that is licensed to conduct real estate brokerage activities in Washington. A firm is authorized to employ managing brokers and brokers. Managing brokers and brokers are sometimes referred to as their firm's **affiliated**

licensees. The law defines affiliated licensees as "the natural persons licensed as brokers or managing brokers employed by a real estate firm and who are licensed to represent the firm in the performance of any of the acts" for which a real estate license is required.

To obtain a license, the firm must disclose the names of all owners and anyone else who has the ability to control the operational and financial decisions of the firm. The firm must also name a designated broker who will have the authority to act for the firm.

Designated broker. As just mentioned, a firm license is issued to a business entity. This may be a corporation, a limited liability company, a general or limited partnership, or a sole proprietorship. The firm must name one individual who will be responsible for all of its real estate activities. This person is called the firm's **designated broker**. A designated broker must be licensed as a managing broker, and she must have a controlling interest in the firm (in other words, authority over the firm's operational and financial decisions). For instance, the designated broker could be an officer in the corporation or a partner in the partnership. A person who owns a real estate firm that is organized as a sole proprietorship would be that firm's designated broker.

The designated broker must obtain a designated broker endorsement for his managing broker's license from the Department of Licensing.

Despite the fact that a managing broker can be the affiliated licensee of only one firm at a time, a managing broker may serve as the designated broker for more than one firm at a time, so long as he has a controlling interest in each of the firms.

A real estate firm's designated broker has the final responsibility for all activities performed by the firm. This includes ensuring that the firm's records are up-to-date and available to state auditors, that trust accounts are accurate and reconciled, and that procedures are in place to ensure compliance with all laws. A designated broker may delegate these duties to managing brokers and branch managers, but these delegations must be in writing and signed. Even if these duties are delegated to another, the designated broker is still responsible for them.

When a firm's designated broker changes, both the outgoing and incoming designated brokers must submit a statement that lists all outstanding client trust fund liabilities, lists pending transactions, and certifies that sufficient funds are held in trust to cover all client liabilities. If a firm closes down, the designated broker is responsible for submitting a closing firm affidavit to the Department.

Regulation of Business Practices

In this section, we'll discuss the many provisions of the license law that regulate the conduct of a brokerage business. (We'll emphasize the impact of these provisions by providing some summaries of recent disciplinary actions taken by the Department of Licensing against real estate agents.) These laws concern:

- the relationship between licensees and their clients and customers;
- the relationship between a firm's designated broker and the affiliated licensees;

- maintaining offices, trust accounts, and business records; and
- how real estate transactions are handled.

Supervision and Licensee Responsibilities

A designated broker is responsible for the proper supervision of all of his firm's licensees (brokers, managing brokers, and branch managers), whether they are independent contractors or employees. For branch offices, both the branch manager and the designated broker are responsible for all licensees working at the branch.

Any licensee who supervises other licensees must be a managing broker. A broker cannot be put in a position of supervising other brokers. For instance, if several licensees form a "team" within a firm, the licensee who supervises the team must be a managing broker, not merely a broker.

Liability for Violations of Affiliated Licensees. A designated broker who fails to supervise his affiliated licensees properly may be held responsible for their actions. If an affiliated licensee violates the license law, the Director may suspend or revoke the designated broker's license. The same sanctions could be imposed on a branch manager or any other managing broker who failed to fulfill supervisory responsibilities in the case.

Broker's Responsibilities. The Director's regulations include lists of specific responsibilities for each type of licensee—broker, managing broker, and designated broker. A broker's responsibilities include (but are not limited to):

- assuring that all brokerage services in which she participated comply with the license law, the Real Estate Brokerage Relationships Act (REBRA), and the Uniform Regulation of Business and Professions Act (URBPA);
- cooperating with the Department of Licensing in an investigation or audit;
- being knowledgeable of the license law, REBRA, and URBPA;
- keeping the Department informed of her current mailing address;
- following her firm's written policy regarding referral of home inspectors;
- being appropriately licensed;
- delivering brokerage service contracts and other transaction documents to the designated broker or another supervising managing broker within two business days of mutual acceptance by the parties; and
- following laws regarding handling of trust funds, advertising, and modifying or terminating contracts on behalf of the firm.

A broker with less than two years of experience is subject to one additional responsibility: working under a heightened degree of supervision. This means the broker must participate in all required reviews of contracts and services by a supervisor (the designated broker, or a managing broker appointed to supervise the broker); obtain a supervisor's advice or assistance regarding matters beyond the broker's expertise; submit evidence of completion of required education courses to a supervisor; and submit all contracts, documents, and funds to a supervisor in accordance with the firm's policies. Brokerage service contracts prepared by a broker with less than two years of experience must be reviewed by a supervisor within five business days after mutual acceptance by the parties.

Managing Broker's Responsibilities. A managing broker has all of the same responsibilities as a broker, and may also have additional ones delegated to him by the designated broker. Delegated responsibilities may include ensuring that:

- monthly trust account reconciliations and trial balances are completed accurately and show that the account(s) are in balance;
- policies and procedures are in place to safely handle trust funds or property;
- affiliated licensees are adequately supervised;
- licensees submit their contracts and other transaction documents as required;
- contracts are reviewed by a supervisor in a timely manner, and records of these reviews are kept;
- all of the firm's records are properly maintained;
- the firm's offices and records are accessible to the Director's representatives; and
- firm policies on referring home inspectors and the supervision of licensees are followed.

A managing broker who has been designated as a branch manager is responsible for all activity within that branch office, including supervision of all brokers and managing brokers, with heightened supervision for brokers with less than two years of experience. The branch manager is responsible for hiring, releasing, and transferring licensees to the branch.

Designated Broker's Responsibilities. A firm's designated broker has additional levels of responsibility beyond those of a managing broker. The designated broker is responsible for ultimate oversight of the entire firm. This includes:

- maintaining up-to-date written agreements detailing any delegation of supervisory authority (such as to a branch manager), signed by all parties to the agreement; and
- maintaining written policies on the referral of home inspectors, the supervision of all affiliated brokers, managing brokers, and branch managers, and the review of brokerage service contracts prepared by brokers with less than two years of experience.

Affiliation with a Firm

A licensed broker or managing broker must be affiliated with a real estate firm in order for his license to be active. A broker or managing broker isn't allowed to engage in real estate activities except as a representative of a firm and under the supervision of a designated broker. The designated broker has custody of the licenses of her affiliated licensees.

The relationship between a firm and an affiliated licensee may be terminated at any time by either party. Upon termination of the relationship, the broker's or managing broker's license remains inactive until the licensee joins a new firm.

Previously, when an affiliation was terminated, the designated broker was required to surrender the broker's or managing broker's license by mailing or delivering it to the Department of Licensing. Now termination of an affiliation is done online. A licensee who is leaving a firm reports the change by updating her license at the Department's website. This immediately places the license on inactive status.

When an inactive licensee is going to join a new firm, the new firm must send an online request to the licensee, who then confirms online that he wishes to become affiliated with that firm. The licensee can begin working for the new firm immediately, though a paper copy of the license showing the new affiliation won't arrive for two to three weeks.

When a broker or managing broker has been terminated because of conduct that would be grounds for disciplinary action, the designated broker must send the Director a statement of the facts surrounding the termination.

If a firm is closing, the designated broker must provide a closing firm affidavit to the Department within five business days. The designated broker must also give written notice to all parties with pending transactions, and ensure that brokerage service contracts are terminated or transferred to another real estate firm with the parties' written permission. All of the former affiliated licensees will be on inactive status until they join other firms.

Office Requirements

A firm licensed in Washington is required to maintain an office or records repository in this state. The location must be accessible to Department of Licensing representatives. The office must be identified by a sign displaying the name of the firm or its assumed name.

The firm's license must be prominently displayed at the address appearing on the license, along with the licenses of all of the firm's affiliated licensees. If the firm has more than one office, the firm's license and the designated broker's license are displayed in the main office, and the licenses of affiliated licensees are displayed in the office where they work (which should be the address shown on the license).

If the location of a firm's office changes, within ten days after the move the designated broker must submit a change of address application, return all licenses (the firm's and those of any affiliated licensees), and pay a fee. The Department will issue licenses for the new address.

Two Businesses in the Same Office. It isn't unusual for a firm to be involved in other business activities that are related to, or at least not in conflict with, its real estate brokerage business. For example, a brokerage firm might also act as an escrow agent or mortgage broker. A firm is allowed to operate two businesses out of the same office if the brokerage business is kept apart from other business activities and has completely separate records.

Branch Offices. There is no limit on the number of branch offices a firm can have, but every branch office must receive a duplicate license. Every branch office is also required to have a branch manager, who must be a managing broker.

A separate license is not required for a branch office where sales activity concerns only a particular subdivision or tract. This exemption applies only if the subdivision is within 35 miles of a licensed office.

Dual-State Licensees. A real estate licensee who is actively licensed in another state as well as in Washington and has an office in that other state isn't required to have her own office here. However, she must maintain a trust account in a Washington depository and keep records of her Washington transactions at a registered location in this state.

The licensee must notify the Department of Licensing of the location of the records and allow representatives of the Department access to them. The licensee is also required to give the parties involved in a transaction access to the records. The license of a dual-state licensee must be displayed at the same place that the records are kept.

If a real estate firm headquartered in another state seeks to operate in Washington, it must obtain a firm license here. As with any other firm, the designated broker must qualify as a managing broker in Washington and have a controlling interest in the firm.

Advertising

The Department of Licensing has published a booklet (available at its website) with guidelines for advertising by real estate licensees. As the booklet explains, advertising isn't only published ads but "any activity, public notice, or representation" that promotes a real estate licensee's services or particular properties. For example, business cards, letterhead, yard signs, and open houses are considered forms of advertising. Advertising by real estate licensees must be truthful and not misleading, and it also must meet the requirements described below.

Firm's Name Required. The license law requires all advertising used by a licensee to include the real estate firm's name as licensed (that is, as it appears on the firm's license) in a clear and conspicuous manner. An ad without the firm's name, which is sometimes called a **blind ad**, violates the license law. There's one exception to this rule: if a licensee is advertising her own property for sale or lease, the firm's name doesn't have to appear in the ad. The ad must disclose that the seller or landlord is a real estate licensee, however.

Before applying for a firm license, the designated broker must obtain approval for the firm's name from the Department of Licensing. A firm may not use a name that is deceptively similar to that of another licensee or firm, or one that creates the impression that the firm is a nonprofit organization, research organization, or public agency.

A firm may use more than one name in conducting its business, as long as it obtains a separate license for each name. To get a license for an additional name, the designated broker submits an assumed name application to the Department of Licensing. (Assumed name licenses expire at the same time as the firm's main license.) When a firm has more than one licensed name, advertising placed by affiliated licensees will be compliant as long as it includes one of those names.

A broker or managing broker may advertise her own practice using a name or brand without obtaining a license for an assumed name. For instance, some brokers create their own "team" under the broader umbrella of the firm for which they work. The team members can use the team name in their advertising if they also include the firm's licensed name (or assumed name) in the advertising. The team name must not suggest that the team is a legal entity separate from the firm; for example, it can't include a designation such as "LLC" or "Inc." or the words "realty," "real estate," or "firm." The firm's designated broker must give written approval for use of the unlicensed name or brand.

Advertising and the Internet. The Department of Licensing's booklet includes guidelines to help licensees use the Internet to promote their business while avoiding violations of the license law's advertising rules.

Licensees are required to fully disclose their licensed status in Internet advertising and other online communications with the public. A full disclosure includes the licensee's own name (as licensed) and the licensed name of the firm with which he is affiliated. If the firm is not licensed in the state of Washington, the disclosure should also include the city and state in which the firm is located.

Note that once a licensee has established an agency relationship with a member of the public, a full disclosure isn't necessary in every online message the licensee sends that person, as long as the licensee made a full disclosure before providing or offering to provide real estate services.

The guidelines include suggestions on how to meet the requirement of full disclosure for the following types of online communications:

- **Website:** Each viewable page on a website owned or controlled by a licensee should include either a full disclosure or a link (via a single click) to a full disclosure.
- **Email, newsgroups, discussion lists, bulletin boards:** These should include a full disclosure at the beginning or end of each message.
- **Instant messages:** A full disclosure is not necessary in this format if the licensee made the disclosure in another format before providing or offering to provide real estate services.
- **Chat:** A full disclosure should be given before providing or offering to provide real estate services during the chat session, or the disclosure should appear in text visible on the same web page that contains the chat session, if the licensee controls the website.
- **Social media:** A full disclosure should be prominently displayed and be no more than one click away from any viewable page.
- **Multimedia advertising (such as executable email attachments):** A full disclosure should be visible as part of the advertising message.
- **Banner ads:** Each ad should link (via a single click) to a website that has a full disclosure, unless the banner ad itself has a full disclosure.

The Department of Licensing's advertising guidelines also offer the following advice on prospecting online:

- If listings are maintained on a website, they should be removed in a timely manner when they have expired.
- If a licensee submits listing information to a third-party site, she should provide written communication of any change of listing status to the publisher in a timely manner.
- A licensee should not advertise the listings of other licensees without their written permission. If permission is given, the licensee should not alter the online display or any informational part of the listing without the written permission of the listing broker.
- Metatags are descriptive words hidden in a website's code that search engines use to index the website. Occasionally, a website owner will insert the name of one or more competitors into the metatags, so that when a potential customer searches for a competitor's site, the owner's site will also come up as a match. Licensees should avoid this practice, as courts have ruled that it may constitute trademark infringement.
- Licensees should periodically review the advertising and marketing information on their website to make sure that it is current and not misleading.

Trust Accounts

Any funds that a licensee temporarily keeps on behalf of clients or customers are considered **trust funds**. They have been entrusted to the licensee and may not be used for personal benefit. Examples include earnest money deposits, tenant security deposits, and advance fees (fees a client pays before the licensee provides the services agreed on).

Unless its affiliated licensees never hold trust funds (for example, if earnest money deposits are delivered directly to escrow instead), a real estate firm must maintain one or more trust accounts in a recognized financial institution in Washington State. Trust funds may never be placed in the firm's general business account or in any licensee's personal bank account, so that they are not **commingled** (mixed) with the firm's or the licensee's own money. A firm's trust account should be opened in the name of the firm as licensed, and specifically designated as a trust account.

All funds given to a real estate firm to hold until a transaction closes (such as earnest money) or until paid to a client (such as rents collected) must be deposited in a trust account no later than the **first banking day after receipt**, unless otherwise specified in the license law. Saturdays, Sundays, and legal holidays are not considered banking days in this context.

Interest-Bearing Accounts. With the exception of property management trust accounts, firms' trust accounts are required to be interest-bearing accounts that allow withdrawals without delay (other than any minimum notice period required by banking regulations).

A firm is required to put deposits of $10,000 or less into a pooled account called a **housing trust fund account**. (It's described as a pooled account because funds from multiple clients or customers are pooled together in a single account.) The interest that accrues on this account, after deducting reasonable bank charges, must be paid to the state Treasurer.

It will be divided between the Washington Housing Trust Fund (which will receive 75%) and the Real Estate Education Account (25%).

For deposits over $10,000, the client or customer who is turning the funds over to the firm has a choice. With the written consent of the parties, the funds can be deposited in the pooled account, in which case the interest will be paid to the state. Alternatively, the firm can establish a separate trust account for the deposit, with the interest to be paid to the client or customer to whom the funds belong. The firm must inform the client or customer of these alternatives in writing.

Property management trust accounts. The rules just outlined do not apply to trust funds that a licensee handles in property management transactions (such as rents or tenant security deposits). Property management trust accounts don't have to be interest-bearing accounts, and property management trust funds don't have to be placed in the firm's pooled account. However, a property management account can be interest-bearing, if the firm's written management agreement with the property owner provides for that, and if the firm follows certain special rules in the license law. If any commissions or property management fees are to be paid out of the trust account directly to the firm, they must be removed from the trust account at least once a month.

A firm that manages several rental properties for different owners does not have to open an individual trust account for each one, if all of the owners assign the interest accruing on their funds to the firm. When the management agreement between the owner and firm terminates, any trust funds associated with that owner that are left in the account will be disbursed according to the agreement's terms; security deposits are disbursed either to the owner or the next property management firm.

Trust Account Procedures. A firm must establish a system of records and procedures that provides an audit trail for all funds received and disbursed, identified to each client. The firm can either follow the procedures that are set forth in the Director's regulations, or submit an alternative system to the Department of Licensing for approval. The system can be either manual or computerized.

Only trust funds may be kept in the trust account, with one exception: a "minimal amount" of firm funds may be used to open the account or maintain a minimum balance to keep the account open. If a client or customer has assigned the interest on a trust account to the firm (in writing), the firm must make arrangements with the financial institution to credit the interest to the firm's general account.

DOL Disciplinary Action Involving Trust Fund Violations

Finding: During the course of an audit, numerous recordkeeping and trust accounting violations were noted, including: shortages in trust accounts, incomplete property management files and failure to maintain trial balances.

Action: License suspended for 2 years (sanction stayed for 3 years) and a $5,000 fine.

Trust Account Disbursements. As a general rule, a firm may not make any disbursements from a trust account before closing, or before a condition in the purchase and sale agreement has been fulfilled. There are three important exceptions to that rule, however. Funds may be disbursed:

1. with the written consent of all parties to the transaction;
2. when the transaction fails to close, if the purchase and sale agreement provides for disbursement without a written release in this situation; or
3. to the closing agent named in the agreement far enough in advance so that the checks will clear by the closing date.

A firm may not pay its own business expenses directly out of a trust account. That includes bank charges for the maintenance of the trust account; these should be paid out of the firm's general business account, not the trust account itself. If a client owes the firm money, the funds must first be transferred from the trust account to the firm's general business account before the firm can use them for business expenses.

If the parties to a transaction cannot agree on who is entitled to the trust funds, the firm must notify all the parties of its intent to disburse the funds. The notice must include names and addresses of the parties, amount of money held, to whom it will be disbursed, and the planned date of disbursement.

Commissions Paid from Trust Accounts. Commissions payable to the firm and to other cooperating firms may be paid directly from the trust account. A separate check must be drawn for each commission after the transaction closes.

Commissions the firm owes to its affiliated licensees may not be paid directly out of the trust account. These commissions are handled the same way as the firm's business expenses. Funds must first be transferred to the firm's general business account, and then the firm can pay its affiliated licensees with checks drawn on that account.

Records

The license law requires a firm to keep adequate records of the real estate transactions its licensees handle for at least **three years** after closing. (However, it's best to keep records for even longer, since the statute of limitations for some claims against a firm may not run out for several more years. In addition, other state laws and regulations might require firms to keep records for longer than three years.)

Although a designated broker may delegate recordkeeping duties to someone else, she is still responsible for the custody and accuracy of the required records. She must make the records available to auditors from the Department of Licensing, and provide copies to the Director upon demand.

The firm must maintain an up-to-date log of all agreements and contracts for brokerage services that are submitted by the firm's licensees, and also retain a copy of these documents on file.

For each transaction, the firm must have a **transaction folder** that includes all of the following that apply:

- the listing agreement,
- the purchase and sale agreement,
- the lease or rental agreement,
- any modifications or addenda to those agreements,
- the settlement statement, and
- all other agreements or documents (such as correspondence and receipts) relevant to the transaction.

As we discussed, brokers with less than two years of experience must have their contracts reviewed by the designated broker or a managing broker. Written records of these reviews must be kept on file.

In addition, the firm is required to keep the following **trust account records**:

- a duplicate receipt book or cash receipts journal showing all receipts;
- prenumbered trust account checks with a check register, cash disbursements journal, or check stubs;
- validated duplicate bank deposit slips;
- a client's ledger summarizing all receipts and disbursements for each transaction, property management account, or contract or mortgage collection account;
- separate ledger sheets for each tenant, lessee, vendee, or mortgagor;
- a ledger for interest on the firm's pooled housing trust fund account; and
- reconciled bank statements and canceled checks, including voided checks. (Trust account checks must be prenumbered, so even voided checks must be kept to show that all checks are accounted for.)

All records for recent transactions must be kept at a licensed office of the firm. Records for transactions that have been closed for at least one year can be kept at one central storage facility, as long as the facility is in Washington. A list of these older transactions must be maintained at a licensed office of the firm, and the records must be retrievable at the request of the Department of Licensing.

Records may be stored electronically, so long as the medium doesn't allow the documents to be modified and is nonerasable. The firm must have equipment available at its office to view, retrieve, and print the documents, if Department representatives show up to inspect them.

DOL Disciplinary Actions Involving Recordkeeping Violations

Spokane

Finding: Several audits found violations of Departmental rules. Licensee was responsible for supervising an office manager who stole cash from rental deposits, which resulted in additional failures to comply with recordkeeping rules.

Action: License suspended for 1 year (stayed for 5 years), and fined $2,500.

Burlington

Finding: Failed to notify department of a civil judgment, change of business address; failed to display her license at her business address or retain real estate records at her business address of record...

Action: License suspended for 6 months.

Tacoma

Finding: Altered rental agreements signed by unlicensed property manager to reflect his name as property manager. Failed to provide office access to the public. Didn't prepare monthly trial balances, ledgers, and reconciliations. Interfered with the DOL investigation by destroying and altering records in anticipation of an audit...

Action: License revoked for 8 years.

Commissions

A valid real estate license is a prerequisite to collecting a commission (or any form of compensation) for brokerage services. A licensee cannot sue for a commission unless there is proof that she was properly licensed before she:

- offered to perform any act or service that requires a license, or
- procured a promise or contract for the payment of compensation for such an act or service.

This rule applies to lawsuits brought by a licensee against a firm (if a broker sues a firm for his share of a commission, for example), and also to lawsuits brought by a firm against a client.

A Washington firm may share a commission with or pay compensation to any firm that is licensed in the United States or in a foreign jurisdiction with a real estate regulatory program (such as Canada). This includes compensation owed due to a transaction with a licensed manufactured or mobile home dealer, where the purchase or lease of land is part of the transaction.

A firm may share commissions with, or pay other compensation to, its own affiliated licensees. However, a firm may not pay any compensation directly to a broker or managing broker licensed with another firm. Payment must be made to the other firm, which then pays its broker or managing broker.

Licensees may receive compensation only from their firm. They cannot collect a commission directly from a client or from another firm. They also are not allowed to share their compensation with other licensees. If two brokers are going to split a commission, for example, the split must be handled by their firm (or firms).

Listing and management agreements are the property of the firm, not the licensee. In other words, a broker who changes to a new firm in mid-transaction cannot bring the agreement to the new firm with her; it belongs to the old firm.

Referral Fees

It's not uncommon for one real estate licensee or firm to pay another licensee or firm for referring a potential customer or client. This type of referral fee between licensees does not violate the license law.

> **Example:** Sheri, a broker with Whitehall Realty, specializes in commercial properties. When a potential client, Jordan, asks her about residential listings, she refers him to Larry, a broker with ABC Homes. In return, Larry agrees to pay Sheri one-third of any commission he receives from working with Jordan. As long as this payment is handled through their firms, it's legal.

Such a payment also does not violate RESPA, the federal Real Estate Settlement Procedures Act (see Chapter 10). Although RESPA generally prohibits referral fees paid by one settlement service provider to another, it specifically exempts referral fees paid by one real estate licensee to another real estate licensee.

A real estate licensee or firm may also pay a referral fee to an unlicensed person in exchange for referring a potential customer or client. However, as we mentioned earlier, the real estate license law prohibits such a fee if it is contingent on the firm actually receiving compensation.

Handling Transactions

The Director's regulations include several rules governing how licensees serve their clients and customers in a real estate transaction, from the negotiation of the purchase and sale agreement through closing.

Offers and Document Copies. When involved in negotiations between a buyer and a seller, a licensee must present all written communications, including offers and counteroffers, from one party to the other.

A licensee is also responsible for providing clients and customers with a copy of any document they sign (the listing agreement, the purchase and sale agreement, escrow instructions, disclosure forms, and so on) within a reasonable time after they sign it.

DOL Disciplinary Actions Involving Failure to Present Offers

Finding: Licensee:
- failed to present several offers to the sellers of property;
- made agency disclosures that were inconsistent and confusing; and
- failed to supervise the activities of an agent in her office.

Action: License revoked for 3 years.

Finding: Licensee:
- failed to present several offers to the sellers of property; and
- made inconsistent and confusing agency disclosures.

Action: License revoked for 3 years.

> **Finding:** Licensee failed to submit an offer to the sellers for the sale of property she listed for them.
>
> **Action:** License suspended for 5 months.

Earnest Money Deposits. A buyer's earnest money deposit may be in the form of a check that's payable to the real estate firm as licensed, so that it can be deposited in the firm's trust account. As explained earlier in the chapter, trust funds, including earnest money, ordinarily must be deposited by the end of the first banking day after receipt. But the firm is allowed to hold an earnest money check without depositing it for a specific length of time or until a particular event occurs (for example, the seller accepts or rejects the offer), if that is what the purchase and sale agreement directs the firm to do.

In some transactions, however, the agreement provides for someone other than the firm to hold the earnest money deposit until closing; that person is usually an escrow agent. In that case, the buyer's check must be promptly delivered to the agreed-upon person as directed in the agreement. A dated receipt documenting the delivery must be included in the transaction folder.

The licensee who first receives the earnest money deposit is responsible for handling the funds in compliance with the license law (although of course the designated broker has ultimate responsibility). This licensee is usually the selling agent, who takes the earnest money check from the buyer. By law, the check should be made out to the licensee's firm unless the parties have agreed that the deposit will be delivered directly to the escrow agent or another party. (Delivery to the escrow agent is the choice in most transactions.)

It is a violation of the license law to accept an earnest money deposit in the form of a promissory note, or some other form that is not considered the equivalent of cash, unless the licensee discloses that fact to the seller before the seller accepts the offer. The purchase and sale agreement must also state the form of the earnest money.

Expeditious Performance. When a purchase and sale agreement or other contract obligates a licensee to perform a certain act (for example, ordering an inspection), that act must be performed as expeditiously as possible. Under the license law, a licensee's intentional or negligent delay is considered to be "conduct...that demonstrates bad faith, dishonesty, untrustworthiness or incompetency," and is therefore grounds for disciplinary action.

Closings. The licensee is responsible for ensuring that the parties to every transaction receive a complete, detailed settlement statement at closing. The licensee isn't required to prepare the statement (most are prepared by escrow agents—see Chapter 10), but making sure the parties receive it is one of the licensee's duties under the license law. The licensee also has to keep a copy of the settlement statement in the transaction folder, even if it was prepared by someone else.

Washington's Escrow Agent Registration Act allows a real estate licensee to close a transaction in which she is already representing the buyer or the seller (or both), if the licensee is designated as the closing agent in the purchase and sale agreement. Unless the licensee is a licensed escrow agent, however, she can't charge either party any fee (beyond her brokerage commission) for closing services. Only licensed escrow agents and attorneys can charge a fee for closing real estate transactions. (See Chapter 10 for information about the Washington Escrow Agent Registration Act.)

Property Management Agreements. A firm must have a written property management agreement with the owner or owners of each property it manages. The license law requires the agreement to state all of the following:

- the property manager's compensation;
- the type of property managed (for example, apartment complex or office building);
- the number of units or square footage;
- whether the firm is authorized to collect and disburse funds, and if so, for what purposes;
- whether the firm is authorized to hold and disburse tenant security deposits, and if so, how; and
- how often the firm is to provide summary statements to the owner.

Note that it isn't necessary to describe the property's physical condition in the agreement.

A **summary statement** is a brief report showing the property's financial status over a certain period of time, such as one month or one quarter. The firm must provide a summary statement to the owner or owners for each property managed as often as the management agreement requires. A summary statement shows:

- the balance carried forward from the last statement;
- the total rent receipts;
- other itemized receipts (for example, from laundry or vending machines);
- contributions from the owner;
- itemized expenditures;
- the ending balance; and
- the number of units or square footage rented.

The firm must keep a copy of the management agreement and all summary statements in its records. The management agreement can be modified only in writing, and the modification must be signed by both the licensee representing the firm and the owner. For all rental properties managed by a firm, the leases or rental agreements must be in writing.

A firm may provide other services to the owner of a property that is being managed, such as janitorial and repair services, with the owner's consent. If the firm uses another company to provide these services, it must make a full written disclosure of its relationship with that company and disclose the fees that are charged.

Disciplinary Action

The Director of the Department of Licensing has the authority to investigate the actions of any real estate licensee and impose penalties, including license suspension or revocation. This is true regardless of whether the licensee was acting on behalf of another or on her own account, and regardless of whether her license is active or inactive.

Grounds for Disciplinary Action

A licensee or a license applicant may be subject to disciplinary action either for engaging in unprofessional conduct in violation of the **Uniform Regulation of Business and Professions Act** (URBPA) or for engaging in one of the activities specifically listed in the license law as grounds for disciplinary action. (The Uniform Regulation of Business and Professions Act applies to all types of professionals licensed by the state of Washington, not just to real estate licensees.)

Unprofessional conduct, as defined in the URBPA, includes any of the following conduct, acts, or conditions:

1. the commission of any act involving moral turpitude, dishonesty, or corruption relating to real estate activities, regardless of whether the act constitutes a crime;
2. misrepresentation or concealment of a material fact in obtaining or reinstating a license;
3. false, deceptive, or misleading advertising;
4. incompetence, negligence, or malpractice that harms another or creates an unreasonable risk of harm;
5. having any business or professional license suspended, revoked, or restricted by any government entity;
6. failure to cooperate with the Department of Licensing in the course of an investigation, audit, or inspection;
7. failure to comply with an order issued by the Director;
8. violating any license law provision or rule made by the Director;
9. aiding or abetting an unlicensed person to perform real estate activities that require a license;
10. practice or operation of a business or profession beyond the scope of practice or operation as defined by law;
11. any type of misrepresentation in the conduct of real estate activities;
12. failure to adequately supervise or oversee staff, whether employees or independent contractors, to the extent that consumers may be harmed or damaged;
13. being convicted of any gross misdemeanor or felony relating to real estate activities;

14. interference with an investigation or disciplinary action by willfully misrepresenting facts, or by threatening, harassing, or bribing customers or witnesses to prevent them from providing evidence; or
15. engaging in unlicensed real estate activities.

DOL Disciplinary Actions Involving Misrepresentation or Concealment

Finding: Licensee:
- failed to advise purchasers of property that a building permit had expired and that there were structural problems with construction; and
- failed to request associated corrections to the Disclosure Form.

Action: License suspended for 90 days.

Finding: Licensee:
- was incompetent and negligent, and failed to exercise reasonable skill and care in rendering real estate services to her client, a purchaser of property; and
- withheld material information from her client which affected the client's decision to proceed with closing.

Action: License revoked for 5 years.

Finding: Licensee:
- failed to conduct herself in an honest and trustworthy manner; and
- failed to act in good faith with regard to a real estate transaction in which she was the listing agent.

Action: License suspended for 2 months.

The license law also lists grounds for disciplinary action. One of the first items on this list is "Violating any provisions of [the real estate license law] or any lawful regulations made by the Director pursuant thereto…" In other words, any violation of the license law is grounds for disciplinary action, and a licensee who fails to comply with any of the rules explained in this chapter could lose his license as a result.

Here is a brief summary of the items listed in the license law that have not been mentioned elsewhere in this chapter. A licensee is subject to disciplinary action for:

- being convicted of forgery, embezzlement, extortion, fraud, or similar offenses;
- making or authorizing statements that she knew (or could have known by the exercise of reasonable care) were false;
- converting trust funds (misappropriating them for his own use);
- failing to disclose information or to produce records for inspection upon request by the Director;
- selling real estate according to a plan that endangers the public interest, after the Director has objected in writing;

- accepting something other than cash (such as a promissory note) as an earnest money deposit unless that fact is stated in the purchase agreement and the seller has been informed;
- accepting money from more than one party in a transaction without first disclosing this to all interested parties in writing;
- accepting a profit on expenditures made for a principal without disclosing it to the principal;
- accepting compensation for an appraisal contingent on reporting a predetermined value;
- issuing an appraisal for property in which she has an interest without disclosing that interest in the appraisal report;
- falsely claiming to be a member of a state or national real estate association;
- directing a client or customer to a lending institution or escrow company in expectation of a kickback or rebate, without disclosing that expectation to the party he is representing;
- buying, selling, or leasing property (directly or through a third party) without disclosing that she holds a real estate license;
- any conduct in a real estate transaction which demonstrates bad faith, dishonesty, untrustworthiness, or incompetency; and
- discriminating against any person in hiring or real estate brokerage services, in violation of antidiscrimination laws.

It is also a prohibited practice, under the license law, for a licensee who has a financial interest in a title insurance company to give a fee or kickback to another real estate licensee for placing business with or referring business to that title insurance company. A licensee may not accept or solicit anything of value from a title insurance company or its representative that it would be illegal for the company to give. Also, a licensee may not require a client to obtain title insurance from a title insurance company in which the licensee has a financial interest.

The Director has the power to suspend the license of any real estate licensee who has been certified by a lending agency for nonpayment or default on a federal or state guaranteed education loan or service-conditioned scholarship. The same applies to any licensee who isn't in compliance with a child support or visitation order, as certified by the Department of Social and Health Services. License reinstatement is automatic upon repayment or compliance.

To conclude our discussion of license law violations, we'll mention that the state licensing law for attorneys prohibits anyone from practicing law who isn't an active member of the state bar association. Practicing law includes drafting contracts and giving legal advice. Thus, real estate licensees who aren't licensed attorneys should never draw up contracts for their clients and customers—or even draft provisions of any complexity. Nor should agents render opinions about the legal import of contract provisions or a party's actions. Engaging in the **unauthorized practice of law** is a gross misdemeanor. Note, however, that the parties themselves may draft provisions for their own transactions without committing an unauthorized practice of law.

Disciplinary Procedures

The procedures for disciplinary action are designed to give the licensee notice of the charges and an opportunity to present a defense. The usual procedures include an investigation, a hearing, and, depending on the outcome of the hearing, either no action or some form of sanctions against the licensee. Either party (the licensee or the Department of Licensing) may appeal the result.

Statement of Charges. If, after investigation, the Director decides there is reason to believe there has been a violation of the license law, the licensee will be served with a statement of charges. The statement of charges must be accompanied by a notice informing the licensee that he may request a hearing to contest the charges. The licensee must file a request for a hearing within 20 days after receiving the statement of charges. If the licensee fails to request a hearing, the licensee will be considered in default and the Director may enter a decision based on the facts available at that time.

Hearing. Once a hearing has been requested, the Director will fix the time for the hearing. The time must be as soon as is convenient, but at least 30 days after the statement of charges was served on the licensee. The only exception to this rule is if the Director issued an immediate suspension or restriction, in which case the hearing may be held sooner.

The hearing may be conducted by the Director, but in most cases the hearing officer is an administrative law judge. The licensee and the Department of Licensing may each be represented by attorneys in the hearing. The Department and the licensee will each have an opportunity to present evidence and testimony, to cross-examine witnesses for the other side, and to present arguments to the hearing officer. A court reporter makes a transcript of the proceedings, just as in a trial.

If the accusation isn't proved by a preponderance of the evidence, no action is taken against the licensee and the case is dismissed. If the accusation is proved, the Director may impose any of the sanctions permitted by law (discussed below). An order imposing the sanctions will be filed with the Director's office and immediately mailed to the licensee. The sanctions called for in the order take effect as soon as the order is received by the licensee.

Appeal. A licensee who is dissatisfied with the outcome of a disciplinary hearing may file an appeal in superior court. The appeal must be filed within 30 days after the date of the Director's decision and order. The licensee will be required to post a $1,000 appeal bond to cover court costs—in case the judge decides against the licensee—and must also pay for a copy of the transcript of the hearing within 15 days after receiving notice of the filing of the transcript. Filing an appeal does not automatically stay the Director's order. In other words, if the Director suspended the licensee's license, it will remain suspended during the appeal process. However, the Director may choose to stay the sanctions during the appeal process, if it is appropriate to do so.

Case Example:

Kimberly Hickethier, a managing broker, received a five-year license revocation from the Department of Licensing for her role in a transaction where she violated a number of license law provisions. In that transaction, in which she represented the buyer, Hickethier recommended a handyman to perform repair work specified in the purchase and sale agreement, without disclosing that she was in a relationship with the handyman. The buyer was not available to conduct a final walk-through inspection before closing; instead, the buyer relied on Hickethier's inspection. Hickethier told the buyer that the repairs were completed, even though her own inspection revealed that significant portions of the work had not been finished. She also was found to have committed a variety of other violations in connection with the transaction, including failure to handle trust funds properly, failure to give the buyer the keys promptly, and appointing an unlicensed person as a rental agent.

Hickethier appealed her license revocation to the court. In addition to arguing that her actions were not negligent, she also claimed that she was denied due process of law because it took five years from the date of the transaction until the time when her disciplinary hearing was held. She also contended that the Department's penalty, five years of license revocation, was arbitrary and capricious.

The court disagreed. It held that the Department's findings of multiple instances of unprofessional conduct were supported by the evidence. The court also found that the delay in holding the hearing did not violate any of Hickethier's rights; the only legal requirements were that the hearing be held "as soon as convenient," but not "earlier than thirty days after service of charges." Finally, the court found that as long as the Department's decision was made honestly and after due consideration, it was not arbitrary and capricious. *Hickethier v. Washington State Department of Licensing* (2011) No. 28776-9-III.

Sanctions for License Law Violations

After a disciplinary hearing, if the licensee (or license applicant) is held to have violated the license law, the Director may impose any or all of the following sanctions:

- revocation of the license for an interval of time;
- suspension of the license for a fixed or indefinite term;
- restriction or limitation of real estate activities;
- satisfactory completion of a specific program of remedial education or treatment;
- monitoring of real estate activities according to the Director's order;
- censure or reprimand;
- compliance with conditions of probation for a designated period of time;
- payment of a fine for each violation found by the Director, of up to $5,000 per violation;
- denial of an initial or renewal license application for an interval of time; or
- other corrective action.

All fines collected are placed in the Real Estate Education Account, to be used for education for the benefit of licensees. If a licensee fails to pay a fine, the Director may enforce the order for payment in superior court.

After a disciplinary hearing, the Director might issue a **cease and desist order** to prevent the continuation of an illegal activity. In special circumstances, the Director can issue a temporary cease and desist order even before a hearing is held. The Director is allowed to do this only when a delay in issuing the order would result in irreparable harm to the public. The temporary order must advise the licensee that she has a right to a hearing to determine if the order should be canceled, modified, or made permanent. If the licensee requests a hearing, one must be held within 30 days (unless the licensee requests more time).

Alternatively, the Director can ask a court to issue an injunction ordering a licensee or an unlicensed person to stop an ongoing violation. The Director can also ask the court to appoint a receiver to take over or close a real estate office operating in violation of the law until a hearing can be held.

Criminal Prosecution. Violations of the license law are gross misdemeanors. If the Director decides that criminal charges should be filed against a licensee, the prosecution would ordinarily be handled by the prosecuting attorney in the county where the violation is alleged to have occurred. If the prosecutor fails to act, the Director can ask the state Attorney General to prosecute instead.

Civil Liability. Anyone who has been injured by a licensee's actions or failure to act can file a civil lawsuit for damages. (See the discussion of tort suits in Chapter 1.) Note, however, that the Director of the Department of Licensing does not have the power to award damages to the victims of wrongful actions, such as real estate fraud. Compensation for injured parties is handled through the court system, not by the Department of Licensing.

Notifying Department of Legal Action. A licensee is required to notify the Department of Licensing within 20 days after learning of:

- any criminal complaint, information, indictment, or conviction in which the licensee is named as a defendant;
- any civil court order, verdict, or judgment entered against the licensee if the case involves any of her real estate or business activities; or
- the suspension or revocation of a professional license or certification held by the licensee (for instance, a real estate license in another state, or a license in another profession such as insurance), or the imposition of a fine connected with a professional license or certification.

Antitrust Laws and
Their Effect on Licensees

In addition to the real estate license law, federal antitrust laws impose certain restrictions on a real estate agent's conduct towards clients, customers, and other agents.

Federal antitrust laws are not new: the **Sherman Act** was passed in 1890, well over a century ago. The Sherman Act prohibits any agreement that has the effect of unreasonably restraining trade, including conspiracies. A **conspiracy** occurs when two or more business entities participate in a common scheme, the effect of which is the restraint of trade.

Antitrust laws are based on the idea that business competition is good for both the economy and society as a whole. The most famous antitrust cases involved giant companies such as Standard Oil or American Telephone and Telegraph, monopolies that dominated or completely controlled a market. But in 1950, antitrust laws were held to apply to the real estate industry as well. In a landmark case, *United States v. National Association of Real Estate Boards*, the U.S. Supreme Court held that mandatory fee schedules established and enforced by a real estate board violated the Sherman Act.

Case Example:

The Washington Real Estate Board adopted standard commission rates and required its real estate broker members to charge these rates. When the board was sued for price fixing, the case eventually reached the U.S. Supreme Court. The court made it clear that the Sherman Antitrust Act applies to real estate brokerage services. The business of a real estate broker is a trade, carried on for profit and commercial purposes. Therefore, the competitive standards addressed by the Sherman Act apply to real estate brokerages, just as to any other commercial activity. The court found that the board's practices constituted a price fixing scheme within the meaning of the Sherman Antitrust Act. *U.S. v. Real Estate Boards* (1950) 339 U.S. 485.

If a real estate agent violates antitrust laws, she (and the firm she works for) may be subject to both civil and criminal actions. If an individual is found guilty of violating the Sherman Act, she can be fined up to one million dollars and/or sentenced to ten years' imprisonment. If a corporation is found guilty of violating the Sherman Act, it can be fined up to one hundred million dollars.

The activities prohibited by antitrust laws can be grouped into four main categories:

- price fixing,
- group boycotts,
- tie-in arrangements, and
- market allocation.

Price Fixing. Price fixing is defined as the cooperative setting of prices or price ranges by competing businesses. To avoid even the appearance of price fixing, two agents from different real estate firms should never discuss their commission rates. It's a discussion between competing agents that is dangerous—licensees affiliated with the same firm, on the other hand, are allowed to discuss commission rates with one another. One exception to this general prohibition is that two competing designated brokers may discuss a commission split in a cooperative sale (the split between the listing agent and the selling agent).

Even a casual announcement that a firm is planning to raise its commission rates could lead to antitrust problems.

> **Example:** Wood, a designated broker, goes to a dinner given by her local MLS. She's called on to discuss current market conditions and, in the middle of her speech, she announces that she's going to raise her firm's commission rate, no matter what anyone else does. This statement could be viewed as an invitation to conspire to fix prices. If any other MLS members raise their rates in response to this announcement, they could be held to have accepted Wood's invitation to conspire.

Real estate licensees must understand that they do not have to actually consult with each other to be charged with conspiring to fix commission rates. The kind of scenario described in the example is enough to lead to an antitrust lawsuit.

Publications that appear to fix prices are prohibited as well. Any MLS or other association that tries to publish "recommended" or "going" rates for commissions could be sued.

Group Boycotts. A group boycott is an agreement between two or more business competitors (such as real estate agents from different firms) to exclude another competitor from fair participation in business activities.

> **Example:** Beckwith and Jordan are the designated brokers of two competing real estate firms. They have lunch together and Beckwith brings up Harley, the designated broker of a third local firm. Beckwith says that Harley is aggressive, dishonest, and unreliable and that she avoids doing business with him. She encourages Jordan to do the same, and they discuss ways in which they can steer around Harley and undermine his firm. Beckwith and Jordan could be found guilty of a conspiracy to boycott.

If a real estate licensee feels that a licensee from another firm is unethical or unprofessional, she may choose not to do business with that person or firm (and perhaps alert the Department of Licensing to suspected misconduct). But agreeing with licensees from other firms to take steps to injure that competitor's business would be an antitrust violation.

Antitrust Enforcement Actions by the Department of Justice

1. The Department of Justice (DOJ) filed an antitrust lawsuit alleging that certain National Association of Realtors® (NAR) policies obstructed real estate brokers who used Internet-based tools to offer better services and lower costs to consumers. The case was scheduled to go to trial in 2008. However, shortly before trial, NAR settled.

The DOJ said of the settlement:

> NAR will enact a new policy that guarantees that Internet-based brokerage companies will not be treated differently than traditional brokers...[and] brokers participating in a NAR-affiliated MLS will not be permitted to withhold their listings from brokers who serve their customers through virtual office websites.

2. In 2005, the DOJ filed a lawsuit challenging Kentucky Real Estate Commission regulations that prohibited Kentucky real estate brokers from offering rebates and other inducements to attract customers. The DOJ alleged that the regulations restricted competition and caused consumers to pay higher prices for real estate services. The Commission settled the case that same year. The DOJ said of the settlement:

> The Commission agreed to cease enforcement of its regulations prohibiting rebates or other inducements. [Further] any disciplinary action initiated by the Commission against any broker for offering a rebate, discount, or other inducement is null and void, and the Commission must note that in its records.

Tie-in Arrangements. A tie-in arrangement is defined as "an agreement to sell one product, only on the condition that the buyer also purchases a different (or tied) product..."

> **Example:** Brown is a subdivision developer and real estate licensee. Tyson, a builder, wants to buy a lot. Brown tells Tyson that he will sell him a lot only if Tyson agrees that after Tyson builds a house on the lot, he will list the improved property with Brown. (This is called a "list-back" agreement.)

The developer's requirement in the example is an illegal tie-in arrangement. Note, however, that a list-back agreement violates antitrust laws only if signing it is a required condition of the sale. Two parties may mutually agree on a list-back agreement without violating antitrust laws.

Market Allocation. Market allocation occurs when competing businesses agree not to sell: 1) certain products or services; 2) in specified areas; or 3) to certain customers in specified areas. Market allocation is illegal because it limits competition.

As with group boycotts, it's collective action by competitors that makes market allocation illegal. An individual real estate firm is free to determine the market areas in which it wants to specialize (if any); similarly, the firm can allocate territory to particular licensees affiliated with the firm. Allocation of territory between competing firms, however, is a violation of antitrust law.

> **Example:** ABC Realty assigns Agent Ava to handle all new customers in the luxury home market, and assigns Agent Paxton to all new customers in the vacant land market. This practice does not violate antitrust law.
>
> However, if ABC Realty and XYZ Realty agree to allocate customers so that ABC Realty will handle all luxury homes and XYZ Realty will handle all vacant land, this would violate antitrust law.

Avoiding Antitrust Violations. To prevent antitrust violations, a real estate firm should establish its fees and other listing policies independently (without consulting competing firms), never use listing forms that contain pre-printed commission rates, and train their affiliated licensees to recognize and avoid actions that violate antitrust laws. For example, real estate agents should never:

- imply to a client that the commission rate is fixed or nonnegotiable; or
- discuss their firm's commission policies and business plans with agents at competing firms.

The Washington Consumer Protection Act

We will end this chapter with a brief discussion of Washington's Consumer Protection Act (CPA). This statute prohibits anyone—including real estate agents—from engaging in unfair or deceptive business practices. Misrepresenting property features, concealing defects, or colluding to provide an inflated appraisal are examples of the types of real estate business practices that could be held to violate the law.

Unfair practices also encompass the same kind of anticompetitive activities that violate federal antitrust law, such as price fixing and tie-in arrangements.

A plaintiff who wins a lawsuit brought under the CPA is generally entitled to more than her actual damages: she may be awarded triple damages (three times the amount of her actual damages) and/or punitive damages, as well as attorney's fees. The increased damages and the award of attorney's fees can make it economically feasible for an individual wronged by an unfair business practice to sue for redress.

A key requirement of the CPA, however, is that the unfair practice must have impacted (or had the potential to impact) the public, not just the individual plaintiff.

> **Example:** A developer and a real estate licensee induce unsophisticated investors to buy into a real estate development on the Olympic Peninsula with the false promise that it's a low-risk investment. Public impact exists because the defendants actively solicited multiple investors.

A purely private dispute won't fall under the CPA.

> **Example:** Bea looks at some property hoping to develop it commercially. Until recently, the seller ran a business on part of the property and now plans to retire. The seller states that commercial development should be possible. Neither party realizes that the property contains wetlands that make development impractical. Bea signs a purchase agreement.
>
> After discovering the wetlands problem, Bea sues to rescind the transaction and claims triple damages against the seller under the CPA. However, the seller doesn't regularly sell property, so it's unlikely that anyone else will be affected by this seller's mistake. A court would probably rule that this dispute must be treated as a simple breach of contract case (meaning no triple damages). Without potential or actual impact on the public, the CPA does not apply.

Conclusion

The Department of Licensing administers Washington's real estate license law, which establishes when a real estate license is required and what the qualifications for licensure are. The license law also regulates the business practices of real estate professionals, controlling how firms form agency relationships, run their offices, supervise their agents, and handle client funds. A thorough understanding of all these requirements will help licensees avoid license law violations and the possibility of disciplinary procedures and penalties. Note that the license law is not the only law that governs business practices in the real estate profession. Other laws, including Washington's Consumer Protection Act and federal antitrust laws, also affect how real estate licensees may carry out their work.

Case Problem

The following is a hypothetical case problem. Most of the facts are taken from a real case. Based on what you have learned from this chapter, make a decision on the issues presented and then check to see if your answer matches the court's decision.

The Facts

Nick Mazza, of Crescent Realty, was the listing agent for the Bolstads. Mazza asked the Bolstads if anything was wrong with their home; the Bolstads said no. Mazza then filed the listing data for his client's home with the MLS. The listing revealed no problems with the property. In reality, the Bolstads' house had chronic sewage and drainage problems and Mazza knew it, having been an agent in the previous sale of the premises to the Bolstads.

The McRaes agreed to buy the property. Before closing and occupancy of the property, the McRaes noticed standing water on the front lawn and a musty smell in the back of the premises. Mazza didn't disclose to the McRaes anything about the property's troubled history (except to say that the Bolstads had abandoned an attempt to build a swimming pool on the property when the hole filled with water, but this was "no problem"). Mazza then told his clients, the Bolstads, to dig drainage ditches as a quick fix.

Three days after the deed was recorded in favor of the McRaes, the toilets in the house erupted with raw sewage.

The McRaes sued Mazza under the Consumer Protection Act. The trial court found in favor of the plaintiffs. On appeal, Mazza argued that his actions did not impact the public interest as required for a CPA claim, and the case against him should be dismissed.

The Question

Did Mazza's various failures to disclose amount to an injury to the public interest, as required for a Consumer Protection Act claim?

The Answer

Yes. Mazza's failure to disclose the property's defects had sufficient potential for repetition so the CPA's requirement of impact on the public interest was satisfied. In the real court case, the court focused on Mazza's submission of the property listing to the MLS. The MLS listing constituted advertising to the public and was therefore potentially misleading to any number of people. The court also suggested that in Mazza's previous sale of the house to the Bolstads, the agent had "presumably" failed to disclose the drainage problems. The court concluded, "The prior instance of possible misrepresentation, in conjunction with the listing. . . establishes the potential for repetition." The decision in favor of the McRaes at the trial court level was upheld on appeal. *McRae v. Bolstad*, 101 Wn.2nd 161, 676 P.2d 496 (1984).

Chapter Summary

- Washington's real estate license law is administered by the Director of the Department of Licensing and the Real Estate Commission.

- It's unlawful to provide real estate brokerage services without a license. There are several important exemptions from the licensing requirement, however, including someone buying or selling on his own behalf, and an uncompensated attorney in fact.

- There are two types of real estate licenses for individuals: broker's licenses and managing broker's licenses. Real estate firms must also be licensed. Brokers and managing brokers may only work for and represent a firm. A managing broker is also authorized to manage a branch office, or to be appointed as a firm's designated broker.

- Any license applicant must be at least 18 years old, have a high school diploma, have completed certain real estate courses, pass an examination, and submit fingerprints. An applicant for a managing broker's license must also have three years of experience as a broker.

- A designated broker is ultimately responsible for the supervision of her affiliated licensees, although supervisory responsibilities may be delegated to managing brokers. When a licensee's affiliation with a firm terminates, the broker's or managing broker's license is inactive until reissued for affiliation with another firm.

- A firm is required to maintain an office in Washington that is open to the public, and may have one or more branch offices. Each branch office must be licensed, and each must be managed by a managing broker. An affiliated licensee's license must be displayed in the office where he works.

- Advertising by real estate licensees must include the firm's name as licensed; blind ads are not allowed. An ad for the licensee's own property does not have to state the firm's name, but it must disclose the licensed status of the seller.

- Trust funds must be placed in an interest-bearing trust account no later than the first banking day after receipt; deposits of $10,000 or less are placed in a pooled account, with interest paid to the state. (Property management trust accounts do not have to be interest-bearing accounts.) A firm may not pay business expenses or an affiliated licensee's share of a commission directly out of a trust account.

- A firm is required to keep records (including a transaction folder and trust account records) for at least three years after a transaction closes.

- A valid real estate license is a prerequisite to payment of a commission or other compensation for brokerage services.

- In handling a real estate transaction, a licensee is required to present all offers and other written communications from one party to the other, provide document copies to the parties, expeditiously perform any acts she is obligated to perform by the purchase and sale agreement, and make sure that the parties receive settlement statements.

- When a licensee is accused of violating the license law, there is an investigation and then a disciplinary hearing. The possible sanctions include license suspension, revocation, or denial; fines; relevant coursework; restrictions on or monitoring of real estate activities; censure or reprimand; probation; or other corrective action. Violation of the license law is a gross misdemeanor and may lead to criminal prosecution.

- Antitrust laws prohibit price fixing, group boycotts, tie-in arrangements, and market allocation. Real estate agents must be especially careful to avoid discussing commission rates with competing agents.

- The Washington Consumer Protection Act prohibits unfair business practices by anyone, including real estate licensees. The act provides for triple damages.

Chapter Quiz

1. The Morenos want to sell their house. They gave their friend Jessica Norwood a power of attorney, authorizing her to represent them in the transaction. Norwood doesn't have a real estate license. It's legal for Norwood to represent the Morenos:

   a. only if she's licensed to practice law
   b. only if she won't be compensated for her services
   c. as long as she obtains a real estate license before the transaction closes
   d. None of the above; it isn't legal for Norwood to represent the Morenos

2. Mark Cutler doesn't have a real estate license. Which of the following activities can he legally do, for a fee?

   a. Advise sellers in a real estate transaction
   b. Issue a broker price opinion
   c. Oversee the management of an apartment building for its owner
   d. Lease units in a property he co-owns

3. Peterson hires an assistant to help him with his real estate business. His assistant answers phones, sets up appointments, and files paperwork. Peterson's assistant:

   a. need not be licensed
   b. must have a real estate license
   c. need not be licensed as long as Peterson has written authorization from his designated broker or branch manager to hire an assistant
   d. must have a special real estate assistant license

4. Although Harper lacked three years' experience as a broker, she was still allowed to take the managing broker's exam because she had other professional experience that was deemed a satisfactory substitute by:

   a. Harper
   b. her firm's designated broker
   c. the Director of the Department of Licensing
   d. the Real Estate Commission

5. Howard Gray, a licensed broker, was involved in a traffic accident. The other driver (who was injured) sued Gray for compensation, and a judgment has just been entered against Gray. He is:

   a. required to notify the Department of Licensing within five days
   b. required to notify the Department of Licensing within 30 days
   c. not required to notify the Department of Licensing, because this was not a criminal charge
   d. not required to notify the Department of Licensing, because the lawsuit didn't involve Gray's real estate or business activities

6. Listing Agent Neely knows that her seller lied on the seller disclosure statement. The seller refuses Neely permission to tell the buyer about the problem. Neely keeps mum. Would a Consumer Protection Act lawsuit by the buyer against Neely be likely to succeed?

   a. Yes, if a court found actual or potential impact on the public
   b. Yes, even without public impact, because Neely's behavior was clearly unfair
   c. No, the CPA exempts real estate licensees
   d. No, the CPA does not permit private lawsuits

7. The license law requires a firm to keep transaction records for:

   a. six months
   b. one year
   c. three years
   d. five years

8. Susan Kurosawa, a licensed broker, is advertising her own house for sale. The license law requires the ad to state:

   a. that the seller is a licensed real estate agent
   b. the name of Kurosawa's firm, as licensed
   c. Both of the above
   d. None of the above

9. A broker may manage a branch office for her firm:

   a. if the broker has at least two years of experience
   b. if the broker has taken an approved course in brokerage management
   c. if the office is in the broker's residence
   d. under no circumstances

10. Which of the following statements is true regarding the supervision of brokers? A managing broker must review documents from:

    a. all brokers within three business days
    b. brokers with less than two years' experience within five business days
    c. all brokers within five business days
    d. brokers with less than two years' experience within three business days

11. If a licensee accused of violating the license law does not request a hearing within 20 days after receiving the statement of charges:

    a. her license is automatically revoked
    b. the Director may enter a decision based on the available facts
    c. a hearing will automatically be scheduled for the licensee
    d. the Director will issue a cease and desist order

12. Barton, a real estate licensee, helps negotiate a sale. The purchase and sale agreement is contingent on a pest inspection, and Barton tells the parties he will arrange for an inspection to be done by August 19. But he forgets to request the inspection before taking his family on a planned vacation. When he gets back into town on August 18, he finally remembers to call the pest inspector. The inspector says she's very busy and won't be able to inspect the home until August 29.

    a. Since the pest inspection wasn't an important term in the purchase agreement, Barton hasn't done anything wrong
    b. Even though Barton was negligent in failing to perform his duty, he hasn't violated the license law
    c. The closing agent will cancel escrow immediately and terminate the sale
    d. Barton has failed to perform expeditiously, and may be subject to disciplinary action

13. Trust funds received by a licensee in a sales transaction must be placed in an:

    a. account that doesn't bear interest, by the third banking day after receipt
    b. interest-bearing account, by the second banking day after receipt
    c. interest-bearing account, by the first banking day after receipt
    d. account that doesn't bear interest, by the first banking day after receipt

14. Great County MLS publishes a monthly list of the commission rates charged by all member firms. The multiple listing association:

    a. could be found guilty of price fixing
    b. isn't guilty of price fixing, because it's simply reporting newsworthy information
    c. isn't guilty of price fixing, because no two competing firms are discussing rates
    d. isn't guilty of price fixing, because only real estate brokers can be guilty of price fixing, not multiple listing associations

15. A designated broker conducts a sales meeting once a week for her licensees. At one meeting, she discusses commission rates at length. She is:

    a. guilty of price fixing
    b. guilty of a tie-in arrangement
    c. guilty of a group boycott
    d. not guilty of any antitrust violation

3 The Nature of Real Property

Outline

B. Water rights
1. Riparian rights
2. Appropriative rights
3. Disappearance of riparian rights
4. Navigable waters
5. Non-navigable waters
C. Mineral rights
D. Support rights
1. Lateral support
2. Subjacent support
E. Oil and gas rights

Key Terms

- Metes and bounds
- Monument
- Course
- Point of beginning
- Compass bearing
- Natural monument
- Government survey
- Meridian
- Base line
- Range line
- Township
- Section

- Government lot
- Lot and block
- Air lot
- Datum
- Bench mark
- Reformation
- Adverse possession
- Attachment
- Boundary line agreement
- Recognition and acquiescence
- Doctrine of emblements

- Fixture
- Constructive annexation
- Annexor
- Trade fixture
- Appurtenance
- Riparian rights
- Appropriative rights
- Navigable waters
- Lateral support
- Subjacent support
- Rule of capture

Chapter Overview

This chapter will give you an overview of basic legal concepts regarding real property. You will learn how real property is described, what is (and isn't) included as part of the real property, and what rights accompany real property ownership. This information will help you understand the obligations of property sellers and agents in a real estate transaction.

Case Example:

In 1983, the Connall family put their property up for sale. They told their agent that the property had been surveyed before they bought it, and that it was five acres. They pointed out the property's boundaries to the agent. The agent later pointed out these same boundaries to potential buyers, the Hoffmans. Part of the property contained a corral, cattle chute, barn, and shed. These were important to the Hoffmans because they owned a horse and wanted to get involved with 4-H activities.

Shortly after the Hoffmans purchased the property, a neighbor told them that a recent survey showed that part of the corral, cattle chute, and horse shed were actually

18 to 21 feet on his property. The Hoffmans brought a lawsuit against the Connalls and the agent for misrepresenting the property's boundaries. *Hoffman v. Connall*, 108 Wn.2d 69, 736 P.2d 242 (1987).

Are the corral, cattle chute, barn, and shed part of the real property? Are the Connalls liable for misrepresenting the boundaries? Should the agent be held liable? Was the agent negligent in not verifying the seller's statements concerning the boundaries? How could the agent have discovered where the real boundaries were located?

After reading this chapter, you will be able to answer these and other questions concerning the nature of real property. The outcome in the case of *Hoffman v. Connall* is given below.

Land Description

Knowing where the boundaries of a piece of property lie is important to the seller, the buyer, and the real estate agent. Boundary problems are one of the most common causes of real estate lawsuits. When people buy property, they want to know exactly what they are buying and how much land is included.

Misrepresenting Boundaries

In *Hoffman v. Connall*, the case described above, the sellers and their agent were sued for misrepresenting the location of the property's boundaries. The Connalls were found liable, but the agent was not.

Seller's Liability. Although the outcome in a specific case may vary depending on its facts, Washington courts typically hold sellers (property owners) liable for misrepresenting the boundaries of their property. This is true even if the misrepresentation was innocent—in other words, even if the seller was simply mistaken, not intentionally deceiving the buyer. Sellers are presumed to know the character and attributes of the property they are conveying. If they give mistaken information about the boundaries, they can be held liable for that mistake.

Agent's Liability. Real estate agents representing sellers have a duty to avoid making misrepresentations to buyers (see Chapter 7). Even so, in Washington agents generally aren't held liable for innocent misrepresentations based on information provided by a seller. A seller's agent isn't expected to verify every claim the seller makes, so an agent who simply passes along incorrect information from the seller usually isn't liable to the buyer.

It's a different matter if the agent knew something that indicated the seller's claim might be false, but failed to investigate further. If anything suggests that the seller's statements may be incorrect, the agent has a duty to verify the information before repeating it to buyers.

In *Hoffman v. Connall*, the court decided there was no evidence to indicate that anything was wrong with the boundaries pointed out by the Connalls, so the agent had no reason to investigate further. Therefore the agent was not held liable to the Hoffmans. However, if the agent had reason to suspect that the Connalls were wrong about the boundaries, yet still did not investigate before repeating the information to the Hoffmans, the agent (as well as the Connalls) would have been liable.

To avoid liability for misrepresenting boundaries, sellers and real estate agents shouldn't claim to know the location of the boundaries with certainty. If buyers specifically ask, it's appropriate to point out where the boundaries are assumed to be, as long as the information is accompanied by a clear disclaimer. For example, the sellers or their agent might tell the buyers that these have been treated as the property lines, but a survey would be necessary to confirm their actual location.

Methods of Description

As you can see, it is extremely important to know a property's true boundaries. Documents such as deeds, mortgages, and purchase and sale agreements must contain complete and accurate descriptions. Ambiguous or uncertain descriptions are not legally adequate and will cause the instrument to be invalid.

There are many methods for describing property, but the three most commonly used systems of land description are:

- metes and bounds,
- government survey, and
- lot and block.

Metes and Bounds Descriptions

The metes (measurements) and bounds (boundaries) system is the oldest of the three methods of describing land. It was used by the original colonists as they settled in this country. This method is still frequently used in rural areas and is especially common in many eastern states.

The **metes and bounds** method of description identifies a parcel of land by describing its outline or boundaries. The boundaries are fixed by reference to three things:

1. **monuments**, which may be natural objects such as rivers or trees, or man-made objects such as roads or survey markers;
2. **courses** or directions, in the form of compass readings; and
3. **distances**, measured in any convenient unit of length.

A **metes and bounds** description gives a starting point and then proceeds around the boundary by describing a series of **courses** (compass readings) and distances. The description continues until the boundary has been described all the way around to the point of beginning.

Fig. 3.1 Metes and bounds description

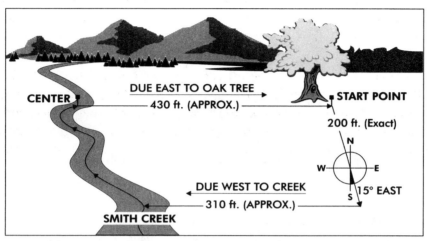

CENTER

DUE EAST TO OAK TREE
430 ft. (APPROX.)

START POINT

200 ft. (Exact)

N
W—E
S
15° EAST

DUE WEST TO CREEK
310 ft. (APPROX.)

SMITH CREEK

A tract of land located in Spokane County, described as follows: "Beginning at the oak tree, thence south 15° east, 200 feet, thence north 90° west, 310 feet more or less to the centerline of Smith Creek, thence northwesterly along the centerline of Smith Creek to a point directly west of the oak tree, thence north 90° east, 430 feet more or less to the point of beginning."

Point of Beginning. A metes and bounds description always starts at some convenient and well-defined point that can be easily identified (such as the oak tree in Figure 3.1). The starting point is referred to as the **point of beginning** or **POB**. The point of beginning is always described by reference to a monument.

> **Examples:** "The SW corner of the intersection of 1st Street and 2nd Avenue," or "200 feet north of the old oak tree."

Note that the point of beginning does not have to be a monument itself; it must simply refer to a monument. In the second example above, the old oak tree is a monument, and the POB is 200 feet north of the tree.

Although older metes and bounds descriptions often refer to natural monuments such as "the old oak tree," present-day descriptions generally refer to government survey lines as monuments. This helps avoid problems that may occur if the original monument is moved or destroyed.

Compass Bearings. In a metes and bounds description, a direction is described by reference to a compass point. The compass directions are described in terms of the degree of deviation from north or south. Thus, northwest or 315° is written as north 45° west, since it is a deviation of 45° to the west of north. Similarly, south southeast or 157½° is written as south 22½° east, since it is a deviation of 22½° to the east of south. East and west are both written relative to north: north 90° east and north 90° west, respectively.

Fig. 3.2 Compass bearings

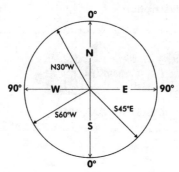

Compass bearings are given by reference to north or south.

Conflicting Elements. In a metes and bounds description, discrepancies sometimes occur between the various elements of the description. This is usually because the original surveyor made a mistake. For instance, if the description calls for a course of "320 feet in a northerly direction to the corner of the Smith farmhouse" and the Smith farmhouse is really in a northwesterly direction, there is a discrepancy that must be resolved. To help surveyors resolve problems like these, an order of priority for the various elements has been set up:

1. natural monuments (for example, "Sanders Creek"),
2. then man-made monuments ("Avondale Road"),
3. then courses ("south 8° east"),
4. then distances ("310 feet"),
5. then names ("the Holden Ranch"), and
6. then the area or quantity of acreage ("80 acres").

> **Example:** A land description reads "east 380 feet to the midpoint of Sanders Creek." It is actually 390 feet to the midpoint of Sanders Creek. The reference to Sanders Creek takes precedence over the distance. The property will extend clear to the middle of the creek, not just 380 feet.

Government Survey Descriptions

A second method of land description is the **government survey** method. This method emerged after the American Revolution, when the federal government owned huge amounts of undeveloped land. Land speculators and settlers were moving into the territories, and Congress was anxious to sell some of the land in order to increase revenues and diminish the national debt. Since using the metes and bounds method of description for all of this property was not feasible, a new system called the government survey method was developed. This method of description is used mainly in states west of the Mississippi.

Fig. 3.3 Lines in a government survey grid

North/South lines	East/West lines
principal meridian	base line
guide meridians	correction lines
range lines	township lines
ranges	township tiers

This system of land description is also called the rectangular survey method because it divides the land into a series of rectangles or grids. Each grid is composed of two sets of lines, one set running north/south and the other east/west.

Meridians and Base Lines. The original north/south line in each grid is called the principal meridian. Each principal meridian is given its own name, such as the Willamette Meridian, which runs through the western part of Oregon and Washington. (See Figure 3.4.) The original east/west line in each grid is called a **base line.**

Additional east/west lines, called **correction lines**, run parallel to the base lines at intervals of 24 miles. Additional north/south lines—called **guide meridians**—are also established at 24-mile intervals. Because of the curvature of the earth, all true north/south lines converge as they approach the North Pole. Therefore, each guide meridian only runs as far as the next correction line. Then a new interval of 24 miles is measured and a new guide meridian is run. This is done to correct for the curvature of the earth, so that the lines remain approximately the same distance apart and do not converge. (See Figure 3.5.)

Fig. 3.4 Principal meridians and baselines in northwestern states

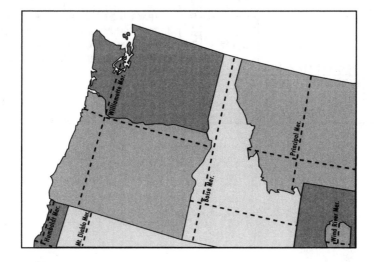

Fig. 3.5 Sections, townships, and ranges in the government survey system

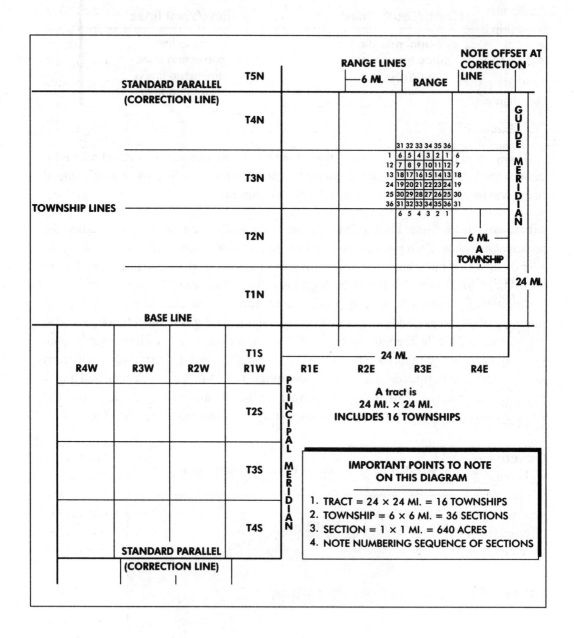

The large squares created by the intersection of guide meridians and correction lines are further divided into smaller tracts of land by additional north/south lines running at six-mile intervals, called **range lines**. These range lines divide the land into columns called **ranges**. Additional east/west lines run at six-mile intervals from the correction lines and are called **township lines**. The east/west lines divide the land into rows or tiers called **township tiers**.

Townships and Sections. The square of land located at the intersection of a range and a township tier is called a **township**. It is identified by its position relative to the principal meridian and base line. (See Figure 3.6.)

> **Example:** The township located in the fourth tier north of the base line and the third range east of the principal meridian is called "township 4 north, range 3 east" or "T4N, R3E."

Each township measures 36 square miles. A township is divided into 36 sections, which are each one square mile (640 acres). The sections are always numbered 1 through 36 in a specified sequence. (See Figure 3.7.) Parcels of land smaller than sections can be identified by reference to sections and partial sections. (See Figure 3.8.)

> **Example:** "The northwest quarter of the southwest quarter of section 12, township 4 north, range 3 east," or "the NW ¼ of the SW ¼ of section 12, T4N, R3E."

Grid systems are identical across the country, so it is necessary to include in the description the name of the principal meridian that is being used as a reference. (Since each principal meridian has its own base line, it is not necessary to specify the base line.) The county and state where the land is situated should also be included, to avoid any possible confusion. Thus, a complete description of a township would be T4N, R3E of the Willamette Meridian, Clark County, State of Washington.

Government Lots. Because of the curvature of the earth, the convergence of range lines, and human surveying errors, it is impossible to keep all sections exactly one mile square. Government regulations provide for any deficiency or surplus to be placed in the north and west sections of a township. These irregular sections are called **government lots** and are referred to by a lot number. Government lots can also result when a body of water or other obstacle prevents an accurate square-mile section from being surveyed. (See Figure 3.9.)

Lot and Block Descriptions (Recorded Plat)

In terms of surface area, more land in the United States is described by the government survey method than by any other land description system. However, in terms of number of properties, the lot and block or recorded plat system is the most important land description method. It is the method used most frequently in metropolitan areas.

Fig. 3.6 Township 4 North, Range 3 East

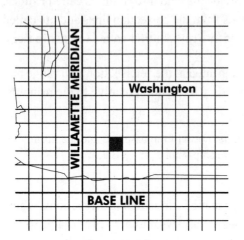

Fig. 3.7 A township contains 36 sections, numbered in this sequence

6	5	4	3	2	1
7	8	9	10	11	12
18	17	16	15	14	13
19	20	21	22	23	24
30	29	28	27	26	25
31	32	33	34	35	36

Fig. 3.8 A section can be divided up into smaller parcels

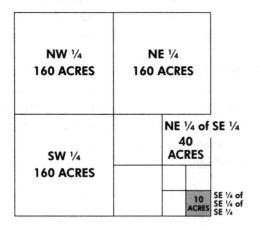

Fig. 3.9 Government lots

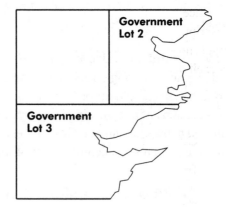

Fig. 3.10 Plat map

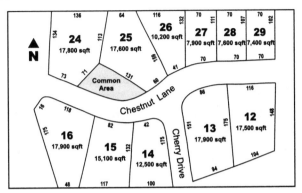

Under this system, land is described by reference to lots and blocks (groups of lots surrounded by streets) that are mapped out by a surveyor on a subdivision **plat** (map) that is subsequently recorded in the county where the land is located. After the map is recorded, any reference to one of the numbered lots on the specified plat will be a sufficient legal description of the lot. (See Figure 3.10.)

> **Example:** A lot and block description might read as follows: Lot 2, Block 4 of Tract number 45, in the city of Everett, county of Snohomish, state of Washington, as per map recorded in Book 22, page 36, of maps, in the office of the recorder of said county.

Since a detailed description of the lot is already on file in the recorder's office, that description may be incorporated into any legal document simply by reference. However, that is not usually done in Washington. Typically, a complete legal description is included in each document. Referring to an attached legal description, but failing to actually attach it, can be a costly error.

Case Example:

The Lees signed a purchase and sale agreement for a home in Bellevue. They made a $50,000 earnest money deposit with John L. Scott Realty. No legal description was attached to the agreement. However, there was a pre-printed provision stating: "Selling Licensee, Listing Agent or Closing Agent to insert, attach or correct the Legal Description of the Property."

The Lees subsequently sought to rescind the purchase and sale agreement after expiration of the financing contingency, but the seller wouldn't agree to return the earnest money. In litigation, the Lees argued that the lack of a property description meant that the contract wasn't enforceable. The seller claimed that a copy of the deed bearing a legal description had been faxed to the buyers. However, the seller couldn't provide a fax cover sheet or other evidence of this transmission.

The court ruled in favor of the buyers. The lack of a property description was fatal; there was no contract and the purchase money had to be refunded. *Home Realty Lynnwood, Inc. v. Walsh*, 146 Wn. App. 231, 189 P.3d 253 (2008).

Plat maps frequently contain a wealth of information above and beyond the detailed description of property boundaries. Other information that may be listed includes:

- measurements of area,
- locations of various easements,
- right-of-way dimensions,
- location of survey markers,
- proposed streets, blocks, and lots of the subdivision,
- records of conditions and restrictions applying to the land,
- topographical details such as elevation, and
- school sites and recreational areas.

However, examination of a plat map is not a substitute for a thorough title search and should not be treated as such.

Air Lots

Not all real property can be described simply by reference to a position on the face of the earth. Some forms of real property, such as condominiums, also require description in terms of elevation above the ground. When describing the location of a condominium or other airspace, you can't simply measure the height from the ground, because the ground is not a stable and exact legal marker.

The United States Geodetic Survey and most large cities have established datums and bench marks as legal reference points for measuring elevation. A **datum** is an artificial horizontal plane, such as sea level. A **bench mark** is a point whose elevation has been officially measured relative to a datum. For example, a bench mark may be a metal or concrete marker, often placed in a sidewalk or other stable position.

> **Example:** A metal disk located in the sidewalk at the corner of Oak and Elm streets has the following words engraved on it: "Bench Mark No. 96, seventeen feet above River City Datum."

Surveyors use the datum or a bench mark as a reference point in describing air lots.

> **Example:** A surveyor plotting a condominium unit on the 16th floor of a new building being built on Elm Street calculates that the floor of the unit will be 230 feet above the sidewalk. He therefore shows in his survey that the floor of the unit is located 247 feet above the River City Datum as established by Bench Mark 96, because Bench Mark 96 is 17 feet above the datum.

Description Problems and Disputes Between Neighbors

A discussion of land description would not be complete without reviewing some of the problems that arise with land descriptions and their possible solutions. Some typical problems that might occur are:

- incorrect descriptions,
- indefinite or ambiguous descriptions,
- omission of part of the description,
- adjoining owners disagreeing over boundary lines, and
- modern surveys that don't match the original survey lines.

These problems can often be cured or resolved by:

- correcting the description,
- possession,
- recognition and acquiescence,
- a boundary line agreement,
- the common grantor theory, or
- litigation and a court decision.

Correcting the Description. When an error occurs in a land description, the problem can often be solved simply by having the party who transferred the property give a new deed with the correct description. When this is not possible, a court order can be obtained to correct the description. This is called a **reformation**.

Possession. Sometimes a description problem or boundary dispute can be resolved by possession.

> **Example:** John Thompson owns property in Lincoln County and Spokane County, and both pieces of property are referred to as the "Thompson Ranch." Thompson conveys property to Maria Alberti. The deed identifies the property as the "Thompson Ranch," but does not specify which county the land is located in.
>
> Such a description is legally insufficient. However, if Alberti occupies the ranch in Lincoln County, the deed could be held valid, since her possession of the Lincoln County ranch makes it obvious which ranch was referred to in the deed.

A boundary dispute may also be resolved by adverse possession. Under the doctrine of **adverse possession**, the claimants must show that they treated the property as if they owned it, in a way that could not escape the true owner's notice. Their possession of the property must be exclusive, actual, open, notorious, hostile, and uninterrupted for a period of ten years. If the adverse possessor is acting under color of title or has paid all taxes on the property, the time limit is only seven years. (Adverse possession is discussed in more detail in Chapter 9.)

Recognition and Acquiescence. Another method of resolving a boundary dispute is called **recognition and acquiescence**. A claimant must show that the boundary is well-defined and has been acquiesced to (accepted or treated as the boundary) for ten years. This method is similar to adverse possession, except that possession is with the true owner's acquiescence instead of being hostile.

Boundary Line Agreement. Parties may also simply agree on a boundary. For example, neighbors may agree to build a fence and have the fence serve as the boundary line. A boundary line agreement will become binding on the parties and all subsequent owners if it is put in writing and signed and acknowledged in the same manner as a deed. The boundary line agreement must use legal descriptions and include a survey map that has been filed in the county where the land is located.

Common Grantor. If a common grantor has clearly designated a boundary, that boundary will be binding on all subsequent owners of the property, even if it was not the true or original boundary.

Case Example:

In 1957, the Corletts purchased a piece of property. In 1958, they bought the neighboring piece of property and built a fence on what they thought was the boundary line between the two properties. In 1970, the Corletts sold the west parcel to the Youngs, and in 1977, the Youngs sold it to the Rosses. Then, in 1978, the Corletts sold the east parcel to the Winanses.

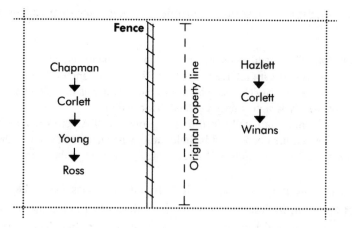

The Winanses had a survey done that showed the fence was not the true property line. The Winanses brought a quiet title action to establish the fence as the property line. The Rosses wanted the original boundary line to be upheld.

The court found that the new boundary (the fence) was established by a common grantor. (Remember that the Corletts originally owned both pieces of property and they put up the fence.) When the Corletts sold the west lot to the Youngs, it was with the understanding that the fence was the boundary. Thus, the court found that the

Corletts and the Youngs had agreed on a new boundary. Visual inspection of the property showed a fence that was clearly meant to be the dividing line. Therefore, the new boundary designated by the common grantor became the true boundary for all subsequent purchasers. *Winans v. Ross*, 35 Wn. App. 238, 666 P.2d 908 (1983).

Court Decision. Problems often arise in connection with the government survey method of land description. When much of the West was originally surveyed, the surveyors worked under harsh conditions, with inadequate tools and equipment by today's standards. Errors were frequently made. When these errors are discovered, the court normally attempts to maintain the line as intended by the original surveyors.

Case Example:

Two parcels of land were designated government lot numbers 5 and 6. They were established as government lots because of the presence of Crescent Lake. The Wicks owned lot 5, and the Ericksons owned lot 6. The original official government plat was produced in 1857 and showed that the lake crossed the north/south line between the lots, as shown in diagram number 1.

A more modern survey showed that the lake was actually 51 feet from the north/south line, as shown in diagram number 2. In a lawsuit concerning ownership of the chunk of property below the rim of the lake, the Wicks attempted to establish that their lot failed to close at the lake and actually continued on past the rim of the lake. They argued that the piece below the rim was actually part of their property.

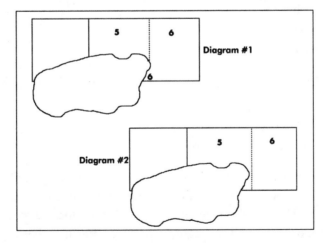

The court stated the intent of a new survey should be to ascertain where the original surveyors placed the boundaries, not where modern surveyors would place them. Therefore, the Wicks' lot should close at a point as near as possible to the one shown on the original government survey. The Wicks did not own property beyond that point, regardless of how a modern survey team would divide the property today. *Erickson v. Wick*, 22 Wn. App. 433, 591 P.2d 804 (1979).

Attachments

You are involved in a real estate transaction. Because the lot has been recently surveyed, you have a clear idea exactly how much property is being conveyed. But the legal description of the lot does not mention the house and garage built on the property, nor the lovely rose garden and collection of gardening tools. Are these included in the sale?

Whenever there is a sale or transfer of land, it is important to be able to distinguish between real property (which is included in the sale) and personal property (which can be removed by the seller). Buyers and sellers, landlords and tenants, owners and creditors often disagree about whether an item is personal property or part of the realty. These disagreements can lead to lawsuits.

> **Example:** A buyer sues a seller because the seller took the built-in washer and dryer with him and the buyer assumed they were included in the purchase price.

When there is a conflict like this, the real estate agent may end up paying for the disputed item out of her own pocket to keep the peace. Thus, it is important for all of the parties (seller, buyer, and agent) to know what things are included in the sale of the real property.

Most people automatically think of the land itself when they hear the term "real property." But real property is more than just rocks and dirt. Things attached to the land (like buildings and fences) and things growing on the land (like trees and shrubs) are called **attachments**, and they are considered part of the real property.

There are two main categories of attachments:

- natural attachments (such as trees and crops), and
- man-made attachments (fixtures).

Natural Attachments

Natural attachments are things growing on the property. There are two types of natural attachments:

- naturally occurring trees and plants; and
- plants grown and cultivated by people.

Traditionally, different legal rules applied to these two types of natural attachments, but those distinctions have largely been eliminated. Both types are considered part of the real property, and they will be included in a sale of the land unless they're specifically excepted from the sale in the purchase and sale agreement. Once they have been severed from the land, natural attachments are personal property.

> **Example:** Standing timber growing on the land is considered part of the real property. However, once cut (severed from the land), it becomes personal property.

Personal property is governed by a different set of rules than real property. Washington has adopted a statute called the **Uniform Commercial Code (UCC)** to deal with the sale of goods. The UCC defines crops as goods and governs their sale.

Under the UCC, crops that are specifically identified in a contract may be considered personal property even before they are actually severed from the land. This is referred to as **constructive severance**.

> **Example:** Farmer Beardsley sells the timber on his east 40 acres to a lumber company. The contract provides that the trees are to be cut. The lumber company owns the trees from the date of the contract, and the trees are considered personal property, even while they are still attached to the land.

Doctrine of Emblements. A special rule called the **doctrine of emblements** applies to crops planted by tenant farmers. If the tenancy is for an indefinite period of time, and the tenancy is terminated (through no fault of the tenant) before the crop is ready for harvest, the tenant has the right to re-enter the land and harvest the crop.

> **Example:** For several years, a farmer has been renting a large field from his neighbor. They have a year-to-year lease; it is automatically renewed each June until one of the parties gives the other notice of termination.
>
> In April, the neighbor tells the farmer the lease will end in June because she's planning to sell her land. The farmer has the right to enter the property in the autumn to harvest the crops he planted, even though the lease has ended.

To fall within this rule, the crop must be produced annually, by the labor and industry of the farmer. For example, if the crop is wild mushrooms, which were not planted or cultivated by the farmer, the rule does not apply. If the crops are an annual product of perennial plants, such as apples or blueberries, the right to re-enter and harvest applies only to the first crop that matures after the tenancy has ended.

Fixtures

Fixtures are man-made attachments. They are items that were once personal property, but are now attached to the real estate in such a way that they are considered part of the real property. For instance, a pile of lumber and a batch of nails are considered personal property. But are they still personal property if they are used to build a barn?

Whether a particular item is a fixture or personal property is a question that real estate agents deal with constantly. Earlier, we referred to a dispute over a built-in washer and dryer. Are these items fixtures? What about a tool shed? A freestanding swimming pool? A swing set?

To avoid controversy, the real estate agent should discuss these kinds of items with the parties, making sure that each person knows what is and is not included in the sale. Of course, to be able to do this, the agent must know what is normally considered a fixture and what is normally considered personal property.

Fig. 3.11 Fixture tests

FIXTURE TESTS

- Method of attachment
- Intention of the annexor
- Adaptation to the realty
- Relationship of the parties
- Evidence of written agreement

The courts have developed a series of tests to apply in deciding whether an item is a fixture. A court will consider the method of attachment, the intention of the annexor, adaptation of the item to the realty, the relationship of the parties, and whether there is a written agreement.

Method of Attachment. When an item is permanently attached to the land, it becomes part of the real estate. An attachment is considered to be permanently attached when it is:

- permanently resting on the land (like houses and barns and other buildings),
- affixed to the land by roots (as with trees and shrubs),
- embedded in the earth (like sewer lines or septic tanks), or
- attached by any enduring method (such as by cement, plaster, nails, bolts, or screws).

Genuine physical attachment (called **actual annexation**) is not absolutely necessary for an item to be considered a fixture.

> **Example:** An outbuilding on the Parkers' property is simply resting on the ground, without any foundation. Even so, it is considered to be a fixture, part of the real property.

An item may also be considered a fixture if it is enclosed within a room or building in such a manner that it cannot be removed without dismantling it or tearing down part of the building.

Constructive annexation. Some completely movable items are regarded as so strongly connected with the property that they are considered fixtures, even though they are not actually attached to the realty. This is called the **doctrine of constructive annexation**.

> **Example:** A firm that manufactures widgets sells its main processing plant. The widget-making machine weighs four tons and is bolted to the floor. It is clearly a fixture. The key to turn on the widget-maker and the specialized tools used to repair the machine, though easily moved, are also considered fixtures.

The doctrine of constructive annexation also applies to items that have been temporarily removed for servicing or repair, such as built-in appliances.

Example: Mr. Adams sells his house to Mr. Brown. At the time of the sale, the built-in dishwasher is at a repair shop. The dishwasher is still considered part of the sale, and its ownership transfers to Mr. Brown at the time of the sale.

Intention of the Annexor. The method of attachment test can be rigid and may lead to inconsistent results. Therefore, the courts have decided that the intention of the annexor is a more important test. (The **annexor** is the person who placed the item on the property.) This test asks this question: "Did the annexor intend the item to become part of the realty or to remain personal property?" If the annexor intended the item to become part of the realty, then the item will generally be considered real property. Conversely, if the annexor didn't intend the item to become part of the real property, the item will be considered personal property.

There must be objective evidence of the annexor's intent; the secret intent of the annexor does not control. Each of the other tests (including the method of attachment) is viewed as objective evidence of the annexor's intent.

Example: A property owner installed a birdbath by embedding it in concrete. This permanent method of attachment is evidence that she intended the birdbath to become part of the realty. Even if the owner claimed she always intended to take the birdbath with her when she moved, a court would be unlikely to rule that it is personal property.

Adaptation to the Realty. When an item is essential to the use and operation of the property, or was designed specifically for use in a particular location, such as pews in a church, it is probably a fixture.

Example: Computers placed in a general purpose office building are normally considered personal property. However, components of a computer system housed in a specially built computer facility have been held to be fixtures.

Relationship of the Parties. When attempting to determine intent, a court considers the relationship of the parties, such as landlord-tenant, seller-buyer, or owner-creditor.

Example: If a tenant screws a lamp fixture into the wall, it is generally assumed that she intends to take the lamp with her when she moves. Items installed by a tenant are usually personal property; both the landlord and the tenant would expect the tenant to remove the item.

However, if an owner installs a similar lamp fixture, it is generally assumed that he is attempting to improve the property, without thought of removing the lamp later. A lamp installed by an owner would probably be considered a fixture, and a buyer could assume that it would stay with the property.

Trade fixtures. A tenant who installs items for the purpose of carrying on a trade or business usually intends to remove the items at the end of the lease. Such items are called

trade fixtures. The general rule is that trade fixtures may be removed unless there is a contrary provision in the lease or the trade fixtures have become an integral part of the property.

Case Example:

Hahn ran an auto painting business in a building leased from the Whitneys. When Hahn left, he removed a furnace that the Whitneys claimed was a fixture. Hahn had installed the furnace to help dry paint and keep the employees warm. The court determined that this was a trade fixture that could be removed by the tenant. *Whitney v. Hahn*, 18 Wn.2d 198 (1943).

If the trade fixture has become an integral part of the property, but the tenant wants to remove it anyway, the tenant has the duty to restore the property to its original condition or compensate the owner for any damage caused by removing the fixture.

> **Example:** A tenant installed refrigeration units in a grocery store. Removing the units created a hole in the roof, ceiling, and wall. The tenant was required to repair the damage to the leased premises.

Allowing tenants to remove trade fixtures encourages efficiency in business. Tenants are more likely to install new equipment if they know they can take the equipment with them when they leave. Trade fixtures that are not removed when the tenant leaves automatically become the owner's property.

A rule similar to the trade fixtures rule applies to items installed by agricultural tenants for the purpose of farming the land. Certain farming equipment and items such as small tool sheds or prefabricated henhouses are called **agricultural fixtures** and may be removed by the tenant farmers when they leave the property.

Written Agreement. Regardless of any of the previously discussed considerations, if there is a written agreement between the parties stipulating how a particular item is to be treated, a court will respect and enforce the written agreement.

> **Example:** A seller planned to take certain shrubs from the property when she left. She informed the buyer of her intention and included a statement in the sales agreement specifying which shrubs she intended to remove. The written agreement allows her to remove the shrubs even though they would normally be considered part of the realty.

Case Example:

Frank Montgomery leased some property from a realty company. The 15-year lease provided that upon its expiration, Montgomery could remove all the structures he had placed on the premises. Montgomery placed a cabin on the property. Although a cabin would normally be a fixture, in this case the cabin was considered Montgomery's personal property because of the specific agreement in the lease. Although this is a New Mexico case, Washington law also recognizes that a written agreement supersedes all other considerations. *Garrison General Tire Service, Inc. v. Montgomery*, 75 N.M. 321, 404 P.2d 143 (1965).

Manufactured Homes. Traditionally, a mobile home or manufactured home was classified as personal property until it was permanently attached to land (for example, by mounting it on a foundation), at which point it became a fixture—part of the real property. Today, Washington has a title registration system for manufactured homes, similar to the one used for motor vehicles. In order for a manufactured home to become real property, it must go through a procedure called **title elimination**. This eliminates the registered title, and the home becomes part of the real property it is located on.

Secured Financing and Fixtures. A special problem with fixtures may arise if they were purchased with secured financing instead of cash. For example, when an appliance is purchased on credit, the creditor often takes a security interest in the appliance. This gives the creditor the right to repossess the appliance if it isn't paid for. In a real estate transaction, the buyer and the buyer's lender need to know whether any of the appliances or other fixtures are still subject to a creditor's security interest.

Article 9 of the Uniform Commercial Code governs secured financing for personal property, including items that will become fixtures. To establish a security interest in an item that will be a fixture, the creditor must have the borrower sign a security agreement that specifies the terms of the loan, and then must also file a brief document called a **financing statement** with the county recorder's office. The financing statement gives constructive notice to the public that a security interest exists in the item. Any later purchasers of the real estate are put on notice by this filing. If the secured creditor hasn't been paid in full, the item could be repossessed.

> **Example:** Dave Roberts owns an office building that is mortgaged to State Bank. He purchases a central air conditioning unit and has it installed on a concrete slab in back of the building. He buys the air conditioner on credit, and the seller files a financing statement to give notice of its security interest.
>
> Dave defaults on his payments to the bank and to the air conditioning company. Normally, a central air conditioner would be considered a fixture, and upon default ownership of the air conditioner would pass to the bank along with the office building. However, since a financing statement has been filed, the air conditioning company can repossess the air conditioner.

In a real estate transaction covered by title insurance (see Chapter 9), the title report should list any unexpired financing statements for fixtures that are part of the property being purchased. Creditors holding a security interest in fixtures are commonly paid off when the real estate transaction closes.

Appurtenances

Once you know the boundaries of the property and what items are included in the sale, you must become familiar with the property rights that transfer with the property ownership.

One of the best ways to understand real property and its accompanying rights is to imagine property as an **inverted pyramid** with its tip at the center of the earth and its base extending out into the sky. A property owner has rights to the surface of the land within the property's boundaries, plus everything under or over the surface that falls within the pyramid. This includes rights to oil and minerals beneath the surface, plus certain air and water rights.

An **appurtenance** is a right or interest that is associated with a piece of real property. Examples of appurtenances are the rights to use air, water, and minerals in or on the land. When real property is sold or transferred, these rights are normally transferred along with the property, but they may be sold separately or limited by past transactions. When you are involved in a real estate transaction, it's important to be aware of these rights and how they can be limited.

Air Rights

According to the inverted pyramid idea, a property owner's rights would theoretically extend to the upper limits of the sky. However, through the Air Commerce Act of 1926 and the Civil Aeronautics Act of 1938, Congress declared that the federal government has complete control over U.S. airspace.

Use of Airspace. Although the federal government has placed restrictions on air rights, property owners still have the exclusive right to use the lower reaches of airspace over their property, so long as they do nothing to impede or interfere with normal air traffic. In addition, property owners have the right not to be harmed or damaged by use of the airspace above their property.

> **Example:** The classic example is an airport built near a chicken farm. The noise of the airplanes flying at low altitude over the chicken farm causes the chickens to stop laying eggs. If the farmer can prove that he has suffered actual harm, he may be able to recover damages for trespass in his airspace.

Sale of Airspace. A property owner may sell rights to the airspace above the property separately from the surface land. As population increases and real estate prices rise, the sale of airspace has become more common, especially in large metropolitan areas.

> **Example:** The New York Central and New Haven railroads had tracks running across real estate in a prime location. They sold rights to the airspace above the tracks for an enormous sum. The purchasers acquired the airspace plus a surface easement necessary for the construction and support of buildings. The Park Avenue Development (a large development of commercial buildings) was subsequently built above the tracks.

> **Example:** In 2005, to prevent possible blocking of views, the developers of Seattle's Four Seasons Hotel and the Harbor Steps building jointly purchased the air rights above an old theater on First Avenue.

Water Rights

Because water is a vital resource, it has been the source of much legislation and litigation in the United States, particularly in the arid parts of the West. Questions arise as to ownership of water, the right to use water, and ownership of a lake or stream bed.

The two main types of water rights are riparian rights and appropriative rights.

Riparian Rights. Riparian rights arise on properties that are bordered or crossed by water, or contain a body of water within their boundaries. Under the riparian rights system, every landowner who has land touching the water (riparian land) has an equal right to use the water.

All riparian owners may use the lake or stream for swimming, boating, or other recreational purposes. They also have the right to take water for domestic uses such as drinking, bathing, and watering a garden. However, a riparian owner may not take so much water that it lowers the level of the lake or diminishes the quantity or velocity of the stream's flow, affecting the other riparian owners. Also, a riparian owner may not divert water for use on non-riparian land (land that does not adjoin the body of water).

> **Example:** Davis and Carleton both own property along Blueberry Creek. Davis, the upstream owner, also owns a field across the road from the creek. He decides to turn the field into a commercial rice paddy. He diverts so much water from the creek to his non-riparian field that there isn't enough water downstream for Carleton's legitimate domestic uses, such as watering her garden. A court could prohibit Davis from using the water in this way, because it is being used on non-riparian land, is not a domestic use, diminishes the flow of water, and interferes with Carleton's right to use the water.

The common law of England recognized riparian rights, so the riparian rights system became law in the American colonies and eventually throughout most of the United States, including the Washington Territory (before Washington became a state). The riparian system is still used to a greater or lesser extent in many parts of the country. However, as water rights and water law became a more significant issue, many western states, including Washington, moved away from riparian rights to a system of appropriative rights.

Appropriative Rights. Under the system of appropriative rights—also called the **prior appropriation system**—the right to use water in a way that diminishes the normal quantity is established by obtaining a water permit from the state government. The permit holder is authorized to take or divert water from a certain lake, river, or sea for the purpose (the beneficial use) specified in the permit application. The water does not have to be used on land adjoining the body of water that it was taken from.

Under the prior appropriation system, if two or more parties have appropriation permits for the same body of water, first in time is first in right. This means that the party who obtained a permit first can use the full amount of water authorized in the permit, even if this leaves too little water for those who obtained permits later.

> **Example:** Continuing with the previous example, now suppose that instead of relying on riparian rights, Davis applies for a permit to use the amount of water necessary to turn his non-riparian field into a rice paddy. The permit is granted because an experiment

to determine the feasibility of growing rice in this area is considered a beneficial use of the water. Davis will be allowed to divert the amount of water specified in his permit, even if that diminishes the normal flow of the creek, and even if (during a drought, for example) that leaves too little water in the creek for those who hold permits issued after Davis's permit.

Washington's Water Code (RCW 90.03) establishes prior appropriation as the dominant water law of the state and specifies the procedure for obtaining an appropriation permit. In Washington, the prior appropriation system applies to underground water as well as surface water.

Disappearance of Riparian Rights. When the Water Code was passed in 1917, it provided that any existing riparian rights that were not put to a beneficial use would be lost. Later case law established 1932 (15 years after enactment of the code) as the date by which unused riparian rights had to be put to use or else would be forfeited. Landowners who were exercising their riparian rights and putting the water to a beneficial use retained those rights.

> **Example:** In 1915, Shoemaker and Bertoldo each purchased a piece of property that bordered on Houseman Lake. When they acquired their properties, they automatically acquired riparian rights to the lake water. Shoemaker and Bertoldo both use the lake for fishing and swimming, and Bertoldo also uses water from the lake to water his garden.
>
> It is now 1932 and the legal deadline has passed, so unused riparian rights have been forfeited. Bertoldo can still take water from the lake to water his garden; but if Shoemaker wants to start a garden and use lake water for it, he will have to apply for a permit. Shoemaker has lost his riparian rights because he was not using them. Now he cannot use any of the lake water in a way that would diminish the quantity unless he obtains a permit. (Note that he can still use the water for recreation or transportation.)

In 1967, a new provision in the Water Code required that all claims to water rights not already certified by the state had to be recorded by July 1974. This meant that any riparian rights (any water rights that were not granted under the permit system) had to be recorded. Riparian owners did not have to get permits; they simply had to record a document claiming their rights. Any water rights not claimed in this way were deemed relinquished.

> **Example:** Returning to the example above, suppose it's now decades later and Bertoldo's granddaughter has inherited his property on Houseman Lake. She still uses water from the lake, but she fails to record her water rights claim before the 1974 deadline. As a result, she loses the right to take water from the lake for domestic purposes. Now if she wants to use the lake water for her garden, she will have to apply for a permit.

As a result of this rule, unless a riparian landowner's water rights were recorded before the 1974 deadline or a permit has been granted, the only rights the owner has to water bordering his property are rights that do not diminish the quantity of water. Those rights include boating, swimming, and other recreational or aesthetic uses. Additional water rights may only be acquired through compliance with the permit system.

In addition to imposing the recording requirement, the 1967 legislation also provided that under certain circumstances a right to take water will be relinquished after five years of nonuse. That rule applies both to riparian landowners and to permit holders under the prior appropriation system.

Navigable Waters. The question of whether or not a body of water is **navigable** is significant because it affects ownership of lake beds, riverbeds, seabeds, and beaches. The Washington Supreme Court has stated that for a particular body of water to be considered navigable, it must be "capable of being used practically for the carriage of commerce."

Large bodies of water like Puget Sound, Lake Chelan, and the Columbia River are obviously considered navigable. With smaller lakes or rivers, navigability can be a more difficult question. In some cases whether a particular body of water is navigable can be determined only when there is a lawsuit concerning the issue and a decision is rendered by the court.

In the U.S., the navigable waterways in each state are owned and managed by the state government (subject to federal regulation of navigation). Each state government holds its navigable waters in trust for the benefit of the public. When a parcel of land borders on an ocean, sea, or navigable lake or river, the landowner's property usually ends at the ordinary high water mark or high tide line. The strip of shoreland or tideland beyond that point, as well as the land that's always submerged, is generally owned by the state government. The state used to convey title to shorelands and tidelands to private parties, but that practice ended in 1971; now private parties can only lease them from the state. (Earlier conveyances weren't invalidated by this change, however.)

There is a public easement for right-of-way on all navigable waters, which means that the public has the right to use the waterways for transportation. The public also has the right to make reasonable use of the surface of the water (for swimming and boating, for example) unless specifically prohibited. Landowners who own property bordering navigable waters may also apply for an appropriation permit that would allow them to take a specified amount of water for a designated beneficial use.

Non-navigable Waters. If a small lake is completely within the boundaries of one landowner's property, the landowner owns the lake bed. If a non-navigable lake or stream is bordered by properties owned by different landowners, ownership of the lake bed or stream bed is generally divided by tracing lines from each property boundary to the center of the lake or stream. Each owner has title to the parcel of the lake bed or stream bed adjoining their land. Each also has the right to the reasonable use of the entire surface of the lake or stream for purposes such as swimming and boating.

Case Example:

A developer attempted to erect an apartment building over a portion of Bitter Lake, a small, non-navigable lake in Seattle. Even though there was no question that the developer was building only on the portion of the lake bed it owned, the court required the building to be removed because it interfered with the rights of the other landowners around Bitter Lake to make reasonable use of the surface of the lake. *Bach v. Sarich*, 74 Wn.2d 575, 445 P.2d 648 (1968).

Mineral Rights

A landowner generally owns all minerals located in or under her property. Minerals are considered real property until they are extracted, at which point they become personal property. A landowner may sell mineral rights separately from the actual land. This type of sale is sometimes called a **horizontal division**. The right to own and use the surface property is divided from ownership of or rights to the subsurface minerals. The four main methods of dividing mineral rights are:

1. **Mineral deed**—A mineral deed transfers all rights to the minerals, and also grants the rights necessary to conduct mining operations to obtain the minerals. This usually includes the rights of access, development, processing, and transportation.
2. **Mineral reservation**—A mineral reservation is similar to a mineral deed, except that the owner sells or transfers the surface property and retains the mineral rights for himself.

Case Example:

Burlington Northern Railroad sold property to the Weyerhaeuser Company but retained the mineral rights for itself. The deed specifically reserved to the railroad "all minerals of any nature whatsoever, including coal, iron, natural gas and oil, upon or in said land. . ." Weyerhaeuser purchased the land and all of its accompanying rights, except the mineral rights, which were kept by the railroad. *Weyerhaeuser Co. v. Burlington Northern, Inc.*, 15 Wn.App. 314, 549 P.2d 54 (1976).

---

3. **Mineral lease**—Under a mineral lease, the lessee is given the right to mine and has title to the minerals obtained, but the lessor retains a future right in the minerals. The property owner is usually compensated by royalty payments based on a percentage of the value of the extracted minerals.
4. **Mineral rights option**—A mineral rights option grants the right to explore for the presence of minerals. After exercising this option, the mining company would then decide whether or not to lease or purchase the mineral rights as stated in the option agreement.

Support Rights

A landowner has the right to the natural support of the land provided by surrounding land. **Lateral support** is the right to support from adjacent land. This right applies not only to land, but also to improvements such as buildings, so long as the added weight of the improvements is not the cause of the problem. To make a case for a violation of lateral support rights, the slipping and sliding of the soil must occur because of the soil's own weight and not because of the superimposed weight of improvements.

Example: Smith and Jones own property next to each other. Smith builds a house on his property. There is no problem with soil slippage. A few years later, Jones decides to level his property before building. He brings in bulldozers and removes several feet of soil near Smith's property line.

The soil on Smith's property begins to slide. This destroys expensive landscaping, and several cracks develop in the foundation of Smith's house. Jones may be liable for the damage to Smith's property, since his bulldozing removed vital lateral support.

Subjacent support is the right to support from the underlying earth. This right is significant when the property is divided horizontally and rights to underlying minerals or oil and gas are transferred to someone else. The underlying owner may be liable for damage to the surface property caused by excavations in the supporting earth.

Oil and Gas Rights

Washington does not produce large quantities of oil or natural gas. However, when the issue arises, Washington follows the non-ownership theory, which holds that underground oil and gas are not subject to ownership, because of their migratory nature. Under this theory, a property owner cannot actually own the oil or gas until it is pumped to the surface, where it becomes personal property.

Oil and gas in their natural states lie trapped under great pressure beneath the surface of the earth. However, once an oil or gas reservoir has been tapped, the oil and gas begin to flow toward the point where the reservoir was pierced by the well, since this is the area of lowest pressure. By drilling a well, a property owner could theoretically drain an oil or gas reservoir that lay beneath his own property and beneath several neighbors' property as well.

Rule of Capture. Once oil or gas has been pumped to the surface, it is governed by the **rule of capture**. This rule specifies that if a property owner drills on his own land, he owns all of the oil or gas produced, even though it may have migrated from under a neighbor's land.

This rule stimulates oil and gas production. If the neighbors want to protect their interests in the oil or gas that lies beneath their property, they must drill offset wells, in order to keep all of the oil or gas from migrating to one well. The outcome is that more oil or gas is produced in a shorter amount of time because more wells are drilled.

Since landowners usually do not have the necessary skill, experience, or equipment to drill for oil or gas themselves, they often enter into lease agreements with oil or gas companies who drill the wells and extract the oil or gas. There is no standard lease form, but oil and gas leases generally include an initial cash amount paid for granting the lease, a specified lease term, a method by which the lease term may be extended if necessary, and the amount of royalties to be paid to the landowner based on the amount of oil or gas actually extracted.

Conclusion

As you can see, a sale or other transfer of real property involves much more than just the land. You need to know where the property boundaries lie, what natural attachments and fixtures are included, and whether any rights that are ordinarily appurtenant to real property have been severed. Knowing how real property is described and what rights go along with real property ownership will help you avoid some of the problems that commonly arise in real estate transactions.

Case Problem

The following is a hypothetical case problem. Most of the facts are taken from a real case. Based on what you have learned from this chapter, make a decision on the issues presented, and then check to see if your answer matches the decision reached by the court.

The Facts

Henry Timm rented a house from his brother from 1948 through 1972. During that time he made many improvements to the home. Upon his brother's death, the house was put up for sale and advertised as "remodeled." Timm participated in the arrangements for the sale and knew that it was being advertised as remodeled.

When the house was sold, Timm moved out, taking with him:

1. a kitchen sink and cabinet combination installed to modernize the kitchen,
2. an exhaust fan constructed in a wall to replace a window,
3. two baseboard heaters, and
4. carpeting attached to the floor by nailing strips and staples.

A dispute developed over whether or not these items were fixtures that should have remained with the house. At the trial, Timm said that he considered these items his personal property and always intended to take them with him. However, he had never previously expressed this intention.

The Question

Which of the items listed above, if any, would be considered fixtures?

The Answer

In the case of *Kane v. Timm*, 11 Wn. App. 910, 527 P.2d 480 (1974), the court found that all of the items were fixtures except for the baseboard heaters.

Consider all of the tests used to determine whether an item is a fixture. The intention of the annexor is the most significant test. Although Timm said that he always intended to take these items with him, he had not previously expressed this intent. A secret intent cannot govern; there must be objective evidence of intent.

The kitchen sink and cabinet unit were installed to modernize the kitchen. This implies an intent for the items to remain in the kitchen. Remember also that Timm knew that the house was advertised as "remodeled." If the updated items were removed, it could hardly be considered remodeled.

The exhaust fan was built into the wall to replace a window. So constructed, it was specifically adapted to this particular realty.

The carpet was attached by nailing strips and staples, fairly permanent methods of attachment. The baseboard heaters were probably resting on the floor, with no actual attachment to the property.

As to the relationship of the parties, although Timm was renting the property from his brother, he lived on the premises for 24 years—longer than many people live in homes they own. It is likely that when Timm improved the property, he intended the improvements to remain with the property.

None of the items were trade fixtures, and there was no written agreement concerning them.

Chapter Summary

- Knowing the correct boundaries of a parcel of real property is important to the buyer, the seller, and the real estate agent. A seller may be held liable for innocently misrepresenting property boundaries. An agent will usually not be held liable for an innocent misrepresentation based on information provided by a seller; but the agent should make a reasonable effort to determine if the seller's statements are accurate.

- The three main methods of land description are metes and bounds, government survey, and lot and block. The lot and block method is the system used most frequently in metropolitan areas.

- The two types of attachments to real property are natural attachments and man-made attachments (fixtures). The tests used to determine whether an item is a fixture include: method of attachment, intention of the annexor, adaptation to the realty, relationship of the parties, and written agreement.

- An appurtenance is a right or interest associated with real property, such as air, water, oil and gas, and mineral rights. These rights are normally transferred along with the property, but they may be severed and sold separately.

- The use of water is regulated by one of two systems: the riparian rights system or the appropriative rights system. Prior appropriation is the dominant water law in the state of Washington. To acquire an appropriative right, you must obtain a permit from the government.

Checklist of Problem Areas

Real Estate Licensee's Checklist

☐ Any sale of property raises questions as to which items are fixtures. A real estate agent should be aware of which items the seller plans to remove and which will remain with the real property. The following are some items that often cause disputes:

- carpeting (in general, unattached rugs are personal property, but wall-to-wall carpeting specially cut to fit the room and tacked to the floor is a fixture);
- drapes and venetian blinds;
- mirrors and chandeliers;
- appliances such as refrigerators, stoves, microwave ovens, and air conditioners (the method of attachment is important here—a freestanding refrigerator or a microwave oven that can be removed by merely disconnecting an electric plug is generally personal property, but a built-in unit may be considered a fixture);
- special landscaping such as expensive trees or shrubs;
- play equipment such as swing sets and slides; and
- birdbaths, sundials, or statues in the garden or yard.

☐ Most listing agreement forms and purchase and sale agreement forms contain a clause that lists included items. The pre-printed list of items is not necessarily the same on all forms, however. An agent should make sure that both the listing agreement and the purchase and sale agreement list the same items, so that problems don't arise later.

☐ If an agent has any reason to doubt a seller's statement regarding the size of the property, or if the seller is not sure of the exact boundaries of the property, the agent should proceed with caution. Some agents put a statement like "Buyer is to verify size of the property" in the MLS listing information, to protect themselves against inaccuracies in both the lot size and the size of the structures. If there are questions concerning the true boundaries of the property, the agent should recommend that the property be surveyed.

☐ An agent should check to see if all appurtenant rights (such as mineral rights or oil and gas rights) pass with the property, or if any rights have already been transferred or sold to another party, or if the seller plans to retain any appurtenant rights. (The title report will indicate whether any rights have been transferred to another party, if the seller isn't sure.)

Seller's Checklist

❑ Unless the property has been surveyed recently, a seller should not claim to know the location of the boundaries with certainty. Remember, a seller can be held liable for making an innocent misrepresentation to a buyer.

❑ If a seller wants to remove items that might be considered fixtures, a written list of excluded items should be incorporated into the purchase and sale agreement. It may also be advisable to simply remove certain items before showing the property. This way there can be no questions later about whether or not a particular item was meant to be included in the sale.

❑ If a seller wants to retain any rights that would ordinarily pass to the buyer (such as mineral rights), there must be a clear provision in the purchase and sale agreement and in the deed that severs these rights from the conveyed property.

Buyer's Checklist

❑ A buyer should ask where the boundaries of the property lie. If the agent or seller is uncertain, the buyer should consider requesting a new survey.

❑ A buyer should ask specific questions concerning whether or not certain items are fixtures that will transfer with the property, and then make sure that the purchase and sale agreement accurately reflects the parties' understanding concerning the fixtures.

❑ It's important for a buyer to know whether financing statements have been filed on any of the property's fixtures. (These would usually be listed in the title report.)

❑ A buyer also needs to know whether the air rights, mineral rights, and oil and gas rights are still appurtenant to the property, or if they have already been severed from the land and sold to another party.

Chapter Quiz

1. A portion of a metes and bounds description states "thence south 275 feet to the edge of the old gravel pit." A recent survey shows that it is actually 280 feet to the old gravel pit. The property:
   a. will end at 275 feet because distances take precedence over monuments
   b. will end at the edge of the gravel pit because monuments take precedence over distances
   c. will have to be resurveyed and a new description provided
   d. None of the above

2. Under the government survey method of land description, a township is divided up into how many sections?
   a. 12
   b. 20
   c. 36
   d. 42

3. New guide meridians are established at each correction line:
   a. because of the curvature of the earth, so that the lines don't converge
   b. because of the curvature of the earth, so that the lines don't convect
   c. because when the surveying was first begun, 24 miles was the largest interval they could survey
   d. Both a) and c)

4. A government lot:
   a. is a lot owned by the government
   b. is a parcel of land of irregular shape or size
   c. must be described using the lot and block system
   d. None of the above

5. The method of land description used most often in large metropolitan areas is:
   a. rectangular survey
   b. lot and block
   c. metes and bounds
   d. government survey

6. If the tenancy is terminated before a crop is ready to harvest, the tenant farmer has the right to re-enter the land and harvest the crop. This rule is known as the doctrine of:
   a. fructus industriales
   b. constructive annexation
   c. emblements
   d. appurtenance

7. Kirk Horton is in the process of selling his house to Susan Bianucci. At the time of closing, the dishwasher is at the repair shop. Under the doctrine of constructive annexation, the dishwasher:
   a. will not be considered part of the sale
   b. is a fixture that will be considered part of the sale
   c. will have to be conveyed under a separate contract since it was not actually present at the time of the sale
   d. None of the above

8. In determining whether or not an item is a fixture, the most important test is the:
   a. relationship of the parties
   b. adaptation to the realty
   c. intention of the annexor
   d. character of the item

9. Trade fixtures:

   a. are considered real property and cannot be removed by the tenant
   b. must be specified in the lease to be removable
   c. are generally removable
   d. None of the above

10. A candy maker has a two-year lease. The lease specifies that any improvements the tenant makes to the property will remain with the property and pass to the owner upon termination of the lease. The candy maker installs a marble counter to roll the candy on. When the lease is up:

   a. the candy maker may remove the marble counter because it is a trade fixture
   b. the candy maker may remove the counter because it is not a fixture
   c. the candy maker may not remove the counter because of the written agreement
   d. the candy maker may not remove the counter because he did not ask the owner if he could install it

11. Western Pacific Railroad has tracks that run through downtown Metropolis. Western Pacific owns the strip of land that the tracks are located on. Megacorp wants to purchase the airspace above the tracks to build a shopping complex. Which of the following is true?

   a. Megacorp must purchase the air rights from the federal government, since it has control over airspace
   b. Megacorp can purchase the air rights from Western Pacific Railroad
   c. Megacorp cannot purchase the air rights; unlike other appurtenant rights, they can't be sold separately from the land
   d. None of the above

12. Abe Harris owns two sections of property. One borders along Red Rock Creek, and the other section is across the road and does not adjoin the creek. Abe uses water from the creek to irrigate his crops on both sections of property. This use of the water:

   a. is illegal
   b. is legal since he has a riparian right to the use of the water
   c. is legal if he has obtained a permit giving him an appropriative right to the water
   d. None of the above

13. Alison Simmons owns property along a navigable river.

   a. Alison owns the section of the riverbed adjoining her property and running to the middle of the river
   b. The government owns and controls the riverbed
   c. Alison is not entitled to any use of the water since it is owned by the government
   d. Both b) and c)

14. Greg Majeski has horizontally divided his property and sold all the mineral rights to a mining corporation along with the necessary rights to obtain the minerals. This type of a mineral sale is called a:

   a. mineral deed
   b. mineral reservation
   c. mineral lease
   d. mineral option

15. In dealing with oil and gas rights, the rule of capture provides that:

    a. a property owner can only own the oil and gas captured from beneath her own land. Oil or gas that migrates from beneath a neighbor's land is owned by the neighbor

    b. a property owner who drills on her own land owns all of the oil or gas produced even though some of the oil or gas may have migrated from under a neighbor's land

    c. oil and gas remain real property even after being captured

    d. None of the above

4 Interests in Real Property

Outline

IV. Liens (Financial Encumbrances)
   A. Mortgages and deeds of trust
   B. Construction liens
   C. Judgment liens
   D. Tax liens
   E. Lien priority
   F. Protecting the debtor

Key Terms

- Freehold estate
- Fee simple estate
- Fee simple absolute
- Fee simple defeasible
- Life estate
- Life tenant
- Pur autre vie
- Estate in remainder
- Remainderman
- Estate in reversion
- Waste
- Leasehold
- Estate for years
- Periodic tenancy

- Tenancy at will
- Tenancy at sufferance
- Wrongful possession
- Encumbrance
- Easement
- Appurtenant
- In gross
- Runs with the land
- Dominant tenement
- Servient tenement
- Estoppel
- Prescription
- Hostile
- Merger

- License
- Encroachment
- Trespass
- Nuisance
- Specific lien
- General lien
- Redemption
- Construction lien
- Foreclosure
- Lien priority
- Judgment lien
- Special assessment
- Homestead exemption

Chapter Overview

Interests in real property refer to the rights or claims people have in property. Do they actually "own" the property or are they simply leasing it? Do they have an immediate interest or a future interest? Do they have the right to possess the property, or is their interest an easement or lien?

The answers to these questions are significant to the seller, the buyer, and the real estate agent, since a person can only sell or transfer the interest that he owns. For example, if you are renting a house, you may assign your lease to someone else, but you can't sell the house because you don't actually own it.

Before purchasing property, a buyer must be sure the seller owns the type of interest that the buyer wants to purchase. It is also important to find out if other people have any interests in the property, such as mortgages, easements, or judgment liens.

This chapter describes the various interests in property, including how they are created and terminated and how they affect the property.

Estates

An **estate** is an interest in land that is—or may become—possessory. In other words, the person who holds the interest currently has, or may have in the future, the right to possess the property. The various types of estates can be distinguished both by their duration and when they may be possessed. A present interest gives a person the right to immediate possession of the property. A future interest gives a person the right to possess the property only at some future date.

Freehold Estates

Under the English feudal system, all land was owned by the king. The king parceled out land to his followers in return for certain services. These men often created subtenancies by renting out portions of their properties. The modern American system that allows several different people to possess interests or estates in the same piece of property grew out of that feudal system. Many of the legal terms still used in discussing real estate came out of that system.

The term "freehold" originally referred to the holdings of a freeman under the English system. A freeman was allowed to sell his rights in the property, as long as the new owner agreed to give the same services to the lord or king, who held a higher interest in the property.

In modern usage, a freehold estate may still be sold, and unless specifically stated otherwise, the new owner acquires the same type of ownership held by the previous owner.

A **freehold estate** is a possessory interest in real property that is of uncertain duration, which means that the length of time of ownership is unspecified and indefinite. There are two main categories of freehold estates:

- the fee simple estate, and
- the life estate.

Fee Simple Estates

Normally, when a person is referred to as the "owner" of property, it is assumed that she holds a fee simple estate. A **fee simple estate** is the highest and best interest that can exist in land. A fee simple is always:

1. inheritable,
2. transferable, and
3. perpetual.

That an estate is **inheritable** means quite simply that it can be inherited—left to someone in a will, or automatically passed to heirs upon death if there is no will. A fee simple estate is also freely **transferable**, which means that it can be sold, divided, or even given away with no restrictions. Finally, a fee simple is **perpetual**, meaning that a person who holds a fee simple estate has the right to possess the property for an indefinite period of time. Since there is no specified termination date, a fee simple estate can theoretically be held forever (in perpetuity) by the titleholder or heirs.

The fee simple estate is divided into two subcategories:

1. fee simple absolute, and
2. fee simple defeasible.

Fee Simple Absolute. A **fee simple absolute** is essentially the same type of fee simple estate described above: inheritable, transferable, and perpetual. In a typical sale of property, the real estate agent and the buyer assume that the seller holds a fee simple absolute title and that this same interest will pass to the new buyer. However, it is important to recognize that not every estate is a fee simple absolute. The grantor of property can qualify the estate being transferred and specify that it is not a pure fee simple absolute. Such qualifications create what are called fee simple defeasible estates.

Fee Simple Defeasible. When transferring property, the grantor may want to include certain conditions on the use of the property. As long as these conditions are met or a specified future event does not occur, the **fee simple defeasible** is also for an indefinite period of time, just like the fee simple absolute. However, a defeasible estate can be defeated, or undone, upon the happening of the future event specified by the grantor.

There are two types of defeasible fees:

- fee simple determinable, and
- fee simple subject to condition subsequent.

A **fee simple determinable** estate will automatically revert back to the grantor, or the grantor's heirs, if certain conditions are not met. This type of estate is usually created by using the words "so long as," "which," "while," "during," or "until."

> **Example:** Wilmington Elementary School was located next to property owned by Mrs. Martin. In 1997, Mrs. Martin transferred her property as a gift to the Mountain View School District. The deed specified "so long as it is used for school purposes." For many years the property was used at recess as a playground by the children at Wilmington Elementary.
>
> In 2018, due to population changes and the failure of school levies, the Mountain View School District closes down Wilmington Elementary. After that point, none of the property is used for school purposes. Mrs. Martin's property automatically reverts back to her, or to her heirs.

A **fee simple subject to condition subsequent** is an estate that may revert back to the grantor if certain conditions are not met. The conditions are usually expressed with the words "if," "provided that," or "on the condition that." When the conditions are not met, the grantor or heirs have the right, at their option, to terminate the estate and reacquire the property. This estate is similar to a fee simple determinable, except that the termination is not automatic. The grantor or heirs must take legal steps to terminate the estate; they are said to have the **power of termination**.

> **Example:** Consider the example used above. Suppose the deed said "provided that it is used for school purposes." When the property was no longer used for school purposes, it would not automatically revert to Mrs. Martin (or her heirs). She would have to take legal steps to terminate the estate.

The fee simple determinable estate can produce harsh outcomes, because if a condition is not met, the property automatically reverts back to the grantor. To avoid this inflexible result, courts generally try to construe the terms of a grant of a defeasible fee as conditional rather than determinable. Automatic reversion is thus avoided; action by the grantor is required to terminate the estate.

Life Estates

A **life estate** is an estate that is based on someone's lifetime. For example, Harrison dies, leaving his farm to a charity, but grants a life estate to his sister. Harrison's sister may possess and live on the property for the remainder of her life, but upon her death, the farm will automatically pass to the charity.

Life estates are often used to simplify the division of property in a will or to avoid the expense of probate. A life estate is usually measured by the life of the holder of the life estate.

> **Example:** To avoid the expense of probating his will after death, Bob deeds his property to his son Stan, but reserves a life estate for himself. Bob has the right to use and possess the property for the rest of his lifetime, but upon his death, the property automatically passes to Stan.

This example describes an **express reservation** of a life estate to the original owner of the property. A life estate may also be created by **express grant** to someone other than the original owner.

A life estate may also be based on the life of someone other than the holder of the life estate. This is called a life estate **pur autre vie** (for another's life). This type of estate is sometimes used to create security for ailing parents or disabled children who are unable to provide for themselves.

> **Example:** Bob's mother is afflicted with Alzheimer's disease, and his sister Charlotte is her caregiver. Bob deeds his property to Charlotte so long as their mother is still alive. Upon their mother's death, the property is to pass to Bob's son Stan.
>
> Charlotte has a life estate based on their mother's life. Charlotte has the right to use and possess the property only so long as their mother is alive. When their mother dies, the property automatically passes to Stan.

Their mother is the **measuring life**. The life estate lasts only as long as her lifetime. Charlotte is the holder of the life estate. She has the right to possess the property and is called the **life tenant**.

The life tenant has an ownership interest in the land that can be sold, leased, or mortgaged. Remember, however, that a person can only sell, lease, or mortgage the interest she owns. In the example above, if Charlotte, the life tenant, sells her interest in the property, the buyers are purchasing only a life estate. The buyers' interest will still terminate when the measuring life ends—that is, when Bob and Charlotte's mother dies—just as it would have if Charlotte still owned the life estate at that point.

Future Possessory Interests. When a life estate is given, an interest also passes to the person who will receive the property when the life estate ends. This is a **future possessory interest**, since he does not have the right to possess the property until sometime in the future (at the death of the measuring life). There are two types of future possessory interests:

- estates in remainder, and
- estates in reversion.

Case Example:

In his will, George left his second wife, Wilma, a life estate in the family home, with the remainder interest to his six adult children from a previous marriage.

After George's death, Wilma had the right to use and possess the property for the rest of her lifetime. Upon her death, the property was to pass automatically to the children. *In re Estate of Campbell*, 87 Wn. App. 506 (1997).

In this case example, George's children hold an **estate in remainder**. Although they do not have the right to possess the property right now, they have a current interest in the remainder of the estate (the estate that will begin when the life estate terminates). George's children are called the **remaindermen**.

When the property is designated to return to the original grantor at the end of the life estate, the grantor has an **estate in reversion**. The grantor (or the grantor's heir) may be known as a reversioner.

A life tenant has certain duties towards the property. A life tenant may not use or abuse the property in any way that would permanently damage the property or reduce its market value. Such abuse is called **waste**. This term implies neglect or misconduct, and does not include ordinary depreciation of property due to age and normal use.

A life tenant must allow for reasonable inspection of the property by the holder of the future possessory interest. He is permitted to check for possible waste. If waste is discovered, the holder of the future possessory interest may bring a legal action for damages. An action for waste may be brought at any time, against either the life tenant, or if the life tenant has died, against the life tenant's estate.

Trusts. In modern practice, life estates are seldom used because trusts provide the same benefits, with the additional safety factor of a trustee who looks out for the interests of the specified party.

When a trust is created, a trustee is given legal title to property that she holds for the life of the beneficiary. Upon the death of the beneficiary, the property is disposed of as provided for by the creator of the trust.

Leasehold Estates

A **leasehold estate** is a more limited interest in property than a freehold estate. The holder of a leasehold estate—the **tenant**—does not own the property but merely leases or rents the property. This gives the tenant the right to exclusive possession of the property for a time.

Although most real estate agents deal with the sale of property, many are also involved in renting or leasing property. Even for an agent who deals only with sales, a knowledge of the different types of leasehold estates is important. If a sale involves rental property, the potential buyer may want to know what kind of leases the current tenants hold, and if or when their leases could be terminated.

In Washington, three different kinds of leasehold estates are recognized:

- tenancy for a specific term (also called estate for years or term tenancy),
- periodic tenancy, and
- tenancy at will.

We'll also discuss the tenancy at sufferance, which is similar to the above tenancies but isn't actually an estate.

Estate for Years

The **estate for years** lasts for a specific time period. Despite its name, this type of estate is not required to have a term of one year or a period of years. It may be for three months, six months and five days, two years, or any period with a specific beginning and ending date.

> **Example:** Ramon is a college student renting an apartment for one semester. The lease gives him the right to possess the apartment from August 20 until December 31. Ramon's tenancy is an estate for years because it is for a specific time period.

With an estate for years, neither party is required to give notice to terminate the lease agreement. The lease terminates automatically at the end of the specified rental period. If the parties want to terminate the lease before the specified end of the lease period, they may do so by mutual consent. The termination of an estate for years by mutual consent is called **surrender**.

Fig. 4.1 Types of estates

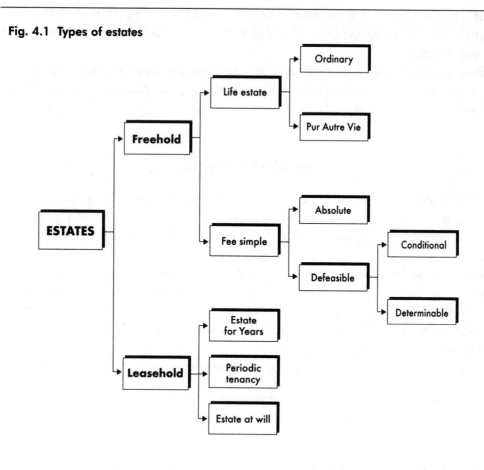

Unless specifically prohibited by the lease, an estate for years is assignable by the tenant. This means that a tenant may sublease or assign the interest in the lease to another party. The lease agreement is not terminated, but is merely taken over by someone else.

Periodic Tenancy

A **periodic tenancy** continues from period to period until terminated by proper notice from one of the parties. The length of the period is usually one month, but may be any specified time period. A periodic tenancy automatically renews itself from period to period, and thus continues for an indefinite length of time. No specific or automatic termination date exists; the tenancy ends only when one of the parties gives proper notice of termination. In Washington, a periodic tenancy may be terminated by written notice from either party (landlord or tenant) 30 days or more before the end of the rental period.

Example: Carl Schmidt is leasing office space on a month-to-month basis. His landlord gives Carl written notice of termination on March 10. Since it is less than 30 days until the end of March, Carl has the right to continue to occupy the space through March and April. The March 10 notice is more than 30 days before the end of the April rental period, so Carl has to vacate the space by the end of April.

If the tenancy is covered by the Residential Landlord-Tenant Act (RLTA), it may be terminated by written notice from either party 20 days or more before the end of the rental period.

> **Example:** Now suppose that Carl Schmidt is renting an apartment on a month-to-month basis. His landlord gives Carl written notice of termination on March 10. Since it is more than 20 days until the end of the month, Carl will have to vacate the apartment by April 1.

Many residential apartment leases begin as estates for years, with a specified time period such as one year or six months. After the specified time period is up, the tenancies often continue as periodic tenancies, usually from month to month.

Tenancy at Will

Under a **tenancy at will**, the tenant is in possession of the property by permission or at the will of the owner. A tenancy at will has no specified termination date and no periodic time limits. Usually no rent is paid, or else rent is given in some form that has no reference to periods of time.

In Washington, a landlord may terminate a tenancy at will at any time, and must simply give the tenant a "reasonable time" in which to vacate.

Case Example:

Paul Najewitz occupied a house on some property in return for keeping the property in repair. This was considered a tenancy at will because it was for an indefinite term and no periodic rent was required.

The tenancy was terminated when demand for possession was made by the owner. The only right Najewitz had after that was a reasonable time in which to vacate. *Najewitz v. Seattle*, 21 Wn.2d 656, 152 P.2d 722 (1944).

Note that unlike the estate for years or the periodic tenancy, a tenancy at will cannot be assigned. Also, the tenancy at will automatically expires upon the death of either the landlord or the tenant.

Tenancy at Sufferance

A **tenancy at sufferance** is created when a tenant comes into possession of a property lawfully and under a valid lease, but then holds over after the lease has expired. The tenant continues in possession of the property, but without the consent of the landlord.

Example: Joe has a one-year lease with Landlord Sam. At the end of the term, Joe refuses to move out. Joe initially obtained possession of the property legally (under a valid lease), but is remaining on the property without Sam's consent.

The tenancy at sufferance technically isn't an estate at all. The tenant, referred to as a **holdover tenant,** has no possessory interest in the property. Even so, the landlord must follow proper legal procedures to evict a holdover tenant, as we explain below. The key difference between a holdover tenant and a trespasser is that a holdover tenant initially occupied the property with the owner's (the landlord's) permission. A trespasser, in contrast, entered the property without the owner's permission. (Trespass is discussed later in this chapter.)

Wrongful Possession

A tenant is in **wrongful possession** of the property if he no longer has the legal right to remain. A landlord may bring an action for unlawful detainer against tenants in wrongful possession. **Unlawful detainer** is the legal action taken to evict a tenant. Evictions will be discussed in more detail in Chapter 13. Some examples of tenants in wrongful possession are:

- tenants who hold over after the expiration of a specific lease term (tenants at sufferance);
- tenants who continue in possession after being given proper notice of termination; and
- tenants who fail to pay the rent and continue in possession after being given notice requiring payment of rent or surrender of the premises.

Encumbrances

A freehold estate is a possessory interest in real property with ownership rights; a leasehold estate is a possessory interest without ownership rights. The third type of interest in real property is a nonpossessory interest. Someone who holds a nonpossessory interest in property has a claim or right concerning the property, but does not have the right to possess the property. Nonpossessory interests are called **encumbrances** because they encumber or burden the title.

Encumbrances may be financial or nonfinancial in nature. Nonfinancial encumbrances, such as easements, affect the use or physical condition of the property. Financial encumbrances, referred to as liens, affect only the title.

Easements (Nonfinancial Encumbrances)

An **easement** is a right owned by one party to use the land of another for a particular purpose. Easements affect the value and use of property, so real estate agents and prospective buyers should find out whether a property is subject to any easements. A standard title insurance report will list the recorded easements, but usually won't list unrecorded easements. Agents and buyers should ask the seller about easements, and should also keep an eye out for any indication that the property is used by someone other than the seller (a neighbor, for instance).

An easement may be either positive or negative. A **positive easement** authorizes a party to do something on another person's land or to take something from the land. The most common example of a positive easement is the right to cross another's land, often called a right-of-way easement or access easement.

> **Example:** Johnson has an easement to cut across the corner of Eldridge's property to reach her mailbox, instead of having to go the long way around by the road. This is a positive easement because it grants Johnson the right to do something on another person's land.

Instead of granting a right, a **negative easement** prohibits a landowner from doing something on her own land.

> **Example:** A planned unit development contains areas that are to be maintained as "greenbelts" (in their natural condition). The property owners in the development are restricted from placing any buildings or cutting down any trees or plants in the greenbelt areas.

The greenbelt rule is a negative easement, because it prevents the owners from doing something on their own property that they would otherwise be permitted to do. "Negative easement" is really just another name for a restrictive covenant. Restrictive covenants are explained in Chapter 11. This chapter focuses on positive easements.

Positive easements are classified as either:

- appurtenant easements, or
- easements in gross.

Appurtenant Easements

An **appurtenant easement** burdens one parcel of land for the benefit of another parcel of land. The parcel that receives the benefit of the easement is called the **dominant tenement**. The burdened parcel over which the easement runs is the **servient tenement**. ("Tenement" is an old property law term that refers to the land and all of the rights that go along with the land.) The owner of the dominant tenement is referred to as the dominant tenant, and the owner of the servient tenement is the servient tenant.

Probably the most common example of an appurtenant easement is a right-of-way easement providing access across one parcel of land to another parcel.

> **Example:** Albright owns a landlocked piece of property with no access to the road. Albright has a right-of-way easement to travel over Schindler's neighboring property to reach the road.

This is a positive easement because it grants Albright the right to do something. The Schindler property is the servient tenement because the easement runs across it. The Albright property is the dominant tenement because it benefits from the easement.

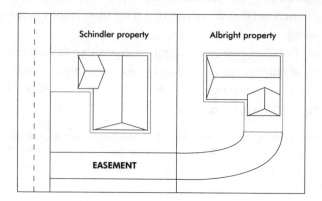

An appurtenant easement **runs with the land**, which means that when either parcel of land—the dominant or the servient tenement—is transferred (sold, inherited, or given away), the benefit or the burden of the easement is also transferred. That's true even if the easement is not mentioned in the deed.

> **Example:** In the example above, if Albright sells her property (the dominant tenement) to Crowley, then Crowley also acquires the easement across the Schindler property. If Schindler sells his property (the servient tenement) to Rodriguez, Rodriguez must allow Crowley, or whoever owns the dominant tenement, to continue using the easement.

Note that an appurtenant easement cannot be sold separately from the land. Whoever owns the dominant tenement also owns the easement.

Easements in Gross

An **easement in gross** belongs to an individual or a commercial entity. Although there is a dominant tenant, there is no dominant tenement involved with an easement in gross. The only parcel of land involved is the servient tenement across which the easement runs.

> **Example:** Andy lives down the road from Carter. Carter grants Andy a personal easement to cross Carter's property and fish in Carter's pond. Andy is the dominant tenant, but there is no dominant tenement. Carter's property is the servient tenement, and if he sold the property, the new owners would still have to allow Andy to fish in the pond.

A personal easement in gross such as the one in the example can't be assigned to another party. In other words, Andy can't sell or give away his easement rights to someone else. If Andy dies, the easement will be extinguished; no one can inherit it from him.

Most easements in gross are commercial rather than personal. Unlike personal easements in gross, commercial easements in gross are freely assignable and transferable.

> **Example:** The Greentown Electric Company has an easement in gross to enter property to install and service its power lines. When Mega-Electric buys Greentown Electric, it also purchases the easement.

Note, however, that a commercial easement for a specific purpose cannot normally be sold for another purpose. For example, the electric company could not sell its easement for power lines to the local sewer district to run sewer lines through the easement.

When showing property to prospective buyers, a real estate agent should be able to explain all utility easements affecting the property. An average residence may be subject to easements for the water company, electric company, gas company, cable company, and telephone company, just to name a few. Utility easements can have an impact on the value of the property.

> **Example:** If the electric company has an easement running through your backyard and installs unsightly power lines, this easement may seriously decrease the value of the property.

Creation of Easements

An easement (whether appurtenant or in gross) may be created in any of the following ways:

- express grant or reservation,
- plat maps,
- implied from prior use or necessity,
- dedication,
- condemnation,
- estoppel, or
- prescription.

Express Easement. An **express easement** is generally written in a deed or other legal document that sets forth the boundaries and specifications of the easement.

The most effective way to create an easement is to describe the easement in a deed. The easement may be described in the deed passing title to the property, or there may be a separate deed describing only the easement.

A deed or other document may create an easement by either express grant or express reservation.

When an easement is created by **express grant**, the property owner expressly grants a specific right to use the property (the easement) to another.

> **Example:** David sells the west half of his property to Martha. In the deed, he expressly grants Martha the right to use the private road located on his half of the property.

An **express reservation** is similar to an express grant, except that instead of giving away the easement, the landowner reserves it for himself or a third party.

> **Example:** David sells the east half of his property to Martha. In the deed, he expressly reserves to himself the right to use the private road now located on Martha's half of the property.

Plat maps. Another way of creating an express easement is by recording a **plat map**. If a landowner subdivides and sells land according to a recorded plat, the purchasers acquire easements to use the roads, alleys, and all common areas shown on the plat. These areas are considered dedicated for public use.

Case Example:

In 1956, Haven Lake Development Company recorded the Haven Lake plat map. Approximately one year later, a map entitled "Access Easement-Lots 251 thru 256" was also recorded, showing an easement access road that originated on lot 255 and crossed lot 254.

Forty years later, the current owner of lot 255 attempted to access his lot via the easement across lot 254. The owners of lot 254 sued to quiet title.

The original plat map did not reflect any easement, and the mere filing of the subsequent document was insufficient to amend the original plat. Therefore, no grant of easement existed. *McPhaden v. Scott*, 95 Wn. App. 431, 975 P.2d 1033 (1999).

Implied Easement. An **implied easement**, or easement by implication, is presumed to exist because of certain facts that tend to show that the parties meant to create an easement. This type of easement arises only when the tract of land was originally under common ownership (owned by the same individual) and then was severed or divided into two or more parcels.

There are two situations in which an easement by implication may develop. An easement may be implied from prior use, or may be implied because of obvious necessity.

For an easement to be **implied from prior use**, the use giving rise to the easement must have been going on for a long time, and must be apparent from a visual inspection of the property at the time of sale. The use must also be reasonably necessary for the enjoyment of the dominant tenement.

Example: John owns two adjacent, heavily forested mountain properties. Parcel A is accessible only by two roads. One road is often impassable due to weather conditions; the other road is located on Parcel B.

John sells Parcel A to Tina, but objects when Tina wants to reach her property using the road located on Parcel B, which John still owns. If a court determines Tina's use of the road is reasonably necessary, she will have an easement by implication.

If the easement is essential to a parcel of property, the court may find an **easement by necessity** even if there is no apparent prior use.

Example: If a lot is completely landlocked with no access to roads, and no express easement has been given, an easement by necessity may be found to provide access to the road.

Dedication. A private landowner may grant an easement to the public to use some portion of his property for a public purpose, such as a sidewalk. The dedication may be expressly stated or it may be implied. It may be philanthropic in nature, or required by a local government as a condition for permission to develop the land.

Condemnation. As we'll discuss in Chapter 9, the government can exercise its power of eminent domain to take ownership of private property and put it to a public use, if compensation is paid to the private owner. This process, called condemnation, can also be used to obtain an easement for a public purpose, such as a road or a bike path.

Estoppel. Easements can also be created by estoppel. The legal doctrine of **estoppel** prevents a person from asserting rights or facts that are contrary to previous acts or conduct.

> **Example:** Bianca has a house on several acres. It is too far out in the country to be connected to the city sewer system, so the house is connected to a large septic system capable of handling several houses. Bianca divides her property and sells half to Carl. No mention is made of the septic system. Carl builds a house on his property. Bianca watches and says nothing as Carl hooks up his plumbing to the septic system on her property.
>
> An easement has been created by estoppel. Because of her failure to object, Bianca cannot now claim that Carl had no right to hook up to the septic system.

Prescription. An **easement by prescription** is created when someone makes long and continuous use of another's property without the permission of the owner. To acquire an easement by prescription, use of the easement must be **open and notorious**. This means that the use must be obvious and visible to any landowner who keeps reasonably well informed about the property.

The use must also be **hostile** or **adverse**, meaning without the permission or consent of the owner, or against the owner's interests. An owner may acquiesce to the use, but not give permission. In other words, if the owner is aware of the use and does not object—but also does not give permission—the use is hostile. But if the owner gives consent or permission, a license has been granted, and an easement by prescription cannot develop.

In Washington, the use must be **continuous and uninterrupted** for ten years. Continuous does not mean constant use, but only a continuous use that is normal for that property.

> **Example:** Mr. Rose and Mr. Green both own summer cottages on a hill above the beach. There are steps to the beach cut into the rocky hillside on Mr. Rose's property. Every summer for the last 12 years, Mr. Green has used these steps to get to the beach. This is a continuous use even though Mr. Green never uses the steps in winter.

Note also that a continuous and uninterrupted use does not necessarily mean use by only one person.

> **Example:** Michael and Patrick own adjoining property. For two years, Michael drives across a corner of Patrick's property without Patrick's permission. Then Michael sells his property to Donovan. For another four years, Donovan drives across the same

corner. Then Donovan sells to Maureen. Maureen drives across Patrick's property for another five years.

Maureen may be able to claim a prescriptive easement. The time periods in which Michael, Donovan, and Maureen drove across the property can be added together to make up the required ten years. This adding of time periods is called **tacking**.

Note that there can be no prescriptive easements against government property.

Maintenance and Repair of Easements

Neither party has a duty to maintain or repair an easement unless this duty is specifically spelled out in the easement grant. However, if an easement is allowed to fall into such a state of disrepair that it is totally unusable, the easement may be lost.

> **Example:** Consider our previous example of the right-of-way easement. Albright has the right to drive across the Schindler property. Unless spelled out in a written agreement, if the Schindlers do not use this driveway, they have no duty to maintain it. They cannot block or obstruct the drive, but they are not responsible for any repairs or upkeep.
>
> The easement holder also has no duty to repair or maintain the driveway. Albright can let it fall into disrepair if she likes. Although Albright has no duty to repair, she has the right to take all steps necessary to make the easement usable. If she chooses, she can repair or maintain it as much as needed.

Where a private road or driveway is used by the landowner and an easement gives another party the right to use the same road or driveway, both parties must divide the cost of repairs in proportion to their use of the road.

Termination of Easements

There are several methods by which easements may be terminated or cease to exist. These correspond roughly to the ways easements are created.

Express Termination. Just as easements may be expressly created, they may be expressly terminated.

Written agreement. The parties may agree on an express termination date that is specified when the easement is granted, or there may be a later written agreement, called a **release**.

Automatic termination. Most easements do not expire automatically. However, if the grant of the easement specifies a time period, the easement expires or automatically terminates at the end of the time period. An easement may be granted for life. This type of easement automatically terminates upon the death of the person who was the measuring life.

Condemnation. As discussed above, an easement can be created through the condemnation process. An easement may also be terminated through condemnation. If the state condemns and takes title to either the dominant or the servient property, the easement may be lost. However, the easement holder (the owner of the dominant property) is entitled to compensation for the value of the easement.

> **Example:** Adams has an easement to maintain a billboard on Barton's property. The state condemns Barton's property because they are going to build a new highway across it. The state compensates Barton for the value of his property, and it must also compensate Adams for loss of the value of her easement.

Implied Termination. An easement may be terminated without any express agreement, by the actions of the parties or by circumstances beyond the control of the parties.

Merger. When the owner of the easement (the dominant property) also becomes the owner of the property subject to the easement (the servient property), the easement is extinguished by **merger**. The need for an easement no longer exists. You cannot have an easement in your own property, since an easement is defined as an interest in another's land.

Necessity ends. If an easement is created by necessity, the easement automatically terminates once the necessity disappears.

Abandonment. An easement may cease to exist if the owner abandons it. Although non-use alone is not enough to terminate an easement, it may be evidence of an intent to abandon. Abandonment is usually proven by a clear act or expression of the owner's intent to abandon.

> **Example:** Abernathy has an easement that allows her to cross Simpson's property to reach the lake. Abernathy has not used the easement for nine years and has planted a rose garden across the area where the path to Simpson's property used to be.

Case Example:

The High Line is a popular tourist attraction in Lower Manhattan, where an old railroad viaduct has been converted to an elevated "linear" park. When the viaduct was built back in the 1930s, the railroad obtained easements allowing the viaduct to be constructed over existing properties. The railroad stopped using the viaduct in the 1970s, and the rails were removed by 1982. The viaduct was converted to a park in 2005, under the authority of the federal National Trails System Act.

In 2011, Romanoff Equities, an owner of property crossed by the viaduct, filed a lawsuit claiming that conversion of the viaduct into a park was a taking of its property, for which it should be compensated. Romanoff argued that the easement over its property was limited to railroad use, and, moreover, the easement had been abandoned when the railroad stopped operating there decades earlier. However, the court held that the 1932 grant of easement was broad enough in nature to allow for non-railroad use. The court also ruled that decades of mere non-use were not enough to terminate the easement, and that the easement holders had taken no affirmative actions to terminate it. The easement was still in effect, the park was a valid use of the easement, and the plaintiffs were not entitled to compensation. *Romanoff Equities, Inc. v. U.S.*, No. 15-5034 (Fed. Cir. 2016).

Fig. 4.2 How easements may terminate

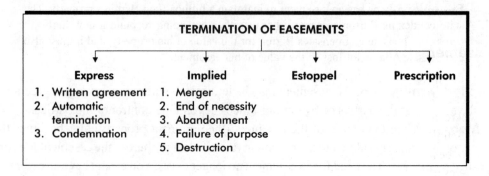

Failure of purpose. If an easement has been created for a particular purpose, it terminates when the purpose ceases or has been fulfilled.

> **Example:** B&D Railroad had an easement for railroad tracks across a corner of Farmer Brown's property. B&D discontinued using this track, removed the rails, and subsequently went bankrupt. The easement terminated because the purpose of the easement ceased.

Destruction of servient tenement. When an easement exists in a building rather than in the land, the involuntary destruction of the building will terminate the easement.

Estoppel. In the same way that they may be created, easements may also be terminated by estoppel. If the conduct of the easement holder (dominant property owner) leads the servient property owner to assume that the easement holder does not intend to use the easement, and the servient property owner takes some action in reliance on this, the easement holder may be prevented from later trying to enforce the easement.

> **Example:** Max sold half of his property to Sylvia but reserved to himself an easement to walk across the corner of Sylvia's property to get to his mailbox. After several years, Max put up a fence blocking off the path to the mailbox.
> Sylvia naturally assumed that Max was no longer going to use the path, so she set up her garden shed in the corner over the path. Two years later Max took down the fence and told Sylvia she would have to move the shed so that he could use the easement to get to his mailbox.
> By building the fence, Max led Sylvia to believe that he did not intend to use the easement. Sylvia reasonably relied on his conduct when she built the shed. Max could be estopped (prevented) from now claiming the right to use the easement.

Prescription. Actions by the owner of the servient property that interfere with the easement could extinguish the easement by prescription. There must be an open, continuous, and uninterrupted interference with the easement for ten years.

> **Example:** Consider the example just above. Now suppose Sylvia (the owner of the servient property) built the fence across the easement. The fence has been in place blocking off the easement for 14 years. Max's easement has probably terminated by prescription.

Easements vs. Licenses

Like an easement, a **license** grants permission to enter another's property for a specific purpose. But a license does not create an interest in the property.

There are several differences between easements and licenses. Easements are often for an indefinite period of time, but licenses are usually more temporary. While an easement cannot be revoked, a license may be revoked by the grantor at any time. If revoked, money damages may have to be paid, but a court could not force the grantor to reinstate the license.

Easements are usually created by written agreement or through action of law, while licenses are often created by simple verbal agreement. A license is a purely personal right that cannot be sold or transferred and becomes invalid if the licensee dies.

> **Example:** Carl is having his driveway repaved, so he makes arrangements with his neighbor Karen to park his car in her driveway for two weeks. After only one week, Carl dies. The license automatically terminates. Carl's son does not have the right to park the car in Karen's driveway for the remaining week unless he makes a new arrangement with Karen.

Note that since a license is revocable by the landowner, it is not actually considered an encumbrance or an interest in the property.

Also, because a license is created through permission of the landowner, the use is not hostile. Therefore, no claim of adverse possession or prescriptive easement can be brought by the licensee.

Encroachments, Trespass, and Nuisance

Disputes between neighbors typically arise in one of three ways: encroachment, trespass, or nuisance.

Encroachment. An **encroachment** is a structure or object, such as a fence or garage, that extends over the property line and intrudes onto an adjacent neighbor's land. Most encroachments are unintentional, resulting from a mistake concerning the exact location of the property line.

A court can order an encroachment to be removed through an ejectment action. Alternatively, if the cost of removal would be too high, the court may order the encroacher to pay damages to the neighbor.

Technically, an encroachment is not an encumbrance because it is not a right or interest held by the encroacher. However, if an encroachment is ignored, it could ripen into a prescriptive easement or even title by adverse possession.

Trespass. A **trespass** is entry onto another's land without permission or legal authority, violating the landowner's right to exclusive possession. (In the case of leased property, it violates the tenant's right to exclusive possession.)

A trespass is a tort—that is, an injury against a person or property. Under certain circumstances, a trespass may also be considered a criminal act.

Climbing over a fence and walking around or engaging in other activities on someone else's land is the simplest example of a trespass. However, trespass also includes the physical invasion of property with an object or a substance.

> **Example:** Glen keeps his RV parked behind his house. He doesn't realize that the vehicle is straddling the property line, so that the back end is on his neighbor's property. The presence of the RV on the neighbor's property is a trespass.

A trespass may be a one-time event, as when hunting without permission on someone's property, or it may be a **continuing trespass**, which occurs when a person fails to remove himself or an object from another's land. The RV parked on the neighbor's property is an example of a continuing trespass. Of course, at this point, the trespass could also be called an encroachment.

Nuisance. A **nuisance** is any activity or conduct that substantially interferes with an owner's use and enjoyment of her property, or with the general welfare of the community. A public nuisance affects a community or neighborhood, or a large number of people. A private nuisance affects only one person or just a few people.

> **Example:** Anthony loves to practice the drums in his garage for hours, often late into the evening. However, since the houses in his neighborhood are very close together, his neighbors can hear every drumbeat. While he's practicing, they can't sleep, read, or watch television. Anthony's drumming could be considered a private nuisance.

It's possible for an activity to be completely legal and nevertheless have the effect of creating a nuisance. As long as Anthony's drumming doesn't violate any laws (such as noise ordinances) or other restrictions, it's not illegal—but it still may be a nuisance. The neighbors could sue and ask the court for an injunction ordering Anthony to stop or limit his drumming.

Private Restrictions

Private restrictions (also known as deed restrictions) are restrictions on the use of a property that were imposed by a previous owner. Like easements, private restrictions are encumbrances that limit a property owner's use of her land. Private restrictions are discussed in Chapter 11.

Liens (Financial Encumbrances)

A **lien** is a financial interest in property that gives a creditor the right to have a debt paid out of the debtor's property if the debtor fails to pay. The lienholder does not own or have a right to possess the property, but could cause the property to be sold to satisfy the lien.

Both buyers and sellers will be concerned about liens against property because liens decrease the property's value. Existing liens against a property will not prevent its transfer or sale, but the transfer does not eliminate the liens. The new owner takes the property subject to those liens. Thus, it is extremely important for a buyer to know what liens are attached to a property before purchasing it.

A real estate agent should always find out if there are any outstanding liens on the property. Liens are generally filed in the office of the county recorder in the county where the property is located.

Voluntary liens are liens the owner places against his own property. These liens are usually placed in order to secure repayment of a debt.

> **Example:** Mortgages and deeds of trust are voluntary liens. A property owner borrows money and provides a lien on specific property as security for the debt.

Involuntary liens (sometimes called statutory liens) arise through operation of law without the property owner's consent. Involuntary liens are created to protect those who have valid financial claims against the owner of the real property.

> **Example:** When taxes are assessed, a tax lien arises against the property. If the taxes are not paid, the property can be sold to satisfy the lien.

Liens are also classified as either general or specific. A **general lien** attaches to all of the debtor's property. A **specific lien** attaches only to a particular piece of property. A deed of trust is an example of a specific lien. It attaches only to the particular property offered as security for the loan.

Some of the most common types of liens against real estate are:

- mortgages and deeds of trust,
- construction liens,
- judgment liens, and
- tax liens.

Mortgages and Deeds of Trust

Mortgages and deeds of trust are voluntary, specific liens created by a contract between a borrower and a lender. The borrower's property is used as security for the loan. If the borrower fails to repay the loan as agreed, the lender can sell the property and use the proceeds to repay the loan.

When property transfers to a new buyer, it remains subject to any existing mortgages or deeds of trust. So whether the seller will pay off an existing mortgage or deed of trust—or whether it is assumable by the buyer—are questions that must be answered before the sale closes.

Construction Liens

A person who supplies materials or performs work on property may be entitled to claim a **construction lien** against the property to secure payment for the labor or materials. For example, if a general contractor is building a house on a site and is not paid for his services, he can obtain a lien against the property for the amount owed. The lien allows the property to be sold to satisfy the debt. A construction lien is created by filing a notice of the claim at the office of the recorder in the county where the property is located.

In addition to (or instead of) filing the lien, a laborer or supplier could sue the property owner for the amount due. However, litigation is time-consuming and expensive, and even if you win, it is sometimes difficult to collect the judgment.

The right to file a construction lien can be waived. When a construction contract is drawn up, it may include a provision that states that liens may not be filed on the property. This type of provision is called a **waiver**. Such a waiver must be stated clearly and unambiguously in the contract.

Every state now has some type of construction lien law. It's important to be aware of the time limits contained in Washington's construction lien law.

Time Limits. Initially, to establish and preserve the right to a construction lien, laborers and suppliers must give the general contractor and property owner a written **pre-claim notice** of the right to claim a lien. This pre-claim notice must be served personally or by certified or registered mail. For new construction of a single-family residence, notice must be given within ten days of first supplying services or materials. For remodels, repairs, or commercial projects, notice must be given within 60 days of beginning work. Pre-claim notices are not required, however, from claimants who have contracted directly with the owner.

A **lien claim** must be filed within 90 days after last performing work or furnishing materials for the project. A lien filed more than 90 days after labor or materials were last furnished is invalid. The 90-day time period starts to run when the particular claimant stops providing labor or supplies, not when the entire project is completed.

Foreclosure. Construction liens must be foreclosed judicially (through the court system). A legal action to foreclose this type of lien must be brought within eight months after the lien was recorded, in the county where the real estate is located.

> **Example:** New plumbing is being put into the Montgomery Building. Karl is the one who supplied the new pipes. The last load of pipes was delivered on January 15. When Karl still had not been paid by March 1, he filed a construction lien against the property.

On November 5, Karl attempts to file a legal action to foreclose. However, Karl will not be successful because it has been just over eight months since the lien was recorded.

Priority. Often, there is more than one construction lien against the same piece of property. If the property is sold to satisfy these liens, the proceeds from the sale will be applied according to the order of priority (see Figure 4.3).

Termination of Construction Liens. A construction lien is terminated by the payment of the debt upon which the lien is based. In Washington, an owner may also release an existing construction lien by giving a bond or paying the amount owed into court to cover any potentially valid claims. The funds are controlled by the court. This system benefits the property owner, since the property is not tied up by a lien. It also benefits the lienholder, since the funds are available to pay any valid claims and cannot be withdrawn by the property owner.

If a lien foreclosure action is filed, but is not prosecuted to judgment within two years, the court has discretion to dismiss the action for want of prosecution. This dismissal cancels the lien. The purpose of this rule is to prevent property from being encumbered by a lien for an unreasonable amount of time.

> **Example:** A contractor filed a construction lien and subsequently filed a legal action for foreclosure on February 4, 2016. However, the foreclosure action still had not been prosecuted by February 5, 2018. Since more than two years have elapsed, the court can dismiss the action.

Judgment Liens

Judgment liens arise from a court's determination that one party owes money to another. The court enters a judgment, and the winner (the judgment creditor) can obtain a **judgment lien** against property owned by the loser (the judgment debtor). This type of lien is involuntary and general. It arises by operation of law and automatically attaches to

---

Fig. 4.3 Construction lien priority

CONSTRUCTION LIEN PRIORITY

1. First, to people who performed labor;
2. Next, any contributions owed to employee benefit plans;
3. Then to people who furnished materials or equipment;
4. Then to the subcontractors; and
5. Finally, to the original or general contractor.

Fig. 4.4 Types of liens

LIENS				
	Voluntary	Involuntary	General	Specific
Mortgages	X			X
Deeds of trust	X			X
Construction liens		X		X
Special assessments		X		X
Judgment liens		X	X	
IRS liens		X	X	

all of the debtor's property in the county where the judgment was entered, except for the debtor's homestead (principal residence). The judgment will attach to homestead property only if the judgment creditor records an **abstract of judgment** with the county recorder.

If the debtor owns property in other counties, the judgment creditor may file an abstract of judgment in other counties and attach those additional properties. The judgment lien also attaches to any property acquired by the debtor during the lien period.

> **Example:** Glen owns two acres of land in Snohomish County. A lawsuit was filed against him. Glen lost the case and a judgment was entered against him. The winner obtained a lien against Glen's property for the judgment amount. Two months later, Glen's father died, leaving Glen ten acres of property, also in Snohomish County. The judgment lien also attaches to this property.

Once a judgment lien has attached to property, the debtor must pay the judgment to free the property from the lien. If it is not paid, the property can be sold to satisfy the judgment.

Termination of Judgment Liens. Like any lien, a judgment lien is terminated by payment of the amount owed. Judgment liens also terminate according to statutory limitations.

In Washington, a judgment lien is generally valid for ten years after the date of entry of the judgment. However, within 90 days before a judgment lien expires, the lienholder can apply for an order extending the period for an additional ten years. The lienholder must apply to the court that issued the judgment and pay a filing fee.

Also, note that a judgment lien for child support lasts for ten years after the child's 18th birthday.

Tax Liens

Tax liens are another common type of lien. Property taxes, special assessments, federal income taxes, and various other taxes create liens against the taxpayer's real property. For the government, these liens are a key tool in tax collection.

Property Taxes. Real property is assessed (appraised) and then taxed according to its value. Property taxes are involuntary and specific liens. In Washington, property taxes become a lien on the first day of January in the year in which the taxes are levied. The levy of property taxes takes place in October.

Therefore, taxes levied in October are actually considered to have become a lien against the property on the previous January 1, even though the taxes are not payable until the next year.

Tax bills are typically mailed around the middle of February. One-half of the property tax is due and payable by April 30, and the second half must be paid by October 31. Delinquent taxes are subject to interest and penalties.

A buyer usually pays all of the real estate taxes that become due in the year following the purchase, even though the lien for these taxes arose prior to the time of purchase.

Taxpayers in Washington are given a three-year grace period before property is foreclosed on because of property tax liens. The owner must be given notice of the impending foreclosure sale. In other words, three years after the taxes became delinquent, the owner is given notice of application for a judgment foreclosing the lien.

The taxpayer has the right to redeem the property at any time up to the date of the foreclosure sale by paying the delinquent amount plus any interest and costs or penalties. Once the foreclosed property has been sold, the purchaser takes title immediately. The former owner has no further redemption rights at that point.

Special Assessments. Municipalities may levy taxes called **special assessments** to pay for local improvements such as road paving or sewer lines. In order to distribute the costs of the improvement fairly, special assessments are levied only against those properties that actually benefit from the improvement. If a special assessment is not paid, it becomes an involuntary, specific lien against the property.

After a special assessment becomes delinquent by two installment payments, or if the final installment is over one year late, the local taxing authority can begin foreclosure proceedings. These proceedings must commence within ten years after the last installment becomes delinquent.

Income Tax Liens. If federal income taxes are not paid, another type of tax lien will arise. Income tax liens are involuntary and general. They apply to all property owned by the taxpayer, both personal and real.

Other Tax Liens. Counties, cities, and nonpolitical units with taxing powers (such as school and irrigation districts) are also authorized to use liens as security devices when taxes are not paid.

Lien Priority

It is not unusual for one piece of property to have several types of liens placed against it. One property may be subject to a mortgage, a construction lien, and a tax lien. Often the total amount of the liens is more than the property will bring at a forced sale, and all the liens cannot be paid in full. Since liens are not paid on a pro rata basis, it must be determined which liens should be paid first.

As a general rule, the priority of liens depends on the order in which they were created. **Lien priority** is established by date of recording. In other words, the lien recorded first gets first priority for payment.

However, there are some exceptions to this rule. Property tax liens and special assessment liens are superior to all other liens against the property. They have first priority, even if another lien was created first. (The lien for general property taxes is superior to a lien for a special assessment, even if the special assessment lien was created first.) Also, the date used to determine the priority of construction liens is the date work first started on the project, rather than the date the lien was recorded.

> **Example:** Margaret Smith's property has the following liens against it:
>
> - a mortgage recorded March 9, 2007;
> - property tax liens that attached January 1, 2016 and January 1, 2017;
> - a lien for a judgment entered June 2, 2016;
> - a special assessment lien that attached July 6, 2016; and
> - a construction lien recorded August 16, 2016 (but work on the project started May 19, 2016).
>
> When the property is sold at a foreclosure sale, the liens would be paid out of the proceeds of the sale in the following order:
>
> 1. property tax liens
> 2. special assessment lien
> 3. mortgage
> 4. construction lien
> 5. judgment lien

Protecting the Debtor

When a creditor forecloses a lien, the amount of money obtained from the foreclosure sale is not always enough to cover the amount owed on the debt. To recover any remaining balance, the creditor may get a **deficiency judgment**, which is a personal judgment against the debtor ordering the debtor to pay the creditor the remaining amount owed.

> **Example:** The Osgoods borrowed money from the bank to buy some property. When the Osgoods defaulted on the loan, the lender foreclosed on the mortgage. The amount owed was $225,000, but the proceeds of the foreclosure sale only came to $215,000. The lender may obtain a deficiency judgment against the Osgoods for the $10,000 shortfall.

There are, however, some limitations on the right to obtain a deficiency judgment. For example, no deficiency judgment is available after a trustee's sale under a deed of trust.

An alternative to foreclosure is a **short sale**, where an owner sells the property for whatever it will bring (something "short" of the amount owed on the mortgage), and the lender accepts the sale proceeds and releases the property from the mortgage lien. In a short sale involving an owner-occupied principal residence, Washington law requires the lender to notify the seller whether it is waiving or retaining the right to collect a deficiency judgment. If retained, the lender's right to collect a deficiency judgment expires three years after the short sale.

Homestead Laws. Another way of protecting debtors is through homestead laws. While homestead laws do not protect family residences from all types of liens, they can sometimes protect families from the forced sale of their homes. Homestead laws reflect a belief by the legislature that a person's obligation to support dependents is as important as the payment of debts.

Washington law provides for an automatic **homestead exemption** for certain property used as a principal residence. Under the law, a **homestead**—a family dwelling, along with the land and any outbuildings—is exempt from the foreclosure of judgment liens for up to the total net value of the property, or $125,000, whichever is less. (The legislature increases the homestead exemption amount periodically.) The exemption begins as soon as the owner begins residing on the property.

Case Example:

In 1995, RMC, a construction company, attempted to foreclose on a judgment lien against a home owned by the Hyppas. At that time, the homestead exemption amount was $30,000. The property, valued at $145,000, was encumbered by liens totaling more than $130,000.

The total of the $30,000 homestead exemption and the $130,000 in liens exceeded the home's market value. The court thus held that there was no net value on which RMC could execute. *Miller Constr. Co. v. Coltran*, 87 Wn. App. 112, 940 P.2d 661 (1997).

An owner can obtain homestead protection in advance, for property he is planning to reside on, by recording a **declaration of homestead** for that property. The declaration of homestead must contain a legal description of the property and an estimate of its cash value. A person can have only one homestead at a time, so if the owner already has a homestead, she must record a declaration of abandonment of homestead on the other property.

Use of the homestead exemption is fairly rare, mainly because the exemption does not protect the debtor against all claims. The homestead exemption does not offer protection against:

- mortgages or deeds of trust,
- construction liens,
- tax liens,

- liens for child support or spousal maintenance obligations, or
- liens imposed by a condominium or homeowners association.

Conclusion

As you can see, many different people may have various interests in the same piece of property. The interests others may have in your property affect your right and ability to use, possess, or sell the property. Encumbrances and conditions on your title affect your right to use your property. And liens affect the value of your property and your ability to sell it quickly and easily.

Case Problem

The following is a hypothetical case problem. Most of the facts are taken from a real case. Using what you've learned from this chapter, make a decision on the issues presented, and then check to see if your answer matches the real decision by the court.

The Facts

Doris Smith and Eugene Breen owned adjoining land. A dirt road leading to the back of both their properties ran astride the boundary line. The road had existed since at least the 1930s and had been used jointly and amicably by the various owners of both pieces of property for over 30 years.

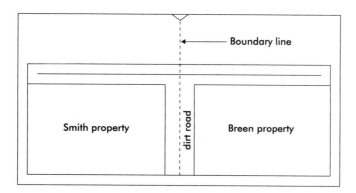

In 1966, Smith and Breen both tried to assert ownership of the entire road. Breen began parking his truck on the road, blocking Smith's passage. Smith's attorney wrote Breen a letter requesting that he not block the road. The letter apparently had no effect, so Smith brought a lawsuit to enjoin Breen from blocking the road, and claiming sole ownership of the road (Smith claimed that she alone maintained the road). Breen counterclaimed, asserting that he had acquired title to the entire roadway by blocking Smith's access.

The Questions

Who was the rightful owner of the road? Had Breen obtained ownership by blocking Smith's use of the road? Could Smith claim sole ownership because she had been the only one to maintain the road? If an easement existed, what type was it and how was it established?

The Answer

Neither party had sole ownership of the road, and both had the right to use it equally. If Breen had successfully blocked the road from use by Smith for over ten years, he might have been able to terminate Smith's easement by prescription. However, Smith objected to the blocking, and the time period was not nearly long enough.

Nor did Smith have a valid claim simply because she maintained the road. There is no specific requirement that the owner of an easement make repairs or perform maintenance.

A prescriptive easement may be acquired by clear proof that the land was used in an open, notorious, continuous, and uninterrupted manner for ten years, that the use was adverse to the owner, and that the owner had knowledge of the use.

In this case, both parties' predecessors had been using the entire width of the roadway as if it belonged to them. For more than 30 years neither asked the other for permission to use the road, and there was no challenge to the use of the road.

In the case of *Smith v. Breen*, 26 Wn. App. 802, 614 P.2d 671 (1980), the court found that the use of Smith's property by Breen and his predecessors, and the use of Breen's property by Smith and her predecessors, had ripened into mutual easements by prescription. Both Smith and Breen had an equal right to use the roadway because both had acquired a prescriptive easement.

Chapter Summary

- An estate is an ownership interest in property that is or may become possessory. The highest and best interest is the fee simple. There are two types of fee simple estates: the fee simple absolute and the fee simple defeasible.

- A defeasible fee may end if certain events occur or conditions are not met. A defeasible fee may be determinable or conditional.

- The duration of a life estate is measured by someone's lifetime. A life estate based on someone else's life is called a life estate "pur autre vie." The person who will receive the property when the life estate ends has an estate in remainder or an estate in reversion. Today, trusts are used more frequently than life estates.

- A leasehold estate is a non-ownership, possessory interest in property. There are three types of leasehold estates: the estate for years, the periodic tenancy, and the tenancy at will. The tenancy at sufferance is not a true leasehold estate.

- An encumbrance is a nonpossessory interest in real property. Encumbrances may be nonfinancial or financial in nature.

- Easements may be appurtenant or in gross. Creation of an easement may be express, implied, by dedication, by condemnation, by estoppel, or by prescription.

- A license is similar to an easement but is not considered an interest in property. A license is usually more temporary than an easement. An encroachment is a structure or object that extends over the property line onto an adjacent property.

- A lien is a financial interest in property that gives a creditor the right to have the property sold upon default and the debt paid out of the sale proceeds. A lien is either specific or general, and either voluntary or involuntary. Some examples of liens are mortgages, deeds of trust, construction liens, judgment liens, and tax liens.

Checklist of Problem Areas

Real Estate Licensee's Checklist

❑ When taking a listing, determine whether the sellers own the property in fee simple absolute. Although they almost certainly do, it's not out of the question that they have a defeasible fee or a life estate instead. If the sellers aren't sure, check their deed for language that could indicate that they have less than a fee simple absolute estate.

❑ Besides the lien for annual property taxes, are there any other liens against the sellers' property?

❑ Look for visible signs of easements on the property and ask the sellers whether there are any. If so, how do the easements affect use of the property?

Seller or Lessor's Checklist

❑ What liens will have to be paid off out of the sale proceeds?

❑ If the property has been leased, does the lease have a specific termination date? If not, how much notice of termination is the tenant entitled to? Does the Residential Landlord-Tenant Act (RLTA) apply to this tenancy? If so, the notice period may be different.

Buyer or Tenant's Checklist

❑ Buyers should verify that the seller will be conveying a fee simple absolute.

❑ Buyers should also find out whether any easements burden the property. If so, what practical and aesthetic impact do they have on the property, and how do they affect its value?

❑ A buyer takes title subject to any valid lease on the property. If a tenant is currently occupying the property, the new owner must comply with the terms of the existing lease. A periodic tenancy can be ended by giving the tenant proper notice of termination, but it's necessary to wait for a term tenancy to expire, unless there are grounds for eviction.

❑ Tenants who have a periodic tenancy should be aware of how much notice they're required to give the landlord in order to end their tenancy. Tenants who don't give sufficient notice could be liable for an additional rent payment, even if they have already vacated the premises. Remember that notice of termination must be in writing.

Chapter Quiz

1. The highest and best interest that can exist in land is called a:

   a. leasehold estate
   b. fee simple estate
   c. conditional fee
   d. life estate

2. The type of estate called a fee simple subject to condition subsequent is based on certain express conditions. If these conditions are not met:

   a. the property will automatically revert back to the grantor
   b. the grantor has the "power of termination" but must take legal steps to terminate
   c. the property automatically reverts to the state
   d. None of the above

3. Jean grants Mary a life estate in some property. Upon Mary's death, the property is to pass to David. David is called:

   a. the reverter
   b. a pur autre vie
   c. the remainderman
   d. the primary holder

4. When discussing life estates, waste is defined as:

   a. the years until the life tenant dies
   b. lost revenue while the property cannot be sold
   c. permanent damage or abuse to property which reduces its market value
   d. None of the above

5. Roger rents a house in Yakima. The lease gives him the right to possess the house for an eight-month period. This type of tenancy is called a:

   a. periodic or month-to-month tenancy
   b. tenancy for a specific term
   c. tenancy at will
   d. tenancy at sufferance

6. Alice is renting an apartment on a month-to-month basis. The tenancy is covered by the Residential Landlord-Tenant Act. If Alice wants to move, she must give her landlord:

   a. 10 days' written notice
   b. 20 days' written notice
   c. 30 days' written notice
   d. No notice is required

7. Lori owns a landlocked piece of property, but she has a right-of-way easement to drive across her neighbor's property. This is a(n):

   a. appurtenant easement
   b. negative easement
   c. easement in gross
   d. None of the above

8. The Riverside Power Company has a commercial easement in gross to run a power line through your backyard. The power company is purchased by Mega-Corp Power. The easement:

   a. is automatically extinguished
   b. may not be sold since it is an appurtenant commercial easement
   c. may be sold since it is a commercial easement in gross
   d. may be sold since it is a negative easement

9. In order to acquire an easement by pre-scription in Washington, the use must be continuous and uninterrupted for:

   a. 5 years
   b. 10 years
   c. 15 years
   d. 20 years

10. Jones owns an easement to walk across Farley's property to reach his mailbox. Then Farley sells his property to Jones. The easement no longer exists because it has terminated through:

   a. merger
   b. abandonment
   c. failure of purpose
   d. destruction of the dominant tenement

11. A mortgage is a(n):

   a. involuntary, specific lien
   b. involuntary, general lien
   c. voluntary, specific lien
   d. voluntary, general lien

12. A construction lien in Washington must be filed within how many days after cessation of work on the project?

   a. 30 days
   b. 45 days
   c. 60 days
   d. 90 days

13. In Washington, one-half of the assessed property tax is due and payable before:

   a. January 1
   b. March 15
   c. April 30
   d. June 1

14. In paying liens:

   a. mortgages always have first priority
   b. lien priority is established by date of recording
   c. property tax liens are superior to other liens
   d. Both b) and c)

15. In Washington, the homestead exemption is:

   a. $30,000
   b. $40,000
   c. $75,000
   d. $125,000

5 Co-Ownership of Real Property

Outline

Key Terms

- Concurrently
- Severalty
- Community property
- Separate property
- Commingling
- Joinder
- Tenancy in common
- Contribution
- Waste
- Partition

- Joint tenancy
- Right of survivorship
- Unity of possession
- Unity of interest
- Unity of time
- Unity of title
- Marketable title
- Severance
- Corporation (domestic or foreign)

- Shareholders
- Nonprofit corporation
- Articles of incorporation
- Partnership (general or limited)
- Partnership property
- Limited liability company
- Joint venture
- Syndicate

Chapter Overview

Ownership of real property is frequently shared by more than one person. Two, ten, or two hundred people can own the same piece of property at the same time (**concurrently**). This chapter explains the forms that concurrent ownership can take.

The first section of the chapter focuses on the various ways in which co-owners can hold title, such as community property or tenancy in common. The second part of the chapter describes ownership by associations of two or more persons, such as partnerships.

Forms of Co-ownership

When one individual or entity owns property, title is held **in severalty**. In Washington, when property is owned by more than one individual, they can hold title in one of three ways:

- community property,
- tenancy in common, or
- joint tenancy.

Many prospective co-owners are unaware of these various forms of co-ownership, and wind up with one or another by default. However, the way in which title is held is very important, as it determines who controls the property. It can also have dramatic repercussions when co-ownership ends, whether voluntarily or through dissolution or death. Co-owners need to understand these potential consequences and deliberately choose the type of ownership they want.

Real estate agents should make sure that buyers realize the importance of the form of co-ownership. However, when an agent raises the subject, buyers often ask for help in choosing how to take title. This is beyond the licensee's area of expertise; at that point, she must advise the buyers to consult a lawyer. Even a well-intentioned licensee who gives buyers friendly advice may end up charged with the unauthorized practice of law,

Fig. 5.1 Forms of ownership

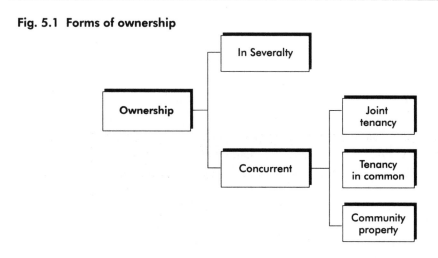

in addition to facing disciplinary action by the Department of Licensing. And if the buyers make the wrong choice based on the agent's advice, the agent could be liable for damages.

Even though a real estate licensee should avoid advising buyers about forms of co-ownership, the licensee nevertheless needs at least a general understanding of the subject. Whenever a legal document is executed, the agent needs to know whether only one co-owner's signature is sufficient, or whether all the co-owners need to sign. For the parties, this can mean the difference between an effective sale and a voidable transaction. For the agent, it can mean the difference between a commission and a lawsuit.

Community Property

Community property is one of the most common forms of co-ownership in this state. Outside of Washington, only Alaska, Arizona, California, Idaho, Louisiana, Nevada, New Mexico, Texas, and Wisconsin have community property systems. In most other states, married couples co-own property as **tenants by the entirety**. Tenancy by the entirety is similar to joint tenancy (discussed below).

The concept of community property is based on Spanish law. Early Washington settlers had little contact with Spain or Spanish culture. However, many of Washington's early laws were patterned after California's laws, and California has a history that is rich with Spanish influence.

When Community Property Rules Apply

Under community property rules, all property owned by a married couple is classified either as the **separate property** of one spouse, or as the **community property** of both spouses. These classifications determine a couple's rights and duties in regard to the property.

Community property rules apply only to property acquired during a marriage. In some states, a couple that has lived together for a certain number of years in a marriage-like relationship is considered legally married, even though there has been no marriage ceremony, and no marriage license has been obtained or signed. This kind of marriage is called a **common law marriage**. Washington law does not provide for common law marriages. However, if a couple has met the common law marriage requirements of another state before moving to Washington, they will be considered legally married when they move to Washington, and the property they acquire while living in Washington will be considered community property.

Unmarried Couples. Although community property laws don't apply to unmarried couples, if a couple has lived together for a significant period of time, Washington courts will examine the nature and extent of the relationship and the property accumulations, and try to make a just and equitable disposition of the property when the couple splits up or one party dies. The court considers a number of factors:

- continuous cohabitation,
- duration of the relationship,
- purpose of the relationship,
- pooling of resources,
- pooling of services for joint projects,
- which party acquired the property,
- monetary and labor contributions,
- whether or not there are children,
- who is to care for the children, and
- the general condition in which each of the parties will be left.

Based on these factors, a court may divide property evenly between the parties, award it to the person whose name is on the title, or award it in some other fair and equitable manner.

Classifying the Property

While problems can arise when dividing property between an unmarried couple, the question of an equitable division of property occurs most frequently when a married couple separates. Who receives what portion of the property depends on whether the property is classified as community property or separate property.

The idea behind the community property system is that a marriage is a partnership. Each spouse works for the good of the partnership. Any money or property acquired through the skill or labor of either spouse during the marriage belongs to the marital community, not just to the individual who earned it. This means that the salaries of both spouses are community property. And even if only one spouse works outside the home for wages (for example, while the other spouse works inside the home raising children), those wages are community property, and belong to both spouses.

In addition, anything purchased with community funds or community credit (for example, an item purchased with a credit card issued to both spouses) is community property.

The principle behind community property is favored so strongly that it is presumed that any property purchased during marriage belongs to the community, even if title is held in the name of only one spouse, unless it can be proven otherwise.

> **Example:** Suppose Tim and Sarah were married for nine years. During their marriage, they bought a house. Title to the house is in Tim's name alone. When they divorce, the house is presumed to be community property even though title is in Tim's name.

On the other hand, everything acquired before marriage remains separate property after marriage. This includes money accumulated before marriage, and items purchased with money accumulated before marriage.

> **Example:** Sarah earns her living as a bus driver. While she was single, she accumulated $15,000 in savings. Even after her marriage to Tim, that $15,000 remained Sarah's separate property. Anything purchased with separate property funds is also separate property. So if Sarah uses her $15,000 to buy a car during her marriage, the car is also her separate property.

Gifts. Property or money acquired by gift, will, or inheritance is also separate property, even if it is received during the marriage. For example, if Veronica's father leaves her $25,000 in his will, that $25,000 is Veronica's separate property, even if she acquired it during her marriage to Phil.

The rationale behind this rule is that a gift, a legacy, or an inheritance is not earned by the skill or labor of a spouse. But if a gift is actually given in exchange for services rendered, either in the past or in the future, it is considered community property rather than separate property.

> **Example:** Phil's elderly mother gives him her sailboat. It is understood between them that the sailboat is Phil's compensation for helping his mother with housekeeping and other chores. The sailboat is not a true gift. Because Phil "earned" it, the sailboat is community property rather than separate property.

Note that a gift purchased with community funds by one spouse for the other spouse is the recipient spouse's separate property.

> **Example:** Veronica buys Phil a Rolex watch with money she has saved from her salary. Even though the watch was purchased with community funds, the watch becomes Phil's separate property.

Fig. 5.2 Community property vs. separate property

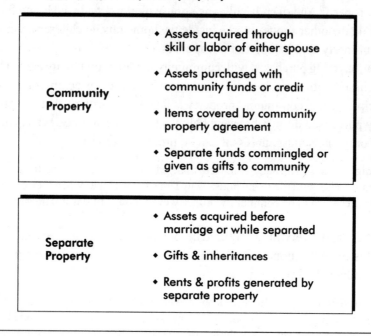

Rents and Profits. Ordinarily, any appreciation in separate property and any rents or profits generated by separate property are also separate property. However, if the appreciation or profits are the result of a spouse's effort, skill, or labor, they are community property instead.

> **Example:** Phil owns an apartment building as his separate property. If he hires a property management company and is not actively involved in managing the building himself, the rents it generates will be his separate property. But if he spends time and energy on maintaining the building and leasing the apartments, the rents will be at least partly community property.

Community Property Agreements. Some couples choose to sign **community property agreements**, which makes all property owned by either of them community property, no matter when or how it was acquired. Most community property agreements provide that:

1. all property owned by either spouse is converted to community property;
2. all property later acquired will be community property; and
3. upon the death of one spouse, all community property will immediately vest in the survivor.

Note that a community property agreement avoids the necessity for probate when one spouse dies. All of the deceased spouse's property has been converted to community property by the agreement, and all community property automatically vests in the surviving spouse. An attorney should be consulted prior to preparing a community property agreement, because the agreement could disrupt more sophisticated estate planning.

Commingling. Even without a community property agreement, separate property will sometimes become community property. This occurs when separate funds are mixed, or **commingled**, with community funds so that they are impossible to distinguish.

> **Example:** Returning to an earlier example, suppose that when Sarah got married she put her $15,000 into a joint checking account. Both she and Tim contributed to the account and used funds from the account. It is no longer clear whether the money remaining in the account is Sarah's $15,000 or community funds.
>
> Under these circumstances, the $15,000 might well be considered a gift to the community and will no longer be considered Sarah's separate property.

Separation. The rules change when a married couple is living separately or if a decree of separation has been issued. Then the income earned and property acquired by each spouse is considered his or her separate property. This rule applies only to a "defunct marriage," and does not apply when the spouses are separated for other reasons.

Case Example:

A husband and wife experienced a long separation due to the wife's confinement in a mental institution outside of Washington. Acquisitions by the husband during the separation were considered community property, not his separate property. *Rustad v. Rustad*, 61 Wn.2d 1176, 377 P.2d 414 (1963).

When a married person wins a personal injury suit, the damages award is community property if it is received while the couple is living together. If the couple is living apart, the damages award is usually the separate property of the injured spouse. Even then, if the injury occurred while the couple was still living together, a portion of the award may be community property.

Case Example:

Ronna and William Brown were married in 1967. In 1979, Ronna was injured in a car accident. Approximately six months later, Ronna instituted a dissolution action. At trial, Ronna had not yet recovered any damages for the accident. The trial court said any recovery should be divided as follows:
- lost earnings and diminished earning capacity from the date of the accident until the date of the separation is community property and should be awarded one-half each to Ronna and William;
- lost earnings and diminished earning capacity after the date of separation is Ronna's separate property;

- out-of-pocket expenses prior to trial had already been reimbursed in full (otherwise, expenses paid by community funds would probably have been reimbursed);
- expenses occurring after trial should be awarded to the party incurring the expense; and
- recovery for all other damages (probably referring to "pain and suffering") is Ronna's separate property.

In re Marriage of Brown, 100 Wn.2d 729, 675 P.2d 1207 (1984).

A different rule applies if the personal injury was inflicted by the other spouse, rather than a third party. Then the damages award is the injured spouse's separate property, regardless of whether the couple is living together.

Separate and Community Property Interests. Sometimes there are both separate and community interests in a single property. This commonly occurs in two situations: when the property is paid for over time, and when the property is improved during the marriage.

When property is paid for over time (as with a deed of trust or an installment contract), some payments may be made with separate funds and some with community funds. This is especially likely to occur with a major purchase, such as a home.

> **Example:** Doreen and Dimitri purchased a residence for $400,000. They used Doreen's separate funds to make the $80,000 downpayment. However, their $320,000 loan was a community obligation (both Doreen and Dimitri signed the loan documents). They proceed to use community funds to make the monthly payments on the loan.
>
> The house is community property, but Doreen has a separate property interest in the house in the same proportion that the downpayment had to the purchase price (20%). If ten years later the property is worth $700,000, Doreen's separate interest has increased to $140,000 (20% of $700,000).

Another common example would be one spouse purchasing a home before the marriage, and then making the mortgage payments on the home after the marriage with community funds. The home would be the purchasing spouse's separate property, but the community would have an interest in it in proportion to the amount of principal payments made with community funds.

Community property—either community funds, or the time, skill, and labor of one of the spouses—is often used to improve separate property. That gives the marital community an interest in the property.

> **Example:** Terri and Sharon are married. Terri inherits a house from her mother. This is Terri's separate property. Since Terri and Sharon already have a home, Terri decides to lease the inherited house to tenants. In preparing the house for rental, Terri spends $10,000 in community funds on repairs and improvements. The house is still Terri's separate property, but Terri and Sharon's marital community now has an interest in it.
>
> This interest is proportionate to the community's contribution (the $10,000 plus Terri's time and efforts). Although most of the rent generated by the property will be Terri's separate property, a portion will be Terri and Sharon's community property.

The same process works in reverse. Let's say Terri's mother left her $10,000, which Terri used to improve the home she and Sharon own as community property. Then Terri would have a separate interest in the home along with the community's interest.

Legal Consequences

The way in which property is classified has a significant bearing on each spouse's rights and interests in that property: each spouse owns his or her separate property in severalty; each has an undivided ½ interest in all community property.

Management and Control. Equal control of community property is the general rule. Equal control means that either spouse can act unilaterally, without the other's consent.

> **Example:** Lowell and Gina own a car as community property. One day a passerby offers Lowell $5,000 for the car. That strikes Lowell as a very good price, so he accepts the offer without consulting Gina.
>
> When Lowell tells Gina he sold the car, she's very annoyed. But it's too late to do anything about it; Lowell's unilateral action was legally binding.

One exception to this rule is that when one spouse operates a business, the other spouse has no right to interfere in its management, even though the business is community property.

Joinder Requirements. There are several important limitations on a spouse's right to unilateral management and control of community property. In certain transactions, both spouses are required to act jointly; this is called a **joinder requirement**.

One spouse can't give away community property without the other's consent. In the example above, if Lowell had given away the car rather than selling it, Gina could have demanded it back. Also, one spouse can't sell, lease, or encumber the couple's household furnishings without the other's consent. And one spouse can't purchase, transfer, or encumber community real property without the other spouse's consent.

It is crucial for real estate agents to remember this joinder requirement and obtain the signature of both spouses on any contract involving community real property. Otherwise, the contract is voidable.

> **Example:** Instead of selling their car, Lowell decides to sell their home without asking Gina. He finds a buyer and signs a purchase and sale agreement. Since Lowell cannot transfer community real property without Gina's consent (and signature), the purchase and sale agreement is not a valid contract.

There are very few exceptions to this joinder requirement. One of the exceptions is that joinder is not required in an estoppel situation. A spouse who accepts benefits from a transaction, or fails to object to it in a timely way, may be estopped from objecting. Also, if another party has acted in reliance on consent given by one spouse, the other spouse may not be allowed to object. For example, suppose a neighbor builds a garage over the property line because Lowell said it was okay. Even though Gina didn't give her approval, a court might not allow her to object to the encroachment, because the neighbor expended significant resources in reliance on her husband's permission.

Remedies for Unauthorized Acts. When only one spouse enters into a transaction regarding community real property, the transaction is not binding on the other spouse. If the nonacting spouse wants to, he or she may void the transaction, even when the other party acted in good faith. Any payment received from the other party (for example, an earnest money deposit) must be refunded.

For real estate agents, buyers, and lienholders, the rule is simple: always determine whether a property owner is married. If so, then the safest course is to have the owner's spouse:

- sign a quitclaim deed transferring any interest he or she might have in the property to the other spouse (the one who's participating in the transaction),
- execute a power of attorney authorizing the other spouse to transfer the property, or
- co-sign all the documents involved in the transaction (the listing agreement, purchase and sale agreement, and deed).

These steps are not necessary if in fact the property being transferred or encumbered is entirely the separate property of the spouse who's participating in the transaction. However, if it turns out that the community has an interest in the property, the buyer could lose the property, and the brokerage could lose the commission.

Case Example:

Roy and Billee Haueter owned an apartment building they wanted to sell. On October 3, 1982, Roy signed an exclusive listing contract with Larry Klaas. Billee testified that she did not know about this listing agreement.

On November 29, 1982, the Haueters sold the apartment house through Dennis Weybright. Weybright received a 6% commission on the sale.

Klaas brought a lawsuit for breach of his exclusive listing agreement. The court entered a judgment against Roy Haueter individually. No judgment was entered against the community because the court found that Billee Haueter had not authorized the listing with Mr. Klaas and did not ratify the contract. *Klaas v. Haueter*, 49 Wn. App. 697, 745 P.2d 870 (1987).

In this case example, the sale itself was valid. The problem arose because an unwary agent did not have both spouses sign an exclusive listing agreement. The fact that Klaas won a judgment against Roy Haueter individually means that he was entitled to the full commission amount from Roy. However, the fact that no judgment was entered against Billee may have made it harder for Klaas to actually collect the money.

Liability for Debts. A creditor's rights against a married person's property are determined by its classification as separate or community property. One spouse's separate property is shielded from liability for the other spouse's premarital debts.

Fig. 5.3 Creditors' claims and community or separate property

	Other Spouse's Premarital Debt	Other Spouse's Debt Incurred During Marriage
Separate Property	SAFE	SAFE*
Community Property	SAFE**	NOT SAFE

* unless debt is for necessities
** except for child support/maintenance, or judgments incurred in three years prior to marriage

Example: When Lois and Joe got married, Lois already owned a home, and Joe owed a large judgment in connection with an automobile accident. Since the home is Lois's separate property, the judgment against Joe cannot become a lien against the home.

Separate property is also protected from debts the other spouse incurs during the marriage, unless the debts were incurred for necessities such as food and clothing. Thus, if Joe's automobile accident occurred during the marriage, Lois's separate property still could not be reached by the judgment creditor.

A spouse's premarital creditors generally cannot reach the couple's community property. There are two exceptions. The community may still be liable for a child support or maintenance obligation from a spouse's previous marriage. The community may also be liable for a judgment debt against one spouse that arose within three years prior to the marriage.

Finally, all community property is subject to liability for the debts either spouse incurs during the marriage. Referring back to the example above, if the home were community property and Joe's accident occurred during the marriage, the judgment lien against Joe would attach to the home, even though Lois had nothing to do with the automobile accident.

Division of the Property on Dissolution. When a marriage is dissolved, the court presiding over the dissolution can divide and award the couple's community property.

Community property is divided between the spouses in a "just and equitable manner." The court may divide the property equally, or it may choose an unequal allocation, based on the economic circumstances of each spouse. Separate property is excluded from this process; the court cannot award one spouse's separate property to the other spouse.

In determining whether property is separate or community property, the court relies on two legal presumptions that strongly favor community property:

1. all property acquired during the marriage is presumed to be community property, unless it was a gift or inheritance, and
2. after several years of marriage, everything the couple owns is presumed to have been acquired during the marriage.

These presumptions apply even if the title to the property states that it is separate property. Either spouse may rebut these presumptions with evidence that the property is actually separate property.

> **Example:** When Todd married Nancy, he owned a car and had $85,000 in savings. The car and the money were his separate property. During the marriage, Todd used his $85,000 to buy some land. The deed to the property says, "Todd Smith, a married man, as his sole and separate property."
>
> In the couple's dissolution proceedings, the court presumes that both the car and the land are community property. It is up to Todd to rebut this presumption by showing that they are his separate property. He must present evidence that he owned the car before the marriage, and that he purchased the land with funds he possessed before the marriage.

It can be especially difficult to prove that property is separate when it has changed form during the marriage (from a grand piano to cash to a motorcycle), or when separate funds have been commingled with community funds. It may be necessary to go through a complicated process of tracing the couple's expenditures. Community expenses are presumed to have been paid out of community funds, and separate expenses are presumed to have been paid out of separate funds.

When there are both separate and community interests in the same piece of property, the court will likely order some form of reimbursement. Typically, a spouse must reimburse the community for contributions to his or her separate property, and the community must reimburse a spouse for separate contributions to community property.

Disposition of Property at Death. When a married person dies, the probate court determines what part of the estate is separate property and what part is community property. The property is then distributed according to the will, or if there is no will, according to the rules of intestate succession. (See Chapter 9 for more information about wills and intestate succession.)

A married person is free to will his or her separate property to anyone. In addition, both spouses have the right to will their undivided ½ interest in all community property to someone other than the surviving spouse.

> **Example:** Jules and Maria own a home as community property. Maria wills her ½ interest in the property to her friend, Josephine. When Maria dies, Jules and Josephine each own an undivided ½ interest in the property as tenants in common.

If a married person dies without having made a valid will, all the community property vests in the surviving spouse.

> **Example:** Bud and Rena had four children. Bud never got around to writing a will. When he dies, Rena receives full title to their home, car, furniture, and other community property. She now owns all of this in severalty, and the children have no rights in it.

The separate property of the intestate spouse (the spouse who died without leaving a will) is divided between the surviving spouse and the deceased's children. The spouse receives an undivided ½ interest in the separate property and the children share the remaining ½ interest. All of these interests are held as tenants in common.

Example: Bud also owned some land as his separate property. When Bud dies, Rena receives an undivided ½ interest in the land. Each of their four children receives an undivided ⅛ interest in the land (a ½ interest divided among four children).

If both spouses die at the same time (in an accident, for example), each spouse's ½ interest in the community property is distributed as if that spouse survived the other spouse.

Tenancy in Common

Tenancy in common is the most basic form of concurrent ownership. It is the residual category: co-ownership that doesn't fit into any of the other categories is a tenancy in common by default. If a deed transferring land to two unmarried individuals doesn't specify how they are taking title, they take title as **tenants in common**.

Co-owners who choose tenancy in common should make that clear in the deed, by adding "as tenants in common" after their names. If they own unequal shares in the property, that should be stated in the deed as well.

Example: When Zowalski and Martinez bought Baker's tract of land, they decided to take title as tenants in common. Zowalski came up with ⅔ of the purchase price, and Martinez contributed ⅓. Their deed reads, "Zowalski, a single woman, with an undivided ⅔ interest, and Martinez, a single woman, with an undivided ⅓ interest, as tenants in common."

When a deed does not state each co-tenant's fractional interest, the law presumes that the interests are equal. In a lawsuit, a tenant in common can overcome that legal presumption by submitting evidence that the contributions to the purchase price were unequal.

Example: Zowalski paid ⅔ of the purchase price, and Martinez paid ⅓. However, their deed simply states, "Zowalski, a single woman, and Martinez, a single woman, as tenants in common."

Zowalski and Martinez subsequently have a serious disagreement, and they take each other to court over the property. Because the deed doesn't state what fractional interest each of them owns, the judge presumes that each has a ½ interest.

But Zowalski presents evidence (a canceled check) showing that she paid ⅔ of the purchase price. This rebuts the presumption that she and Martinez have equal shares. Now the judge is likely to rule that Zowalski has a ⅔ interest in the property and Martinez has only a ⅓ interest, unless Martinez presents persuasive evidence to the contrary.

Rights and Duties of Tenants in Common

In principle, there's no limit to how many tenants in common can share a property. There are also no restrictions on how they divide up the ownership. One tenant in common might own a ½ interest, and 50 others might each own a ¹⁄₁₀₀ interest.

The interests owned by tenants in common are always **undivided**: each tenant has a right to possess and occupy the whole property, no matter how small his or her share of ownership is. Similarly, no co-tenant can exclude another co-tenant from any portion of the property. This rule is referred to as **unity of possession**. This concept is best illustrated by contrasting tenancy in common with ownership in severalty.

> **Example:** Abernathy owns a large tract of land. She deeds the east ⅔ of it to Bernstein, and the west ⅓ to Corman.
>
> Bernstein and Corman each own their portion of the tract in severalty. They are not co-owners; they are sole owners of two separate properties. Each holds the entire bundle of rights to his portion, and has the right to exclude all others from his portion. Bernstein can exclude Corman from the east ⅔ and Corman can exclude Bernstein from the west ⅓.
>
> On the other hand, suppose Abernathy deeds her entire tract to Bernstein and Corman as tenants in common, with Bernstein taking an undivided ⅔ interest and Corman taking an undivided ⅓ interest. Now they are co-owners of a single property, sharing a single bundle of rights. Both have the right to possess and occupy the whole tract; neither can exclude the other from any part of it. Even though Bernstein's interest in the property is twice as great as Corman's, Bernstein can't fence off ⅔ of the property and tell Corman to keep out.

One tenant in common does not have a right to charge another co-tenant rent. If Bernstein chooses to live on the property while Corman chooses not to, Corman is not entitled to collect rent from Bernstein. But Corman may be allowed to offset the rental value of the property against his share of the property's expenses.

As an extension of the unity of possession rule, each co-tenant has a right to an equal share of any products or income generated by the property. Diamonds from a mine or apples from an orchard belong to all the tenants in common. If they lease out the property to someone else, the co-tenants share the collected rent equally.

Contribution. All tenants in common are required to share the property's expenses, such as maintenance, insurance, taxes, and mortgage payments. Unless otherwise agreed, each tenant's share of expenses is proportionate to his or her ownership interest. Thus, Bernstein is liable for ⅔ of the expenses, and Corman is liable for ⅓ of the expenses.

A co-tenant who pays more than his share of the expenses can demand reimbursement from the other tenants in common. This is called the **right to contribution**.

The right to contribution also applies to property improvements, but only when the other tenants in common have agreed to the improvement.

> **Example:** Armstrong, Bennett, and Crane own a house as tenants in common. Armstrong and Bennett want to add a deck, but Crane is opposed to the project. Armstrong pays a carpenter to build the deck. Armstrong is entitled to reimbursement from Bennett, but not from Crane.

As you might guess, this rule often leads to disputes over whether a particular project (a new cedar roof, for example) was an improvement or necessary maintenance.

Waste. A tenant in common is liable to the other tenants for any waste she commits on the property (just as a life tenant is liable to a remainderman for waste). For instance, if Armstrong drives a car through the garage wall, she will have to compensate Bennett and Crane for the damage.

Transfer and Encumbrance

A tenant in common is free to sell, will, or encumber his undivided interest without the consent of the other tenant(s). A tenant in common's interest can also be transferred involuntarily, by foreclosure or bankruptcy.

> **Example:** Drew, Giles, and Magraw are tenants in common. Drew mortgages her undivided ⅓ interest, but that mortgage doesn't encumber Giles's or Magraw's interest.
>
> Drew dies, leaving all her property to her friend, Lohr. Now Giles, Magraw, and Lohr are tenants in common, and Lohr's undivided ⅓ interest is encumbered by the mortgage.
>
> Lohr can't make the mortgage payments, so eventually the bank forecloses. Warner purchases Lohr's ⅓ interest at the foreclosure sale. Now Giles, Magraw, and Warner are tenants in common.

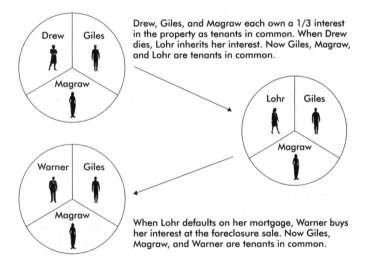

Drew, Giles, and Magraw each own a 1/3 interest in the property as tenants in common. When Drew dies, Lohr inherits her interest. Now Giles, Magraw, and Lohr are tenants in common.

When Lohr defaults on her mortgage, Warner buys her interest at the foreclosure sale. Now Giles, Magraw, and Warner are tenants in common.

To transfer or encumber the whole property, all the tenants in common must sign the deed, deed of trust, or other instrument.

> **Example:** Williams, McNeil, Pohto, and Starbuck are tenants in common. Investments, Inc. offers them a great deal of money for their land. Williams, McNeil, and Pohto leap at the offer. But Starbuck (who holds an undivided $1/16$ interest) turns it down, because of his sentimental attachment to the property.
>
> Williams, McNeil, and Pohto can sell their combined undivided $15/16$ interest in the property without Starbuck's consent, but they can't sell the whole property. Investments, Inc. insists on all or nothing. The others plead with Starbuck, but he won't budge. Investments, Inc. withdraws its offer.

What if Williams, McNeil, and Pohto all signed a deed that purported to convey the whole property to Investments, Inc.? The deed would effectively convey their undivided $^{15}/_{16}$ interest, but not the whole property. Investments, Inc. could withdraw from the transaction or sue for damages.

The real estate agent who represented Investments, Inc. in the sale might be in trouble. She probably relied on the title insurance company to figure out who owned the property and who needed to sign the deed. The title officer slipped up—it happens, though not often. By failing to double check, the real estate agent exposed herself to liability for negligence. She might even be accused of participating in a fraud, if she knew about Starbuck's interest.

Terminating a Tenancy in Common

A tenancy in common can be terminated by agreement or by judicial partition.

Agreement. All the tenants in common can agree to terminate the tenancy. The co-tenants can agree to change their tenancy in common to one of the other forms of concurrent ownership (joint tenancy or community property, if they are married). Or they can agree to divide their property, so that each owns a portion of the property in severalty. This division by agreement is called voluntary partition.

> **Example:** Ames wills 20 acres of vacant land to Bakke and Church as tenants in common. Bakke and Church agree that they'd each rather have half the property instead of sharing the whole property.
>
> They have the land surveyed and divided into two ten-acre parcels. Bakke deeds her undivided ½ interest in the east ten acres to Church, and Church deeds his undivided ½ interest in the west ten acres to Bakke. Now each owns a ten-acre tract in severalty.

Judicial Partition. A tenancy in common can also be terminated by the unilateral action of one of the co-tenants, without the consent of the other(s). If Bakke wants to end the tenancy in common, but Church does not, Bakke can file a **partition action** in superior court.

Everyone with a recorded interest in the property (co-tenants and lienholders) is brought into the partition suit as a defendant. The judge determines the status and priority of all the liens against the property, and what interest each party holds. Then the judge terminates the tenancy in common by partitioning the property. Each former co-tenant is granted a share proportionate to her ownership interest.

Whenever possible, the judge will order the property to be physically divided. But physical division often won't work. For example, if the property Bakke and Church owned as tenants in common included a house, it would not be practical to divide it in half.

When physical partition is impractical or inequitable, the judge can order the property sold. The sale proceeds are then divided among the former co-tenants according to their ownership interests. Or, in some cases, a judge may order part of the property sold and part of it physically divided.

A tenant in common may oppose a physical division of the property. She can present evidence to show that the divided property would be worth substantially less than the proceeds from a sale of the whole property. In this case, the judge should order the property sold instead of physically divided.

Joint Tenancy

Joint tenants have a relationship similar to that of tenants in common: each joint tenant has an undivided interest in, and shares possession of, the whole property.

But the distinguishing feature of joint tenancy—the **right of survivorship**—comes into play if one of the joint tenants dies. When a joint tenant dies, his interest in the property passes automatically to the surviving joint tenant(s).

> **Example:** Craft, Kaskell, and Rusnak buy a vacation home together. Sometime later, Craft dies. If Craft, Kaskell, and Rusnak were tenants in common, Craft's undivided interest would pass to his heirs. Kaskell, Rusnak, and Craft's heirs would then own the property as tenants in common.
>
> But if Craft, Kaskell, and Rusnak were joint tenants, from the moment of Craft's death, Kaskell and Rusnak own the whole property. Because of the right of survivorship, Craft cannot will his interest to his heirs.

Creating a Joint Tenancy

Since joint tenancy has such a radical effect on the disposition of property, it isn't something co-owners can slip into by default. Specific rules exist for creating and maintaining a joint tenancy. If these rules are not followed when the property is acquired, or if they are broken during the period of ownership, the joint tenancy fails and the right of survivorship is lost. Instead of a joint tenancy, the co-owners will either have a tenancy in common or, if they're a married couple, community property.

The Four Unities. To create a joint tenancy, the **four unities of title** must exist:

1. unity of possession,
2. unity of interest,
3. unity of time, and
4. unity of title.

Unity of possession means that all co-owners have the right to occupy the whole property. A tenancy in common also requires the unity of possession.

Unity of interest means that all the joint tenants must have an equal interest in the property. If there are two joint tenants, each must have a ½ interest; if there are three joint tenants, each must have a ⅓ interest; and so on. If Scovel has a ¼ interest and Dimarco has a ¾ interest, they aren't joint tenants.

Unity of time means that all of the joint tenants must acquire their interests in the property at the same moment.

Unity of title means that the joint tenants all must take title through the same deed or will.

> **Example:** Connelly deeds an undivided ½ interest in his property to Dreyer. Two months later, Connelly deeds an undivided ½ interest in the same property to Cree. Dreyer and Cree cannot be joint tenants, because they acquired title at two different times, through two different deeds. Although there is unity of interest and unity of possession, there is no unity of time and no unity of title. As a result, there is no joint tenancy.

However, it is possible for a property owner to create a joint tenancy by deeding the property to herself and others.

> **Example:** Karen has owned some land for many years. When her children, Bill and Clarisse, reach adulthood, Karen deeds the property "to Karen, Bill, and Clarisse, as joint tenants."
> This new deed satisfies the unity of time and the unity of title requirements, even though Karen originally acquired the property long before and through a different deed than Bill and Clarisse.

Note that joint tenants may agree among themselves to give one joint tenant exclusive possession of the property. Such an agreement does not destroy the joint tenancy. The agreement can even be entered into at the same time that the co-owners acquire the property, without preventing the creation of a joint tenancy.

Other Requirements. A joint tenancy can only be created in writing. The deed or will must expressly state the intention to create a joint tenancy. It's best to have the deed or will state that title is held either "as joint tenants" or "in joint tenancy."

Courts have disagreed over whether any other language is sufficient evidence of an intent to create a joint tenancy. However, it is clear that the phrase "with the right of survivorship" will not create a joint tenancy by itself. And even the words "as joint tenants" or "in joint tenancy" only establishes a presumption that there was an intent to create a joint tenancy. A court will consider evidence presented to rebut the presumption: for example, evidence showing that the grantor, the testator, or the new co-owners had confused joint tenancy with tenancy in common.

Rights and Duties of Joint Tenants

Once co-owners manage to establish a joint tenancy, they have similar rights and duties as tenants in common: the right to contribution, the right to the products and rents from the property, and the duty to avoid waste. A joint tenant can also encumber his own interest without the others' consent. But in addition, joint tenants have a right that tenants in common don't have: the right of survivorship.

Right of Survivorship. As explained earlier, when a joint tenant dies, her interest in the joint tenancy property passes directly to the surviving joint tenants.

Example: Kunz, Dodd, and King are joint tenants. Because of the unity of interest rule, each has an undivided ⅓ interest in the joint tenancy property.

When King dies, Dodd and Kunz still own the property as joint tenants, but now each has an undivided ½ interest, since they automatically acquired King's interest.

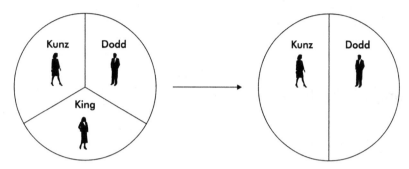

A joint tenancy interest cannot be willed or inherited, because it no longer belongs to the joint tenant at the moment of her death. As a result, joint tenancy property does not need to go through the probate process. This can spare the surviving joint tenants considerable expense and delay. However, joint tenancy property doesn't escape federal estate taxes. The deceased joint tenant's interest is treated as part of her estate for federal estate tax purposes.

Making the Title Marketable. Although surviving joint tenants acquire the deceased joint tenant's interest automatically at the moment of death, they must take steps to clear their title.

This can be accomplished by recording proof of the death, such as a court decree or a certified copy of the death certificate. The survivors should also record a sworn statement (an affidavit) that identifies the deceased as one of the property's joint tenants and identifies themselves as the surviving joint tenants. It may also be necessary to record certificates of state or federal estate tax lien releases.

Until these steps have been taken, the surviving joint tenants' title is not **marketable**. That means the public record presents some question about the validity of their title.

A title company will refuse to insure a title unless it is marketable. Here again, however, a real estate agent can't rely absolutely on the title company. The agent needs to know the rules and double check to make sure they've been followed. When surviving joint tenants sell property, the buyer should not go through with the transaction until the proof of death, affidavit, and tax releases have all been recorded.

Simultaneous Death. If all the joint tenants die at once, each tenant's interest in the joint tenancy property passes according to his or her will. Each joint tenant's interest is probated separately and the heirs of each joint tenant receive their interests as tenants in common.

Example: Debra and Tim own property as joint tenants. They are killed at virtually the same moment when an earthquake hits their house.

Debra's undivided ½ interest in the property passes to her heirs, Samuel and Zeke, by intestate succession. Tim had written a will leaving all his property to his friend Cliff, so Cliff takes Tim's undivided ½ interest in the joint tenancy property.

After the probate process is completed, Samuel, Zeke, and Cliff are tenants in common. Samuel and Zeke each have an undivided ¼ interest, and Cliff has an undivided ½ interest.

Terminating a Joint Tenancy

Partition. Just like tenants in common, joint tenants can agree to partition their property, or one joint tenant can bring suit for judicial partition. Either way, by breaking the unity of possession, partition eliminates the right of survivorship and ends the co-ownership.

Merely filing a partition action does not terminate the joint tenancy; it ends only when the court's partition judgment is entered. Thus, if one of the joint tenants dies during the trial, the right of survivorship is still effective.

Severance. A joint tenancy is also terminated when it is **severed**. Severance may occur as a result of transfer, declaration, or agreement. Severance ends the joint tenancy and eliminates the right of survivorship, but unlike partition, it does not terminate the co-ownership. Instead, severance changes a joint tenancy into a tenancy in common or community property.

Each joint tenant has the power to sever the joint tenancy by transferring his or her interest. A transfer severs a joint tenancy by breaking the unities of time and title.

Example: Adams and Buzzell own some land as joint tenants. Buzzell sells her undivided ½ interest in the property to Wall. Now Adams and Wall each own an undivided ½ interest, but they are tenants in common, not joint tenants.

An involuntary transfer of a joint tenant's interest also severs the joint tenancy. This includes transfers due to bankruptcy or foreclosure.

A transfer (either voluntary or involuntary) severs the joint tenancy only in regard to the transferred interest. When there are just two joint tenants, that ends the joint tenancy altogether. When there are more than two joint tenants, however, the co-owners who did not transfer their interests remain joint tenants in relation to one another.

Example: Kennedy, Jordan, and Chin are joint tenants. Kennedy deeds her interest to her friend, Peabody. That severs the joint tenancy as far as Kennedy's undivided ⅓ interest is concerned, so Peabody is not a joint tenant. Peabody is a tenant in common in relation to Jordan and Chin. But Jordan and Chin are still joint tenants in relation to one another.

If Peabody were to die, her interest would pass to her heirs, since the right of survivorship does not apply to her.

But if Jordan dies, Chin (rather than Jordan's heirs) acquires Jordan's interest, because the right of survivorship was still effective between Jordan and Chin. On Jordan's death,

Chin has an undivided ⅔ interest, and Peabody still has an undivided ⅓ interest. Chin and Peabody are tenants in common.

In Washington (and most other states), a joint tenant may sever the joint tenancy simply by deeding her interest in the property to herself.

Transferring the property is not the only way to sever a joint tenancy. One of the co-owners can simply declare in writing that the joint tenancy is severed. And executing any written instrument that shows an intention to sever the joint tenancy also may be held to sever it.

> **Example:** Kunz and Lambert own a house as joint tenants. They enter a written agreement stating that Lambert is to have the right to will his interest in the property to his heirs.
>
> This agreement suggests an intention to sever the joint tenancy, since the right of survivorship is a basic characteristic of a joint tenancy. For that reason, a court would probably hold that the agreement caused a severance.

In this example, it is the written document that caused the severance, because it was evidence of an intention to sever. Note that a joint tenant's unilateral attempt to will the joint tenancy property will not automatically cause a severance (although it may be used as evidence of an intent to sever).

Recording requirement. Unless all the joint tenants have agreed to the severance, a deed, declaration, or other document severing the joint tenancy must be recorded to be effective. If the severance document has not yet been recorded and the severing joint tenant dies, the property will still pass to the surviving joint tenants as required by the right of survivorship.

Agreement requiring consent to sever. Joint tenants may agree among themselves that their joint tenancy can only be severed by mutual consent, and not by the unilateral action of one tenant. If one joint tenant later deeds his or her interest to someone else, the transfer will not be effective, and the joint tenancy won't be severed.

> **Example:** Ramsey and Pomerenke agree that their joint tenancy can be severed only by mutual consent. Later Ramsey deeds his undivided ½ interest to Thorne. Because of the mutual consent agreement, the deed to Thorne is invalid, and the joint tenancy is not severed.

There's an important exception to this rule. If Thorne was a good faith purchaser, received the interest in exchange for value, and was not aware of the mutual consent agreement, the deed is valid and the joint tenancy is broken.

Advantages and Disadvantages of Joint Tenancy

Co-owners who take title as joint tenants usually choose to do so to avoid probate, and to enable the surviving tenant to take the property free of the other's liens and debts. These are substantial advantages, if in fact one of the parties dies during the period of co-ownership.

But the right of survivorship is very easily lost through severance. Although a severance document must be recorded to be effective, a co-owner who has no reason to suspect that the joint tenancy has been severed is not likely to check the public record. He may be in for a shock if the other co-owner dies and the deceased's interest in the property becomes part of the deceased's estate.

As mentioned above, co-owners can prevent this kind of surprise by agreeing that their joint tenancy cannot be severed except by mutual consent. But that arrangement can create the opposite problem, making it difficult to get out of the joint tenancy. If one of the joint tenants is unwilling to consent to a severance, the others must file a partition action. Like any lawsuit, a partition action can be expensive, time-consuming, and stressful.

Co-ownership and Married Couples

Spouses may share title to property as joint tenants or as tenants in common, rather than holding it as community property. For example, a married couple may choose to own their home in joint tenancy: that way, if one spouse dies, his or her interest is automatically transferred to the other spouse, without having to wait for probate to be completed.

However, in Washington, there is a very strong presumption in favor of community property. There must be conclusive evidence showing that a couple understood the various forms of ownership and specifically wanted a form other than community property. Otherwise, the court will presume that the property is community property.

Fig. 5.4 Characteristics of different forms of co-ownership

	Joint Tenancy	Tenancy in Common	Community Property
Creation presumed	No	Yes	Yes
Equal right to possession	Yes	Yes	Yes
Equal interests required	Yes	No	Yes
Right of survivorship	Yes	No	No
Each co-owner can unilaterally convey undivided interest	Yes	Yes	No
Each co-owner can will undivided interest	No	Yes	Yes

Statutory law provides that property co-owned by spouses is presumed to be community property, even if the deed states that it is owned in joint tenancy. If a married couple wants to own property as joint tenants, they must take other steps (such as stating in the deed that the property is not intended to be community property) to be sure that the presumption of community property can be refuted.

In dissolution proceedings, real estate held in joint tenancy is presumed to be community property, regardless of what the deed says. The spouse who objects to this classification must present evidence to rebut the presumption, showing that the couple truly intended a joint tenancy and not community property.

A joint tenancy between spouses is not severed by dissolution of the marriage, and the court does not have the power to award joint tenancy property in the property settlement.

When a spouse dies, the deceased spouse's interest in property held in joint tenancy with the other spouse vests automatically in the survivor. But the heirs and devisees of the deceased spouse may try to establish that it really was community property, rather than a joint tenancy.

> **Example:** The deed to Rick and Samantha's home says, "Richard Fitch and Samantha Walters, a married couple, in joint tenancy." Rick dies, and his will provides that his undivided ½ interest in the home goes to Denise, his daughter by a previous marriage.
>
> If the home was truly owned in joint tenancy, Rick's interest in it could not be willed. Upon Rick's death, the right of survivorship would automatically vest Rick's interest in Samantha. (Rick's attempt to will his interest would not have severed the joint tenancy.)
>
> But Denise wants to establish that the home was really held as community property, not in joint tenancy. In the probate court, she may argue that Rick and Samantha didn't really understand what a joint tenancy was and didn't intend to create one. Denise can use her father's attempt to will his interest to her as evidence that there wasn't a joint tenancy, along with the absence of language in the deed stating that the property should not be considered community property.
>
> If Denise succeeds in proving that the home was community property, the court will award her Rick's undivided ½ interest, in accordance with his will. Denise and Samantha would then own the home as tenants in common. (And then, because of hard feelings generated by the lawsuit, either Denise or Samantha would probably bring a partition action to end the co-ownership.)

Ownership by Associations

The second aspect of real property co-ownership is ownership by associations—businesses, nonprofit groups, and other organizations—rather than individuals. Depending on its form, an association may be a legal entity separate from its individual members or owners.

Title to property can be held in an association's name. Ownership by associations overlaps with the different forms of co-ownership discussed in the first part of the chapter. For example, a business organization may hold property in severalty, or it may be a tenant in common with other organizations or individuals.

A business organization generally can't be a joint tenant, however, since the right of survivorship is the key trait of a joint tenancy. Artificial entities such as corporations potentially have perpetual existence, which would prevent a joint tenant from acquiring any genuine survivorship right.

A real estate agent should understand when and how an association can hold title to real property. Most importantly, she needs to know who can sign (and who must sign) on behalf of an association to enter into contracts and transfer property.

Corporations

The most sophisticated form of association is the **corporation**. The ownership interests in a corporation are divided into **shares**. The corporation is owned by **stockholders** or **shareholders**, individuals who purchase shares in the company as an investment. The money invested provides the corporation with operating capital.

A corporation may have only a few shareholders, or it may have hundreds. The shareholders may simply be several members of a family—as with many closely held corporations—or they may have purchased publicly traded shares on a stock exchange. But the corporation is legally a separate entity from its shareholders. The law treats it as an artificial individual: it can enter into contracts, own property, incur debts, sue and be sued. Because of this special legal status, corporations are tightly regulated by state and federal laws.

Creation. To start a corporation in Washington, its organizers (the **incorporators**) file **articles of incorporation** with the secretary of state's office. The articles establish the corporation's name, list the name and address of each incorporator, explain the share structure, and include a general statement of purpose.

A **domestic corporation** is one organized in compliance with Washington law. A **foreign corporation** is one organized under the laws of another state, or in another country. A foreign corporation involved in Washington real estate transactions must be registered by the secretary of state to do business in Washington.

Management. A corporation's shareholders may have very little direct involvement in its management. They receive an annual report and may inspect the corporate records. They may also attend an annual meeting and vote on some major issues.

The real power behind a corporation is its **board of directors**. The directors govern the corporation's affairs in accordance with its bylaws. They appoint corporate **officers**—for example, the president or chief executive officer (CEO), one or more vice presidents, a treasurer or chief financial officer (CFO), and a corporate secretary—who run the business on a day-to-day basis.

The officers are not automatically authorized to convey or encumber the corporation's real property. These actions must be expressly authorized by a resolution of the board. A title company will usually require proof of the authorization before insuring a transaction.

Liability. The primary advantage of the corporate form of organization is that shareholders are protected from liability for the corporation's debts.

Example: A few years ago, Mendez spent $3,000 on stock in the ABC Corporation. His shares are now worth $3,600.

The ABC Corporation is found liable for an injury caused by a defective product it manufactured, and a $250,000 judgment is entered against the corporation. The judgment creditor can file a lien against the corporation's assets if the judgment is not paid.

However, the creditor cannot proceed against Mendez to collect the judgment. His home, bank accounts, and other property are protected from liability, because the corporation is a separate legal entity. Mendez may lose his original $3,000 investment if the corporation goes out of business because of the judgment, but that is the extent of his liability.

In theory, all stockholders have this protection from liability. But in fact, creditors often require the personal guaranties of the major stockholders before they will make large loans to or enter into a lease with a corporation.

Taxation. One potential drawback to the corporate form of organization is the problem of "double taxation," where income is taxed twice, first at the corporate level and then at the individual level for shareholders. However, not all corporations face this problem; most small businesses organized as corporations are set up as **S corporations**, where the income flows through to the shareholders without first being taxed at the corporate level. An S corporation can have no more than 100 individual shareholders and only one class of stock. Larger corporations, known as **C corporations**, are subject to corporate tax.

Nonprofit Corporations. Until now, our discussion of corporations has been limited to for-profit corporations—businesses organized for the purpose of generating a profit that is distributed to its shareholders. Now let's take a moment to discuss **nonprofit corporations**, which are subject to some different rules.

Nonprofit corporations may be organized for charitable, political, social, religious, or professional purposes. Examples of nonprofit corporations include homeowners associations, social clubs, charities, and service organizations. Note that labor unions and cooperative organizations are excluded from nonprofit corporation status, as are organizations subject to state banking or insurance laws.

In contrast to a for-profit corporation, a nonprofit corporation must be structured so that it shares neither ownership nor revenues with individuals or other corporations. So a nonprofit corporation cannot issue stock or distribute income to its members, directors, or officers. It is also prohibited from lending money or extending credit to directors or officers.

However, nonprofit corporations are permitted to earn revenues, and may pay reasonable compensation to or confer benefits on members, directors, or officers for services rendered.

General Partnerships

A **general partnership** is simply an association of two or more individuals as co-owners of a business run for profit. It doesn't have the formal structure of a corporation or other business organization. Although a partnership can own property, for most other purposes the law does not recognize a general partnership as an entity independent from its members.

Creation. General partnerships are usually created by express agreement (either oral or written). In Washington, they can also be created by implied agreement, based on the actions of the parties. However, having a common interest in a business transaction doesn't automatically create a partnership. The parties must intend to carry on a definite, ongoing business as co-owners, sharing the management and profits. When that is their intention, they have a partnership, whether they call it that or not.

In Washington, general partners are not required to file any paperwork to form a partnership. However, an affidavit of partnership may be filed in the county recorder's office. Although this is not a legal requirement, some lenders or title insurance companies may require such a filing before participating in any transactions with the partnership.

Management and Profits. A general partnership agreement can provide for almost any allocation of rights and duties between the partners. If the agreement doesn't address an issue (or if it is an implied agreement), then the allocation will be according to statute. The rules outlined here are the statutory rules; most of them can be altered in a partnership agreement.

All general partners have an equal voice in the management and control of the business. The partnership is legally bound by the actions of one partner, as long as the partner is acting within the scope of his authority. (Each partner is an agent and a fiduciary of the partnership, so the agency rules explained in Chapters 6 and 7 apply.)

Unless otherwise agreed, the partners all share in the profits equally, even if their contributions to the business are unequal. In fact, some partners may contribute only skill or labor, without making any capital contributions at all. Partners usually divide losses in the same way they share profits.

Liability. General partners have unlimited liability for the acts of the partnership. Each partner can be made to pay the full amount of any partnership debts out of her own pocket.

> **Example:** Power, Quen, and Roberts own the PQR Company, a general partnership. Both the PQR Company and the individual partners are sued for breach of a construction contract, and a judgment is entered against them for $95,000. Neither the individual partners nor the PQR Company pay the judgment, so the judgment creditor claims a lien against Power's home. Power ends up paying the entire $95,000 to protect his home from foreclosure.

Power can then demand reimbursement from Quen and Roberts for their share of the judgment, and can sue them if they don't pay. This personal liability is the main disadvantage of a general partnership. It contrasts sharply with the protection enjoyed by a corporate shareholder, for example.

Partnership Property. All property that general partners bring into the business at the outset, and all that they later acquire for the business, is **partnership property**. Anything purchased with partnership funds is presumed to be partnership property.

Real estate may be acquired in the partnership name. If title is acquired in the partnership name, it can be conveyed only in the partnership name. Note that partnership property can be encumbered or conveyed in the name of the partnership with the signature of any authorized partner. When there are several partners and they live in different cities, this can save a lot of time and expense.

Every partner is an agent of the partnership, and thus the acts of any partner will bind the partnership. However, a partner cannot bind the partnership by acts that exceed his authority if the third party knows that the partner is acting beyond his authority.

> **Example:** Tom, Dick, and Harry own TDH Enterprises, a general partnership. The partnership owns some land, but the title to the land is in Tom's name. Tom sells the land to his brother. Tom and his brother are trying to cheat the partnership out of the property. They both know that the land is actually partnership property and that Dick and Harry would not approve of the sale.
>
> The sale does not bind the partnership. When Dick and Harry find out about the sale, they can recover the land from Tom's brother.

On the other hand, if a partner conveys partnership property to a good faith purchaser who doesn't realize that the partner is not authorized to sell it, the partnership can't recover the property.

> **Example:** Returning to the example above, suppose that Tom sells the land to Arthur, who is an innocent, good faith purchaser. Because Arthur believes that Tom has authority to sell the land, the partnership will be bound by the sale. Dick and Harry can sue Tom for violating his duties to the partnership, but they can't get the land back from Arthur.

Unless otherwise agreed, each partner has a right to possess all partnership property for partnership purposes. A partner has no right to possess partnership property for any other purpose, except with the consent of the other partners.

A partner can't transfer her interest in partnership property to someone outside the partnership, except when all of the partners assign the whole property. But (unless otherwise agreed) one partner may assign her interest in the partnership itself to an outsider. That gives the assignee a right to share in the partnership's profits. It does not make the assignee a partner, however, or give her the right to interfere in the management of the business.

Also, if a judgment is entered against a partner personally, the judgment creditor can't claim a lien against the partnership property in order to enforce the judgment.

> **Example:** Abernathy and Bowen own A&B Company, a general partnership. They also own a building as partnership property.
>
> Bowen is involved in an automobile accident, and a judgment is entered against her. The judgment creditor is entitled to liens against Bowen's house and other real property that she personally owns, and the creditor can foreclose if the judgment isn't paid. But the creditor cannot claim a lien against A&B Company's building, since that's partnership property. (The creditor could claim a lien against the building if the judgment were against the partnership rather than Bowen.) However, the creditor could collect the judgment by garnishing Bowen's share of the profits from the partnership.

When a partner dies, his interest in partnership property vests in the surviving partners. The deceased partner's estate has a right to an accounting and a share of the partnership profits, but it does not have an interest in the partnership property.

Fig. 5.5 Partnership liability

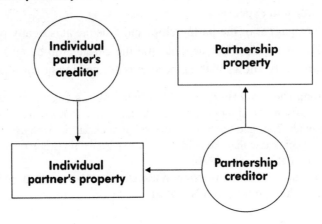

Limited Partnerships

A **limited partnership**, like a general partnership, is an association of two or more persons as co-owners of a business. A limited partnership has one or more general partners, plus one or more limited partners. The rights and duties of general partners in a limited partnership are the same as in a general partnership, but the limited partners have only limited liability.

Think of a limited partnership as a compromise between a general partnership and a corporation. Limited partners generally don't participate in the management of the business to the extent that general partners do, although they may have a greater role than corporate shareholders. Like corporate shareholders, limited partners are protected from the business's debts. As a result, limited partnerships are more strictly regulated than general partnerships.

Unlike a general partnership—which can be formed without filing any particular document, or even without any written agreement at all—a limited partnership can be formed only by filing a certificate of limited partnership at the office of the secretary of state. This form includes the name and address of all general partners. It must also include an address where the names and addresses of all limited partners may be found. The names and addresses of the limited partners do not have to be filed with the secretary of state, but they must be available for inspection at the address listed in the form. If the certificate of limited partnership is not filed, or the names and addresses are not available as required, all of the partners may be considered general partners.

A limited partner has no control over partnership property, which is controlled solely by the general partners.

Limited Liability Companies

Owners and investors, especially real estate owners and investors, often choose the **limited liability company (LLC)** form of business for its many advantages. First, there is great flexibility in structuring the management of a limited liability company. Second, members of an LLC are subject only to limited liability for the company's obligations. And last, an LLC can be set up so that it is taxed as a partnership. Limited liability companies in Washington are governed by the state Limited Liability Company Act.

Creation. An LLC is created when an LLC agreement is drawn up and a certificate of formation is filed with the state. In the LLC agreement, members can choose virtually any manner of allocating income, losses, or appreciation among themselves. Once the LLC is created, initial and annual reports must be filed with the state and an annual fee must be paid.

Management. LLCs have the flexibility of a general partnership when it comes to managing the business. Management of the LLC is placed in the hands of its members, unless the certificate of formation assigns management to one or more managers.

In a **member-managed** limited liability company, every member has agency authority; that is, all managing members can bind the LLC with their actions. Unless the LLC agreement provides otherwise, all decisions are made by the majority of LLC members. However, the LLC agreement may create a structure in which certain persons or classes of members have different management powers, duties, and voting rights.

In a **manager-managed** limited liability company, ordinary members do not act as agents of the LLC. Unless the LLC agreement provides otherwise, designated managers may be appointed or removed by a majority of the members and do not need to be members of the LLC.

Liability. An attractive aspect of the LLC form is that its members enjoy limited liability like that of corporation shareholders or limited partners. However, members and managers will be liable for any acts or omissions on behalf of the LLC that constitute gross negligence, intentional misconduct, or a knowing violation of the law.

Taxation. As we previously discussed, a major disadvantage to the corporate form of ownership is the double taxation imposed on large, publicly traded corporations and their shareholders. Income is first taxable at the corporate level, and is then taxable at the shareholder level when it is distributed as dividends. Income earned by an LLC, on the other hand, is taxed at only one level—the member level. LLC income is taxed as the personal income of each member, in the same manner as partnership income.

As you can see, LLCs offer a unique combination of advantages. By using this form of business entity, an owner can take advantage of the best attributes of both a corporation and a partnership.

Joint Ventures

A **joint venture** is similar to a partnership, but is formed for a single transaction or a related series of transactions, not as an ongoing business. There are no formal requirements for the creation of a joint venture. The parties simply agree to work together on a project and to share the profits or losses.

A joint venture is not an entity separate from its individual members; however, title to property can be held in the joint venture's name.

Syndicates

A **syndicate** is not a recognized legal entity. Like "company," the term "syndicate" can be used to refer to virtually any business organization. The XYZ Syndicate might be a corporation, general partnership, limited partnership, or trust, and it would hold title accordingly.

Conclusion

In Washington, ownership of real property by married persons is subject to community property laws. There is a very strong presumption in favor of community property. Property is presumed to belong to the marital community unless specific evidence shows otherwise. Certain transactions concerning community property require the consent and signature of both spouses. This requirement is especially significant to a real estate agent, since neither spouse can transfer or encumber community real property unless the other spouse also consents to the transaction.

Co-ownership of property also includes tenancy in common and joint tenancy. The biggest difference between tenancy in common and joint tenancy is the right of survivorship enjoyed by joint tenants.

Many legal presumptions exist in the area of co-ownership. If they want a form of co-ownership that differs from the applicable presumptions, co-owners must clearly and specifically set out their intentions in writing.

Real estate agents also need to be familiar with property ownership by associations such as corporations, partnerships, and limited liability companies. Each type of entity has different characteristics in terms of organizational structure, personal liability, and taxation.

Case Problem

The following is a hypothetical case problem. Most of the facts are taken from a real case. Make a decision on the issues presented and then check to see if your answer matches the decision reached by the court.

The Facts

Jeanette Borghi purchased a property in 1966, using a real estate contract. She married Robert Borghi in March 1975. In July 1975, the Borghis paid off the real estate contract; they received a special warranty deed to the property executed to "Robert G. and Jeanette L. Borghi, husband and wife." However, they did not record the 1975 deed until 1979, when they also used the property as security for a loan to purchase a mobile home to place on the property.

Jeanette Borghi died intestate (without a will) in 2005. Robert was still alive, and he was appointed personal representative of Jeanette's estate. Arthur Gilroy, Jeanette's son from a previous marriage, claimed that he was entitled to a one-half interest in the property because it was Jeanette's separate property at the time of her death.

The superior court held that the property was the Borghis' community property and would pass to Robert under the rules of intestate succession. Gilroy appealed, and the state Court of Appeals reversed the lower court's decision, holding that the property was Jeanette's separate property. The estate then appealed the Court of Appeals decision to the Washington Supreme Court.

The Questions

Was the property separate or community property at the time of Jeanette's death? Is it more important that she owned the property prior to her marriage, or that the Borghis received a deed with both their names on it?

The Answer

The Washington Supreme Court held that the property was Jeanette's separate property, so her son was entitled to a partial interest under the rules of intestate succession. The deed issued in the name of both spouses, received years after the property was first acquired by Jeanette, did not create a presumption that it was community property.

The supreme court stated that property's character as either community property or separate property is determined on the date of acquisition. Under the theory of "inception of title," when property is purchased through a real estate contract, the property is acquired when the contract obligations are first undertaken.

To establish that the property had stopped being Jeanette's separate property, the estate would have had to present evidence of the Borghis' intent to transmute the separate property into community property. The estate had argued that a deed that included Robert's name on it acted as a transfer of the property, as a gift, to the marital community. However, the supreme court suggested that a more affirmative act, in writing, would be necessary to accomplish that—for example, Jeanette executing a quitclaim deed transferring the property to the marital community, or the Borghis entering into a community property agreement. Robert's name on the deed only expressed the Borghis' intent to jointly take title, not necessarily to turn the property into community property. *In the matter of the Estate of Borghi,* 167 Wn.2d 480, 219 P.3d 932 (2009).

Chapter Summary

- All property owned by a married couple in Washington is either the separate property of one spouse or the community property of both. Both spouses have equal control over the community property. The joinder requirement prevents the transfer or encumbrance of community real property without the signature of both spouses. An unauthorized transfer is voidable by the nonconsenting spouse. Community property is not subject to partition.

- A tenancy in common is the most basic form of co-ownership. Tenants in common may have unequal interests, their interests are undivided, and they share possession of the whole property. A tenant in common's interest can be freely transferred or willed. A tenancy in common may be terminated by partition, either voluntarily or by court order.

- A joint tenancy requires the four unities (time, title, interest, and possession). The key characteristic of joint tenancy is the right of survivorship. It prevents a joint tenant from willing her interest, but makes probate of the property unnecessary. The transfer of a joint tenant's interest severs the joint tenancy by breaking the unities of time and title. Severance does not terminate the co-ownership, but changes it to tenancy in common or community property.

- Title to real property can be held by associations of individuals: corporations, general partnerships, limited partnerships, or limited liability companies. Each form of organization has advantages and disadvantages in terms of management, taxation, regulation, and liability.

- General partners have equal rights of possession and control of partnership property. One partner cannot transfer or encumber his undivided interest in the property separately from the other partners' interests.

- A limited liability company has the flexibility and tax advantages of a partnership, but LLC members have limited liability, like corporate shareholders.

Checklist of Problem Areas

Real Estate Licensee's Checklist

❑ Have both spouses signed the listing agreement and the purchase and sale agreement?

❑ What kind of interest does the seller have in the property? Is it owned in severalty, or is the seller a tenant in common or joint tenant?

❑ If the seller is a tenant in common or a joint tenant, are the other owners aware of the sale? Will the buyer be an owner in severalty or will she be a co-owner?

Seller's Checklist

❑ Are you selling separate or community property? If it is community property, has your spouse agreed to the sale and signed the listing agreement and the purchase and sale agreement?

❑ If you are a tenant in common or a joint tenant, you may sell your interest in the property without your co-tenants' consent. However, you may sell only your portion, not the entire property.

❑ If you hold property as a joint tenant, selling your interest separately will sever the joint tenancy. Severance changes a joint tenancy into a tenancy in common. Does the buyer realize that she is purchasing only an undivided interest in the property?

❑ If you hold property as a joint tenant, have you signed any kind of agreement specifying that the property may only be severed by mutual consent?

Buyer's Checklist

❑ Are you purchasing property as your separate property or as community property? If it will be community property, has your spouse signed the purchase and sale agreement? If you intend for it to be separate property, is this clearly specified in the agreement and the deed, and are you paying for the property with your separate funds?

❑ Will you hold title in severalty or as a tenant in common or joint tenant? If you're attempting to create a joint tenancy, has the four unities requirement been met?

Chapter Quiz

1. Anderson and Baker own a house in Seattle. Anderson has an undivided ¾ interest in the property and Baker has an undivided ¼ interest. They hold the property as:

    a. tenants in common
    b. joint tenants
    c. tenants by the entirety
    d. community property

2. In Washington, a married person cannot hold title to real property:

    a. as separate property
    b. in a partnership
    c. as a tenant by the entirety
    d. as a joint tenant

3. When title to property is held in severalty:

    a. the property cannot be transferred or encumbered without the consent of a majority of the co-owners
    b. the property is owned by one individual
    c. none of the owners can be a corporation
    d. the property cannot be willed

4. The only one of the four unities required for a tenancy in common is the unity of:

    a. time
    b. title
    c. interest
    d. possession

5. When Schultz and White took title to the house as joint tenants, they agreed that only White would live there. What effect did this agreement have on the joint tenancy?

    a. It severed the joint tenancy; unity of possession is essential
    b. It did not sever the joint tenancy if Schultz and White stated that they did not intend to sever it
    c. It did not sever the joint tenancy as long as Schultz is charging White rent
    d. It severed the joint tenancy by partitioning the property

6. Adams, Kester, and Calhoun own some land as tenants in common. Adams and Kester each have an undivided ¼ interest, and Calhoun has an undivided ½ interest. Calhoun wills all his property to Davis. When Calhoun dies, who owns the land?

    a. Adams and Kester each have an undivided ½ interest
    b. Adams and Kester each have an undivided ¾ interest
    c. Adams and Kester each have an undivided ¼ interest, and Davis has an undivided ½ interest
    d. Adams, Kester, and Davis each have an undivided ⅓ interest

7. Ayers, Burns, and Cervas own some land as joint tenants. When Cervas dies, Ayers and Burns each have a ½ undivided interest, because of:

    a. the right of survivorship
    b. unity of possession
    c. the rules of intestate succession
    d. the doctrine of severalty

8. Alton, Barrett, and Carter own a house as tenants in common. Alton and Barrett want to sell the property to a developer; Carter refuses. Alton and Barrett would like a court to order the sale of the property and distribution of the proceeds among the three co-owners. To request such a court order, they will file a:

   a. foreclosure action
   b. interpleader action
   c. quiet title action
   d. partition action

9. Ames, Barry, and Carlson own some land as joint tenants. Carlson sells his interest in the property to Delaney. Which of the following is true?

   a. Ames and Barry each hold an undivided ⅓ interest as joint tenants, and Delaney holds an undivided ⅓ interest as a tenant in common
   b. Ames and Barry each hold an undivided ¼ interest as joint tenants, and Delaney holds an undivided ½ interest as a tenant in common
   c. Ames, Barry, and Delaney each hold an undivided ⅓ interest as joint tenants
   d. Ames, Barry, and Delaney each hold a ⅓ interest in severalty

10. A married couple might choose to hold real property in joint tenancy rather than as community property in order to:

    a. avoid paying property taxes
    b. avoid the probate process
    c. prevent one spouse from conveying his or her interest in the property without the other's consent
    d. prevent a mortgage foreclosure

11. Harry and Wilma are a married couple; they own some land as community property. Harry wills all his property to Annette. When Harry dies, who owns the land?

    a. Wilma owns the land in severalty
    b. Wilma has an undivided ⅔ interest and Annette has an undivided ⅓ interest
    c. Wilma and Annette each have an undivided ½ interest
    d. Wilma, Annette, and Harry's minor child each have an undivided ⅓ interest

12. Which of these is a spouse's separate property?

    a. A house she bought before the marriage
    b. A house purchased during the marriage using her own earnings as a downpayment
    c. A house he received during the marriage in exchange for services rendered to a family member
    d. None of the above; all real property owned by a married person is community property

13. Fong did not consent to any of these transactions involving community property. He can void the transfer or encumbrance in each case except one. Which one?

    a. His wife sold the couple's boat to a neighbor
    b. His wife gave the couple's boat to a neighbor
    c. His wife sold the couple's vacant lot to her cousin
    d. His wife mortgaged the couple's residence

14. The ZAP Corporation owns some land in severalty. In order to sell the land, who must sign the sale documents?

  a. The CEO and at least one member of the board of directors
  b. A majority of the directors
  c. A majority of the stockholders
  d. Corporate officers authorized to sell it by a resolution of the board of directors

15. The LMNOP company is a general partnership. Partnership funds were used to purchase a building for the company's offices. The building is partnership property:

  a. only if the deed lists all the partners and expressly states that they are tenants in partnership
  b. even though the title is in one partner's name alone
  c. only if the title was acknowledged by all the general partners
  d. as long as none of the partners is a married person

6 Introduction to Agency

Outline

Key Terms

- Agent
- Principal
- Subagent
- Universal agent
- General agent
- Special agent
- Actual authority
- Express authority
- Implied authority
- Apparent authority
- Ostensible agency
- Vicarious liability
- Imputed knowledge
- Ratification
- Agency by estoppel
- Renunciation
- Revocation
- Implication
- Independent contractor
- Retainer
- In-house transaction

Chapter Overview

The term "real estate agent" is commonly used, but few people stop to think about what the "agent" part really means. This chapter explains what an agent is, discusses how an agency relationship is created and terminated, and describes the specific agency relationships that exist in the real estate business.

Rules defining and governing agency relationships are found in general agency law, a body of law that applies to agency relationships in nearly any context, such as between lawyer and client, or between trustee and beneficiary. Since 1997, real estate agency relationships have also been subject to Washington's real estate agency statute: the Real Estate Brokerage Relationships Act. This statute has its roots in general agency law, but contains important changes that address agency issues that are specific to the real estate field.

Basic Agency Definitions

An **agent** is someone who is authorized to represent or act for someone else—the **principal**—in dealings with other parties. In the real estate business, the agent is the real estate licensee and the principal may be a property seller, a buyer, a landlord, or a tenant. Persons outside the agency relationship who deal with the principal through the agent are called **third parties**.

A **subagent** is an agent (or representative) of the agent. For example, a listing agreement is a contract that creates an agency relationship between a property seller and a brokerage firm (see Chapter 8). Under the agreement, the seller is the principal and the brokerage is the seller's agent. The listing agent—the affiliated licensee who takes the listing and markets the property—carries out the work as an agent of the brokerage and as a subagent of the principal (the seller).

Agency Authority

In an agency relationship, the agent receives authority from the principal to perform certain actions, and the agent also takes on certain duties and responsibilities. The amount and type of authority determines what type of agency relationship is created, and what liability the agency assumes. Note that an agent may be liable for any harm caused by actions that exceed the authority granted by the principal.

Types of Agents

A **universal agent** is authorized by the principal to do everything that can be done by a lawfully designated representative. This type of agent has the highest degree of authority.

> **Example:** A guardian charged with the care of someone who is mentally incompetent to manage his own affairs is a universal agent.

A **general agent** has authority to handle all matters for the principal in certain specified areas.

> **Example:** A property manager is a general agent if she has the authority to market and maintain the property, hire and fire maintenance personnel, enter lease agreements on the owner's behalf, and take full responsibility for managing property on behalf of the owner.

A **special agent** has limited authority to do a specific thing or conduct a specific transaction. Most real estate agents are special agents. Their authority is usually limited by the principal to a single function or transaction.

> **Example:** A seller hires an agent to find a buyer for a particular piece of property. The agent is authorized to negotiate with third parties—but not to sign a contract on the seller's behalf.

Types of Authority

There are two types of authority: actual and apparent.

Actual Authority. Authority specifically given by the principal is called **actual authority**. Actual authority may be either express or implied.

Express authority is specifically communicated by the principal to the agent, either orally or in writing. **Implied authority** is the authority necessary to carry out the duties expressly authorized by the principal. Implied authority does not have to be expressed, because it is required by the agent to fulfill her responsibilities.

> **Example:** A listing agreement gives a real estate agent express authority to find a ready, willing, and able buyer for a property. The agent is generally assumed to have the implied authority to do what is necessary to find that buyer. This includes activities

Fig 6.1 Types of agency authority

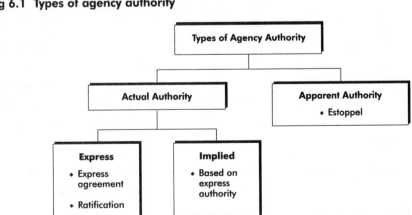

such as advertising, placing "for sale" signs on the property, showing the property, and negotiating and transmitting offers.

Apparent Authority. In contrast to actual authority, an agent may have only **apparent authority** to do something. This situation may occur when a person has no actual authority to act, but the principal's words or conduct lead a third party to believe that this person's actions are authorized. In other words, the principal negligently or deliberately allows it to appear that the person (the **apparent agent** or **ostensible agent**) has authority to act on behalf of the principal. As a general rule, the principal is bound by acts performed within the scope of an ostensible agent's apparent authority.

Agency Liability Issues

As we said earlier, agency authority carries with it certain duties and responsibilities. If an agent fails to live up to those duties and responsibilities, he can be held liable for any harm he causes. Washington's real estate agency statute significantly changed a real estate agent's level of liability in two areas (compared with how these were traditionally handled under general agency law). The two areas are vicarious liability and imputed knowledge.

Vicarious Liability. A **tort** is a negligent or intentional wrongful act that causes injury or financial harm to another person. Someone who commits a tort may be sued by the injured party and required to compensate her.

In some states, a principal may be held liable for his agent's torts under the legal theory of **vicarious liability**. But Washington's real estate agency statute eliminated most vicarious liability between a real estate agent and his principal. This means that a seller or buyer is generally not liable for an act, error, or omission by his agent or the agents of other brokerages.

Exceptions. Two exceptions do exist to this exclusion from liability. A principal may be liable for her real estate agent's actions if:

1. the principal participated in or authorized the act, error, or omission; or
2. the principal benefited from the act, error, or omission, and a court determines that it is highly probable that the injured party would be unable to enforce a judgment against the agent or subagent.

Likewise, an agent will not be held vicariously liable for the act, error, or omission of a subagent, unless the agent participated in or authorized the act, error, or omission. Note, however, that a brokerage may still be held liable for the actions of its affiliated licensees.

Imputed Knowledge. Previously, under general agency law, a principal was considered to have notice of any information that his agent had—even if the agent never actually told the principal. In other words, the agent's knowledge was automatically **imputed** to the principal. As a result, the principal could be held liable for failing to disclose a problem to a third party, even if the agent never informed the principal of the problem.

However, Washington's real estate agency statute eliminated the imputed knowledge rule. A principal in a real estate transaction is no longer automatically held to have notice of facts known by his real estate agent.

Creating an Agency Relationship

It is important for both the principal and the agent to understand how and when an agency relationship is created. Under general agency law, an agency relationship may originate in several different ways: express agreement, ratification, estoppel, and implication.

Express Agreement

Most agencies are created by **express agreement**: the principal appoints someone to act as her agent and the agent accepts. An express agency agreement may be written or oral.

Although agency relationships are usually created in writing, a written agreement is not required. An oral agreement will create an agency just as effectively. The agent will be held to the same degree of responsibility and must perform all the agency duties owed to the principal. If the agent is negligent or does not carry out the required duties, the principal may sue the agent for damages.

Ratification

Even without a specific understanding or agreement, an agency relationship may still be created. An agency is created by **ratification** when the principal gives approval after the fact to acts performed by:

- a person who is without authority to act for the principal, or
- an agent whose actions exceed the authority granted by the principal.

The principal may ratify unauthorized acts expressly. Alternatively, if the principal is aware of the acts, does nothing to stop them, and accepts the benefit of these acts, an agency relationship is created by ratification.

Estoppel

Estoppel is a legal doctrine under which a person is prevented from asserting rights that are inconsistent with previous representations or actions. A situation may occur where the principal has not authorized an agency, but the principal's acts or behavior mislead someone into believing that an agency exists (see the discussion of apparent authority, above). The principal's previous acts—conduct, words, or even silence in not disavowing the agency—prohibit her from denying the existence of an agency relationship. This is called an **agency by estoppel**.

Agency by estoppel protects innocent third parties who have reasonably assumed that a person acting like an agent was an agent. The principal is held responsible because he allowed such a belief, or failed to advise the third party that the agent was acting without authority.

It's important to note that the estoppel doctrine will not be used against a principal who has no knowledge of someone claiming agency. Note also that a third party has a duty to make a reasonable effort to discover the scope of the agent's authority. A principal won't be estopped from denying an agency relationship when a reasonable effort by the third party would have shown that the degree of agency claimed did not exist.

Implication

An agency may be created by **implication** when one person behaves toward another in a way that suggests or implies that she is acting as that person's agent. If the other person reasonably believes an agency relationship exists, and the supposed agent fails to correct that impression, he may owe the other person agency duties.

Agency by implication resembles agency by estoppel, but there's a significant difference. An agency by estoppel requires the principal to acknowledge that an agency relationship exists, to protect the interests of a third party. An agency by implication requires the agent to acknowledge that an agency relationship exists, to protect the principal's interests.

Creating a Real Estate Agency

In Washington, the Real Estate Brokerage Relationships Act imposed new rules concerning how agency relationships are created in real estate transactions. Under this statute, an agency relationship between a real estate licensee and a client begins when the licensee undertakes to provide real estate brokerage services for the client. The agency relationship begins regardless of whether or not any fee has been paid to the agent.

An agency relationship with a seller typically begins with the execution of a written listing agreement. On the other hand, an agency relationship with a buyer begins automatically when a licensee performs real estate brokerage services for the buyer.

> **Example:** A prospective buyer visits a real estate brokerage and tells a broker that he's interested in buying a home. The broker asks the buyer about his price range and the type of house he's interested in. The buyer and broker then go look at some homes listed for sale that may fit the buyer's needs.
>
> Under the real estate agency statute, the broker and her brokerage have automatically become agents for the buyer, since the broker is performing brokerage services for the buyer.

There is an important exception to this rule concerning buyer agency. A licensee working with a buyer does not automatically become the buyer's agent if a written agreement exists to the contrary, such as a listing agreement with the seller, a written dual agency agreement with both parties, a written subagency agreement with the seller, or a written non-agency agreement.

Example: Returning to the previous scenario, suppose the broker shows the buyer one of her own listings. Because the brokerage already has a written agreement with the seller, the broker and brokerage won't be representing the buyer if she decides to buy this house. They will represent the seller.

Terminating an Agency Relationship

Now that you are familiar with how an agency is created, it is important to understand how and when an agency relationship will end. Once the agency is terminated, the agent is no longer authorized to represent the principal.

Under general agency law, an agency may be terminated either by operation of law or by the acts of the parties.

Termination by Operation of Law

An agency relationship may be terminated by operation of law. This means the agency will automatically end upon the occurrence of certain specified events. An agency is terminated by operation of law in the following situations:

- expiration of the agency term,
- fulfillment of the agency's purpose,
- death, incapacity, or bankruptcy of either party, and
- extinction of the subject matter.

Expiration of the Agency Term. If no specific termination date is included in the listing agreement, the listing is considered terminated after a "reasonable time." If a dispute arises over when the listing agreement expired, the court will determine what is considered reasonable under the circumstances of the particular case.

Fulfillment of Agency's Purpose. Perhaps the most common reason for termination is that the purpose of the agency has been accomplished.

Example: A property owner hires a real estate agent to sell some property. Once the property is sold and all of the details addressed, the agency relationship terminates.

Death, Incapacity, or Bankruptcy. Generally, an agency relationship will be terminated by the death or bankruptcy of either the agent or the principal. In addition, most states (including Washington) provide that the agency terminates if either party becomes mentally incompetent. Generally, the agent has no authority to act after either the death or incompetence of the principal, even if the agent is unaware of the principal's death or incompetence. However, these common law rules have only limited application to real estate agents, as we'll discuss in a moment.

Extinction of Subject Matter. If the subject matter of an agency is extinguished, the agency automatically terminates. The subject matter of a real estate agency is the property in question—if it is extinguished (e.g., sold, condemned, or destroyed), the agency is terminated.

Termination by Action of the Parties

An agency may also be terminated through action of the parties, by:

- mutual agreement,
- renunciation by the agent, or
- revocation by the principal.

Mutual Agreement. An agency is a consensual relationship, which means that it is entered into by the consent of both parties. If both parties agree, the agency may be terminated by mutual agreement, with no liability or obligation to either party.

Renunciation. Because of the consensual nature of agency, each party in an agency relationship has the power to terminate the agency. The agent may **renounce** his or her agency at any time. However, if a contract exists and the agent renounces it, the agent may be liable to the principal for damages resulting from breach of the contract.

When a real estate agent signs a contract with a principal, she agrees to provide personal, professional skills. Since this is a personal services contract, the principal cannot demand specific performance as a remedy (see Chapter 8). A court cannot force a person to perform personal services, because that would violate the constitutional prohibition against involuntary servitude. Therefore, only monetary damages are awarded.

Revocation. A principal may **revoke** the grant of agency powers at any time by firing the agent. However, if revoking the agency breaches a contractual agreement, the principal may be liable for any damages suffered by the agent because of the breach.

> **Example:** Alan Bertoldo is planning to sell his house. He signs an exclusive listing agreement with Yamamoto Brokerage. In the meantime, he starts dating a real estate agent who convinces him to switch the listing to her brokerage company. Alan revokes his grant of agency to Yamamoto Brokerage and then switches firms.

Alan has the right to revoke the agency, but he is also liable for the consequences. For instance, he could end up having to pay the full commission amount to Yamamoto Brokerage because he breached the exclusive listing agreement. Alan's new agent may also be in trouble because of her actions. She interfered with another agent's exclusive listing, and convinced Alan to breach his agreement. (This type of problem is discussed in Chapter 8.)

An exception to the usual rules about revocation occurs when an agent has an interest in the property. When agency is coupled with an interest, the principal does not have the right to revoke the agency. Also, in this situation, the death, incompetence, or bankruptcy of the principal does not terminate the agency.

Example: An agent loans funds to a contractor to complete the building of a home. In addition to agreeing to repay the loan, the contractor agrees to give the agent an exclusive right to sell the property when the home is completed. Before the home is sold, the contractor dies. The agency is not automatically terminated by the contractor's death, because the agent has an interest in the property.

Terminating a Real Estate Agency

Under Washington's Real Estate Brokerage Relationships Act, a real estate agency relationship ends when one of the following occurs:

1. Completion of performance by the licensee (the terms of the agency agreement are fulfilled).
2. Expiration of the agency term as agreed by the parties. (Note that an exclusive listing agreement should always specify a termination date. That is a legal requirement in some states, although it is not required in Washington.)
3. Termination of the relationship by mutual consent.
4. Notification from one party to the other that the agency is terminated.

In addition, if the brokerage loses its license, the agency will terminate. (In contrast, an agency won't terminate if the designated broker or an affiliated licensee loses his license, dies, or suffers incapacity—the firm can simply appoint another licensee to take her place.)

Once an agency relationship has terminated, the agent can no longer represent the principal. However, under the agency statute, the agent still owes two duties to the principal even after the relationship has ended:

1. The agent must account for all money and property received during the relationship.
2. The agent must not disclose confidential information about the principal that was learned during the agency relationship.

Real Estate Agency Relationships

Washington's Real Estate Brokerage Relationships Act fundamentally changed how real estate agency relationships work. To better understand agency relationships under this statute, we'll first take a look at how they worked under the old rules.

Agency Relationships: Historical Background

Previously, under general agency law, buyers and sellers were often confused about which party each of the various real estate agents were representing in their transaction. In particular, buyers often believed that the agent they were working with was representing them, when in fact the agent was almost always representing the seller.

Unilateral Offer of Subagency. This confusion stemmed from a standard provision found in most listing agreements, called a "unilateral offer of subagency." This provision stated that any member of the multiple listing service who found a buyer for a listed property automatically represented the seller. In other words, the selling agent became a subagent of the seller.

This provision made it difficult to create a buyer agency. In order to represent a buyer in a particular sale, a licensee had to reject the offer of subagency and enter into a separate written agreement with the buyer. Thus, nearly all licensees represented the seller.

Inadvertent Dual Agency. Under the circumstances, it was easy for a buyer to assume—incorrectly—that the selling agent represented the buyer. After all, the selling agent often worked with the buyer on a continuous and friendly basis, encouraging the buyer's loyalty by going out of his way to meet the buyer's needs. As a result, the buyer often told the selling agent confidential information.

But the selling agent represented the seller and had a duty to pass that confidential information along to the seller—which came as an unpleasant surprise to the buyer. And often the selling agent would let his natural desire to help the buyer interfere with the fiduciary duties owed to the seller. This confusion caused trouble for everyone, and sometimes resulted in the creation of an inadvertent dual agency.

> **Example:** Mattucci worked for Fairfield Realty. Over the course of several weeks, he showed the Kaplans many homes. He liked the Kaplans and worked hard to find them the right house. He gave them tips on buying and discussed their finances with them at length. Understandably, the Kaplans believed that Mattucci was their agent. But Mattucci did not have an agency agreement with the Kaplans, and so (under the traditional presumption) he was acting in the capacity of a seller's agent.
>
> The Kaplans decided to make an offer on a house listed by Agent Eisner. They told Mattucci they were willing to pay the full listing price, but wanted to make an initial offer of $5,000 less.
>
> If Mattucci failed to disclose to the seller that the Kaplans were willing to pay full price, he would be breaching his duty of loyalty to the seller. However, his conduct had caused the Kaplans to believe that he was representing them. Thus, if Mattucci did disclose this information to the seller, the Kaplans could claim that he had breached his duty of loyalty to them. And because he was inadvertently acting as agent for both parties, both could claim that he acted as a dual agent without their consent.

Offer of Cooperation. In the 1990s, as buyers became more interested in having their own agents to represent them, many multiple listing services replaced the unilateral offer of subagency in their listing agreements with an "offer of cooperation." Under this provision, other members of the MLS acted only as cooperating agents, not as subagents. A cooperating agent was simply any member of the MLS who attempted to find a buyer. Each individual cooperating agent could decide whether he would represent the seller or the buyer in a given transaction.

Despite this change, many cooperating agents continued to act as the seller's agent. They did not offer to represent the buyer or enter into an agency agreement with the buyer, so the traditional presumption that they were representing the seller continued.

Real Estate Agency Statute. To help eliminate confusion over agency representation, many states (including Washington) passed agency disclosure laws in the early 1990s. These laws require real estate agents to disclose to both the buyer and the seller, in writing, the identity of the party they represent. Some states later went further and adopted comprehensive real estate agency statutes. The Washington State Legislature passed the Real Estate Brokerage Relationships Act, which became effective in 1997.

Under this statute, a real estate licensee who works with a buyer is presumed to be the buyer's agent, unless a written agreement to the contrary exists. This rule has two important benefits. First, it turns the buyer's natural assumption—that the licensee working with the buyer is acting as the buyer's agent—into reality. Second, it significantly reduces the danger of inadvertent dual agency. Because a licensee represents the buyer she's working with, there is no conflict between the licensee's desire to help the buyer and the licensee's agency duties.

Types of Real Estate Agency Relationships

Under the Real Estate Brokerage Relationships Act, there are four types of real estate agency relationships:

- seller agency,
- buyer agency,
- dual agency, and
- non-agency.

The rules concerning seller agency also apply when representing a landlord, and the buyer agency rules apply when representing a tenant.

Note that which type of agency relationship a real estate agent has in a transaction (which party or parties the agent is representing) does not depend on which party pays the agent's compensation. For example, a buyer's agent may accept compensation from the seller without creating an agency relationship with the seller, and without compromising her agency relationship with the buyer.

Seller Agency. Although traditionally real estate agents nearly always represented the seller, under the real estate agency statute the only licensees representing the seller are the listing brokerage, its designated broker, and the affiliated license who is handling the transaction. The listing agreement creates a seller agency relationship.

Under the terms of the listing agreement, the primary task of a seller's agent is to find a buyer for the seller's property at a price that is acceptable to the seller. To accomplish this, the seller's agent advises the seller about preparing the property for sale, helps the seller decide on the listing price, markets the property appropriately, and negotiates on the seller's behalf with selling agents and buyers.

Seller's agents and buyers. Throughout a transaction, a seller's agent must use her best efforts to promote the interests of the seller. Yet the seller's agent may also provide some services to a prospective buyer.

> **Example:** Susie is the seller's agent. A prospective buyer, Bart, doesn't have his own agent but wants to make an offer on the house. Susie helps Bart fill out a purchase offer form and apply for financing.
>
> These services are considered to be in the best interests of the seller, and thus do not violate Susie's duties to the seller. Of course, Susie must disclose to Bart that she is acting as the seller's agent, not his agent.

A seller's agent must be very careful to treat the buyer fairly, but must not act as if she is representing the buyer. In other words, the agent must fully disclose all known material facts and answer the buyer's questions honestly—but should not give the buyer negotiating advice, such as how much to offer for the listed property.

> **Example:** Sanjay lists Giselle's house for sale. The listing price is $299,000 but Sanjay believes Giselle will be willing to accept an offer of $290,000. Sanjay shows the house to a prospective buyer who asks him, "How low do you think the seller will go?"
>
> Sanjay must make it clear that he represents Giselle and cannot divulge confidential information to any prospective buyer. If he were to divulge such information, Giselle could sue for breach of agency duties.

In some cases, the seller's agent has had a previous relationship with the buyer. In this situation it may be difficult for the agent to represent the seller's interests without feeling some loyalty to the buyer as well.

> **Example:** Returning to the previous example, suppose Giselle is pleased with how Sanjay handled the sale of her home and subsequently asks Sanjay to help her find a new home. Sanjay shows Giselle one of his own listings.
>
> Under the circumstances, Giselle may believe that Sanjay is acting as her agent. However, because of the listing agreement, Sanjay is the seller's agent and he must make that fact clear to Giselle. Furthermore, he needs to remind Giselle that he is obligated to disclose to the seller any material information Giselle tells him and that in all negotiations, he will be representing the seller's best interests.
>
> Remember that a real estate agent cannot disclose confidential information about a principal even after an agency terminates. So Sanjay cannot disclose to the seller anything confidential about Giselle that he learned during his agency relationship with her.

In transactions like this, where the listing agent is also the selling agent, the agent may still come up against the problem of inadvertent dual agency. But aside from that situation, a seller's agent will rarely face that problem under current law.

Buyer Agency. Under Washington's real estate agency law, a buyer is automatically represented by the agent she is working with (unless there is a written agreement to the contrary). Although this relationship is created automatically, a buyer and a brokerage may enter into a written **buyer representation agreement**, which typically includes the following provisions:

- the duration of the agency,
- the general characteristics of the property the buyer wants,

- the price range,
- the conditions under which a fee will be earned,
- who will pay the fee, and
- a description of the brokerage's duties.

The advantages of buyer agency include confidentiality and loyalty, objective advice, and help with negotiations.

Confidentiality and loyalty. A buyer's agent owes agency duties to the buyer, including the duties of confidentiality and loyalty.

> **Example:** Malia has shown Tony two homes he likes. The first is a large fixer-upper listed for $560,000. The other is a smaller, newer house priced at $541,000. If Tony bought the larger house, Malia would receive a larger commission. But the smaller house better suits Tony's needs, and since Malia must put Tony's interests before her own, she advises him to purchase the smaller house.
>
> Malia suggests Tony start with an offer of $537,000. Tony agrees, but tells Malia he is willing to pay full price. Because Malia is Tony's agent, she cannot tell the seller that Tony is willing to pay full price. Had she been the seller's agent instead, she would have been required to disclose that information to the seller.

Objective advice. A seller's agent will present the property in the most positive light and may use expert sales techniques to convince the buyer to sign on the dotted line. But a buyer's agent can be relied upon to give the buyer objective advice about the pros and cons of a particular home. For example, the buyer's agent will point out various issues important to the buyer, such as energy costs, the need for future repairs, and property value trends.

Help with negotiating. Buyers often feel uncomfortable negotiating for a property, especially one they really want to buy. They may be afraid to make a mistake through ignorance, or they may feel pressured to make a high offer quickly before someone else snaps up the property. A buyer's agent can use her negotiating skills and knowledge of the real estate market to help the buyer get the property on the best possible terms.

Buyer's agent's compensation. A buyer's agent may be compensated in a variety of ways. The three most common are:

- a retainer,
- a seller-paid fee, and/or
- a buyer-paid fee.

A **retainer** is a fee paid up front before services are provided. Some buyer's agents collect a retainer when a buyer agency relationship begins, to ensure that their services won't go entirely uncompensated. The retainer is usually nonrefundable but will be credited against any fee or commission the agent earns.

In many cases, a buyer's agent is paid by the seller through a commission split. In a **commission split**, a cooperating agent who procures a buyer is entitled to the selling agent's portion of the commission, regardless of which party the cooperating agent represents. Note that accepting a seller-paid fee does not create any agency duties toward the seller.

> **Example:** Shelley lists her property with Sato Realty and agrees to pay a commission of 6% of the sales price. The listing agreement includes a clause that entitles any cooperating agent who procures a buyer to the selling agent's portion of the commission.
> An agent working for Ross Realty has a buyer agency agreement with prospective buyer Graham, who offers $250,000 for Shelley's house. Shelley accepts the offer. When the transaction closes, Shelley pays a $15,000 commission; $7,500 goes to Sato and $7,500 goes to Ross.

Most buyer representation agreements also provide for compensation by means of a commission split when the buyer purchases a home listed through an MLS. However, a buyer representation agreement may provide for a **buyer-paid fee** instead. The buyer-paid fee might be based on an hourly rate, essentially making the agent a consultant. Alternatively, a buyer's agent may charge a percentage fee, so that the commission is a percentage of the purchase price. A third possibility is a flat fee—a specified sum that is payable if the buyer purchases a property found by the agent.

Some buyer agency agreements provide that the buyer's agent will accept a commission split if one is available; otherwise the buyer will pay a fee. Providing the alternative of a buyer-paid fee frees the buyer's agent to show properties where there is no commission split available, such as FSBOs, open listings, and properties in foreclosure or probate.

Dual Agency. A **dual agency** relationship exists wherever a licensee represents both the seller and the buyer in the same transaction. Because the interests of the buyer and seller usually conflict, it's hard to represent them both without being disloyal to one or both.

> **Example:** Buyer Brant and Seller Amy are both represented by Agent Tyler. Amy tells Tyler that she's in a hurry to sell and will accept any reasonable offer. Brant tells Tyler that he's very interested in the house and is willing to pay the full asking price.
> Should Tyler tell Brant how eager Amy is to sell? And should Tyler tell Amy that Brant is willing to pay full price?

Clearly, it's impossible for a dual agent to fully represent both parties. Thus, instead of the duty of loyalty, Washington law imposes on a dual agent the duty to refrain from acting to the detriment of either party. The dual agent must do his best to act impartially and treat both clients equally.

The dual agent must inform both parties that neither will receive full representation. Certain facts must necessarily be withheld from each party; the dual agent cannot divulge confidential information about one party to another party.

> **Example:** Returning to the previous scenario, Agent Tyler must not tell Brant that Amy will accept any reasonable price. Similarly, Tyler must not tell Amy how much Brant is willing to pay.

Both parties must give their informed written consent to the dual agency. A licensee who acts as a dual agent without full disclosure and written consent has violated the real estate license law and is subject to disciplinary action.

In-house transactions. Dual agency occurs most often in in-house transactions. An **in-house transaction** is a sale in which both the listing agent and the selling agent work for the same brokerage. In this situation, under Washington law, the listing agent represents only the seller, the selling agent represents only the buyer, and the brokerage is a dual agent, representing both parties. The dual agency at the brokerage level must still be disclosed, even though each party is represented by a licensee who works exclusively for them.

> **Example:** Agent Paul works for Excellent Realty. Paul has shown Buyer Wanda several houses over the course of a few weeks. Finally, Paul shows Wanda a house listed by Agent Philip, who also works for Excellent Realty. Wanda decides to make an offer on this house.
>
> This is an in-house transaction. Paul, the selling agent, is the buyer's agent. Philip, the listing agent, is the seller's agent. And Excellent Realty is a dual agent.

Non-Agency. In some transactions, a real estate licensee might choose to act only as a facilitator and refuse to assume any agency duties at all. This arrangement is called non-agency and is legal under Washington's real estate agency law.

A non-agent will still owe general statutory duties to any party he works with. (These duties are discussed fully in Chapter 7.) There is no way for a licensee to opt out of the duties of disclosure, reasonable skill and care, honesty and good faith, and so on.

Employee vs. Independent Contractor

One final aspect of real estate agency relationships to consider is whether or not a licensee acting as an agent is considered an employee of either the principal or the brokerage firm.

Relationship between Licensee and Principal. When an agency relationship has been created between a real estate brokerage firm and a seller or buyer, one of the firm's affiliated licensees is working for or on behalf of the principal, but is not considered the principal's employee. Instead, a real estate licensee is usually regarded as an independent contractor in relation to the principal. The factors used to determine whether someone is an independent contractor or an employee include:

- the principal's degree of supervision and control,
- whether the work schedule is set by the principal,
- who decides how the job will be carried out, and
- whether the principal withholds taxes and social security contributions.

An **independent contractor** is generally hired to perform a particular job and to use his own judgment as to how the work will be done. In contrast, an **employee** is hired to perform whatever tasks the employer requires and is given guidelines and instructions as to how to perform each task.

Real estate licensees generally decide what hours they will work and use their own judgment as to the best methods for accomplishing the principal's goals, whether that's selling the principal's property or searching for property that meets the principal's needs. A licensee is not controlled by the principal, and the principal does not withhold income taxes or make contributions to social security for the licensee. Therefore, a real estate licensee is almost always an independent contractor, not an employee, in relation to the principal.

Relationship between Licensee and Brokerage. Although some real estate licensees are employees of the brokerage firm they're affiliated with, most are independent contractors in relation to their firm. The Internal Revenue Service considers a real estate agent to be an independent contractor if:

1. the individual is a licensed real estate agent;
2. compensation is directly related to sales rather than to hours worked; and
3. the services are performed pursuant to a written contract that states the individual will not be treated as an employee for federal tax purposes.

In Washington, there is usually a written contract between the brokerage and each affiliated licensee. This contract should specify whether the licensee is working as an employee or as an independent contractor.

A brokerage generally does not exercise the same degree of control over independent contractors as over employees. However, the firm and its designated broker are still liable for the actions of affiliated licensees, since the licensees are agents of the firm. As explained in Chapter 2, Washington license law requires designated brokers (and any managing brokers with a supervisory role) to adequately supervise their sales agents or risk disciplinary action. Note that this supervision requirement does not turn a licensee into an employee.

State laws differ in regard to the treatment of independent contractors in the area of unemployment and workers' compensation. In Washington, independent contractors licensed

Fig. 6.2 Distinction between employee and independent contractor

Employee	Independent Contractor
• Firm withholds taxes, social security	• Pays own taxes, social security
• Firm controls activities	• Controls own activities
• May receive employee benefits	• Does not receive employee benefits

to sell real estate are not eligible to receive unemployment compensation. However, they are eligible to receive workers' compensation, and the brokerage is responsible for paying premiums for their coverage to the Washington Department of Labor and Industries (see Chapter 15).

Conclusion

Real estate licensees work as agents: the brokerage firm is the agent of the principal, and the affiliated licensee handling the transaction is an agent of the brokerage and a subagent of the principal. To understand their duties and responsibilities, licensees should be aware of how their agency relationships were created, how much authority they've been given, and when the relationships will terminate. For licensees in Washington, it's necessary to be familiar with both general agency law and the Real Estate Brokerage Relationships Act.

Case Problem

The following is a hypothetical case problem. Most of the facts are taken from a real case. Make a decision on the issues presented and then check to see if your answer matches the decision reached by the court.

The Facts

In August 1983, Holst listed her property for sale with Fear, an agent with Fireside Realty. Rader was interested in the property. He contacted Fireside Realty and spoke with Bourgeois, another agent. Bourgeois showed Rader the property and answered questions about its condition.

Rader told Bourgeois he would offer $250,000 for the property. Bourgeois said Holst would probably not accept that price, and asked what Rader's highest offer would be. Rader responded $300,000 and Bourgeois wrote up an offer for that amount.

On October 19, Holst accepted the $300,000 offer and the parties signed a purchase and sale agreement. The agreement stated that the "Listing Agent" was "Charles Fear of Fireside Realty" and the "Selling Agent" was "Art Bourgeois of Fireside Realty."

The agreement was subject to the property being staked by a surveyor, to an inspection of the buildings, and to marketable title. At Rader's request, Bourgeois obtained survey bids as well as bids for removing timber from the property. He also took Rader through the buildings for inspection and discussed the issue of marketable title with Rader and the closing agent. Bourgeois did not tell Holst about the timber bids.

After the sale closed, Holst brought a lawsuit against Fireside Realty, Fear, and Bourgeois. The suit alleged that Bourgeois had acted as Rader's agent and that Fireside Realty had acted as a dual agent without informing Holst or obtaining her consent. Fireside denied that Bourgeois had agreed to represent Rader, and that even if it had acted as a dual agent, it had adequately disclosed the dual agency in the purchase and sale agreement.

The Questions

Did Fireside Realty act as a dual agent in the transaction? And if so, did it adequately disclose its dual agency to the parties involved?

What if the current real estate agency law is applied (as opposed to common law agency rules, which were in effect at the time the events in this case took place)?

The Answer

The court held that when a brokerage lists a property for sale, it owes a duty to the seller not to act as the buyer's agent without the seller's consent. The court found that it was reasonable to infer that Bourgeois had acted as Rader's agent. It also found that it was reasonable to infer that Fireside had breached its duty to Holst by not adequately disclosing the existence of a dual agency. *Holst v. Fireside Realty*, 89 Wn. App. 245, 948 P.2d 858 (1997).

Under the current real estate agency statute, it's clear that Bourgeois became Rader's agent as soon as he began providing brokerage services to Rader, such as showing Rader the property and answering questions about it. Fireside Realty would have been acting as a dual agent. Fear and Bourgeois would have been required to disclose this fact and obtain the parties' written consent to the dual agency.

Chapter Summary

- An agent may be universal, general, or special. Most real estate agents are special agents.

- An agent may have actual or apparent authority. Actual authority may be express or implied.

- An agency relationship may be created by express agreement, ratification, estoppel, or implication. Under Washington's real estate agency statute, an agency relationship between a licensee and a client is generally created when the licensee begins providing real estate services for the client.

- An agency relationship may be terminated by expiration of the term, operation of law, mutual agreement, renunciation, or revocation.

- The real estate agency statute defines four types of real estate agency relationships: seller agency, buyer agency, dual agency, and non-agency.

- Under general agency law, buyer agency was rare. Under the real estate agency statute, however, a buyer agency is usually created as soon as a licensee begins working with a buyer.

- A real estate agent is an independent contractor in relation to the principal. Most affiliated licensees also work as independent contractors rather than as employees of their brokerage firm.

Checklist of Problem Areas

Real Estate Licensee's Checklist

❑   How much authority have you and your brokerage firm been given by the principal?

❑   What type of agent are you?

❑   Have you signed a written listing agreement or buyer representation agreement? Remember that you can become a buyer's agent without a written agreement.

❑   What circumstances will cause your agency to terminate?

Seller's Checklist

❑   How much authority have you given to the agent?

❑   Have any of your actions created an agency relationship by ratification or estoppel, even if there is no express agency agreement?

❑   Do you know when the agency will terminate, or what consequences you may suffer if you revoke the agency agreement?

Buyer's Checklist

❑   Do you understand how your agent will be compensated?

Chapter Quiz

1. Most real estate agents are considered:

   a. general agents
   b. universal agents
   c. special agents
   d. total agents

2. An apparent agent is one who:

   a. has actual authority from the principal
   b. appears to be the agent of another but does not have actual authority
   c. is an agent working for the buyer instead of the seller
   d. None of the above

3. A real estate agency agreement:

   a. is usually in writing
   b. may be oral
   c. may be created by estoppel
   d. All of the above

4. A real estate agent who decides what hours she will work, is compensated solely by commission, and pays her own social security contributions would be considered:

   a. an ostensible broker
   b. an independent contractor
   c. an employee
   d. None of the above

5. Once an agency relationship has been created, the agency may terminate when:

   a. both parties agree
   b. the agent renounces
   c. the principal revokes
   d. Any of the above

6. An example of something that will cause the agency relationship to terminate by operation of law is the:

   a. death of the principal
   b. bankruptcy of the brokerage
   c. incapacity of the principal
   d. All of the above

7. After an agency relationship terminates, the agent still owes the principal the duty of:

   a. disclosure of material facts
   b. confidentiality
   c. reasonable care and skill
   d. loyalty

8. An agency relationship can be created in any of the following ways, except:

   a. ratification
   b. verification
   c. estoppel
   d. oral agreement

9. Dual agency is:

   a. legal as long as the agent consents to the arrangement in writing
   b. legal as long as both principals give their informed consent to the arrangement in writing
   c. legal as long as the agent receives equal compensation from both principals
   d. illegal in Washington State

10. In Washington, a real estate agency relationship is created when a licensee:

    a. obtains an acceptance to a valid offer
    b. makes an appointment to meet with a seller
    c. first undertakes to provide brokerage services
    d. places an advertisement for buyers or sellers in the newspaper

11. To create an agency relationship, all of the following are necessary, EXCEPT:

    a. in writing
    b. lawful objective
    c. competent parties
    d. mutual agreement

12. In a typical designated broker/broker relationship, which of the following is true?

    a. The broker is licensed to represent members of the public directly
    b. The broker is classified as an independent contractor, responsible for paying her own taxes
    c. The brokerage is required to withhold unemployment and industrial accident insurance premiums from the broker's paychecks
    d. The brokerage is required by law to withhold income and social security taxes from the broker's paychecks

13. Under Washington law, a seller is not vicariously liable for the actions of his real estate agent unless:

    a. the agent has a bad reputation in the community and the seller should have known the agent would do something illegal
    b. the seller is bankrupt
    c. the seller knew that the agent had a grudge against the buyer and might do something to harm her
    d. the seller benefitted from the act and the brokerage is bankrupt

14. Which of the following would not result in the termination of a listing?

    a. Owner revokes agent's authority
    b. Brokerage goes bankrupt
    c. Property owner is declared incompetent before property is sold
    d. Broker dies before property is sold

15. Renunciation of an agency occurs:

    a. automatically, when the agency term expires
    b. after a reasonable time
    c. when the agent unilaterally terminates the agency
    d. when the agency contract is breached before the term expires

7 Agent's Duties and Responsibilities

Outline

I. Agent's Duties to the Principal
   A. Loyalty
   B. Conflicts of interest
   C. Confidentiality
   D. Expert advice
   E. Good faith and continuous effort
II. Agent's Duties to All Parties
   A. Reasonable care and skill
   B. Honesty and good faith
   C. Present written communications
   D. Disclosure of material facts
   E. Accounting
   F. Real estate agency law pamphlet
   G. Agency disclosure
III. Dealing Ethically with Clients, Customers, Colleagues, and Competitors
IV. Errors and Omissions Insurance and Breach of Duties

Key Terms

- Fiduciary
- Secret profit
- Conflict of interest
- Confidential information
- Reasonable care and skill
- Actual fraud

- Constructive fraud
- Misrepresentation
- Puffing
- Material fact
- Latent defect
- Agency disclosure

- Unprofessional conduct
- Seller disclosure statement
- Lead paint disclosure
- Codes of ethics
- E&O insurance

Chapter Overview

In Chapter 6 you learned what an agent is and how an agency relationship is created and terminated. In this chapter, you will learn about the duties involved in an agency relationship. Under Washington's real estate agency statute, an agent owes certain duties to all parties she works with, such as prospective buyers. An agent also owes specific duties to her principal.

Agent's Duties to the Principal

As we discussed in the previous chapter, agency relationships in Washington used to be governed solely by general agency law. A real estate agent owed certain duties to his principal, called **fiduciary duties**. A **fiduciary** is someone who occupies a position of special trust in relation to another person. The fiduciary duties owed to the principal included loyalty, reasonable care and skill, obedience and good faith, and disclosure of material facts.

In 1997, Washington's Real Estate Brokerage Relationships Act went into effect, replacing the fiduciary duties of general agency law with **statutory duties**. Specifically, an agent in a real estate transaction now owes her principal the following duties:

- loyalty,
- disclosing conflicts of interest,
- confidentiality,
- advising the principal to seek expert advice, and
- good faith and continuous effort.

Loyalty

A real estate agent owes the principal a duty of **loyalty**, which means that the principal's interests must be put above the interests of the agent or any other party. For example, an agent cannot make a **secret profit**, which is any profit or financial benefit from a transaction that is obtained by the agent without the knowledge or authorization of the principal. So if an agent accepts a kickback for referring the principal's business, he will have breached his duty of loyalty.

> **Example:** Amy is helping Saul find a home. She shows him a home that he likes, but it needs some repairs. Saul asks Amy to recommend a contractor for the repairs and she gives him the name of Braeburn Construction. She doesn't tell Saul that she is friends with the owner.
>
> When Saul hires Braeburn to do the repairs, the owner gives Amy a small percentage of the contract price. Amy has breached her duty of loyalty to Saul.

Conflicts of Interest

Closely related to the duty of loyalty is the duty to disclose any conflicts of interest to the principal. A **conflict of interest** is a circumstance that could tempt the agent to put someone else's interests (a third party's or the agent's own) above the principal's interests, such as a relationship between the agent and the other party in the principal's transaction. So, for example, if the buyer is a friend, relative, or business associate of the seller's agent, or a company in which the agent has an interest, the agent must disclose this fact to the principal (the seller). The disclosure must take place before the principal decides whether to accept the buyer's offer.

> **Example:** Kroeger signs a 30-day exclusive listing agreement with Treeline Realty. Stoddard, an agent with Treeline, shows the property to his mother, who makes an offer

on the house. Stoddard is in a hurry when he presents the offer, and he neglects to tell Kroeger that the potential buyer is one of his own relatives. Kroeger accepts the offer.

Even if Kroeger suffers no financial harm as a result of the transaction and neither Stoddard nor his mother gains any unfair advantage from it, the duty to disclose conflicts of interest has been breached.

Confidentiality

The duty of **confidentiality** prohibits an agent from disclosing any confidential information about the principal, even after the agency has ended. Washington's real estate agency law defines **confidential information** as information from or concerning a principal that:

1. was acquired by the licensee during the course of an agency relationship with the principal;
2. the principal reasonably expects to be kept confidential;
3. the principal has not disclosed or authorized to be disclosed to third parties;
4. would, if disclosed, operate to the detriment of the principal; and
5. the principal personally would not be obligated to disclose to the other party.

For example, a seller's agent must not reveal to potential buyers the fact that the seller is willing to accept less than the listing price, unless the seller has authorized such a disclosure. On the other hand, the agent would need to disclose a leaking roof to buyers, even if the seller tells her to treat that as confidential information, because it's something that the principal himself would be obligated to disclose.

Expert Advice

Real estate agents must be careful not to perform any acts beyond their skill and ability. An agent has a duty to advise the principal to **seek expert advice** on any matters relating to the transaction that are beyond the agent's expertise.

Agents should never claim to have expertise in areas in which they have no special training or skills. For example, if questions arise as to a home's structural soundness, the agent should advise the principal to contact a home inspector.

Example: Pat lists his house for sale with Celina. An interested buyer approaches Pat and proposes a seller-financed transaction. Pat asks his agent, Celina, for advice in structuring the financing. Although Celina is familiar with seller-financed transactions, she must advise Pat to seek the advice of an attorney.

Good Faith and Continuous Effort

A real estate agent has a duty to make a **good faith and continuous effort** to fulfill the terms of the agency agreement. A seller's agent must make a good faith and continuous effort to find a buyer for the property; a buyer's agent must make a good faith and continuous effort to find a suitable property to purchase.

Note that once a seller has entered into a purchase and sale agreement, the seller's agent is not required to seek out additional buyers. And once a buyer has entered into a purchase and sale agreement, the buyer's agent need not search for additional properties to show the buyer.

Agent's Duties to All Parties

Although a real estate agent's main responsibilities are to her principal, the agent also owes certain duties to other parties. Under general agency law, real estate agents owed third parties only the duty of honesty and fair dealing. Washington's real estate agency law replaced that with seven statutory duties that an agent owes to anyone she renders real estate services to, including her principal. In fact, a real estate licensee owes these duties even if she is acting as a non-agent and not representing any of the parties. The duties are:

- reasonable care and skill,
- honesty and good faith,
- presenting all written communications,
- disclosure of material facts,
- accounting,
- providing a pamphlet on agency law, and
- disclosing any existing agency relationship.

The real estate agency statute (RCW 18.86) provides that a breach of any of these statutory duties is grounds for disciplinary action under the real estate license law (RCW 18.85).

Reasonable Care and Skill

In performing their duties, real estate agents must use the degree of care and skill ordinarily employed by others competently engaged in the same business. This means that an agent's actions will be compared to what is expected of other competent real estate agents. Failing to act competently, reasonably, or carefully may be considered negligence.

Honesty and Good Faith

A real estate agent has the duty to act with honesty and good faith toward any party. **Misrepresentations**—false or misleading statements, either spoken or written—are a breach of this duty. So are concealment and other deceptive conduct.

> **Example:** The foundation of the house is settling rapidly, and a large crack has opened up in the wall of the finished basement. Instead of telling potential buyers about the crack or leaving it in plain view for buyers to see, the seller's agent decides to move a large bookcase in front of the crack, completely hiding it. This action is a breach of the agent's duty of honesty and good faith.

Fig. 7.1 Types of fraud

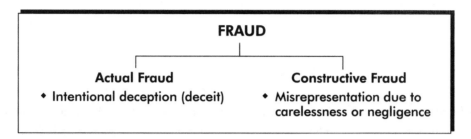

As we'll discuss in Chapter 8, a misrepresentation or concealment by an agent—or by a principal—may amount to **fraud** if a third party acts in reliance on the incorrect information (for example, if a buyer signs a contract he would not have entered into if he had not been misled by the seller's agent and/or the seller).

Fraud can be classified as either actual or constructive. **Actual fraud** (also called deceit) involves an intentional deception. This is usually accomplished by deliberately misrepresenting or concealing a material fact.

> **Example:** Although the house appears sound, there is a serious dry rot problem in the walls. The sellers tell their agent about it but ask her not to mention it to potential buyers. When a buyer asks if there are any structural problems, the seller's agent replies that the house is in excellent condition. This deliberate misrepresentation is actual fraud.

On the other hand, **constructive fraud** does not involve a deliberately misleading statement or act, but a misrepresentation made through carelessness or negligence, as in the following case example. Here the agent innocently passed on incorrect information from the seller; but the seller had specifically asked the agent to check it, and the agent didn't do that.

Case Example:

Dorothy was selling some vacant land. She told her listing agent that the land had passed a percolation test. Actually, Dorothy was confused—it was some adjoining property that she had already sold that had passed the test. Dorothy gave her agent some official paperwork that she erroneously believed applied to the subject property. However, she was worried about expiration dates on the documents, so she asked her agent to check on the validity of the paperwork. The listing agent failed to do so, and proceeded to tell a couple named the Tennants that the land had passed a perc test. The Tennants bought the property, believing it was suitable for a septic tank and could be easily built upon. That turned out not to be the case. When the Tennants discovered the true situation, they sued the agent.

The court found that the listing agent had made an innocent mistake. However, the agent had been instructed to check the paperwork and failed to do so. This was negligence, making the agent liable for the damages that the buyers suffered. *Tennant v. Lawton*, 26 Wn. App. 701, 615 P.2d 1305 (1980).

A buyer who signs a purchase and sale agreement based on misrepresentations generally has the right to rescind the transaction and/or sue for damages, whether the misrepresentations were intentional or unintentional. Ordinarily, a seller is liable for her own misrepresentations, but not for her agent's (see Chapter 6). The seller's agent and the brokerage firm may be liable to the buyer for any misrepresentations by the agent. However, the agent and the brokerage generally won't be held liable if the agent innocently passed along incorrect information from the seller, unless the agent was negligent, as in the *Tennant* case above.

All of the examples we've discussed in this section so far have involved misrepresentations made to buyers by a seller's agent. Of course, real estate agents can also be held liable for making misrepresentations to sellers. In the case example below, a listing agent is sued by his own clients.

Case Example:

The Farrells listed their laundromat for sale with Score, a real estate agent. Score located a potential buyer named Robinson.

Score told the Farrells that Robinson had a good job with Standard Oil, which he would retain after the purchase while his wife managed the laundromat. He also said that Robinson had sufficient stock in Standard Oil to buy out the Farrells, but since Robinson didn't want to cash in the investment at that time, he would require seller financing. Based on these representations, the Farrells accepted Robinson's offer (which was contingent on the seller financing arrangement) and executed a promissory note to Score for his commission.

Robinson took possession of the laundromat and made payments for seven months. He was unable to make any further payments. After negotiating with the Farrells, the contract was rescinded and Robinson returned the laundromat business to the Farrells.

The Farrells sued Score to cancel the promissory note for his commission. The court found that Score had known Robinson could raise the downpayment funds only by resigning from Standard Oil and thereby receiving an annuity benefit. Score also knew that Robinson possessed only a small amount of stock worth approximately $320.

The court held that a principal is entitled to rely on representations made by an agent concerning the financial ability of the intended purchaser. Intentional misrepresentation of the potential buyer's financial condition constitutes fraud. Since the Farrells' acceptance of Robinson as a purchaser was induced through the agent's misrepresentation as to his financial condition, they were entitled to cancellation of the note. *Farrell v. Score*, 67 Wn.2nd 957, 411 P.2d 146 (1966).

Puffing, Predictions, and Opinions. Misrepresentations that can give rise to legal action should not be confused with mere opinions, predictions, or puffing.

- Opinion—"I think this is the best buy on the market."
- Prediction—"This house could double in value over the next ten years."
- Puffing—"This is the finest house in the neighborhood; it has a fantastic view."

As we said earlier, to prove fraud based on a misrepresentation, it is necessary to show that someone relied on the misrepresentation. Statements that are mere opinions, predictions, and puffing are not considered the types of statements that a reasonable person would rely on in making a decision to buy property, because of their nonfactual or exaggerated nature.

> **Example:** The agent tells a buyer, "This is a great little house; you'll be very happy here." After purchasing the house, the buyer is not happy. He discovers several problems and decides it is not a great house at all.
>
> Even if it isn't a great house, the agent is not liable for his statement because it was mere puffing—a statement of opinion made to induce the purchaser to buy, but not relating to any specific material fact.

In general, recovery is not available for fraud or misrepresentation based on statements of opinion. However, an agent should be very cautious in voicing unsubstantiated opinions or predictions. If a statement is considered a professional or expert opinion, it could lead to liability for negligence.

Present Written Communications

Any type of written communication to or from either party, including all written offers and counteroffers, must be presented to the other party in a timely manner. Even if an offer seems totally unacceptable, the agent must present it to the principal, because the principal—not the agent—decides which offer is acceptable. The agent must relay an offer to the principal even if its acceptance is not in the agent's best interest, because the agent's first loyalty is to the principal.

> **Example:** An agent was aware of two potential purchasers for a property. The first party offered $400,000 and the second party offered $425,000. Instead of telling the seller about the $425,000 offer, the agent arranged two sales: a sale from the seller to the first buyer for $400,000 and a second sale from that buyer to the second buyer for $425,000. In this way, the agent earned two sales commissions.
>
> The original seller sued the agent, accusing him of failing to let the seller know there was a higher offer for the property. The court awarded the seller the amount of the second commission plus other damages.

Disclosure of Material Facts

A real estate agent has the duty to disclose a **material fact** to a party if the agent is aware of the fact, and it is not apparent or readily ascertainable by the party. Washington's real estate agency law defines a "material fact" as information that:

1. has a substantial negative impact on the property's value or on a party's ability to perform, or
2. defeats the purpose of the transaction.

For example, the property's true value is a material fact that the agent must disclose to the principal. Misleading the principal as to the value of the property or withholding information that affects its value would be a breach of the licensee's duty to disclose material facts. A licensee should also inform the principal of any information or recent events that may affect the value of the property, such as zoning changes or plans to build a new school in the neighborhood.

For a seller's agent, the buyer's financial position may be material information that must be disclosed. Financial information regarding the buyer is considered material if the seller would have refused to enter into the agreement if the information were known at the time the contract was made. If the agent misrepresented or failed to disclose detrimental financial information concerning the buyer, the agent may lose the right to a commission. Essentially, the agent failed to produce a buyer who was financially able to complete the sale.

> **Example:** A buyer made an offer on a property that complied with all the terms desired by the seller. However, the agent failed to disclose to the seller that the buyer did not make enough money to keep up with the monthly payments. At the last minute, the seller began to have doubts about the transaction and refused to sign the purchase and sale agreement.
>
> The agent was not entitled to the commission. Even though the buyer's offer met the terms required by the seller, the buyer was not a "ready, willing, and able" buyer.

Latent Defects. A common example of a material fact that must be disclosed is a latent defect. A **latent defect** is one that would not be discovered through ordinary inspection. A licensee must disclose any known latent defect to the parties.

> **Example:** When taking a listing from a seller, the agent notices a crack in the home's foundation that is almost entirely hidden from view. This is a latent defect and must be disclosed to the seller as well as to any potential buyers.

What is Not Material. The real estate agency law excludes certain types of information from the material fact disclosure requirement. Specifically, it isn't considered material if the property (or a neighboring property) was the site of a violent crime, suicide, or other death, drug- or gang-related activity, political or religious activity, or any other occurrence that doesn't adversely affect the physical condition of or title to the property.

> **Example:** An agent is showing a buyer a home in which a brutal homicide occurred three years ago. This information is not considered a material fact and need not be disclosed to the buyer.

Note, however, that if the buyer asked the agent whether any crimes had occurred on the property, the agent would have to answer honestly. Regardless of whether or not the information requested is a material fact, the agent is obligated to answer questions honestly and in good faith.

Criminal activity will be considered a material fact if it affects the property's physical condition.

> **Example:** A house for sale previously contained an illegal drug lab. It's possible that the house may be contaminated by dangerous chemical residues left behind that

substantially affect the condition of the property. This is a material fact and must be disclosed to prospective buyers.

The Washington State Human Rights Commission has stated that questions about Acquired Immune Deficiency Syndrome (AIDS) or any of its related conditions are improper questions by any prospective landlord, tenant, home buyer, or seller.

The guidelines specifically prohibit an agent from engaging in a discussion about or disclosing whether a tenant, owner, or resident had AIDS. AIDS is considered a disability under the Washington State Law Against Discrimination. It is an unfair practice for an appraiser to lower the value of real property because a person with AIDS resides in the property or is a neighbor to the property. The presence of AIDS is not a factor that should be discussed or disclosed during a real estate transaction.

Seller Disclosure Statement. In Washington, a seller of real property must provide the buyer with a disclosure statement. Different disclosures are required for various types of property, such as commercial real estate and unimproved property. A seller disclosure form for improved residential property is shown in Figure 7.2.

Note that certain kinds of transactions are exempt from the disclosure requirement, including foreclosures, gifts to family members, transfers by personal representatives in settling estates, and transfers of less than fee simple estates. Unimproved timber or agricultural land may also be exempt from disclosure requirements.

Disclosure statement contents. The purpose of the disclosure statement is to disclose the seller's knowledge regarding the condition of the property, including the condition of the buildings and utilities, the existence of any easements and encumbrances, and other material information.

The disclosure form states that the disclosures are made by the seller only. The disclosures can't be treated as representations made by the real estate licensees involved in the transaction. The form also states that the statement isn't a warranty from either the seller or the real estate agents; the disclosures are purely informational. Further, the form states that the seller agrees to defend and hold the licensees harmless if the buyer brings a legal claim that the statement contains inaccuracies. Note that by law, the agents aren't liable for errors or omissions in the statement, unless they knew the disclosures were wrong.

Deadlines and right of rescission. The seller must give the buyer the disclosure statement within **five business days** after a purchase and sale agreement is signed, unless the parties agree in writing to another time frame, or the buyer signs a written waiver of the right to receive the statement. However, a waiver is not allowed for the Environmental section of the form, if that section reveals potential environmental issues (that is, the seller checked the "Yes" answer box to any of the questions).

Within **three business days** after receiving the statement (or another time frame agreed to in writing), the buyer can either "approve and accept" the disclosure statement or rescind the purchase and sale agreement. The choice between acceptance and rescission is completely up to the buyer. If the buyer doesn't like something revealed in the disclosure statement, however trivial, the buyer can rescind the agreement. In fact, the buyer can

Fig. 7.2 Seller disclosure statement

Form 17 Seller Disclosure Statement Rev. 7/15 Page 1 of 6	**SELLER DISCLOSURE STATEMENT** **IMPROVED PROPERTY**	©Copyright 2015 Northwest Multiple Listing Service ALL RIGHTS RESERVED

SELLER: _____ 1
            Seller   Seller

To be used in transfers of improved residential real property, including residential dwellings up to four units, new construction, 2
condominiums not subject to a public offering statement, certain timeshares, and manufactured and mobile homes. See RCW 3
Chapter 64.06 for further information. 4

INSTRUCTIONS TO THE SELLER 5
Please complete the following form. Do not leave any spaces blank. If the question clearly does not apply to the property check 6
"NA." If the answer is "yes" to any asterisked (*) item(s), please explain on attached sheets. Please refer to the line number(s) of 7
the question(s) when you provide your explanation(s). For your protection you must date and initial each page of this disclosure 8
statement and each attachment. Delivery of the disclosure statement must occur not later than five (5) business days, unless 9
otherwise agreed, after mutual acceptance of a written purchase and sale agreement between Buyer and Seller. 10

NOTICE TO THE BUYER 11
THE FOLLOWING DISCLOSURES ARE MADE BY THE SELLER ABOUT THE CONDITION OF THE PROPERTY LOCATED AT 12
_____ , CITY _____ , 13
STATE _____ , ZIP _____ , COUNTY_____ ("THE PROPERTY") OR AS 14
LEGALLY DESCRIBED ON THE ATTACHED EXHIBIT A. 15

SELLER MAKES THE FOLLOWING DISCLOSURES OF EXISTING MATERIAL FACTS OR MATERIAL DEFECTS TO BUYER BASED 16
ON SELLER'S ACTUAL KNOWLEDGE OF THE PROPERTY AT THE TIME SELLER COMPLETES THIS DISCLOSURE 17
STATEMENT. UNLESS YOU AND SELLER OTHERWISE AGREE IN WRITING, YOU HAVE THREE (3) BUSINESS DAYS FROM 18
THE DAY SELLER OR SELLER'S AGENT DELIVERS THIS DISCLOSURE STATEMENT TO YOU TO RESCIND THE AGREEMENT 19
BY DELIVERING A SEPARATELY SIGNED WRITTEN STATEMENT OF RESCISSION TO SELLER OR SELLER'S AGENT. IF THE 20
SELLER DOES NOT GIVE YOU A COMPLETED DISCLOSURE STATEMENT, THEN YOU MAY WAIVE THE RIGHT TO RESCIND 21
PRIOR TO OR AFTER THE TIME YOU ENTER INTO A PURCHASE AND SALE AGREEMENT. 22

THE FOLLOWING ARE DISCLOSURES MADE BY SELLER AND ARE NOT THE REPRESENTATIONS OF ANY REAL ESTATE 23
LICENSEE OR OTHER PARTY. THIS INFORMATION IS FOR DISCLOSURE ONLY AND IS NOT INTENDED TO BE A PART OF 24
ANY WRITTEN AGREEMENT BETWEEN BUYER AND SELLER. 25

FOR A MORE COMPREHENSIVE EXAMINATION OF THE SPECIFIC CONDITION OF THIS PROPERTY YOU ARE ADVISED 26
TO OBTAIN AND PAY FOR THE SERVICES OF QUALIFIED EXPERTS TO INSPECT THE PROPERTY, WHICH MAY INCLUDE, 27
WITHOUT LIMITATION, ARCHITECTS, ENGINEERS, LAND SURVEYORS, PLUMBERS, ELECTRICIANS, ROOFERS, 28
BUILDING INSPECTORS, ON-SITE WASTEWATER TREATMENT INSPECTORS, OR STRUCTURAL PEST INSPECTORS. 29
THE PROSPECTIVE BUYER AND SELLER MAY WISH TO OBTAIN PROFESSIONAL ADVICE OR INSPECTIONS OF THE 30
PROPERTY OR TO PROVIDE APPROPRIATE PROVISIONS IN A CONTRACT BETWEEN THEM WITH RESPECT TO ANY 31
ADVICE, INSPECTION, DEFECTS OR WARRANTIES. 32

SELLER ❑ IS/ ❑ IS NOT OCCUPYING THE PROPERTY. 33

I. SELLER'S DISCLOSURES: 34
*If you answer "Yes" to a question with an asterisk (*), please explain your answer and attach documents, if available and not 35
otherwise publicly recorded. If necessary, use an attached sheet. 36

	YES	NO	DON'T KNOW	N/A	
1. TITLE					37 38
A. Do you have legal authority to sell the property? If no, please explain. ......❑	❑	❑	❑	39
*B. Is title to the property subject to any of the following?					40
(1) First right of refusal ....❑	❑	❑	❑	41
(2) Option ....❑	❑	❑	❑	42
(3) Lease or rental agreement ....❑	❑	❑	❑	43
(4) Life estate? ....❑	❑	❑	❑	44
*C. Are there any encroachments, boundary agreements, or boundary disputes? ....❑	❑	❑	❑	45
*D. Is there a private road or easement agreement for access to the property? ....❑	❑	❑	❑	46
*E. Are there any rights-of-way, easements, or access limitations that may affect the Buyer's use of					47
the property? ....❑	❑	❑	❑	48
*F. Are there any written agreements for joint maintenance of an easement or right-of-way? ....❑	❑	❑	❑	49
*G. Is there any study, survey project, or notice that would adversely affect the property? ....❑	❑	❑	❑	50
*H. Are there any pending or existing assessments against the property? ....❑	❑	❑	❑	51

SELLER'S INITIALS	Date	SELLER'S INITIALS	Date

Form 17	**SELLER DISCLOSURE STATEMENT**	©Copyright 2015	
Seller Disclosure Statement	**IMPROVED PROPERTY**	Northwest Multiple Listing Service	
Rev. 7/15		ALL RIGHTS RESERVED	
Page 2 of 6	*(Continued)*		

	YES	NO	DON'T KNOW	N/A	
					52
					53
*I. Are there any zoning violations, nonconforming uses, or any unusual restrictions on the property that would affect future construction or remodeling?	❑	❑	❑	❑	54 / 55
*J. Is there a boundary survey for the property?	❑	❑	❑	❑	56
*K. Are there any covenants, conditions, or restrictions recorded against the property?	❑	❑	❑	❑	57

PLEASE NOTE: Covenants, conditions, and restrictions which purport to forbid or restrict the conveyance, encumbrance, occupancy, or lease of real property to individuals based on race, creed, color, sex, national origin, familial status, or disability are void, unenforceable, and illegal. RCW 49.60.224.

58
59
60
61

2. WATER
62

A. Household Water
63

   (1) The source of water for the property is: ❑ Private or publicly owned water system   ❑ Private well serving only the subject property   *❑ Other water system
64
65

	YES	NO	DON'T KNOW	N/A	
*If shared, are there any written agreements?	❑	❑	❑	❑	66
*(2) Is there an easement (recorded or unrecorded) for access to and/or maintenance of the water source?	❑	❑	❑	❑	67 / 68
*(3) Are there any problems or repairs needed?	❑	❑	❑	❑	69
(4) During your ownership, has the source provided an adequate year-round supply of potable water?	❑	❑	❑	❑	70
If no, please explain: _____					71
*(5) Are there any water treatment systems for the property?	❑	❑	❑	❑	72
If yes, are they: ❑ Leased ❑ Owned					73
*(6) Are there any water rights for the property associated with its domestic water supply, such as a water right permit, certificate, or claim?	❑	❑	❑	❑	74 / 75
(a) If yes, has the water right permit, certificate, or claim been assigned, transferred, or changed?	❑	❑	❑	❑	76
*(b) If yes, has all or any portion of the water right not been used for five or more successive years?	❑	❑	❑	❑	77
*(7) Are there any defects in the operation of the water system (e.g. pipes, tank, pump, etc.)?	❑	❑	❑	❑	78

B. Irrigation Water
79

	YES	NO	DON'T KNOW	N/A	
(1) Are there any irrigation water rights for the property, such as a water right permit, certificate, or claim?	❑	❑	❑	❑	80 / 81
*(a) If yes, has all or any portion of the water right not been used for five or more successive years?	❑	❑	❑	❑	82 / 83
*(b) If so, is the certificate available? (If yes, please attach a copy.)	❑	❑	❑	❑	84
*(c) If so, has the water right permit, certificate, or claim been assigned, transferred, or changed?	❑	❑	❑	❑	85
*(2) Does the property receive irrigation water from a ditch company, irrigation district, or other entity?	❑	❑	❑	❑	86

    If so, please identify the entity that supplies water to the property:
87
88

    _____

C. Outdoor Sprinkler System
89

	YES	NO	DON'T KNOW	N/A	
(1) Is there an outdoor sprinkler system for the property?	❑	❑	❑	❑	90
*(2) If yes, are there any defects in the system?	❑	❑	❑	❑	91
*(3) If yes, is the sprinkler system connected to irrigation water?	❑	❑	❑	❑	92

3. SEWER/ON-SITE SEWAGE SYSTEM
93

A. The property is served by:
94

   ❑ Public sewer system ❑ On-site sewage system (including pipes, tanks, drainfields, and all other component parts)
95
96

   ❑ Other disposal system

   Please describe:_____
97

_____   _____
SELLER'S INITIALS   Date   SELLER'S INITIALS   Date

Form 17
Seller Disclosure Statement
Rev. 7/15
Page 3 of 6

SELLER DISCLOSURE STATEMENT
IMPROVED PROPERTY

(Continued)

©Copyright 2015
Northwest Multiple Listing Service
ALL RIGHTS RESERVED

	YES	NO	DON'T KNOW	N/A	
					98
					99

B. If public sewer system service is available to the property, is the house connected to the sewer main? ....☐ ☐ ☐ ☐ 100
   If no, please explain:_____ 101

*C. Is the property subject to any sewage system fees or charges in addition to those covered 102
   in your regularly billed sewer or on-site sewage system maintenance service?...............☐ ☐ ☐ ☐ 103

D. If the property is connected to an on-site sewage system: 104
   *(1) Was a permit issued for its construction, and was it approved by the local health 105
        department or district following its construction?..☐ ☐ ☐ ☐ 106
   (2) When was it last pumped? _____ 107
   *(3) Are there any defects in the operation of the on-site sewage system? ....☐ ☐ ☐ ☐ 108
   (4) When was it last inspected? _____ ☐ ☐ 109
        By whom: _____ 110
   (5) For how many bedrooms was the on-site sewage system approved? _____ bedrooms ☐ ☐ 111

E. Are all plumbing fixtures, including laundry drain, connected to the sewer/on-site 112
   sewage system? ....☐ ☐ ☐ ☐ 113
   If no, please explain:_____ 114

*F. Have there been any changes or repairs to the on-site sewage system? ....☐ ☐ ☐ ☐ 115

G. Is the on-site sewage system, including the drainfield, located entirely within the 116
   boundaries of the property? ....☐ ☐ ☐ ☐ 117
   If no, please explain:_____ 118

*H. Does the on-site sewage system require monitoring and maintenance services more frequently 119
   than once a year? ....☐ ☐ ☐ ☐ 120

NOTICE: IF THIS RESIDENTIAL REAL PROPERTY DISCLOSURE IS BEING COMPLETED FOR NEW CONSTRUCTION 121
WHICH HAS NEVER BEEN OCCUPIED, SELLER IS NOT REQUIRED TO COMPLETE THE QUESTIONS LISTED IN ITEM 4 122
(STRUCTURAL) OR ITEM 5 (SYSTEMS AND FIXTURES). 123

4. STRUCTURAL 124

*A. Has the roof leaked within the last 5 years?..☐ ☐ ☐ ☐ 125

*B. Has the basement flooded or leaked? ....☐ ☐ ☐ ☐ 126

*C. Have there been any conversions, additions or remodeling? ....☐ ☐ ☐ ☐ 127
   *(1) If yes, were all building permits obtained?...☐ ☐ ☐ ☐ 128
   *(2) If yes, were all final inspections obtained? ....☐ ☐ ☐ ☐ 129

D. Do you know the age of the house? ....☐ ☐ ☐ ☐ 130
   If yes, year of original construction:_____ 131

*E. Has there been any settling, slippage, or sliding of the property or its improvements? ...☐ ☐ ☐ ☐ 132

*F. Are there any defects with the following: (If yes, please check applicable items and explain) ....☐ ☐ ☐ ☐ 133

☐ Foundations	☐ Decks	☐ Exterior Walls	134
☐ Chimneys	☐ Interior Walls	☐ Fire Alarms	135
☐ Doors	☐ Windows	☐ Patio	136
☐ Ceilings	☐ Slab Floors	☐ Driveways	137
☐ Pools	☐ Hot Tub	☐ Sauna	138
☐ Sidewalks	☐ Outbuildings	☐ Fireplaces	139
☐ Garage Floors	☐ Walkways	☐ Siding	140
☐ Wood Stoves	☐ Elevators	☐ Incline Elevators	141
☐ Stairway Chair Lifts	☐ Wheelchair Lifts	☐ Other _____	

*G. Was a structural pest or "whole house" inspection done?.......................................☐ ☐ ☐ ☐ 142
   If yes, when and by whom was the inspection completed? 143
   _____ 144

H. During your ownership, has the property had any wood destroying organism or pest infestation?........☐ ☐ ☐ ☐ 145

I. Is the attic insulated?...☐ ☐ ☐ ☐ 146

J. Is the basement insulated? ....☐ ☐ ☐ ☐ 147

_____ _____   _____ _____
SELLER'S INITIALS   Date   SELLER'S INITIALS   Date

Form 17	**SELLER DISCLOSURE STATEMENT**	©Copyright 2015
Seller Disclosure Statement	**IMPROVED PROPERTY**	Northwest Multiple Listing Service
Rev. 7/15		ALL RIGHTS RESERVED
Page 4 of 6	*(Continued)*	

	YES	NO	DON'T KNOW	N/A	
					148
					149

5. SYSTEMS AND FIXTURES

*A. If any of the following systems or fixtures are included with the transfer, are there any defects? — 150

If yes, please explain: _____ — 151

	YES	NO	DON'T KNOW	N/A	
Electrical system, including wiring, switches, outlets, and service	❑	❑	❑	❑	152
Plumbing system, including pipes, faucets, fixtures, and toilets	❑	❑	❑	❑	153
Hot water tank	❑	❑	❑	❑	154
Garbage disposal	❑	❑	❑	❑	155
Appliances	❑	❑	❑	❑	156
Sump pump	❑	❑	❑	❑	157
Heating and cooling systems	❑	❑	❑	❑	158
Security system: ❑ Owned ❑ Leased	❑	❑	❑	❑	159
Other_____	❑	❑	❑	❑	160

*B. If any of the following fixtures or property is included with the transfer, are they leased? — 161
(If yes, please attach copy of lease.) — 162

	YES	NO	DON'T KNOW	N/A	
Security System: _____	❑	❑	❑	❑	163
Tanks (type): _____	❑	❑	❑	❑	164
Satellite dish: _____	❑	❑	❑	❑	165
Other: _____	❑	❑	❑	❑	166

*C. Are any of the following kinds of wood burning appliances present at the property? — 167

	YES	NO	DON'T KNOW	N/A	
(1) Woodstove?	❑	❑	❑	❑	168
(2) Fireplace insert?	❑	❑	❑	❑	169
(3) Pellet stove?	❑	❑	❑	❑	170
(4) Fireplace?	❑	❑	❑	❑	171

If yes, are all of the (1) woodstoves or (2) fireplace inserts certified by the U.S. Environmental — 172
Protection Agency as clean burning appliances to improve air quality and public health? — ❑ ❑ ❑ ❑ 173

D. Is the property located within a city, county, or district or within a department of natural — 174
resources fire protection zone that provides fire protection services? — ❑ ❑ ❑ ❑ 175

E. Is the property equipped with carbon monoxide alarms? (Note: Pursuant to RCW 19.27.530, Seller — 176
must equip the residence with carbon monoxide alarms as required by the state building code.) — ❑ ❑ ❑ ❑ 177

F. Is the property equipped with smoke alarms? — ❑ ❑ ❑ ❑ 178

6. HOMEOWNERS' ASSOCIATION/COMMON INTERESTS — 179

A. Is there a Homeowners' Association? — ❑ ❑ ❑ ❑ 180
Name of Association and contact information for an officer, director, employee, or other authorized — 181
agent, if any, who may provide the association's financial statements, minutes, bylaws, fining policy, — 182
and other information that is not publicly available: _____ — 183

B. Are there regular periodic assessments? — ❑ ❑ ❑ ❑ 184
$ _____ per ❑ month ❑ year — 185
❑ Other: _____ — 186

*C. Are there any pending special assessments? — ❑ ❑ ❑ ❑ 187

*D. Are there any shared "common areas" or any joint maintenance agreements (facilities — 188
such as walls, fences, landscaping, pools, tennis courts, walkways, or other areas — 189
co-owned in undivided interest with others)? — ❑ ❑ ❑ ❑ 190

7. ENVIRONMENTAL — 191

*A. Have there been any flooding, standing water, or drainage problems on the property — 192
that affect the property or access to the property? — ❑ ❑ ❑ ❑ 193

*B. Does any part of the property contain fill dirt, waste, or other fill material? — ❑ ❑ ❑ ❑ 194

*C. Is there any material damage to the property from fire, wind, floods, beach movements, — 195
earthquake, expansive soils, or landslides? — ❑ ❑ ❑ ❑ 196

D. Are there any shorelines, wetlands, floodplains, or critical areas on the property? — ❑ ❑ ❑ ❑ 197

*E. Are there any substances, materials, or products in or on the property that may be environmental — 198
concerns, such as asbestos, formaldehyde, radon gas, lead-based paint, fuel or chemical — 199
storage tanks, or contaminated soil or water? — ❑ ❑ ❑ ❑ 200

*F. Has the property been used for commercial or industrial purposes? — ❑ ❑ ❑ ❑ 201

SELLER'S INITIALS	Date	SELLER'S INITIALS	Date

Form 17
Seller Disclosure Statement
Rev. 7/15
Page 5 of 6

SELLER DISCLOSURE STATEMENT
IMPROVED PROPERTY

(Continued)

	YES	NO	DON'T KNOW	N/A	
					202
					203
*G. Is there any soil or groundwater contamination?...	❑	❑	❑	❑	204
*H. Are there transmission poles or other electrical utility equipment installed, maintained, or					205
buried on the property that do not provide utility service to the structures on the property?............	❑	❑	❑	❑	206
*I. Has the property been used as a legal or illegal dumping site?	❑	❑	❑	❑	207
*J. Has the property been used as an illegal drug manufacturing site?	❑	❑	❑	❑	208
*K. Are there any radio towers in the area that cause interference with cellular telephone reception?..........	❑	❑	❑	❑	209

8. **LEAD BASED PAINT** (Applicable if the house was built before 1978). 210

   A. Presence of lead-based paint and/or lead-based paint hazards (check one below): 211

      ❑ Known lead-based paint and/or lead-based paint hazards are present in the housing 212
         (explain). _____ 213

      ❑ Seller has no knowledge of lead-based paint and/or lead-based paint hazards in the housing. 214

   B. Records and reports available to the Seller (check one below): 215

      ❑ Seller has provided the purchaser with all available records and reports pertaining to 216
         lead-based paint and/or lead-based paint hazards in the housing (list documents below). 217

         _____ 218

      ❑ Seller has no reports or records pertaining to lead-based paint and/or lead-based paint hazards in the housing. 219

9. **MANUFACTURED AND MOBILE HOMES** 220

   If the property includes a manufactured or mobile home, 221

*A. Did you make any alterations to the home?	❑	❑	❑	❑	222
If yes, please describe the alterations: _____					223
*B. Did any previous owner make any alterations to the home?	❑	❑	❑	❑	224
*C. If alterations were made, were permits or variances for these alterations obtained?	❑	❑	❑	❑	225

10. **FULL DISCLOSURE BY SELLERS** 226

   A. Other conditions or defects: 227
   *Are there any other existing material defects affecting the property that a prospective 228

buyer should know about?..	❑	❑	❑	❑	229

   B. Verification 230
   The foregoing answers and attached explanations (if any) are complete and correct to the best of Seller's knowledge and 231
   Seller has received a copy hereof. Seller agrees to defend, indemnify and hold real estate licensees harmless from and 232
   against any and all claims that the above information is inaccurate. Seller authorizes real estate licensees, if any, to deliver a 233
   copy of this disclosure statement to other real estate licensees and all prospective buyers of the property. 234

      235

   _____   _____   _____   _____
     Seller   Date   Seller   Date 236

If the answer is "Yes" to any asterisked (*) items, please explain below (use additional sheets if necessary). Please refer to the line 237
number(s) of the question(s). 238

   239
   240
   241
   242
   243
   244
   245
   246
   247
   248
   249
   250
   251

Form 17
Seller Disclosure Statement
Rev. 7/15
Page 6 of 6

SELLER DISCLOSURE STATEMENT
IMPROVED PROPERTY
(Continued)

II. NOTICES TO THE BUYER 252

1. SEX OFFENDER REGISTRATION 253

INFORMATION REGARDING REGISTERED SEX OFFENDERS MAY BE OBTAINED FROM LOCAL LAW ENFORCEMENT AGENCIES. THIS NOTICE IS INTENDED ONLY TO INFORM YOU OF WHERE TO OBTAIN THIS INFORMATION AND IS NOT AN INDICATION OF THE PRESENCE OF REGISTERED SEX OFFENDERS. 254 255 256

2. PROXIMITY TO FARMING 257

THIS NOTICE IS TO INFORM YOU THAT THE REAL PROPERTY YOU ARE CONSIDERING FOR PURCHASE MAY LIE IN CLOSE PROXIMITY TO A FARM. THE OPERATION OF A FARM INVOLVES USUAL AND CUSTOMARY AGRICULTURAL PRACTICES, WHICH ARE PROTECTED UNDER RCW 7.48.305, THE WASHINGTON RIGHT TO FARM ACT. 258 259 260

III. BUYER'S ACKNOWLEDGEMENT 261

1. BUYER HEREBY ACKNOWLEDGES THAT: 262

A. Buyer has a duty to pay diligent attention to any material defects that are known to Buyer or can be known to Buyer by utilizing diligent attention and observation. 263 264

B. The disclosures set forth in this statement and in any amendments to this statement are made only by the Seller and not by any real estate licensee or other party. 265 266

C. Buyer acknowledges that, pursuant to RCW 64.06.050(2), real estate licensees are not liable for inaccurate information provided by Seller, except to the extent that real estate licensees know of such inaccurate information. 267 268

D. This information is for disclosure only and is not intended to be a part of the written agreement between the Buyer and Seller. 269

E. Buyer (which term includes all persons signing the "Buyer's acceptance" portion of this disclosure statement below) has received a copy of this Disclosure Statement (including attachments, if any) bearing Seller's signature(s). 270 271

F. If the house was built prior to 1978, Buyer acknowledges receipt of the pamphlet *Protect Your Family From Lead in Your Home*. 272 273

DISCLOSURES CONTAINED IN THIS DISCLOSURE STATEMENT ARE PROVIDED BY SELLER BASED ON SELLER'S ACTUAL KNOWLEDGE OF THE PROPERTY AT THE TIME SELLER COMPLETES THIS DISCLOSURE. UNLESS BUYER AND SELLER OTHERWISE AGREE IN WRITING, BUYER SHALL HAVE THREE (3) BUSINESS DAYS FROM THE DAY SELLER OR SELLER'S AGENT DELIVERS THIS DISCLOSURE STATEMENT TO RESCIND THE AGREEMENT BY DELIVERING A SEPARATELY SIGNED WRITTEN STATEMENT OF RESCISSION TO SELLER OR SELLER'S AGENT. YOU MAY WAIVE THE RIGHT TO RESCIND PRIOR TO OR AFTER THE TIME YOU ENTER INTO A SALE AGREEMENT. 274 275 276 277 278 279

BUYER HEREBY ACKNOWLEDGES RECEIPT OF A COPY OF THIS DISCLOSURE STATEMENT AND ACKNOWLEDGES THAT THE DISCLOSURES MADE HEREIN ARE THOSE OF THE SELLER ONLY, AND NOT OF ANY REAL ESTATE LICENSEE OR OTHER PARTY. 280 281 282

283

_____   _____
Buyer   Date   Buyer   Date 284

2. BUYER'S WAIVER OF RIGHT TO REVOKE OFFER 285

Buyer has read and reviewed the Seller's responses to this Seller Disclosure Statement. Buyer approves this statement and waives Buyer's right to revoke Buyer's offer based on this disclosure. 286 287

288

_____   _____
Buyer   Date   Buyer   Date 289

3. BUYER'S WAIVER OF RIGHT TO RECEIVE COMPLETED SELLER DISCLOSURE STATEMENT 290

Buyer has been advised of Buyer's right to receive a completed Seller Disclosure Statement. Buyer waives that right. However, if the answer to any of the questions in the section entitled "Environmental" would be "yes," Buyer may not waive the receipt of the "Environmental" section of the Seller Disclosure Statement. 291 292 293

294

_____   _____
Buyer   Date   Buyer   Date 295

_____   _____   _____   _____
SELLER'S INITIALS   Date   SELLER'S INITIALS   Date

rescind the agreement simply because he's decided he doesn't want the property after all, even if the decision isn't actually based on information disclosed by the seller.

If the buyer wants to rescind the agreement, he must send a rescission notice to the seller before the three-day period expires. The buyer will then be entitled to a refund of the earnest money deposit.

If the buyer accepts the disclosure statement, information may later come to light that makes the disclosure statement inaccurate.

> **Example:** The seller filled out the seller disclosure statement and gave it to the buyer within the five-day time frame. The buyer examined the statement, was satisfied with it, and waived the right to rescind the agreement. One week later (but before closing), the roof starts leaking. The disclosure statement given to the buyer is no longer accurate.

When this happens, the seller must either give the buyer an amended disclosure statement or else take corrective action so that the original disclosure statement is accurate again. If an amended statement is provided, the buyer has three business days to either accept the amended statement or rescind the purchase and sale agreement.

> **Example:** The seller in the previous example gives the buyer an amended disclosure statement noting the roof leak. The buyer, who has had second thoughts about buying the property anyway, decides to rescind the purchase and sale agreement.

If the seller neither provides an amended statement nor takes corrective action—or if the seller never provided a disclosure statement in the first place—the buyer can rescind the contract at any time before closing. Once the sale closes, however, the buyer's right of rescission ends. Even if new information comes to light after closing, the buyer doesn't have the right to rescind the transaction.

No Duty to Investigate. Some states require licensees to inspect the property and report their findings to the buyer. In Washington, however, the real estate agency law provides that an agent has no duty to investigate anything unless she specifically agrees to do so. The agent is not required to inspect the property, investigate either party's financial position, or independently verify statements made by either party or any reasonable source.

> **Example:** A seller tells his agent that the house has never had any problems with termites. The agent has no duty to verify the seller's statement. When a potential buyer then asks the agent if the house has ever had termite problems, the agent says no. If it turns out that the house does in fact have termite problems, the agent is not liable for passing the seller's statement on to the buyer.

Lead-Based Paint. The final issue regarding disclosure of material facts that we will discuss is lead-based paint. When a transaction involves a home built before 1978, the federal Residential Lead-Based Paint Hazard Reduction Act requires the owner to provide prospective buyers or tenants with information about lead-based paint.

A seller must disclose the location of any known lead-based paint on the property and, if the home has been inspected for this hazard, provide a copy of the inspector's report. The seller must also give a buyer ten days to inspect for lead-based paint or associated hazards. Finally, the seller has to provide the buyer with a booklet called *Protect Your Family From Lead In Your Home*.

Accounting

A real estate licensee must be able to account for any trust funds she accepts in a transaction. Trust funds are funds and other valuables that the licensee receives on behalf of a client. Trust funds must not be mixed, or commingled, with the licensee's own funds. In addition, the licensee must report to the client on the status of the trust funds on a regular basis.

Like the duty of confidentiality, the duty of accounting continues after the transaction has concluded. If an agent continues to hold trust funds after closing, the agent still has the same obligations regarding the funds.

Real Estate Agency Law Pamphlet

A real estate agent must give each party he renders services to a pamphlet containing the provisions of Washington's real estate agency law, the Real Estate Brokerage Relationships Act. This pamphlet must be given to each party before the party signs an agency agreement, consents to a dual agency, or waives any agency rights.

Agency Disclosure

Before a party signs an offer in a real estate transaction that is being handled by a real estate agent, the agent must disclose whether she represents the buyer, seller, both parties, or neither. This disclosure must be made to the party in writing.

Dealing Ethically with Clients, Customers, Colleagues, and Competitors

The various laws that we've discussed in this chapter set forth minimum legal standards for a licensee's behavior. However, an agent can and should ask more of herself than simply meeting minimum legal requirements. Successful agents make conforming to ethical standards a central part of their practice.

Ethical standards are found in the codes of professional organizations and also come from personal sources. Whatever the source of your ethical rules or guidelines, treating the people you work with ethically will build your reputation and help ensure that clients return, customers become clients, and colleagues (and even competitors) consider referring business your way.

Professional Codes of Ethics. If you are considering taking an action that isn't illegal but raises fairness concerns, check to see if there's a provision in a professional association's code of ethics that's relevant to the situation.

The best-known code of ethics in the real estate industry is the Code of Ethics and Standards of Practice of the National Association of REALTORS®. Although only NAR® members must follow this code, its rules are helpful to anyone weighing the ethics of a particular action in a real estate transaction. In fact, the NAR® Code of Ethics is sometimes cited in court decisions, as support for the judge's ruling that a real estate licensee's conduct was inappropriate.

We'll only mention a couple of provisions of the NAR® Code of Ethics here. For example, Article Three requires agents to cooperate with other real estate professionals when it will help advance their clients' best interests. This ethical mandate is really just an extension of the legal duty to serve one's client competently. Another NAR® Code provision requires a listing agent to continue submitting all offers and counteroffers to the seller up until closing (unless the seller has waived this obligation). Note that the seller must be advised to seek legal advice before accepting a subsequent offer, unless it is simply a backup offer.

Most brokerages make a commitment to follow standards of conduct that exceed the minimum legal requirements. Ideally, the brokerage incorporates these standards into its policies and procedures manual, although those standards may instead be passed along more informally while training new licensees.

Personal Ethics. As a real estate professional, you will have your own personal code of ethics. This personal code may tell you that a given action is wrong even though it is technically legal or conforms to a professional code. In this case, it's best to trust your instincts. An agent who cuts ethical corners will eventually pay the price. Treat everyone the way you would wish to be treated.

Errors and Omissions Insurance and Breach of Duties

Over the course of a career, any real estate agent could face a claim by a customer or client that the agent violated her legal duties. And most branch managers and designated brokers will sooner or later have to deal with claims stemming from the actions of the licensees working under them.

Errors and omissions insurance, like the malpractice insurance carried by other types of professionals, helps cover the costs that arise from such a lawsuit. E&O insurance, as it's commonly called, pays claims that result from a licensee's **error**, **omission**, or **negligence** relating to his agency duties. The insurance company will cover the costs of the licensee's defense, and pay any settlement or judgment up to the limit stated in the policy.

However, like most insurance policies, E&O insurance has a deductible, so a portion of the costs will not be covered.

It's generally advisable for all licensees to have E&O coverage, either under their brokerage firm's policy or by obtaining their own individual policy.

Conclusion

Most real estate agents are honest and hardworking, and very few intentionally commit fraud. But only the very lucky get through a lengthy real estate career without some problems arising, often because of carelessness or mistakes.

Washington's real estate agency statute spells out a licensee's duties to his principal and to third parties. Make sure you're familiar with all of the requirements and keep up to date with any changes in the law. Also, a professional association's code of ethics can provide useful guidance to help you avoid legal trouble and build a stronger practice.

Case Problem

The following is a hypothetical case problem. Most of the facts are taken from a real case. Based on what you have learned from this chapter, make a decision on the issues presented, and then check to see if your answer matches the court's decision.

The Facts

Marjorie Belote and a co-owner owned over 1,000 acres of wheat land in Whitman County. On May 19, 1970, a written 90-day listing on the property was given to agent Owen Koller at a listing price of approximately $500,000.

Koller telephoned the owners to see if they would be interested in trading the farm for a building in Lewiston, Idaho, owned by Gerald Anderson. For purposes of a trade, this building and the adjacent parking lot were worth approximately $400,000. The owners said they were not interested in a trade, but wanted an outright sale.

In June, Koller contacted the owners several times about the exchange and sent them a brochure on the building. After much insistence by Koller, the owners finally flew to Lewiston to inspect the building and arranged to have the building appraised.

Without the owners' approval, Koller obtained a copy of their appraisal of Anderson's building and gave it to Anderson. The owners were very upset when they learned that Anderson had a copy of the appraisal, because they had paid $300 for it and considered it privileged information. Some negotiation concerning the trade occurred, but the trade never took place. The listing agreement expired and the owners had no further contact with Koller.

In October, Anderson began to negotiate with the owners for the direct purchase of the property without a trade. Anderson eventually purchased the property in January.

The owners later learned that their agent, Koller, had been a friend of Anderson for several years and had made a number of sales on his behalf. They discovered that Koller and Anderson had agreed that if a trade of the building for the property were made, Koller would receive a commission from Anderson of approximately $24,000.

Koller never disclosed to the owners that this agreement existed. It further appeared that Anderson was willing to make a direct sale at any time if a trade could not be arranged. It was clearly always the owners' preference to make a direct sale, but Koller never disclosed this possibility to the owners.

On the brochures of the building that Koller sent to the owners, the following information appeared:

> "FARM & BUSINESS REALTY INC."
> Suite 209 Davenport Hotel, Spokane, Wash. 99201
> MA4-2121
> Owen F. Koller—Broker

Koller brought a lawsuit against the owners claiming that he was entitled to a commission, since they sold the property to a purchaser whom he introduced to the property during the term of the exclusive listing agreement.

The Questions

Is Koller entitled to the commission? Did Koller breach any duty? Was the information printed on the brochure enough to inform the owners that Koller was also an agent for Anderson, and their subsequent negotiation proof that they approved of the dual agency?

The Answer

In the case of *Koller v. Belote*, 12 Wn. App. 194, 528 P.2d 1000 (1974), the court held that Koller was not entitled to a commission. The court also awarded $1,071 to the owners for transportation costs and expenses in visiting Lewiston at Koller's insistence.

The court found that Koller had failed to disclose the existence of a dual agency relationship and obtain the parties' consent. The mere transmittal of a brochure upon which the agent's name was listed was not enough to satisfy this duty of disclosure.

In addition, Koller failed to disclose a potential conflict of interest: his long-standing friendship with the prospective buyer. Furthermore, he placed his own interests above those of the principals by pushing the trade over a direct sale, which was clearly contrary to the express desires of the owners.

The court also found that Koller had breached his duty to the sellers by transmitting confidential information (the appraisal) to Anderson.

Note that this case was decided prior to the enactment of Washington's Real Estate Brokerage Relationships Act. Under the current law, Koller would also have been required to give a real estate agency law pamphlet to each of the parties and make a written agency disclosure to each party before the sales contract was signed.

Chapter Summary

- Real estate agency relationships in Washington are governed by general agency law and the real estate agency statute.

- A real estate agent must put her principal's interests above her own and those of third parties, and must also disclose any conflicts of interest. She may not disclose her principal's confidential information, even after the agency ends. She must advise the principal to seek expert advice when necessary. She must also make a good faith and continuous effort to fulfill the agency agreement's terms.

- A secret profit is any financial benefit obtained by the agent as a result of the agency that was not authorized by the principal.

- When dealing with any party in a transaction (including the principal), a real estate agent must use reasonable care and skill, act with honesty and good faith, present all written communications in a timely manner, disclose all material facts, and properly account for all funds received in a transaction. The agent must also give a real estate agency law pamphlet to every party to whom he provides services, and must make a written agency disclosure to each party in a transaction before that party signs an offer.

- An agent or principal who makes misrepresentations or conceals information may be held liable for fraud if a third party acts in reliance on the misinformation. Fraud may be actual (intentional) or constructive (negligent). Puffing, predictions, and opinions are generally not actionable.

- Unless otherwise agreed, an agent has no duty to inspect the property or independently investigate or verify information provided by either party or any reasonable source. However, an agent can be held liable for failing to verify information after having agreed to do so, or for negligently disregarding indications that the information is incorrect.

- A material fact is one with a substantial negative impact on the property's value or a party's ability to perform, or one that would defeat the purpose of the transaction. A latent defect is one that would not be discovered through an ordinary inspection. Any known latent defects must be disclosed to the parties.

- In Washington, a seller of real property generally must provide the buyer with a seller disclosure statement within five business days after their agreement is signed. The buyer then has three business days to decide whether to rescind or proceed with the transaction. If a new problem comes to light before closing, the seller must take corrective action or amend the disclosure statement.

- Adhering to personal and professional ethical standards will help a real estate agent avoid legal problems, and it makes good business sense over the long run. But it's also advisable for an agent to have errors and omissions coverage.

Checklist of Problem Areas

Real Estate Licensee's Checklist

❑ Have you provided the real estate agency law pamphlet to all appropriate parties?

❑ Have you disclosed which party or parties you're representing in the transaction and included written confirmation in the purchase and sale agreement?

❑ Have all of your statements to the seller and to the buyer been truthful and accurate?

❑ Have you fully disclosed all known material facts to the seller and to the buyer, while also protecting your principal's confidential information?

❑ If you and/or your firm are acting as dual agent(s), have you disclosed that to both parties and obtained their written consent?

❑ If the potential purchaser is your friend, relative, or business associate, have you disclosed that to the seller in writing?

Seller's Checklist

❑ Have you been truthful with your agent and with potential buyers concerning all material facts about the property, and have you filled out the required disclosure statement?

❑ Have you made clear to your agent what terms of sale are acceptable to you? Does your agent know what information you want kept confidential?

❑ Have you asked your agent for relevant financial information about the buyer?

Buyer's Checklist

❑ Make sure you know who the real estate agent who's helping you is working for. Even though the agent is showing you property and answering your questions, she may be the seller's agent.

❑ Remember that you can't rely on puffing, opinions, or predictions. Such statements, even if untrue, are generally not actionable.

❑ Ask questions; the agent or the seller may simply forget to tell you certain things if you don't ask. (However, the agent and the seller have a legal obligation to disclose all known material facts even if you don't ask.)

❑ Do you understand your rights under Washington's seller disclosure law? Have you examined the seller's disclosure statement carefully?

Chapter Quiz

1. A listing agent should disclose all of the following to a purchaser, EXCEPT:

   a. the listed property has a latent defect

   b. the agent is aware of some problems with the septic tank

   c. the property owner has expressed a willingness to accept less than the asking price

   d. the property is currently classified as a nonconforming use

2. Without the seller's permission, an agent tells a potential buyer that her client is experiencing financial difficulties and needs to sell immediately at any cost. The agent:

   a. was obligated to disclose this information to the buyer

   b. has breached the duties of loyalty and confidentiality by disclosing this information to the buyer

   c. should have disclosed this information if it helped to close a sale

   d. was right to disclose this information only if the buyer had already made an offer

3. A property is listed for $208,950. The agent finds an interested buyer who wants to offer $183,000, which is well below what the agent knows the seller will accept. What should the agent do?

   a. Write the offer and submit it to the seller as is

   b. Write the offer but don't submit it to the seller

   c. Refuse to write the offer because, as agent for the seller, the licensee is authorized to reject unacceptable offers

   d. Refuse to write the offer and notify the seller in writing of that refusal

4. It is 28° in January in Spokane. The furnace in a seller's house is broken. He has been heating the house by using the oven and several portable heaters. Right before a buyer comes to look at the house, the seller shuts off the oven and hides the heaters. He tells the buyer that the furnace works great. The seller is guilty of:

   a. constructive fraud

   b. actual fraud

   c. puffing

   d. negligence

5. A real estate agent tells potential buyers, "This is a great old house. They just don't build them like they used to." This statement would be considered:

   a. a misrepresentation

   b. constructive fraud

   c. self-dealing

   d. puffing

6. A buyer tells the listing agent in confidence that there are going to be some zoning changes that will have a favorable effect on the property. The listing agent passes this information on to the seller. The agent:

   a. has fulfilled his fiduciary duty to the seller

   b. has violated the license law

   c. may owe damages to the buyer

   d. has committed a crime

7. Harold wants to list his house with Angela. He asks her what the property is worth. Angela says she is no expert, but the house is probably worth $275,000 and he should consider listing it at $278,500. However, she warns him that if he wants an accurate, professional assessment of the home's value, he should ask an appraiser. Harold relies on Angela's estimate and lists the house at $278,000. He turns down three offers for $262,000, thinking the price is too low. He later discovers his house is really worth $260,000. Before Harold can relist it at the lower price, the stock market crashes, interest rates go sky-high, and Harold's property value decreases by $20,000. Harold sues Angela for breach of her fiduciary duty, asking for $20,000 in damages.

   a. Angela will be held liable because she misrepresented Harold's property value
   b. Angela will probably not be liable because she did not hold herself out as an expert and recommended that Harold ask an appraiser
   c. Angela will not be held liable because it is not her fault that the economy suffered such a severe setback
   d. Angela will be held liable because she was not able to find a ready, willing, and able buyer at her suggested listing price

8. Cheryl Burgess hired agent Tom Osling to sell her property. Tom is a limited partner in a local land development company that purchased the property. Tom did not tell Cheryl that he had any interest in the company that purchased the property.

   a. Tom did not need to disclose this information, since he was only a limited partner and not a general partner
   b. Tom breached his duty to Cheryl by not disclosing this information, and may be considered a dual agent
   c. Tom did not need to disclose this information since it was only a business relationship
   d. Tom could not be charged with dual agency, since he received no commission from the development company

9. Agent Bob has a listing to sell Sam's house for $519,000. Bob's sister is interested in purchasing the house. Bob tells Sam that the purchaser is his sister and that her offer is $517,000. Sam says he doesn't care who the buyer is, but he won't go below $518,000. They close the deal at $518,000.

   a. The sale is invalid because an agent can't sell to a member of his family
   b. Bob adequately fulfilled his duty by disclosing who the buyer was to Sam
   c. The sale is valid, but Bob cannot earn any commission on the transaction
   d. Bob should have told his sister that she would have to work through another agent

10. Who must follow the National Association of REALTORS® Code of Ethics?

    a. All U.S. real estate agents
    b. All NAR members
    c. All Washington real estate licensees
    d. No one; the Code is optional

11. Should a brokerage's code of ethics exceed the requirements imposed by the state's real estate license law?

    a. No, that would be illegal
    b. No, that would be impossible; state law specifies the highest possible ethical standards
    c. Yes, creating higher standards is the main reason for an independent code of ethics
    d. Yes, state license law doesn't touch on ethical concerns for agents

12. The letters E and O in the phrase "E&O insurance" stand for:

    a. executives and officers
    b. easements and other encumbrances
    c. ethics and omissions
    d. errors and omissions

13. E&O insurance is mainly designed to protect against the cost of:

    a. property damage
    b. professional negligence
    c. theft from the brokerage
    d. workplace injuries

14. Babette has a listing on a charming 1930s Craftsman bungalow. Are there any particular disclosures to buyers that are required simply because of the house's age?

    a. Yes, a termite disclosure
    b. Yes, an asbestos disclosure
    c. No, just the usual latent defect disclosures
    d. Yes, a lead paint disclosure

15. Emilio makes an offer on a house and the seller accepts. Emilio receives the seller disclosure statement on Friday. He reads it over and on Monday talks to a contractor about the costs of repairs. He thinks things over. On Tuesday he notifies the seller that he's rescinding the transaction. The seller says Emilio can't do this. Who is right?

    a. The seller; the buyer has just three days to rescind
    b. The seller; if everything is disclosed, there is no right of rescission
    c. The buyer; only business days are counted in determining when the right of rescission ends
    d. The buyer; the right of rescission lasts five days

8 Contract Law

Outline

VI. Real Estate Contracts
  A. Licensee affiliation agreements
  B. Listing agreements
    1. Types of listing agreements
    2. Basic elements
  C. Purchase and sale agreements
    1. Parties, property, and terms of sale
    2. Contingencies
    3. Other common provisions
    4. Acceptance or counteroffer
  D. Options
    1. Consideration for an option
    2. Relation back
    3. Assignment
    4. Termination
    5. Right of first refusal

Key Terms

- Express/implied contract
- Executory/executed contract
- Valid contract
- Void
- Voidable
- Unenforceable
- Disaffirm
- Capacity
- Emancipated minor
- Offer
- Acceptance
- Objective intent
- Revocation
- Mailbox rule
- Counteroffer
- Fraud
- Undue influence
- Duress
- Business compulsion
- Unilateral mistake
- Consideration
- Severable
- Statute of frauds
- Promissory estoppel
- Detrimental reliance
- Assignment
- Novation
- Accord and satisfaction
- Material breach
- Substantial performance
- Time is of the essence
- Contingency clause
- Tender offer
- Anticipatory repudiation
- Mandatory arbitration
- Contractual arbitration
- Statute of limitations
- Parol evidence rule
- Damages
- Mitigation
- Liquidated damages
- Equitable remedies
- Injunction
- Rescission
- Cancellation
- Specific performance
- Integration clause
- Extender clause
- Bump clause
- Option
- Relation back
- Right of first refusal

Chapter Overview

A **contract** is an agreement to do (or not do) a certain thing. It doesn't have to be a legal document; a spoken promise, a bus pass, and a movie ticket are all examples of contracts. To be enforced by a court, a contract must be made according to the rules of contract law. These rules are designed to protect the parties against misunderstandings and false claims.

A typical real estate sales transaction involves a number of contracts: a listing agreement; a purchase and sale agreement; a title insurance policy; an escrow agreement; and a security instrument, such as a deed of trust. Because contracts are such an integral part of real estate transactions, it's essential for real estate agents to understand basic contract law.

This chapter discusses forming and modifying a contract, the remedies available when a contract is breached, and several specific types of contracts used in real estate transactions.

Contract Classifications

There are several fundamental ways of classifying all contracts. Every contract is:

- express or implied,
- executory or executed, and
- valid, voidable, void, or unenforceable.

Express vs. Implied. An **express** contract is an agreement that has been expressed in words, either spoken or written. If Miller asks Simpson, "Will you cut my hair for $10?" and Simpson says, "OK," they have an express contract. An **implied** contract, on the other hand, hasn't been put into words. Instead, the agreement is implied by the actions of the parties.

> **Example:** Ferris offers to mow George's lawn for $25. George accepts and is pleased with the work. Without being asked, Ferris begins coming on the first Saturday of every month to mow George's lawn. George pays Ferris in cash after each job is finished.
> One Saturday Ferris shows up to mow the lawn and is greeted by a housesitter who says George is on vacation for a few days. Ferris goes ahead and mows the lawn anyway. Under their implied contract, George is obligated to pay for the mowing job.

Some contracts are partly express and partly implied. When you order a meal in a restaurant, it's understood that you agree to pay the price on the menu, although you don't actually say that to the waiter.

Executed vs. Executory. An **executed** contract is one that has been fully performed—both parties have done what they promised to do. An **executory** contract has not yet been fully performed. One or both of the parties have not begun to carry out their promises, or are in the process of carrying them out. Contracts start out executory and end up executed.

Valid, Void, Voidable, or Unenforceable. A **valid** contract is an agreement that meets all the legal requirements for contract formation outlined in the next section of this chapter. If one of the parties doesn't fulfill his side of the bargain (**breaches** the contract), the other can sue to have the contract enforced.

But many agreements don't meet one or more of the requirements for contract formation. These agreements are usually considered legally void. In the eyes of the law, a **void** contract is actually not a contract at all; it can't be enforced in court. If both parties fulfill

Fig. 8.1 Agreements may or may not be legally binding

Status of Contract	Legal Effect	Example
Void	No contract at all	An agreement for which there is no consideration
Voidable	Valid until rescinded by one party	A contract with a minor
Unenforceable	Party may not sue for performance	A contract after the limitations period has expired
Valid	Binding and enforceable	An agreement with all the requirements for a valid contract

their promises, all is fine. But if one breaches and the other sues, the judge will rule that no contract was formed, and will refuse to enforce the agreement.

In certain situations, an agreement that is missing a legal requirement is not void, but rather **voidable** by one party. This generally occurs when one party has taken advantage of the other in some way. For example, if someone has signed a contract as a result of undue influence exerted by the other party, the injured party can choose whether or not to go through with the contract. The injured party can **disaffirm** the contract—that is, ask a court to terminate it. If the injured party chooses not to disaffirm, the agreement will be enforceable. In the next section, we'll cover the various situations in which a contract is voidable rather than void.

Finally, some contracts are **unenforceable** even when they are not void or voidable. For example, a valid contract becomes unenforceable when the statute of limitations runs out. Or maybe all the requirements for contract formation were met, but there isn't proper evidence to prove that in court. (This problem often occurs with oral contracts.) A contract is also likely to be unenforceable if it is vaguely worded.

Contract Formation

A valid contract must have these four elements:

- capacity to contract,
- mutual consent,
- consideration, and
- a lawful purpose.

These requirements apply to all contracts. In addition, certain contracts (especially real estate contracts) must be in writing and signed to be enforceable.

Capacity

To enter into a valid contract, a person must be at least **18 years old** and must also be legally **competent**. This requirement protects minors and the mentally disabled, who otherwise might enter into contracts without understanding the consequences. Only the legal guardian can enter into a valid, binding contract on behalf of a minor or an incompetent person.

Minority. If a minor enters into a contract, the contract is voidable, but only by the minor. The minor can decide whether he wants to go through with the transaction. If not, the minor can go to court to disaffirm the contract. But if the minor does want to go through with it, the other party is bound.

> **Example:** Martinson, who is only 17, signs a contract to buy some property from Stuart. A week later, Stuart decides it wasn't a very good deal. However, only Martinson can disaffirm the contract. Stuart must fulfill the terms of the contract if Martinson chooses to go through with it.

A minor must disaffirm a voidable contract before he turns 18, or within a reasonable time after turning 18.

Note, however, that a contract with an emancipated minor is valid. An **emancipated minor** is a person under 18 who:

- is or has been married,
- is on active duty in the armed forces, or
- has a declaration of emancipation from a court.

Incompetence. A person who is entirely without understanding cannot make a contract. After a person has been declared incompetent by a court (because of mental disability or senility), any contract she enters into is void. If the person made a contract before the declaration of incompetence but while of unsound mind, the court-appointed guardian can ask the court to have that contract set aside.

In a few cases, if a person was under the influence of alcohol or other drugs at the time of entering into a contract, it will be voidable. But to disaffirm the contract, the person will usually have to prove that he was involuntarily intoxicated.

Necessities Exception. An exception to these capacity rules applies to a minor or an incompetent person who contracts to buy necessities (such as food, clothing, shelter or medicine). In this situation, the contract is not voidable and she must pay the reasonable value of those items.

Note that this exception applies only to necessities and not to items such as a car, a video game system, or sports equipment.

> **Example:** Jenelle, who is 16, goes on a spending spree at the mall. She buys a $900 stereo system, paying $100 cash and signing a contract agreeing to pay the balance over the next six months. When she goes home, her parents take one look at the stereo and tell her to take it back. Because Jenelle is a minor, she can return the stereo, disaffirm the contract, and get her money back.

Mutual Consent

For a contract to be a binding obligation, all the parties must consent to its terms. This mutual consent is sometimes referred to as a "meeting of the minds." It is achieved through **offer and acceptance**.

Offer. The process of forming a contract begins when one person (the **offeror**) makes an offer to another (the **offeree**). To be the basis for a contract, an offer must:

- express an intent to contract, and
- have definite terms.

The intent to contract must be **objective intent** (what the offeror says and does) rather than **subjective intent** (what the offeror is actually thinking). If you say or do something that a reasonable person could interpret as a serious expression of the intention to make a contract ("I'll sell you a dozen roses for $15"), that may be a legally binding offer even if you don't have any roses and never really intended to come up with them.

On the other hand, a casual remark or a joke is not a binding offer. Because of the nature of the remark, the tone of voice, or the situation, a reasonable person should not interpret the statement as a serious offer.

> **Example:** Rico has just paid $65,000 for a sports car. After it breaks down for the second time in a week, Rico tells Paulson, "I'm so tired of this piece of junk I'd sell it for ten bucks." Paulson pulls out her wallet and hands Rico a ten-dollar bill.
>
> Rico is not required to sell Paulson the car for ten dollars, because his statement was not a binding offer. A reasonable person would not have interpreted his remark as a serious expression of an intent to contract.

Here's how this issue played out in one Washington court case.

Case Example:

Warren Treece, vice president of Vend-A-Win (a corporation that distributed punchboards), spoke before the Washington State Gambling Commission in support of punchboards. During his speech, Treece offered to pay $100,000 to anyone who could find a crooked punchboard. His statement brought laughter from the audience.

Vernon Barnes heard a news report of Treece's statement. Several years earlier, Barnes had purchased two fraudulent punchboards. Barnes telephoned Treece, told him that he had two crooked punchboards and asked if Treece's offer was serious. Treece told Barnes the offer was serious, that the money was being held in escrow, and asked Barnes to bring in the punchboards for inspection.

The punchboards were inspected and found to be rigged and dishonest. However, Treece refused to pay Barnes the $100,000. Barnes brought a breach of contract action against Treece.

In his defense, Treece argued that his statement was made in jest, and could not be construed as an offer that could be accepted to form a contract.

The court found that although the original statement drew laughter from the audience, Treece's subsequent statements and conduct showed a serious intent.

The court found that there was a binding contract: Treece had promised to pay $100,000 to anyone who found a crooked board, and Barnes had found two crooked boards. The court awarded judgment for Barnes in the amount of $100,000. *Barnes v. Treece*, 15 Wn. App. 437, 549 P.2d 1152 (1976).

An offer must have **definite terms**—it won't be binding if it is too vague. It should state at least such basic terms as the subject matter, the time for performance, and the price. In some cases, a court will fill in the blanks with a reasonable time or a reasonable price.

Example: A waiter describes the day's "Seafood Special" without stating the dish's price. A restaurant diner orders and eats the dish without knowing its price. Unless the restaurant charges an unreasonably high price for the dish, a contract has been formed and the diner is obligated to pay for his meal.

However, if too many terms are left unspecified (for example, during preliminary negotiations for a contract), no contract has been formed.

If an offer to purchase involves financing, terms such as the interest rate or length of the loan term must be included in the offer.

Case Example:

The Setterlunds signed a purchase and sale agreement to buy some commercial real estate from the Firestones. The agreement provided that the sellers were to accept a promissory note and deed of trust as security for the $205,000 balance of the purchase price. However, a note and deed of trust were never attached to the agreement.

The Firestones did not go through with the sale and the Setterlunds sued for specific performance of the purchase contract. In other words, the Setterlunds asked the court to order the Firestones to complete the sale and transfer title to them.

The Firestones argued that the purchase and sale agreement was too indefinite to permit specific performance because the note and deed of trust were not attached. Thus, essential terms and conditions were missing. Since no note was attached, the parties had never agreed on an interest rate (a very important point with a balance of $205,000).

Preliminary agreements (such as purchase and sale agreements) must be definite enough to allow the court to enforce the agreement without having to supply important missing terms. In this case, the court would have needed to supply the missing interest rate.

The court found that the purchase and sale agreement was not definite enough to be enforced by specific performance. The Firestones could not be forced to go through with the sale. *Setterlund v. Firestone*, 104 Wn.2d 24, 700 P.2d 745 (1985).

Using pre-printed forms for real estate contracts such as listing agreements and purchase and sale agreements helps eliminate the possibility of vagueness. The pre-printed forms have spaces to fill in the contract's essential terms, making it less likely that a term will be overlooked.

Termination. An offer is not legally binding until it is accepted by the offeree. It can be accepted at any time before it terminates. An offer can be terminated by one of four events:

- lapse of time,
- death or incapacity of one of the parties,
- revocation by the offeror, or
- rejection by the offeree.

Lapse of time. Many offers state that they will expire at a certain time, such as "after five days" or "on March 30." When an offer doesn't specify an expiration date, a court will generally rule that it expired after a reasonable time. But even when an offer includes an expiration date, it may end sooner, through one of the other methods of termination.

Death or incapacity. An offer is terminated if either of the parties dies or becomes incompetent before it is accepted. A party's bankruptcy may also have this effect.

Revocation. If an offeror revokes the offer before the offeree accepts it, it is terminated—the offeree has lost the chance to accept it. This is true even if the offer stated that it was irrevocable, or that it would not expire until a particular date.

Case Example:

In July 1975, Seattle First National Bank foreclosed against the Knights' property. On December 16, 1976, the Knights learned that the bank was negotiating with Johnston to buy the property. At a meeting with the bank's attorney, Mrs. Knight was told that the bank would sell the property back to the Knights for the amount then owing (approximately $22,000). Mrs. Knight claimed that the bank told her it would not conclude the sale with Johnston for two or three weeks.

On December 22, with Johnston's approval, the bank entered into an agreement to sell the property to Patrick.

The Knights brought a lawsuit against the bank and argued that the offer by the bank to sell to them was an oral agreement to extend the time for redemption and that it was a binding agreement.

The court held that the bank's offer to Mrs. Knight was an offer that could be revoked or withdrawn any time before acceptance. The bank withdrew its offer when it sold to Patrick. *Knight v. Seattle First National Bank,* 22 Wn. App. 493, 589 P.2d 1279 (1979).

Note that the result would have been different if the Knights had paid the bank to keep the offer open for a few weeks. When an offeree pays or gives something to the offeror in exchange for holding an offer open, the offer cannot be revoked during the specified period. (See the discussion of options at the end of this chapter.) But without such a payment, an offer can be revoked at any time before it is accepted.

A revocation is effective as soon as it is communicated to the offeree. When it is not communicated directly (in person or over the telephone), the revocation is effective at the time it is received by the offeree. So if a notice of revocation is mailed to the offeree, the offer is not revoked until the revocation is delivered.

Rejection. An offer is also terminated when it is rejected by the offeree. If I reject your offer on Monday, I can't change my mind and call back on Tuesday to accept it. If you're still interested in the deal, we can start the process of offer and acceptance over again. But your original offer was terminated by my rejection, and if you've lost interest, I can no longer hold you to your offer.

Acceptance. When an offer is accepted, a contract is formed. At that point, the parties are legally bound. Neither party can back out unless the other is willing to call off the contract.

There are four basic requirements for acceptance:

- an offer can only be accepted by the offeree,
- an acceptance must be communicated to the offeror,
- an acceptance must be made in the manner specified, and
- an acceptance must not vary the terms of the offer.

Accepted by the offeree. The first of these requirements—that an offer can be accepted only by the offeree—may sound obvious. But it means that if Jeremy makes an offer to Arthur and Arthur decides not to accept it, Amy can't accept the offer and force Jeremy to deal with her. Of course, Jeremy may be willing to work with Amy, but in legal terms any contract between Jeremy and Amy is based on a new offer, not on the offer Jeremy made to Arthur.

Communicated to the offeror. An acceptance must be communicated to the offeror. You may already have decided to accept my offer, but until you let me know that you've accepted it, I can still revoke it.

> **Example:** Seller is selling waterfront property. Seller's agent tells Buyer that the frontage is about 800 feet. Buyer signs a purchase and sale agreement offering to buy the property and the agent delivers it to Seller. In the meantime, Buyer discovers that the frontage is only 700 feet. Buyer notifies Seller that he will not go through with the purchase.
>
> Seller sues. Seller claims that he signed the purchase and sale agreement the day he received it. But since he hadn't sent it back to Buyer yet, the acceptance was not communicated and Buyer still had the right to revoke.

Fig. 8.2 Offer and acceptance

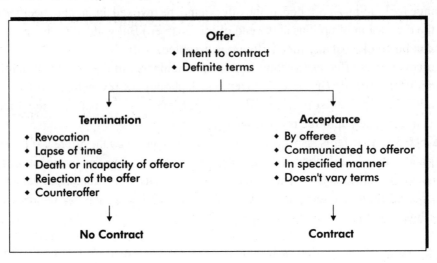

Mailbox rule. When an acceptance is not communicated directly (in person or over the telephone), it is effective as soon as the message is sent, even though the offeror may not receive it immediately. This is called the **mailbox rule**: the acceptance creates a binding contract when the offeree drops it in the mailbox. The mailbox rule may also be applied to communication of an acceptance by fax or email.

Manner of acceptance. As mentioned earlier, certain types of contracts (including most contracts concerning real property) are required by law to be in writing and signed. For those contracts, only a written, signed acceptance will bind the offeree.

> **Example:** Adams writes Bing a letter offering to sell him her house for $250,000. It's an excellent offer, so Bing calls Adams on the phone and says he's accepting it.
> Two hours later, Bing changes his mind. He can call Adams back and withdraw his acceptance, because it wasn't in writing.

However, other types of contracts do not necessarily require a written acceptance. Any reasonable method of acceptance will usually be effective, unless the offer specifies how it is to be accepted. If the offer specifies a particular method (such as "in writing," "by registered mail," or "by delivering a cashier's check"), the acceptance will not bind the offeror unless those instructions are followed.

> **Example:** Wallace offers to sell his antique car to Savala. The offer states it is to be accepted by registered mail. Savala drops by Wallace's office and tells him that she's accepting the offer. Wallace can still revoke the offer, because Savala did not accept the offer in the manner specified.

Of course, an offeror can waive this requirement. If Wallace chooses to treat Savala's spoken acceptance as effective, a contract is formed.

Note that generally, silence cannot be the specified manner of acceptance.

> **Example:** Xavier writes Zigler a letter offering to buy her sailboat for $2,000. The letter says, "If you have not rejected this offer by Saturday, I will consider it accepted." Zigler receives the letter but never replies.
>
> Xavier goes to Zigler's house with $2,000 and demands the boat. Zigler is not required to let him have it. Her silence in response to Xavier's letter was not an acceptance, and no contract was formed.

But if the offeree accepts the benefits of the offer, silence may be construed as acceptance. If Xavier had enclosed a $2,000 check with his letter and Zigler cashed it, she would be deemed to have accepted his offer and would be required to let him have the boat.

Acceptance must not vary terms of offer. To create a contract, the offeree must accept the terms exactly as offered. The offeree can't modify the terms of the offer or add any new terms.

Case Example:

The Flerchingers listed their ranch for sale with a brokerage and the listing expired without a sale. Koller, an agent at the brokerage, later went into business for himself and continued to seek a buyer for the Flerchinger property without the owners' knowledge.

Koller contacted Watson, who offered $150,000 for the property. Koller then attempted to get the Flerchingers to sign a purchase and sale agreement under which Koller would receive a $7,000 commission upon closing.

The Flerchingers signed the purchase and sale agreement, but only after the price was raised to $155,000 and a provision was added giving them the buildings and pasture for their cattle until October and possession of the current hay crop. After the Flerchingers signed the agreement, Koller edited out the new clause.

Koller never obtained Watson's signature to this agreement and after May 26, all parties treated the agreement as terminated.

The next month, Watson approached the Flerchingers directly and they reached a new agreement. Upon learning of the sale, Koller sued for a commission and lost. Although the Flerchingers eventually sold to Watson, it was not an acceptance of the original offer. Each change constituted a new offer or counteroffer. *Koller v. Flerchinger*, 73 Wn.2d 857, 441 P.2d 126 (1968).

Because the Flerchingers added terms (the additional $5,000 and retention of hay and pasture until October), they technically did not accept Watson's offer. Instead, they made a counteroffer. A **counteroffer** is essentially a new offer, so the Flerchingers became the offerors, and Watson became the offeree. To create a binding contract, Watson would have had to accept the Flerchingers' counteroffer (which he didn't do). Further negotiations took place before an agreement was finally reached.

A counteroffer terminates the original offer, just as a rejection would. If your counteroffer is rejected, it's too late to go back and accept the original offer. You can start again with a new offer identical to the original offer. But if the original offeror has had a change of heart, you can no longer hold him to the original offer. It's important to keep this in mind, since a real estate transaction often involves a series of offers and counteroffers. Each counteroffer terminates the previous offer.

Consent Freely Given. Offer and acceptance are the expression of mutual consent to the terms of an offer. But to create a binding contract, consent must be freely given. It is not freely given when it is the result of one of these negative influences:

- fraud,
- undue influence,
- duress, or
- mistake.

Any of these makes a contract voidable by the party who was harmed. The injured party may choose to go ahead with the contract or disaffirm it. To disaffirm, the victim must be able to show that the negative influence was the key to his consent.

Fraud. A victim of fraud must prove that she would not have entered into the contract if the other party had not misrepresented the effect of the agreement or made false promises. Recall from our discussion of fraud in Chapter 7 that fraud may be actual or constructive. For example, a seller who intentionally hides cracks in the basement and assures the buyer the foundation is sound is committing actual fraud. A seller who innocently points out incorrect lot boundaries may be committing constructive fraud.

It's also important to distinguish between fraud in the inducement and fraud in the execution of the contract. When **fraud in the inducement** occurs, a party understands what he is signing, but his signature is induced by fraud. The contract is voidable by the defrauded party.

> **Example:** A real estate agent convinces an owner to sign a listing agreement by falsely claiming the house is worth $100,000 more than its true value. This is fraud in the inducement.

When **fraud in the execution** is committed, the defrauded party does not know what he is signing and did not intend to enter into such a contract at all.

> **Example:** Two days before a sale closes, the listing agent hands his client a stack of papers, telling him that his signature is needed on each document for closing purposes. The client signs the documents, without realizing that one of the documents is actually a deed granting his property to the agent. This is fraud in the execution.

Undue influence. Taking unfair advantage of another person by using your influence over them is considered **undue influence**. A contract is voidable if you persuade someone to sign it by taking advantage of her trust in you, her weakness of mind (due to senility or exhaustion, for example), or her necessities or distress (drug addiction, for example). Undue influence often involves telling the victim that documents must be signed immediately, and that there's no time to consult a lawyer.

Case Example:

In 1972, John F. Jeanes was a Christian Science practitioner who met Nancy Ferguson when she was considering making a full commitment to Christian Science. They fell in love and began considering marriage. During their relationship, Nancy received treatment from John several times a week. At trial, she testified that she exalted practitioners in her mind and that she trusted John because of her affection for him and because of his role as a practitioner.

When Nancy decided to purchase an apartment building, John helped her locate some suitable property and began to encourage Nancy to take him on as a partner in the purchase. When Nancy declined, John became angry, telling her she was ungrateful and that her refusal violated the tenets of Christian Science. He also told her she was financially, intellectually, and emotionally incapable of buying and operating the property alone.

Nancy finally agreed to accept John as an equal partner. Nancy advanced nearly $13,000, while John provided less than $3,000, saying he had other immediate obligations and would pay more later. John later paid another $500 but never made any more payments. Whenever Nancy brought up the subject, he would assure her that he would pay later, and frequently became angry with her for bringing it up. Because of their close relationship, Nancy tolerated the delay and was confident that John would ultimately pay.

The relationship between Nancy and John ended in 1975. John subsequently refused to help pay an upcoming balloon payment on the apartment building's mortgage. Nancy also unsuccessfully attempted to secure a quitclaim deed from John. Nancy attempted to buy John out, but he refused to respond.

In 1978, Nancy filed an action to quiet title. The court found that John's performance as a practitioner had an immense influence upon Nancy, causing her to have an extraordinary amount of trust and confidence in him. It further found that John's emotional and spiritual influence over Nancy made her particularly susceptible to his influence. Where one party is under the domination of another, a transaction induced by unfair persuasion is the result of undue influence and is voidable.

The court found that the partnership agreement in the apartment house between Nancy and John was subject to rescission for undue influence. John was awarded the amount of his contribution plus interest, and title to the apartment house was quieted in Nancy's name alone. *Ferguson v. Jeanes*, 27 Wn. App. 558, 619 P.2d 369 (1980).

Duress. Illegal imprisonment or confinement, threats of bodily harm, threats of injury to a person's reputation, or the use of other means to coerce a person into doing what she otherwise would not do are all examples of **duress**. Any contract that is signed under duress is voidable by the injured party. This is true even if the actions or threats are taken against a third party, such as the person's spouse, child, or parent.

Washington courts have extended the concept of duress to include business compulsion. **Business compulsion** is a form of duress in which a person is threatened with a serious business loss. Entering into a disadvantageous contract because of financial necessity does not constitute business compulsion. For the doctrine to apply, the victim must prove that the offending party caused or contributed to the problem and exerted the pressure that brought about the decision to enter into the agreement.

For example, it is a form of business compulsion to coerce someone into signing a contract by threatening to take some action that will be financially disastrous for the victim, such as withholding a payment owed to the victim, or starting a groundless lawsuit in bad faith. However, the acts or threats of one party cannot amount to duress if there is a legal right to do the threatened act. For instance, threatening to bring a valid lawsuit is not duress.

Mistake. Unlike the other negative forces that can make a contract voidable, mistake does not usually involve any bad faith or villainy. If both parties are mistaken about some fact or law that is important to their contract, either of them may disaffirm the contract. This is known as **mutual mistake**.

Case Example:

Simonson and Teeter formed Northwest Furnace & Equipment Company. Teeter supplied the business expertise and Simonson supplied the capital. Fendell was hired as the general manager.

Simonson became disenchanted with the business and offered to sell his interest to Teeter and Fendell. Fendell wanted proof of the business's financial condition before negotiating to buy out Simonson. The parties conducted a complete inventory and the company accountant prepared a financial statement. The statement indicated the business was solvent and operating at a profit; all three believed this to be accurate.

The parties signed a contract in which Fendell and Teeter agreed to buy Simonson's interest for $75,000 by December 30, 1978.

In mid-December Fendell and Teeter discovered that $48,000 in accounts payable had been mistakenly omitted from the financial statement. The business was not making a profit and was actually insolvent.

Simonson brought a lawsuit seeking enforcement of the contract. Fendell and Teeter argued for rescission of the contract due to mutual mistake.

The court found that all parties believed the business was solvent and operating at a profit when the contract was signed. Since the contract would not have been formed but for the mutual mistake, Fendell and Teeter were entitled to rescission and the contract was not enforceable. *Simonson v. Fendell*, 101 Wn.2d 88, 675 P.2d 1218 (1984).

When only one of the parties to a contract is mistaken (**unilateral mistake**), the contract is not voidable unless the other party knew about the mistake and did nothing to correct it.

Trusts, Estates, and Other Entities as Parties. To conclude our discussion of the mutual consent element of contract formation, let's consider how a trust, estate, or other entity (e.g., a corporation or LLC) indicates consent to a contract. Specifically, if your client or customer is an entity instead of an individual, who exactly has authority to sign real estate agreements and related documents—such as deeds and promissory notes—on behalf of the entity?

Someone signing a document on behalf of an entity must be authorized to do so. For example, the executor of an estate in probate who wants to sell the deceased's home will have court papers showing that he is, in fact, the executor and that the sale has been authorized by the court (wills and probate are discussed further in Chapter 9).

> **Example:** Alan, an agent at Barrow Brokerage, makes a practice of scouring the obituaries for listing leads. Alan finds an executor named Sheila who is willing to sell a probate property through Barrow Brokerage.
>
> Alan's designated broker reviews a court-certified copy of the court order naming Sheila as the executor and any paperwork authorizing this specific sale. The designated broker also has the brokerage attorney examine these documents. (Note that brokerage policies may vary and may be a good deal more complex than this.)

Similarly, you may encounter a trustee who wants to sell the real estate of a deceased person ("living trusts" are often used as an alternative to a will and probate). The typical living trust provides that on the death of whoever created the trust, the trustee (essentially, the equivalent of the executor of a will) may sell or distribute the trust property. Again, your brokerage's practices will vary, but basically the trustee will have to produce the trust document that names her as trustee and grants her the power to sell, and also provide a copy of the death certificate to prove that the trust's creator is actually dead.

Finally, let's very briefly discuss how corporations and other business entities delegate authority to execute real estate transactions. Usually a corporate officer, often the president, will sign real estate agreements and related documents on behalf of the corporation. As a general rule, the officer must have specific written authorization for the transaction from the corporation's board of directors. A partnership is similar. While generally any partner has authority to enter into contracts on behalf of the partnership, for a major transaction like the sale or purchase of real estate, a document signed by all the partners authorizing the particular partner to carry out the transaction is usually required.

Consideration

Even after an offer has been accepted, there is no valid contract unless it is supported by consideration. **Consideration** is something of value exchanged by the parties. A contract can't be a one-way street: each party must give something to the other. The exchange of consideration is what distinguishes a contractual promise from the promise of a gift.

> **Example:** If Alan promises Barry his sweater in exchange for Barry's wheelbarrow, they have a contract. Each has given the other some consideration: Alan gave Barry a promise, and Barry gave Alan a promise.
>
> But if Alan promises Barry his sweater and Barry promises Alan nothing in return, there is no contract. The sweater is a gift.
>
> The distinction becomes important if, after making the promise, Alan fails to give Barry the sweater. In the first case, where Alan received consideration for his promise (Barry's promise to give him the wheelbarrow) Barry can sue Alan to enforce the promise.
>
> But in the second case, Barry can't sue Alan. The courts will not enforce a promise that is not supported by consideration. It wasn't nice of Alan to break his promise, but since the sweater was a gift instead of a contractual obligation, the law won't get involved.

Consideration can be anything of value—a sweater, $10, or a split-level ranch house. The consideration for most contracts is a promise to give something of value, as in the example above. For this reason, the parties to a contract are sometimes referred to as the **promisor** (the party making a promise) and the **promisee** (the party who is to receive the benefit of a promise).

In a typical real estate contract, the buyer promises to pay the seller money, and the seller promises to transfer title to the buyer. By exchanging promises they create an executory contract; when they fulfill their promises (when the buyer actually pays the seller and the seller actually gives the buyer the deed) the contract is executed.

To provide consideration for a contract, a promisor must either do something that benefits the promisee, or give something up. Promising to not do something can be consideration—for example, promising to stop smoking. Or if you don't smoke, promising never to start can be consideration.

But an empty promise is not consideration for a contract: if you've never smoked, promising to quit can't be consideration. And something that you've already done can't be consideration.

> **Example:** Andrew quit smoking, and Aunt Bernice is very pleased. Aunt Bernice says to Andrew, "Because you quit smoking, I'm going to buy you a yacht." This is not a contract; since Andrew had already quit smoking, he didn't really give Aunt Bernice anything (or give up anything) in exchange for Aunt Bernice's promise.

Also, promising to do something that you're already legally obligated to do (or promising to refrain from doing something that you're obligated to refrain from doing) is not consideration.

> **Example:** Williams agrees to build a house for Kessner for $200,000. When the house is over halfway done, Williams says, "You're going to have to pay me another $30,000 if you want me to finish this project." Kessner meekly agrees. This is not an enforceable contract; Williams can't sue Kessner for the additional $30,000, because Williams was already obligated to finish the house for $200,000.

Fig. 8.3. Requirements for a valid real estate contract

A Valid Real Estate Contract
◆ Capacity
◆ Mutual consent
◆ Lawful purpose
◆ Consideration
◆ In writing

Adequacy. It's important to understand that the value of the consideration one party gives doesn't have to equal the value of what the other gives. In other words, even though one party struck a bad bargain, the contract is still enforceable.

> **Example:** Peterson's house was appraised at $300,000. He's anxious to sell it very quickly, because he thinks he may have to leave the country in a hurry. When Marshall offers $215,000 for the house, Peterson accepts, and they execute a written contract.
>
> As it turns out, Peterson won't have to leave the country. He wants to back out of the sale, but Marshall wants to go through with it. Although Peterson's consideration is worth much more than what Marshall is giving, their contract is binding.

Of course, when the consideration is grossly unequal, that may be a sign that there was fraud, undue influence, duress, or mistake involved in the contract negotiations. But unless one of those negative forces is proven, the contract is enforceable.

Lawful Purpose

The purpose of a contract (sometimes called the objective or the object of the contract) must be lawful at the time the contract is made. If one person promises to pay another for committing an illegal act, their contract is void and cannot be enforced by a court. This may seem obvious; a hit man is unlikely to take his employer to court to collect his fee, and the employer is unlikely to sue him for failing to carry out the murder. But the requirement has a considerably broader application. Even when a contract's purpose does not violate an express provision of the law, a court may refuse to enforce it if it is contrary to public policy or accepted morals.

> **Example:** Lara asks Kerr, a contractor, to remodel her basement. Lara wants the job completed as soon as possible and Kerr offers to do the work without obtaining the required construction permits. Lara agrees and they sign a contract. This contract is void for lack of a lawful purpose.

Many contracts have more than one purpose, and they are often **severable**—it's possible to enforce one part without the rest. When one part of a contract is legal and another part is illegal, a court may set aside the illegal part and enforce the remaining provisions. But when a contract has a single purpose and that purpose is unlawful, then the entire contract is void.

The Statute of Frauds

The law that requires certain contracts to be in writing and signed is commonly known as the **statute of frauds**. As the name suggests, the writing requirement is intended to prevent fraudulent claims. The parties to an unwritten contract are likely to disagree later about what each agreed to do or whether they agreed to do anything. Putting a contract in writing helps eliminate that kind of dispute, because the document is solid evidence of the existence of an agreement and its essential terms.

The statute of frauds applies to any agreement that, by its terms, will not be performed within one year from the time it is made. It also applies to a promise to pay another's debt, or guarantee payment of another's debt.

Most importantly for licensees, the statute of frauds applies to any agreement authorizing or employing an agent to sell or purchase real estate for a commission or other compensation, and to any agreement for the purchase and sale of real estate. To be enforceable, these contracts must be in writing and signed.

The statute of frauds does not apply to a commission-splitting agreement between two brokerages. If a designated broker orally agrees to share a commission with another brokerage, there is a valid contract even if this agreement is never written down. The cooperating agent can sue the listing agent to collect his share.

The writing required by the statute of frauds doesn't have to be a formal legal document. A note or memorandum is enough, if it indicates there is an agreement between the parties and it is signed.

Case Example:

Seck, a real estate agent, had known Foulks for a long time. Foulks asked Seck to help him sell his ranch in Sacramento County, and Seck agreed.

However, Foulks refused to give Seck a formal listing agreement. "You know doggone well, you know me, I'm not going to cheat you out of a commission," Foulks said. But Seck took out one of his business cards and jotted down the basic terms of the listing on the back of the card. It looked like this:

310 M/L
2000 per acre
½ down
bal. 5 years
5% int
quarterly with int

keep taxes up to date
½ mineral rights
6% comm
10/1/65

Seck then asked Foulks to initial and date the card. Foulks wrote, "3/24/65 GWF."

Seck found a buyer for the ranch, but Foulks refused to pay Seck a commission. When Seck sued, Foulks argued that the notes on the business card weren't enough to comply with the statute of frauds. But the court disagreed. The court said that all Seck needed was a written, signed memorandum indicating the fact of employment. This requirement was fulfilled by "6% comm" and Foulks's initials on the business card. *Seck v. Foulks*, 25 Cal. App. 3d 556, 102 Cal. Rptr. 170 (1972).

This case clearly shows that in order to satisfy the statute of frauds, the writing doesn't have to be very formal. Although this is a California case, Washington also follows the rule that a writing is sufficient to satisfy the statute of frauds if it clearly indicates the agreement between the parties and is signed.

To comply with the statute of frauds, a contract only needs to be signed by "the party to be charged"—that is, the one who's being sued. For example, it didn't matter that Seck hadn't signed the business card, as long as Foulks had. A full signature is unnecessary; initials are enough. In fact, anything that the signer intends as a signature will do. But it may be difficult to prove that a wavy line or an "X" was someone's signature if that person later denies it.

Once you've signed a contract, you're bound by its terms, even if you claim you never read it. An illiterate person should ask someone trustworthy to explain all the terms of a written agreement before signing it. The same is true for a person signing a document written in a foreign language. Of course, if someone convinces another person to sign a document by misrepresenting its contents, fraud has occurred and the contract is voidable.

Here's another point about written contracts. Many standard contract forms include a paragraph stating that the document represents the entire agreement between the parties. This is called an **integration clause**. When a contract contains an integration clause, neither party can rely on any oral promises or side agreements that the other makes. Any terms that are not included in the written document are unenforceable.

Promissory Estoppel

Many people don't know what the requirements for a valid contract are, and as a result they are surprised to discover that a promise someone made to them is unenforceable. The outcomes of some contract lawsuits can seem very unfair.

To prevent unfairness in at least some cases, the courts have developed the doctrine of **promissory estoppel** (also called the doctrine of **detrimental reliance**). Under this doctrine, a court may enforce a promise that is lacking consideration, a signed writing, or some other contract requirement.

A party attempting to enforce a promise under the theory of promissory estoppel must show the court that the following type of situation exists:

1. Able made a promise to Brown;
2. Able should have expected that his promise would cause Brown to take some action;
3. Brown did take action, in reasonable reliance on Able's promise; and
4. as a result, Brown will be harmed if Able's promise is not enforced.

In such a case, a court may decide to enforce the promise, even though no valid contract exists.

> **Example:** Martha, Stan's mother, bought a large tract of land and promised to give it to Stan. Stan cleared and fenced the land, built a house on it, and moved in with his wife.
> Two years later, Martha and Stan have a fight. Martha tells Stan and his wife to get off her property, but they refuse to leave. Martha sues to regain possession of her land.
> Martha's promise to Stan was not originally enforceable, since Stan did not give Martha any consideration in exchange for her promise, and there was no signed writing. But the court uses the doctrine of promissory estoppel to rule in Stan's favor. Martha should have realized that her promise would induce action by Stan, and she was in fact aware of all his work on the property. Stan's reliance on Martha's promise was reasonable, so the court rules that Stan and his wife are entitled to possession of the property.

Note that the doctrine of promissory estoppel will be applied only when the promisee's reliance on the promise was reasonable. For example, a real estate agent who does not have a written listing cannot use promissory estoppel to collect a commission. The agent should know that a written agreement is necessary—it is not reasonable for the agent to rely on a client's oral promise.

Modification of a Contract

When both parties agree that their written contract contains an error or omission, they can simply correct it. But to make a more substantial change in the contract, they usually must exchange additional consideration. In effect, the modification is a separate contract; like any other contract, it must be supported by consideration or it is unenforceable.

Assignment or Novation

When one party transfers his rights and duties under a contract to another person, it is either an **assignment** or a **novation**.

As a general rule, either party to a contract may **assign** her contractual rights to another party. But this right may be limited by the contract itself: a contract often provides that one party can't assign it without the other party's consent.

Example: Lightfoot and Tanner sign a two-year residential lease. It provides that Tanner, the tenant, cannot assign her rights under the lease (the right to live on the property) to anyone else without Lightfoot's permission.

However, the contract doesn't prevent Lightfoot from assigning his rights to someone else without Tanner's permission. Lightfoot assigns the lease to Clarke; Lightfoot is the assignor and Clarke is the assignee. Now Tanner is required to pay rent to Clarke.

Even without a provision prohibiting assignment, a contract for personal services, such as a listing agreement, cannot be assigned without consent. If I contract to have you play the piano at a party, you can't send your sister over instead of showing up yourself. A contract also can't be assigned without consent if the assignment would significantly change the other party's duties or increase her risks.

It's important to keep in mind that an assignor isn't relieved of all liability under the contract. Suppose the assignee doesn't carry out his contractual duties. The other party sues, but the assignee turns out to be judgment-proof (has no money or assets). The assignor is **secondarily liable**, and can be required to pay the other party if the assignee doesn't.

To avoid secondary liability, a party who wants to withdraw from a contract should request a novation instead of an assignment. In a **novation**, a new person takes the place of one of the parties, and the withdrawing party is completely relieved of liability connected with the contract.

But a novation can be arranged only with the other original party's consent. A novation is essentially a new contract, so it must comply with all the rules for contract formation, including the mutual consent requirement.

Note that the term "novation" doesn't necessarily refer to the substitution of a new party. It can also refer to the substitution of a new obligation in place of the original one. If the original parties tear up a two-year lease and execute a five-year lease, a novation has occurred.

Accord and Satisfaction

Sometimes a promisee agrees to accept something different or less than what the original contract required the promisor to provide. This kind of agreement is called an **accord**; it does not have to be supported by separate consideration. To extinguish the promisor's original obligation, the promisee executes a **satisfaction**—a document expressly stating that the promisor's performance has been accepted in satisfaction of the obligation.

Release

A contractual obligation can be eliminated altogether if the promisee grants the promisor a release. An oral release is valid if the promisee receives some new consideration; a written release doesn't have to be supported by new consideration. If the contract had to be in writing because of the statute of frauds, the release should also be in writing.

Breach of Contract

Now that you are familiar with how contracts are created and modified, let's take a look at what happens when a contract is breached.

If one party to a contract performs his side of the bargain, the other party is required to perform, too. But if one party fails to perform (**breaches** the contract), the other is not required to perform. If I agree to build you a house for $250,000 and I don't build the house, you don't owe me $250,000.

Substantial Performance vs. Material Breach

In most cases, each party carries out the promised performance to the other's satisfaction. And in certain cases, one party clearly fails to do what she promised. But sometimes it's not so clear-cut.

> **Example:** One party to a contract, Abernathy, does everything he promised, but the other party, Bono, feels that the quality of Abernathy's work was substandard. Or Abernathy does nearly everything promised, but some details are overlooked. Or Abernathy does everything promised, but takes longer to do it than agreed. In these cases, there is room for argument about whether or not the contract was breached. Is Bono required to perform his side of the bargain?

The answer to that question depends on whether there has been substantial performance or a material breach. If Abernathy hasn't fulfilled every detail of the contract but has carried out its main objectives, that may be treated as **substantial performance**. Although Bono may be able to sue for damages because of the unfulfilled details, they don't excuse Bono from performing his side of the bargain.

If Abernathy fails to perform some important part of the contract, or performs very badly, that will be treated as a **material breach**. If Abernathy commits a material breach, Bono is excused from fulfilling his promises. If Bono doesn't perform, he won't be liable to Abernathy for breach of their contract, because Abernathy already breached it. (If Bono has already fully performed, Abernathy will be required to pay him damages for breach of contract.)

What provisions of a contract are so important that failure to fulfill them amounts to a material breach? That depends on all the circumstances of each case. If the promisee emphasized to the promisor that a particular detail of the contract was especially important, failure to comply with that detail may be a material breach. On the other hand, if the promisee acted as though a detail was unimportant, failure to comply with it isn't a material breach.

> **Example:** Grace hires Jorgen to build her a house based on her design. According to the plans, the hallways are to be a standard three feet wide. After construction is completed, Grace inspects the house and determines that the hallways are a half inch too wide. She is angry and withholds her final payment to Jorgen, who in turn sues for payment on their contract. A court would likely find that Jorgen has substantially performed and no material breach has occurred.

Time is of the Essence. Many standard contract forms state that "time is of the essence of this agreement." The purpose of including that phrase is to emphasize that timely performance is crucial. That makes failure to meet a deadline a material breach. Otherwise, a delay isn't a material breach, as long as performance is completed within a reasonable time after the deadline. However, note that the phrase often doesn't have any real effect. Unless the parties actually insist on timely performance, a court is likely to hold that the "time is of the essence" clause has been waived. Don't let deadlines slip by if timely completion of the transaction is important to you.

Conditions

Contracts often include one or more **conditions** (sometimes called **contingency clauses**). A **condition** makes the promisor's obligation depend on the occurrence of a particular event. If the event does not occur, the promisor can withdraw without liability for breach of contract. For example, many purchase and sale agreements are contingent on the buyers qualifying for financing, or on the results of an appraisal, termite inspection, or soil test.

When a contract is conditional, the promisor must make a good faith effort to fulfill the condition. He can't deliberately prevent its fulfillment in order to get out of the contract.

Case Example:

The Egberts agreed to buy a 98-acre field from Mrs. Way. The offer to purchase was conditional on Mrs. Way clearing flaws in the title within one year. Encumbrances on the title included state inheritance tax and federal estate tax liens.

Within the next year, Mrs. Way failed to file tax returns necessary to release the encumbrances on the property. The Egberts filed suit for specific performance.

The court found that Mrs. Way had an obligation to make a good faith effort to clear the tax liens on the property. By her own admission, she had done nothing to pay these taxes. The court ordered Mrs. Way to perform her part of the contract. *Egbert v. Way*, 15 Wn. App. 76, 546 P.2d 1246 (1976).

A condition can be waived by the party it was intended to benefit or protect.

Example: A purchase and sale agreement is contingent on a satisfactory termite inspection. If the results of the inspection are unsatisfactory, the buyer can withdraw from the purchase unless the seller corrects the problems revealed.

The inspection shows that the house is infested with termites. The seller informs the buyer that she is not going to correct the problem, but the buyer decides to go ahead with the purchase. The buyer has a right to waive the condition, because it was included in the contract for his protection.

When a condition is included for the benefit of both parties, however, neither one can waive it without the other's consent.

Tendering Performance

In many cases, Party A has reason to believe that Party B is not going to fulfill the contract. The time for performance has arrived, and Party B hasn't taken any steps toward carrying out her side of the bargain. Before Party A can sue Party B for breach of contract, Party A must offer to perform his side of the bargain. This offer of performance is called a **tender offer** or simply a **tender**.

> **Example:** Lin contracted to buy Maxwell's house, but Maxwell suspects Lin doesn't plan to go through with the purchase. Maxwell must offer to deliver the deed to Lin as promised in their contract. If Lin refuses to pay Maxwell and accept the deed, Lin is in default, and Maxwell may sue.

A tender must be made in good faith. In other words, the tendering party must be willing and able to perform everything he promised, fully and immediately. The tender must be unconditional, unless the contract contained a condition that the other party hasn't fulfilled yet.

It is not necessary to tender performance when there has been an **anticipatory repudiation**. If Lin repudiates the contract by notifying Maxwell that she won't perform, Maxwell can file suit for breach without making a tender. The tender would be a waste of time. But an anticipatory repudiation must be a clear, unequivocal statement. Maxwell can't infer repudiation from Lin's behavior or from a vague remark.

Remedies for Breach

When a promisor has performed badly, or has refused to perform at all (either by anticipatory repudiation or by rejecting the tender offer), she has breached the contract. Then the promisee can turn to the legal system for help in enforcing the contract.

Arbitration

As we discussed in Chapter 1, it can take many months for a case to get to trial. The complexity of a trial also increases legal costs. To expedite dispute resolution and lower the cost, more and more contracts include an arbitration provision.

Arbitration is an alternative to the court system. An arbitrator performs the functions of a judge, reviewing the evidence and resolving the dispute. Arbitration is usually much more informal than a trial; the discovery process is limited and the rules of evidence are relaxed. Thus, arbitration is typically faster and less expensive than a trial.

Arbitration is generally required by Washington law if the amount of damages is less than a certain amount (between $15,000 and $50,000, depending on the county) and the only relief sought is money damages. This is called **mandatory arbitration** and is designed to ease court congestion. In other cases, parties to a dispute can agree to submit to arbitration instead of going to court. Parties to a contract may include an arbitration provision in the contract, agreeing in advance to arbitrate if a dispute arises. This is called **contractual arbitration** and is intended to save the parties time and money.

Unless otherwise agreed, the arbitrator's decision will be legally binding on the parties—the loser can't just shrug it off. The results of mandatory arbitration may be appealed in superior court. But parties agreeing to contractual arbitration typically give up the appeal right, in the effort to save time and money.

As you can see, an arbitration provision in a contract has a significant effect on the parties' rights in the event of a breach. An arbitration clause should be clearly explained to any party signing a contract. Otherwise, parties to a real estate transaction might sign a contract containing an arbitration provision without truly understanding the legal consequences.

Lawsuit

A breach of contract often is the first step towards a lawsuit. A lawsuit must be brought within a certain specified time period. The laws that set forth the time period requirements are known as **statutes of limitations**. In Washington, a lawsuit based on a written contract must be filed within six years after the breach occurred. An action based on an oral contract generally must be brought within three years.

The parties to a contract can agree to a shorter limitation period than the one prescribed by statute, but the period must not be unreasonably short.

These limitation periods apply even when the suing party was not aware of the breach at the time it occurred. But there's an exception for cases involving fraud or mistake: time doesn't start to run until the injured party discovers the fraud or mistake.

Interpretation of the Contract. In order to decide whether a contract has been breached (and if it has, what the plaintiff's remedy should be), the court must interpret the parties' agreement. In doing so, the court tries to determine (and enforce) what the parties intended at the time they entered the contract.

When the contract is in writing, the court is supposed to determine the parties' intention from the written document alone. If the language in the document is clear and unambiguous, the court will not hear evidence about the contract negotiations or any oral agreements that contradict the terms of the written agreement.

> **Example:** Tiokasin is going to lease a townhouse from Lane for nine months. The written lease form clearly states that rent is due on the first of each month. Before signing the lease, Tiokasin asks Lane if she can pay the rent on the fifteenth of each month instead, and Lane agrees. However, they don't change the lease form to reflect this agreement.
>
> Later Tiokasin and Lane wind up in court. Tiokasin wants to testify that Lane agreed to accept the rent on the fifteenth of each month. But this testimony will not be allowed, because it contradicts the written agreement between the parties.

This is known as the **parol evidence rule**. ("Parol" is a legal term that means "spoken.") This rule, like the statute of frauds, is intended to cut down on false claims and prevent people from weaseling out of what they agreed to do.

If the written contract is ambiguous, the judge will let the parties testify about their contract negotiations to shed light on the meaning of the document. Often the evidence presented doesn't clear up the ambiguity. In that case, the court will interpret the contract against the party that was responsible for the ambiguity—usually the one that drafted the document. If neither party is to blame, the court will interpret the provision in favor of the promisor: at the time the contract was made, what did the person making the promise believe that the other person understood?

Damages

Once the court has concluded that a breach of contract has occurred, it must decide on a remedy. The most common remedy for breach of contract is a **damages** award: the breaching party is ordered to pay a sum of money to the nonbreaching party. How much? The award is supposed to be the amount that will put the nonbreaching party in the position she would have been in if the other party had fulfilled the contract.

> **Example:** Perkins contracted to clear Hanawalt's property for $10,000, but he quit the project soon after starting. So Hanawalt hired Lopez to carry out the job. Lopez charged her $12,000.
>
> Hanawalt sues Perkins for breach of contract, and Perkins is ordered to pay her $2,000. If Perkins had not breached the contract, it would have cost Hanawalt only $10,000 (rather than $12,000) to have her property cleared. The $2,000 judgment against Perkins represents the difference between what the job actually cost Hanawalt and what it would have cost her if Perkins hadn't breached: $12,000 – $10,000 = $2,000.

However, if Lopez had charged Hanawalt only $9,000 to clear the property, Hanawalt would actually have been better off as a result of Perkins's breach. The job would have cost her $1,000 less than it would have if Perkins had fulfilled their contract. In that case, Hanawalt would not be entitled to a judgment against Perkins, because she wasn't damaged by his breach. The purpose of a contract lawsuit is to compensate the promisee for actual damages, not to punish the promisor for breaching.

Certainty Requirement. To be the basis for a damages award, a loss resulting from breach of contract must be proven with certainty. Occasionally a damages award includes lost profits: "If Harrison hadn't breached the contract, I could have opened my store a month earlier, and I would have made at least $1,000 in profit during that month." But in most cases, lost profits are considered too uncertain to be included in the judgment. Who knows whether the store would have turned a profit if it had been open that month? It might even have lost money. Unless the evidence proves that there would have been a profit, and that it would have been at least a certain amount, lost profits are not awarded.

Mitigation Requirement. The nonbreaching party in a contract dispute is required to **mitigate** damages. That means the nonbreaching party must do what he can to reduce losses resulting from the other party's breach.

Example: Hernandez leases an apartment to Tyler for one year; Tyler has agreed to pay $1,000 a month. Two months later, Tyler decides she doesn't like the place, so she moves out and doesn't make any further rent payments. That's clearly a breach of contract.

But Hernandez can't simply sue Tyler and expect a judgment for $10,000 (the additional amount she would have received if Tyler had honored the lease). Hernandez is required to mitigate her damages by trying to rent the apartment again.

If Hernandez immediately finds a new tenant for $1,000 a month, Tyler will not be liable for any of her unpaid rent. However, Tyler might be required to reimburse Hernandez for expenses incurred in renting the apartment again, such as any leasing fee and the cost of cleaning, painting, advertising, etc.

Suppose no one will rent the apartment for $1,000 a month, but someone rents it for $900 a month. Then Tyler will be liable to Hernandez for the difference between what Hernandez actually collects and what she would have collected if Tyler hadn't breached: $100 per month, for 10 months. The damages award would be $1,000 ($100 × 10 = $1,000), plus any expenses Hernandez incurred in renting the apartment.

Liquidated Damages. To lessen the possibility of expensive litigation, some contracts include a **liquidated damages** provision. The parties agree in advance that if there is a breach, the damages will be set at a specified sum or calculated according to a specified formula. The nonbreaching party will accept the liquidated damages instead of suing for actual damages.

As a general rule, a court will enforce a liquidated damages provision if the amount is reasonable and does not constitute a penalty, and the type of harm is such that it is difficult to ascertain or estimate the actual damages accurately.

There are restrictions on liquidated damages for certain types of contracts. In the case of a residential lease, a liquidated damages clause is void unless it would be extremely difficult to calculate the actual damages after a breach of the contract. The same rule applies to a consumer loan for the purchase of personal property. That standard is hard to meet, so a liquidated damages provision in a residential lease or a consumer loan contract is rarely enforceable.

In a real estate purchase and sale agreement, the parties typically agree that all or a portion of the buyer's earnest money deposit will be treated as liquidated damages if the buyer defaults. Under Washington law, the amount that can be forfeited is limited to no more than 5% of the purchase price. In other words, although the earnest money deposit may be any amount that the parties agree to, no more than 5% of the price may be treated as liquidated damages.

Example: The buyer agrees to purchase the property for $300,000 and gives the seller an earnest money deposit of $18,000 (6% of the price). Under the terms of their contract, the entire deposit will serve as liquidated damages if the buyer backs out of the transaction.

Three weeks after the contract is signed, the buyer defaults. Washington law allows the seller to keep only $15,000 (5% of the price) as liquidated damages. Even though the contract provided for the entire deposit to be forfeited, the seller is required to refund $3,000 to the buyer.

Note that the 5% limit on liquidated damages in purchase and sale agreements applies to both residential and nonresidential transactions.

Equitable Remedies

A damages award—a sum of money intended to compensate the nonbreaching party—is the standard remedy in a contract dispute. But money doesn't always do the trick. In some cases, alternative remedies are available.

Injunctions. An **injunction** is a court order directing a person to do something or refrain from doing something (see Chapter 1). Sometimes one party to a contract can obtain an injunction to prevent the other party from breaching.

To get an injunction, it's usually necessary to convince the court that the other party is about to breach the contract, and that the breach will cause **irreparable harm**. That doesn't actually mean it has to cause harm that could never be fixed; it simply must be harm that can't be adequately redressed by a damages award.

> **Example:** A restrictive covenant in Nelson's deed protects the enormous oak tree that has stood for 150 years on the boundary between her property and Locke's property. Locke learns that Nelson is planning to chop down the tree in spite of the restrictive covenant. He obtains an injunction to prevent Nelson from breaching the covenant.
>
> An injunction is an appropriate remedy because a damages award would not compensate Locke for the loss of a tree that took 150 years to grow.

Rescission. Sometimes one party to a contract doesn't want to enforce the other party's promise. Instead, he just wants to undo the contract completely, as if it never happened. In that case, he may ask a court to **rescind** the contract. When a contract is rescinded, each party returns any consideration the other has given. All of their contractual obligations are terminated.

Fig. 8.4 Suing for breach of contract

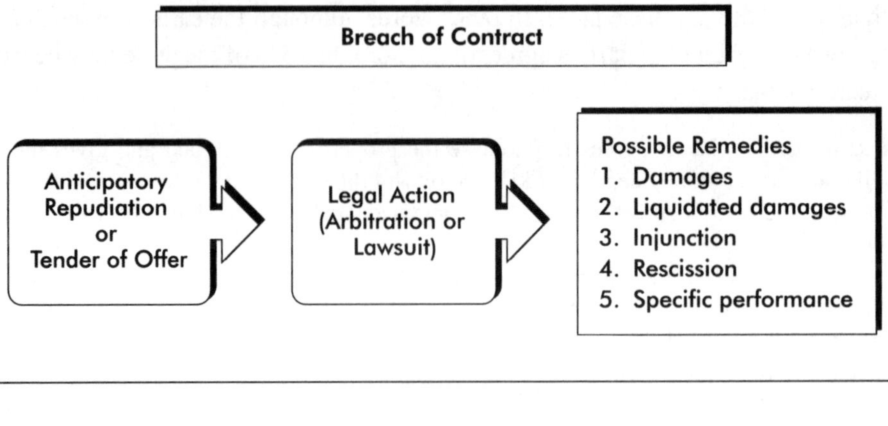

Rescission is available under a variety of circumstances. Whenever a voidable contract is disaffirmed—because of lack of capacity, fraud, undue influence, duress, or mistake—the court will rescind it. A contract can also be rescinded without going to court, if both parties agree. One party can request court-ordered rescission if the other party failed to provide the promised consideration, or if that consideration turned out to be void. A court will also rescind an unlawful contract (unless the unlawfulness was clear from the contract's terms and the parties were equally at fault—then a court will refuse to become involved in any way).

In some situations, the parties may prefer to **cancel** their contract instead of rescinding it. When a contract is canceled, all further obligations are terminated, but the parties aren't required to return what they've already received under the contract.

Specific Performance. Sometimes the nonbreaching party to a contract doesn't want to be compensated for the harm that resulted from the other's breach. Instead, the nonbreaching party wants to make the other party do what he or she promised to do. This is called **specific performance**: the court orders the breaching party to carry out the performance she promised in the contract.

Specific performance is generally not granted when a damages award will be just as effective. For example, a car dealer won't be ordered to sell you a particular car when you could get an identical one from another dealer. (If you have to pay more at the second dealer, the first dealer will be ordered to pay you the difference as a damages award.) But if the subject of a contract is unique, then specific performance is an appropriate remedy. A damages award won't enable you to buy an identical item, because there isn't another just like it.

Specific performance is most often used in enforcing real estate contracts, because a piece of real property is generally unique. A damages award may not be sufficient compensation for breach of an agreement to transfer real property.

A preference in favor of specific performance exists where the agreement is in writing, is certain in its terms, is fair and just, is for valuable consideration, and is capable of being enforced without hardship to either party.

In many circumstances, a court cannot grant specific performance. For example, it can never be a remedy for breach of a personal services contract, because no one can be forced to work for someone or to employ someone. Specific performance also can't be ordered for an agreement to procure the act or consent of another person, such as when a husband has agreed to persuade his wife to sign a document.

You can't be ordered to perform a contract if it wasn't just and reasonable, or if you didn't receive legally adequate consideration. For example, if you agreed to sell your $250,000 house for $175,000, the contract is enforceable even though the consideration is inadequate. But although you may be required to pay damages to the buyer, you can't be forced to complete the sale. Furthermore, a buyer can't be ordered to complete a purchase of real property when the seller doesn't have marketable title.

You also can't be ordered to perform if the other party hasn't fulfilled all the conditions he agreed to. And finally, you can't be ordered to perform if your consent to the contract was obtained by misrepresentation or unfair practices, or if your consent was given because of mistake, misapprehension, or surprise.

In spite of all these restrictions, specific performance is a common remedy when a seller breaches a purchase and sale agreement.

Interference with Contract

Sometimes one of the parties to a contract is persuaded to breach it by a third party that is outside the contractual relationship. For example, another real estate agent might convince your client to breach the listing agreement he has with you. Or a real estate agent might persuade a seller to breach a binding sales contract and accept a better offer.

These acts may constitute a tort called **interference with contractual relations**. The nonbreaching party can file a tort lawsuit against the third party, in addition to filing a contract lawsuit against the breaching party. To win the tort suit, the plaintiff must show that the defendant (the third party):

1. was aware of the contract,
2. intentionally interfered with the contract,
3. causing a breach of the contract,
4. that resulted in damages.

A tort called **interference with prospective economic advantage** is similar to interference with contractual relations, but the plaintiff doesn't need to show that he or she had a binding contract with another person. It's only necessary to prove that they had an economic relationship and the defendant was aware of that relationship.

Real Estate Contracts

A real estate agent is expected to be familiar with several different types of contracts. Each of these real estate contracts is simply a particular application of the basic rules of contract law outlined in the first part of this chapter.

As you've seen, the statute of frauds requires most of the contracts used in a real estate transaction to be in writing. Even when a signed written document isn't required by law, it's always wise to have one. The parties to a contract can draft a document for themselves, but it's much safer to use standard forms or to have lawyers do the drafting. A real estate agent preparing a contract must use approved forms, with minimal additions and changes, or risk liability for the unauthorized practice of law.

Whenever a document is executed in the course of a real estate transaction, the agent must see to it that each party receives a copy at the time of signing. That includes copies of any modifications of the agreements, too. Under the real estate license law, a brokerage must keep copies of all documents pertaining to a transaction for at least three years.

Some of the contracts commonly used in real estate transactions will be discussed in later chapters: title insurance policies (Chapter 9); escrow instructions (Chapter 10); and leases (Chapter 13).

This section examines licensee affiliation agreements, listing agreements, purchase and sale agreements, and options. Forms for each of these types of contracts are published by a number of different companies. Although the forms are standardized in a general sense, their details vary. Keep in mind that the provisions discussed here are not necessarily required by law, and are not necessarily included in every form. Also remember that the parties may choose to alter some of the pre-printed provisions in a form.

Licensee Affiliation Agreements

It's a good business practice for a brokerage to have a written contract with each affiliated licensee who works for the firm. This agreement should be signed by the designated broker or another managing broker representing the firm, and also by the licensee. It should state the main terms of the employment relationship, such as duties, supervision, compensation, and termination.

The Northwest Multiple Listing Service Firm/Associate Agreement form is shown in Figure 8.5 as an example. Like most contracts of this type, it provides that the licensee will work for the firm as an independent contractor, as opposed to an employee (see Chapter 6). It has detailed provisions concerning what resources the firm will provide and which expenses are the licensee's responsibility.

The compensation arrangements appear at the end of the form. Among other things, this agreement provides that the licensee is entitled to receive his share of a commission from the firm only if the firm has actually been paid in the transaction (see paragraph B in the final section of page 3). So if a difficult client refused to pay the commission and the firm decided not to take legal action to collect the money, the licensee would not have a claim against the firm.

Listing Agreements

A **listing agreement** is a contract between a seller (a property owner who wants to list the property for sale) and a brokerage. As we discussed earlier, a brokerage cannot sue for a commission unless the listing is in writing and signed by the client. The listing agreement need not be a formal legal document, but it must indicate the fact of employment—either expressly, with a statement indicating that the signer is employing the brokerage, or by implication, through a reference to the firm's compensation.

Remember that even without an enforceable listing agreement, a real estate licensee may owe agency duties to the client. Those duties are based on agency law, not on contract law.

Fig. 8.5 Licensee affiliation agreement

Form 127A
Firm/Associate Agreement
Rev. 7/10
Page 1 of 3

FIRM / ASSOCIATE AGREEMENT
(Independent Contractor Agreement)

© Copyright 2010
Northwest Multiple Listing Service
ALL RIGHTS RESERVED

IT IS AGREED by and between _____ ("Firm")

and _____ ("Associate"), as follows:

1. **LICENSES:** Each of the parties hold appropriate real estate licenses issued by the State of Washington.

2. **OFFICE ASSOCIATION:** Associate agrees to use his/her best efforts to promote Firm's and Associate's reputation and business.

3. **INDEPENDENT CONTRACTOR STATUS:** The parties agree that Associate is an independent contractor for federal tax and all other purposes and is not an employee of, or partner with, Firm. Under federal law, remuneration paid Associate must be directly related to sales or other production rather than to salary or the number of hours worked, or the independent contractor status will be lost for federal income tax purposes. Notwithstanding the foregoing, RCW 18.85 requires Firm to supervise associate's real estate activities. Associate agrees to comply with Firm's directions and procedures in this regard.

4. **FIRM TO PROVIDE OFFICE AND OFFICE PROCEDURES:** Firm shall, in common with other Associates of the office, make available office space, office equipment, local telephone service, receptionist, business secretarial assistance, office signs, office advertising, membership in listing and/or referral services selected by Firm, and use of maps and other sales materials. To allow Associate an equal opportunity in the matter of customers, sales and listings, and to promote the image of the Associate and Firm, Firm agrees to maintain rules regarding use of the office: days it will be open; office procedures; floor time; inquiries; leads; and other sales opportunities.

5. **ASSOCIATE RESPONSIBILITY - BUSINESS EXPENSES:** Associate shall be responsible to pay for his/her own license and business fees; automobile and other transportation; long distance phone charges; entertainment; insurance; and other business expenses. From time-to-time, unusual expenses involved in listing and/or sale, such as out-of-town travel, extended long distance charges, and brochures, may, by advance agreement of the parties, be deducted from a commission prior to division between Firm and Associate.

6. **ASSOCIATE'S ADVERTISING:** Associate is responsible to pay for his/her own advertising, over and above general office advertising by Firm. Associate shall abide by RCW 18.85 and WAC 308-124, including, without limitation, restrictions on advertising and signs. Associate agrees not to utilize any advertising, signs, brochures or other solicitation materials without Firm's advance approval thereof.

7. **ASSOCIATE'S AUTO INSURANCE:** Associate agrees to at all times maintain, at Associate's expense, automobile liability and property damage insurance covering Associate's own car and any other car that may be used in conduct of Associate's business. The limits on said policy shall be as approved by Firm. In the absence of such approval the policy limits shall be at least $1,000,000 single limit. Firm shall be named co-insured and a copy of the policy shall be given to Firm.

8. **ASSOCIATE'S TAXES:** Associate shall file and pay quarterly estimated, and annual federal income tax returns; and any other taxes required of an independent contractor. Firm will file any required notices or returns (such as IRS Form 1099) on all monies received by Associate through Firm. Firm shall pay any applicable State, County and/or City Business & Occupation Taxes on the entire commission, and the amount of such tax shall be deducted from the commission prior to division between Firm and Associate. At Firm's request, Associate will pay one-half of the medical aid and supplemental retirement portions of any industrial insurance premiums which Washington law requires Firm to pay on independent contractors.

9. **DELIVERY AND OWNERSHIP OF CLIENT PROPERTY AND RECORDS:** Associate shall timely provide to Firm all earnest money or other deposits, transaction documents and correspondence as required by RCW 18.85 and WAC 308-124. All maps, manuals, log books, printed materials, and supplies; client records, customer records, and transaction records, electronic or printed; and any other records, related to or received through the Firm's office (collectively the "Firm's Property") are the exclusive property of and remain owned by Firm. Any amount paid by Associate for the Firm's Property shall be for use of the Firm's Property and shall create no ownership interest therein.

INITIALS: FIRM _____ DATE _____ ASSOCIATE _____ DATE _____

Reprinted with permission, Northwest Multiple Listing Service. No endorsement implied.

Form No. 127A
Firm/Associate Agreement
Rev. 7/10
Page 2 of 3

FIRM / ASSOCIATE AGREEMENT
(Independent Contractor Agreement)
Continued

10. **ASSOCIATE TO RETURN FIRM'S PROPERTY:** Associate shall return all of Firm's Property described in Paragraph 9, above, to Firm prior to separating from Firm (including transfer to another real estate firm).

11. **MULTIPLE LISTING SERVICE:** Associate shall be responsible for paying all membership fees and costs for joining the multiple listing service (the "MLS") (or other real estate associations). Associate acknowledges that all proprietary information, passwords, keys, keyboxes, forms, and other services and information provided by the MLS are furnished for the use of Associate only and may not be disclosed, loaned, or distributed to anyone except in accordance with MLS Rules and agreements. Associate shall indemnify, defend, and hold Firm harmless from any liability, including MLS fines and damage suits, resulting from violation of MLS rules, misuse of MLS property and disclosure or distribution of passwords or other proprietary information in violation of MLS rules and breach of agreements with third parties, including without limitation moving companies, insurance companies, oil companies, clients, customers, employees, assistants, and licensees, or anyone else.

12. **COMPLIANCE WITH BYLAWS & RULES:** Firm and Associate shall comply with all rules and regulations and agreements of the MLS, Board of Realtors or other real estate associations to which either or both of the parties may belong. Each party hereby agrees to hold the other harmless from violation of any such Rules or Regulations or breach of any agreements each of them may enter with the MLS, Board, or association.

13. **MANDATORY MEMBERSHIP:** If Firm (now or in the future) belongs to any MLS, Board of Realtors, or association which requires that (as a condition of Firm's membership) all of those associated with Firm must belong, then Associate agrees to immediately apply for and maintain membership and pay (when due) all dues or other charges levied. In the event of Associate's failure to do so, Firm may terminate this Agreement and/or deduct required dues or charges from the next commission or other monies due to Associate.

14. **PROPERTY INVESTMENT:** Associate may acquire, for personal investment or residence, property listed with Firm's office or through the MLS, provided that Firm and any other Associate's portion of the commission provided in the listing is paid at closing. Firm or Firm's other Associate(s) may likewise acquire property listed by Associate, provided that the Associate's portion of the commission provided in the listing is paid at closing.

15. **OWNERSHIP - LISTINGS:** All listings, sales and other agreements obtained or negotiated by Associate shall, in accordance with state law, be in the name of and be the property of Firm, subject to Associate's share of any commission. Earnest money, lease deposits and other money; Purchase and Sale Agreements; Listing Agreements; Leases; and any other wholly or partially executed instruments or documents shall be immediately delivered to Firm in accordance with state law. Associate shall be entitled to copies thereof for his/her own records.

16. **TERMINATION:** This Agreement may be terminated, at any time, without cause, by either party giving notice to the other. If Associate contemplates termination of this Agreement, Associate will make reasonable efforts to close any pending sales in which Associate is interested. In the event that any such sale does not close prior to termination of this Agreement and, in Firm's discretion, it is necessary or appropriate for Firm to assign another broker(s) to attend to any matters concerning the sale (including changes in financing; securing of occupancy agreements; removal of contingencies; and any other usual or unusual matters required to close the sale), then Firm is authorized to deduct up to 50% of the Associate's share of the commission and pay the same to another broker(s) according to their participation in the matters necessary to close the sale. Associate agrees not to, in any way, induce or encourage an owner to terminate a listing (or sale) following termination of this Agreement.

17. **ARBITRATION:** Any and all disputes between Associate and Firm, or between Associate and other Associates in Firm's office, arising from matters occurring, all or in part, prior to termination of this Agreement, shall be resolved by arbitration, rather than suit. Each of the parties shall, within five days of being requested to do so by the other, name one arbitrator. The two arbitrators shall within five days of their appointment, appoint a third arbitrator. The dispute shall be heard within thirty days thereafter, in accordance with state statutes governing arbitration, and the decision of the arbitrators shall be final and binding upon the parties subject only to statutory review by the Superior Court. Alternatively, the parties may agree to submit the dispute to a Board of Realtors, which may offer such arbitration services.

Form No. 127A
Firm/Associate Agreement
Rev. 7/10
Page 3 of 3

FIRM / ASSOCIATE AGREEMENT
(Independent Contractor Agreement)
Continued

18. COMMISSIONS: The parties shall share commissions in accordance with the Addendum attached hereto.

19. ATTORNEY'S FEES AND COSTS: If either party to this Agreement shall bring any action or commence any proceeding to enforce the provisions of this Agreement, the prevailing party in such action or proceeding shall be entitled to recover all reasonably incurred costs and expenses, including attorney fees, incurred by such party in connection with such action or proceeding.

DATED this_____ day of _____ , _____ .

_____   _____
FIRM SIGNATURE   ASSOCIATE SIGNATURE

COMMISSION AGREEMENT ADDENDUM TO FIRM / ASSOCIATE AGREEMENT

IT IS AGREED by and between _____ ("Firm")

and _____ ("Associate").

A. Associate shall not be entitled to any salary, draws or compensation of any nature other than the listing fees and commission shares set forth hereinafter.

B. Associate shall have no claim to a listing fee or commission share except from money actually received by Firm.

C. All commissions and other monies must be paid to Firm alone. State law prohibits Associate from receiving commissions other than from the Firm holding his/her license.

D. MLS dues, listing fees owed Associate or others, Business and Occupation Taxes, Industrial Insurance, and other expenses, shall be deducted from the commission prior to determining Firm's and Associate's shares. In addition, Firm shall be entitled to deduct, from Associate's commission share, unpaid amounts owed Firm or the MLS or Board of Realtors for dues or any other reason. The net amount is the "commission" below.

E. Commissions shall be divided _____ % to the Associate and _____ % to the Firm.

F. Associate shall be entitled to the following listing fee (both before and after termination of this Agreement) for each exclusive listing obtained by Associate for Firm and sold by Associate or by others:

DATED this_____ day of _____ , _____ .

_____   _____
FIRM SIGNATURE   ASSOCIATE SIGNATURE

And these agency duties are in addition to—and independent of—the contractual duties the brokerage firm takes on in a listing agreement.

Because a listing agreement is a personal services contract, it can be assigned to another brokerage only with the client's consent. The assignment, like the original contract, must be in writing. It should be signed by the assignor and the assignee, as well as the client.

Types of Listing Agreements. A brokerage's right to a commission also depends on the type of listing agreement used. Under an **exclusive right to sell listing**, the owner agrees to list the property with only one brokerage. That brokerage is entitled to a commission if the property sells during the listing term, regardless of who sells it (even if the one who sells it is the owner). Most agents prefer this type of listing. The Northwest Multiple Listing Service form shown in Figure 8.6 is an example of an exclusive right to sell listing agreement.

In an **exclusive agency listing**, the owner agrees to list with only one brokerage but retains the right to sell the property herself without being obligated to pay the brokerage a commission. The brokerage is entitled to a commission if it or any other licensee sells the property, but not if the owner sells it.

Whenever an agent takes an exclusive agency or exclusive right to sell listing, the beginning and ending dates for the listing period should be stated in the listing agreement. (That isn't a legal requirement in Washington, though; a listing agreement without a termination date will expire after a reasonable length of time.)

Under an **open listing** agreement, the owner is only obligated to pay a commission to the agent who sold the property or was the procuring cause of the sale. To be the **procuring cause,** the brokerage must be primarily responsible for the parties' agreement. Since an open listing is a non-exclusive agreement, the seller is free to give listings to other brokerages as well. The sale of the property terminates all open listings.

If two firms contribute to a particular sale, a dispute may arise over which one was the procuring cause. Whether a brokerage was the procuring cause is a question of fact that is determined by examining all of the circumstances surrounding the particular transaction.

> **Example:** The principal gave open listings to agents from three different brokerages, Aimes Realty, Baker Land Co., and Kimoto Realty. Aimes and Baker both showed the property to the same buyer. The Aimes agent brought the buyer to the property for the first time, but it was the Baker agent who successfully negotiated the offer that the principal accepted.
>
> Aimes Realty claims that it should receive at least part of the commission. But the agent who effectuated the sale is considered the procuring cause, so Baker Land Co. is the one entitled to the commission.

Basic Elements. A listing agreement must identify the property to be sold or leased. The street address is generally useful, but is not enough to identify the property with certainty. That usually isn't an issue, but it can become one if the client decides not to sell and tries to avoid paying a commission. It's a good practice to attach a legal description of the property

Fig. 8.6 Listing agreement

Form 1A
Exclusive Sale
Rev. 7/15
Page 1 of 2

EXCLUSIVE SALE AND LISTING AGREEMENT

©Copyright 2015
Northwest Multiple Listing Service
ALL RIGHTS RESERVED

_____ ("Seller") hereby grants to,   1

Seller   Seller

_____ ("Firm") from date hereof until midnight of   2

_____ ("Listing Term"), the exclusive right to sell the real property ("the Property")   3

commonly known as _____, City _____ ,   4

County _____, WA, Zip _____; and legally described on Exhibit A.   5

1. **DEFINITIONS.** For purposes of this Agreement: (a) "MLS" means the Northwest Multiple Listing Service; and (b) "sell"   6
    includes a contract to sell; an exchange or contract to exchange; an option to purchase; and/or a lease with option to   7
    purchase.   8

2. **AGENCY/DUAL AGENCY.** Seller authorizes Firm to appoint _____   9
    as Seller's Listing Broker. This Agreement creates an agency relationship with Listing Broker and any of Firm's brokers   10
    who supervise Listing Broker's performance as Seller's agent ("Supervising Broker"). No other brokers affiliated with   11
    Firm are agents of Seller, except to the extent that Firm, in its discretion, appoints other brokers to act on Seller's behalf   12
    as and when needed. If the Property is sold to a buyer represented by one of Firm's brokers other than Listing Broker   13
    ("Buyer's Broker"), Seller consents to any Supervising Broker, who also supervises Buyer's Broker, acting as a dual   14
    agent. If the Property is sold to a buyer who Listing Broker also represents, Seller consents to Listing Broker and   15
    Supervising Broker acting as dual agents. If any of Firm's brokers act as a dual agent, Firm shall be entitled to the entire   16
    commission payable under this Agreement plus any additional compensation Firm may have negotiated with the buyer.   17
    Seller acknowledges receipt of the pamphlet entitled "The Law of Real Estate Agency."   18

3. **LIST DATE.** Firm shall submit this listing, including the Property information on the attached pages and photographs of   19
    the Property (collectively, "Listing Data"), to be published by MLS by 5:00 p.m. on _____ ("List Date"),   20
    which date shall not be more than 30 days from the effective date of the Agreement. Seller acknowledges that exposure   21
    of the Property to the open market through MLS will increase the likelihood that Seller will receive fair market value for   22
    the Property. Accordingly, prior to the List Date, Firm and Seller shall not promote or advertise the Property in any   23
    manner whatsoever, including, but not limited to yard or other signs, flyers, websites, e-mails, texts, mailers, magazines,   24
    newspapers, open houses, previews, showings, or tours.   25

4. **COMMISSION.** If during the Listing Term (a) Seller sells the Property and the buyer does not terminate the agreement   26
    prior to closing; or (b) after reasonable exposure of the Property to the market, Firm procures a buyer who is ready,   27
    willing, and able to purchase the Property on the terms in this Agreement, Seller will pay Firm a commission of (fill in   28
    one and strike the other) _____% of the sales price, or $ _____ ("Total Commission"). From the   29
    Total Commission, Firm will offer a cooperating member of MLS representing a buyer ("Selling Firm") a commission of   30
    (fill in one and strike the other) _____% of the sales price, or $ _____. Further, if Seller shall, within   31
    six months after the expiration of the Listing Term, sell the Property to any person to whose attention it was brought   32
    through the signs, advertising or other action of Firm, or on information secured directly or indirectly from or through   33
    Firm, during the Listing Term, Seller will pay Firm the above commission. Provided, that if Seller pays a commission to a   34
    member of MLS or a cooperating MLS in conjunction with a sale, the amount of commission payable to Firm shall be   35
    reduced by the amount paid to such other member(s). Provided further, that if Seller cancels this Agreement without   36
    legal cause, Seller may be liable for damages incurred by Firm as a result of such cancellation, regardless of whether   37
    Seller pays a commission to another MLS member. Selling Firm is an intended third party beneficiary of this Agreement.   38

5. **SHORT SALE / NO DISTRESSED HOME CONVEYANCE.** If the proceeds from the sale of the Property are insufficient   39
    to cover the Seller's costs at closing, Seller acknowledges that the decision by any beneficiary or mortgagee, or its   40
    assignees, to release its interest in the Property, for less than the amount owed, does not automatically relieve Seller of   41
    the obligation to pay any debt or costs remaining at closing, including fees such as Firm's commission. Firm will not   42
    represent or assist Seller in a transaction that is a "Distressed Home Conveyance" as defined by Chapter 61.34 RCW   43
    unless otherwise agreed in writing. A "Distressed Home Conveyance" is a transaction where a buyer purchases   44
    property from a "Distressed Homeowner" (defined by Chapter 61.34 RCW), allows the Distressed Homeowner to   45
    continue to occupy the property, and promises to convey the property back to the Distressed Homeowner or promises   46
    the Distressed Homeowner an interest in, or portion of, the proceeds from a resale of the property.   47

6. **KEYBOX.** Firm is authorized to install a keybox on the Property. Such keybox may be opened by a master key held by   48
    members of MLS and their brokers. A master key also may be held by affiliated third parties such as inspectors and   49
    appraisers who cannot have access to the Property without Firm's prior approval which will not be given without Firm   50
    first making reasonable efforts to obtain Seller's approval.   51

_____   _____   _____   _____
Seller's Initials   Date   Seller's Initials   Date

Reprinted with permission, Northwest Multiple Listing Service. No endorsement implied.

Form 1A
Exclusive Sale
Rev. 7/15
Page 2 of 2

EXCLUSIVE SALE AND LISTING AGREEMENT
Continued

7. **SELLER'S WARRANTIES AND REPRESENTATIONS.** Seller warrants that Seller has the right to sell the Property on 52
the terms herein and that the Property information on the attached pages to this Agreement is correct. Further, Seller 53
represents that to the best of Seller's knowledge, there are no structures or boundary indicators that either encroach on 54
adjacent property or on the Property. Seller authorizes Firm to provide the information in this Agreement and the 55
attached pages to prospective buyers and to other cooperating members of MLS who do not represent the Seller and, 56
in some instances, may represent the buyer. If Seller provides Firm with any photographs of the Property, Seller 57
warrants that Seller has the necessary rights in the photographs to allow Firm to use them as contemplated by this 58
Agreement. Seller agrees to indemnify and hold Firm and other members of MLS harmless in the event the foregoing 59
warranties and representations are incorrect. 60

8. **CLOSING.** Seller shall furnish and pay for a buyer's policy of title insurance showing marketable title to the Property. 61
Seller shall pay real estate excise tax and one-half of any escrow fees or such portion of escrow fees and any other 62
fees or charges as provided by law in the case of a FHA or VA financed sale. Rent, taxes, interest, reserves, assumed 63
encumbrances, homeowner fees and insurance are to be prorated between Seller and the buyer as of the date of 64
closing. Seller shall prepare and execute a certification (NWMLS Form 22E or equivalent) under the Foreign Investment 65
in Real Property Tax Act ("FIRPTA") at closing. If Seller is a foreign person or entity, and the sale is not otherwise 66
exempt from FIRPTA, Seller acknowledges that a percentage of the amount realized from the sale will be withheld for 67
payment to the Internal Revenue Service. 68

9. **MULTIPLE LISTING SERVICE.** Seller authorizes Firm and MLS to publish the Listing Data and distribute it to other 69
members of MLS and their affiliates and third parties for public display and other purposes. This authorization shall 70
survive the termination of this Agreement. Firm is authorized to report the sale of the Property (including price and all 71
terms) to MLS and to its members, financial institutions, appraisers, and others related to the sale. Firm may refer this 72
listing to any other cooperating multiple listing service at Firm's discretion. Firm shall cooperate with all other members 73
of MLS, or of a multiple listing service to which this listing is referred, in working toward the sale of the Property. 74
Regardless of whether a cooperating MLS member is the agent of the buyer, Seller, neither or both, such member shall 75
be entitled to receive the selling firm's share of the commission. MLS is an intended third party beneficiary of this 76
agreement and will provide the Listing Data to its members and their affiliates and third parties, without verification and 77
without assuming any responsibility with respect to this agreement. 78

10. **PROPERTY CONDITION AND INSURANCE.** Neither Firm, MLS, nor any members of MLS or of any multiple listing 79
service to which this listing is referred shall be responsible for loss, theft, or damage of any nature or kind whatsoever to the 80
Property, any personal property therein, or any personal injury resulting from the condition of the Property, including entry by 81
the master key to the keybox and/or at open houses. Seller is advised to notify Seller's insurance company that the Property is 82
listed for sale and ascertain that the Seller has adequate insurance coverage. If the Property is to be vacant during all or part of 83
the Listing Term, Seller should request that a "vacancy clause" be added to Seller's insurance policy. Seller acknowledges that 84
intercepting or recording conversations of persons in the Property without first obtaining their consent violates RCW 9.73.030. 85

11. **FIRM'S RIGHT TO MARKET THE PROPERTY.** Seller shall not commit any act which materially impairs 86
Firm's ability to market and sell the Property under the terms of this Agreement. In the event of breach of the foregoing, 87
Seller shall pay Firm a commission in the above amount, or at the above rate applied to the listing price herein, 88
whichever is applicable. Unless otherwise agreed in writing, Firm and other members of MLS shall be entitled to show 89
the Property at all reasonable times. Firm need not submit to Seller any offers to lease, rent, execute an option to 90
purchase, or enter into any agreement other than for immediate sale of the Property. 91

12. **SELLER DISCLOSURE STATEMENT.** Unless Seller is exempt under RCW 64.06, Seller shall provide to Firm 92
as soon as reasonably practicable a completed and signed "Seller Disclosure Statement" (Form 17 (Residential), Form 17C 93
(Unimproved Residential), or Form 17 Commercial). Seller agrees to indemnify, defend and hold Firm harmless from and 94
against any and all claims that the information Seller provides on Form 17, Form 17C, or Form 17 Commercial is inaccurate. 95

13. **DAMAGES IN THE EVENT OF BUYER'S BREACH.** In the event Seller retains earnest money as liquidated 96
damages on a buyer's breach, any costs advanced or committed by Firm on Seller's behalf shall be paid therefrom and 97
the balance divided equally between Seller and Firm. 98

14. **ATTORNEYS' FEES.** In the event either party employs an attorney to enforce any terms of this Agreement and 99
is successful, the other party agrees to pay reasonable attorneys' fees. In the event of trial, the successful party shall be 100
entitled to an award of attorneys' fees and expenses; the amount of the attorneys' fees and expenses shall be fixed by 101
the court. The venue of any suit shall be the county in which the Property is located. 102

Are the undersigned the sole owner(s)? ❑ YES ❑ NO 103

_____ 104

_____ _____   _____
Seller's Signature   Date   Real Estate Firm

_____ 105

_____ _____   _____
Seller's Signature   Date   Broker's Signature   Date

to the contract as an exhibit. Any pages attached to a contract should be dated and initialed by the parties, to show that the attachments were intended to be part of the agreement.

A provision stating the amount (or rate) of the real estate commission is another key part of every listing agreement. Remember that because the amount or rate is always negotiable as a matter of law, it must not be pre-printed on the listing agreement form. The figure has to be filled in for each transaction.

Provisions affecting the commission. A listing agreement should state the sales price and terms that the client is willing to accept. The client can refuse any offer that doesn't meet these terms without being liable for a commission. Of course, if the agent presents an offer that doesn't meet the listing terms and the client accepts it anyway, he is liable for the commission.

Generally, a brokerage is hired to find a **ready, willing, and able** buyer who meets the specific requirements established by the seller. A buyer is considered ready and willing if the buyer makes an offer that meets the terms stipulated by the seller. A buyer is considered able if she has the financial ability to complete the purchase. This means that the buyer must have one of the following:

1. enough cash to complete the sale;
2. a strong enough credit rating and enough personal assets to ensure that she can complete the sale; or
3. a binding commitment for a loan to finance the purchase.

Under the terms of most listing agreement forms, the brokerage is entitled to a commission even if the transaction never closes, as long as the client and a ready, willing, and able buyer have agreed on the essential terms of a sale. It doesn't have to work that way, however. The seller can add a condition to the listing agreement, making liability for the commission depend on the sale actually closing, or on some other event.

Even under a standard listing agreement, if the contract between the buyer and seller is conditional (contingent on the results of an inspection, for example) the seller isn't liable for a commission unless the condition is either fulfilled or waived by the parties.

Most exclusive listing forms make the client liable for a commission if he withdraws the property from sale or does anything to make it unmarketable.

Extender clause. Exclusive listing forms usually include an extender clause (also called a safety clause or carryover clause). An **extender clause** makes the client liable for a commission during a specified period after the listing expires, if the property is sold to someone an agent from the brokerage dealt with during the listing term. This makes it difficult for a buyer and seller to conspire to deprive the brokerage of a commission by waiting until the listing expires before signing a purchase and sale agreement.

In some forms, the extender clause requires the client to pay the commission if the agent merely introduced the buyer to the property during the listing term. In other forms, the extender clause has a stricter requirement, so that the client has to pay the commission only if the agent was the procuring cause of the sale.

An extender clause often includes some safeguards for the seller. It may require the agent to provide a list of the people she negotiated with, so the seller won't become liable for a commission without realizing it. It may also state that if the seller signs a listing agreement with another brokerage during the carryover period, the seller will not be liable for a commission to the first brokerage. Without that provision, the seller could become liable for two commissions on the same sale, one to the first brokerage and one to the second brokerage. Some forms do not include these safeguards, so a seller should beware.

Purchase and Sale Agreements

The general term for a contract between a buyer and a seller of real property is **purchase and sale agreement**, or something similar. In Washington, purchase and sale agreements are sometimes called **earnest money agreements**. (This is because in most transactions, the buyer commits to making an earnest money deposit at the same time he makes an offer to purchase.)

If the seller decides to accept the offer, she signs the form, and it becomes the parties' contract. A residential purchase and sale agreement form from the Northwest Multiple Listing Service is shown in Figure 8.7 as an example.

The basic elements of a purchase and sale agreement are fairly simple. The agreement must:

- identify the parties and the property,
- state the price and the method of payment, and
- state the time for delivery of title and possession.

Most purchase and sale agreements are quite detailed. It's very important for the contract to state all the terms of the parties' agreement clearly and accurately. The closing of the transaction will follow the terms set forth in the agreement. Who is required to do what and when depends on the purchase and sale agreement. Anything that isn't clear can lead to a dispute.

The Parties. When a purchase and sale agreement is being signed, ask two key questions regarding the parties:

- Does everyone who is signing have the capacity to contract?
- Is everyone with an ownership interest signing?

If any of the parties is underage or incompetent, the contract will be voidable or void.

Property Description. A full legal description of the property should be attached as an exhibit to the contract. Include a reference to the attachment in the space provided for the description (for example, "see Exhibit A"). The parties must initial and date each page of the attachment to incorporate it into their agreement.

Terms of Sale. The purchase and sale agreement should state all the terms of the sale as clearly as possible: what is and isn't included in the sale, the total price, and whether any contingencies are involved (contingencies are discussed below).

Any personal property that will be included in the sale should also be listed. Some forms have a paragraph entitled "Included Items," which lists personal property included in the sale. This list should be reviewed and items deleted or added as necessary. When adding included items, be specific: write in "washer, dryer, refrigerator" rather than "all major appliances."

The seller doesn't warrant the condition of the personal property, but he does promise that it is free of liens. If the seller wants to exclude any fixtures from the sale, they must also be listed.

Contingencies. Most agreements between buyers and sellers are conditional. Any conditions or contingencies must be spelled out in the purchase and sale agreement or in an attached addendum. This section should state exactly what must occur in order to fulfill each condition. It should explain how one party is to notify the other when a condition has been fulfilled or waived. It should also state a time limit; if the condition is not fulfilled by that date, the contract will be void. Finally, it should explain the parties' rights in the event that the condition is not met or waived.

If a real estate agent believes that a contingency clause in a purchase and sale agreement may affect the date of closing or the date that possession will transfer, the agent should explain this to the parties.

Financing. Nearly all residential transactions are contingent on the buyer's ability to obtain financing. The buyer is required to make a diligent, good faith effort to obtain financing on the terms stated in the purchase and sale agreement, but if no lenders are willing to make a loan on those terms, the buyer can terminate the agreement without forfeiting the deposit. That's why it's particularly important to describe the financing arrangements in detail in a payment terms addendum. If the buyer must obtain financing within a specific time period, he must notify the seller in a timely manner of the failure to obtain the financing or risk losing the deposit.

If seller financing is going to be used for part of the purchase price, it is imperative to refer to and attach the appropriate finance documents to the purchase and sale agreement. If the real estate contract or note and deed of trust are not referred to and attached to the agreement, the agreement will not be enforceable.

Sale of buyer's home. Many purchases are contingent on the buyer's ability to sell her current home. In fact, even when that isn't an express condition, it may be a hidden condition. Often a buyer won't have enough money for a downpayment unless the current home is sold. As a result, she can't qualify for the loan described in the financing contingency without selling the current home.

If the buyer will not be able to obtain financing unless her current home is sold, it's best to make the sale of the current home an express condition in the purchase and sale agreement. Otherwise, the seller may be misled into believing that the buyer has a much

Fig. 8.7 Purchase and sale agreement

Residential Purchase & Sale Agreement
Rev. 2/17
Page 1 of 5

Northwest Multiple Listing Service
ALL RIGHTS RESERVED

RESIDENTIAL REAL ESTATE PURCHASE AND SALE AGREEMENT
SPECIFIC TERMS

1. **Date:** _____ **MLS No.:** _____ **Offer Expiration Date:** _____

2. **Buyer:** _____
   Buyer   Buyer   Status

3. **Seller:** _____
   Seller   Seller

4. **Property:** Legal Description attached as Exhibit A. Tax Parcel No(s).: _____, _____, _____,
   _____
   Address   City   County   State   Zip

5. **Included Items**: ❑ stove/range; ❑ refrigerator; ❑ washer; ❑ dryer; ❑ dishwasher; ❑ hot tub; ❑ fireplace insert;
   ❑ wood stove; ❑ satellite dish; ❑ security system; ❑ attached television(s); ❑ attached speaker(s); ❑microwave;
   ❑ generator; ❑ other _____

6. **Purchase Price: $** _____ Dollars

7. **Earnest Money: $** _____ ❑ Check; ❑ Note; ❑ Other _____ (held by ❑ Selling Firm; ❑ Closing Agent)

8. **Default:** (check only one) ❑ Forfeiture of Earnest Money; ❑ Seller's Election of Remedies

9. **Title Insurance Company:** _____

10. **Closing Agent:** _____
    Company   Individual (optional)

11. **Closing Date:** _____; **Possession Date:** ❑ on Closing; ❑ Other _____

12. **Services of Closing Agent for Payment of Utilities:** ❑ Requested (attach NWMLS Form 22K); ❑ Waived

13. **Charges/Assessments Levied Before but Due After Closing:** ❑ assumed by Buyer; ❑ prepaid in full by Seller at Closing

14. **Seller Citizenship (FIRPTA):** Seller ❑ is; ❑ is not a foreign person for purposes of U.S. income taxation

15. **Agency Disclosure:** Selling Broker represents: ❑ Buyer; ❑ Seller; ❑ both parties; ❑ neither party
    Listing Broker represents: ❑ Seller; ❑ both parties

16. **Addenda:** _____
    _____
    _____
    _____

Buyer's Signature	Date	Seller's Signature	Date
Buyer's Signature	Date	Seller's Signature	Date
Buyer's Address		Seller's Address	
City, State, Zip		City, State, Zip	
Phone No.	Fax No.	Phone No.	Fax No.
Buyer's E-mail Address		Seller's E-mail Address	
Selling Firm	MLS Office No.	Listing Firm	MLS Office No.
Selling Broker (Print)	MLS LAG No.	Listing Broker (Print)	MLS LAG No.
Firm Phone No. / Broker Phone No.	Firm Fax No.	Firm Phone No. / Broker Phone No.	Firm Fax No.
Selling Firm Document E-mail Address		Listing Firm Document E-mail Address	
Selling Broker's E-mail Address		Listing Broker's E-mail Address	
Selling Broker DOL License No. / Selling Firm DOL License No.		Listing Broker DOL License No. / Listing Firm DOL License No.	

Reprinted with permission, Northwest Multiple Listing Service. No endorsement implied.

RESIDENTIAL REAL ESTATE PURCHASE AND SALE AGREEMENT
GENERAL TERMS
Continued

a. Purchase Price. Buyer shall pay to Seller the Purchase Price, including the Earnest Money, in cash at Closing, unless 1
otherwise specified in this Agreement. Buyer represents that Buyer has sufficient funds to close this sale in accordance 2
with this Agreement and is not relying on any contingent source of funds, including funds from loans, the sale of other 3
property, gifts, retirement, or future earnings, except to the extent otherwise specified in this Agreement. 4

b. Earnest Money. Buyer shall deliver the Earnest Money within 2 days after mutual acceptance to Selling Broker or to 5
Closing Agent. If Buyer delivers the Earnest Money to Selling Broker, Selling Broker will deposit any check to be held by 6
Selling Firm, or deliver any Earnest Money to be held by Closing Agent, within 3 days of receipt or mutual acceptance, 7
whichever occurs later. If the Earnest Money is held by Selling Firm and is over $10,000.00 it shall be deposited into an 8
interest bearing trust account in Selling Firm's name provided that Buyer completes an IRS Form W-9. Interest, if any, 9
after deduction of bank charges and fees, will be paid to Buyer. Buyer shall reimburse Selling Firm for bank charges 10
and fees in excess of the interest earned, if any. If the Earnest Money held by Selling Firm is over $10,000.00 Buyer 11
has the option to require Selling Firm to deposit the Earnest Money into the Housing Trust Fund Account, with the 12
interest paid to the State Treasurer, if both Seller and Buyer so agree in writing. If the Buyer does not complete an IRS 13
Form W-9 before Selling Firm must deposit the Earnest Money or the Earnest Money is $10,000.00 or less, the Earnest 14
Money shall be deposited into the Housing Trust Fund Account. Selling Firm may transfer the Earnest Money to Closing 15
Agent at Closing. If all or part of the Earnest Money is to be refunded to Buyer and any such costs remain unpaid, the 16
Selling Firm or Closing Agent may deduct and pay them therefrom. The parties instruct Closing Agent to provide written 17
verification of receipt of the Earnest Money and notice of dishonor of any check to the parties and Brokers at the 18
addresses and/or fax numbers provided herein. 19

Upon termination of this Agreement, a party or the Closing Agent may deliver a form authorizing the release of Earnest 20
Money to the other party or the parties. The party(s) shall execute such form and deliver the same to the Closing Agent. 21
If either party fails to execute the release form, a party may make a written demand to the Closing Agent for the Earnest 22
Money. Pursuant to RCW 64.04, Closing Agent shall deliver notice of the demand to the other party within 15 days. If 23
the other party does not object to the demand within 20 days of Closing Agent's notice, Closing Agent shall disburse the 24
Earnest Money to the party making the demand within 10 days of the expiration of the 20 day period. If Closing Agent 25
timely receives an objection or an inconsistent demand from the other party, Closing Agent shall commence an 26
interpleader action within 60 days of such objection or inconsistent demand, unless the parties provide subsequent 27
consistent instructions to Closing Agent to disburse the earnest money or refrain from commencing an interpleader 28
action for a specified period of time. Pursuant to RCW 4.28.080, the parties consent to service of the summons and 29
complaint for an interpleader action by first class mail, postage prepaid at the party's usual mailing address or the 30
address identified in this Agreement. If the Closing Agent complies with the preceding process, each party shall be 31
deemed to have released Closing Agent from any and all claims or liability related to the disbursal of the Earnest 32
Money. If either party fails to authorize the release of the Earnest Money to the other party when required to do so 33
under this Agreement, that party shall be in breach of this Agreement. For the purposes of this section, the term Closing 34
Agent includes a Selling Firm holding the Earnest Money. The parties authorize the party commencing an interpleader 35
action to deduct up to $500.00 for the costs thereof. 36

c. Included Items. Any of the following items, including items identified in Specific Term No. 5 if the corresponding box is 37
checked, located in or on the Property are included in the sale: built-in appliances; wall-to-wall carpeting; curtains, 38
drapes and all other window treatments; window and door screens; awnings; storm doors and windows; installed 39
television antennas; ventilating, air conditioning and heating fixtures; trash compactor; fireplace doors, gas logs and gas 40
log lighters; irrigation fixtures; electric garage door openers; water heaters; installed electrical fixtures; lighting fixtures; 41
shrubs, plants and trees planted in the ground; and other fixtures; and all associated operating remote controls. Unless 42
otherwise agreed, if any of the above items are leased or encumbered, Seller shall acquire clear title before Closing. 43

d. Condition of Title. Unless otherwise specified in this Agreement, title to the Property shall be marketable at Closing. 44
The following shall not cause the title to be unmarketable: rights, reservations, covenants, conditions and restrictions, 45
presently of record and general to the area; easements and encroachments, not materially affecting the value of or 46
unduly interfering with Buyer's reasonable use of the Property; and reserved oil and/or mining rights. Monetary 47
encumbrances or liens not assumed by Buyer, shall be paid or discharged by Seller on or before Closing. Title shall be 48
conveyed by a Statutory Warranty Deed. If this Agreement is for conveyance of a buyer's interest in a Real Estate 49
Contract, the Statutory Warranty Deed shall include a buyer's assignment of the contract sufficient to convey after 50
acquired title. 51

e. Title Insurance. Seller authorizes Buyer's lender or Closing Agent, at Seller's expense, to apply for the then-current 52
ALTA form of Homeowner's Policy of Title Insurance for One-to-Four Family Residence, from the Title Insurance 53
Company. If Seller previously received a preliminary commitment from a Title Insurance Company that Buyer declines 54
to use, Buyer shall pay any cancellation fees owing to the original Title Insurance Company. Otherwise, the party 55
applying for title insurance shall pay any title cancellation fee, in the event such a fee is assessed. If the Title Insurance 56
Company selected by the parties will not issue a Homeowner's Policy for the Property, the parties agree that the Title 57
Insurance Company shall instead issue the then-current ALTA standard form Owner's Policy, together with 58
homeowner's additional protection and inflation protection endorsements, if available. The Title Insurance Company 59

Buyer's Initials	Date	Buyer's Initials	Date	Seller's Initials	Date	Seller's Initials	Date

Form 21
Residential Purchase & Sale Agreement
Rev. 2/17
Page 3 of 5

RESIDENTIAL REAL ESTATE PURCHASE AND SALE AGREEMENT
GENERAL TERMS
Continued

shall send a copy of the preliminary commitment to Seller, Listing Broker, Buyer and Selling Broker. The preliminary 60
commitment, and the title policy to be issued, shall contain no exceptions other than the General Exclusions and 61
Exceptions in the Policy and Special Exceptions consistent with the Condition of Title herein provided. If title cannot be 62
made so insurable prior to the Closing Date, then as Buyer's sole and exclusive remedy, the Earnest Money shall, 63
unless Buyer elects to waive such defects or encumbrances, be refunded to the Buyer, less any unpaid costs described 64
in this Agreement, and this Agreement shall thereupon be terminated. Buyer shall have no right to specific performance 65
or damages as a consequence of Seller's inability to provide insurable title. 66

f. **Closing and Possession.** This sale shall be closed by the Closing Agent on the Closing Date. If the Closing Date falls 67
on a Saturday, Sunday, legal holiday as defined in RCW 1.16.050, or day when the county recording office is closed, 68
the Closing Agent shall close the transaction on the next day that is not a Saturday, Sunday, legal holiday, or day when 69
the county recording office is closed. "Closing" means the date on which all documents are recorded and the sale 70
proceeds are available to Seller. Seller shall deliver keys and garage door remotes to Buyer on the Closing Date or on 71
the Possession Date, whichever occurs first. Buyer shall be entitled to possession at 9:00 p.m. on the Possession Date. 72
Seller shall maintain the Property in its present condition, normal wear and tear excepted, until the Buyer is entitled to 73
possession. Seller shall either repair or replace any system or appliance (including, but not limited to plumbing, heat, 74
electrical, and all Included Items) that becomes inoperative or malfunctions prior to Closing with a system or appliance 75
of at least equal quality. Buyer reserves the right to walk through the Property within 5 days of Closing to verify that 76
Seller has maintained the Property and systems/appliances as required by this paragraph. Seller shall not enter into or 77
modify existing leases or rental agreements, service contracts, or other agreements affecting the Property which have 78
terms extending beyond Closing without first obtaining Buyer's consent, which shall not be unreasonably withheld. If 79
possession transfers at a time other than Closing, the parties shall execute NWMLS Form 65A (Rental 80
Agreement/Occupancy Prior to Closing) or NWMLS Form 65B (Rental Agreement/Seller Occupancy After Closing) (or 81
alternative rental agreements) and are advised of the need to contact their respective insurance companies to assure 82
appropriate hazard and liability insurance policies are in place, as applicable. 83

RCW 19.27.530 requires the seller of any owner-occupied single-family residence to equip the residence with a carbon 84
monoxide alarm(s) in accordance with the state building code before a buyer or any other person may legally occupy 85
the residence following the sale. The parties acknowledge that the Brokers are not responsible for ensuring that Seller 86
complies with RCW 19.27.530. Buyer and Seller shall hold the Brokers and their Firms harmless from any claim 87
resulting from Seller's failure to install a carbon monoxide alarm(s) in the Property. 88

g. **Section 1031 Like-Kind Exchange.** If either Buyer or Seller intends for this transaction to be a part of a Section 1031 89
like-kind exchange, then the other party shall cooperate in the completion of the like-kind exchange so long as the 90
cooperating party incurs no additional liability in doing so, and so long as any expenses (including attorneys' fees and 91
costs) incurred by the cooperating party that are related only to the exchange are paid or reimbursed to the cooperating 92
party at or prior to Closing. Notwithstanding the Assignment paragraph of this Agreement, any party completing a 93
Section 1031 like-kind exchange may assign this Agreement to its qualified intermediary or any entity set up for the 94
purposes of completing a reverse exchange. 95

h. **Closing Costs and Prorations and Charges and Assessments.** Seller and Buyer shall each pay one-half of the 96
escrow fee unless otherwise required by applicable FHA or VA regulations. Taxes for the current year, rent, interest, 97
and lienable homeowner's association dues shall be prorated as of Closing. Buyer shall pay Buyer's loan costs, 98
including credit report, appraisal charge and lender's title insurance, unless provided otherwise in this Agreement. If any 99
payments are delinquent on encumbrances which will remain after Closing, Closing Agent is instructed to pay such 100
delinquencies at Closing from money due, or to be paid by, Seller. Buyer shall pay for remaining fuel in the fuel tank if, 101
prior to Closing, Seller obtains a written statement from the supplier as to the quantity and current price and provides 102
such statement to the Closing Agent. Seller shall pay all utility charges, including unbilled charges. Unless waived in 103
Specific Term No. 12, Seller and Buyer request the services of Closing Agent in disbursing funds necessary to satisfy 104
unpaid utility charges in accordance with RCW 60.80 and Seller shall provide the names and addresses of all utilities 105
providing service to the Property and having lien rights (attach NWMLS Form 22K Identification of Utilities or 106
equivalent). 107

Buyer is advised to verify the existence and amount of any local improvement district, capacity or impact charges or 108
other assessments that may be charged against the Property before or after Closing. Seller will pay such charges that 109
are or become due on or before Closing. Charges levied before Closing, but becoming due after Closing shall be paid 110
as agreed in Specific Term No. 13. 111

i. **Sale Information.** Listing Broker and Selling Broker are authorized to report this Agreement (including price and all 112
terms) to the Multiple Listing Service that published it and to its members, financing institutions, appraisers, and anyone 113
else related to this sale. Buyer and Seller expressly authorize all Closing Agents, appraisers, title insurance companies, 114
and others related to this Sale, to furnish the Listing Broker and/or Selling Broker, on request, any and all information 115
and copies of documents concerning this sale. 116

_____	_____	_____	_____	_____	_____	_____	_____
Buyer's Initials	Date	Buyer's Initials	Date	Seller's Initials	Date	Seller's Initials	Date

RESIDENTIAL REAL ESTATE PURCHASE AND SALE AGREEMENT
GENERAL TERMS
Continued

j. **Seller Citizenship and FIRPTA**. Seller warrants that the identification of Seller's citizenship status for purposes of U.S. 117
income taxation in Specific Term No. 14 is correct. Seller shall execute a certification (NWMLS Form 22E or equivalent) 118
under the Foreign Investment in Real Property Tax Act ("FIRPTA") at Closing and provide the certification to the Closing 119
Agent. If Seller is a foreign person for purposes of U.S. income taxation, and this transaction is not otherwise exempt 120
from FIRPTA, Closing Agent is instructed to withhold and pay the required amount to the Internal Revenue Service. 121

k. **Notices and Delivery of Documents**. Any notice related to this Agreement (including revocations of offers or 122
counteroffers) must be in writing. Notices to Seller must be signed by at least one Buyer and shall be deemed delivered 123
only when the notice is received by Seller, by Listing Broker, or at the licensed office of Listing Broker. Notices to Buyer 124
must be signed by at least one Seller and shall be deemed delivered only when the notice is received by Buyer, by 125
Selling Broker, or at the licensed office of Selling Broker. Documents related to this Agreement, such as NWMLS Form 126
17, Information on Lead-Based Paint and Lead-Based Paint Hazards, Public Offering Statement or Resale Certificate, 127
and all other documents shall be delivered pursuant to this paragraph. Buyer and Seller must keep Selling Broker and 128
Listing Broker advised of their whereabouts in order to receive prompt notification of receipt of a notice. 129

Facsimile transmission of any notice or document shall constitute delivery. E-mail transmission of any notice or 130
document (or a direct link to such notice or document) shall constitute delivery when: (i) the e-mail is sent to both Selling 131
Broker and Selling Firm or both Listing Broker and Listing Firm at the e-mail addresses specified on page one of this 132
Agreement; or (ii) Selling Broker or Listing Broker provide written acknowledgment of receipt of the e-mail (an automatic 133
e-mail reply does not constitute written acknowledgment). At the request of either party, or the Closing Agent, the 134
parties will confirm facsimile or e-mail transmitted signatures by signing an original document. 135

l. **Computation of Time**. Unless otherwise specified in this Agreement, any period of time measured in days and stated 136
in this Agreement shall start on the day following the event commencing the period and shall expire at 9:00 p.m. on the 137
last calendar day of the specified period of time. Except for the Possession Date, if the last day is a Saturday, Sunday 138
or legal holiday as defined in RCW 1.16.050, the specified period of time shall expire on the next day that is not a 139
Saturday, Sunday or legal holiday. Any specified period of 5 days or less, except for any time period relating to the 140
Possession Date, shall not include Saturdays, Sundays or legal holidays. If the parties agree that an event will occur on 141
a specific calendar date, the event shall occur on that date, except for the Closing Date, which, if it falls on a Saturday, 142
Sunday, legal holiday as defined in RCW 1.16.050, or day when the county recording office is closed, shall occur on the 143
next day that is not a Saturday, Sunday, legal holiday, or day when the county recording office is closed. If the parties 144
agree upon and attach a legal description after this Agreement is signed by the offeree and delivered to the offeror, then 145
for the purposes of computing time, mutual acceptance shall be deemed to be on the date of delivery of an accepted 146
offer or counteroffer to the offeror, rather than on the date the legal description is attached. Time is of the essence of 147
this Agreement. 148

m. **Integration and Electronic Signatures**. This Agreement constitutes the entire understanding between the parties and 149
supersedes all prior or contemporaneous understandings and representations. No modification of this Agreement shall 150
be effective unless agreed in writing and signed by Buyer and Seller. The parties acknowledge that a signature in 151
electronic form has the same legal effect and validity as a handwritten signature. 152

n. **Assignment**. Buyer may not assign this Agreement, or Buyer's rights hereunder, without Seller's prior written consent, 153
unless the parties indicate that assignment is permitted by the addition of "and/or assigns" on the line identifying the 154
Buyer on the first page of this Agreement. 155

o. **Default**. In the event Buyer fails, without legal excuse, to complete the purchase of the Property, then the following 156
provision, as identified in Specific Term No. 8, shall apply: 157

    i. **Forfeiture of Earnest Money**. That portion of the Earnest Money that does not exceed five percent (5%) of the 158
Purchase Price shall be forfeited to the Seller as the sole and exclusive remedy available to Seller for such failure. 159

    ii. **Seller's Election of Remedies**. Seller may, at Seller's option, (a) keep the Earnest Money as liquidated damages 160
as the sole and exclusive remedy available to Seller for such failure, (b) bring suit against Buyer for Seller's actual 161
damages, (c) bring suit to specifically enforce this Agreement and recover any incidental damages, or (d) pursue 162
any other rights or remedies available at law or equity. 163

p. **Professional Advice and Attorneys' Fees**. Buyer and Seller are advised to seek the counsel of an attorney and a 164
certified public accountant to review the terms of this Agreement. Buyer and Seller shall pay their own fees incurred for 165
such review. However, if Buyer or Seller institutes suit against the other concerning this Agreement the prevailing party 166
is entitled to reasonable attorneys' fees and expenses. 167

q. **Offer**. Buyer shall purchase the Property under the terms and conditions of this Agreement. Seller shall have until 9:00 168
p.m. on the Offer Expiration Date to accept this offer, unless sooner withdrawn. Acceptance shall not be effective until a 169
signed copy is received by Buyer, by Selling Broker or at the licensed office of Selling Broker. If this offer is not so 170
accepted, it shall lapse and any Earnest Money shall be refunded to Buyer. 171

Buyer's Initials	Date	Buyer's Initials	Date	Seller's Initials	Date	Seller's Initials	Date

Form 21
Residential Purchase & Sale Agreement
Rev. 2/17
Page 5 of 5

RESIDENTIAL REAL ESTATE PURCHASE AND SALE AGREEMENT
GENERAL TERMS
Continued

r. **Counteroffer**. Any change in the terms presented in an offer or counteroffer, other than the insertion of or change to 172
Seller's name and Seller's warranty of citizenship status, shall be considered a counteroffer. If a party makes a 173
counteroffer, then the other party shall have until 9:00 p.m. on the counteroffer expiration date to accept that 174
counteroffer, unless sooner withdrawn. Acceptance shall not be effective until a signed copy is received by the other 175
party, the other party's broker, or at the licensed office of the other party's broker. If the counteroffer is not so accepted, 176
it shall lapse and any Earnest Money shall be refunded to Buyer. 177

s. **Offer and Counteroffer Expiration Date**. If no expiration date is specified for an offer/counteroffer, the 178
offer/counteroffer shall expire 2 days after the offer/counteroffer is delivered by the party making the offer/counteroffer, 179
unless sooner withdrawn. 180

t. **Agency Disclosure**. Selling Firm, Selling Firm's Designated Broker, Selling Broker's Branch Manager (if any) and 181
Selling Broker's Managing Broker (if any) represent the same party that Selling Broker represents. Listing Firm, Listing 182
Firm's Designated Broker, Listing Broker's Branch Manager (if any), and Listing Broker's Managing Broker (if any) 183
represent the same party that the Listing Broker represents. If Selling Broker and Listing Broker are different persons 184
affiliated with the same Firm, then both Buyer and Seller confirm their consent to Designated Broker, Branch Manager 185
(if any), and Managing Broker (if any) representing both parties as dual agents. If Selling Broker and Listing Broker are 186
the same person representing both parties then both Buyer and Seller confirm their consent to that person and his/her 187
Designated Broker, Branch Manager (if any), and Managing Broker (if any) representing both parties as dual agents. All 188
parties acknowledge receipt of the pamphlet entitled "The Law of Real Estate Agency." 189

u. **Commission**. Seller and Buyer shall pay a commission in accordance with any listing or commission agreement to 190
which they are a party. The Listing Firm's commission shall be apportioned between Listing Firm and Selling Firm as 191
specified in the listing. Seller and Buyer hereby consent to Listing Firm or Selling Firm receiving compensation from 192
more than one party. Seller and Buyer hereby assign to Listing Firm and Selling Firm, as applicable, a portion of their 193
funds in escrow equal to such commission(s) and irrevocably instruct the Closing Agent to disburse the commission(s) 194
directly to the Firm(s). In any action by Listing or Selling Firm to enforce this paragraph, the prevailing party is entitled to 195
court costs and reasonable attorneys' fees. Seller and Buyer agree that the Firms are intended third party beneficiaries 196
under this Agreement. 197

v. **Cancellation Rights/Lead-Based Paint**. If a residential dwelling was built on the Property prior to 1978, and Buyer 198
receives a Disclosure of Information on Lead-Based Paint and Lead-Based Paint Hazards (NWMLS Form 22J) after 199
mutual acceptance, Buyer may rescind this Agreement at any time up to 3 days thereafter. 200

w. **Information Verification Period**. Buyer shall have 10 days after mutual acceptance to verify all information provided 201
from Seller or Listing Firm related to the Property. This contingency shall be deemed satisfied unless Buyer gives notice 202
identifying the materially inaccurate information within 10 days of mutual acceptance. If Buyer gives timely notice under 203
this section, then this Agreement shall terminate and the Earnest Money shall be refunded to Buyer. 204

x. **Property Condition Disclaimer**. Buyer and Seller agree, that except as provided in this Agreement, all representations 205
and information regarding the Property and the transaction are solely from the Seller or Buyer, and not from any Broker. 206
The parties acknowledge that the Brokers are not responsible for assuring that the parties perform their obligations 207
under this Agreement and that none of the Brokers has agreed to independently investigate or confirm any matter 208
related to this transaction except as stated in this Agreement, or in a separate writing signed by such Broker. In 209
addition, Brokers do not guarantee the value, quality or condition of the Property and some properties may contain 210
building materials, including siding, roofing, ceiling, insulation, electrical, and plumbing, that have been the subject of 211
lawsuits and/or governmental inquiry because of possible defects or health hazards. Some properties may have other 212
defects arising after construction, such as drainage, leakage, pest, rot and mold problems. Brokers do not have the 213
expertise to identify or assess defective products, materials, or conditions. Buyer is urged to use due diligence to 214
inspect the Property to Buyer's satisfaction and to retain inspectors qualified to identify the presence of defective 215
materials and evaluate the condition of the Property as there may be defects that may only be revealed by careful 216
inspection. Buyer is advised to investigate whether there is a sufficient water supply to meet Buyer's needs. Buyer is 217
advised to investigate the cost of insurance for the Property, including, but not limited to homeowner's, flood, 218
earthquake, landslide, and other available coverage. Buyer and Seller acknowledge that home protection plans may be 219
available which may provide additional protection and benefit to Buyer and Seller. Brokers may assist the parties with 220
locating and selecting third party service providers, such as inspectors or contractors, but Brokers cannot guarantee or 221
be responsible for the services provided by those third parties. The parties shall exercise their own judgment and due 222
diligence regarding third-party service providers. 223

Buyer's Initials	Date	Buyer's Initials	Date	Seller's Initials	Date	Seller's Initials	Date

better chance of obtaining the necessary loan than she actually has. The contingency clause should state whether it will be fulfilled once the buyer accepts an offer, or whether the sale of the current home must actually close.

Inspections. The transaction will likely be made dependent on one or more satisfactory property inspections, such as a physical inspection, a geological inspection, or a pest control inspection. The lender may require certain inspections before it will fund the loan.

Bump clause. Including a **bump clause** enables the seller to keep the property on the market pending the fulfillment of a condition. While bump clauses are used when there's a good chance that any condition won't be fulfilled on time, they are most often used when a transaction depends on the sale of the buyer's home. If the seller receives another offer before the buyer's home is sold, the seller can demand that the buyer waive the condition or cancel their contract.

Release of contract. When one transaction fails because a condition is not met, the seller may want to enter into another agreement with a second buyer. In this situation, it's advisable for the seller to include an express condition in the second purchase and sale agreement, making it contingent on the failure of the first agreement and on the first buyer's release of all claims. The seller should not proceed with the second transaction without first clearly establishing that the first agreement is terminated and the first buyer has no right to enforce it. The best way to accomplish this is by asking the first buyer to execute a release of contract form in which the parties agree to rescind the contract.

Encumbrances and Condition of Title. A seller generally agrees to provide marketable title, free of undisclosed encumbrances or defects. The seller usually agrees to obtain a title insurance policy for the buyer.

Closing and Date of Possession. The purchase and sale agreement should provide a specific date for closing. Possession of the property is usually transferred to the buyer on the closing date, but the parties can make other arrangements. The seller may want a few extra days for vacating the property. Or the buyer may want to take possession before closing. In either case, the parties should execute a separate rental agreement in addition to the purchase and sale agreement.

Escrow and Closing. Most purchase and sale agreements include arrangements for the escrow. When the parties set the closing date, they should take into account the time needed for fulfilling any conditions. If the closing date is approaching and an inspection report is not yet available, or it looks like some other contingency won't be met on time, the parties may want to move the closing date by executing a written extension agreement.

Deposit. The buyer's deposit is an expression of good faith; it is evidence of a serious intention to buy the property. Instructions for handling the deposit should be specified in the buyer's offer (the purchase and sale agreement). The funds may be immediately deposited in an escrow account, or (if the offer so directs) the brokerage may temporarily hold the deposit check uncashed. Then if the seller rejects the offer, the check can easily be returned to the buyer.

The purchase and sale agreement should also explain the circumstances under which the deposit will be refunded or forfeited. The parties have the option of treating the deposit as liquidated damages. If the buyer defaults, the seller will keep all or part of the deposit as liquidated damages instead of suing for actual damages. (As we discussed earlier, no more than 5% of the purchase price may be forfeited as liquidated damages for breach of a purchase and sale agreement.)

Funds deposited in escrow are not released automatically if there is a dispute. If the seller wants to retain the deposit as liquidated damages, the escrow agent will usually not release that money to the seller without the buyer's consent. It may be necessary to sue or submit the matter to arbitration in order to establish that the buyer is in default and the seller is entitled to liquidated damages. If the brokerage has possession of disputed funds, it may distribute the funds to one or more of the parties after giving a notice of intent to do so.

Agency Disclosure. An agency disclosure clause must be included in the purchase and sale agreement, unless the parties are also signing a separate disclosure document. The listing agent states which party (or parties) he is representing in the transaction. When there is a selling agent in addition to the listing agent, the selling agent must also indicate which party he represents. By signing the purchase and sale agreement, the seller and buyer accept these characterizations of the agency relationships. (See Chapter 6.)

Other Provisions. Additional provisions may be included, such as what utilities the property is connected to, whether there are any leased fixtures, the condition of a well or septic tank, and type of insulation.

Acceptance. The seller accepts the buyer's offer as set forth in the document. The seller also agrees to compensate the brokerage.

In most cases, the seller's agreement to pay the brokerage is merely a reaffirmation of the commission agreement in an earlier written listing. But if the brokerage has taken the risk of operating under an oral or implied listing agreement, this written provision will satisfy the statute of frauds.

Under the compensation provision of the purchase and sale agreement, if the buyer defaults, the brokerage is usually entitled to half of the damages the seller receives. In practice, this generally means that the brokerage will take half of the forfeited deposit. However, the brokerage is not allowed to receive more in damages than it would have received as a commission if the transaction had closed.

Counteroffers. Often a seller is unwilling to accept the buyer's offer as written, but would accept slightly different terms. Remember that when an offeree varies any terms in an offer, it becomes a counteroffer instead of an acceptance. The original offeror (the buyer) is not bound unless he chooses to accept the seller's counteroffer.

When a seller wants to make a counteroffer, some agents simply cross out the appropriate terms on the buyer's purchase and sale agreement and replace them with the seller's new terms. The seller signs the agreement and initials and dates the changes. Then if the buyer is willing to accept the counteroffer, she also initials and dates the changes. This approach may work if the changes are minor and there is enough space to indicate them clearly. But the agreement may become difficult to read. Sometimes an agent fails to get every change initialed, so that it isn't clear whether the parties ever reached an agreement on all of the terms.

It's clearer and more professional to write any counteroffer on another form or a separate attachment. There are many forms specifically designed for this purpose.

Options

An **option** is a contract that gives one party the right to do something, but not the obligation to do it. In real estate, the most common type of option is an option to purchase. An option to purchase gives one party (the **optionee**) the right to buy the property of the other (the **optionor**) at a designated price within a specific time period. Within that period, the optionee may choose to exercise the option—that is, enter into a contract to buy the property. But the optionee is under no obligation to exercise the option.

> **Example:** Sullivan is interested in buying Hubbard's house, but hasn't quite made up his mind. He asks Hubbard to grant him an option to purchase the house for $250,000. Hubbard agrees and writes up an option agreement in which Sullivan agrees to pay $250 to keep the option open for two weeks.
> A week later, while Sullivan is still making up his mind, he hears that Pirandello is planning to offer Hubbard $275,000 for the house. Sullivan decides he does want to buy the house, so he exercises his option. Hubbard is bound to sell her house to Sullivan for $250,000, instead of selling it to Pirandello for $275,000.

Note that an option to purchase real property must be in writing and signed. The written option agreement should be as specific as possible, identifying the parties and the property, and stating all the terms of the potential sale. The option must also be exercised in writing.

Consideration for an Option. Consideration paid for an option contract is not refundable. If the optionee decides not to exercise the option, she can't demand that the optionor return the consideration. In the previous example, if Sullivan had decided not to buy the house, he would have lost the $250. If consideration is paid for an option, then the option cannot be revoked. Sullivan paid consideration of $250, so Hubbard could not revoke the option.

To make an option irrevocable, very little consideration is necessary. But if the consideration is not legally adequate, the optionee will not be able to sue for specific performance.

> **Example:** Hubbard granted Sullivan an option to purchase her house for $250,000. Sullivan gave Hubbard $15 to keep the option open for two weeks. During that period, Pirandello offers Hubbard $275,000 for the house. Hubbard can't revoke Sullivan's option because he gave her consideration.
> However, Hubbard decides to breach the option contract and sell the house to Pirandello. When Sullivan sues Hubbard for breach of contract, the court rules that $15

was not adequate consideration for a two-week option on a $250,000 house. Sullivan is entitled to damages for breach of contract, but not specific performance. The court cannot order Hubbard to sell the house to Sullivan for $250,000.

Relation Back. When an option is exercised, the interest the optionee acquires in the property **relates back** to the time the option was granted. In the eyes of the law, it's as though the optionee purchased the property when the option was granted, rather than when the option was exercised.

> **Example:** Entwhistle gave an exclusive listing on her house to B&D Realty. This listing was to expire on July 15. On May 20, Entwhistle gave Sumner an option to purchase her house for $340,000. Both parties agreed that the option would not be exercised until after B&D's listing expired.
>
> Sumner exercised his option and purchased the house on August 20. B&D Realty sued for its commission. Entwhistle would be required to pay the commission.
>
> Even though the option was not exercised until August, it was entered into in May. When Sumner exercised the option, his interest in the property related back to the time the option was granted. In effect, he is held to have purchased the property in May rather than in August. Since the listing agreement was still in effect in May, B&D is entitled to the commission.

Assignment. An option agreement can generally be assigned, unless the contract states that assignment is prohibited. An option to purchase may be included in a lease. If the lease is assigned, the option is assigned too, even when the assignment doesn't specifically mention the option.

Termination. When an optionee has given consideration for the option, the death of the optionor does not terminate the option. The option contract is binding on the optionor's heirs, and the optionee can still exercise it.

An option terminates automatically if it is not exercised before its expiration date. But if the option agreement was recorded, it can still be a cloud on the title after it has expired. A title insurance company will not simply ignore a recorded option after its expiration date—they can't be sure that the optionor didn't grant an extension. So when a recorded option is no longer effective, a document canceling the option should be recorded. To make absolutely sure that the optionee doesn't have any claim on the property, title insurers often require a quitclaim deed from the optionee to the optionor.

Right of First Refusal. A right of first refusal (sometimes called a **right of preemption**) is not the same thing as an option. Someone who holds a **right of first refusal** has the right to buy the property only when and if the owner decides to sell it. The owner can't be required to sell the property against her will.

Rights of first refusal are sometimes included in leases for office space. If adjacent space on the same floor becomes vacant, the lessor must offer the lessee the chance to expand into that space before it can be offered to a new tenant. Co-owners of property sometimes grant each other the right of first refusal; if one co-owner decides to sell his share, the other has the right to buy it instead of letting it go to a stranger.

Homeowners associations occasionally use rights of first refusal to maintain some control over who moves into the area. When a homeowner decides to sell, the association can buy the property to prevent its sale to someone the members consider undesirable. In this way, preemption rights have sometimes been used as a tool for racial discrimination. That practice is illegal (see Chapter 12).

Conclusion

Anyone participating in real estate transactions should have a general knowledge of how contracts are formed, and what is required for them to be valid and enforceable. It's also important to know what kinds of things cause a contract to be void, and what actions or problems would be considered a breach of contract.

If you participate in many transactions, you're likely to encounter situations where one party does not fulfill the terms of a contract. It then becomes important to know what the possible solutions are. A contract may be rescinded or canceled. The contract may provide for liquidated damages, or a court (or arbitrator) may order one party to pay the other a certain amount of damages. In some instances, the court may even order specific performance.

Virtually all real estate transactions involve at least one contract of one type or another. An understanding of contract law can help you deal more competently and securely with all of the contracts used in the industry.

Case Problem

The following is a hypothetical case problem. Most of the facts are taken from a real case. Based on what you have learned from this chapter, make a decision on the issues presented and then check to see if your answer matches the court's decision.

The Facts

Kreger entered into a purchase and sale agreement with Hall for the purchase of 15 acres of land, making a $1,000 initial deposit. The agreement provided that upon Hall furnishing title clear of encumbrances, Kreger would pay $11,500 in cash at closing on February 1, 1965. The agreement specified that Hall could use the cash received at closing to pay off encumbrances. The balance of the purchase price was to be paid in annual installments.

The property was encumbered by a $10,000 mortgage. Hall told Kreger he intended to pay off the mortgage with funds he expected to receive in a fire insurance claim settlement.

On January 28, 1965, Hall wrote to Kreger demanding that Kreger deposit the $11,500 downpayment for closing of the sale by February 1. Otherwise, Hall stated that all rights of the purchaser would be terminated.

Kreger responded that he was ready, willing, and able to make the downpayment, upon the furnishing of title clear of encumbrances, and that if the mortgage was not yet satisfied, it should be paid out of the downpayment. In the alternative, Kreger offered to assume the mortgage and remit to Hall any balance remaining over the amount of the encumbrance.

Hall did not want to use the downpayment for this purpose, and intended to satisfy the mortgage from the fire insurance payments. However, payment of the insurance settlement was taking longer than expected.

On January 29, 1965, Hall entered into a purchase and sale agreement for the sale of the property to Parker, upon the same terms as the agreement with Kreger, except that the Parker agreement did not require that the encumbrance be satisfied out of the downpayment.

Upon discovering that Hall had entered into an agreement with someone else, Kreger filed a lawsuit for specific performance of his purchase and sale agreement. Kreger claimed that he was ready, willing, and able to make the downpayment, but that the seller failed to deliver a report showing clear title.

Hall alleged that the contract with Kreger was forfeited, since Kreger failed to pay the sum required on February 1, 1965.

The Questions

Was the purchase and sale agreement forfeited? Was Kreger entitled to specific performance of the agreement? What happens to Parker (the second purchaser)?

The Answer

The trial court found that there was no forfeiture of the agreement by Kreger. The agreement provided for payment on February 1. Kreger was ready, willing, and able to pay on this date, but Hall had not provided clear title. Even though Kreger knew that Hall intended to pay off the mortgage with the fire insurance money, this did not change the terms of the agreement. The contract provided that title was to be free of encumbrances, and Kreger was not required to pay until presented with clear title. Kreger had not forfeited the agreement because he was at all times ready to perform.

Kreger was entitled to specific performance of the agreement. The court directed Kreger to deposit into court the sum of $10,500 ($11,500 minus Kreger's earnest money deposit of $1,000). Payment from this amount was used to satisfy the encumbrance. Hall was then required to execute a contract for the balance of the sales price as provided for in the purchase and sale agreement.

The alleged sale to Parker was junior to the prior rights of Kreger. Hall had no right to sell the property to Parker while there was still an enforceable agreement with Kreger. If Parker was damaged, he might have a cause of action against Hall. *Kreger v. Hall*, 70 Wn.2d 1002, 425 P.2d 638 (1967).

Chapter Summary

- An express contract has been put into words, either spoken or written. An implied contract is not put into words, but rather is implied by the actions of the parties.

- A valid contract meets all legal requirements and therefore is legally binding. If the contract does not meet one or more of the legal requirements, it is void. When a contract is voidable, one of the parties has the right to choose whether to proceed with the agreement or withdraw from it without penalty. Sometimes a contract is simply unenforceable due to lack of evidence or vague or ambiguous wording, or because the statute of limitations has run out.

- The four essential elements for a valid contract are capacity to contract, mutual consent (offer and acceptance), consideration, and lawful purpose.

- An offeree's acceptance must not vary the offer's terms. If it does, it is a counteroffer, not an acceptance of the offer.

- In order to create a binding contract, consent must be given freely. A contract may be voidable if consent was obtained by fraud, undue influence, duress, or mistake.

- The statute of frauds provides that certain contracts must be in writing, such as contracts for the purchase and sale of real estate, real estate agency agreements, contracts which cannot be performed within one year, and agreements to pay another's debt or assume another's obligation.

- There are many remedies for breach of contract. The dispute may be resolved through arbitration or a civil lawsuit. Damages may be ordered, or the breaching party may be required to pay the amount specified in a liquidated damages provision. There are also equitable remedies that might be granted, such as injunctions, rescission, or specific performance.

Checklist of Problem Areas

Real Estate Licensee's Checklist

❑ Does the listing agreement or purchase and sale agreement meet all of the requirements for a valid contract?

❑ If a party to an agreement is an entity, such as an estate, trust, or business entity, is the individual signing on behalf of the entity legally authorized to do so?

❑ If the buyer has made an offer, did the seller accept the offer—or make changes in the acceptance so that it is actually a counteroffer? You are only entitled to a commission if you find a buyer who meets the seller's terms, or whose offer is accepted by the seller.

❑ Is the contract, including all of its terms, clear to both parties? Remember that a contract is voidable for mutual mistake.

Seller's Checklist

❑ Is the listing agreement, option, or purchase and sale agreement you signed a valid contract?

❑ If you breach the contract, what kind of damages could you be liable for? Is there a provision for liquidated damages? Could specific performance be required?

Buyer's Checklist

❑ Has there been actual acceptance of your offer, or merely a counteroffer?

❑ Does the seller have the capacity to contract? In other words, is she 18 or older and mentally competent?

❑ If the seller breached the contract, what kind of damages would you be entitled to?

❑ If you breach the contract (refuse to buy after signing a purchase and sale agreement), what kind of damages could you be liable for?

Chapter Quiz

1. Sam tells his teenage neighbor, "I'll pay you $10 if you mow my lawn on Saturday." The teenager mows the lawn. What is the status of the contract?

   a. Incompetent
   b. Executed
   c. Void
   d. Implied

2. On May 15, Sharon offers to sell her property to Bill. The offer provides for acceptance by mail. On May 18, Bill mails a letter to Sharon accepting the offer. On May 19, before receiving Bill's letter, Sharon calls Bill on the phone to tell him that she is revoking the offer. Which of the following is true?

   a. Sharon can still revoke because she notified Bill before she received the acceptance
   b. Sharon can still revoke because Bill should have accepted by telephone
   c. Sharon cannot revoke because acceptance is held to be communicated as soon as it is sent, even though not yet received
   d. Sharon cannot revoke because it has been more than three days since she made the offer

3. Art offers to buy Kevin's house for $235,000. Kevin says "I'll accept your offer, but at $238,000." This is known as a/an:

   a. partial acceptance
   b. unilateral acceptance
   c. implied offer
   d. counteroffer

4. White owns some beautiful beachfront property. He is a reputable businessman with a wife and children. Many years ago, White was involved in a scandal involving drugs. The whole thing was hushed up at the time and White has since mended his ways.

   Johnson was White's roommate in college. He is now a struggling real estate agent. Johnson visits White and tells him that unless White gives him an exclusive listing on the beachfront property, he will tell everyone about White's past. This is an example of:

   a. duress
   b. business compulsion
   c. mutual mistake
   d. unlawful purpose

5. Smith agrees to sell his property to Carlucci. The property is worth approximately $500,000. Smith says he will give it to Carlucci for $250,000 and some cocaine. This contract:

   a. is enforceable
   b. is not entirely void; just the illegal part is void
   c. lacks adequate consideration
   d. is void

6. The statute of frauds requires:

   a. that all contracts be in writing
   b. that certain contracts be in writing
   c. that a contract is not enforceable if it is fraudulent
   d. None of the above

7. Tom and Val have been neighbors for 20 years. Both have five acres of property on which they grow apples and peaches. For the last few years, Val has been severely crippled with arthritis. She promised Tom that if he would work her property and harvest the fruit along with his own for five years, she would sell the property to him for half its market value. Tom works as promised and starts to make arrangements to purchase the property. But Val changes her mind and refuses to sell the property to Tom unless he pays full market value.

a. Tom has no recourse because there was no written contract

b. This is still a valid contract even though it is not in writing

c. Even though no written contract exists, Tom may still have an action against Val based on promissory estoppel

d. Even though no written contract exists, Tom may still have an action against Val based on accord and satisfaction

8. The purchase and sale agreement contains a clause providing that it will not be binding unless the buyers qualify for financing. This type of clause is known as a:

a. repudiation clause
b. contingency clause
c. declaratory clause
d. None of the above

9. When comparing arbitration to an action that goes to trial:

a. arbitration is usually cheaper but takes longer

b. arbitration is usually faster, but costs much more

c. arbitration is usually both faster and cheaper

d. arbitration is usually slower and more expensive

10. In Washington, a lawsuit based on breach of a written contract generally must be filed within how many years after the breach occurred?

a. Two years
b. Four years
c. Six years
d. Eight years

11. A contract contains a provision stating how much each party will have to pay in the event of a breach. This is called:

a. a liquidated damages provision
b. an equitable remedy
c. a personal injunction
d. None of the above

12. Krebs breaches a contract to sell his property to Barkley. Barkley decides that he doesn't want to try to enforce the contract. He just wants to undo the contract and get his earnest money deposit back. This is called:

a. an injunction
b. rescission
c. specific performance
d. mitigation

13. Woods agrees to sell his $200,000 house to Yatz for only $90,000. When the time comes, Woods suddenly refuses to perform. Yatz brings a lawsuit against Woods asking for specific performance.

a. Specific performance will probably be granted because real property is unique

b. Specific performance will probably not be granted because the consideration is inadequate

c. Specific performance will probably be granted because the amount of consideration is irrelevant

d. Specific performance will probably not be granted because it is hardly ever granted in cases involving real estate

14. Which of the following is not a contract?

    a. A listing agreement
    b. A purchase and sale agreement
    c. An option
    d. None of the above

15. An option:

    a. must be supported by consideration
    b. obligates the optionee to exercise the option
    c. is an implied contract if supported by consideration
    d. is revocable by the optionor

9 Title to Real Property

Outline

Key Terms

- Alienation
- Deed
- Grantor/grantee
- Conveyance
- Granting clause
- Power of attorney
- Attorney in fact
- Acknowledgment
- Donative intent
- Acceptance
- General warranty deed
- Covenant of seisin
- Covenant of right to convey
- Covenant against encumbrances
- Covenant of quiet enjoyment
- Covenant of warranty
- Bargain and sale deed
- Quitclaim deed

- Cloud on title
- After-acquired title
- Will
- Testament
- Testator
- Bequeath
- Codicil
- Legatee
- Devise
- Devisee
- Executor
- Probate
- Nuncupative will
- Testamentary capacity
- Holographic will
- Involuntary alienation
- Intestate succession
- Escheat
- Foreclosure
- Suit for partition

- Quiet title action
- Adverse possession
- Tacking
- Color of title
- Condemnation
- Eminent domain
- Dedication
- Recording
- Book of plats
- Actual notice
- Constructive notice
- Race-notice statute
- Bona fide purchaser
- Torrens system
- Title insurance
- Standard coverage
- Extended coverage
- Homeowner's coverage

Chapter Overview

The process of transferring ownership of real property from one person to another is called **alienation**. A property owner may voluntarily transfer property by a number of different methods, such as selling it to a buyer or leaving it to friends in a will. Property may also be transferred involuntarily (against the owner's wishes), as in a foreclosure sale or when the property is condemned. This chapter describes the various types of transfers. It also explains title insurance and the recording system.

Voluntary Alienation

Deeds

The most common method of voluntary alienation is by deed. A **deed** is a document used by an owner of real property (the **grantor**) to transfer all or part of an interest in the property to another party (the **grantee**). This process of transferring (alienating) real property by deed is called **conveyancing**.

In order to be valid, a deed must meet specific requirements and contain certain elements. It must:

1. be in writing,
2. contain words of conveyance and a description of the property,

3. identify the grantee,
4. be signed and acknowledged by a competent grantor, and
5. be delivered to and accepted by the grantee.

Written. The statute of frauds requires any transfer of an interest in real property to be in writing. A transfer of real property cannot be accomplished orally.

Words of Conveyance. The core of a deed is the granting clause. This is the portion of the deed that sets forth words that actually convey the property to the new owner. The **granting clause** must express the intention to transfer ownership of the property or an interest in the property.

The requirement for words of conveyance is easily satisfied. Usually one word, such as "convey," is sufficient. However, deeds often contain several words of conveyance. (Attorneys sometimes like to use five or six words when one would do.) A typical granting clause might state:

> "Grantors . . . do hereby give, grant, bargain, sell, and convey unto the said grantees forever . . ."

Description of Property. The property being conveyed must be adequately described in the deed. A legal description should always be included.

Identifiable Grantee. For a deed to transfer title, it must name an existing and identifiable grantee.

> **Example:** A deed to "Tom Jones and his wife" is adequate to transfer the property to Tom and his wife. Even though the wife was not actually named in the deed, she was identifiable as Tom's wife.

Note that the grantee does not have to be competent. Property can be transferred to someone who is a minor or mentally incompetent. Essentially, the only requirement is that the grantee be alive and identifiable.

> **Example:** John executes a deed to transfer his property to Mary. Unknown to John, Mary had recently passed away. Mary's heirs argue that they are entitled to the property. However, they have no legal right to the property because it never transferred to Mary. A deed cannot transfer property to a dead grantee. The deed is void and the property remains John's. If he wishes it to go to Mary's heirs, he must deed it to them.

The grantee may be a corporation or other legal entity (such as a partnership or trust), rather than a human being. Normally, these entities are adequate grantees so long as they legally exist. In other words, they must meet the requirements for incorporation, or be licensed, or have the proper certificates on file, so that they can be recognized as an existing legal entity.

Competent Grantor. Every deed must name an identifiable grantor. The grantor is the person who conveys or transfers the property or an interest in the property. If a mistake is made in the spelling of the grantor's name or it is spelled differently in different parts of the deed, it will not invalidate the deed, as long as it is clear who the grantor is meant to be.

> **Example:** In the body of the deed the name of the grantor is spelled "Reily," but the signature at the bottom of the deed is spelled "Reilly." A deed names the grantor as "Jane Elizabeth Hawthorne," but the signature is written as "Jane E. Hawthorne." Both of these deeds would probably be valid.

In addition to being clearly identifiable, the grantor must also be competent (of legal age and sound mind). If the grantor is mentally incompetent or under legal age, the deed is void or voidable by the grantor.

Marital status. Marital status can affect the grantor's right to convey the property, since Washington is a community property state. So it's a good idea to state clearly in the deed whether the grantor is married or single, although that is not a legal requirement.

Corporate grantor. Under the law, a corporation is considered a person for certain purposes. A corporation has the right to transfer real property. There are specific rules governing the transfer of real property by a corporation. Normally, a resolution of the board of directors is required before a corporate officer can execute a deed.

Signature of Grantor. To be valid, a deed must be signed by the grantor. (The grantee's signature is not required.) Although the grantor's signature is not required to be in any certain place, it is important to make it clear that the signature applies to the entire document. Usually the signature is found at the end of the document.

In certain situations, the deed may be signed by a mark. A mark may be used if the grantor is illiterate or physically disabled and cannot write his own name. If the grantor signs by a mark, his name should be written or typed near the mark, and the act of making the mark should be witnessed.

Power of attorney. A deed may be signed by the grantor's **attorney in fact**: someone the grantor has authorized to act on her behalf. The grantor gives the attorney in fact (not necessarily a lawyer) this authority to act in a written document called a **power of attorney**. A power of attorney may be revoked by the grantor at any time.

When the attorney in fact is signing a deed or other document for the grantor, she usually prints the grantor's name and then signs her name beneath it.

> **Example:** *Andrew C. Thompson*
> by *Margaret L. Pierson*, his Attorney in Fact

A power of attorney is automatically revoked if the principal dies. It's also automatically revoked if the principal becomes mentally incompetent, unless it's a **durable power of attorney**—one that specifically provides that it will remain effective despite the principal's incompetence. Before accepting a deed signed by an attorney in fact, the grantee should make sure that the power of attorney is still in effect and that the grantor is still alive.

Fig. 9.1 Requirements for a valid deed

A VALID DEED	
I hereby grant	words of conveyance
Greenacres Farm	adequate description of property
To Harry Carter	identifiable, living grantee
(signed) Sam Smith	signature of competent grantor

In Chapter 8, we explained that an individual who is representing an entity, such as a trust or estate, must be properly authorized to sign a contract involving real estate. That is also true when an entity wishes to convey property. The entity's representative must be properly authorized to sign the deed.

Acknowledgment. A legal document is **acknowledged** when the person executing it makes a formal declaration that he has signed it voluntarily. Acknowledgment of a deed usually occurs when the grantor signs the document in front of a notary public, but certain other officers or public officials (such as a judge, court clerk, or county auditor) are also authorized to take acknowledgments.

In Washington, a deed can be valid and effective—transferring title to the property—even though it hasn't been acknowledged by the grantor. However, an unacknowledged deed cannot be recorded to provide constructive notice of the transfer to other parties. (Recording and notice are discussed later in this chapter.)

When a deed is acknowledged, the notary or other official who takes the acknowledgment fills in a **certificate of acknowledgment**, which states that the grantor appeared and acknowledged that she executed the instrument as a free and voluntary act.

Someone who has an interest in the property may not take the acknowledgment. For instance, if you are deeding property to your nephew (who is a notary public), he may not acknowledge the deed, because he is the grantee and therefore has an interest in the property.

The document must be read to a blind grantor before the acknowledgment is taken. Similarly, if the grantor does not speak or understand English, the acknowledgment should not be taken until it is clear that the document has been translated into a language that the grantor understands.

Delivery, Donative Intent, and Acceptance. Even if a deed contains all of the required elements, it will not transfer title until it is delivered by the grantor, with the intent to pass title, and is accepted by the grantee. Actual physical delivery of the deed is usually necessary, although the grantee may accept delivery of the deed through an agent.

Valid delivery cannot occur without **donative intent**: the grantor must intend to pass title to the grantee and surrender control. It is the grantor's intention that governs.

Case Example:

Norman Proctor, a married man, ran a real estate brokerage. In 1964, he hired Zee Forsythe as an agent, and they became personally involved. In 1967, Forsythe signed a contract for the purchase of a parcel of land, and Proctor supplied the downpayment. They planned to construct a home there. Forsythe also signed a $10,000 mortgage; the loan funds were paid to Proctor, who applied the money to construction costs. He also contributed $12,000 to the construction and made the mortgage payments.

Proctor asked Forsythe to marry him, told her he loved her, gave her a variety of gifts, and purchased a plaque to be installed in the home which read, "From Norman to Zee with love."

During their relationship, there were several dealings by Proctor on Forsythe's behalf that required her to sign lots of papers, some of them in blank (in other words, even though they had not been completely filled out yet).

At some point the relationship soured, and a dispute arose concerning ownership of the property. Proctor claimed ownership based on two quitclaim deeds and a mortgage bearing Forsythe's signature, which showed that she had transferred ownership of the property from herself to Proctor. Forsythe claimed that she had not intentionally or knowingly signed these documents, and she requested that they be set aside. On one of the quitclaim deeds, two typewriters were used at separate times to complete the instrument, evidence supporting Forsythe's claim that she had signed it in blank.

The court found an express intent by Proctor to make a gift of the home to Forsythe. It further found a lack of intent by Forsythe to convey title back to Proctor, because the documents were not knowingly or intentionally signed. This lack of donative intent rendered the deeds to Proctor void, so the court ruled that Forsythe was the owner of the property. *Proctor v. Forsythe*, 4 Wn. App. 238, 480 P.2d 511 (1971).

Case Example:

Susan Fenich quitclaimed 80 acres to her granddaughter, Helene Bull. The purpose of this deed was to transfer the property to Helene if Helene's mother (Mary) predeceased the grandmother (Susan). The deed was given to an attorney for safekeeping.

Susan died in 1949, while Mary was still living. Susan's will left almost all of her property to Mary. A lawsuit arose regarding the 80 acres. One of the issues was whether the quitclaim deed from Susan to Helene was valid and properly delivered.

The court found that at the time the deed was given to the attorney, Susan did not intend to make a present transfer of title to Helene, because the instrument was to be effective only if Mary predeceased Susan. Since the deed from Susan to Helene was not delivered to Helene with donative intent, it did not transfer title to Helene. Thus, Susan still owned the property at the time of her death, and ownership of the 80 acres passed to Mary under the terms of Susan's will. *Bull v. Fenich*, 34 Wn. App. 435, 661 P.2d 1012 (1983)

Although it is rare, a court may rule that a deed was delivered constructively or by implication, if the intention of the grantor can be adequately shown. Also, as was mentioned earlier, a deed may be properly delivered if it is given to an agent of the grantee rather than directly to the grantee, as long as the grantor has donative intent at that time.

> **Example:** Appleby signs a deed to Bertinelli as grantee and hands the deed to Bertinelli's lawyer, with the intention of transferring ownership to Bertinelli here and now. This is delivery to an agent of the grantee, and it is effective to transfer title.

Putting a deed in escrow is also a form of delivery. For escrow to be valid, complete and irrevocable delivery must occur. When a deed is placed in escrow, the depositor must give up possession and all control over the deed.

As a general rule, delivery of a deed must occur while the grantor is alive.

> **Example:** After Garrett dies, a properly executed deed is found in his safe deposit box. The deed grants title to Garrett's land to his niece. The deed is void for lack of delivery, since Garrett was dead before his niece received the deed.

However, Washington law now allows transfer on death deeds. A **transfer on death deed** will transfer title to the grantee automatically and without probate when the grantor dies. The deed must state that the transfer will take place upon the grantor's death, and it must be recorded. The grantor can revoke the deed at any time before dying.

As we said, even when a grantor delivers a valid deed with donative intent, in order for ownership to transfer it's also necessary for the grantee to accept the deed. If there is a dispute concerning acceptance, the courts generally try to find in favor of acceptance. But in some circumstances the grantee may not want to accept, either for personal reasons or because it would not be in his best interest.

> **Example:** Moynihan owns property worth $10,000 that she wants to deed to her son. However, the property has a tax lien on it for $12,000. The son does not want to accept ownership of the property because of the tax liability.

Other Elements. Many deeds contain other elements that seem to be standard, but actually are not required. For instance, almost all deeds are dated, but it is not a legal requirement that the deed contain the date of conveyance.

Another item occasionally included is the grantee's signature. Although a deed must contain the grantor's signature, the grantee does not need to sign.

The deed also does not have to contain a recital of the specific consideration for which the property is being transferred. However, it is helpful to include a recital of consideration to show that a transaction was a purchase rather than a gift, since the grantee of a gift deed may be vulnerable to claims by the grantor's creditors. The recital of consideration generally does not contain the actual purchase price, but may simply state: ". . . for $10.00 and other valuable consideration." Consideration can take forms other than money, such as waiver of a right or performance of a service.

Types of Deeds

There are three main types of deeds used in Washington: the general warranty deed, the bargain and sale deed, and the quitclaim deed.

General Warranty Deed. A **general warranty deed** is also called a statutory warranty deed, or just a warranty deed. This is the type of deed most commonly used in Washington real estate transactions. Compared to other deeds, a general warranty deed provides the grantee with the most comprehensive protection. It contains these **covenants** (assurances or guarantees) by the grantor:

1. The grantor has good title to the land conveyed: at the time of executing and delivering the deed, the grantor actually owned the land. This is called the **covenant of seisin**.
2. The grantor has the right to convey the land: the grantor either has title to the land or is an agent of the owner with the authority to transfer the interest. This is called the **covenant of right to convey**.
3. The property is free from undisclosed encumbrances. This is called the **covenant against encumbrances**.
4. The grantor promises quiet and peaceable possession of the premises: the grantee's possession will not be threatened by any lawful claim made by a third party. This is called the **covenant of quiet enjoyment**.
5. The grantor is required to defend the title against anyone who may lawfully have a claim to it. This is called the **covenant of warranty**.

If the grantee suffers financial harm or even loses the property because the title was not as promised (covenanted), the grantee may sue the grantor for damages. For instance, if there was an undisclosed encumbrance such as a tax lien that the grantee had to pay to avoid foreclosure, the grantee could sue the grantor for the amount paid and other costs incurred.

Note that in a 2011 Washington Supreme Court decision, *Edmonson v. Popchoi*, the court held that the covenant of warranty requires a grantor to actively defend the grantee's title against a third party's claim. The grantor in that case chose to settle a third party's adverse possession claim and pay the grantee damages for breach of the covenant, since that was less expensive than defending the grantee's title in court. The supreme court ruled that this was not adequate to fulfill the grantor's duty to the grantee under the covenant of warranty.

Bargain and Sale Deed. The next type of deed is the **bargain and sale deed** (sometimes called a **special warranty deed**). In this type of deed, the grantor only guarantees her own actions. Essentially, the grantor conveys the same interest in property and quality of title as acquired from the last owner. The grantor promises:

1. Nothing the grantor has done has encumbered the property.
2. The grantee's possession of the property won't be disturbed by claims of ownership brought by the grantor's heirs or assigns.

Under a bargain and sale deed, the grantor is liable if the grantee is disturbed by some claim arising through an act of the grantor. However, if an outstanding title is asserted by an outside third party, the grantor is not liable.

> **Example:** Roberts purchased property from Fenniman. Roberts then sold the property to Yamagato. Roberts gave Yamagato a bargain and sale deed.
> Unknown to Roberts, Fenniman was a clever crook who had sold the same property to several people. One of these other people appeared and claimed title to the property. Roberts cannot be held liable.

Quitclaim Deed. A **quitclaim deed** simply conveys whatever interest the grantor has. It contains no warranties of any sort. A quitclaim deed will convey nothing at all if the grantor had no interest in the property when the deed was executed.

> **Example:** Able and Baker are neighbors and good friends. They don't know where the boundary line is between their property. A fence runs between the properties 30 yards from Baker's house. Baker thinks his true property line is actually 32 yards from the house. Able and Baker both want to sell their property, but don't want to hire a surveyor. Baker gives Able a quitclaim deed for the two yards of property on the other side of the fence.
> Years later, when a survey is done, it is found that the fence is right on the true boundary line. Baker's quitclaim deed didn't actually transfer any interest, since Baker didn't really own the two yards on the other side of the fence.

A common reason for using a quitclaim deed is to cure **clouds on the title.** These could be defects or technical flaws in an earlier conveyance, such as a misspelling of one of the parties' names, or an error in the description of the estate.

A quitclaim deed is also used when the grantor is unsure of the validity of her title and wants to avoid any warranties.

> **Example:** A grantor holds title to the property by virtue of an inheritance that is being challenged in probate court. If the grantor wants to transfer the property, she will probably use a quitclaim deed.

After-Acquired Title. Sometimes a grantor may acquire good title after previously attempting to convey good title to a grantee. When the grantor obtains good title, it will automatically pass to the grantee by operation of law, if the transfer was by a general warranty deed or a bargain and sale deed. This is referred to as **after-acquired title**.

> **Example:** Seller conveyed her property to Buyer on June 1, by a general warranty deed. However, Seller did not have valid title to the property on June 1, because she held title under a forged deed. On August 12, Seller received good title to the property under a properly executed deed. Buyer automatically acquired good title to the property on August 12.

After-acquired title normally does not pass to a grantee under a quitclaim deed. A quitclaim deed transfers only the grantor's current interest. If the grantor did not have valid title at the time of the quitclaim deed, the grantee could not receive title then, and would not receive any after-acquired title. (However, title would pass if the quitclaim deed included a clause specifically expressing an intent to pass after-acquired title.)

Wills

A **will** (or testament) is a common form of voluntary alienation. Before discussing wills, it is helpful to know the general terminology. The person making out the will is called the **testator**. A testator **bequeaths** personal property (known as a **bequest**) to a **legatee** and **devises** real property to a **devisee**. An amendment to a will is called a **codicil**. The **executor** is named in the will and is the person who carries out the directions in the will, under the supervision of the probate court. **Probate** is the process by which a will is proved valid and its directions are carried out.

Requirements for a Valid Will. In Washington, any person of sound mind who is at least 18 years old may make a will leaving personal and real property to others. To be valid, a will generally must be:

1. in writing,
2. signed by a competent testator, and
3. attested to by two or more competent witnesses.

In writing. Generally, a will must be in writing to be valid. Under limited circumstances, Washington will recognize a **nuncupative** (oral) will used to dispose of personal property. However, real estate can never be devised by a nuncupative will.

Signature. Except for nuncupative wills, a will must be signed by the testator in order to be valid. However, as with deeds, a will may be signed by a mark or by someone acting for the testator. In Washington, if the will is signed by someone other than the testator, it must be signed under the direction of or at the request of the testator and in the testator's

---

Fig. 9.2 Will terminology

WILL TERMINOLOGY

Testator: one who makes a will

Bequeath: to transfer personal property by will

Devise: to transfer real property by will

Codicil: an amendment to a will

Executor: carries out directions in the will

Probate: procedure to prove a will's validity

---

presence. The person who signs for the testator must also sign his own name and state that the testator's name was subscribed at the testator's request.

Just as the grantor of a deed must be competent, so must a person making out a will. The test for **testamentary capacity** is whether the party has sufficient mind and memory to understand the transaction, comprehend the nature and extent of the estate property, and recollect the "objects of her bounty."

The law presumes the validity of a will. However, if the person making the will was incompetent when the will was executed, the will is invalid. To invalidate a will, the evidence of incompetency must be clear, cogent, and convincing.

Case Example:

Ernest and Elva Eubank had an estate worth approximately $500,000. They had no children. In 1977, they executed wills that left $20,000 to Kermit Lighter (Elva's brother), along with other smaller bequests. The residuary estate was bequeathed half to J.E. Marvin (Ernest's cousin) and the remaining half to Marvin's six children.

On September 8, 1984, Ernest and Elva executed a new will that made Kermit Lighter residuary legatee, and gave only $40,000 to Marvin and $10,000 to each of the Marvin children.

The Marvins petitioned to invalidate the 1984 will, claiming lack of capacity and also undue influence by Kermit Lighter.

Dr. Ebert had treated both Ernest and Elva since 1955. He testified that he had diagnosed Elva in 1981 as suffering from senile dementia or an Alzheimer's-like syndrome. He testified that by June 1984, he felt she was unable to care for herself and was not oriented as to time, place, or self. In his opinion, she was not competent to understand a legal document or to comprehend the nature and extent of her holdings, and he was not confident that Elva could know the objects of her bounty.

Dr. Ebert and Dr. Murphy, a neurologist, also testified that Ernest was not competent.

James Simonton, the Eubanks' trust officer at the bank, visited the Eubanks in September of 1984. Although he had seen them approximately every two months, neither Ernest nor Elva recognized him. Simonton, who is an attorney, testified that in his opinion, neither of the Eubanks had sufficient mind or memory to understand a complicated legal document, to know the extent of their property, or to know the objects of their bounty.

The trial court found testamentary incapacity to execute the 1984 wills. *Matter of Estate of Eubank*, 50 Wn. App. 611, 749 P.2d 691 (1988).

Witnesses. Washington requires two or more competent witnesses to sign their names to the will in the presence of the testator. To validate the will, the witnesses must be able to testify that the testator signed the will or acknowledged the signature in their presence.

Any competent adult may act as a witness. Someone who is a beneficiary under the will should not act as a witness, however. Although a will can still be valid if someone named as a beneficiary is also one of the witnesses, that person might not be allowed to benefit under the will. If a beneficiary acts as a witness, all devises, legacies, and gifts made to him may be void, unless there are two other competent witnesses.

> **Example:** Ethel Crabtree signs her will and has it witnessed by her chauffeur and her cook. Ethel bequeaths $10,000 to the chauffeur in the will and leaves the remainder of her estate to a charitable organization. The will is valid because it was attested to by two witnesses; the chauffeur can testify as a witness to establish the validity of the will. However, the bequest to the chauffeur is probably void, because he is a beneficiary acting as a witness and there is only one other witness.
>
> Now suppose instead that the same will is witnessed by Ethel's gardener in addition to the chauffeur and the cook. In this case Ethel's bequest to the chauffeur is valid, because there are two other witnesses besides the chauffeur (the beneficiary).

Foreign wills. If a will is made by someone in another state in a manner that meets the laws of that state, Washington will recognize the will as valid, even if it does not meet all of Washington's requirements.

> **Example:** Some states recognize holographic wills, even though they are not witnessed. A **holographic will** is a will written entirely in the testator's handwriting, typically without being witnessed. Washington, however, does not recognize holographic wills. Taylor lives in a state where holographic wills are valid, and he writes a holographic will. He later moves to Washington and does not make a new will. When he dies, Washington will recognize the holographic will, since it was valid in the state where it was executed.

Revocation of a Will. A will may be revoked by a subsequent written will, or by being burnt, torn, canceled, obliterated, or destroyed with the intent and for the purpose of revoking the will. This destruction may be done directly by the testator, or by another person in the testator's presence and at the testator's direction.

If a will is lost or destroyed inadvertently or as a result of fraud, the court may still take proof of the will and establish it. A will must be proved by at least two witnesses.

Family Rights Under a Will. In Washington, when a married person (or registered domestic partner) dies, one-half of any community property goes to the surviving spouse. The other one-half of the community property and any of the deceased's separate property may be disposed of by will. Children do not have an absolute right to inherit and may be disinherited in a will.

Involuntary Alienation

Involuntary alienation is any transfer of ownership or an interest in property that occurs without any action by the owner or against the owner's wishes. In several instances involuntary alienation occurs automatically, such as when a person dies without leaving a will, or dies without leaving any heirs. Property ownership may also be transferred due to

Fig. 9.3 Transfer of a deceased person's property

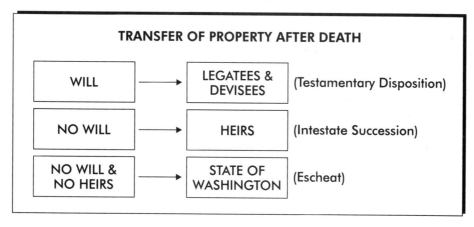

adverse possession, a court decision, or government action. And finally, ownership may change due to environmental or geological changes in the land itself.

Intestate Succession

Someone who dies without leaving a valid will is said to have died **intestate**. Intestate succession is the method of distributing the property of a person who dies without leaving a will (or whose will is invalid). The people who take property by intestate succession are called **heirs**. Intestate succession is strictly governed by statute and is supervised by the probate court. The probate court normally appoints an administrator to carry out the statutory distribution of the property.

Escheat

When a person dies intestate and without leaving any heirs, his property **escheats** to the state. The state acquires title to all of the deceased person's property.

Case Example:

John Adomaitis died intestate and without leaving any heirs. John died a resident of Illinois, but he left approximately $7,500 on deposit at the Seattle First National Bank.

A dispute arose concerning whether Illinois or Washington was entitled to this money. The court found that when a person dies without surviving heirs, leaving personal property located in the state of Washington, that property escheats to the state of Washington. *O'Keefe v. State Department of Revenue*, 79 Wn.2d 633, 488 P.2d 754 (1971).

In order for a person to die without leaving any heirs, there must be no living **issue** (issue includes children, grandchildren, great-grandchildren, and so on), and no parents, issue of the parents, grandparents, or issue of the grandparents. Obviously, this doesn't happen often.

If no heirs have appeared within four months after the decedent's death, the court may order payment of claims and expenses out of the estate. After ten months, if no heirs have appeared, personal property may be sold under order of the court. Real property cannot be sold to satisfy any debts until all of the proceeds of the personal property have been used up.

Court Decisions

Another form of involuntary alienation occurs when title to property is conveyed by court order. The most common forms of involuntary alienation by court action are foreclosure, partition, and quiet title actions. Title to property may also change hands due to adverse possession. A claim of adverse possession is often settled by the court in a quiet title action.

Foreclosure Actions. Someone who has a lien on a property may force the sale of the property if the underlying debt is not paid. **Foreclosure** is available for any type of lien against real property, including mortgages, construction liens, tax liens, and judgment liens.

In some foreclosure actions, the court will order the sheriff to seize the debtor's property and sell it at an auction (sheriff's sale, tax sale, or execution sale). The buyer at the auction receives a certificate of sale that ripens into title if the debtor does not redeem the property within eight months (or within one year in some cases, depending on certain statutory requirements). There is no redemption period after a foreclosure action under a deed of trust.

Suit for Partition. A **suit for partition** is a means of dividing property held by more than one person when the owners cannot agree among themselves how to divide it. The decision of the court is conclusive as to the parties involved. Frequently the court will order the property sold and the proceeds divided among the co-owners.

Case Example:

In 1973, Patty and Wally were planning to get married. They bought a purchaser's interest in a contract for the sale of a house. They paid $2,500 for the assignment of the purchaser's interest. The assignment was made to Wally and Patty as tenants in common. Both of them contributed to the downpayment and they intended to contribute equally in the purchase of the property. The contract called for monthly payments of $150.

In 1974, Patty and Wally were married. They lived in the house together for only seven months, until Patty moved out. She was granted a default dissolution in 1975. Wally remained in the house and continued to make the payments. Patty made no further payments after she moved out.

Patty brought a suit for partition claiming a one-half interest in the purchaser's equity on the house. Wally claimed that she had abandoned her interest and was not entitled to any interest in the house.

The court found that originally they had intended to share equally. However, after Patty moved out, Wally made all of the payments. Since they contributed unequally to the purchase price, a presumption arose that they intended to share the property proportionately to their contributions.

The court held that Patty had an equity in the property bearing the same relationship to the total equity as the ratio of her investment to the total investment of the parties. (For instance, if the amount she had paid was one-sixth of the total amount invested, she would have a one-sixth interest in the property.)

Once Wally paid Patty an amount sufficient to compensate her for her interest in the property, he had clear title to the property. *Cummings v. Anderson*, 94 Wn. 2d 135, 614 P.2d 1283 (1980).

Quiet Title Action. A **quiet title action** is used to remove a cloud on the title when the title cannot be cleared by the more peaceable means of a quitclaim deed. The court makes a binding determination of the various parties' interests in a particular piece of real estate.

A **cloud on the title** occurs whenever doubt exists as to the validity of a seller's title. The property is unmarketable as long as the cloud exists. To clear the cloud, the seller may have to bring a quiet title action to get a judicial ruling on the title.

> **Example:** The seller has found a potential buyer for his property. A search of the recorded documents shows a gap in the title. (A gap occurs when the recorded documents don't indicate who owned the property for a certain time period.)
>
> The seller brings a quiet title action. The defendants in the action are all parties who have a potential interest in the land. (This includes the mystery person who held title during the gap, even though this person's name is unknown.)
>
> The seller asks the court to declare his title valid, thereby "quieting title" to the land. If no defendants appear to challenge the seller's title, the court will grant the seller's request. The buyer can then rely on the validity of the seller's title and purchase the property.

Adverse Possession

Adverse possession is a statutory process by which possession and use of property can mature into title to the property. Adverse possession is based on the idea that it is better to give title to someone who makes good use of the property, rather than leaving title with someone who makes no attempt to use the property for a long period of time.

Owners of vacant property (for instance, owners of land held for future sale or development) should periodically inspect their property to check for any signs of adverse possession. The mere posting of "no trespassing" signs may not be sufficient to prevent a claim of adverse possession.

Public Lands. Adverse possession cannot be claimed against public lands, such as any land owned by the United States or Washington State, or land that a city, county, or other municipal district holds in a governmental capacity, such as public school lands, or public parks.

Requirements. In Washington, there are five basic requirements for adverse possession. Possession of the land must be:

1. actual,
2. open and notorious,
3. hostile,
4. exclusive, and
5. continuous and uninterrupted for a specified period of time.

Actual. Actual possession requires occupation and use of the property in a manner appropriate to the type of property. Residing on the property is not required unless residence is an appropriate use.

> **Example:** Actual possession of farmland may be achieved by fencing the land and planting crops.

Open and notorious. Possession must occur in a manner that would put a reasonable owner on notice that her ownership of the property was being threatened. An adverse possessor couldn't live in a hidden underground cave for ten years and then claim adverse possession, since her possession was not open enough to give the real owner notice.

Case Example:

The Butlers purchased property on Lake Sammamish in 1927. They believed their property line ran from a piling in the lake to the southwesterly corner of the lot. Pursuant to this belief, they planted lawn to the water line and planted a holly hedge in line with the piling. For many years they mowed the lawn, trimmed the hedge, and planted other trees, berry vines, and flowers.

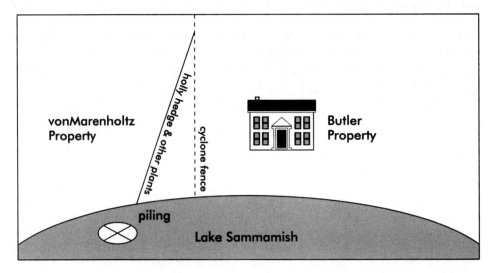

In 1958, the vonMarenholtzes bought the property next to the Butlers. By this time, the Butlers' holly hedge had become overgrown and was not very well kept up, due to Mr. Butler's advanced age.

A survey by the vonMarenholtzes showed an encroachment by the holly hedge. Nothing was done about it until 1964, when they hired a contractor to erect an eight-foot cyclone fence between the properties.

In constructing the fence, the contractor bulldozed down the line to the waterfront, removing all growth on both sides of the line to a width of 15 to 20 feet. No consent was obtained from the Butlers for this bulldozing and removal of the hedge.

The Butlers brought an action to quiet title, claiming adverse possession of the narrow strip in dispute between the adjacent properties.

The court found that the Butlers' improvements on the strip of property were actual, open, exclusive, and continuously adverse for the statutory period, long before the vonMarenholtzes even acquired possession of the adjoining property.

The court not only gave title to the strip of property to the Butlers, but also awarded damages for the reasonable expense of restoring the destroyed hedge and plantings. *Butler v. Anderson*, 71 Wn.2d 60, 426 P.2d 467 (1967).

Many adverse possession claims involve narrow strips of land between adjoining properties. As the example shows, planting and maintaining plants and hedges can be enough to meet the requirements for adverse possession. Note, however, that just mowing the lawn on a disputed strip is probably not enough to claim actual possession.

Hostile. Hostile possession requires the occupant to treat the property as his own as against all other parties.

If the owner has given another party permission to use the property, this use can never develop into adverse possession. Use of the property must be open enough for the true owner to be aware of the use, and must be without permission.

Exclusive. Possession of the land must be exclusive, meaning that the adverse possessor may not share possession with the true owner.

> **Example:** Johnson is the true owner of beachfront property. Abbott owns the property next to Johnson and believes that his boundary extends across Johnson's lot clear to the beach.
>
> Abbott uses the beach several weekends each month. Johnson also uses the beach sometimes. He works weekends, so he typically uses the property during the week.
>
> When a dispute arises as to ownership of the beachfront property, Abbott claims the property as an adverse possessor. But his claim of adverse possession would fail because he did not have exclusive use of the property.

Continuous and uninterrupted. Under the Washington statute, the adverse possessor must be in possession of the land for ten successive years (or seven years if under color of title and taxes have been paid). Uninterrupted means that there cannot be a significant break in the period of possession. Minor breaks, such as going away on vacation for two weeks, will not end the possession period.

Fig. 9.4 Requirements for adverse possession

ADVERSE POSSESSION	
10 YEARS	**7 YEARS**
1. actual, open, notorious 2. hostile 3. continuous & uninterrupted 4. exclusive	1. actual, open, notorious 2. hostile 3. continuous & uninterrupted 4. exclusive 5. good faith color of title 6. payment of taxes

The requirement that possession be continuous does not mean that the adverse possessor must use the property throughout the year. Continuous use means normal continuous use that a true owner would make of the property.

> **Example:** Returning to the previous example, now suppose Johnson does not live on the property but is merely holding it as an investment. He never uses the beach; in fact he has not been out to look at the property in 12 years.
>
> During that time, Abbott has used the beach almost every weekend all summer long. Abbott seldom uses the property in winter because it is too cold and rainy.
>
> Abbott's use of the property is continuous enough to meet the requirement because it was normal use for this type of property.

The continuous and uninterrupted requirement can be met by tacking. **Tacking** is the joining together of periods of adverse possession by different parties, to make one long period.

> **Example:** Davis possessed certain property for six years before his death. In his will, he left all of his property to his son, Brent. Brent continued possession of the property for six more years. When a dispute arose, Brent claimed he had met the time period requirements for adverse possession. Brent's six years of possession may be tacked on to his father's six years for a total of twelve years.

If the possessor claims a right to the property in good faith under color of title and pays taxes on the property, the required period of continuous possession is only seven years instead of ten. A party is said to have **color of title** when she appears to have title, or believes she has valid title, but in fact her title is not valid. Failure of the title may be due to a defect such as a forged deed or an erroneous land description.

In order to fall under the seven-year limit, the person claiming adverse possession under color of title must not have been aware that the deed was defective. The claim to the property must be made in good faith. In other words, the possessor must actually believe that he has a right to the property.

Under the seven-year rule, the possessor must also have paid all taxes legally assessed on the property during the time of possession.

Condemnation

Condemnation of private property by the government is another form of involuntary alienation. Under the U.S. Constitution, the government has the power to acquire private property for public use, without the owner's consent. This power is called the power of **eminent domain**. The procedure for exercising the power of eminent domain is called **condemnation**. Based on language in the Constitution, condemnation is often referred to as a "taking" of private property. After a taking, the Constitution requires the government to pay **just compensation** to the property owner (see Chapter 1). Just compensation is ordinarily the fair market value of the property.

The power of eminent domain can be exercised by any government entity (the state, a city, a school district, and so on). Limited use of the power can be delegated to certain private entities. For example, privately owned utility companies may be authorized to condemn property for utility purposes. Whether the entity is public or private, the intended use of the property must benefit the public.

When the government (or other authorized entity) determines it needs a particular piece of property, it first offers to purchase it. If the owner rejects the offer, the government files a condemnation lawsuit. The court considers evidence concerning the fair market value of the property, and directs the government to compensate the owner. Then the court orders the property condemned.

Dedication

Another method of transferring the ownership of real property is by dedication. **Dedication** is the transfer of privately owned land to the public without compensation. Dedication may sometimes be voluntary, as when a wealthy philanthropist dedicates a portion of her estate as a public park.

More frequently, dedication is by developers or subdividers. If a developer wants government approval for a planned subdivision, he may be required to dedicate certain areas for public use, such as streets, sidewalks, play areas, and so forth.

Natural Changes

Sometimes the land itself changes shape, thereby changing ownership of some portions of the soil. **Accretion** is the gradual build-up of soil caused by water-borne soil deposits. These soil deposits are called **alluvion** (or alluvium). A key feature of accretion is that the build-up must be gradual and almost imperceptible. When the land is changed by accretion, the boundary line may change to include the new soil deposits.

When property is enlarged by the retreat of a body of water, the landowner acquires title to the newly exposed land. This is called **reliction** (or dereliction). As with accretion, the retreat of the waterline must be gradual and imperceptible.

Avulsion is the violent tearing away of land by flowing water or waves. The land severed by avulsion does not change title; it still legally belongs to the original owner. Avulsion must be more sudden and violent than simple erosion, which is the gradual wearing away of soil due to the action of wind or water.

Avulsion may also result from a sudden change in a watercourse, as in the following case example.

Case Example:

The Sheldons and the Stroms owned property on opposite sides of a small stream known as "Whiskey Slough." The original deeds to both properties described the boundary as being the center or thread of the slough. In 1954, the Sheldons dredged the slough in order to widen it. The Sheldons used the enlarged slough to moor barges and trollers.

As a result of the dredging, a significant portion of the stream shifted onto the Sheldons' property, leaving the original boundary line on dry land. For many years, neither property owner was concerned about the change in the center line of the slough. Upon request from the Stroms, the Sheldons would move any craft that obstructed the Stroms' side of the slough.

In 1972, however, the Sheldons asserted a claim to the entire slough and refused to move barges from the Stroms' half. The Stroms brought an action to quiet title to the portion of land running from the original boundary to the present thread (middle of the slough).

The Sheldons argued that the sudden change in the boundary was avulsive, and that therefore the property boundary should not change. They claimed title clear up to the former boundary line, which was now on dry land on the other side of the slough.

The court found that a person may not induce an artificial change in water boundaries, and then claim whatever advantage that change produced. Therefore, the boundary line between the property was held to be the present thread or middle of Whiskey Slough, and the Stroms' action to quiet title was granted. *Strom v. Sheldon*, 12 Wn. App. 66, 527 P.2d 1382 (1975).

Recording

The fact that someone offers to sell real property is no assurance that the seller actually owns the property. The seller simply may be lying about owning the property, or the seller's title may be defective in some way. In order to limit these potential dangers, every state has recording laws. The purpose of the **recording system** is to protect purchasers by providing a method of determining who owns what interest in a particular piece of property.

A real estate agent is not required to verify a seller's title or perform a title search. However, it's helpful to know as much as possible about the property being sold. By using the recording system, an agent can find out useful information about the property, such as:

1. who is listed as the present owner of the property,
2. the legal description of the property,
3. whether there are any liens against the property, and
4. whether there are any easements or restrictive covenants that affect the property.

Recording Procedure

Many types of legal instruments affecting real property can and should be recorded. Some of the most common are deeds, easements, covenants, certain long-term leases, mortgages and releases of mortgages, agreements relating to community property or separate property, and powers of attorney to convey real estate. Purchase and sale agreements, however, are ordinarily not recorded.

To **record** a document, you simply deposit it with the recorder and pay a nominal fee. The document is then said to be filed for record. As we noted earlier, in Washington a deed cannot be recorded until it is acknowledged.

Once a document has been given to the recorder, it is copied and placed in the public record in chronological order based on the filing date, to establish the priority of the interest described in the document. It may be copied by transcription, or by any photographic or photomechanical process (photocopiers, microfilm, etc.) that produces a clear, legible, and durable record. After being recorded, the original document is returned to the party named on the document as entitled to possession of it.

Usually the county auditor has the duty of recording instruments. In this capacity, the auditor is often referred to as the **county recorder** or **county clerk**.

Access to Recorded Documents

Each county recorder's office must maintain indexes of recorded documents. Documents can be searched for by:

1. grantor name,
2. grantee name,
3. filing date,
4. recording number,
5. document type (for instance, deed or mortgage), and
6. legal description and other information.

Almost every recorder's office maintains a website where the public can search for property records. Typically, however, the online database only includes transactions from more recent decades. Earlier records are on microfilm or in bound volumes at the recorder's office.

Recorder's offices also keep books containing plat maps of all platted (subdivided) land within the county. An index to the plat maps is maintained, listing the name of each subdivision or addition.

Notice

One of the purposes of recording deeds and other documents is to provide notice of the transaction. **Notice** is knowledge of information about the property. Every purchaser or mortgagee of land is charged with notice of all prior recorded documents concerning that property.

Actual Notice. When information is acquired personally by a party, she is said to have actual notice. Actual notice may be gained from the seller, from other parties, or from inspection of the property.

> **Example:** Ashworth tells Simpson that he wants to sell his house. Simpson is interested in buying it.
>
> When Simpson goes to look at the property, she notices that there's a large power transformer located at the back of the property and power cables extending across the property. When she asks Ashworth about this, he tells Simpson that the power company has an easement across the property. Simpson has actual notice of the power company's interest in the property.

Constructive Notice. Notice may be imparted by operation of law as a result of recording. A court will not allow a party to claim ignorance of a recorded document. Even if the purchaser was not actually aware of the document, if it was in the public record the purchaser is deemed to have had constructive notice of it. The document (and the interest set forth in it) would have been discovered if the purchaser had checked the public record.

> **Example:** Smith grants an easement across his property to Jones. Jones records the grant of easement.
>
> Smith then sells his property to King. King claims that the easement is extinguished because he could not tell that it existed simply by looking at the property, and Smith never told him about it.
>
> The easement is still valid. Even though he had no actual notice of it, King is deemed to have constructive notice of the easement. If he'd checked the recorded documents pertaining to the property, he would have found a record of the easement.

Washington Recording Law

Although the rules differ somewhat, every state has **recording statutes**. Generally, these laws provide that a deed, mortgage, or other instrument is ineffective as to subsequent purchasers of the same property unless it is recorded (or unless the purchaser had actual notice of the instrument or interest). Purchasers should be able to rely on the public record, and the law protects them against any secret, unrecorded instruments.

Document Format. The recording statute contains very specific format requirements for any document submitted for recording. Among other requirements, the document must contain an abbreviated legal description and the county assessor's tax parcel number, and each page must have margins of a certain size. Documents failing to conform to these format requirements will incur an additional fee and may be subject to a delay. If you need to record anything, check the statutory requirements and make sure your documents are in the proper format.

Washington's type of recording statute is called a **race-notice statute**, meaning that there is a race to record. Whoever records first wins, if he has no notice of any previous conveyances.

> **Example:** Connelly sells his property to O'Donnell and gives him a deed on June 10. O'Donnell fails to record his deed. Connelly later sells the same property to McMurphy on August 15. McMurphy has no knowledge of the sale to O'Donnell. McMurphy records her deed on August 15.
>
> McMurphy would win an action to determine ownership of the property even though O'Donnell purchased the property first. McMurphy "won the race" by recording first, and she had no notice of the previous sale. (She had no actual notice, and could not be deemed to have constructive notice because O'Donnell's deed had not yet been recorded.)

In the example, McMurphy is what is known as a **subsequent bona fide purchaser**—someone who pays for an interest in land that has already been sold to another, without any knowledge (actual or constructive notice) of the previous sale.

A mortgagee who loans money in reliance on the public record is considered a **bona fide encumbrancer** and is likewise protected by the recording laws.

However, a subsequent purchaser who has notice of a previous conveyance can never win, even if she records first. Someone with notice of a previous sale is not a bona fide purchaser.

> **Example:** Majeski and Yancey are both house hunting. They have bumped into each other several times at the brokerage office and have chatted about the kind of house they are looking for.
>
> Nomiama sells her property to Majeski and gives her a deed on September 6. Majeski moves onto the property on October 1. Yancey hears about Nomiama's property, and when he goes out to look at it he discovers that Majeski is living on the property. Majeski tells Yancey about the great deal she made. Yancey casually asks if Majeski has recorded her deed yet and Majeski tells him no.
>
> Yancey then purchases the property from Nomiama and records the deed on October 12. Majeski doesn't record her deed until October 20.
>
> Even though Yancey recorded first, his claim will not prevail, since Yancey had actual notice of the prior conveyance to Majeski.

An unrecorded deed or mortgage is valid between the parties, but not as to subsequent bona fide purchasers.

Example: Smith sells his property to Jones and gives Jones a deed. Jones never records the deed. Even though unrecorded, the deed is valid between Smith and Jones. Smith later sells the property to White and gives White a deed. White has no knowledge of the sale to Jones. White records the deed.

In a lawsuit to determine ownership of the property, White will prevail. The deed between Smith and Jones is ineffective as to the subsequent purchaser (White) because it was never recorded.

Of course, Smith's action in selling the property twice was illegal and Jones could try to obtain damages from Smith, but Smith has probably skipped town by now.

The recording statutes are meant to protect purchasers. Someone who inherits property or receives it as a gift may not be protected.

Example: Fritzley mortgages his land to the bank, but the bank fails to record the mortgage document.

Sometime later, Fritzley deeds the land to his son as a gift. The son records his deed. The son is not protected against the bank's claim, however, because he is not a bona fide purchaser. The bank can still enforce the mortgage.

However, if the son sold the property to McGillicuddy and McGillicuddy recorded the deed, McGillicuddy would get good title, free of the unrecorded mortgage, because McGillicuddy is a bona fide purchaser without notice.

Torrens System

Washington adopted the Torrens system of land registration in the early twentieth century. However, even though it is available, Torrens registration is not commonly used here.

Under the Torrens Act, title to a parcel of real property can be registered through the county recorder's office. Once the property is registered, any interests in the property or claims against the title must also be registered in order to have legal effect. So, for example, a mortgage against the property must be added to the Torrens register in order for the lender to have a valid lien. (There's one exception to that rule: construction liens against a Torrens property do not have to be registered to be valid.)

The status of title to registered property may be determined by examining the Torrens register alone; it generally isn't necessary to search the public record in the usual way. A purchaser of property registered under the Torrens system is not held to have constructive notice of interests or claims that were recorded through the ordinary recording system.

Title Insurance

Title insurance is a contract in which the title insurance company agrees to indemnify (reimburse) the policy holder for possible financial losses that could occur due to undiscovered defects in a property's title, such as an undisclosed lien or a forged deed. Title insurance coverage is typically obtained by a buyer or lender when a piece of real property is purchased or mortgaged. It generally protects the buyer or lender from losses caused by title defects (clouds on title) that are unknown at the time the transaction closes but discovered at some later point, typically when a third party makes a claim against the property.

The title insurance company will handle the legal defense of any claim by a third party that is based on a defect covered by the policy. If the third party prevails in the lawsuit, the company will pay the policy holder's damages, up to the policy's coverage limit.

Obtaining Insurance

When an application for title insurance is received, the title insurance company's first step is to conduct a **title search**. An employee of the company searches the public record for documents concerning the property in question. Next, the company prepares a **title report** (also called a preliminary title report), which lists items that were discovered in the title search and that will be excepted from coverage if a policy is issued.

This list of exceptions from coverage includes the recorded encumbrances—liens, easements, and private restrictions—that currently affect title to the property, in the opinion of the insurer. If it someday turns out that there is an encumbrance or a title defect that was not listed as an exception, the policy will cover problems resulting from that.

> **Example:** There's an easement on the property, but the title searcher accidentally overlooked the recorded grant of easement during the title search. As a result, the easement wasn't listed in the title report or excepted from coverage when the title insurance policy was issued. The buyer doesn't learn about the easement until six months after the sale closes. This problem is covered by the policy.

The parties to the transaction may arrange to have some of the items listed in the title report cleared from the title. For example, a property seller is usually expected to pay off liens before the sale closes.

If the party requesting the insurance (the buyer or lender) is satisfied with the condition of the property's title, the transaction proceeds to closing. When the required premium is paid, the title company issues the title insurance policy. (A single premium payment provides coverage for as long as the policy holder continues to have an interest in the property.)

Hidden Title Defects

Sometimes a property has title defects that are not plainly shown by the recorded documents concerning the property. Examples of hidden defects include a forged signature on a previous deed in the chain of title, a deed or release of mortgage executed by a minor or mentally incompetent person, a deed or mortgage that incorrectly states marital status, or a deed that was not properly delivered. Problems like these can't be discovered through a standard search of the public record and an ordinary examination of the documents. This type of hidden defect usually is covered by a title insurance policy; the company assumes the risk that there may be something like this lurking in the property's history.

Case Example:

W & A Development Company negotiated the sale of some of its property. Transamerica Title Insurance Company issued a preliminary title report showing W & A as the owner and also showing that the property was subject to a mortgage. Allen Bowden, an attorney and controlling owner of W & A, forged a satisfaction of the mortgage and had it recorded.

When Transamerica issued its title insurance policy, it did not list the mortgage as an exception from coverage, since the forged satisfaction made it appear that the mortgage was no longer a lien against the property.

Sometime later, the mortgage holder initiated foreclosure proceedings. The title company had to pay damages to the policy holder because the still-valid mortgage was not excepted from coverage in the policy. *Securities Services, Inc. v. Transamerica Title*, 20 Wn. App. 664, 583 P.2d 1217 (1978).

Types of Coverage

There are three main types of title insurance coverage: standard coverage, extended coverage, and homeowner's coverage.

A **standard coverage policy** is used to insure an owner or lender against title problems related to matters of public record. If there is a recorded document that the title searcher failed to find, or if there is a hidden problem with a recorded document, such as a forged signature, those will be covered. However, standard coverage does not insure against the interests of a person in actual possession of the property, or against other problems that could only be discovered through an inspection or a survey of the property, not from the public record.

An **extended coverage policy** insures against all matters covered by the standard coverage policy, plus matters that could be discovered through an inspection or survey, such as an unrecorded easement, an unrecorded construction lien, an encroachment, or adverse possession.

> **Example:** There are adverse possessors living on the property, but the inspector from the title insurance company fails to notice the indications of their presence. The company issues an extended coverage policy without listing that problem as an exception from coverage.
>
> Several months after the transaction closes, the adverse possessors file a lawsuit claiming that they have met the legal requirements for adverse possession of the property and asking the court to quiet title in their names. Under the extended coverage policy, the title company is required to handle the defense of this lawsuit. The policy will also cover the policy holder's damages if the court rules that the adverse possessors now own the property.

Although an extended coverage policy can be purchased to protect a buyer, it is typically purchased to protect the buyer's lender; this is referred to as a **mortgagee's policy**.

A buyer is ordinarily required to pay the premium for the mortgagee's extended coverage policy as a condition for obtaining the loan.

In Washington, most residential purchase and sale agreements require the seller to pay for a **homeowner's coverage policy** protecting the buyer. This kind of coverage is available in transactions involving residential property with up to four units. It protects the buyer against most of the same title problems as an extended coverage policy, plus some additional ones.

Coverage of certain items not ordinarily included in a particular type of policy may be obtained by purchasing an **endorsement** to cover them.

As a general rule, title insurance will not protect a landowner from losses due to government action. If the property is condemned, or if there is a change in the law that reduces the property's value, that won't be covered by the title policy.

Conclusion

One of the basic rights inherent in property ownership is the right to transfer the property to another party. Property can also change hands without the consent of the owner, through operation of law, as with intestate succession, foreclosure, or partition.

When property is sold and ownership is transferred, the new owners can safeguard their interest in the property by recording the deed and purchasing title insurance.

Owners should be certain of their property's true boundaries and inspect the property regularly to prevent a possible claim of adverse possession. A real estate agent should also be alert to the possibility of adverse possession.

Case Problem

The following is a hypothetical case problem. Most of the facts are taken from a real case. Based on what you have learned from this chapter, make a decision on the issues presented and then check to see if your answer matches the court's decision.

The Facts

John Mayes owned some unimproved land. Upon his death, the land was inherited by several heirs. They each received a percentage interest in the property, which they held as tenants in common. Maude Hamilton, one of the heirs, owned a ¼ interest in the property. In 1936, she executed a quitclaim deed to the property to L. E. Palm. Palm subsequently sold the property to the McGills, giving them a warranty deed that purported to convey the land in its entirety. This deed was recorded in 1936. Since 1936, the McGills have paid all of the taxes on the property.

The McGills erected fences and a goat shed on the property and used it for grazing purposes for several years. Sometime after 1940, the grazing was discontinued, and the land lay vacant and unused except as a source of firewood.

From 1936 to 1955, none of the other heirs of John Mayes made any claim to the land or attempted to occupy or use the land.

In 1955, the heirs executed quitclaim deeds to the Shugartses. When the Shugartses entered the land and cut and removed timber, the McGills brought an action to quiet title.

The Questions

When Maude Hamilton executed the quitclaim deed, what was transferred? When Palm sold to the McGills, what was transferred? Have the McGills met the requirements for adverse possession, even though they did not live on the property or even use it for many years except to cut firewood? Did the Shugartses acquire any interest in the property by the quitclaim deeds given by the heirs?

The Answer

When Maude Hamilton executed the quitclaim deed, she could only transfer the interest she possessed, which was a ¼ interest. This means that Palm only received a ¼ interest and could only transfer a ¼ interest. Since he gave the McGills a warranty deed to all of the property, he could be liable to them because he only had clear title to a ¼ interest.

However, the McGills adversely possessed the property under color of title. They had a deed that purported to transfer all of the property to them. In addition, and probably most convincing, they paid all taxes on the property since 1936. None of the heirs had paid any taxes, made any claim to the property, or attempted to occupy or use it.

By the time the heirs attempted to convey the property to the Shugartses, they had no interest to convey. The McGills had already acquired the property by adverse possession. Since a quitclaim deed only transfers the interest the grantor possesses, the Shugartses gained no interest in the property.

Title to the property was quieted in the McGills, and the McGills were awarded damages for the Shugartses' trespass and the cutting of timber. *McGill v. Shugarts*, 58 Wn.2d 203, 361 P.2d 645 (1961).

Chapter Summary

- Transferring (or alienating) real property by deed is called conveyancing. Three main types of deeds are used in Washington: the general warranty deed, the bargain and sale deed, and the quitclaim deed.

- To be valid, a deed must have an identifiable grantee, be in writing, contain words of conveyance and an adequate description of the property, and be signed by a competent grantor. It must also be delivered to and accepted by the grantee. A deed can be recorded in Washington only if it has been acknowledged by the grantor.

- A valid will in Washington generally must be executed by a competent testator, be in writing, and be signed by the testator, and the signature must be attested to by two or more competent witnesses.

- Intestate succession is the method of distributing the property of someone who dies without a valid will. If a person dies intestate without any heirs, the property will escheat to the state.

- Property ownership may be transferred by court decisions such as foreclosure actions, suits for partition, and quiet title actions.

- Property ownership may also be acquired through adverse possession. The requirements for adverse possession are that possession be actual, open, notorious, hostile, continuous, uninterrupted, and exclusive for ten years. If the claim of adverse possession is made in good faith under color of title and the adverse possessor has paid taxes on the property, the time requirement is only seven years.

- Other methods of transferring the ownership of real property include dedication, condemnation, and natural changes such as accretion, reliction, or avulsion.

- When a document is recorded, a copy is placed in the public record, in chronological order based on the date it was filed for recording. Recorded documents can generally be searched for online using the database maintained by the county recorder.

- Every purchaser or mortgagee of land is charged with notice of all prior recorded documents concerning the property in question. Even without actual notice, a party will be deemed to have constructive notice if the information has been recorded.

- Washington has a race-notice type of recording statute. When a dispute occurs as to ownership, the party who filed first, with no notice of previous conveyances, wins.

- Title insurance is purchased to protect the policy holder against losses caused by defects in title. Common policies include the standard coverage policy, the extended coverage policy, and the homeowner's coverage policy.

Checklist of Problem Areas

Real Estate Licensee's Checklist

❑ Does the title report confirm that the seller is the current owner of the property?

❑ Are there any encumbrances or problems with the seller's title that might block the sale?

Seller's Checklist

❑ Are you aware of the warranties you are making in the deed when you transfer the property to the buyer?

❑ Has title insurance been purchased for the buyer?

Buyer's Checklist

❑ Are there any clouds on the title?

❑ Does anyone have a possible claim to the property based on adverse possession?

❑ Has title insurance been purchased for the lender?

❑ What type of deed are you receiving, and what warranties or guarantees does this type of deed give you?

❑ Has the deed been signed by the grantor and does it indicate the grantor's marital status?

❑ Was the deed acknowledged and properly delivered?

❑ Has the deed been recorded?

Chapter Quiz

1. Johnson sells her property to Eibert. Johnson is 23 and Eibert is 17. Eibert signs the deed but Johnson does not. The deed does not specify the amount of the purchase price. Eibert never records the deed. The deed between Johnson and Eibert is invalid because:

   a. Eibert is only 17
   b. Johnson did not sign the deed
   c. the amount of the purchase price was not specified
   d. the deed was never recorded

2. A deed grants property to "Jonathan Searl Meachan and his brother Ed."

   a. The deed is invalid because it does not specify Ed's full name
   b. The deed is valid as to Jonathan but not as to Ed
   c. The deed is valid because it adequately identifies Ed even though it doesn't give his full name
   d. None of the above

3. A deed does not indicate whether the grantor is married or single. Which of the following is true?

   a. The deed is invalid because it must specify marital status
   b. Marital status is irrelevant in a deed
   c. Stating marital status is not required but is helpful and strongly recommended
   d. None of the above

4. Celia Johnson executes (but does not record) a deed granting her property "to my niece upon my death" and places it in her safe deposit box. She has several nieces, although only one ever comes to visit her. The deed is discovered after Celia dies. The deed does not transfer title, because:

   a. it was not properly delivered before Celia died
   b. a transfer on death deed must be recorded
   c. the grantee is not adequately identified
   d. All of the above

5. Barbara has been appointed as the attorney in fact for her grandmother. When she executes a deed conveying an interest in real property held by her grandmother, she should:

   a. sign her grandmother's name only
   b. sign her own name only
   c. write her grandmother's name, followed by her own signature as attorney in fact
   d. None of the above

6. A quitclaim deed conveys:

   a. whatever interest the grantor has
   b. only a portion of the interest held by the grantor
   c. only property acquired by adverse possession
   d. None of the above

7. A will:

   a. is a form of involuntary alienation
   b. is a form of voluntary alienation
   c. may be made out by anyone, regardless of age, if adequately witnessed
   d. must be witnessed by a notary public

8. A nuncupative will:

   a. must be entirely handwritten
   b. is invalid in Washington
   c. is an oral will
   d. can be used to convey real property

9. Which of the following is true regarding witnesses to a will?

   a. A beneficiary may never be a witness
   b. There must be at least three witnesses
   c. The witnesses must be notary publics
   d. The witnesses must be mentally competent

10. Which of these is not a requirement for adverse possession?

   a. Continuous and uninterrupted possession
   b. Exclusive possession
   c. Constructive possession
   d. Open and notorious possession

11. Under a race-notice statute, the person who wins is the:

   a. last to purchase the property, with notice of all previous conveyances
   b. first to record, without notice of any previous conveyances
   c. first to purchase the property, without notice of all subsequent conveyances
   d. first to record, with notice of all previous conveyances

12. In Washington, when someone with color of title has paid all taxes on property, the time limit required for adverse possession is:

   a. five years
   b. seven years
   c. ten years
   d. None of the above

13. A flash flood changes the course of a small river and leaves it in a new position. This type of change is known as:

   a. reliction
   b. accretion
   c. avulsion
   d. alluvion

14. Which type or types of title insurance protect against adverse possession?

   a. Only the standard coverage policy
   b. Both the extended coverage policy and the homeowner's coverage policy
   c. Both the standard coverage policy and the extended coverage policy
   d. Neither the standard coverage policy nor the extended coverage policy

15. A deed has been recorded but the prospective purchaser has not checked the public record. The purchaser is said to have what type of notice of this document?

   a. Actual notice
   b. Constructive notice
   c. Implied notice
   d. The purchaser has no notice until the document is discovered

10 Closing and Escrow

Outline

Key Terms

- Escrow
- Closing
- Escrow (closing) agent
- Delivery
- Escrow instructions
- Like-kind exchange
- Relation back doctrine
- RESPA
- Federally related loan
- Kickback
- Unearned fee
- TRID
- Form 1099-S reporting
- Form 8300 reporting
- FIRPTA

Chapter Overview

A seller listed her property with a real estate firm, and an agent from the firm began marketing the property. An interested buyer was found and a purchase and sale agreement was signed. Now the process of closing the sale begins. In most transactions, escrow is opened to facilitate the closing. This chapter discusses how escrow works and when title to the property actually passes to the new owner. It also covers federal disclosure and tax-reporting laws that an escrow agent or other closing agent is required to comply with.

Preparing for Closing

All of the preliminary work must be done and a clear agreement reached between the parties before a transaction is ready for closing. **Closing** is the consummation of the transaction, when the seller delivers title to the buyer in exchange for the purchase price. Typically, closing is not official until all of the documents are recorded.

When the purchase and sale agreement is signed, the real estate agent usually helps the parties set a **closing date**. This is the legal closing date on which the documents transferring title from the seller to the buyer are delivered and recorded.

One of the most significant factors to consider when estimating a closing date is the current volume of mortgage lending. If many people are seeking financing, lenders and appraisers may be too busy to act immediately, and a fairly long closing period may be necessary. However, if lenders aren't particularly busy and everything goes smoothly, it may be easy to close the transaction in less than a month. Of course, the closing date stated in the purchase and sale agreement can be postponed if both parties agree to an extension.

Escrow

A property buyer seldom hands the seller cash in exchange for title to the property. Usually an escrow is opened to handle the details of the closing process.

Escrow is an arrangement in which money and/or documents are held by a third party—an **escrow agent** (also called a **closing agent**)—on behalf of the buyer and seller. The money and documents are then transferred or distributed by the escrow agent, according to instructions from the buyer and seller.

Purpose of Escrow

Escrow is used to ensure that the concerns of the buyer, the seller, and the lender will all be met. A buyer is often reluctant to invest more than the initial earnest money deposit in the property until she is certain that the seller can convey title as agreed. And a seller

Fig. 10.1 How escrow works

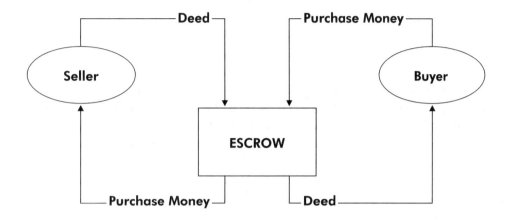

doesn't want to deliver the deed until he receives the purchase price. Escrow ensures that the seller receives the purchase price, the buyer receives clear title to the property, and the lender's security interest in the property is perfected, all at the same time.

Escrow protects the parties against a one-sided change of mind. For example, after escrow has been opened, the seller cannot change his mind and refuse to deliver the deed to the buyer. Once a deed is deposited with an escrow agent, the seller no longer has any control over the deed. When the buyer meets the specified conditions (such as paying the purchase price), the escrow agent must deliver the deed.

Escrow is also a great convenience when the parties are located in different states (or even countries), travel extensively, or are occupied with other business. The use of escrow allows the closing process to continue even if both parties are not readily available to meet in person.

> **Example:** John is being transferred from Cleveland, Ohio, to the Seattle office of his corporation. He has already made several trips to Seattle and has found a house he wants to buy. He has signed the purchase and sale agreement and escrow has been opened. John agreed to and signed the escrow instructions.
>
> John has to return to Cleveland to finish up some business in that office. He doesn't have the time to fly out to Seattle again, and he doesn't plan to return to Seattle until he moves into his new house. Therefore, the rest of the closing is handled by mail with the escrow company.
>
> The seller delivers into escrow a fully executed deed. Once the financing goes through and John delivers the purchase price into escrow, the escrow company delivers the deed to John. (Delivery is usually accomplished by recording the deed, with the document sent to the grantee after recording.)

Escrow Agents

An escrow agent may be a bank or other financial institution, a title insurance company, an independent escrow firm, a mortgage broker, or an attorney. In eastern Washington, attorneys frequently close real estate transactions. In the western half of the state, attorneys are not as commonly used.

State Licensing Requirements. Washington's Escrow Agent Registration Act requires companies providing escrow services to be registered and licensed as **escrow agents** by the Department of Financial Institutions. The individuals that a licensed escrow agent employs to handle transactions must be licensed **escrow officers**, and they must be supervised by the company's **designated escrow officer**. The designated escrow officer is a licensed escrow officer and is usually also one of the company's partners or corporate officers, or a sole proprietor, depending on how the company is organized.

Licensed escrow agents must keep records of all transactions. When handling funds on behalf of a buyer or seller, an escrow agent must place the funds in a trust account maintained in a recognized Washington depository. If a licensed escrow agent or escrow officer converts trust funds to personal use, or commits any other dishonest or prohibited acts, the Director of the Department of Licensing may temporarily suspend or permanently revoke the license.

Exemptions. Certain entities are exempt from the escrow registration and licensing requirements: attorneys, title companies, banks, savings and loans, credit unions, insurance companies, federally approved lenders, and those acting under the supervision of a court, such as receivers, trustees in bankruptcy, guardians, executors, and probate administrators. Real estate agents handling escrow for their own transactions are also exempt, as long as they don't charge an additional fee for escrow services.

All escrow agents, including those exempt from the Escrow Agent Registration Act's licensing and registration requirements, are required by the law to act fairly and honestly in dealings with clients and third parties.

Limited practice officers. In Washington, limited practice officers (LPOs) may prepare certain escrow documents and perform routine closing functions. LPOs are certified and regulated by the state supreme court.

Escrow Agent's Duties. An escrow agent acts as a special agent, with authority limited to the escrow transaction. He is considered the agent or trustee for both parties and is essentially acting as an authorized dual agent, with duties to both parties.

An escrow agent is bound by the terms of the escrow agreement and must follow its specific instructions. If the agent acts contrary to the instructions, she may be liable for any resulting damages.

> **Example:** Seller delivers a deed to the closing agent. Buyer delivers the purchase price to the agent. Among other things, the escrow instructions provide that the escrow agent

is to deliver the purchase price to Seller after receiving the title insurance report and pest inspection report.

The escrow agent delivers the money after receiving the title insurance report, but before receipt of the pest inspection report. Seller accepts the money and moves to Rio. It turns out that the house is infested with termites. The escrow agent would be liable to Buyer for damages.

The Escrow Process

An escrow agent plays a key role in the closing process. One of the agent's first steps is to review the purchase and sale agreement and/or loan commitment to determine whether there is a valid agreement that can be closed. The escrow agent also orders title insurance and helps the parties clear up title defects or unexpected encumbrances revealed in the title report.

The escrow agent prepares and explains the escrow instructions, and arranges for the execution, recording, and delivery of all necessary documents. She collects the funds necessary to close and prepares the closing statements. A critical condition of most real estate closings in Washington is the issuance of the title insurance policy or policies.

Choosing the Escrow Agent. Theoretically, the choice of an escrow agent is a subject for agreement between the parties. In actual practice, the decision is often made by the real estate agent handling the sale, or by the lender.

Most modern escrow agents do more than simply receive deposits. They usually create or obtain the documents required to close the transaction (for example, by ordering title insurance and preparing settlement statements).

Originally, the escrow agent was required to be a disinterested third party, independent of the seller or the buyer. Today, the closing agent must still be a third party. The seller or buyer cannot act as the escrow agent. However, it is not a specific requirement that the escrow agent be completely neutral and disinterested. (Although not a requirement, it is usually the wisest choice.) If both parties agree, the closing agent may be an attorney or real estate agent of the seller or buyer, as long as serving as the escrow agent involves no violation of his duty to the principal.

Opening Escrow. Escrow may be opened by any of the people involved in the sale transaction. It is usually opened when the real estate agent delivers a copy of the purchase and sale agreement to the closing agent specified in the agreement. It may also be opened when the lender delivers a copy of the purchase and sale agreement or a loan commitment to its escrow department or escrow subsidiary.

Enforceable contract. There must be an underlying enforceable contract between the parties before escrow can be opened. This is usually a purchase and sale agreement. Since the sale of real estate is governed by the statute of frauds, the contract must be in writing. An oral contract for the sale of real estate cannot be the basis of an escrow.

Case Example:

McLain entered into an oral agreement to exchange his land with land owned by Morgan and Pepper. Healy, an attorney, prepared the respective deeds. The deeds were executed by all of the parties except Mrs. McLain, who was out of town.

The parties agreed that Morgan and Pepper would deposit their deed with Healy. As soon as the McLain deed was executed by Mrs. McLain, it would be deposited with Healy. Healy would then deliver the deeds to the respective parties.

After depositing their deed with Healy, Morgan visited the McLain property. Dissatisfied with the land, he told Healy not to deliver their deed to McLain.

Healy received the McLain deed duly executed by Mrs. McLain. However, under the instructions from Morgan, he refused to deliver the Morgan and Pepper deed to McLain.

McLain brought an action to compel delivery of the deed. The court declined, holding that an enforceable escrow must rest upon an enforceable contract, and an enforceable contract for the exchange of real property must be in writing to meet the requirements of the statute of frauds. *McLain v. Healy*, 98 Wash. 489, 1168 P. 1 (1917).

The purchase and sale agreement must also contain all the required terms of the underlying transaction. For example, if the sale involves seller financing, the appropriate forms (the note and deed of trust or real estate contract) must be mentioned in and attached to the contract. Otherwise the sales agreement will be unenforceable, and therefore the escrow will be invalid. (See the discussion of purchase and sale agreements in Chapter 8.)

Where there is a binding and enforceable contract between the parties, a deposit into escrow becomes irrevocable and neither party can remove any deposits until the conditions are satisfied.

Delivery. In order for escrow to be valid—legally binding on both parties—there must be complete and irrevocable delivery of the documents (such as a valid deed), funds, and other items deposited into escrow. This means that the party who deposits an item has to relinquish all rights of possession or control over it. If the depositor retains the legal power to retrieve a deposit, the escrow fails.

> **Example:** Maxwell deposits a deed into escrow with the instruction that it isn't to be delivered to the purchaser until Maxwell notifies the escrow agent that it's okay to deliver it.
>
> Maxwell has retained control of the deed because it is to be delivered only under her direction. Since she has retained control, the deed is not validly delivered into escrow.

Neither party may withdraw documents or money unless the escrow conditions are satisfied or terminated, or both parties consent to the withdrawal.

Escrow Instructions. The obligations of the parties and the conditions that must be fulfilled are set forth in written **escrow instructions**. Escrow instructions are typically prepared by the escrow agent.

Fig. 10.2 Escrow requirements

REQUIREMENTS FOR VALID ESCROW

- a valid deed,
- an enforceable contract,
- delivery,
- an escrow agent,
- instructions, and
- conditions that must be met.

Joint instructions—one set of instructions that applies to both parties—is the norm. Joint instructions eliminate the risk of conflicting instructions. However, in some cases (usually commercial transactions) the buyer and seller may execute separate escrow instructions. In that case, a set of instructions from each of them would be given to the closing agent.

A problem arises if the terms of the escrow instructions are inconsistent with the terms of the purchase and sale agreement. As a general rule, if two consecutive contracts involving the same subject matter are inconsistent, the two are interpreted together to determine the whole contract. If the two contracts have material terms that are inconsistent and cannot be reconciled, the latter contract supersedes the former. So in this situation, the terms of the escrow instructions will control the outcome of the conflict.

> **Example:** The purchase and sale agreement states that Seller will pay for the pest inspection report. However, the escrow instructions provide that Buyer will pay for the pest inspection.
>
> Since the two are inconsistent, the later contract controls. The parties must follow the terms in the escrow instructions. Buyer pays for the pest inspection report.

No specific legal requirements control what must be included in escrow instructions. However, some provisions are typically included in the instructions.

Parties and property. Escrow instructions identify all of the parties by name and address. A description of the property involved is also included. There should be a statement of the nature of the transaction and the purpose of the escrow.

Obligations. A significant section of the instructions describes the obligations of the parties. There should be a list of all deposits to be made by the seller. This might include the deed, bill of sale, leases, paid tax statements, service contracts, insurance policies, warranty contracts, and pest or other inspection reports. The items to be deposited by the buyer are usually the purchase price and purchase money mortgage or deed of trust, and proceeds of the mortgage or deed of trust loan. This section may also describe the duties and liabilities of the closing agent.

General instructions. A section should be included with general instructions, including when the deed is to be recorded, when deposits are to be made, and when and where those items are to be delivered. This passage should also include provisions for the return of deposits (documents and funds) if the conditions are not met.

Fees and costs. The fees and costs each party will pay must be included in the instructions. This includes directions for payment of escrow, title, and recording charges, the real estate commission, and attorney's fees. Also included is a list of items to be prorated or apportioned between the parties, and the basis for such proration.

Conditions. One of the most important sections of the instructions is the portion that describes the conditions that must be met before the deposits may be delivered to the respective parties.

Even if a condition has been included in the instructions, it may be waived by the party who imposed the condition as long as it was not included for the benefit of both parties. And if escrow closes without strict compliance with the terms of the condition, a party may be held to have waived the condition by failing to make a timely objection.

> **Example:** One of the terms of the escrow instructions provides that Seller will repair or replace a broken light on the back porch. All of the other terms are met, but Seller has not yet fixed the light. Buyer is aware that the light is still broken. The parties go ahead with closing and Buyer does not raise any objection concerning the broken light. Buyer moves into the house.
>
> Buyer will probably be held to have waived the condition that Seller must repair or replace the light.

Time limits. Often an instruction is included that provides that the terms and conditions must be performed within a certain time limit. To be enforceable, the time limit must be clearly specified. Washington courts have held that if time has specifically been made "of the essence," the agreement becomes defunct when the time limit expires and performance has not been completed.

Case Example:

On July 26, 1965, Seller and Buyer entered into a purchase and sale agreement. The agreement expressly stated that time was of the essence and provided that the sale was to be closed "in any event not later than 120 days from date of this Agreement, which shall be the termination date."

Buyer delivered a promissory note in the sum of $5,000, dated July 23, 1965, payable in 60 days. This note was not paid when due and on September 25, Seller notified the escrow agent and real estate agent in writing that he did not wish to proceed with the sale. There was no response to this letter.

On November 26, 1965, Buyer tendered the full purchase price into escrow. The real estate agent and escrow agent mistakenly believed this met the specified deadline, but they had erroneously computed the time limit based on four 30-day months. Actually, the deposit was made 123 days after the date the purchase and sale agreement was signed.

Seller refused to accept Buyer's tender on the grounds that it was over 120 days, and therefore the closing period had expired and the agreement had terminated.

Buyer brought a lawsuit requesting specific performance. The court found that time was of the essence in the agreement and a specific termination date was fixed that Buyer did not meet. Seller was not required to accept the tender and Buyer's lawsuit was dismissed. *Nadeau v. Beers*, 73 Wn.2d 608, 440 P.2d 164 (1968).

Specific time limits are a tricky area, and courts do not always adhere to such a strict rule. In some situations, a court may consider the intent of the parties, whether the parties have extended the time for performance, and surrounding circumstances (such as fluctuating property values) in order to decide if the agreement is defunct or not.

Delay may sometimes be found to be a waiver of the time limit. If one party is the cause of the delay, that party cannot hold the other party to the time limit.

Case Example:

Huffacker agreed to sell her property to Langston. On the scheduled closing date, July 25, 1980, neither party had performed. Huffacker's title had not been cleared, and Langston had not deposited the purchase price. The closing agent finally received the documents necessary to clear title on August 20. On October 9, Langston was asked to deposit a check for closing, and he immediately did so.

Huffacker refused to close the transaction because the July 25 closing date had passed.

Langston brought a lawsuit requesting specific performance of the purchase and sale agreement. The court found that Huffacker had a legal duty to clear title in a timely manner. Diligent attention to her duty to clear title would have made it possible to close the transaction on July 25. The failure to meet the time limit was the result of her lack of diligence.

Langston was ready, willing, and able to close the transaction on July 25. Langston had no duty to perform until the title was clear and Huffacker was able to perform.

Langston was entitled to specific performance of the purchase and sale agreement. *Langston v. Huffacker*, 36 Wn. App. 779, 678 P.2d 1265 (1984).

When one party has performed within the required time limit and the other has not, the performing party may cancel escrow and withdraw its deposits without any liability to the other party. If no time limit is specified, the parties have a reasonable time period in which to perform.

Termination of Escrow

Escrow terminates in one of three ways: the transaction closes, the parties agree to terminate it, or one party defaults.

Upon Closing. Upon fulfillment of all conditions and transfer of all deposits, termination of escrow is automatic. Escrow is set up for a particular transaction—when that transaction concludes, the escrow terminates.

Before authorizing the escrow agent to close the sale, a buyer would be wise to inspect the property again personally. By the time escrow is ready to close, the buyer may not have seen the property for weeks. The buyer should make sure that all of the property items are in the same condition now as they were in when the sales agreement was signed.

Sometimes after closing there is money still left in escrow. This usually happens when a sum was deposited for a specific item (such as a pest inspection) and the cost of the item was less than the amount deposited. Often the parties are so concerned with all of the technicalities of closing that they forget about this leftover sum. The parties should review their closing statements to see that all amounts have been removed from escrow when escrow is closed.

Mutual Agreement. Escrow may be terminated at any time by mutual consent of the parties, even if all of the conditions have not been fulfilled and the transaction does not close. This might happen if unforeseen circumstances cause both parties to decide not to go through with the transaction.

> **Example:** The sellers were a couple that planned to retire, sell the house, and spend the next year traveling through Europe. After opening escrow, the husband died and the wife decided she would rather keep the house and not go traveling alone.
>
> At the same time, the buyers decided to get a divorce. Neither of them wants to go ahead with the purchase of the new house. The seller and the buyers discuss their situations and decide to cancel the agreement and return all deposits. (Remember that even though the parties have agreed to cancel the sale, the seller may still be liable for the real estate commission.)

If both parties agree to cancel, the escrow agent is notified of the cancellation. The agent will usually send a rescission or cancellation agreement to all of the parties involved so that everyone knows what's going on and any questions or disagreements may be resolved. This agreement should state what is to happen to the funds already in escrow and who is required to pay accumulated bills such as the cost of the pest control report. The escrow company itself may also charge a cancellation fee covering the cost of work already completed.

Default. What if both parties don't agree to cancel escrow? Often one party still wants to go through with the sale, but the other party has changed her mind, or has defaulted and not fulfilled the required conditions.

In many cases, the purchase and sale agreement or the escrow instructions include provisions that specifically state how the funds in escrow will be handled in the event of default by either party. For example, escrow instructions might provide that if the buyer does not deposit the remainder of the purchase price in escrow by the closing date, the escrow agent is authorized to release the earnest money deposit to the seller.

When neither the purchase agreement nor the escrow instructions specifically authorize the release of deposited funds in the event of default, the closing agent cannot simply release the funds to one party without the other's permission, even if the funds are returned to the party who deposited them, and even if that party appears to be entitled to them.

> **Example:** The buyer's $10,000 earnest money check is deposited into escrow. The closing date arrives, but the seller has not cleared her title as agreed; in fact, she hasn't even attempted to clear title.
>
> A week later, the buyer calls the transaction off. He asks the escrow agent to return his $10,000. It is clear to the escrow agent that the seller has defaulted, and the buyer is legally entitled to the $10,000. The agent calls the seller and asks for authorization to return the money to the buyer. The seller refuses to authorize the release of the funds. Without the seller's written permission, the closing agent cannot release the funds.

Of course, when one of the parties in a real estate transaction defaults, the other party may decide to sue. (In the example just given, the buyer could sue the seller for specific performance or for return of the earnest money.) When that happens, the escrow agent can **interplead** the disputed funds into the court where the lawsuit was filed. In an interpleader action, the escrow agent turns the funds over to the court. The agent has no further responsibility for the money, and the court will decide which party is entitled to it. An escrow agent can also turn disputed funds over to a court without waiting for one of the parties to sue the other.

Closing Like-Kind Exchanges

To conclude our discussion of escrow, we'll take a brief look at like-kind exchanges (also known as tax-deferred exchanges or Section 1031 exchanges) and the rules that apply to the closing of this kind of transaction.

In a **like-kind exchange**, an investor sells a piece of property that has appreciated, but she is able to postpone taxation of the gain by having the proceeds from the sale used to purchase a replacement investment property. (The replacement property must be of the same general type, or "like kind," as the original property.) The investor must identify the replacement property within 45 days of selling the original piece of property, and then close the sale on the second piece of property within 180 days of the first sale.

To close a like-kind exchange, a special kind of escrow agent, called an **exchange facilitator**, is needed. The facilitator is necessary chiefly because in a like-kind exchange the investor can never take possession of the sale proceeds from the first sale. Instead, the proceeds must be held by a neutral third party—the facilitator—and then used to purchase the replacement property. Washington state law imposes particular bonding requirements and other rules on exchange facilitators. These transactions are complicated and legal advice is strongly advised.

When Title Passes

In most circumstances, title to property or deposited funds remains with the grantor or depositor until performance of all the conditions specified in escrow. For example, the seller generally remains in possession of the property, collects any rents, and pays taxes until the day of closing.

> **Example:** Seller and Buyer agree on escrow instructions that provide that Seller will deposit the deed to the property and Buyer will deposit the purchase price with an escrow agent. Seller deposits the deed on May 15. Buyer deposits the purchase price on June 4.
>
> Although Seller has relinquished possession of the deed as of May 15, title does not pass to Buyer until June 4, when Buyer performs the required condition of paying the purchase price.

The time at which title actually passes to the buyer becomes especially important if the property is damaged or something happens to the deposited funds. The risk of loss regarding property or funds delivered into escrow follows legal title. This means, for example, that if the escrow agent absconds with the deposited funds, the party who suffers from the loss is the one who holds title to the funds.

Case Example:

The conditions of escrow provide that Seller will deposit a deed and Buyer will deposit the purchase price. Buyer has deposited the money, but Seller has not yet deposited the deed. The escrow agent absconds with the money. The loss falls on Buyer because the conditions of escrow had not yet been fulfilled, which means that Buyer was still the legal owner of the funds. The escrow agent was merely holding the funds until the deed was deposited. *Angell v. Ingram*, 35 Wn.2d 582, 213 P.2d 944 (1950).

Unauthorized Delivery

If the escrow agent delivers deposited funds or a deed before all the conditions are fulfilled, title does not pass unless ratified by the depositor. Delivery to one who has failed to perform the required conditions constitutes **conversion**. The injured party may recover damages from the escrow agent or from the party who has participated in the wrongful delivery.

Relation Back Doctrine

In certain circumstances, a deed may be considered delivered as of the date it was deposited into escrow, instead of the date the conditions were performed. In other words, the date of delivery **relates back** to the date of deposit. The relation back doctrine applies if, after a deed has been delivered into escrow, any of the following events occurs:

- the seller dies, marries, or becomes legally incompetent; or
- the buyer dies.

In each case, if the other party fulfills the requirements set forth in the escrow instructions, the transaction will relate back to the date the deed was delivered into escrow. (Note that the buyer's mental competence and marital status don't matter, since taking title doesn't raise the same legal issues as transferring title.)

Case Example:

McKinnon entered into a contract to sell his property to Mallonee. In June 1950, a warranty deed, the purchase money receipt, and the escrow instructions were deposited with the Washington Escrow Company.

McKinnon died July 9, 1950. In August, Mallonee paid the balance of the purchase price to the escrow holder, who then recorded the deed to Mallonee.

Where justice requires it, a legal fiction holds that the title of the grantee (the buyer) relates back to the time of the original delivery of the deed to escrow.

If necessary, a court could find that Mallonee's title related back to the date of deposit of the deed. Thus, Mallonee may be held to have title to the property as of June, when the deed was delivered to escrow. *Washington Escrow Co. v. Blair*, 40 Wn.2d 432, 243 P.2d 1044 (1952).

Closing and Federal Laws

The rules concerning escrow and closing that we've discussed so far are from state law (Washington statutes or court cases). There are also important federal laws that affect closing, which we'll cover here in the final section of the chapter. These include the Real Estate Settlement Procedures Act and a number of income tax-related requirements.

RESPA

We can't complete our discussion of closing and escrow without examining a significant piece of federal legislation called the **Real Estate Settlement Procedures Act (RESPA).** In the early 1970s, there was concern about widespread problems in the residential mortgage and escrow industry—problems with fees and services (such as confusing or unexplained charges), mistakes in calculating impound account payments, and failures to notify borrowers when their loans were transferred from one lender to another. Congress enacted reform measures by passing RESPA in 1974. RESPA requires disclosure of closing costs to borrowers and prohibits practices that unnecessarily inflate the cost of settlement services (closing services). Since its passage more than 40 years ago, the act has sparked a great deal of industry debate, private litigation, and government enforcement action.

Who needs to worry about RESPA? Everyone who works with residential loans and escrows. If a mortgage falls within RESPA's scope, then the lender and every other **settlement service provider** involved in the transaction is subject to the act's prohibitions. This would include the escrow agent, the title company, the credit reporting agency, the appraiser, the pest inspector, and so on. In addition, RESPA's definition of settlement services specifically includes "services rendered by a real estate agent or broker." This means the act's rules concerning settlement service providers also apply to real estate agents.

Covered and Exempt Transactions. RESPA applies only to transactions involving federally related loans, but this hardly limits the extent of its coverage. A loan is federally related if it meets both of the following criteria:

1. it is secured by a mortgage or deed of trust against:
   - property on which there is (or on which the loan will be used to build) a one- to four-unit dwelling;
   - a condominium unit or cooperative apartment; or
   - a lot with (or on which the loan will be used to place) a mobile home; and
2. the lender:
   - is federally regulated;
   - has federally insured accounts;
   - makes loans in connection with a federal program;
   - sells loans to Fannie Mae, Ginnie Mae, or Freddie Mac; or
   - makes more than $1 million in real estate loans per year.

RESPA does not apply to seller-financed transactions, since sellers aren't federally regulated lenders. And certain types of loans made by institutional lenders are exempted from RESPA. Loans are exempt if used for: 1) the purchase of 25 acres or more; 2) a purpose that is primarily business, commercial, or agricultural; or 3) the purchase of vacant land (unless there will be a one- to four-unit dwelling built on it or a mobile home placed on it). Temporary financing, such as a construction loan, is also exempt from RESPA.

Although loan assumptions are subject to RESPA, there is an exemption for assumptions that don't require the lender's approval (for instance, because the original loan agreement did not include a due-on-sale clause). This type of assumption doesn't involve closing costs or the negotiation of terms with an institutional lender, so there would be little point in imposing RESPA requirements.

Settlement Service Providers and Referrals. As we said, in RESPA, the professionals involved in closing a real estate transaction—including the mortgage lender and the real estate agent(s)—are called settlement service providers. Some of the statute's key provisions concern referrals between settlement service providers, as when a mortgage lender recommends or even requires that a borrower use a particular title insurance company, for example. These referrals are not illegal under RESPA, but compensating a service provider for such a referral is strictly prohibited.

Section 8 violations. Under RESPA, it is illegal for one settlement service provider to pay a referral fee (a kickback) or an unearned fee to another settlement service provider. Kickbacks and unearned fees are often called "Section 8 violations," since the RESPA rules concerning them are in Section 8 of the act.

For RESPA purposes, a **kickback** is not necessarily a monetary payment. It can be anything of value given in exchange for referrals—a gift, for instance, or services provided without charge or at a discounted rate. Both the person offering the kickback and the person accepting the kickback are in violation of the law. Also, a payment or gift can be illegal even if neither party openly acknowledges that it has anything to do with the referral of business; an unspoken understanding can be enough to violate RESPA.

> **Example:** A real estate agent routinely recommends to all his buyers that they apply to Acme Mortgage for their financing. These referrals aren't illegal, but it would be illegal for loan officers at the mortgage company to pay the real estate agent a fee for each customer referred. It would also be illegal to send the real estate agent concert tickets, restaurant gift certificates, or other presents to encourage more referrals.

Kickbacks were an entrenched practice in the real estate industry before RESPA, and since the law went into effect many people have tried to get around its anti-kickback rules. One common subterfuge is to pay someone a fee that's ostensibly compensation for a service but is actually a disguised kickback for referrals.

> **Example:** A real estate agent recommends Acme Mortgage to his buyers and provides them with a blank copy of the uniform residential loan application form. Acme pays the agent a $100 "application service fee" for each of his buyers who ends up applying for a loan with the company.

The payments in the example run afoul of RESPA's prohibition against unearned fees, so this would be a Section 8 violation. A payment is considered an **unearned fee** if the recipient has performed no significant service, or if the payment amount does not bear a reasonable relationship to the services provided.

Note that RESPA's rules against kickbacks and unearned fees do not apply to fees paid by one real estate broker to another for the referral of brokerage business. Brokerage referrals don't involve settlement services, and RESPA specifically provides that fees paid for those referrals don't violate the act.

Required service providers. If the lender (or any other settlement service provider) requires the borrower to use a particular appraiser, title company, or other service provider, that requirement must be disclosed to the borrower when the loan application or service agreement is signed.

Affiliated business arrangements. If a settlement service provider refers a customer to an affiliated service provider, the relationship between the providers must be disclosed to the customer. The disclosure should take place at or before the time of referral. A relationship between two service providers counts as an affiliated business arrangement if one of them has more than a 1% ownership interest in the other company.

In addition to the disclosure requirement, there are two other rules concerning referrals to an affiliated business. First, the customer can't be required to use the services of the affiliated provider. Second, the first provider can't receive anything of value from the affiliated provider other than a return on his ownership interest.

> **Example:** A real estate broker owns 5% of the stock in Termitron, Inc., a pest inspection business. It's legal for the broker to refer her sellers and buyers to the pest inspection company if she discloses that she has an ownership interest in it. But she may not refuse to provide brokerage services unless they agree to use Termitron instead of another pest inspection company. Termitron may pay corporate dividends to the broker, as long as they do not exceed the appropriate return on her investment in the company.

Closing Cost Disclosures. In addition to the requirements we've just discussed, RESPA requires lenders to disclose detailed information about closing costs after someone applies for a mortgage loan and again right before the transaction closes. Until recently, these disclosure requirements overlapped with—and in some cases, were inconsistent with—similar requirements under the Truth in Lending Act, another federal law that applies to most residential mortgage transactions. In 2015, Congress combined the disclosure rules under the two laws. These new disclosure requirements are known as the TILA-RESPA Integrated Disclosure (TRID) rule.

Under the TRID rule, lenders must provide consumers with two disclosure forms, the **loan estimate form**, which is associated with the loan application, and the **closing disclosure form**, which is associated with closing the transaction. Previously, RESPA required lenders to provide a good faith estimate of closing costs upon application and a uniform settlement statement at closing; the information from those forms is incorporated into the new loan estimate and closing disclosure, respectively.

Loan estimate. A lender must give a loan applicant the loan estimate form within three days of receiving a loan application. The loan estimate provides detailed information to help the applicant understand the loan's features and costs.

Closing disclosure. If the loan is approved and the transaction proceeds, the lender must provide the borrower with a closing disclosure form (see Figure 10.3) at least three business days before the closing date. The property seller is also entitled to receive a closing disclosure form no later than the closing date. Although the borrower's and seller's information may be combined on a single closing disclosure form, for privacy reasons the escrow agent often prepares a separate closing disclosure for each party.

Fig. 10.3 Closing disclosure form

Closing Disclosure

This form is a statement of final loan terms and closing costs. Compare this document with your Loan Estimate.

Closing Information		Transaction Information		Loan Information	
Date Issued	4/15/20XX	**Borrower**	Michael Jones and Mary Stone	**Loan Term**	30 years
Closing Date	4/15/20XX		123 Anywhere Street	**Purpose**	Purchase
Disbursement Date	4/15/20XX		Anytown, ST 12345	**Product**	Fixed Rate
Settlement Agent	Epsilon Title Co.	**Seller**	Steve Cole and Amy Doe		
File #	12-3456		321 Somewhere Drive	**Loan Type**	☒ Conventional ☐ FHA
Property	456 Somewhere Ave		Anytown, ST 12345		☐ VA ☐ _____
	Anytown, ST 12345	**Lender**	Ficus Bank	**Loan ID #**	123456789
Sale Price	$180,000			**MIC #**	000654321

Loan Terms

		Can this amount increase after closing?
Loan Amount	$162,000	**NO**
Interest Rate	3.875%	**NO**
Monthly Principal & Interest *See Projected Payments below for your Estimated Total Monthly Payment*	$761.78	**NO**

		Does the loan have these features?
Prepayment Penalty		**YES** • **As high as $3,240** if you pay off the loan during the first 2 years
Balloon Payment		**NO**

Projected Payments

Payment Calculation	Years 1-7		Years 8-30	
Principal & Interest		$761.78		$761.78
Mortgage Insurance	+	82.35	+	—
Estimated Escrow *Amount can increase over time*	+	206.13	+	206.13
Estimated Total Monthly Payment	**$1,050.26**		**$967.91**	

		This estimate includes	In escrow?
Estimated Taxes, Insurance & Assessments *Amount can increase over time* *See page 4 for details*	$356.13 a month	☒ Property Taxes	YES
		☒ Homeowner's Insurance	YES
		☒ Other: Homeowner's Association Dues	NO
		See Escrow Account on page 4 for details. You must pay for other property costs separately.	

Costs at Closing

Closing Costs	$9,712.10	Includes $4,694.05 in Loan Costs + $5,018.05 in Other Costs – $0 in Lender Credits. *See page 2 for details.*
Cash to Close	$14,147.26	Includes Closing Costs. *See Calculating Cash to Close on page 3 for details.*

CLOSING DISCLOSURE

PAGE 1 OF 5 • LOAN ID # 123456789

Source: Consumer Financial Protection Bureau

Closing Cost Details

Loan Costs		Borrower-Paid		Seller-Paid		Paid by Others
		At Closing	Before Closing	At Closing	Before Closing	
A. Origination Charges		**$1,802.00**				
01 0.25 % of Loan Amount (Points)		$405.00				
02 Application Fee		$300.00				
03 Underwriting Fee		$1,097.00				
04						
05						
06						
07						
08						
B. Services Borrower Did Not Shop For		**$236.55**				
01 Appraisal Fee	to John Smith Appraisers Inc.					$405.00
02 Credit Report Fee	to Information Inc.		$29.80			
03 Flood Determination Fee	to Info Co.	$20.00				
04 Flood Monitoring Fee	to Info Co.	$31.75				
05 Tax Monitoring Fee	to Info Co.	$75.00				
06 Tax Status Research Fee	to Info Co.	$80.00				
07						
08						
09						
10						
C. Services Borrower Did Shop For		**$2,655.50**				
01 Pest Inspection Fee	to Pests Co.	$120.50				
02 Survey Fee	to Surveys Co.	$85.00				
03 Title – Insurance Binder	to Epsilon Title Co.	$650.00				
04 Title – Lender's Title Insurance	to Epsilon Title Co.	$500.00				
05 Title – Settlement Agent Fee	to Epsilon Title Co.	$500.00				
06 Title – Title Search	to Epsilon Title Co.	$800.00				
07						
08						
D. TOTAL LOAN COSTS (Borrower-Paid)		**$4,694.05**				
Loan Costs Subtotals (A + B + C)		$4,664.25	$29.80			

Other Costs		Borrower-Paid		Seller-Paid		Paid by Others
E. Taxes and Other Government Fees		**$85.00**				
01 Recording Fees	Deed: $40.00 Mortgage: $45.00	$85.00				
02 Transfer Tax	to Any State			$950.00		
F. Prepaids		**$2,120.80**				
01 Homeowner's Insurance Premium (12 mo.) to Insurance Co.		$1,209.96				
02 Mortgage Insurance Premium (mo.)						
03 Prepaid Interest ($17.44 per day from 4/15/13 to 5/1/13)		$279.04				
04 Property Taxes (6 mo.) to Any County USA		$631.80				
05						
G. Initial Escrow Payment at Closing		**$412.25**				
01 Homeowner's Insurance $100.83 per month for 2 mo.		$201.66				
02 Mortgage Insurance per month for mo.						
03 Property Taxes $105.30 per month for 2 mo.		$210.60				
04						
05						
06						
07						
08 Aggregate Adjustment		– 0.01				
H. Other		**$2,400.00**				
01 HOA Capital Contribution	to HOA Acre Inc.	$500.00				
02 HOA Processing Fee	to HOA Acre Inc.	$150.00				
03 Home Inspection Fee	to Engineers Inc.	$750.00			$750.00	
04 Home Warranty Fee	to XYZ Warranty Inc.			$450.00		
05 Real Estate Commission	to Alpha Real Estate Broker			$5,700.00		
06 Real Estate Commission	to Omega Real Estate Broker			$5,700.00		
07 Title – Owner's Title Insurance (optional) to Epsilon Title Co.		$1,000.00				
08						
I. TOTAL OTHER COSTS (Borrower-Paid)		**$5,018.05**				
Other Costs Subtotals (E + F + G + H)		$5,018.05				
J. TOTAL CLOSING COSTS (Borrower-Paid)		**$9,712.10**				
Closing Costs Subtotals (D + I)		$9,682.30	$29.80	$12,800.00	$750.00	$405.00
Lender Credits						

Calculating Cash to Close

Use this table to see what has changed from your Loan Estimate.

	Loan Estimate	Final	Did this change?
Total Closing Costs (J)	$8,054.00	$9,712.10	**YES** · See **Total Loan Costs (D)** and **Total Other Costs (I)**
Closing Costs Paid Before Closing	$0	– $29.80	**YES** · You paid these Closing Costs **before closing**
Closing Costs Financed (Paid from your Loan Amount)	$0	$0	**NO**
Down Payment/Funds from Borrower	$18,000.00	$18,000.00	**NO**
Deposit	– $10,000.00	– $10,000.00	**NO**
Funds for Borrower	$0	$0	**NO**
Seller Credits	$0	– $2,500.00	**YES** · See Seller Credits in **Section L**
Adjustments and Other Credits	$0	– $1,035.04	**YES** · See details in **Sections K and L**
Cash to Close	$16,054.00	$14,147.26	

Summaries of Transactions

Use this table to see a summary of your transaction.

BORROWER'S TRANSACTION

K. Due from Borrower at Closing	**$189,762.30**
01 Sale Price of Property	$180,000.00
02 Sale Price of Any Personal Property Included in Sale	
03 Closing Costs Paid at Closing (J)	$9,682.30
04	
Adjustments	
05	
06	
07	
Adjustments for Items Paid by Seller in Advance	
08 City/Town Taxes to	
09 County Taxes to	
10 Assessments to	
11 HOA Dues 4/15/13 to 4/30/13	$80.00
12	
13	
14	
15	

L. Paid Already by or on Behalf of Borrower at Closing	**$175,615.04**
01 Deposit	$10,000.00
02 Loan Amount	$162,000.00
03 Existing Loan(s) Assumed or Taken Subject to	
04	
05 Seller Credit	$2,500.00
Other Credits	
06 Rebate from Epsilon Title Co.	$750.00
07	
Adjustments	
08	
09	
10	
11	
Adjustments for Items Unpaid by Seller	
12 City/Town Taxes 1/1/13 to 4/14/13	$365.04
13 County Taxes to	
14 Assessments to	
15	
16	
17	

CALCULATION	
Total Due from Borrower at Closing (K)	$189,762.30
Total Paid Already by or on Behalf of Borrower at Closing (L)	– $175,615.04
Cash to Close ☒ From ☐ To Borrower	**$14,147.26**

SELLER'S TRANSACTION

M. Due to Seller at Closing	**$180,080.00**
01 Sale Price of Property	$180,000.00
02 Sale Price of Any Personal Property Included in Sale	
03	
04	
05	
06	
07	
08	
Adjustments for Items Paid by Seller in Advance	
09 City/Town Taxes to	
10 County Taxes to	
11 Assessments to	
12 HOA Dues 4/15/13 to 4/30/13	$80.00
13	
14	
15	
16	

N. Due from Seller at Closing	**$115,665.04**
01 Excess Deposit	
02 Closing Costs Paid at Closing (J)	$12,800.00
03 Existing Loan(s) Assumed or Taken Subject to	
04 Payoff of First Mortgage Loan	$100,000.00
05 Payoff of Second Mortgage Loan	
06	
07	
08 Seller Credit	$2,500.00
09	
10	
11	
12	
13	
Adjustments for Items Unpaid by Seller	
14 City/Town Taxes 1/1/13 to 4/14/13	$365.04
15 County Taxes to	
16 Assessments to	
17	
18	
19	

CALCULATION	
Total Due to Seller at Closing (M)	$180,080.00
Total Due from Seller at Closing (N)	– $115,665.04
Cash ☐ From ☒ To Seller	**$64,414.96**

Additional Information About This Loan

Loan Disclosures

Assumption

If you sell or transfer this property to another person, your lender

☐ will allow, under certain conditions, this person to assume this loan on the original terms.

☒ will not allow assumption of this loan on the original terms.

Demand Feature

Your loan

☐ has a demand feature, which permits your lender to require early repayment of the loan. You should review your note for details.

☒ does not have a demand feature.

Late Payment

If your payment is more than *15* days late, your lender will charge a late fee of *5% of the monthly principal and interest payment.*

Negative Amortization (Increase in Loan Amount)

Under your loan terms, you

☐ are scheduled to make monthly payments that do not pay all of the interest due that month. As a result, your loan amount will increase (negatively amortize), and your loan amount will likely become larger than your original loan amount. Increases in your loan amount lower the equity you have in this property.

☐ may have monthly payments that do not pay all of the interest due that month. If you do, your loan amount will increase (negatively amortize), and, as a result, your loan amount may become larger than your original loan amount. Increases in your loan amount lower the equity you have in this property.

☒ do not have a negative amortization feature.

Partial Payments

Your lender

☒ may accept payments that are less than the full amount due (partial payments) and apply them to your loan.

☐ may hold them in a separate account until you pay the rest of the payment, and then apply the full payment to your loan.

☐ does not accept any partial payments.

If this loan is sold, your new lender may have a different policy.

Security Interest

You are granting a security interest in

456 Somewhere Ave., Anytown, ST 12345

You may lose this property if you do not make your payments or satisfy other obligations for this loan.

Escrow Account

For now, your loan

☒ will have an escrow account (also called an "impound" or "trust" account) to pay the property costs listed below. Without an escrow account, you would pay them directly, possibly in one or two large payments a year. Your lender may be liable for penalties and interest for failing to make a payment.

Escrow		
Escrowed Property Costs over Year 1	$2,473.56	Estimated total amount over year 1 for your escrowed property costs: *Homeowner's Insurance Property Taxes*
Non-Escrowed Property Costs over Year 1	$1,800.00	Estimated total amount over year 1 for your non-escrowed property costs: *Homeowner's Association Dues* You may have other property costs.
Initial Escrow Payment	$412.25	A cushion for the escrow account you pay at closing. See Section G on page 2.
Monthly Escrow Payment	$206.13	The amount included in your total monthly payment.

☐ will not have an escrow account because ☐ you declined it ☐ your lender does not offer one. You must directly pay your property costs, such as taxes and homeowner's insurance. Contact your lender to ask if your loan can have an escrow account.

No Escrow		
Estimated Property Costs over Year 1		Estimated total amount over year 1. You must pay these costs directly, possibly in one or two large payments a year.
Escrow Waiver Fee		

In the future,

Your property costs may change and, as a result, your escrow payment may change. You may be able to cancel your escrow account, but if you do, you must pay your property costs directly. If you fail to pay your property taxes, your state or local government may (1) impose fines and penalties or (2) place a tax lien on this property. If you fail to pay any of your property costs, your lender may (1) add the amounts to your loan balance, (2) add an escrow account to your loan, or (3) require you to pay for property insurance that the lender buys on your behalf, which likely would cost more and provide fewer benefits than what you could buy on your own.

Loan Calculations

Total of Payments. Total you will have paid after you make all payments of principal, interest, mortgage insurance, and loan costs, as scheduled.	$285,803.36
Finance Charge. The dollar amount the loan will cost you.	$118,830.27
Amount Financed. The loan amount available after paying your upfront finance charge.	$162,000.00
Annual Percentage Rate (APR). Your costs over the loan term expressed as a rate. This is not your interest rate.	4.174%
Total Interest Percentage (TIP). The total amount of interest that you will pay over the loan term as a percentage of your loan amount.	69.46%

 Questions? If you have questions about the loan terms or costs on this form, use the contact information below. To get more information or make a complaint, contact the Consumer Financial Protection Bureau at **www.consumerfinance.gov/mortgage-closing**

Other Disclosures

Appraisal
If the property was appraised for your loan, your lender is required to give you a copy at no additional cost at least 3 days before closing. If you have not yet received it, please contact your lender at the information listed below.

Contract Details
See your note and security instrument for information about
• what happens if you fail to make your payments,
• what is a default on the loan,
• situations in which your lender can require early repayment of the loan, and
• the rules for making payments before they are due.

Liability after Foreclosure
If your lender forecloses on this property and the foreclosure does not cover the amount of unpaid balance on this loan,

☒ state law may protect you from liability for the unpaid balance. If you refinance or take on any additional debt on this property, you may lose this protection and have to pay any debt remaining even after foreclosure. You may want to consult a lawyer for more information.

☐ state law does not protect you from liability for the unpaid balance.

Refinance
Refinancing this loan will depend on your future financial situation, the property value, and market conditions. You may not be able to refinance this loan.

Tax Deductions
If you borrow more than this property is worth, the interest on the loan amount above this property's fair market value is not deductible from your federal income taxes. You should consult a tax advisor for more information.

Contact Information

	Lender	Mortgage Broker	Real Estate Broker (B)	Real Estate Broker (S)	Settlement Agent
Name	Ficus Bank		Omega Real Estate Broker Inc.	Alpha Real Estate Broker Co.	Epsilon Title Co.
Address	4321 Random Blvd. Somecity, ST 12340		789 Local Lane Sometown, ST 12345	987 Suburb Ct. Someplace, ST 12340	123 Commerce Pl. Somecity, ST 12344
NMLS ID					
ST License ID			Z765416	Z61456	Z61616
Contact	Joe Smith		Samuel Green	Joseph Cain	Sarah Arnold
Contact NMLS ID	12345				
Contact ST License ID			P16415	P51461	PT1234
Email	joesmith@ ficusbank.com		sam@omegare.biz	joe@alphare.biz	sarah@ epsilontitle.com
Phone	123-456-7890		123-555-1717	321-555-7171	987-555-4321

Confirm Receipt

By signing, you are only confirming that you have received this form. You do not have to accept this loan because you have signed or received this form.

_____   _____   _____   _____
Applicant Signature   Date   Co-Applicant Signature   Date

CLOSING DISCLOSURE

The closing disclosure reiterates much of the information from the loan estimate form, replacing estimates with the actual charges. (The lender's own charges, such as the origination fee and discount points, may not be more than the figures given on the loan estimate form, and there are limits on how much certain other charges can increase over the estimated figures.) The "Closing Cost Details" section of the form serves as a settlement statement, listing all of the charges and credits that apply and the exact amount that each party must pay or will receive at closing.

If the amounts listed in the closing disclosure change, the lender generally must provide the borrower with a revised closing disclosure form at or before closing. If the borrower requests it, the lender must make the revised form available for inspection one business day before closing.

RESPA Enforcement. The government agency charged with enforcing RESPA is the Consumer Financial Protection Bureau (CFPB). The CFPB investigates complaints from consumers (borrowers), and also complaints from settlement service providers, such as title and escrow companies seeking to stop unfair practices by their competitors. Much of the enforcement activity involves Section 8 violations. Each violation can bring a fine of up to $10,000, as well as up to a year in prison.

Tax-Related Requirements for Closing

The laws we've discussed so far in this chapter are aimed at creating a secure, orderly escrow process and protecting the interests of the parties in a real estate transaction. Real estate escrows are also affected by federal laws designed to prevent parties from avoiding payment of income taxes.

Form 1099-S Reporting. The IRS requires an escrow agent to report the gross proceeds from a real property sale on Form 1099-S. However, the form doesn't have to be filed for the sale of a principal residence if: 1) the seller certifies in writing that none of the gain is taxable; and 2) the sale is for $250,000 or less ($500,000 or less for a married couple filing a joint return).

Form 8300 Reporting. An escrow agent who receives more than $10,000 in cash is required to report the payment on Form 8300, in order to help detect money laundering. This rule applies whether the cash was received in a single transaction or a series of related transactions. The escrow agent must file Form 8300 within 15 days of receiving the cash. A copy of the form should be kept on file for five years.

FIRPTA. Congress passed the **Foreign Investment in Real Property Tax Act (FIRPTA)** because it was concerned that foreign investors were selling U.S. real estate holdings without paying income taxes on their profits. The act requires the buyer to determine if the seller is a "foreign person" (neither a U.S. citizen nor a resident alien). If the seller is a foreign person, the buyer must withhold 15% of the amount realized from the transaction and send it to the IRS. (The amount realized is usually the sales price.) In practice, the obligation to check the seller's citizenship or residency status and withhold funds is assumed by the escrow agent. The withheld funds must be paid to the IRS within 20 days after the transfer date (closing).

Some real property sales are exempt from FIRPTA, such as the sale of a home to be occupied by the buyer for under $300,000. Sales of homes to be occupied by the buyer where the amount realized is between $300,000 and $1 million require only a 10% withholding amount.

Conclusion

Once all of the escrow conditions and disclosure requirements have been met, the transaction is ready to close. All of the paperwork is reviewed and signed, and the escrow agent delivers the deed to the buyer and the net sale proceeds to the seller. Key transaction documents (the deed, the buyer's new mortgage, and releases for the seller's mortgage and other liens that have been paid off) are filed for recording, and the buyer's and lender's title insurance policies are issued. The transaction has closed, and the buyer is now the new owner of the property.

352 ■ Chapter 10

Chapter Summary

- Escrow is an arrangement in which money and/or documents are held by a third party on behalf of the buyer and seller. The purpose of escrow is to ensure that the concerns of the buyer, the seller, and the lender will all be met.

- An escrow agent may be a bank, some other financial institution, a title insurance company, an independent escrow firm, a mortgage broker, or an attorney.

- A real estate agent may offer escrow services for transactions in which the agent is already providing brokerage services, as long as no additional fee is charged for the escrow services.

- The requirements for valid escrow include an enforceable contract, a valid deed, delivery, an escrow agent, instructions, and conditions.

- Escrow instructions set out the obligations of the parties and the conditions that must be met in order for the transaction to close.

- Escrow is terminated when all of the conditions have been met and the transaction concludes; it can also terminate by mutual agreement of the parties, or when there is a default.

- Title does not pass to the new owner until performance of all of the conditions specified in escrow. However, the relation back doctrine provides that in certain situations, the date of delivery of the deed to the new owner relates back to the original date of its deposit in escrow.

- Under the Real Estate Settlement Procedures Act, lenders must make disclosures concerning closing costs to residential loan applicants. RESPA also prohibits kickbacks between settlement service providers.

Checklist of Problem Areas

Real Estate Licensee's Checklist

❑ Are you monitoring the closing process? If the buyer or seller asks you what is happening, can you explain what still needs to be done before escrow will close?

❑ Has a provision for the payment of your commission been included in the escrow instructions? Is there an instruction regarding payment if the transaction never closes?

❑ Do you have a good understanding of RESPA's rules concerning referrals between settlement service providers and how they apply to you?

Seller's Checklist

❑ Have you and the buyer agreed on who will be the escrow agent, or is the buyer's lender handling escrow?

❑ Do you understand that when you deposit the deed into escrow, you're relinquishing control of it?

❑ Before signing escrow documents, read them carefully. Among other things, check to see that:
  • the deed is correct;
  • the closing date stated in the escrow instructions is correct;
  • the conditions in the escrow instructions correctly reflect the terms of sale;
  • the sales price, loan payoff amount, and other figures are correct in the closing disclosure you're given.

Buyer's Checklist

❑ When you receive the closing disclosure, compare it to the loan estimate form you received when you applied for the loan. Do you understand the reasons for any differences between the estimated charges and the actual charges?

❑ Before signing escrow and loan documents, read them carefully. Among other things, check to see that:
  • your full name (and spouse's name) is included and spelled correctly;
  • the legal description of the property is correct;
  • title has been cleared;
  • you have been credited for all loan amounts and other deposits placed in escrow;
  • the promissory note is properly filled out, with the correct loan amount, interest rate, due date, and prepayment terms.

Chapter Quiz

1. The period between the date the purchase and sale agreement is signed and the closing date:

   a. is ordinarily 30 days

   b. must be no more than 90 days

   c. depends on the status of the finance market and the agreement of the parties

   d. None of the above

2. Escrow is opened by:

   a. the seller or buyer

   b. an attorney

   c. the real estate agent

   d. Any of the above

3. A real estate agent may unilaterally extend the escrow period without notice for:

   a. seven days

   b. 30 days

   c. 60 days

   d. None of the above; an agent may not do this

4. An escrow agent may be:

   a. a company licensed as an escrow agent

   b. a title company

   c. an attorney

   d. Any of the above

5. Escrow instructions:

   a. are directions to the escrow agent

   b. are based on the purchase agreement

   c. may be joint instructions from both the seller and the buyer

   d. All of the above

6. In Washington, courts have generally held that when the statement "time is of the essence" is specifically included in the escrow agreement:

   a. the agreement becomes defunct when the time limit expires and performance has not been carried out

   b. it is mere rhetoric and has no particular effect on the agreement

   c. the circumstances are examined, but it is very rare that the agreement will be considered defunct

   d. None of the above

7. Escrow may be terminated by:

   a. allocation

   b. mutual agreement

   c. redemption

   d. All of the above

8. Title normally passes to the new owner:

   a. as soon as the deed is deposited in escrow

   b. once title insurance has been purchased

   c. upon performance of all of the conditions specified in escrow

   d. None of the above

9. If an escrow agent wrongfully delivers a deposit before all of the specified conditions have been performed:

   a. the loss usually falls on the seller

   b. the loss usually falls on the buyer

   c. the injured party may recover damages from the escrow agent

   d. None of the above

10. The relation back doctrine provides that a deed may be considered delivered as of the date of deposit into escrow if:

   a. the seller delivers a deed to escrow and then dies
   b. the buyer dies after the deed has been delivered to escrow
   c. the seller marries or becomes insane after delivery of the deed to escrow
   d. All of the above

11. Under RESPA, a loan is considered federally related if:

   a. it will be used to finance the purchase of real property
   b. it is secured by a mortgage
   c. the lender is federally regulated
   d. All of the above factors are met

12. Under RESPA, settlement service providers:

   a. may not pay referral fees to or accept referral fees from other settlement service providers
   b. are allowed to pay or accept referral fees, as long as the fees are not kickbacks
   c. are allowed to pay referral fees but not to accept them
   d. are entirely prohibited from making referrals to other settlement service providers

13. IRS Form 1099-S is used to report the:

   a. taxes due on a sale of real property
   b. gross proceeds from a sale of real property
   c. net proceeds from a sale of property
   d. amount withheld from a sale proceeds when the seller is a foreign person

14. What federal law might require a certain percentage of a seller's net proceeds to be withheld and sent to the Internal Revenue Service?

   a. RESPA
   b. Foreign Investment in Real Property Tax Act
   c. Truth in Lending Act
   d. All of the above

15. In Washington, escrow agents are licensed and regulated by the:

   a. Department of Licensing
   b. Department of Financial Institutions
   c. Insurance Commissioner
   d. None of the above

11 Restrictions on Land Use

Outline

Key Terms

- Police power
- Eminent domain
- Zoning ordinance
- Nonconforming use
- Variance
- Conditional use
- Rezone
- Spot zone
- Certificate of occupancy
- Subdivision
- Plat
- Planned unit development
- Growth Management Act
- Comprehensive plan
- Urban growth area
- Concurrency requirement
- CERCLA
- Model Toxics Control Act
- National Environmental Policy Act
- Environmental impact statement
- State Environmental Policy Act
- Determination of nonsignificance
- Shoreline Management Act
- Clean Air Act
- Clean Water Act
- Open space
- Right to farm laws
- Ad valorem
- True and fair value
- Special assessment
- Condition
- Covenant
- CC&Rs

Chapter Overview

This chapter discusses the public and private restrictions that may limit the use of real property. Public restrictions are laws or regulations, such as a zoning ordinance; private restrictions are encumbrances on title, such as a restrictive covenant in a deed. Both types of restrictions can have a tremendous impact on how a piece of property may and may not be used, and that in turn can have a tremendous impact on the property's value.

For example, suppose an older house is for sale in an area that has recently experienced a lot of residential growth. The owners used to run a small grocery store out of the first floor of the house. They closed the store several years ago because they were getting too old to run it by themselves.

A young couple is interested in buying the house and would like to reopen the store. Can they? Just because there was a store here once does not necessarily mean that a store can be legally operated on the property now.

A real estate agent would be negligent if she told the prospective buyers that they would be able to reopen the store, unless the agent has first checked the local land use laws and any private restrictions that might apply.

Public Land Use Restrictions

During colonial times, landowners could do whatever they liked with their property. They could build a house or raise pigs or run a blacksmith shop, or even do all three on the same piece of property. But as the population grew and towns became crowded cities, people began to object to pig farms right next to shopping districts. To alleviate these types of problems and to ensure that landowners did not interfere with each other's use of property, local governments began enacting zoning ordinances.

Today, zoning ordinances are the primary type of public restriction on land use. Building codes, comprehensive planning laws such as Washington's Growth Management Act, and other regulations also serve to restrict land use in ways that benefit the public.

Power to Regulate Land Use

The power to regulate land use is rooted in the state's police power. **Police power** is a state government's power to adopt and enforce laws for the protection of the public health, safety, morals, and general welfare. (A state may delegate the police power to its local governments.) Because land use laws prevent overcrowding and its accompanying sanitation, fire protection, and law enforcement problems, they protect the public health, safety, and welfare. So as a general rule, land use laws are a legitimate use of the police power, and not an unconstitutional interference with private property rights. The U.S. Supreme Court upheld the constitutionality of zoning in a landmark case decided in 1926 (*Village of Euclid v. Ambler Realty Co.*, 272 U.S. 365).

Nevertheless, the constitutionality of a particular land use law can still be challenged if it imposes excessive restrictions on a landowner's use of his property. In severe cases, an **inverse condemnation** lawsuit may be filed: the landowner sues the government, claiming that the restrictions amount to a "taking" of the property. That means that the restrictions limit development of the property to such an extent that it is equivalent to the government exercising its power of eminent domain and condemning the property for public use (see Chapter 9). As a result, the landowner argues, the government is constitutionally required to pay just compensation for the property. If the court agrees, the government will be ordered either to compensate the landowner, or to repeal or modify the land use law.

To successfully challenge a land use law, the landowner must do more than simply prove that the law has lowered the value of the property. The landowner ordinarily must prove that the law makes the property virtually useless, by preventing the only kind of development it was suited for.

Zoning

The purpose of zoning is to control and regulate growth and building in a way that serves the public's best interests. **Zoning ordinances** partition a community into areas or zones and specify the uses allowed in each zone. In this way, compatible uses are located in the same area. Zoning ordinances are detailed, specific land use laws enacted by the county or city council.

Zoning Categories. Early zoning regulations used only four categories—residential, commercial, industrial, and agricultural/rural. Today's zoning regulations are much more complicated. The four basic categories may still be used, but there are numerous subcategories as well.

A residential zone may be divided into areas for single-family housing, duplexes, apartments, condominiums, or mobile homes. Industrial zones may be divided into sections for light and heavy industry. There may even be a mixture allowed (for instance, a certain percentage of multifamily housing and commercial uses in the same zone).

In addition to specifying uses, zoning ordinances may also regulate the height, size, and shape of buildings, as well as their locations on a lot.

> **Example:** A city ordinance provides that office buildings located in a commercial area may not be more than ten stories high.

Zoning ordinances are also used to control population density, and to ensure adequate open spaces and access to air and daylight. They may even provide guidelines concerning specific matters such as vehicle parking.

> **Example:** A city ordinance allows storage of recreational vehicles (RVs) and boats only on the side or back of a lot, in a front yard if the vehicle is fully screened from view, or in an extra-long driveway.

Ordinances concerning items such as the storage of vehicles are often enforced on a complaint-only basis. For example, a property owner could probably park her RV on the street in front of her house until a neighbor complained; at that point, the city would require her to move the RV.

Zoning for Aesthetics. In many areas, there is a concern that the attractiveness of the community not be marred by developments that are ugly or cheap or that simply do not fit in with the general character of the other buildings in the neighborhood.

This is a difficult area to regulate, since personal tastes vary: what one person considers beautiful might be hideous to another. However, there are certain qualities that most people can agree on. For instance, a landscaped parking lot is more attractive than one that is completely asphalt with no plants or trees in sight.

When a proposal for new development is made, it must go through a plan review process to make sure that it meets all building code and zoning requirements. Many communities now also have a design review process that assesses the aesthetic quality of the buildings and landscaping.

Exceptions to Zoning Regulations. In Washington, zoning ordinances are only adopted after a public hearing has been held. This gives members of the public the opportunity to express their opinions and to state any objections.

When an area is rezoned, there are usually at least some properties that don't comply with the new zoning restrictions, or some landowners who want to make a different use of their property than the one allowed. These conflicts are resolved by seeking exceptions to the zoning rules.

Nonconforming uses. A land use that violates current zoning but was legal prior to a zoning change is called a **nonconforming use**. Typically, the owners of nonconforming

Fig. 11.1 Zoning map

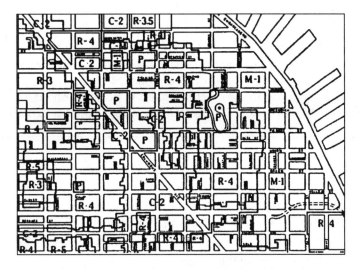

use property are not required to immediately discontinue the use, because such a requirement could be considered a "taking" of the property (and the government would then be required to compensate them). Instead, the use is permitted to continue even though it does not comply with the new or revised ordinance.

> **Example:** McGillicuddy lawfully owns and operates a bakery at the time his property is included in a rezone that changes the area to single-family residential use only. The bakery will be allowed to remain as a nonconforming use.

Although nonconforming uses are allowed to continue, they are usually subject to certain limitations or restrictions. For instance, the use may not be enlarged. (McGillicuddy can continue to run the bakery, but cannot expand or add on to the bakery.)

Also, if the use is discontinued, it cannot be resumed later on. (So if McGillicuddy closed the bakery down for a year, it could not be reopened.) However, a temporary cessation of business due to war or other causes over which the owner has no control does not constitute a discontinuance or abandonment. Most courts require proof of an intent to abandon the use.

Case Example:

The Raging River Quarry has been used as a rock quarry since about 1935. It existed prior to the adoption of the King County zoning code in 1958. The administrative department of King County determined that the quarry was a valid nonconforming use. That decision was appealed by property owners who lived near the quarry.

To qualify as a nonconforming use, the use must lawfully exist on the date specified in the zoning code. If a nonconforming use is abandoned or discontinued, the right to continue as a nonconforming use comes to an end.

It is the nature of rock quarries to operate only when there is a need for material sufficient to justify quantity production. When the need is not present, quarry operations may cease for as long as a year or more.

Just because the quarry was not actively in use at all times did not necessarily mean the quarry had been discontinued or abandoned. Instead, it was necessary to find an intent to abandon or an overt act or failure to act that carried the implication of abandonment. *Andrew v. King County*, 21 Wn. App. 566, 586 P.2d 509 (1978).

Some ordinances place a time limit on nonconforming uses. In other words, they will be allowed to continue only for a certain amount of time. So long as the time limit is reasonable, it will generally be upheld by the courts. A factor in determining reasonableness is the life expectancy of the nonconforming building. If the life expectancy of the bakery building from the earlier example is thirty years, the ordinance may require that the nonconforming use be discontinued in thirty years.

Some ordinances forbid the rebuilding of a nonconforming structure that has been destroyed by earthquake, fire, or other casualty. Any new structure built must comply with the current zoning regulations. In our example, if McGillicuddy's building burned down, a house could be built on the property, but the bakery could not be rebuilt.

Nonconforming uses usually run with the land. This means that if the property is sold, the new owner can continue the nonconforming use. However, all of the same restrictions that applied to the previous owner would also apply to the new owner. A potential purchaser of property that is a nonconforming use should check whether there is a time limit or other restrictions on enlarging or rebuilding the structures.

Variances. A **variance** permits an owner to build a structure or conduct a use not otherwise allowed. Even well-planned zoning ordinances may cause unintentional hardship to certain property owners. A variance is a built-in safety valve that gives community officials flexibility when the injury to the property owner would outweigh the benefit of strict zoning enforcement.

Where peculiarities of a specific property make it difficult or impossible to meet the zoning guidelines, a variance can be granted. Generally, a variance allows only a minor deviation from the requirements of the zoning ordinance.

Example: Judith's property is located in a single-family residential zone that requires all structures to be set back at least 20 feet from the road. Judith's lot is an odd-shaped end lot. No matter how the plans are oriented, Judith finds it impossible to build her house 20 feet from the road. Judith applies for and obtains a variance to build her house only 18 feet from the road.

When a variance is sought, the proposed use must not change the essential character of the area, or reduce the value of the surrounding properties.

Case Example:

The Stromgrens owned a large, woodsy lot (36,840 square feet) in an area zoned RE (residential estate), which required a minimum lot size of 20,000 square feet. The Stromgrens' lot was not only oversized but uniquely positioned, with extensive roadside frontage that required more upkeep than the Stromgrens could handle.

Their home was located in one corner of the lot. They wanted to short plat the land and create a second lot. However, the zoning ordinance prohibited any change that would establish a new lot smaller than the permitted 20,000 square feet.

The Stromgrens applied for a variance, but several neighbors opposed it. The board of adjustment held two full hearings concerning the issue.

Evidence showed that the Stromgren lot was one of only four oversized corner lots in the zone. It was bounded on two sides by land zoned with a minimum lot size of only 7,300 square feet. In addition, 25 of the lots in the zone were smaller than 20,000 square feet because they were platted before the zoning ordinance. Therefore a smaller lot would not substantially change the character of the neighborhood. The Stromgrens' variance was granted. *Martel v. City of Vancouver Board of Adjustment*, 35 Wn. App. 250, 666 P.2d 916 (1983).

To obtain a variance, a property owner applies to the local zoning authority. As in the case example above, there may be an administrative hearing, which is similar to a court proceeding but less formal. Notice of the hearing is given to neighboring property owners. If the requested variance is minor and there are no objections, the hearing is perfunctory and the variance is easily granted. If the variance is a large deviation from the zoning requirements and there are objections, the hearing may be quite lengthy. Expert witnesses or neighbors may be called to testify.

In some communities, routine variances are handled by a board of adjustment, and a hearing is held only if there are objections to the requested variance.

In any case, certain factors must be present before a variance is granted. The owner must show that the zoning causes undue hardship. The hardship suffered must be that reasonable use cannot be made of the land, not simply that more money could be made by devoting the land to another use.

Fig. 11.2 Basic requirements for a variance

VARIANCE
♦ Owner must show undue hardship
♦ Must not change character of area
♦ Must not reduce value of surrounding property

Fig. 11.3 Types of zoning exceptions

```
┌─────────────────────────────────────────┐
│   EXCEPTIONS TO ZONING REGULATIONS        │
├─────────────────────────────────────────┤
│         ◆ Nonconforming Use               │
│         ◆ Variance                        │
│         ◆ Conditional Use                 │
│         ◆ Rezone                          │
└─────────────────────────────────────────┘
```

Personal hardship such as the owner's age or physical condition cannot justify a variance. And the hardship claimed cannot be the result of the owner's own action.

> **Example:** Johnson departs from the plans and specifications attached to his building permit and intentionally builds his house five feet closer to the road than the zoning ordinance allows. The building inspector spots the deviation. Johnson then seeks a variance.
>
> Johnson will not be granted the variance, because it's clear that his hardship was self-created. He intentionally departed from the permitted plans. An owner cannot knowingly build a structure that does not comply with the zoning ordinance and then seek a variance.

Conditional uses. A common provision in zoning ordinances allows the zoning board to issue special permits for certain uses that are inconsistent with the designated zone, but are necessary or beneficial to the community. Such **conditional uses** (also called **special exceptions**) include schools, hospitals, churches, cemeteries, public utility structures, and parks. These uses must be located somewhere, but they are controlled to ensure proper placement in the community and limit possible adverse effects on neighboring property. Most people would be dismayed to learn that the vacant lot next door is going to be developed as a cemetery.

In contrast to the requirements for variances, evidence of hardship in developing the property is not required for a conditional use permit. However, the use must meet a specific need of the community. As long as the proposed location meets the requirements detailed in the zoning code, the owner will generally be granted a permit to construct the special use.

Case Example:

The state Department of Corrections applied for a conditional use permit for a prison work release facility in downtown Kennewick. The location was chosen in part due to its proximity to businesses that would provide employment opportunities for inmates.

Under the city's zoning laws, a conditional use permit could be issued only if the use would not be materially detrimental to the public welfare or injurious to local property or improvements. In addition, a conditional use permit for a penal institution located near facilities serving children or the elderly could be granted only if the city planning director made specific findings justifying the location, and found that the location was not detrimental to those uses.

Kennewick's city planning director found that the site conformed to the requirements of the code, and issued the permit. Neighboring property owners appealed to the city planning commission, which reversed the director's decision. The Kennewick City Council upheld the commission's reversal, stating that the fear of increased crime constituted a material detriment to the value of local businesses and properties. The Department of Corrections sought judicial review.

The court ordered the City of Kennewick to issue the conditional use permit, holding that unsubstantiated, generalized community fear was an irrelevant consideration when deciding where to build essential public facilities, and an improper basis for denying a land use permit. *DOC v. Kennewick*, 86 Wn. App. 521 (1997).

Rezones. If someone believes that the zoning classification applied to a particular property or neighborhood is inappropriate or out of date, they may petition to have the zoning ordinance amended. This is called a **rezone**. Generally the party seeking the change is a landowner or developer who wants to make a different use of the land than is permitted under its current zoning classification. Rezones may also be initiated by the local government based on recommendations from citizens' advisory committees or planning officials.

Notice must be given to surrounding property owners and a hearing must be held before a rezone can occur. The change must be justified by the current needs of the community; it can be made only if it makes more sense than the current zoning category and will not damage the rights of those relying on the current zoning. The community should look to its overall plan to determine what use would best serve future as well as present owners.

Case Example:

In 1964, the city of Redmond zoned an area in the Sammamish River Valley for light industrial use. Valley View Industrial Park was a general partnership formed to develop a specific parcel of land located in this zone.

During the 1970s, the farmlands preservation movement began applying pressure for agricultural zoning of the parcel. In 1977, a citizens' advisory committee was formed to make recommendations on the land use plan. The committee conducted numerous public hearings and meetings.

In September 1978, Valley View submitted a preliminary site plan for its proposed development.

In June 1979, based on the citizens' advisory committee's findings, the Redmond City Council enacted a revised zoning code that rezoned the Valley View property from light industrial to agricultural use.

Valley View filed a lawsuit claiming that the rezone was unconstitutional or, in the alternative, that it was an uncompensated taking requiring the payment of damages.

The court found that the zoning change was unconstitutional. A property owner has a right to use property under the terms of the current zoning ordinance. This right vests or accrues at the time the building permit is applied for.

In other words, Valley View applied for approval for industrial development while the land was zoned for industrial use. If the permit application is complete and complies with the existing zoning ordinance and building codes, the developer has the right to rely on the current zoning.

Once a proper building permit is filed, the zoning classification it carries at the moment of the filing is fixed on the property. The city could no longer simply change the category. *Valley View Industrial Park v. City of Redmond*, 107 Wn.2d 621, 733 P.2d 182 (1987).

Spot zoning. Some forms of zoning changes are illegal. For instance, **spot zoning**—when one piece of property is singled out and rezoned without any clear justification for the change—is illegal.

> **Example:** A rich developer owns property in an area classified as residential. He does favors for several members of the local zoning authority, and his property alone is re-zoned light industrial. (Industrial property can be much more profitable than residential property.) This type of spot zoning is illegal.

Some legitimate zoning changes may appear to be spot zoning. If the rezone of a single property or a few selected parcels is based on sound planning policy and is clearly justified, the change is not illegal.

> **Example:** A new area on the outskirts of the city is zoned residential. Because residents complain about having to travel all the way into the city to find a gas station or convenience store, four corner lots in the developing neighborhood are rezoned for commercial use. This would probably be considered a justifiable reclassification.

In deciding whether or not a particular rezone is spot zoning, a court considers several factors:

- the size of the area rezoned,
- the character of the surrounding areas,
- whether the new use meets community needs or fits into the comprehensive plan, and
- whether the rezone benefits the individual owner without any corresponding benefit to the community.

Case Example:

In July 1979, Snohomish County adopted a comprehensive plan that designated an area near Lake Stevens as a suburban residential zone. This area included property known as the Soper Hill site. In August 1979, the Hewlett-Packard Company proposed development of an electronics manufacturing facility on the Soper Hill site. Hewlett-Packard suggested amending the comprehensive plan to provide for a business park zone.

In 1980, the county council formally enacted the plan amendment. Save Our Rural Environment (SORE), a nonprofit corporation organized to oppose the rezone, filed a lawsuit charging that the Soper Hill rezone constituted a spot zone.

In deciding to uphold the rezone, the court noted that environmental impact statements were prepared and the county planning commission conducted public hearings on the proposal. The county took traffic counts and arranged for road improvements to the area. The county also imposed certain conditions to mitigate the environmental impact on the area.

The rezone was found to bear a substantial relationship to the general welfare of the community. The court found the rezone valid and not an illegal spot zone. *Save Our Rural Environment v. Snohomish County*, 99 Wn.2d 326, 662 P.2d 816 (1983).

Enforcement of Zoning Ordinances. In Washington, zoning ordinances may be enforced by either city or county officials, depending on where the property is located. Fines or other penalties may be imposed on parties who violate zoning regulations. In addition, neighbors or the local government may bring court actions seeking to enjoin a particular use of the property.

One of the best methods for enforcing zoning regulations is a system of building codes and permits, which we'll discuss next. If a proposed use is in violation of the zoning ordinance, a building permit simply will not be granted. If construction begins without a permit, the owner and the builder may be penalized.

Building Codes and Permits

Like zoning laws, **building codes** are intended to protect public health and safety. Building codes are generally divided into specialized areas, such as the fire code or the plumbing code. They set minimum standards for construction methods and for the materials used in construction, as well as other safety requirements. Washington has a state building code, and there are also local building codes. A city or county's building code may set higher standards, but not lower standards, than the state code.

A structure that was built before a new building code standard is implemented may still be required to meet the new standard. For example, a provision was added to Washington's building code in 2009 requiring residential properties to have carbon monoxide detectors. By 2011, all new residential construction and all existing residential rental units had to be in compliance. So even if an apartment building had been built decades earlier, its owners had to install detectors in all units. Owner-occupied single-family homes that were legally occupied before July 2009 are exempt from the requirement, but only until they are sold; carbon monoxide detectors must be installed before such a home can be legally occupied by a buyer.

The primary way that building codes (and zoning rules) are enforced is by requiring a **building permit** to be obtained before a building can be built, repaired, or altered. Before issuing a permit, local officials inspect the construction plans to verify that they comply with the applicable building codes and zoning ordinances. With luck, any problems will be recognized at the planning stage and corrected before the actual construction begins.

After construction is under way, building inspectors may visit the property periodically to examine various phases of the construction. If there are problems, they must be resolved before construction can continue. Once the building is completed, it is inspected again. If the construction is found to be satisfactory, a **certificate of occupancy** is issued.

It's a good idea for real estate agents or prospective buyers to check with the building department to verify that the structures on a property have been inspected and approved, and that a certificate of occupancy has been issued. Most building departments also have records showing any improvements made to a building (such as a new roof, decks, or room additions). Some building departments have records showing where the sewer and utility lines run.

Subdivision Regulations

There are two types of subdivision regulations in Washington. The first type is concerned with the physical aspects of subdivisions, such as provisions for streets and utilities, the size of lots, and locations of schools, parks, and other community services, and these determine the procedures for subdividing and developing land. The second type of subdivision regulation is concerned with protecting the interests of consumers in real estate transactions.

Procedural Requirements. Regulations that set forth the procedures for subdividing land are adopted and administered by each county. Before subdividing, a landowner generally must notify the officials of the county where the property is located. If the property is within one mile of a city or within city limits, notice must also be given to city officials (usually the planning commission).

Notice is usually given by filing a map called a **plat**. A plat is a type of map that shows the location and boundaries of the proposed lots within the subdivision and the location of streets and public areas, and provides information about public services, such as utilities, schools, and parks.

Most city and county regulations provide that a developer may not divide and sell or make improvements to the land until the proposed design of the subdivision has been approved by the planning authority. This often means that the developer must submit a preliminary plat for consideration. After any required changes or improvements have been made, the subdivider files a final plat for approval.

Subdivision regulations may control the size of the individual lots, the location of streets and sidewalks, the placing of sewer and water lines, and the presence of open spaces and recreation areas.

Washington Land Development Act. The Washington Land Development Act is a consumer protection law that applies to sales of land subdivided into 26 or more vacant lots and sold or advertised to the general public.

Requirements. Under the act, a subdivision developer is required to provide prospective lot buyers with a **public offering statement** at least two days before the sale of the lot closes. The public offering statement discloses detailed information about the development, such as:

- the name and address of the developer and the development;
- a brief description of the permitted uses and use restrictions pertaining to the development and the purchaser's individual lot;
- the number of existing lots in the development and the maximum number of lots that may be added to it;
- a list of the principal common amenities in the development; and
- any owners association dues or other charges the purchaser will be obligated to pay.

In addition, the public offering statement must include copies of relevant documents such as surveys and plat maps, CC&Rs (covenants, conditions, and restrictions), and the articles of incorporation, bylaws, and current or proposed budgets for the owners association (if there is or will be one).

The Land Development Act also makes it unlawful to sell a lot that is subject to a blanket encumbrance unless the purchaser of the lot will obtain legal title, free and clear of the blanket encumbrance. This means that if the developer has financed the development by using all of the parcels as security for the loan, the lender must be obligated to release each individual lot from the lien when it is purchased by the individual buyer. This way, the purchasers will be able to obtain title to the individual lots free and clear of the developer's debt.

A developer's failure to comply with any of these requirements may lead to:

1. liability for actual damages,
2. an injunction prohibiting future sales, and
3. cancellation of any sales agreements made with purchasers who did not receive a copy of the public offering statement.

Exemptions. The Land Development Act has several exemptions. For example, the act does not apply if all of the lots in the development are at least five acres. A subdivision is also exempt if the lots have buildings on them or if the developer has a legal obligation to construct buildings on them within two years. And a subdivision that is entirely within the limits of a city is not subject to the act.

Planned Unit Developments. Some communities use **planned unit developments (PUDs)** to provide flexibility in zoning requirements. PUDs differ greatly from each other, but usually have certain characteristics in common. Generally, PUDs are larger than traditional subdivisions, and houses are clustered closely together on slightly undersized lots in order to provide more open space to all of the residents.

A developer may also be able to mix residential and retail uses, single-family and multi-family uses, or some other combination of uses that would not normally be permitted in one area. In return, the developer must usually provide more open space, dedicate more land to the public, or take other actions beneficial to the public welfare.

Some communities designate specific areas as PUD zones. More commonly, a floating zone system is used, which means that a PUD could be put in any area if an adequate proposal is made and approved by the community and the local zoning authority.

To get approval for a PUD, a developer must submit detailed plans of the proposed development to the planning authority. The planning authority may require additional concessions to the community before approval for the PUD is granted.

Historic Preservation

Throughout the United States, and particularly in older urban areas, certain buildings, properties, or districts have been designated as historic sites under federal, state, or local historic preservation laws. This affects land use because the designation protects buildings from destruction. In addition, a special permit must be obtained before any significant changes can be made to historic buildings.

Land Use Planning and Administration

In Washington, land use planning and administration changed dramatically with the passage of the **Growth Management Act** (GMA) in 1990, and its subsequent amendments. The GMA has four major goals:

1. to change Washington's previous patterns of "sprawling settlement" by concentrating new development in already existing urban growth areas;
2. to ensure adequate public facilities are available to serve all new development by requiring thorough infrastructure planning;
3. to protect critical areas from environmentally harmful activities, and to protect natural resource lands from incompatible development; and
4. to encourage regional responsibility by coordinating the plans and regulations of neighboring communities.

The GMA created a framework for land use planning, outlining the steps local governments must take to achieve the goals of the act. The GMA also contains deadlines for compliance, and it established three regional hearing boards to adjudicate disputes under the act. However, the act leaves the bulk of land use planning to the local governments themselves.

Comprehensive Plans. All states—not just Washington—have adopted legislation authorizing or requiring local governments to develop comprehensive plans. A **comprehensive plan** (sometimes referred to as a comp plan) sets forth general guidelines for development in a community, to prevent the problems caused by haphazard and unplanned growth. A comprehensive plan addresses many issues affecting land use, such as building intensity, affordable housing, utility services, and roads and transportation. A comp plan is usually developed by a **planning commission** appointed by the local legislative body (the county council or city council).

In Washington, the land use planning objectives of the GMA are achieved using comprehensive plans. The GMA requires most counties in Washington, as well as the cities within those counties, to prepare a plan. Other local governments may choose whether or not to prepare one.

Requirements. The Growth Management Act requires comprehensive plans to be:

1. internally consistent;
2. coordinated and consistent with the plans of adjacent counties and cities within a region; and
3. implemented by development regulations (such as zoning ordinances) that are consistent with those plans.

Under the GMA, comprehensive plans must specifically address a number of land use issues. Among other things, a plan must:

- include comprehensive information on required land uses, especially housing;
- address the housing needs of all economic segments of society, by providing for low-income housing, government-subsidized housing, manufactured housing, group homes, and foster care facilities;
- explore the relationship between land use and transportation, inventory current transportation facilities, forecast future transportation needs, and plan the financing of future transportation facilities;
- determine the location and distribution of various land uses, set forth the appropriate population densities and building intensities in relation to the various land uses, and project future population growth; and
- provide for the protection of ground water quality and quantity, and the management of drainage, flooding, and storm water run-off.

Generally, comprehensive plans are implemented by zoning ordinances. Local zoning ordinances can never conflict with the goals set forth in a comp plan. Amendments to the plan can only be considered once a year.

In a large city, in addition to a planning commission, there are often several agencies that administer the zoning ordinances and other land use laws. There may be a board of adjustment that grants variances and conditional use permits, a hearing examiner who decides quasi-judicial disputes, a board for subdivision approval, a department that issues building permits, and an enforcement division. In a small town, the town council may handle all of those matters and also serve as the planning commission.

Urban Growth Areas. The Growth Management Act requires new development to be concentrated in compact **urban growth areas** that are contiguous with presently urbanized areas. Counties and cities planning under the GMA must designate the areas to which new urban growth will be limited. Urban growth areas must consist of areas that are or will be adequately served by public facilities and services, and must contain greenbelt and open space areas. Each county's urban growth area must contain enough space to accommodate the county's projected 20-year population growth.

The resulting high density in urban growth areas minimizes the number of areas that will be developed and helps protect natural resource areas and critical areas. Using urban growth areas also helps ensure that public facilities are provided more efficiently and with less environmental damage.

Concurrency Requirement. Another important element of the Growth Management Act is its **concurrency** requirement. Under this requirement, public facilities that are adequate to serve new development must be made available when the impact of development occurs and without decreasing current service levels below certain minimum standards. This means that development cannot take place unless it is accompanied by sufficient public facilities and services.

Case Example:

In 1996, Mason County adopted a comprehensive plan and accompanying development regulations. Members of a local community group filed a petition with the local Growth Management Hearings Board, challenging the plan. The board determined that the comp plan and regulations failed to comply with several GMA requirements.

First, the board found that the county had used the wrong population growth projections and had therefore allocated too much land for urban growth areas. The comp plan also provided for density levels in rural areas that were high enough to be essentially "urban in nature." These density levels would allow excessive population growth and prevent growth from concentrating in urban growth areas.

In addition, the comp plan did not meet the GMA's concurrency requirement: the plan used inaccurate growth projections, contained no rural transportation plan, and failed to discuss the future levels of service that would be required from major public facilities.

The board also found that the comp plan did not make adequate provisions for affordable housing and failed to identify open space areas and greenbelts.

The board ordered Mason County to re-evaluate the comp plan and regulations and bring them into compliance with the GMA. When the county appealed, the court upheld the board's order. *Diehl v. Mason County*, 94 Wn. App. 645 (1999).

Environmental Legislation

The federal and state governments have enacted environmental legislation to preserve and protect the natural environment and the health and welfare of their citizens. These laws affect land use in a number of ways.

Comprehensive Environmental Response, Compensation and Liability Act (CERCLA)

The Comprehensive Environmental Response, Compensation and Liability Act is a federal law that concerns liability for environmental cleanup costs. This act is responsible for dramatically changing the way property owners view potential environmental liability.

CERCLA is well known for its creation of the **Superfund**, a multibillion dollar fund used to clean up hazardous waste dumps and respond to spills of hazardous materials. CERCLA also created a process that is used to identify liable parties and make them responsible for cleanup costs.

The Environmental Protection Agency (EPA) is responsible for enforcing CERCLA. Once the EPA determines that a release of hazardous materials has occurred, it can begin remedial action. First, the EPA determines who is responsible for the release of hazardous materials. These parties, which may include present and previous landowners as well as industrial generators of waste, are referred to as "potentially responsible parties." If the potentially responsible parties fail to cooperate voluntarily in the cleanup, the EPA can begin the cleanup work itself. The EPA will then charge the cleanup costs to the responsible parties. Cleanup costs may include both the cost of cleaning up that particular property and the cost of cleaning up any neighboring property that may have been contaminated by the hazardous substances.

Liability under CERCLA is **joint and several**: any one property owner can be held responsible for the entire cost of the cleanup, regardless of the liability of any other owners. If only one owner can afford the cleanup, she must pay for it, and can then try to get reimbursed by the other owners.

In some cases, the current owners of contaminated property may be required to pay for the cleanup even if they did not cause the contamination. This kind of liability is referred to as **retroactive liability**, and does not depend on any findings of fault.

Model Toxics Control Act

Washington's Model Toxics Control Act (MTCA) is a state law analogous to CERCLA. Like CERCLA, MTCA imposes joint and several liability for hazardous waste cleanup on "potentially liable parties" that include past and present landowners and waste generators. Cleanup under MTCA is coordinated by the state Department of Ecology and is funded in part through taxation of hazardous materials.

Potentially liable parties may conduct cleanup without the assistance and oversight of the state, but the cleanup results must still be reported to the Department of Ecology. If the potentially liable parties do not begin cleanup voluntarily, the department may handle the cleanup and then recover up to three times the amount spent from the responsible party.

National Environmental Policy Act

The National Environmental Policy Act (NEPA) requires federal agencies to provide an **environmental impact statement** (EIS) for any action that would have a significant effect on the environment.

NEPA applies to all types of federal development, such as construction projects, the building of highways, and waste control. NEPA also applies to private actions when the use or development requires the approval of a federal agency in the form of licenses, permits, or even federal loans. In these cases, federal agencies may require submission of an EIS before approving the use or development.

An EIS should disclose the impact of the proposed development on energy consumption, sewage systems, school population, drainage, water facilities, and other environmental, economic, and social factors.

State Environmental Policy Act

Many states have developed specific state versions of NEPA—sometimes known as "little NEPAs." Washington's "little NEPA" is the State Environmental Policy Act (SEPA). It is similar to the federal legislation in that it requires the issuance of an environmental impact statement for all acts of local and state agencies that may have a significant effect on the quality of the environment.

SEPA applies to all state and local developments and also to private developments that require the approval of state, city, or county government agencies. For instance, SEPA requirements must be met before a city or county can give approval for rezones, variances, conditional use permits, or building permits.

SEPA Procedures. When a government agency is considering its own project or whether to issue a permit for a private project, the agency must review the environmental considerations. This review is based on information found in an **environmental checklist**, which is provided by the project applicant. After reviewing the checklist, the agency decides if the project may have significant environmental effects that would require the preparation of an environmental impact statement.

If the proposal will have only a moderate or minor effect on the environment, the agency may issue a **determination of nonsignificance**. When a determination of nonsignificance is issued, additional SEPA procedures do not have to be met, and an environmental impact statement does not have to be prepared.

When the effect is deemed significant, an environmental impact statement is required. The state or local agency may prepare the statement itself. But commonly, the developer provides the necessary environmental information to the agency, or may even be involved in the actual preparation of the EIS. The agency makes its decision to approve or deny the proposed project after considering the findings in the EIS.

If a buyer is purchasing property with plans to improve it, the buyer needs to consider what impact the improvements will have on the surrounding environment. Even if the proposed development meets all zoning and building code requirements, a building permit may still be refused based on adverse information in an environmental impact statement.

Case Example:

Polygon Corporation applied for a permit to build a 13-story condominium in an area of Seattle zoned "Multiple Residence High Density." The city's building department determined that the proposed project was a major action with significant environmental impacts. An environmental impact statement was prepared.

The EIS disclosed a number of adverse impacts, including "view obstruction, excessive bulk and excessive relative scale, increases in traffic and noise, and shadow effect." The EIS also contained comments of numerous local residents who opposed the project.

The Superintendent of Buildings denied Polygon's permit application, stating that the project was inconsistent with SEPA's goals. Polygon appealed the denial, arguing that its project complied with existing zoning regulations.

The court held that since SEPA "overlays" existing local ordinances, the city could deny the permit even though the project conformed to local zoning laws. SEPA gives a municipality the discretion to deny a building permit application on the basis of adverse environmental impacts disclosed by an EIS. *Polygon Corp. v. Seattle*, 90 Wn.2d 59 (1978).

Shoreline Management Act

Washington's Shoreline Management Act protects shorelines by regulating development within 200 feet of high water marks. The act applies to coastal shorelines, to the shores of lakes larger than 20 acres, and to streams that flow at a rate in excess of 20 cubic feet per second. Since there is so much water in the state, the Shoreline Management Act affects quite a large amount of property. Anyone purchasing shoreline property needs to consider what impact this law may have on the use they hope to make of the property.

Structures existing at the time the law took effect get special treatment. Provisions in the law allow existing structures (including houses, fences, bulkheads, and docks) to be maintained and repaired. And if an existing structure burns down, a replacement can be built in the same footprint. But buyers who want to build a new home or other structure—or add on to an existing one—may face problems.

Developers of shoreline property are required to obtain a **substantial development permit** from their city or county before beginning any work. A development is considered "substantial" if it would materially interfere with the normal public use of the water or shoreline, or if its value exceeds $7,047. (This threshold value is adjusted for inflation every five years; the current value will be adjusted again in 2022.)

The Shoreline Management Act also requires cities and counties to adopt **shoreline master programs**. These programs regulate development in shoreline areas, and preempt other zoning laws that may apply to shoreline regions.

Case Example:

Clam Shacks of America, Inc., leases approximately 1,500 acres of mud-flat tidelands in Skagit Bay, where it harvests clams. In 1983, Clam Shacks planned to begin harvesting clams with a newly developed hydraulic clam rake. The rake injects salt water into the sand, which causes the clams to break free and float to the surface.

The Skagit County Planning Department placed certain conditions on Clam Shacks concerning the use of the clam rake. Clam Shacks filed a petition seeking a determination that it was not subject to the regulatory requirements of the Shoreline Management Act or the Skagit County Shoreline Master Program because its use of the clam rake was not a "development."

The court determined that the Shoreline Management Act should be construed to provide the greatest protection to the shoreline environment and concluded that a permit may be required for an activity affecting the shoreline even though it is not a "development." *Clam Shacks of America v. Skagit County*, 45 Wn. App. 346, 725 P.2d 459 (1986).

Violation of the Shoreline Management Act may result in fines and damages. A court may also order that the shoreline be restored to its original condition—even if this means the complete removal of any buildings or improvements.

Clean Air Act

The federal Clean Air Act requires the Environmental Protection Agency (EPA) to control the emission of air pollutants that are harmful to the public health and welfare. National standards have been issued for certain pollutants. Each state is required to prepare a **state implementation plan** (SIP) for meeting the national standards.

The air quality of an area can have a significant effect on land use and development. A state must be concerned with how any new development or use of the property will affect the air quality. Refusal to grant a building permit may be based on how the proposed use would adversely affect air quality.

Developers of projects that will cause direct emissions of pollutants into the air must obtain permits from the State Department of Ecology or from regional air pollution control authorities.

Clean Water Act

The federal Clean Water Act is meant to safeguard water and prevent water pollution. Water quality standards may affect land use by prohibiting the construction of certain

Fig. 11.4 Federal and state environmental laws

ENVIRONMENTAL REGULATIONS
CERCLA
NEPA
SEPA
Shoreline Management Act
Clean Air Act
Clean Water Act

industrial uses that would discharge an unacceptable level of water pollutants. Permits are required for the discharge of pollutants into a lake, stream, or other waterway.

The Clean Water Act also regulates wastewater treatment systems. It encourages local governments to investigate new technology and alternatives to the traditional sewage treatment plants. The wastewater facilities available may have a significant effect on the type and amount of new construction permitted. New construction will not be permitted in an area that does not have adequate sewage treatment facilities.

Other Legislation

A number of other federal statutes may also affect land use, including the Endangered Species Act, the Coastal Zone Management Act, the Resource Conservation and Recovery Act, and the Noise Control Act. Washington also has some similar state statutes.

In addition, other laws that don't immediately seem to apply to real estate may also have an effect on land use.

> **Example:** Due to a declining population in the district, an old grade school building has been closed and unused for several years. The school district is anxious to sell the building. An agent has a client who is interested in purchasing the building and turning it into offices.
>
> Unfortunately, many of the construction materials used in the building contain asbestos. The Occupational Safety and Health Act (OSHA) provides health and safety standards to protect employees in the workplace. It has set specific asbestos standards that must be met. The building cannot be approved for use as offices until the asbestos has been removed.

A real estate agent should advise his clients that there may be significant expenses above and beyond the price of the property. In the example above, substantial renovations may have to be made before the school can be approved and used as office space. (In addition to this concern, the agent would need to know the zoning regulations in this area. Is it zoned for office space? Most schools are located in residential areas.)

Taxation

Although taxes are not levied primarily to control land use, the tax liability that attaches to certain properties can affect their use. For instance, high taxes on farmland in an urban area may encourage or even force the owner to convert the land to nonagricultural use. Conversely, an agricultural or forestland tax exemption may encourage a property owner to keep the land undeveloped.

We'll discuss the two main types of taxes on real property: general real estate taxes and special assessments.

General Real Estate Taxes

General real estate taxes are levied annually and used to support the government's general operations and services. For example, police and fire protection are usually paid for out of general tax revenues.

General real estate taxes are sometimes referred to as **ad valorem taxes** because the amount of the tax is calculated based on the value of the property. (*Ad valorem* means "according to value" in Latin.) The taxable value is periodically determined by a county assessor.

Assessing Value. In Washington, real property is valued at its "true and fair value" unless otherwise specifically provided by law. **True and fair value** means market value. In other words, how much would the property sell for if it were currently on the market? For assessment purposes, land is valued as if vacant and available for development to its highest and best use. **Highest and best use** means the use of the property that would produce the highest net return.

> **Example:** Property located in the middle of the downtown business district is used as a parking lot. The highest and best use of the lot is as a site for an office building.
>
> The property taxes are based on the lot's value to someone who wants to purchase a site for an office building—not the lot's value to someone who wants to continue operating the parking lot.

Thus, a property owner generally pays taxes based on the highest and best use of the land rather than the use to which it is actually devoted. However, the projected use must be legal and in compliance with zoning regulations and other city or county ordinances.

> **Example:** A parcel of property would be worth a great deal of money if its owner could use it as a site for an office building. However, the lot is in an area that is zoned for single-family residences.
>
> The value of the lot will be assessed according to its value as a building site for single-family homes. This is the highest and best use of the lot because it is the only use permitted under current zoning regulations.

The value of improvements to property (such as office buildings, houses, etc.) is assessed separately from the value of the land.

Example: A residential property is assessed for tax purposes. The lot is valued at $80,000; the house itself is valued at $100,000. Thus, the total assessed value of the property is $180,000.

Exceptions. Some specific types of property are not taxed at their highest and best use. For example, the Washington legislature passed the Open Space Taxation Act because it decided that it was in the best interest of the state to maintain and preserve open space for the production of food, fiber, and forest crops, and to assure the use and enjoyment of natural resources and scenic beauty for the well-being of its citizens.

Under the Open Space Taxation Act, open space is taxed on the basis of its current use rather than its highest and best use. For instance, if agricultural property is used for farming but is located in an area that is experiencing suburban growth, the land will be taxed on its value as agricultural property, not its value as if subdivided for residential use. (The Open Space Taxation Act will be discussed in more detail in the next section.)

The legislature has also declared that it is in the public interest to encourage the preservation of historic landmarks. Therefore it has provided a special tax valuation for improvements to historic property.

Exemptions. Certain types of property are exempt from general real estate taxes. Some of the most important exemptions include publicly owned property, church property, cemeteries, property owned by nonprofit organizations and veterans' organizations, libraries, health care facilities, schools, and museums.

Tax Amounts. In Washington, the total amount of all general taxes on real and personal property in any year cannot exceed 1% of the true and fair value of the property. (This limit does not apply to port district or public utility district levies, or to special levies voted for by the people.)

In most taxing districts the rate is set at a certain number of dollars per thousand dollars of value. That rate is then applied to the assessed value of each taxpayer's property.

Collection of Taxes. Tax bills are usually mailed in the middle of February. Payment of one-half of the tax is due on April 30 and the balance is due on October 31.

Special Assessments

Special assessments (also called **improvement taxes**) are levied to pay for public improvements that benefit specific pieces of property. These taxes are usually a one-time expense to pay for particular improvements, such as installing street lights or sewers.

Only those pieces of property that benefit from the improvement are taxed. The theory behind this rule is that the value of these properties will increase because of the improvements, so the property owners should bear the cost of the improvements.

Case Example:

Samis owned over 200 platted, undeveloped lots in Soap Lake. The city imposed an annual $60 "standby" charge on any vacant, unimproved land that abuts but is not connected to a water or sewer line. Samis challenged the fee as an unconstitutional property tax. The city argued the charge was a regulatory fee assessed in exchange for benefits conferred.

Based on the following considerations, the court held that the charge was an illegal property tax. First, the primary purpose of the charge was to raise revenue and not to regulate the fee payers. Second, the collected funds were not segregated and used to benefit the parties being assessed, but rather were used to pay the cost of general utility improvements. And last, there was no relationship between the fee charged and any service received by the lots.

The $60 charge therefore constituted a property tax. Because the tax was imposed selectively and without regard to property value, it was unconstitutional. *Samis Land Co. v. Soap Lake*, 143 Wn.2d 798 (2001).

Open Space and Agricultural Properties

In the last section, we discussed how agricultural properties are sometimes taxed at a lower rate as an incentive for property owners to preserve open space and traditional farms. In this section, we'll take a closer look at what buyers and sellers need to know when transferring ownership of property that has been classified as open space, agricultural property, or timber land. We'll also look at how the state's Right to Farm law has attempted to address conflicts that arise when the needs of residential property owners and agricultural property owners collide.

Open Space Taxation Act

As we mentioned earlier, the Open Space Taxation Act allows property owners to have certain property valued (and taxed) based on its current use, rather than its highest and best use. This law has the effect of lowering—sometimes drastically—the tax bills of property owners who use their property for certain beneficial purposes.

Property Classifications. The law applies to three classifications of property: open space land, farm and agricultural land, and timber land.

Open space. Open space land includes lands that are preserved in their natural state. This means that the current use of the land conserves and enhances natural or scenic resources; protects streams or water supplies; promotes conservation of soils, wetlands, beaches or tidal marshes; or preserves archaeological and historic sites.

Farm or agricultural land. To be classified as farm or agricultural land, a property must be devoted primarily to livestock or agricultural production for commercial purposes. If the property is smaller than 20 acres, it must meet minimum revenue guidelines to qualify. For instance, if a parcel is between five and 20 acres, it will qualify as farm land as long as it has earned a gross income of at least $200 per acre per year for three of the preceding five calendar years.

Timber land. Finally, a parcel of land that is five or more acres may be classified as timber land if it is devoted primarily to the growth and harvest of timber for commercial purposes.

Current Use Status. Once property is classified as open space, agricultural land, or timber land, it must maintain that use for at least 10 years. An owner can withdraw the property from the classification early, but it will cost a significant amount of money to do so. The property owner will have to pay the difference between the classified tax rate and the normal tax rate for up to the previous seven years, plus interest on that amount. There is also a penalty equal to 20% of the total amount owed.

There are some exceptions to this rule. For example, owners can reclassify property from one open space category to another without penalty, such as from timber land to farm land. Also, land use is allowed to change without penalty if the change is due to a natural disaster.

Classified property can be sold (or transferred) at any time, but the seller (or transferor) becomes liable for the additional tax, interest, and penalty at the time of sale (or transfer), unless the new owner agrees to preserve the property's current open space use.

Right to Farm Law

As suburbs have pushed further and further into what were once rural and farming areas, conflicts have developed. After buying a home in a new subdivision in an apparently idyllic rural community, former city dwellers may be in for a shock when the odor of manure from nearby farms fills the air on a sunny day.

Usually, such an offensive odor would meet the statutory definition of a nuisance—something which interferes with an owner's use and enjoyment of her property. But many states have attempted to balance the needs of farmers against the needs of homeowners with statutes known as right to farm laws.

Washington's Right to Farm Act protects not just agricultural activities, but also forest practices (such as a tree farm's clear cutting). In general, if the agricultural property's use is consistent with good agricultural (or forestry) practices, and was established prior to the surrounding nonagricultural property use, then the use is presumed to be reasonable and will not be considered a nuisance.

Certain counties in Washington, such as Snohomish and Skagit, require sellers to give potential buyers a mandatory Right to Farm disclosure form when a property is within a certain distance of designated farmland. This disclosure informs potential buyers that they may be subject to unpleasant odors, pesticide-spraying, noise, dust, and similar agricultural activities from nearby farms.

The purpose of Washington's right to farm law is to promote forestry practices and protect farming from nuisance laws. In essence, it gives the agricultural property owner the right to say "I was here first."

Private Restrictions

So far this chapter has discussed only governmental or public restrictions on land use. However, there may also be private restrictions on a property. Private restrictions are agreements between a seller and a buyer or between neighbors. Private restrictions are usually found in the deed to the property, and they generally run with the land. If the land is transferred or sold, the new owner is also bound by the restrictions.

Covenants and Conditions

Private restrictions may be either covenants or conditions. A **covenant** is a promise to do or not do something. A **condition** in a deed places a restriction on the owner's title. A condition is much more serious than a covenant: a breach of a condition can result in forfeiture of the owner's title through a reversion clause (see Chapter 4).

Since forfeiture is an extremely harsh punishment, if there is any ambiguity in the wording of the clause, a court will usually construe a restriction as a covenant rather than a condition. Almost all private restrictions (especially those found in subdivision restrictions) are covenants.

The violation of a covenant can lead to a court order requiring compliance with the covenant, or a judgment for money damages. Failure to abide by the court order can result in punishment for contempt of court, which is usually time spent in jail.

> **Example:** Leonard purchased a one-story home with a view overlooking Lake Sammamish. All building lots in this subdivision were bound by a restrictive covenant stating that no structure should exceed one story in height, except that the architectural control committee could grant a special variance if the proposed building or addition would not restrict the view for others within the area.
>
> Several years later, Leonard added a second story addition to his house that blocked his neighbor Winston's view of the lake. Winston brought a lawsuit requesting that his view be restored.
>
> Leonard argued that Winston was only entitled to money damages. The court determined that a view is a unique asset for which a monetary value is very difficult to determine. Winston testified that one of the main reasons he bought this particular house was because of the view.
>
> Leonard was required to remodel or remove the addition in its entirety so as to restore Winston's view.

Termination of Restrictions

Most restrictive covenants have no time limit and may be enforced indefinitely. However, some restrictive covenants include a time limit. If a covenant contains a time limit, the covenant simply terminates at the end of the specified time period.

A few states impose time limits on restrictive covenants even if no time limit is specified in the covenant itself. For example, in New York private restrictions terminate automatically after thirty years, unless formally renewed. However, Washington and most other states impose no time limitations.

A restrictive covenant may also terminate by abandonment.

> **Example:** A developer planned to create a residential subdivision and placed a restrictive covenant in some of the deeds. Then the developer's plans changed and the remaining portions of the subdivision were used for commercial buildings. The restrictive covenant for residential use was abandoned.

Similarly, a restrictive covenant may no longer be enforceable if the nature of the restricted neighborhood has changed.

> **Example:** All of the deeds in a particular neighborhood contained a restrictive covenant restricting the properties to residential use. Over the years, however, several other uses crept in.
> Now the neighborhood includes a gas station, a convenience store, and several restaurants. A property owner would have difficulty enforcing the restrictive covenant because the neighborhood has changed so much. The covenant may be deemed inoperative because it is no longer appropriate or suited to the neighborhood.

Subdivision Restrictions

Probably the most common example of private land use regulation is the list of restrictions placed by a subdivider on lots within a subdivision. The restrictions may be referred to as a **declaration of restrictions** or as **CC&Rs** (covenants, conditions, and restrictions).

Subdivision restrictions usually cover matters such as the permitted uses of the property (e.g., single-family detached dwellings for residential use only), and may specify items such as minimum square footage, maximum height, setback requirements, and permitted exterior materials. They may also address aesthetic concerns, such as limiting overnight parking on the streets, and may even limit the types of pets or other animals the property owners may keep.

> **Example:** Although all the lots in a particular subdivision are at least one acre, the CC&Rs prohibit property owners from keeping horses on their property, because the neighborhood is essentially residential rather than rural in character.

> **Example:** A particular subdivision in the Snoqualmie Valley consists of two- to four-acre lots, and many families keep horses and small farm animals on their properties for their own enjoyment. However, the CC&Rs prohibit property owners from keeping animals for commercial purposes. One property owner decided to operate an ostrich farm on the property, keeping ten to twenty ostriches on the land and selling their eggs and offspring.
> Several other property owners sued the ostrich farmer, claiming that the nine-foot birds were nuisances (because of the resulting odor and noise) and a violation of the CC&Rs.
> Even though ostrich farming in this area does not violate any zoning ordinance, health laws, or other public regulations, the property owner will probably have to give up the ostriches to comply with the CC&Rs in effect in the neighborhood.

General Plans. Often subdividers or other land developers devise a general plan for uniformity among all of the lots in the development. The most common way of setting up restrictions in this type of development is with a recorded plat or map of the area that lists all of the uniform restrictions that will apply to every lot. The individual deed to each lot then states that the lot is subject to the restrictions in the recorded plat. The recorded restrictions are incorporated by reference in each individual deed, and the title conveyed is subject to those restrictions.

Enforcement. If there is a general plan, any lot owner may enforce the restrictions in the plan against any other owner. Some developers create a homeowners association made up of the lot owners. The association has the right to enforce the restrictions or bring a lawsuit if the restrictions are violated.

> **Example:** The CC&Rs of a subdivision imposed strict aesthetic requirements on the property owners. The owners of one home repainted it mauve and eggplant. The subdivision homeowners association insisted that they repaint the house in more traditional colors. The owners refused, claiming the mauve and eggplant color scheme was contemporary, yet tasteful. The homeowners association sued the owners and won, forcing them to repaint their house.

Restrictions that violate public policy will not be enforced. For example, a restriction prohibiting the sale of the property to members of a particular race or religion is unenforceable.

Any doubts about the meaning or application of a restriction are usually resolved in favor of the free use of the land, rather than a more restrictive use.

Private Transfer Fees. When ownership of a property in a subdivision is transferred by sale, gift, or inheritance, or even when a property is leased, some homeowners associations require the payment of a fee to the association. In 2011, the Washington legislature passed a law effectively prohibiting these **private transfer fees** as an unreasonable restraint on alienation of real property.

Under this law, private transfer fees cannot run with the land, which means they are not binding on subsequent owners or purchasers of property. Private transfer fee obligations recorded before April 13, 2011 may be enforceable in certain cases, but are not presumed to be. Obligations recorded or entered into after that date are void.

Conclusion

Private property is subject to a considerable variety of public restrictions. Before developing or building on their property, landowners generally must comply with applicable zoning ordinances, building codes, subdivision regulations, and environmental laws. Property taxation also affects land ownership and may have an impact on land use.

In addition to the laws and regulations that apply to a property, there may be private restrictions limiting how it can be used. Prospective property buyers should always make sure that there are no restrictions prohibiting the use they plan to make of the property.

Case Problem

The following is a hypothetical case problem. Most of the facts are taken from a real case. Based on what you have learned from this chapter, make a decision on the issues presented, and then check to see if your answer matches the court's decision.

The Facts

The Wilhelms owned a lot in a residential subdivision that was partially surrounded by adjoining lots. In 1980, the Wilhelms began construction of an enclosure for their swimming pool so that it could be used year-round. (The Wilhelms filed an application and received a building permit for the addition to their home.)

The enclosure was sided with cedar drop siding the same color as the siding on the house, with windows, doors, and trim similar to the house. It was entered through a recreation room in the house, with no separation between the house and the pool enclosure. The back portion of the enclosure was less than 15 feet from the rear property line.

The Dixons and the Whites (neighbors of the Wilhelms) objected to the construction of the pool enclosure and claimed that it violated the subdivision covenants.

When the subdivision was developed in 1962, the developers filed an instrument containing residential area covenants. They also formed an architectural control committee to approve building plans prior to construction, but by 1980 the committee had not functioned for several years.

The neighbors claimed that building the swimming pool enclosure violated the following three covenants:

1. No building shall be erected other than one detached single-family dwelling and a private garage.
2. No building shall be erected until the construction plans and specifications have been approved by the architectural control committee.
3. No dwelling shall be located on any interior lot closer than 15 feet to the rear lot line.

The Questions

Was the construction of the pool enclosure a violation of the restrictive covenants? Should the structure be allowed to remain?

The Answer

The pool enclosure did not violate restriction number one, because it was not a separate building. An addition to a home does not violate a restrictive covenant against building more than one building on the lot.

The pool enclosure was technically a violation of restriction number two, which required approval by the architectural control committee before building. However, the committee had not been operating for several years. If a covenant is habitually and substantially violated so as to create the impression that it has been abandoned, it will not be enforced.

Furthermore, the Whites and the Dixons had also violated this covenant. The Dixons' house was actually built without approval of the committee, and the Whites had altered a deck and added a storage shed without approval of the committee. Someone who has violated a building restriction cannot enforce the same restriction against others.

The court decided that restriction number three was ambiguous because it did not define an "interior lot." The Wilhelms' lot was only partially surrounded by adjoining lots. Any doubts about restrictions should be resolved in favor of the free use of land.

In this case, the Wilhelms' pool enclosure was allowed to remain. *White v. Wilhelm*, 34 Wn. App. 763, 665 P.2d 407 (1983).

Chapter Summary

- Police power is a state's power to adopt and enforce laws and regulations necessary to protect the public health, safety, morals, and general welfare. The state delegates this power to local governments.

- Local governments use zoning ordinances to separate incompatible land uses by creating residential, commercial, industrial, and agricultural zones. Zoning ordinances also regulate the height and size of buildings and where they may be located on a site.

- A nonconforming use is a use that was already legally in place when a new zoning ordinance came into effect, and which does not comply with the requirements of the new ordinance. Nonconforming uses are generally allowed to remain but may be subject to certain restrictions.

- A variance is a permit to build a structure or conduct a use that would not otherwise be allowed. In order to receive a variance, a property owner must show undue hardship.

- Conditional use or special exception permits are generally granted for schools, hospitals, churches, cemeteries, public utility structures, and parks.

- If a property owner believes a zoning classification is incorrect, a rezone may be requested. However, spot zoning—a change in zoning category for a single piece of property without clear justification—is illegal.

- Building codes establish minimum construction standards to protect public health and safety. A building permit must be granted before construction can begin. The completed building must pass an inspection before a certificate of occupancy is issued.

- The Growth Management Act is intended to concentrate development into already existing urban growth areas, help protect environmentally critical areas and natural resource areas, and increase the efficiency of community transportation systems, utilities, and other services. The GMA requires most counties and cities in Washington to adopt a local comprehensive plan.

- Taxation of real property can have an effect on land use by promoting or discouraging certain uses of property. Most real estate is taxed based on the assessed value of its highest and best use. There are some exceptions and exemptions, however.

- Environmental legislation that affects land use includes CERCLA, the Model Toxics Control Act, the National Environmental Policy Act, the State Environmental Policy Act, the Shoreline Management Act, the Clean Air Act, and the Clean Water Act.

- Most private restrictions are covenants rather than conditions. Subdividers commonly impose restrictions (CC&Rs) on the entire subdivision. Violation of private restrictions may result in a court order to comply or a judgment for money damages.

Checklist of Problem Areas

Real Estate Licensee's Checklist

❑ If you're listing a property, have you checked what zoning restrictions apply to it?

❑ If you're working with a buyer, are the buyer's plans for the property compatible with the zoning? Are there private restrictions on the property that could interfere with the buyer's plans?

❑ If a house has an addition or there are other signs of remodeling, was that construction properly permitted and inspected? Are there unpermitted outbuildings that might be unsafe as well as illegal?

❑ Has the property been designated as a historical site? If so, the building is protected from destruction, and the owner would need a special permit before any significant changes could be made to it. Is the potential buyer aware of this?

❑ Is the property close to the water? It may be subject to the Shoreline Management Act, which could affect how the buyer can build on the property.

❑ Are there aspects of the property (such as wetlands) that could be environmentally sensitive, preventing or limiting development or other uses?

Buyer's Checklist

❑ What is the zoning designation of the neighborhood where the property is located? Is the character of the neighborhood consistent with that designation?

❑ Have you read any private restrictions that apply to the property, such as the subdivision's CC&Rs? Does it appear that those restrictions have been enforced?

❑ If you are planning to remodel a structure or develop the property, consider whether your plans could be prevented or adversely affected by:

- the zoning restrictions, including height limits and setback requirements;
- the CC&Rs or other private restrictions;
- a historic preservation law;
- the Shoreline Management Act; and/or
- laws concerning toxic waste (CERCLA and MTCA), air and water quality, noise, habitat protection, or other environmental issues.

❑ Do you understand that there can be retroactive liability for the cost of toxic waste cleanup? Could you be held liable for cleanup costs if you purchase this property, even though you weren't responsible for the contamination?

Chapter Quiz

1. Which of the following has the power to regulate and restrict the use of private property?

   a. The federal government
   b. State governments
   c. Local (city or county) governments
   d. All of the above

2. An area of the city has recently been rezoned residential. John McAllister has been operating a retail upholstery shop in this zone. He will be allowed to continue using his property for commercial purposes. This is known as a:

   a. variance
   b. nonconforming use
   c. spot zone
   d. conditional use

3. In order to be granted a variance, you must show that:

   a. the proposed use will result in a financial benefit
   b. the proposed use will change the character of the area
   c. a hardship will be suffered if the variance is not granted
   d. All of the above

4. A wealthy, philanthropic landowner owns property in a residential area. He is a member of the First Presbyterian Church and wants to build a new church building on the lot as a charitable gift to the church. Will he be allowed to build the church on this lot?

   a. No, because it is zoned residential
   b. Yes, if he is granted a conditional use permit
   c. No, he will not be granted a variance, since he has suffered no true hardship
   d. Yes, because it is a nonconforming use

5. Johnson owns property in a large commercial zone. His property alone is rezoned for industrial use, and he builds a lucrative industrial plant on the property. This is an example of:

   a. a spot zone
   b. a variance
   c. justified zone modification
   d. comprehensive planning

6. Subdivision regulations may control:

   a. lot size
   b. location of streets and sidewalks
   c. provisions for public services such as utilities
   d. All of the above

7. Generally, comprehensive plans are implemented by:

   a. inverse condemnation
   b. variances
   c. building codes
   d. zoning ordinances

8. A planned unit development (PUD):

   a. is generally smaller than most subdivisions
   b. usually places houses on larger than average lots
   c. generally clusters houses close together on undersized lots
   d. may only be located in a commercial zone

9. One of the main methods of enforcing zoning ordinances is:

   a. through the use of building permits
   b. by bringing criminal charges for violations
   c. neighborhood watch programs
   d. None of the above

10. A new addition to the plumbing code requires the use of non-lead pipes in daycare facilities because of the harmful effects of lead on children. The Kiddie Care Center has been located in the Hansen Building for 15 years. The Hansen Building has lead pipes. The Kiddie Care Center:

    a. doesn't have to comply with this requirement because the plumbing code only applies to new buildings
    b. may be required to meet the new standard
    c. is not the only tenant in the Hansen Building, so the plumbing code requirement does not apply
    d. must have non-lead pipes to meet the new standard within 90 days

11. Once a building is completed, if a building inspector finds it satisfactory:

    a. a building permit will be issued
    b. a certificate of occupancy will be issued
    c. an environmental impact statement will be prepared
    d. None of the above

12. General real estate taxes:

    a. are also called ad valorem taxes
    b. are assessed annually
    c. pay for police and fire protection and other public services
    d. All of the above

13. In Washington, the value of agricultural property may be assessed for tax purposes:

    a. based on its current use
    b. every six months
    c. based on its highest and best use
    d. None of the above

14. Under the State Environmental Policy Act (SEPA):

    a. every building project must submit an environmental impact statement
    b. environmental impact statements are only required for state or federal projects
    c. no environmental impact statement is required if there has been a determination of nonsignificance
    d. None of the above

15. If there is ambiguity in the wording of a private restriction, a court will usually construe the restriction as a:

    a. covenant rather than a condition because a condition can result in forfeiture
    b. covenant rather than a condition because a covenant can result in forfeiture
    c. condition rather than a covenant because a condition can result in forfeiture
    d. condition rather than a covenant because a covenant can result in forfeiture

12 Civil Rights and Fair Housing

Outline

I. State Action vs. Private Action
II. Federal Laws
    A. Civil Rights Act of 1866
        1. Application
        2. Enforcement
    B. Fair Housing Act
        1. Application
        2. Exemptions
        3. Prohibited acts
            a. Steering
            b. Blockbusting
            c. Redlining
        4. Disabilities and housing
        5. Enforcement
    C. Fair lending laws
        1. Equal Credit Opportunity Act
        2. Home Mortgage Disclosure Act
    D. Americans with Disabilities Act
        1. Application
        2. Exemptions
        3. Enforcement
III. State and Local Laws
    A. Washington Law Against Discrimination
        1. Unlawful discriminatory practices
        2. Exemptions
        3. Enforcement
    B. Washington Fairness in Lending Act
    C. Washington Real Estate License Law
IV. Effects of Antidiscrimination Legislation
    A. Selling and renting
    B. MLS membership and practices
    C. Employment by brokerage firms
    D. Advertising
    E. Lending practices
    F. Zoning and other municipal regulations
V. The Right to Sue

Key Terms

- State action
- Civil Rights Act of 1866
- Fair Housing Act
- Mrs. Murphy exemption
- Blockbusting
- Steering
- Redlining
- Reasonable accommodations and modifications

- Equal Credit Opportunity Act
- Home Mortgage Disclosure Act
- Americans with Disabilities Act
- Public accommodation
- Readily achievable modification

- Washington Law Against Discrimination
- Washington Fairness in Lending Act
- Disparate impact
- Actual damages
- Punitive damages
- Civil penalty
- Testers

Chapter Overview

Federal and state statutes prohibit discrimination in many contexts, including real estate transactions and related activities. These laws apply to sellers and buyers, landlords and tenants, and real estate agents. Real estate agents who violate antidiscrimination laws could have their licenses suspended or revoked, and could also be subject to a lawsuit.

This chapter discusses the most important federal and Washington state antidiscrimination laws that apply to real estate transactions, including the fair housing laws that govern the day-to-day relationships of residential real estate agents and their clients and customers.

State Action vs. Private Action

The first federal civil rights laws in the U.S. were passed more than 150 years ago. These laws were originally interpreted to forbid discrimination only if it involved "state action"—action by federal, state, or local government entities or officials. For instance, if a city law prohibited loitering, but only African-Americans were arrested for loitering (even though white people were doing exactly the same thing), the police could be accused of discrimination. Examples of discriminatory state action include discriminatory laws and regulations, discriminatory enforcement of the law by police or courts, and court orders to enforce discriminatory private covenants or restrictions.

Case Example:

A party brought suit to enforce private covenants that restricted ownership of property based on race and/or religion. The Supreme Court held that it was unconstitutional to enforce such restrictive covenants. The covenants themselves were not unlawful at that time, but the government could not enforce them (by issuing orders prohibiting their violation or by hearing lawsuits for damages based on their violation). That would be discriminatory state action. *Shelley v. Kraemer*, 334 U.S. 1 (1948).

In the last half-century, however, the courts and legislatures have extended antidiscrimination laws to purely private acts, as well as state action. The right to buy or lease property can be impaired just as effectively by sellers or landlords as by the state or local government. It is now unlawful to include discriminatory covenants in deeds or other documents, to honor or attempt to honor similar provisions in existing documents, or for county recorders to even record documents containing such covenants.

As you read the following discussion of federal discrimination laws, keep in mind that Washington state laws are often stricter than federal laws, prohibiting more types of discrimination in more transactions and with fewer exceptions. It is always the stricter law that must be followed, so you should treat the material covering exemptions from the federal Fair Housing Act as general background information, recognizing that for the most part, those exemptions do not exist under Washington law.

Federal Laws

The effort to eradicate discrimination began on the federal level with the Thirteenth and Fourteenth Amendments to the Constitution. These amendments, passed shortly after the Civil War, abolished slavery and guaranteed equal protection under the law.

Federal laws prohibiting discrimination include the Civil Rights Act of 1866, Title VIII of the Civil Rights Act of 1968 (usually referred to as the Fair Housing Act), the Equal Credit Opportunity Act, and the Home Mortgage Disclosure Act. For the most part, these laws are based on the Thirteenth and Fourteenth Amendments.

Civil Rights Act of 1866

Suppose Mr. and Mrs. Jones try to buy a home in a subdivision. Their offer is refused because they are African-American. What can Mr. and Mrs. Jones do? What can the agent who is representing the Joneses do? What kind of liability, if any, would the sellers have? The agent of the sellers?

The Civil Rights Act of 1866 prohibits discrimination based on race in any property transaction in the United States. The act states, ". . . all citizens of the United States shall have the same right, in every state and territory as is enjoyed by white citizens thereof to inherit, purchase, lease, sell, hold and convey real and personal property."

Application. The 1866 Civil Rights Act contains no exceptions and applies to all property, whether real or personal, residential or commercial, improved or unimproved. However, this act applies only to discrimination based on race.

The constitutionality of the 1866 Act was challenged in *Jones v. Mayer*, a landmark case decided by the U.S. Supreme Court just a few weeks after Congress passed the 1968 Civil Rights Act.

Landmark Case:

Mr. and Mrs. Joseph Jones tried to buy a home, or to have one built for them, in a subdivision being developed by the Mayer Company near St. Louis. When their offer was refused, they brought suit against the Mayer Company based on the 1866 Civil Rights Act, claiming the refusal was evidence of racial discrimination. The court ruled in favor of the Joneses and held that the 1866 Act was constitutional. *Jones v. Alfred H. Mayer Co.*, 392 U.S. 409 (1968).

The Supreme Court's decision in *Jones v. Mayer* established three important precepts:

1. The 1866 Act prohibits all racial discrimination in the sale and rental of property, whether through private or state action, because the right to buy or lease property can be impaired as effectively by those who place property on the market as by state or local governments.

2. The act is constitutional under the Thirteenth Amendment to the U.S. Constitution. This amendment abolished slavery and also gave Congress the power to enforce the amendment through appropriate legislation.

    The 1866 Civil Rights Act is "appropriate legislation." The Thirteenth Amendment was intended to eliminate not only slavery but also the various conditions and aspects associated with slavery, often referred to as "badges of slavery." One of these "badges" was the inability to own or exchange property. Therefore, it was proper for Congress to eliminate this badge of slavery through legislation authorized by the Thirteenth Amendment.

3. The provisions of the 1866 Act are independent of and not superseded by the 1968 Civil Rights Act. The Court noted that the 1866 Act is not a comprehensive fair housing law. It does not address discrimination on grounds other than race; it does not deal with discrimination in services or facilities connected with housing, financing, advertising, or brokerage services; and it does not provide for any federal agency to assist aggrieved parties or for intervention by the attorney general. The 1866 Act is a general statute, enforceable only by private parties bringing their own private lawsuits.

In contrast, the Fair Housing Act of 1968 is a detailed housing law covering a great variety of discriminatory practices and enforceable by the complete range of federal authorities.

Enforcement. You are a real estate agent representing a party whose offer is rejected because of her race. What remedies does she have?

The injured party can bring a lawsuit against the seller. Anyone who is unlawfully discriminated against under the 1866 Act may bring a lawsuit in federal district court. The federal law does not specify a time limit for filing an action, so the lawsuit must be filed within the time limit specified by state law for similar claims.

Fig. 12.1 Civil Rights Act of 1866

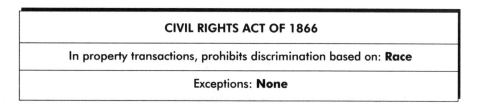

CIVIL RIGHTS ACT OF 1866
In property transactions, prohibits discrimination based on: **Race**
Exceptions: **None**

If the plaintiff wins the discrimination suit, the following remedies are available:

- injunctive relief,
- actual damages, and
- punitive damages.

Injunctive relief is a court order (an injunction) requiring the defendant to do or refrain from doing a particular act. For example, the court might order the owner to sell the house to the plaintiff.

Actual (compensatory) damages is a money award that will compensate the plaintiff for the damages caused by the discrimination. This may include out-of-pocket expenses (such as rent or transportation payments) or compensation for emotional distress. In some cases, awards for actual damages can total thousands of dollars, and in exceptional cases even hundreds of thousands of dollars.

Punitive damages are intended to punish the wrongdoer and discourage others from engaging in similar behavior. There is no limit to the amount of punitive damages that may be awarded for claims brought under the 1866 Act. As we'll discuss later in the chapter, awards of punitive damages can be substantial.

Fair Housing Act

Another federal act prohibiting discrimination is Title VIII of the Civil Rights Act of 1968 (commonly referred to as the Fair Housing Act), which states: "It is the policy of the United States to provide, within constitutional limitations, for fair housing throughout the United States."

The act prohibits discrimination based on **race, color, national origin, religion, sex, disability, or familial status** (families with children) in the sale or lease of residential property or vacant land intended to be used for residential purposes. The law also prohibits discrimination in advertising, lending, real estate brokerage, and certain other services in connection with residential transactions.

Application. Most sales, rentals, and exchanges of residential property are covered by the act. Unless specifically exempt, the law covers transactions involving:

1. any building or structure, or portion of a building or structure that is occupied as, or designed or intended to be occupied as, a residence; and
2. vacant land offered for sale or lease for the construction of any building(s) or portion(s) of building(s) to be used for residential purposes.

Exemptions. Although the act covers the majority of residential transactions, it does contain several exemptions. The provisions regarding discrimination based on familial status generally don't apply to retirement communities. And there are strictly limited exemptions for persons owning up to three homes, owner-occupants of small rental properties, private clubs, and religious, educational, and charitable organizations. Here are the details of those exemptions:

1. The law doesn't apply to a single-family home sold or rented by a private individual owner, provided that:
   - the owner owns no more than three such homes,
   - no discriminatory advertising is used, and
   - no real estate agent (or anyone else in the business of selling or renting homes) is employed.

   If the owner is not the occupant or most recent occupant, she may use this exemption only once every 24 months.

2. The law doesn't apply to the rental of a room or unit in a dwelling with up to four units, provided that:
   - the owner occupies one unit as his residence,
   - no discriminatory advertising is used, and
   - no real estate agent is employed.

   This is sometimes referred to as the **Mrs. Murphy exemption**.

3. In dealing with their own property in noncommercial transactions, religious organizations or societies or affiliated nonprofit organizations may limit occupancy to or give preference to their own members, provided that membership isn't restricted on the basis of race, color, or national origin.

4. Private clubs with lodgings that aren't open to the public and that aren't operated for a commercial purpose may limit occupancy to or give preference to their own members.

These limited exemptions apply very rarely. Remember, the 1866 Civil Rights Act prohibits discrimination based on race in any property transaction, regardless of any exemptions available under the Fair Housing Act. Also, there is no exemption for any transaction involving a real estate licensee. Finally, and most importantly for Washington residents, these exemptions do not exist at all under Washington law. The Washington Law Against Discrimination has no exemptions.

Fig. 12.2 Fair housing poster

U. S. Department of Housing and Urban Development

EQUAL HOUSING OPPORTUNITY

We Do Business in Accordance With the Federal Fair Housing Law

(The Fair Housing Amendments Act of 1988)

It is illegal to Discriminate Against Any Person Because of Race, Color, Religion, Sex, Handicap, Familial Status, or National Origin

- In the sale or rental of housing or residential lots

- In advertising the sale or rental of housing

- In the financing of housing

- In the provision of real estate brokerage services

- In the appraisal of housing

- Blockbusting is also illegal

Anyone who feels he or she has been discriminated against may file a complaint of housing discrimination:
    1-800-669-9777 (Toll Free)
    1-800-927-9275 (TTY)
    www.hud.gov/fairhousing

U.S. Department of Housing and Urban Development
Assistant Secretary for Fair Housing and Equal Opportunity
Washington, D.C. 20410

Previous editions are obsolete

form HUD-928.1 (6/2011)

Prohibited Acts. Under the Fair Housing Act, the following acts are unlawful if based upon race, color, religion, sex, national origin, disability, or familial status:

1. refusing to rent or sell residential property after receiving a bona fide offer;
2. refusing to negotiate for the sale or rental of residential property;

3. any action that would make residential property unavailable or deny it to any person (under this general clause, actions such as steering and redlining are prohibited, as well as many other discriminatory practices and marketing methods);

4. discriminating in the terms or conditions of any sale or rental of residential property or in providing any services or facilities in connection with such property;

5. discriminatory advertising or any other notice that indicates a limitation or preference or intent to make any limitation, preference, or discrimination;

6. making any representation that property is not available for inspection, sale, or rent when it is in fact available;

7. inducing or attempting to induce, for profit, any person to sell or rent property based on representations regarding entry into the neighborhood of persons of a particular race, color, religion, sex, or national origin (**blockbusting**);

8. discrimination by a commercial lender in making a loan for buying, building, repairing, improving, or maintaining a dwelling, or in the terms of such financing;

9. denying access to a multiple listing service or any similar real estate brokerage organization or discriminating in the terms or conditions for access to the organization;

10. coercing, intimidating, threatening, or interfering with anyone on account of his or her enjoyment, attempt to enjoy, or encouragement or assistance to others in enjoying the rights granted by the Fair Housing Act.

Three terms that frequently arise in discussions of fair housing and fair lending laws are:

- steering,
- blockbusting, and
- redlining.

Steering. The term **steering** refers to the channeling of prospective buyers or renters to specific neighborhoods, based on race or other protected classes. For instance, white customers might be shown homes only in white neighborhoods and black customers shown homes only in black neighborhoods.

> **Example:** In some areas, it used to be a widespread practice to code listing agreements with an "X" or some other mark to indicate that the home could be shown to African-American prospects. Unmarked listings could not be.

Case Example:

A real estate brokerage in the Detroit area used a separate phone number when advertising properties located in African-American neighborhoods. The person answering the phone could tell if the call was coming in on the special line, and could direct the caller to one of the African-American agents working in the office. This and other business practices at the brokerage had "a discernible steering effect." *U.S. v. Real Estate One*, 433 F. Supp. 1140 (E.D. Mich. 1977).

In most states, a real estate agent's good faith answer to a buyer's question about a neighborhood's composition (the race, religion, ethnicity, or other protected characteristics of the residents) would not violate antidiscrimination laws if there was no intent to discriminate. However, an agent may not advise or encourage someone to buy or not buy a home based on the composition of the neighborhood.

Example: The following statements could be construed as steering:

"You probably wouldn't be interested in looking at that house; it's in a Latino neighborhood."

"You wouldn't want to buy in this area—it's a changing neighborhood."

Since it's difficult to disprove discriminatory intent, it's generally advisable for agents to avoid making statements regarding the racial, ethnic, or religious composition of a neighborhood.

Blockbusting. The act of blockbusting, or panic selling, occurs when someone (often a real estate agent) predicts the entry of minorities into a neighborhood and forecasts lower property values, higher crime rates, a decline in schools, or some other undesirable consequence. As a result of these statements, panicked property owners list and sell their property in a hurry, often at reduced prices. This allows the person making the statements to make a quick profit on the transactions.

Many blockbusting "techniques" have been cited in various court cases, including:

- passing out literature stating that a member of a minority group has purchased a home nearby;
- "wrong number" phone calls where the callers pretend that they thought they were calling "the minority family that just moved in";
- purchasing a home in the area and then selling it on contract to a minority buyer in order to frighten local residents into selling;
- telling owners that the influx of minorities will adversely affect the schools; and
- implying that because homes are being sold to minorities, the police will no longer be able to patrol the neighborhood effectively.

These are blatant examples of blockbusting. Of course, more subtle blockbusting methods must not be practiced or condoned either.

Redlining. A lender's refusal to make loans on property located in a particular neighborhood will be considered **redlining** if the refusal is for discriminatory reasons. Many lenders used to assume that property values in any predominantly African-American or integrated neighborhood were automatically declining. They would then refuse to make loans in those neighborhoods. Frequently, this was a self-fulfilling prophecy. The inability to obtain purchase or renovation loans made it difficult to sell, maintain, or improve homes in the neighborhood, which caused property values to decline.

Lenders may still refuse to lend money for a property in a neighborhood where values are declining. However, the refusal must be based on objective, economic criteria concerning the condition and value of the property and surrounding neighborhood, without regard to the racial composition of the neighborhood. A lender may not simply equate a minority or integrated neighborhood with declining values.

Disabilities and Housing. An important element of the Fair Housing Act is its inclusion of the disabled as a protected class. The act requires landlords to make reasonable accommodations and permit reasonable modifications necessary for a disabled person to fully use and enjoy a housing unit.

Under the act's **reasonable accommodations** requirement, it is unlawful to refuse to make reasonable accommodations in rules, policies, practices, or services if the accommodations are necessary for a disabled person to have an equal opportunity to use and enjoy a housing unit. This requirement applies to public and common use areas as well as individual living areas.

> **Example:** Bonnie is blind and uses a trained guide dog. She applies to live in an apartment building that does not allow pets. The landlord must allow Bonnie to keep her guide dog because the dog is necessary for Bonnie to have an equal opportunity to use and enjoy the apartment.

Under the Fair Housing Act's **reasonable modifications** requirement, a landlord must permit a disabled tenant to make reasonable modifications to the premises if the modifications are necessary for the tenant's full enjoyment of the property. The tenant may be required to pay for the modifications. The landlord may also require the tenant to return the premises to their original condition, but only if it is reasonable to require that.

> **Example:** A family moves into an apartment and finds that the bathroom doorway is too narrow for their daughter's wheelchair. They ask the landlord for permission to widen the doorways, at their expense. This is a reasonable modification and the landlord must allow it. The landlord cannot require the family to change the doorway back when they move out, unless the wider doorway would somehow interfere with future tenants' use and enjoyment of the apartment.

Multifamily construction. The Fair Housing Act contains several specific design and construction requirements that apply to multifamily dwellings (buildings with four or more residential units) built after 1991.

- All public and common use areas must be accessible and usable by disabled persons.
- Doors must be wide enough for wheelchairs to pass through.
- There must be an accessible route into and through the dwelling unit.
- Light switches, outlets, and thermostats must be placed in accessible locations.
- Bathroom walls must be reinforced, to allow for the installation of grab bars.
- Kitchens and bathrooms must be designed so that a person in a wheelchair can maneuver about the space.

Fig. 12.3 Fair Housing Act

FEDERAL FAIR HOUSING ACT
Prohibits discrimination based on race, color, religion, sex, disability, or national origin, or against families with children

Exemptions:
1. Single-family home sold/rented by owner if:
   a. owner owns no more than three homes
   b. no discriminatory advertising
   c. no real estate agent
   If owner is not the most recent occupant, only one transaction every 24 months.
2. Mrs. Murphy Exemption
3. Religious groups preferring their own members
4. Private clubs preferring their own members
5. Retirement communities excluding children

These requirements apply to the ground floor units in buildings without elevators, and to all units in buildings with elevators. In other words, they apply to all units that are accessible by wheelchair.

Enforcement. An individual unlawfully discriminated against under the Fair Housing Act may file a complaint with the Office of Fair Housing and Equal Opportunity of the Department of Housing and Urban Development (HUD), or may file a lawsuit in federal or state court. HUD may also file a complaint on its own initiative. A complaint must be filed with HUD within one year of the discriminatory conduct; a lawsuit must be brought within two years.

If a complaint is filed with HUD, agency employees will negotiate for "voluntary" compliance. If that is unsuccessful, the case will be decided by HUD or by a federal district court. A defendant may be required to pay actual damages to compensate the victim, plus a civil penalty ranging from a maximum of $20,111 for a first offense to $100,554 for a third offense. (A **civil penalty** is a fine paid to the government.) The judge may also issue an injunction requiring the defendant to cease certain activities or take affirmative steps to redress or prevent harm.

In states such as Washington where there are state or local fair housing laws similar to the federal law, HUD may refer complaints to the equivalent state or local agency. (In Washington, this agency is the Human Rights Commission.)

A suit may be filed in federal district court or in the state trial court having general jurisdiction (in Washington, this would be superior court). The court may grant an injured party a temporary restraining order, a permanent injunction, actual damages, punitive damages, and/or attorney's fees. The defendant may also be ordered to take certain steps to prevent future discrimination.

The U.S. Attorney General may bring a civil suit in federal district court if there is evidence of a pattern of discriminatory activities, or if there is a group of people who have been denied their rights in such a way as to raise an issue of public importance. The Attorney General may request temporary or permanent injunctions or other orders necessary to insure that everyone receives the rights granted under the act. The court may also impose a civil penalty of up to $102,606 for a first offense or up to $205,211 for a subsequent offense.

Fair Lending Laws

In addition to real estate agents and sellers, lenders must also avoid discriminatory activities. The following federal laws target discrimination in lending:

- the Fair Housing Act (discussed above),
- the Equal Credit Opportunity Act, and
- the Home Mortgage Disclosure Act.

The Fair Housing Act prohibits discrimination in home loans and other aspects of residential financing. It does not apply to any other credit transactions.

The **Equal Credit Opportunity Act (ECOA)** applies to all credit transactions, including mortgage lending. The act prohibits lenders, loan originators, mortgage brokers, and others involved in financing from discriminating based on race, color, religion, national origin, sex, marital status, age (as long as the applicant is of legal age), or because the applicant's income is derived partly or wholly from public assistance.

The **Home Mortgage Disclosure Act** addresses whether lenders are fulfilling their obligation to serve the housing needs of the communities where they are located. The act facilitates the enforcement of federal laws against redlining.

Under the Home Mortgage Disclosure Act, large institutional lenders in metropolitan areas must make annual reports on residential mortgage loans (both purchase and improvement loans) that were originated or purchased during the fiscal year. The information is categorized as to number and dollar amount, type of loan (FHA, VA, or other), and geographic location by census tract or county (for small counties with no established census tracts). The reports disclose areas where few or no home loans have been made and alert investigators to potential redlining.

Americans with Disabilities Act

The **Americans with Disabilities Act (ADA)**, which became effective in 1992, is a federal law that was passed to ensure that disabled persons have equal access to public facilities. The ADA requires any business or other facility open to the public to be accessible to the disabled.

Under the ADA, no one can be discriminated against on the basis of disability in places of public accommodation. A **disability** is defined as any physical or mental impairment that substantially limits one or more of the individual's major life activities. A **place of public**

accommodation is defined to include any nonresidential place that is owned, operated, or leased by a private entity and is open to the public, as long as the operation of the facility affects commerce.

Real estate offices are considered to be places of public accommodation, along with hotels, restaurants, retail stores, shopping centers, banks, convention centers, museums, parks, schools, and the offices of attorneys, accountants, and doctors.

The ADA requires each of the following to be accomplished, as long as they are readily achievable:

- Reasonable modifications must be made in policies, practices, and procedures in order to make goods or services accessible to individuals with disabilities.
- Architectural barriers, structural communication barriers, and transportation barriers must be removed so that goods and services are accessible to the disabled.
- Auxiliary aids and services must be provided so that no disabled person is excluded, denied services, segregated, or otherwise treated differently than other individuals.

Readily achievable is defined by the ADA as action that can be easily accomplished, without much difficulty or expense. Here are two examples of readily achievable modifications:

- The owner of an older downtown building with professional offices on the second floor, but no elevator, installs automatic entry doors and a buzzer at street level so that customers of second-floor businesses can ask for assistance.
- The owner of a restaurant in an older building remodels its restrooms to make them more accessible, repositioning paper towel and soap dispensers, adding grab bars to the stalls, and widening a doorway.

In addition, all new commercial construction must be accessible to the disabled, unless structurally impractical. (This requirement applies to the construction of any type of commercial facilities, whether or not they are places of public accommodation.)

Exemptions. Private clubs and religious organizations are exempt from the public accommodation requirements of the ADA.

Enforcement. An individual who is being discriminated against, or who reasonably believes she is about to be discriminated against, may bring a civil action and obtain a temporary or permanent injunction or restraining order from the court. An individual may also file a complaint with the U.S. Attorney General, who will investigate the alleged violation.

If the Attorney General finds that a case of general public importance exists, or that a person is engaging in a pattern or practice of discrimination under the ADA, the Attorney General may file a lawsuit seeking injunctive relief, monetary damages for the victim(s), and civil penalties.

State and Local Laws

Agents, sellers, and landlords must also comply with state laws prohibiting discrimination. The Washington Law Against Discrimination, the Fairness in Lending Act, and the Washington Real Estate License Law all include provisions designed to promote fair housing within the state. In addition, many local jurisdictions have their own regulations barring discrimination in housing.

Washington Law Against Discrimination

The Washington Law Against Discrimination declares that discrimination is a matter of state concern because it threatens the rights and privileges of state inhabitants and the foundations of a free democratic society. The Washington statute is more comprehensive than any of the federal laws discussed above, both as to the types of activities covered and the classes of persons protected from discrimination.

This law prohibits discrimination based on **race, creed, color, national origin, sex, sexual orientation, marital status, familial status; sensory, physical, or mental disability; use of a trained guide dog or service dog;** or **honorably discharged veteran or military status**. Note that those infected or perceived to be infected with HIV are protected from discrimination in the same manner as those suffering from any other sensory, physical, or mental disability.

To further the purposes of the Washington Law Against Discrimination, the Human Rights Commission was created and given the mission of eliminating and preventing discrimination in this state.

Unlawful Discriminatory Practices. The Washington Law Against Discrimination is not just a fair housing law. It prohibits a wide range of discriminatory practices in employment, insurance and credit transactions, places of public accommodation and amusement (such as restaurants, movie theaters, hotels, beauty shops, and most other commercial enterprises), and in regard to all types of real property.

The law prohibits unfair practices with respect to real estate transactions. This means discrimination is prohibited in any real estate transaction, including the sale, appraisal, brokering, exchange, purchase, rental, or lease of real property; transacting or applying for a real estate loan; and the provision of brokerage services.

If based on discrimination against a protected class, it is an unlawful practice to:

1. refuse to engage in a real estate transaction;
2. discriminate in the terms or conditions of a transaction;
3. discriminate in providing services or facilities in connection with a real estate transaction;
4. refuse to receive or fail to transmit a bona fide offer;
5. refuse to negotiate;

6. represent that property is not available for inspection, sale, rental, or lease when it is in fact available;

7. fail to advise a prospect about a property listing or refuse to allow her to inspect the property;

8. discriminate in the sale or rental of a dwelling or otherwise make a dwelling unavailable to any person;

9. publish any advertisement, notice, or sign which indicates, directly or indirectly, an intent to discriminate;

10. use any application form or make any record or inquiry which indicates, directly or indirectly, an intent to discriminate;

11. offer, solicit, accept, or retain a listing with the understanding that a person may be discriminated against;

12. expel a person from occupancy;

13. discriminate in negotiating, executing, or financing a real estate transaction;

14. discriminate in negotiating or executing any service or item in connection with a real estate transaction (such as title insurance or mortgage insurance);

15. induce or attempt to induce, for profit, anyone to sell or rent by making representations regarding entry into the neighborhood of a person of a particular race, creed, color, or national origin, or with a sensory, mental, or physical disability (blockbusting);

16. insert into a written instrument relating to real property, or honor or attempt to honor, any condition, restriction, or prohibition based on race, creed, color, national origin, or sensory, mental, or physical disability; or

17. discriminate in any credit transaction (whether or not real estate related) in denying credit, increasing fees, requiring collateral, or in any other terms or conditions.

In short, just about every form of discrimination in real estate transactions or any services associated with real estate transactions is unlawful if it is because the person is a member of any of the protected classes.

Exemptions. The Washington law has very few exemptions. Educational institutions may discriminate based on sex or marital status in student housing, and private clubs and certain cemeteries and mausoleums operated by religious or sectarian institutions are also exempt as to religious preference. Discrimination based on familial status is allowed in connection with property that qualifies as housing for older persons under the Fair Housing Act.

There are no general exemptions for the typical seller or lessor of real property in ordinary transactions. There is one very limited exemption for some private parties: they are not required to comply with the Washington Law Against Discrimination when they're arranging to share the dwelling unit they occupy. In other words, a homeowner who rents a room in her own house, or a tenant who advertises for a roommate, is allowed to discriminate.

The Washington law has no exemptions for real estate licensees engaged in professional activities.

Enforcement. A party injured by discrimination in a real estate transaction may file a complaint with the Human Rights Commission within one year after the alleged discrimination took place. The Commission will then conduct an investigation. If the investigation reveals a reasonable basis for a belief that discrimination occurred, the Commission will act on the complaint. First, the Commission will try to eliminate the unlawful discrimination by conference, conciliation, and persuasion.

If that is unsuccessful, the Commission may schedule a hearing before an administrative law judge. If the judge finds unlawful discrimination, a cease and desist order will be issued. The judge may require affirmative relief, such as requiring an apartment owner to give the next available apartment to the victim or to solicit minority tenants for future vacancies. The judge may also award damages to the victim. In addition, a civil penalty may be imposed. For a first offense, the maximum penalty is $10,000. For a second offense within five years, the penalty may be up to $25,000. If two or more other unfair practices have been committed in the previous seven years, or if the offender has previously been found guilty of the same act, the penalty may be as much as $50,000.

The outcome of the administrative hearing may be appealed to the superior court by filing an appeal within 30 days after being served with the final order.

As an alternative to an administrative hearing, the injured party may choose to have the state Attorney General bring a civil action against the alleged discriminator.

Washington Fairness in Lending Act

The Washington Fairness in Lending Act prohibits redlining. Under this act, financial institutions may not deny single-family home loan applications because the home is located in a particular geographic area. In addition, they may not vary the terms of the loan (such as by requiring a higher downpayment, higher interest rate, or shorter amortization term, or by deliberately under-appraising the value of the property).

The act does not prevent a lending institution from using sound underwriting practices (including considering the borrower's creditworthiness and the market value of the property), but it outlaws the use of lending standards that have no financial basis.

Washington Real Estate License Law

In addition to complying with the federal and state laws already discussed, real estate licensees must also adhere to the provisions of the license laws and regulations.

According to the license law, violating any fair housing or civil rights laws or regulations is grounds for disciplinary action. If a real estate licensee discriminates in sales or hiring activity on the basis of a protected class, his license could be suspended or revoked. Furthermore, the licensee could face a fine of up to $5,000 for each offense, and/or be required to complete an educational course in civil rights laws and nondiscriminatory real estate practices. Violations of the license law are also punishable as gross misdemeanors.

Effects of Antidiscrimination Legislation

In all property transactions, discrimination based on race is prohibited, with no exceptions. Generally, discrimination based wholly or even partly on any of the other specified classes (creed, color, national origin, sex, familial status, or sensory, physical, or mental disability) is also prohibited in Washington.

In most cases, discrimination by an owner, real estate brokerage, or licensee violates one or more of the laws we have discussed. Some examples of violations are briefly discussed below to give you an idea of the types of practices that have violated civil rights laws in renting and selling real property, MLS membership and practices, brokerage employment and business practices, advertising, lending, municipal zoning, and other regulatory actions.

Selling and Renting

Refusing to sell or rent after receiving a bona fide offer is prohibited if it can be shown that race (or some other class such as religion, national origin, or disability) is a factor, even if it is not the only reason for refusing to sell or rent. In one case, a landlord claimed that a sublessee was an unacceptable tenant. Despite the fact that there were a number of legitimate reasons for rejecting the tenant, a federal court held that the tenant could not be turned down if race was one of the factors for the denial.

Refusal to negotiate for a sale or rental may be a straightforward refusal to talk to or deal with a potential purchaser or renter. Or the lessor or seller simply may refuse to answer the door or to act on an application.

Case Example:

The manager's apartment was located so that she could observe the front door of the building from her own apartment door. When the buzzer rang, she looked down the hall and if the person standing at the door was African-American, she simply went back inside and refused to answer the door. Since she was visible by persons ringing the buzzer, this practice was easily discovered and a complaint was filed with the Human Rights Commission.

After the complaint was filed, the owners installed a peephole in the manager's door. Although the owner maintained this was for the manager's safety, at least one member of the hearing tribunal thought that it could also be for the purpose of allowing the manager to continue her practice without being seen by persons ringing the buzzer. *Skold v. Johnson*, 29 Wn. App. 541, 630 P.2d 456 (1981).

Another method of discrimination involves ignoring rental applications. A property manager takes the rental application and tells the minority applicant that she will be contacted later, or when a vacancy arises. Instead, the manager throws away the application, or never contacts the minority applicant.

In one case, it was the owner's practice not to process rental applications that were not accompanied by a deposit. White applicants were told of this procedure and, accordingly, made a deposit with their applications. African-American applicants were not informed; therefore, few made deposits with their applications, and so their applications were never processed.

The methods used to discriminate can be simple or complex. For example, the salespeople in a model home might dash out the back door when an "undesirable" potential purchaser drives up or approaches the front door. Or a developer might discriminate in the terms or conditions of a sale by making minority purchasers pay higher closing costs. Discrimination can also entail an elaborate scheme, as illustrated by the following case example.

Case Example:

A house was for sale in an exclusive residential district near Chicago. The asking price was $850,000, but after some negotiation, the seller and a African-American couple signed an agreement with a sales price of $675,000. The buyers made an earnest money deposit of $75,000.

News spread that an African-American couple had bought the home, upsetting a number of the community residents. Covenants in the community required all sales to be reported to the homeowners association. The association had a 30-day assignable option to buy the property. In an unprecedented action, the president of the association called a special meeting to discuss the situation. In 16 or 17 previous sales, the option right had been routinely waived without discussion.

At the meeting, talk centered on the buyers' race and occupation (they operated a number of car washes) and ways to prevent the sale. Although the seller was a member of the board of governors and vice president of the association, he was not told of the meeting.

The association's attorney suggested that it might not be advisable for the association itself to buy the property to frustrate the sale, but that perhaps they could form a separate syndicate or find another buyer. Shortly before the 30-day period expired, another buyer (a white person) who had viewed the home earlier was contacted and agreed to buy the association's option.

The African-American buyers brought suit against the homeowners association and against the white buyer alleging a conspiracy to deny them housing based on their race. The court found in favor of the African-American buyers.

While the white buyer claimed ignorance as to the race of the first buyers, the court did not believe her. It also did not believe that the failure to notify the seller of the meeting was an oversight, or that the association's main concern was that the low sales price would lessen the value of other properties in the community. The court noted that price had not been discussed at all at the meeting and that the association had entered into an agreement to have another buyer purchase the property at exactly the same price.

The court noted that the only difference between the second deal and the first was that the second buyer was a white professional businesswoman and the first buyer was an African-American car wash owner.

The court entered judgments in favor of the African-American buyers against both the association and the white buyer for out-of-pocket expenses, emotional distress, and punitive damages. The total judgment was $288,691. *Phillips v. Hunter Trails*, 785 F.2d 184 (7th Cir. 1982).

MLS Membership and Practices

Discrimination has also been found in the denial of access to a multiple listing service and in the practices of MLS members.

Case Example:

A case from Indiana concerned the efforts of a number of brokers in a large city to gain access to multiple listings. The chain of events began in early 1973 and eventually led to several interrelated lawsuits.

In 1973, there was a multiple listing service called Northwest MLS operating in the city, serving the local Board of Realtors. The board was made up of 40 white brokers and four African-American brokers. The MLS had 26 broker members, all of whom were white. The four African-American members of the board repeatedly applied for membership in the MLS but were denied. Towards the end of the year, Northwest MLS ceased operations but was soon replaced by another multiple listing service. This MLS was made up of 18 white brokers and three African-American brokers. At the same time, eight white brokers in the city MLS joined an MLS and local board in a neighboring suburb.

All of the members of the suburban MLS and board were white. The eight white brokers who belonged to both the metropolitan and the suburban multiple listing services began directing all listings they obtained to the suburban MLS, even though they continued doing most of their business in the city.

Since the African-American brokers were not members of the suburban MLS, they were unable to obtain access to those listings. Sometime in the middle of 1977, the white brokers withdrew from the metropolitan MLS altogether and operated solely out of the suburban MLS, although most of their business continued to be with properties located in the city.

The drastic reduction in the number of brokers and listings in the city MLS caused it to cease operations almost immediately. Seven African-American brokers then attempted to join the suburban MLS but were unable to do so. To qualify for membership, it was necessary to belong to the local board, and to qualify for membership in the board, a broker was required to maintain an office in the suburban area.

The African-American brokers alleged that although they attempted to do so, they were unable to rent office space in that suburb because of discriminatory racial attitudes prevalent in the area. They were therefore unable to gain admission to the only operating MLS in the area and were denied access to a majority of the real estate listings in the area.

They sued the multiple listing service, the local board, and eight individual white brokers. They were able to obtain a consent order in federal district court in which the board waived the requirement that members maintain an office within the suburban area. *U.S. v. South Suburban MLS*, and *Wilkes Realty, Inc. v. South Suburban MLS*, No. H77-417 and No. 80-307 (N.D. Ind. 1984).

Employment by Brokerage Firms

It is a violation of antidiscrimination laws and the Washington real estate license law for a brokerage firm to discriminate based on race or any other protected class in hiring affiliated licensees or in determining compensation, work assignments, or other terms and conditions of employment.

Case Example:

A large metropolitan brokerage corporation with over 20 offices and over 300 salespeople had a policy of nondiscrimination in hiring and, in fact, took affirmative steps to recruit, train, and keep licensed African-American salespersons. Several of its officers were recognized leaders throughout the city and state in educating real estate salespeople regarding fair housing laws and the necessity of complying with those laws.

When the lawsuit began, the company was the only real estate firm in the state that operated on a large scale both in predominantly white suburban neighborhoods and in predominantly African-American urban neighborhoods with a biracial sales force.

The problem arose because almost all of the African-American salespeople were assigned to offices located in predominantly African-American urban neighborhoods and almost all of the white salespeople were assigned to offices located in predominantly white suburbs. The judge felt that this practice had the effect of racial steering because:

1. an all-African-American office has a tendency to attract African-American buyers and discourage white buyers;
2. an all-white office has a tendency to attract white buyers and discourage African-American buyers; and
3. agents tend to sell homes in the area near their offices.

The judge believed that an integrated sales staff would foster racially integrated neighborhoods. The brokerage was ordered to give all salespeople information about all offices and neighborhoods served by the firm. Sales associates were to be allowed to visit other offices and typical homes listed by each office, and African-American salespeople were to be encouraged to work out of suburban offices on a full- or part-time basis, without losing the right to be reassigned to the offices in the city if they desired. *U.S. v. Real Estate One, Inc.*, 433 F. Supp. 1140 (E.D. Mich. 1977).

Advertising

Both federal and Washington state law prohibit any advertising that indicates a restriction, preference, or intent to discriminate based on race or other protected class. Discriminatory advertising or solicitations may be very subtle, and apparently innocent statements may sometimes be intended or interpreted as discriminatory.

> **Example:** In some areas of the country, an advertisement that states "Near schools and churches" may be taken to mean that Jewish people (who attend temple or synagogue, not church) are not welcome.

Many agents send advertisements to the neighbors of listed homes in search of potential buyers. While such solicitations are not necessarily discriminatory, they can have a discriminatory effect when:

1. the solicitations are used only in neighborhoods where the residents are predominantly of the same race and/or religious or ethnic background;
2. persons in the neighborhood of a particular race or ethnic background are not sent copies of the solicitation; or
3. the solicitation suggests that the recipient can control the type or character of the person who will buy the property. For example, if the solicitation suggests that a neighbor can, by referring potential buyers, "uphold the standards of the community" (when the "standards" are unspecified), the neighbor is likely to infer that she is being invited to control the race or ethnic background of the buyer.

Solicitations used under these circumstances are considered an unfair practice and a violation of licensing regulations, as are solicitations that invite or provoke discriminatory feelings or actions.

Newspaper advertising is often used by real estate licensees. In certain circumstances, even the choice of newspapers used for advertising purposes may be deemed to have the effect of racial steering.

Case Example:

A real estate brokerage in a large metropolitan area advertised listed properties in two newspapers that were distributed over the entire area, a number of smaller newspapers that were circulated primarily in certain communities or neighborhoods, and in a weekly newspaper circulated primarily in African-American neighborhoods and sold primarily to African-American readers.

The practice that attracted the attention of the attorney general was the company's standard policy of advertising listings in the so-called "changing" areas of the city in the African-American newspaper and not regularly advertising those homes in the newspapers of general distribution.

The court believed this had an impermissible steering effect because, for the most part, only persons who read the African-American newspaper (mostly African-Americans) were made aware of available homes in the "changing" neighborhoods. The judge believed this would have the effect of accelerating the change from a mixed neighborhood to an all or predominantly African-American neighborhood. This would create a segregated neighborhood in violation of the government's policy of fostering integrated neighborhoods.

The company was ordered to maintain the same level of advertising in the newspaper circulated primarily to African-Americans and at the same time advertise the same homes in the two newspapers of general distribution, with some advertising in the smaller community papers nearby. *U.S. v. Real Estate One, Inc.*, 433 F. Supp. 1140 (E.D. Mich. 1977).

The type of models used in advertising can also lead to charges of discrimination.

Example: Ralph is the listing agent for a large, exclusive housing development. He advertises homes for sale on a website he maintains for the development. Every page of the website features professional photography with models representing happy buyers and homeowners at the development. In every one of the photos, all of the people are white, even though 30% of the city's population is non-white. The use of only white models could be the basis for a discrimination lawsuit.

Lending Practices

Discrimination in lending includes unequal treatment at any stage of the loan application and underwriting process, charging applicants or borrowers different fees or rates, and differences in debt collection and foreclosure practices.

Of course, lending discrimination also includes redlining, discussed earlier in the chapter. A lender who has been charged with redlining may be ordered (or may voluntarily agree) to undertake affirmative lending activities to increase lending in neighborhoods where few loans have been made.

These affirmative activities may include:

- setting goals for the number of mortgage loans to be made in particular areas;
- consulting with minority advertising and marketing experts to implement advertising programs in the target areas;
- appointing a bank officer to institute and oversee an affirmative lending program; and
- conducting regular fair lending training seminars for personnel.

In one case, a lender hired two additional loan agents to serve the targeted areas; paid them a guaranteed minimum salary (which was not paid to agents outside the target areas); and paid them a higher rate of commission on the loans they made (because the average amount of those loans was lower than the average amount of loans made in other areas, since property values tended to be lower). [Settlement agreement, *United Neighbors in Action v. American Savings*, No. C-78-1799 (N.D. Calif. 1979).]

Zoning and Other Municipal Regulations

Antidiscrimination laws prohibit zoning practices that have the effect of denying housing to minorities. Since it is unlikely that any state or municipality would currently enact a blatantly racist ordinance, these cases normally involve arguments based on the concept of **disparate impact**. This means that even though the ordinance or regulation may be neutral on its face, its effect is discriminatory because the impact of the law falls more heavily on a particular class than it does on others.

For example, in the field of employment discrimination there have been a number of cases alleging that height restrictions for police or fire departments discriminated against women and certain minorities because these groups tended to be shorter than white males and because there was no evidence to indicate that the height restriction was related to job requirements.

Discriminatory or **exclusionary** zoning cases usually arise out of zoning practices that prohibit or unreasonably restrict zones or permits for multifamily or low-income housing. The argument is that since far more minorities are low-income, any ordinance that limits or restricts lower-cost housing has the effect of excluding minorities or severely restricting their ability to live in the community.

Case Example:

A city was found liable for discrimination based on its practice of approving low-income housing in only one (predominantly African-American) section of the city.

The court found this had the discriminatory effect of preventing African-Americans from moving into predominantly white sections of the city, since there was little or no housing available in those areas for low- or middle-income residents. *U.S. v. Yonkers Board of Education*, 624 F. Supp. 1276 (S.D.N.Y. 1985).

The Right to Sue

As the case examples show, the scope of civil rights laws and the potential consequences of a violation are greater than is immediately obvious from the language of the statutes. Depending on the case, successful plaintiffs may be entitled to:

- actual damages,
- punitive damages,
- attorneys' fees, and
- costs.

As we discussed earlier, actual damages (also called compensatory damages) are intended to reimburse the plaintiff for expenses caused by the discrimination—such as additional rent, or transportation, storage, or moving costs. They also provide compensation for mental distress resulting from the humiliation or embarrassment of discrimination. Punitive damages are intended both to punish the wrongdoer and to serve as a deterrent to others.

Awards for compensatory damages and punitive damages can be substantial in discrimination lawsuits, as in the following case.

Case Example:

This case arose out of what is probably the most common violation of fair housing laws: telling a minority applicant that no apartment is available for rent when in fact there is an available apartment.

The plaintiffs were two African-American women employed as air traffic controllers by the FAA. They attempted to rent apartments at a complex near their jobs at MacArthur Airport on Long Island after reading advertisements for the complex. Both were repeatedly told over a period of several months that no apartments were available for rent. However, the complex continued to run newspaper advertisements for available apartments, and white "testers" who visited the apartments were shown vacant apartments and told space was available. The plaintiffs themselves were told apartments were available when they called on the phone and did not identify themselves.

The jury had no trouble finding the defendant, a realty company, liable for discriminatory conduct. The jury entered a verdict for the following damages: compensatory damages of $40,000 for one plaintiff and $25,000 for the other, and punitive damages of $250,000 for each plaintiff, for a total damages award of $565,000. *Grayson v. Rotundi & Sons Realty Co.*, CV 83-0844 (E.D.N.Y. 1984).

Note that in Washington, punitive damages are generally not available unless expressly authorized by statute. The Washington Law Against Discrimination does not authorize punitive damages. However, punitive damages are available under the federal Fair Housing Act.

It is important to understand that a housing discrimination case may involve many more people as plaintiffs than just the one denied housing, and more defendants than just the one who actually denied the housing. For example, **testers** may also become plaintiffs in a discrimination case.

One of the most common methods of proving violations of fair housing laws is through the use of testers. When a person feels that he has been lied to about the availability of housing, he complains to a government agency, an attorney, or a community fair housing organization. This entity then sends out testers. These testers may be volunteers, although they are more often paid expenses and a nominal fee.

The most frequent type of test is the so-called **sandwich test** in which a white tester (or couple) asks to see available apartments and is shown available space. Immediately after this tester's departure, a minority tester (or minority or mixed-race couple) appears and asks to see available apartments. The minority tester is told that there are no vacancies. Immediately after the minority tester's departure, a second white tester (or couple) appears, asks to see available apartments, and is shown space. This sort of test is generally successful in proving that the property owner or agent is discriminating based on race or some other prohibited grounds.

Obviously, the original applicant (the one who made the complaint) is entitled to damages upon proving that he was discriminated against. What might not be so obvious is that all of the testers as well as the fair housing organization may also be entitled to sue and recover damages from the agent and/or property owner.

Case Example:

An African-American man inquired about available apartments at a complex near Richmond, Virginia. He was told there were no vacancies. He complained to a local nonprofit organization whose purpose was to promote equal housing opportunities. The organization sent out an African-American tester and a white tester. On four different occasions, the African-American tester was told that no apartments were available yet. The white tester was shown vacant apartments.

The realty corporation was then sued by the original rental applicant, the African-American tester, the white tester, and the fair housing organization. The court allowed them all to proceed with their lawsuits for damages.

The rental applicant's claim was based on straightforward allegations of racial steering and denial of housing based on race.

The African-American tester's claim was based on a provision of the Fair Housing Act that makes it unlawful for anyone to misrepresent that housing is not available when it is in fact available. To recover under that provision, it is not necessary to be actually seeking housing. Even testers who expect to be lied to have a right to sue.

The white tester was truthfully told that apartments were available. His claim was based on a right to enjoy the benefits of an integrated society. The prohibited activities of the defendants interfered with that right.

The fair housing organization's claim was based on the theory that the discriminatory activities of the defendant interfered with the organization's efforts to provide housing counseling and referral services, with a resulting drain on its financial resources. *Havens Realty v. Coleman*, 455 U.S. 363 (1982).

In short, there are often many people who are impacted by an act or practice of unlawful discrimination, and they all could sue those connected with the violation. Those sued often include a property manager or real estate agent, a brokerage firm, and an owner, based on their own acts or on the basis of agency liability (see Chapter 6).

If a seller refuses to go through with a transaction because the buyer is a minority, the broker may sue the seller for the commission.

Fig. 12.4 Overview of civil rights laws

	Civil Rights Act of 1866	Federal Fair Housing Act	Washington Law Against Discrimination
Race	X	X	X
Color	X	X	X
Religion (creed)		X	X
Sex		X	X
National origin		X	X
Disability		X	X
Use of guide dog			X
Familial status		X	X
Marital status			X
Sexual orientation			X
Veteran or military status			X
All property	X		X
Housing only		X	

A minority-owned brokerage firm who sues an MLS and member firms for denying it membership could even sue brokerages who refuse to cooperate after the lawsuit.

Case Example:

After several African-American brokers brought suit against an MLS and its members for denying them membership, a number of the white brokers refused to split commissions or co-broker any transactions with the plaintiff African-American brokers.

The African-American brokers then sued the white brokers in a separate lawsuit alleging that the refusal to cooperate was in retaliation for their lawsuit under the Fair Housing Act. The white brokers freely admitted that they refused to cooperate because of the lawsuit, stating that they did not want to work with or share commissions with anyone who was suing them.

Their position may seem reasonable. After all, who wants to do business with someone who is suing you? In this case, though, it was a violation of the Fair Housing Act, which includes a provision that makes it unlawful to "interfere" with the rights guaranteed under the act.

The original lawsuit was based on the African-American brokers' rights under the law. The court held the refusal by the white brokers to cooperate was in retaliation for the lawsuit to enforce rights guaranteed under the Fair Housing Act, and was therefore "interference" with the exercise of their rights under the law. *U.S. v. South Suburban MLS*, No. H 80-307 (N.D. Ind. 1984).

Conclusion

As you've seen, damages awards in discrimination lawsuits can run into hundreds of thousands of dollars, and real estate licensees may be subject to license suspension or revocation for violating fair housing laws or other antidiscrimination laws. Licensees need to understand the application, requirements, and consequences of state and federal antidiscrimination laws, both for their own protection and to provide more professional service to their clients and customers. Promoting fairness in society is also an end in itself.

Case Problem

The following is a hypothetical case problem. Most of the facts are taken from a real case. Based on what you have learned from this chapter, make a decision on the issues presented and then check to see if your answer matches the court's decision.

The Facts

Starrett City is one of the largest rental housing developments in the nation, consisting of 46 high-rise buildings containing over 5,000 apartments in Brooklyn, New York. The project was originally going to be cooperative apartments, but that plan was abandoned.

Starrett City Associates then proposed to construct rental units on the condition that the city real estate tax abatement granted to the original project be transferred to Starrett. This transfer created a great deal of community opposition because of the fear that rental apartments (rather than co-ops) would make Starrett City an overwhelmingly minority development. The community was concerned about "white flight." The transfer was approved only upon assurances that Starrett City was intended to be a racially integrated community.

Starrett City began renting apartments in 1973. Starrett sought to maintain a tenant racial distribution that was approximately 64% white, 22% African-American, and 8% Hispanic. All eligible applicants were told that no apartments were available, but their application would be placed in the active file and they would be notified when a unit became available. When an apartment became available, applicants of a race or national origin similar to that of the departing tenants were selected from the active file and offered the apartment.

Starrett maintained that these procedures were adopted solely to achieve and maintain integration and were not motivated by any racial animus.

Experts at trial testified concerning "white flight" and the "tipping" phenomenon, in which white residents leave a community as the minority population increases, resulting in a predominantly minority community. (The experts disagreed about what the tipping point would be for a particular development.) Starrett claimed that its use of quotas kept the number of minorities in Starrett City low enough to avoid setting off a wave of "white flight." However, Starrett City's quota system also meant that minority applicants waited up to ten times longer than the average white applicant before they were offered an apartment.

The Question

Was Starrett City's quota system a violation of Title VIII of the Civil Rights Act of 1968 (the Fair Housing Act)?

The Answer

Yes. Housing practices that are unlawful under the Fair Housing Act include not only those motivated by a racially discriminatory purpose, but also those that disproportionately affect minorities.

In the real case of *U.S. v. Starrett City Associates*, 840 F.2d 1096 (2nd Cir. 1988), the court said that although quotas promote the Fair Housing Act's integration policy, they contravene its antidiscrimination policy.

In efforts to promote integrated housing, race may sometimes be an appropriate consideration. A race-conscious affirmative action plan does not necessarily violate the Fair Housing Act. However, a race-conscious plan should not use rigid racial quotas of indefinite duration to maintain a fixed level of integration.

In other words, it may have been all right for Starrett to attempt to achieve a certain level of racial integration when the apartments were first rented. It is also legitimate to continue to promote an integrated community. However, strict racial quotas that seriously disadvantage minorities are not an acceptable method for attempting to maintain integration.

Chapter Summary

- Real estate licensees must be aware of both state and federal antidiscrimination laws. The earliest of these is the federal Civil Rights Act of 1866, which prohibits racial discrimination in all property transactions, without exception.

- The federal Fair Housing Act prohibits discrimination based on race, color, religion, sex, national origin, disability, or familial status in the sale or lease of residential property. It prohibits a wide range of discriminatory actions, including steering, blockbusting, and redlining. There are some exemptions from the Fair Housing Act, but no transaction involving a real estate agent is exempt. (The exemptions are also essentially irrelevant in Washington, due to state law.)

- Federal laws that prohibit discrimination in credit transactions include the Fair Housing Act, the Equal Credit Opportunity Act, and the Home Mortgage Disclosure Act.

- The Americans with Disabilities Act prohibits discrimination against disabled people in any place of public accommodation. Under the ADA, a property owner may be required to modify the property to make its facilities accessible to the disabled.

- Washington state law prohibits discrimination not just in housing, but also in employment, insurance, and credit transactions, places of public accommodation and most other commercial enterprises, and all types of real property transactions. There are very few exemptions.

Checklist of Problem Areas

Real Estate Licensee's Checklist

❑ At your brokerage firm, has there been discrimination in hiring agents or working with other firms? Are there other discriminatory practices, such as assigning minority licensees to work only with minority clients or only in minority neighborhoods?

❑ Is your advertising free of language that could suggest an intent to discriminate? Do you advertise all properties in a variety of local and online media, rather than selecting certain properties to be advertised only in certain publications or on certain websites for reasons that are or could be seen as discriminatory?

❑ If you have sent out letters of solicitation, is there anything in the wording that could be interpreted as discriminatory? Were the letters sent out to everyone in the neighborhood, regardless of race, religion, national origin, etc.?

❑ Remember that even though there are some exemptions under the federal Fair Housing Act, these exemptions are generally not available under Washington law and are never available to real estate licensees.

Seller or Landlord's Checklist

❑ Keep in mind that Washington's antidiscrimination law is much more comprehensive than the federal Fair Housing Act. Under Washington law, there are more protected classes and almost no exemptions, not even for sellers of single-family residences who do not use a real estate agent.

❑ If you refuse to go through with a sale or lease and the potential buyer or tenant belongs to a protected class, what is your reason for refusal? You may be liable under federal or state law if the refusal has a discriminatory basis.

Buyer or Tenant's Checklist

❑ If you are told that an apartment is not available or that a house has already sold, is there any reason to suspect otherwise?

❑ Have you been shown houses primarily in one area of town? When you ask about houses in a different area, has the agent tried to steer you away from that area?

❑ If you suspect you have been discriminated against, you can contact local nonprofit housing organizations, the Washington Human Rights Commission, the Department of Licensing (Real Estate Section), the Attorney General's Office, or the Office of Equal Opportunity at HUD.

Chapter Quiz

1. Under the Washington law relating to discrimination in housing, complaints are taken to the:
   a. Department of Fair Employment and Housing
   b. state Human Rights Commission
   c. state Housing Council
   d. Washington Association of Realtors®

2. Title VIII of the Civil Rights Act of 1968 is also called the:
   a. Voting Rights Act
   b. Fair Housing Act
   c. Equal Opportunity in Housing Act
   d. Washington Law Against Discrimination

3. Which of the following is declared to be a national policy in the Fair Housing Act?
   a. Building housing for minority groups throughout the U.S.
   b. Guaranteeing separate but equal housing in all states
   c. Providing fair housing throughout the U.S.
   d. Eliminating prejudice throughout the U.S.

4. Title VIII of the Civil Rights Act of 1968 prohibits:
   a. discrimination in housing
   b. discrimination in residential lending
   c. Both a) and b)
   d. Neither a) nor b)

5. Which of the following is a protected class under Washington's antidiscrimination law but not under the federal Fair Housing Act?
   a. Sex
   b. Familial status
   c. Disability
   d. Veteran or military status

6. Which of the following is exempt from the Fair Housing Act?
   a. A licensee selling vacant lots in a subdivision
   b. An agent helping to sell a single-family home
   c. An owner selling his six-unit apartment house
   d. None of the above

7. Under the Fair Housing Act, a person who feels she has been unlawfully discriminated against can:
   a. seek injunctive relief and sue for damages in state or federal court
   b. file criminal charges in a federal court
   c. file criminal charges in the state supreme court
   d. only sue for damages in federal court

8. The Home Mortgage Disclosure Act helps to enforce the prohibition against:
   a. redlining
   b. steering
   c. blockbusting
   d. None of the above

9. Under Washington law, it would be permissible for a landlord to refuse to rent to a prospective tenant because the tenant:
   a. has a child
   b. was born in Ireland
   c. has a low income
   d. None of the above

10. How long does an aggrieved person have to file a complaint concerning an alleged act of discrimination with the Department of Housing and Urban Development?

    a. 6 months
    b. 12 months
    c. 18 months
    d. 24 months

11. Generally speaking, the Washington Law Against Discrimination:

    a. is broader in application, with fewer exemptions, than the federal Fair Housing Act
    b. is narrower in scope than the Fair Housing Act
    c. provides exactly the same coverage as the federal legislation because of the principle of federal supremacy
    d. is enforceable only insofar as it provides the same protection against discrimination that the federal legislation provides

12. Blockbusting is an acceptable practice:

    a. only under the supervision of licensed real estate brokerage firms
    b. only with prior approval from HUD
    c. only if the buyer and seller are notified and agree
    d. under no circumstances

13. The term "racial steering" refers to:

    a. directing licensees to minority prospects
    b. directing prospects toward housing choices based on the racial composition of the neighborhoods
    c. directing minority prospects toward affordable property, based on their income and assets
    d. None of the above

14. All of the following would be considered public accommodations under the ADA except:

    a. the office of the local credit union
    b. a lab in the home of a self-employed scientific researcher who uses it to complete tests for a well-known company
    c. a real estate office
    d. a property management office that only has one employee

15. An investor owns a five-story office building. She ramped the curb and the steps leading to the office building, altered the height of a pay phone in the lobby, widened restroom doors throughout the building, and added grab bars in certain restroom stalls. The investor did this in an effort to comply with the:

    a. Fair Housing Act
    b. Americans with Disabilities Act
    c. Civil Rights Act of 1866
    d. Civil Rights Act of 1964

13 Landlord/Tenant Law

Outline

D. Eviction
  1. Retaliation
  2. Unlawful detainer
  3. Self-help eviction
  4. Constructive eviction
  5. Personal property
E. Destruction of the premises
F. Tenant rights in foreclosure

Key Terms

- Leasehold estate
- Lease
- Gross (fixed or flat) lease
- Graduated lease
- Net lease
- Percentage lease
- Ground lease
- Assignment

- Sublease
- Novation
- Residential Landlord-Tenant Act (RLTA)
- Covenant of quiet enjoyment
- Implied warranty of habitability

- Common areas
- Surrender
- Abandonment
- Eviction
- Retaliatory eviction
- Unlawful detainer
- Self-help eviction
- Constructive eviction

Chapter Overview

One of the most common of all real estate transactions is the rental or lease of a place to live or work. Someone who rents an apartment, home, office, or business property—a **tenant**—acquires an interest in the property called a **leasehold estate** (see Chapter 4). The fee simple owner of the property—the **landlord**—allows the tenant to take temporary possession of it, usually in exchange for payment of rent. The relationship between landlord and tenant is governed partly by the terms of their lease agreement and partly by the body of legal rules known as landlord/tenant law.

Real estate agents should have a basic knowledge of landlord/tenant law for a number of reasons. Sometimes when property is listed for sale but a buyer can't be found immediately, the seller decides to rent the property with an option to buy, or until a buyer is found; the listing agent often acts as a rental agent in this situation. Many people own rental properties for investment purposes, and they may hire an agent to help them buy or sell those properties. In addition, many real estate agents are involved in property management for rental properties.

This chapter explains the different types of leases and the rights, duties, and liabilities of the landlord and tenant. Both commercial and residential landlord/tenant law are covered, although particular attention is paid to the state Residential Landlord-Tenant Act. Note that some local jurisdictions have additional landlord/tenant rules that are not covered in this book.

Leases

A **lease**, also called a **rental agreement**, transfers the right of possession and use of real property from the owner or landlord to the tenant. A lease is both a conveyance and a contract. As a conveyance, it transfers the right of possession or occupancy. As a contract, it provides for the payment of rent and sets forth the other rights and duties of the landlord and tenant. The parties are free to bargain or negotiate the terms of the contract.

Requirements

Since a lease is a contract, the basic requirements of a contract must be met. First, a valid lease is an agreement between parties who are legally capable of entering into a contract: the parties must not be mentally incompetent or under age.

The lease must also be supported by consideration. The landlord supplies the premises, and the tenant's consideration is typically a set dollar amount that is paid as rent, most often on a monthly basis.

The purpose of the lease must be legal. For instance, in Washington prostitution is illegal. Therefore, it would be illegal to lease a house for that purpose, and the lease would be invalid.

Under Washington law, a lease for over one year must be in writing and acknowledged. A lease for a specific term of one year or less must also be in writing, but does not need to be acknowledged. Other leases, such as periodic (month-to-month) tenancies or tenancies at will, do not have to be in writing to be enforceable. (See Chapter 4.)

If a lease has been put into writing, it must be signed by the landlord. A tenant usually signs the lease as well, but the tenant's signature is not required. If the tenant takes possession of the leased property and pays rent, those actions are considered to constitute acceptance of the lease, even without a signature.

Terms in a Lease. Certain basic information, such as identification of the parties, a description of the premises, the duration of the lease, and the rental amount, should be included in all leases.

Most leases also contain provisions concerning acceptable uses of the property, the right to assign or sublet, the security deposit, and responsibility for repairs and maintenance. In addition, there may be provisions concerning the landlord's access to the premises, the consequences of default by the tenant, and various other issues.

Types of Leases

Gross Lease. Most residential leases are gross leases. Under a **gross lease** (which may also be called a fixed, flat, or straight lease), the tenant pays a set rent amount, and the landlord pays all additional expenses such as maintenance and repairs, taxes, special assessments, and insurance. Most tenants under a gross lease still pay for their utilities, such as electricity and water.

Graduated Lease. A **graduated lease** is similar to a gross lease except that it includes periodic increases in the rental amount. These increases are usually set at specific future dates and are often based on the cost-of-living index.

Net Lease. Many commercial leases are net leases. In a **net lease**, a tenant pays rent plus maintenance and operating expenses, such as utilities, taxes, insurance, and repairs.

There are different gradations of net leases. The terms of a particular lease will vary, but generally under each type of lease a tenant pays a base rent plus the following:

- **net lease**: some maintenance and operating expenses;
- **net-net lease** (also called a double net lease or an NN lease): property taxes, insurance premiums, and some other maintenance and operating expenses; and
- **net-net-net lease** (also called a triple net lease or an NNN lease): property taxes, insurance premiums, and all other maintenance and operating expenses.

Percentage Lease. Some commercial leases are percentage leases. In a **percentage lease**, the rental amount is usually based on a percentage of the tenant's monthly or annual gross sales. Percentage leases are common for retail stores, especially in large shopping centers.

There are many types of percentage leases. For instance, under a pure percentage lease, the entire rental amount is a percentage of the tenant's gross sales. Under the most common type of percentage lease, a fixed minimum rental amount is required along with a percentage of gross sales (or a percentage of gross sales above a certain specified amount).

> **Example:** Dapper Dan, a men's clothing outlet, rents a retail location in a large mall. The lease agreement provides for a minimum rent of $1,500 per month, plus an additional rental amount of 4% of all gross sales above an annual amount of $200,000.

The percentage varies based on the business involved. For instance, parking lots make a much higher percentage of profit on every dollar earned than other businesses. A parking lot might pay a percentage rental of 50% or 60%, while a grocery store would probably pay only 1% or 2%.

A problem with percentage leases is that disagreement often arises concerning what is meant by the term "gross sales." Does it include mail orders, sales and excise tax, credit sales, inter-store transactions, or income from vending machines? The lease should clearly define what is included under the term "gross sales," so that there is no question about the amount the percentage is based on.

Ground Lease. In a **ground lease**, the landowner leases vacant land to a tenant who wants to erect a building on the property. This type of lease is popular in large metropolitan areas and is usually long-term in order to make the construction of a building desirable and profitable.

For example, a tenant might lease a parcel of land and build a 20-story office building on it. Then the tenant would lease office space to different tenants. This creates a **sandwich lease**. The original tenant who constructed the building is both a tenant (as to the land) and a landlord (as to the building).

Transferring Leased Property or a Leasehold

Sale. A landlord is free to sell the leased property at any time. The buyer takes the property subject to existing leases (see the discussion at the end of the chapter for rules about residential foreclosure sales). The new owner must honor the terms of the current lease agreements.

Once the current tenants have been notified of the sale, the new owner has the right to collect all rents. A problem sometimes arises when a tenant has prepaid rent and then the property is sold. The new owner assumes that he is entitled to certain rent, but the tenant has already paid the former owner and does not want to pay again.

Courts disagree on how to handle this situation. Sometimes the new owner is simply out of luck and the prepaid rent remains with the former owner. Sometimes the former owner is required to turn over prepaid rent to the new owner. And sometimes, if there is no record of the prepaid rent and the former owner is unavailable, the unfortunate tenant may be required to pay the rent again, this time to the new owner.

If a tenant prepays rent, she should be sure to get a receipt for the amount paid. A purchaser acquiring property with a pre-existing lease should find out what rent has already been paid, and how much is currently owing.

Assignment. Unless the lease provides otherwise, a tenant may assign the lease to someone else. An **assignment** transfers the tenant's entire interest in the leased property to a new party for the entire remaining portion of the lease term.

> **Example:** Kirk leases an apartment for a one-year period, beginning October 1. In March, Kirk changes jobs and wants to move to a new area of the city. He assigns the remainder of the lease to Mary Alice. Mary Alice agrees to pay the rent to the landlord from April 1 through September 30, the last day of the leasehold.

In an assignment situation, the original tenant becomes secondarily liable for the rent. In the example above, this means that Mary Alice has the primary responsibility for paying the rent. If Mary Alice does not pay, Kirk is still liable to the landlord for payment of the rent.

Sublease. A **sublease** is similar to an assignment except that it does not transfer the tenant's entire interest under the lease. In some cases the tenant is going to share possession of the leased premises with the new party (the subtenant). In other cases the tenant is relinquishing possession to the subtenant, but for a shorter period than the entire remainder of the lease term. In a sublease, the subtenant pays rent to the original tenant rather than to the landlord.

> **Example:** Kirk leases an apartment for a one-year period, beginning October 1. In March, Kirk's employer gives him a three-month assignment in Taiwan. He subleases

his apartment to Mary Alice for the three months he will be gone. Mary Alice agrees to pay rent to Kirk from April 1 through June 30. Kirk continues to pay rent to the landlord.

A sublease does not alter the original landlord-tenant agreement. The original tenant is still primarily liable for payment of rent to the landlord.

Tenants generally have a right to assign their interest or enter into a sublease unless the original lease agreement says otherwise. In practice, though, most leases prohibit both assignment and subleasing without the landlord's consent. This type of consent provision may go on to say that the landlord cannot withhold consent unreasonably. That's especially likely to be true in a commercial lease, as in the following case example.

Case Example:

Ernst Home Center leased commercial space in a mall. The lease stated that the tenants could not assign or sublet the premises without the written consent of the lessors, "whose consent shall not be unreasonably withheld."

Ernst decided to close its store and requested permission to assign the lease to Value Village, a retailer selling used clothing that had been donated to charities. The landlord did not consent and Ernst sued for breach of the lease.

At trial, the court found that the landlord withheld consent because it objected to the type of merchandise sold by Value Village and the "tone" the store presented. No consideration had been given to the financial stability of Value Village.

The lease contained no restrictions as to the nature of the business to be operated on the leased premises. The court held that consent to the assignment was unreasonably withheld. The landlord was ordered to allow assignment of the lease to Value Village. *Ernst Home Center Inc. v. Sato*, 80 Wn.App. 473, 910 P.2d 486 (1996).

In general, courts do not favor restrictions on the right to transfer real property. A landlord must be careful in drafting a limitation on assignment or subleasing. If there is any question or ambiguity, a court will generally favor the right to assign or sublease.

Novation. In a **novation**, a new contract is created and the old contract is extinguished. The purpose of a novation is to terminate the liability of the tenant under the terms of the

Fig. 13.1 Transfer of leased property or a leasehold

SALE	New owner takes subject to existing leases
ASSIGNMENT	Original tenant becomes secondarily liable
SUBLEASE	Original tenant remains primarily liable
NOVATION	Liability of original tenant is completely terminated

original lease. A novation may occur when the tenant and landlord negotiate and replace the original lease with a new one, or when the landlord agrees to release the tenant from the lease and create a new lease with a third party.

> **Example:** Kirk leases an apartment for a one-year period, beginning January 1. In March, Kirk is transferred by his firm to their Taiwan office. His friend Mary Alice likes Kirk's apartment and wants to rent it when he leaves.
>
> Kirk explains his situation to the landlord. After running a background check on Mary Alice, the landlord agrees to terminate the lease with Kirk and enter into a new lease with Mary Alice. Kirk's lease and liability terminate on March 31, and Mary Alice and the landlord sign a new lease that will last from April 1 through March of the following year.
>
> Kirk no longer has any responsibility to the landlord. Even if Mary Alice doesn't pay the rent, Kirk is not liable, because his lease has been terminated and replaced with Mary Alice's new lease.

Residential Landlord-Tenant Act

In 1973, Washington adopted the Residential Landlord-Tenant Act (RLTA). The act's basic purpose is to protect residential tenants from unfair practices and poor living conditions. It imposes a number of duties on residential landlords that other landlords aren't required to fulfill. Nonresidential (commercial or industrial) tenants are presumed to be more sophisticated than residential tenants, and better able to protect their interests during lease negotiations.

The remainder of this chapter focuses mainly on residential tenancies and the rights and duties of landlords and tenants under the RLTA.

Application and Exemptions

Although the RLTA applies to the rental of almost any form of housing, a number of exemptions exist:

1. residents of public or private medical, religious, educational, recreational, or correctional institutions, including correctional facilities, nursing homes, monasteries and convents, and hospitals (but not college dormitories);
2. tenants under a purchase and sale agreement to buy the dwelling;
3. residents of a hotel, motel, or other transient lodging;
4. temporary tenants of property condemned for public use, where the tenant is the owner;
5. residents of land rented incidental to land leased for agricultural purposes;
6. residents of housing for seasonal agricultural employees;
7. tenants leasing public lands from the state of Washington;
8. tenants employed by the landlord, where the right to occupy is conditioned on employment on the property; and
9. tenants in a single-family dwelling with a lease for one year or more, or with an option to purchase, as long as their attorney has approved the lease.

In addition, relationships between landlords and tenants of mobile or floating homes and agricultural properties may be subject to different or additional rules.

Manufactured/Mobile Homes. Washington also has a Manufactured/Mobile Home Landlord-Tenant Act (MHLTA). In a mobile home park, tenants usually own their mobile homes and rent a space from the park owners. It's often difficult for a mobile home owner to move. In many communities, there are few mobile home parks and few vacancies in those parks.

To address this problem, some provisions in the MHLTA differ from the RLTA. For instance, a landlord may not offer a mobile home lot for rent for less than one year. If a tenant wishes to rent a lot for less than a year, or on a month-to-month basis, the tenant must waive the right to a one-year lease in writing.

When a tenant is renting the mobile home itself (rather than just the lot), the RLTA applies instead of the MHLTA.

Floating Homes. In Washington, especially around the Seattle area, many people own floating homes. Specific city ordinances have been passed concerning floating homes. For instance, six months' notice is required for termination of a floating home moorage in Seattle. These specific ordinances override any differing provisions in the RLTA involving floating homes.

Agricultural Leases. Sometimes a residential lease is incidental to an agricultural lease. For instance, a farm is rented and a farmhouse goes along with the farm. The tenant moves into the farmhouse and farms the property. Even though the farmhouse is a residence, if its rental is part of the agricultural lease, it may be excluded from the RLTA.

Rights, Duties, and Liabilities

Whenever two parties enter into a contractual agreement, they agree to certain terms and obligations. Since a lease is a contract, the parties to a lease are bound by the terms agreed to in the lease. Under the RLTA, the parties are also required to fulfill certain other duties and obligations, even if these duties are not specifically mentioned in the lease.

Duties of Landlord Prior to Possession. There are certain restrictions on what a landlord can require of a prospective tenant prior to occupancy. For example, a landlord cannot require a prospective tenant to pay a fee for the privilege of being placed on a waiting list to be considered as a tenant for a dwelling unit.

A landlord who has offered a prospective tenant a unit may charge a fee to help ensure that the prospective tenant will actually move into that unit. However, the landlord must provide the prospective tenant with a receipt, along with a statement describing the conditions under which the fee is refundable. If the tenant does move in, the landlord must credit the fee against the first month's rent or the required security deposit. If the tenant does not move in, the landlord may keep the full amount of the fee if so agreed. This fee cannot include any amount used to pay for a screening service or background check.

If the landlord uses a **tenant screening service**, the landlord may charge the tenant no more than the actual cost of the service. If the landlord screens tenants herself (or has her property manager do the screening), the tenant may be charged for the landlord's actual costs, as long as they do not exceed the customary fee charged by a screening service.

Before charging a tenant a screening fee, the landlord must provide a written notice that: 1) describes what tenant screening entails; 2) lists the criteria that could result in denial of an application; 3) explains the tenant's right to dispute the accuracy of the reported information; 4) provides the name and address of the screening service, if one is being used; and 5) indicates whether the landlord will accept portable tenant screening reports.

Traditional tenant screening reports cannot be shared among landlords, so a prospective tenant applying to several rental properties can end up paying for multiple reports. For this reason, portable tenant screening reports (also called comprehensive reusable screening reports) have become increasingly popular among applicants. A portable screening report, which includes an applicant's credit report, criminal background check, and eviction history, is ordered and paid for by the applicant. The report is made available directly to prospective landlords at no charge.

Landlords are not required to accept portable screening reports. However, they are required to indicate upfront in the application process whether or not they will accept them. This information must appear in the rental application and on any website used to market the property, as well as in the written notice mentioned above.

Possession. A tenant has the right to possession of the rented premises on the agreed date. Implied in every lease is a covenant to deliver possession to the tenant. If the tenant is prevented from gaining possession, this implied covenant has been breached and the tenant may be excused from paying some or all of the rent.

The general rule is that if the covenant to deliver possession is breached, the tenant may rescind or cancel the agreement. But if the tenant elects not to rescind and merely waits for the landlord to clear the premises, the tenant may request only compensatory damages.

For instance, suppose a lease calls for the new tenant to take possession on April 1, but the old tenant does not leave until April 5. The new tenant moves in on April 6. Since the new tenant did not rescind the lease, but merely waited for the premises to be vacated, the new tenant must still pay rent, but may request damages. In this case, the rent would probably be prorated to subtract the amount for April 1 through April 5. In addition, the new tenant might also claim damages for storage fees or additional rent in another location for the extra five days.

Case Example:

Hagbert agreed to rent a piece of property from Draper from July 1, 1980, through June 30, 1983. Hagbert paid a security deposit and the first one-half month's rent.

At the time the lease began, trucks owned by the prior tenant were still using part of the property. There was some disagreement about how long the trucks remained (possibly several weeks). Although Hagbert moved onto the premises, he did not pay any additional rent.

Draper sent Hagbert a notice to pay rent. When Hagbert did not pay, Draper filed a lawsuit. Hagbert claimed that he did not have to pay rent because Draper had breached the implied covenant to deliver possession.

Draper did breach the implied covenant to deliver full possession (because of the presence of the former tenant's trucks). However, Hagbert did not exercise his option to rescind the lease but continued in possession of the property until at least October. Therefore, he only had a claim for damages.

In other words, Hagbert could not completely avoid paying rent, because he took possession of the property. However, he could request damages for the time period between when he was supposed to take complete possession and when the former tenant's trucks were removed. *Draper Mach. Works, Inc. v. Hagbert*, 34 Wn. App. 483, 663 P.2d 141 (1983).

Covenant of Quiet Enjoyment. The landlord's covenant of quiet enjoyment promises that the tenant shall enjoy possession of the premises in peace and without disturbance. This doesn't refer to a noisy neighborhood, but to the right to undisturbed possession.

Under the covenant of quiet enjoyment, a tenant is protected from intrusion by the landlord or anyone else claiming a right to the property. This covenant is breached upon **eviction** of the tenant (either **actual** or **constructive eviction**).

> **Example:** Mother Goose Day Care Center rented a portion of the Talmadge Building. A chemical company rented another section of the building. An accident in the chemical company caused a harmful chemical spill. Environmental guidelines required the whole building to be shut down while the extent of the danger was investigated. Mother Goose was forced to vacate the building and had to rent a new location. The covenant of quiet enjoyment was violated.
>
> Mother Goose has effectively been evicted from the building. Even if it is only a temporary situation, Mother Goose may have a claim against the landlord for breach of the covenant of quiet enjoyment and constructive eviction. (Note that depending on the specific facts of the case, both Mother Goose and the landlord may also have claims against the chemical company.)

Privacy. Once a tenant has taken possession of the property, he has a right of privacy. The landlord may not enter the property without the tenant's consent, except in an emergency. An emergency is any sudden and unexpected threatened or actual injury to property or people.

> **Example:** A water pipe bursts and begins flooding a tenant's apartment. The tenant is not at home. This is an emergency in which the landlord would be authorized to immediately enter the apartment to attempt to stop the flood.

> **Example:** Several apartments have had trouble with bathroom ceiling fans that turn off-center, causing a loud noise when the fan is used. The landlord decides to have a repairman inspect all of the fans in the building. This is not an emergency. The landlord must give the tenants notice and request consent for this inspection.

When requesting entry to inspect the unit, make non-emergency repairs, or provide other services, the landlord must give the tenant two days' notice. The landlord may enter the unit to show it to a prospective buyer or new tenant at a specified time, after giving the current tenant one day's notice. The landlord has a right of access only at times that are reasonable for the tenant. (For instance, the landlord could not request access at two o'clock in the morning.) If the landlord has complied with these requirements, the tenant may not unreasonably withhold permission to enter.

Rent. Not surprisingly, the tenant's most important duty is to pay the rent on time. Most rental agreements specify when rent is due (usually the first day of the month). If there is no agreement as to when rent is due, the common law provides that rent is due at the end of the rental term.

A landlord has the right to terminate a lease or evict a tenant for nonpayment of rent. Many landlords impose a late charge if the rent is not paid by a certain date. A late charge is enforceable only if the lease provides for it.

Security Deposits. A tenant should leave the property in essentially the same condition that it was in at the beginning of the tenancy. The tenant is liable for any alterations made to the property without the landlord's approval, and for any damage beyond normal wear and tear. The tenant cannot be charged for reasonable wear and tear caused by normal use of the premises.

A **security deposit** (also called a **damage deposit**) is money paid by the tenant over and above rent, for the security of the landlord. A typical security deposit is about one month's rent, although there is no specific dollar requirement or limit in Washington. This deposit secures the landlord against the cost of repairing damage caused by the tenant, or against a tenant who abandons the property before the term of the lease is up or without paying all the rent that's owed.

No security deposit may be collected by a landlord unless the rental agreement is in writing and a written checklist is provided that specifically describes the current condition and cleanliness of the premises and furnishings. This checklist must be signed and dated by both the landlord and the tenant, and a copy must be given to the tenant.

Under the RLTA, a landlord must return a security deposit to the tenant within 21 days after termination of the tenancy. (Mailing the deposit within the 21-day period is sufficient, even if the tenant doesn't receive it until a few days later.) The landlord may retain no more of the deposit than is needed to pay for property damage or overdue rent. If any portion of the deposit is retained, the landlord must give the tenant a written statement explaining why it was retained (also within the 21-day window). A court may award the tenant up to twice the amount of the deposit if the landlord intentionally refuses to provide the required written statement or pay the refund due.

Nonrefundable fees. Any nonrefundable amounts required by the landlord (such as a carpet cleaning fee) must be designated in writing as nonrefundable. These amounts may not be taken out of a deposit or designated as a deposit.

Additional damages. If a tenant has caused severe damage and the cost to repair is greater than the amount of the security deposit, the landlord may bring an action against the former tenant for the amount exceeding the deposit. The fact that a security deposit was paid does not protect the tenant from liability for additional damages.

Case Example:

Charron rented a luxury apartment for more than a year. Upon renting the apartment, he paid a security deposit of $225. When he vacated the apartment, the manager discovered that the living room carpet was damaged by rust or mildew stains from plant containers, and the area in front of the wet bar was described as "mutilated." There were also cigarette burns in the carpet in the den. Carpeting in the bedroom and hallway was undamaged.

The manager made inquiries about cleaning or repairing the carpeting but was told that it could not be restored. This particular pattern of carpet had been discontinued, so the damaged areas could not be replaced.

The owners ended up replacing all of the carpeting throughout the entire apartment. The total cost of replacement was $2,723.19. The owners requested additional damages from Charron, over and above the security deposit. Charron argued that he could not be required to pay more than the security deposit.

At trial, the court determined that (especially in light of the fact that this was a luxury apartment) it was reasonable to replace all of the carpeting. The court also found that payment of a security deposit does not protect a tenant from additional liability. The court ordered Charron to pay damages of $1,200. *James S. Black & Co. v. Charron*, 22 Wn. App. 11, 587 P.2d 196 (1978).

Locks. A landlord must provide tenants with reasonably adequate locks and furnish keys for the locks. The landlord must also reasonably safeguard any master or duplicate keys. Some local housing codes contain more specific requirements for locks.

> **Example:** In Seattle, landlords are required to provide dead-bolt locks on all buildings other than detached single-family houses.

Criminal Acts. At one time, landlords had no duty to protect tenants against criminal acts of third parties. However, some courts have imposed liability on landlords for "failure to protect" if the act was foreseeable. This is especially true if the landlord has advertised security protection or if the building is in a high-crime area where criminal activity is likely and foreseeable.

Case Example:

A tenant was assaulted inside her apartment by a neighboring tenant, who entered the victim's apartment through a hole in the wall separating the attic space of the two apartments. The assailant had previously entered the victim's apartment in the same manner. The victim had complained to the landlord, who had merely nailed a piece of lumber over the hole.

The victim sued her landlord for negligence. The court held the landlord liable, holding that a residential landlord has a duty to protect its tenants against foreseeable criminal acts of third parties. *Griffin v. West RS, Inc.* 97 Wn. App. 557 (1999).

The Residential Landlord-Tenant Act provides that another tenant's threatening behavior can be grounds for terminating a lease. If a tenant is threatened by another tenant with a deadly weapon, that other tenant is arrested as a result of the threatening behavior, and the landlord fails to file an unlawful detainer action against that tenant, then the threatened tenant may immediately terminate the tenancy and move out without any further liability for rent.

The RLTA also allows a tenant to terminate a tenancy because of threats from someone who is not a tenant or under the landlord's control (such as an ex-spouse or a stalker). If a tenant or a member of a tenant's household has a valid protection order, the order is violated while the tenant is occupying the rental unit, and the tenant notifies the proper authorities of the violation, then the tenant may terminate the tenancy and quit the premises (move out) without further obligation under the lease. An official report signed by a police officer, health care provider, or other authorized person may substitute for the protection order. A copy of the order or report must be made available to the landlord.

On the other hand, a landlord may not terminate or fail to renew a tenancy simply because the tenant or a household member is a victim of domestic violence, sexual assault, or stalking. Similarly, a landlord cannot refuse to enter into a rental agreement based on the fact that an applicant is a victim of (or has previously terminated a rental agreement due to) domestic violence, sexual assault, or stalking.

If a tenant or a household member is a victim of sexual assault, stalking, or unlawful harassment by the landlord (or someone under the landlord's control, such as an employee), the tenant may terminate the tenancy and move out. Within seven days after leaving, the tenant must provide the landlord with a copy of a protection order or an official report concerning the incident. A tenant in this situation who can't move out immediately is allowed to change the locks, at the tenant's expense, if certain procedures are followed.

Codes and Rules. A landlord must maintain the premises in compliance with all state and local statutes and ordinances that substantially affect the tenant's health and safety. This includes ensuring that the building meets all building code requirements.

In order to enforce a code or regulation, a tenant must show that the violation poses a threat to health or safety. Violations based on faulty wiring or plumbing will be much easier to enforce than something that is not life-threatening like a door that is inches narrower than the code requirement.

Along with the landlord, the tenant must also comply with obligations imposed by municipal, county, and state codes, statutes, ordinances, and regulations. For example, a tenant is required to keep all smoke alarms in proper working order and refrain from dangerous and threatening behavior. In addition, a tenant has a duty to obey any reasonable rules or obligations imposed by the landlord that are noted upon moving in or later adopted with proper written notice from the landlord. All rules brought to the tenant's attention at the beginning of the tenancy automatically become part of the rental agreement. The landlord has the right to terminate the lease or evict the tenant for violating those rules or the terms of the lease.

Pests. A landlord must provide a reasonable program for the control of insects, rodents, and other pests. However, there is no obligation to control infestation in a single-family residence if the problem did not arise until after the tenancy began. The landlord also has no duty when the infestation is caused by the tenant.

> **Example:** Tenant consistently leaves food uncovered on counters and in cabinets. This attracts ants. It will be Tenant's responsibility to get rid of the ants.

Maintenance. The landlord has a duty to maintain any shared or common areas in a reasonably clean, sanitary, and safe condition. This includes keeping them free from anything that would increase the hazard of fire or accident, such as old rags at the bottom of a stairwell, or snow and ice on an entryway. Common areas are those areas of a building that are used by all of the tenants or by the public. Typical common areas include entries, elevators, hallways, stairways, and lobbies.

Case Example:

Lulu Geise, a tenant in a mobile home park, injured herself by slipping on snow and ice that had accumulated in a common area of the park. She brought a lawsuit against the Lees, owners of the Lazy Wheels Mobile Home Park.

The Lees had actual notice of the dangerous icy condition because they had been informed by several tenants and because other residents of the park had already fallen, one even having to go to the hospital.

The court stated that a landlord has an obligation to keep common areas in a reasonably safe condition for the tenants' use. This doesn't mean that the landlord guarantees the tenants' safety. It simply means that the landlord must exercise reasonable care in keeping all common areas reasonably safe from hazards likely to cause injury, if the landlord has actual or constructive notice of the danger. *Geise v. Lee*, 84 Wn.2d 866, 529 P.2d 1054 (1975).

While a landlord must keep the common areas clean and safe, the tenant must keep his private portion of the premises clean and safe. This rule requires the tenant to maintain cleanliness standards that will not cause health problems, attract pests, or interfere with other tenants' use or enjoyment of the property. A tenant must properly dispose of all waste and eliminate pest infestations caused by the tenant.

Case Example:

Richard Taylor, who resided in the Gill Street Apartments, was served with a notice of termination. The notice stated that he had breached the rental agreement because he did not keep his apartment in a clean and safe condition, he did not properly dispose of garbage, and he unreasonably disturbed his neighbors' peaceful enjoyment of the premises.

Taylor did not move by the stated deadline, and filed a complaint against the apartment owners protesting the eviction notice. In the court proceeding, there was testimony that Taylor's apartment badly needed cleaning and exuded a very bad odor. Taylor essentially admitted that he left his drapes open when he walked around his apartment in the nude (this apartment was near the children's play area). Additional testimony revealed that Taylor had refused to move his car to permit snow removal when requested to do so, and that he would sit in the parking lot blowing his horn for an extended period of time if his parking place was occupied. Several witnesses also testified to seeing Taylor frequently intoxicated and driving while intoxicated, and one tenant testified that he had seen Taylor hit a parked car while intoxicated.

Based on this evidence, the court agreed that Taylor had breached the rental agreement. The court entered a writ of eviction ordering Taylor to leave the premises. *Taylor v. Gill Street Investments*, 743 P.2d 345 (Alaska 1987).

Habitability. In all residential rental agreements, there is an **implied warranty of habitability**. This warranty places a duty on the landlord to keep the premises fit for human habitation at all times during the tenancy. Any clause in a lease in which the tenant waives this right is against public policy and will not be enforced. A breach of this warranty may relieve the tenant from the obligation to pay rent.

Case Example:

Ronald Foisy rented a house from Richard Wyman. Foisy signed a six-month lease that required payment of $300 ($50 per month). During the term of the lease, Foisy only paid $95, leaving $205 still owing.

Wyman brought a lawsuit seeking unpaid rent and damages. In his defense, Foisy argued that Wyman had breached the implied warranty of habitability.

The house contained a number of severe defects, including: no heat, no hot water tank, broken windows, a broken door, water running through the bedroom, an improperly seated and leaking toilet, a leaking sink, broken water pipes, and termites in the basement.

Foisy knew about most of these problems when he signed the lease. In fact, because of these defects, the rent was reduced from $87 per month to $50 per month. (As a side note, the court stated that this type of bargaining is contrary to public policy and to the purpose of the doctrine of the implied warranty of habitability. A disadvantaged tenant should not be placed in a position of agreeing to live in an uninhabitable dwelling.)

The court stated that if the premises were found to be totally uninhabitable because of these defects, Foisy's obligation to pay rent could be relieved by the landlord's breach of the implied warranty of habitability. However, if the premises were found to be partially habitable, Foisy would be liable for the reasonable rental value of the house in its substandard condition. *Foisy v. Wyman*, 83 Wn.2d 22, 515 P.2d 160 (1973).

Utilities and Appliances. Facilities adequate to supply heat and hot and cold water as reasonably required by the tenant must be provided. This does not mean that the landlord must pay for these services, but merely that the facilities must be available.

It is unlawful for a landlord to intentionally cause the termination of utility services, except for a reasonable time in order to make repairs. A landlord who unlawfully terminates utilities may be liable to the tenant for any actual damages sustained, plus up to $100 for each day the tenant was deprived of service.

The landlord must maintain all electrical, plumbing, heating, and other facilities and appliances supplied by the landlord. The landlord has no responsibility to maintain any appliances supplied by the tenant. For instance, if the tenant owns and installs her own washer and dryer, the landlord is not responsible if the washer malfunctions and overflows. The tenant is responsible for all of her own appliances. Fixtures and appliances supplied by the landlord must be properly used and maintained by the tenant. A tenant may be responsible if an appliance has problems caused by the tenant's misuse.

> **Example:** Tenant does not own a washer and dryer, but hates going to the laundromat. Tenant has been washing dishrags in the dishwasher along with the dishes. One of the dishrags gets caught in the dishwasher motor. Tenant will be responsible for the cost of repairs to the dishwasher, because her improper use of the dishwasher was the cause of the problem.

Except in the case of a single-family residence, the landlord must provide garbage cans and arrange for regular trash removal.

Structural Components. A building must be kept in a reasonably weathertight condition, and all structural components of the building (the chimney, roof, floors, etc.) must be maintained by the landlord. It is not required that the components be in perfect condition, but merely that they be in reasonably good repair to safely perform the function for which they were intended.

Repairs. Under the RLTA, the landlord has a duty to make repairs to keep the premises habitable. If the premises were substandard to begin with, it is not enough simply to maintain the status quo. Repairs must be made to bring the residence up to a habitable standard.

When a repair needs to be made, the tenant must give the landlord written notice and allow a reasonable time for the repair. In general, a landlord has 24 hours to begin to restore heat, hot or cold water, or electricity, or to repair a hazardous condition. If the tenant is deprived of the use of the refrigerator, range, oven, or a major plumbing fixture supplied by the landlord, repairs must be started within 72 hours. In all other cases, the landlord must begin repairs within 10 days after receiving notice of the problem.

A landlord has no duty to repair a defective condition caused by the conduct of the tenant. This includes the conduct of the tenant's family or guests. A landlord is also not responsible for repairs when the tenant refuses to allow the landlord access for repairs.

Fig. 13.2 Deadlines for making repairs

REPAIR DEADLINES	
24 HOURS	Heat, hot or cold water, electricity, or hazardous condition
72 HOURS	Refrigerator, range, oven, or major plumbing fixture
10 DAYS	All other non-urgent repairs

If a landlord has a duty to repair but does not begin repairs within the applicable statutory time limit, the tenant has several possible remedies:

- The tenant may notify the landlord of intent to vacate and then move out, without further obligation and without forfeiting any prepaid rent or deposit.
- The tenant may arrange to have the repairs performed by a competent third party, after providing the landlord with an estimate of the cost. The tenant may then pay the third party and deduct the cost from the rent. The deduction cannot exceed one month's rent, and if the tenant uses this remedy more than once, the deductions in any 12-month period cannot exceed two months' rent. The landlord must be given an opportunity to inspect the repair work.
- When repairs will cost no more than half of one month's rent, the tenant may choose to perform them (as long as no license is required for the type of work involved). The tenant must make the repairs in a workmanlike manner and allow the landlord to inspect the repairs. The tenant may then deduct the cost of materials and labor from the next month's rent. A tenant may not deduct more than half of one month's rent per repair, or more than one month's rent in any 12-month period.
- A tenant may ask a court or arbitrator to determine that the rent should be reduced until the defect is corrected or repaired.
- When a dangerous problem exists, and the repair and deduct remedy is not adequate to correct it, the tenant can establish a rent escrow. The tenant must first arrange with the local government to have the property inspected. If the inspector certifies that the problem threatens the tenant's health or safety, the tenant may deposit rent into an escrow account when it is due, instead of paying it to the landlord. The tenant must send the landlord written notice of the deposit and disclose the location of the account.

To get the funds released from the escrow account, the landlord must provide a certification from the local government that the defective condition has been repaired. Or the landlord may file a court action for release of the funds, or to have the property's mortgage, insurance, utilities, and the necessary repairs paid out of the escrow account.

Access to Landlord. A landlord must provide a tenant with the name and address of the landlord. A tenant must also be immediately notified of any change of landlord. Many of the tenant's remedies or obligations require giving notice to the landlord. Therefore, the landlord must be available to receive notice, or must appoint someone to receive it on her behalf.

Smoke Detector and Mold Notices. Landlords must give tenants a notice that the dwelling unit is equipped with smoke detectors and disclose the type of detector (battery or hardwired), along with a description of what the tenant must do to maintain the detector in working order. The notice must also address several other fire safety issues, such as emergency preparedness.

Landlords also have to provide tenants with information approved by the department of health concerning the hazards of mold. The mold information notice doesn't have to be given to the tenant personally; it may be posted at a visible location on the property.

Termination of a Tenancy

A tenancy may end in a variety of ways, including notice of termination, expiration of the lease term, surrender, abandonment, eviction, or destruction of the premises. The rights of the parties will vary depending on the reason for termination.

Notice of Termination

As discussed in Chapter 4, if a lease creates a periodic (month-to-month) tenancy, either party may terminate the tenancy with proper notice of termination. As a general rule, the written notice of termination must be given to the other party at least 30 days before the end of the rental period. However, if the tenancy is covered by the Residential Landlord-Tenant Act, either party may terminate the tenancy with only 20 days' notice instead.

In special situations, a residential tenant may terminate a month-to-month tenancy without giving 20 days' notice. That's true if a tenant is in the armed forces and receives reassignment or deployment orders that do not allow for 20 days' notice. The 20-day notice requirement also does not apply to tenants who are terminating their tenancy because of criminal acts by the landlord or others, as described earlier.

Also note that a month-to-month tenant is usually entitled to 30 days' notice before the landlord can increase the rent or change the lease terms or other rules that apply to the tenancy (such as rules concerning pets or smoking).

Expiration of Term

A lease for a specific term ends automatically when the agreed term expires; no notice is required. As a general rule, neither the landlord nor the tenant can unilaterally terminate the lease early (before the end of the term) unless the other party breaches the lease agreement or violates the law. However, a term lease may be terminated early by a tenant in the armed forces who is reassigned or deployed.

Also, the landlord and tenant may mutually agree to terminate the lease at any time. Such a termination is called a **surrender**.

Sometimes when a lease is nearing its expiration date, the parties agree to renew the lease. Upon renewal, the lease may be renegotiated and the rent increased or decreased. (During the term of a lease, the rent and other lease provisions cannot be changed except by mutual agreement.)

Another possibility when a term lease expires is that the landlord may allow the tenant to stay on without signing a new lease agreement for another fixed term. If the landlord continues to accept monthly rent from the tenant, that will create a month-to-month tenancy.

Abandonment

Abandonment is defined as an absolute relinquishment of the premises by the tenant before the end of the lease. When a tenant abandons the leased property, the landlord usually wants to retake possession of the property without waiting until the end of the lease term. Most leases contain a clause permitting reentry by the landlord after abandonment, but reserving the right to collect rent from the absent tenant.

When the tenancy is month-to-month, the tenant is liable for rent for the 30 days following the date the landlord learns of the abandonment, or the date the next regular rental payment would have become due, whichever occurs first.

When the tenancy is for a term greater than one month, the tenant is liable for either the entire rent for the remainder of the term, or the rent accrued during the period reasonably necessary to rent the premises again, plus additional costs.

The landlord has a duty to try to mitigate the damages by renting the property to a new tenant as soon as possible. However, if a new tenant cannot be found after reasonable attempts by the landlord, the original tenant remains liable for damages caused by the abandonment.

> **Example:** Landlord and Tenant enter into a year-long lease for an apartment; the term begins on June 1. Tenant abandons the apartment in October. Landlord retakes possession and attempts to rent the apartment. However, with Christmas coming up, most people don't want to move until after the first of the year. Although Landlord advertises extensively, he is unable to find a new tenant until January 15.

The original tenant is liable for the rent owed for October, November, December, and half of January. Since the landlord found a new tenant, the original tenant is not required to pay rent from mid-January through May, even though this was the original lease agreement. However, the original tenant may also be liable for expenses incurred in finding a new tenant. He could be required to pay for the cost of advertising and any additional work necessary to rent the apartment.

Case Example:

The Meyers owned and leased business premises to Western Farmers Association. The lease was then assigned to Higgins. Without any notification, Higgins abandoned the premises. The Meyers attempted, without success, to find another tenant for the building. The Meyers brought a lawsuit against Western Farmers for the unpaid rent and for reimbursement for repairs.

Western Farmers brought a cross-complaint charging that the Meyers failed to mitigate their damages by leasing to a new tenant. The court found that the Meyers had tried to mitigate but no new tenant was found. An honest and reasonable effort is all that is required.

Western Farmers was therefore liable for unpaid rent and for repairs. *Meyers v. Western Farmers Association*, 75 Wn.2d 133, 449 P.2d 104 (1969).

Eviction

Almost all leases provide that the lease may be forfeited and the tenant evicted for non-payment of rent or for violation of the terms of the lease. However, if the tenant fails to pay the rent, the lease is not automatically terminated. The landlord must first give notice to the tenant of the nonpayment. If the tenant still fails to pay, the landlord may begin legal proceedings to recover rent payments or evict the tenant.

If the tenant breaches the terms of the lease or uses the premises in a manner not authorized by the lease, the landlord may require the activity to stop or terminate the lease and evict the tenant. For example, if the tenant uses the premises for illegal activity, the landlord may demand that the tenant cease the illegal activity or vacate the premises.

Washington's Residential Landlord-Tenant Act specifically allows a landlord to evict a tenant based upon a reasonable belief that illegal drug activity is taking place in the unit.

> **Example:** Landlord discovers that Tenant is using his apartment to manufacture and sell drugs. Landlord may begin eviction proceedings to remove the tenant from the premises, and notify law enforcement agencies that illegal drug activity is taking place.

Retaliation. When a landlord evicts a tenant in response to complaints made by the tenant, it is considered **retaliatory eviction**. Under the RLTA, a landlord cannot retaliate against a tenant simply because that tenant has requested necessary repairs or has complained in good faith to the proper authorities concerning violations of health or building code regulations.

Retaliatory action includes eviction, increasing the rent, reduction of services, or increasing the obligations of the tenant.

Presumptions. If a landlord initiates any of the actions listed above within 90 days after the tenant's complaint or after inspection by an agency resulting from the tenant's complaint, it creates a presumption that the landlord's action was retaliatory. This presumption may be rebutted by evidence from the landlord showing that the action was not retaliatory.

It is sometimes difficult to judge whether an action is retaliatory or not. For instance, raising a particular tenant's rent as a punishment for the tenant's complaints is unlawful. However, raising all tenants' rents in order to pay for necessary repairs complained about by a tenant is acceptable.

A landlord may not single out and evict one tenant who has made complaints. However, if code violations or necessary repairs are so extensive that the landlord cannot afford to bring the building up to the required standards, the landlord may take the entire building off the rental market.

Costs and attorney's fees. In any lawsuit or eviction proceeding where the tenant prevails on a claim of retaliatory action, the tenant is entitled to recover costs and attorney's fees. If the landlord prevails by showing that the action was not retaliatory, the landlord may recover costs and attorney's fees. In fact, the prevailing party in any action brought under RLTA is generally entitled to recover costs and fees.

Unlawful Detainer. An action in unlawful detainer is the most common procedure used by a landlord to recover possession of property from a **defaulting** tenant (a tenant who has failed to pay rent when due). The landlord must give the tenant proper notice of default and allow an opportunity to cure the default. If the tenant fails to **cure** (pay all rent owed), the landlord may file an unlawful detainer action. If the court finds the tenant in default, it issues a **writ of possession**, which requires the tenant to leave the premises or be forcibly removed by the sheriff.

Self-Help Eviction. The process of legal eviction is often slow. However, a landlord should be warned against any attempt at self-help eviction. A landlord may not remove or exclude a tenant without a court order. Sometimes a landlord attempts to force a tenant to leave by cutting off utilities. This is illegal, and the landlord may be fined $100 for each day the tenant is without utility service, plus damages and reasonable attorney's fees.

Lockouts. A **lockout** is another method of self-help eviction: the landlord locks the tenant out of the rental unit by changing the locks while the tenant is out. Lockouts are generally prohibited. If a lockout is prohibited by a local ordinance, the police may assist a tenant who has been locked out.

> **Example:** In Seattle, police enforce the section of the housing code prohibiting lockouts. The police may arrest or issue a citation to a landlord who has unlawfully locked out a tenant.

Constructive Eviction. Eviction can occur when the landlord causes or permits a substantial interference with the tenant's possession of the property. **Constructive eviction** happens when an act materially disturbs the tenant's use or enjoyment of the premises so that the tenant is forced to move out.

> **Example:** Tenant rents a small studio apartment from Landlord in August. Landlord tells Tenant that the apartment is heated by radiant heat. Tenant notices an old-fashioned

radiator along one wall. When winter arrives, Tenant discovers that the radiator is broken and produces no heat. Landlord fails to repair the radiator or supply any heat.

Tenant has been constructively evicted because of lack of heat. Tenant can terminate the lease without liability for any further rent.

In the past, a tenant was required to actually move out before being entitled to claim constructive eviction. However, this rule has been somewhat relaxed. In these days of tight housing markets, high rent, and high deposit requirements, it is often hard or even impossible for a tenant to immediately find a new apartment to move into. Therefore even though a tenant has not actually moved from the premises, the tenant may sometimes claim constructive eviction and sue for damages or an abatement of rent.

Personal Property. A residential landlord may not take or detain a tenant's personal property unless the tenant has been evicted by a court order or the premises have been abandoned. If a landlord takes personal property in any other circumstances, or refuses to return property after a written demand by the tenant, the landlord may be liable for the value of the property, actual damages, and up to $500 per day for each day that the tenant is deprived of his property, up to $5,000.

If a tenant abandons the premises or is evicted and leaves personal property behind, it must be stored by the landlord and can be sold only after written notice is given to the former tenant or mailed to the tenant's last known address. If the property is sold, any proceeds in excess of the landlord's claim against the tenant (for unpaid rent or property damage) must be held by the landlord for at least one year. After one year, if the tenant has not claimed the balance of the proceeds, the money becomes the property of the landlord.

Property of deceased tenant. The personal property of a deceased residential tenant who lived alone is handled differently from that of an evicted or abandoning tenant. The RLTA has detailed rules for this situation; this is just an overview.

While a tenant is still living, the landlord may ask the tenant to designate someone to act on the tenant's behalf in case the tenant dies. The designated person will be allowed to enter the deceased tenant's unit, remove personal property, and distribute and dispose of it properly, and is also authorized to receive any money (such as prepaid rent or the security deposit) that the landlord is required to refund. The tenant's designation of this person must be in writing, signed, and separate from the lease agreement. It can be revoked at any time.

Whether or not the tenant has made such a designation, when a landlord learns that a tenant who was the sole occupant of a unit has died, the landlord is allowed to enter the unit to remove any pets and to dispose of perishable food, hazardous materials, and garbage.

Next, the landlord is required to send a notice concerning the deceased tenant's personal property to any known designated person, emergency contact, or court-appointed personal representative. If one of these parties responds by the deadline stated in the notice, this tenant representative may claim and remove the personal property. The representative is responsible for moving and storage costs.

If no one responds to this initial notice, the landlord must send the same parties a second notice stating that the landlord may sell or dispose of the property on or after the date through which rent has been paid or at least 45 days after the second notice, whichever is later.

If no one responds to the second notice, the landlord can sell or dispose of everything except for personal papers and photographs, which must be kept for at least 90 days and then may be destroyed.

If the landlord estimates that the remaining property is worth $1,000 or less, he may donate it to charity or otherwise dispose of it. If he estimates it is worth more than $1,000, he is required to sell it. Proceeds from the sale may be used to offset moving, storage, and sale costs; anything left over must be put into a bank account. If the money isn't claimed by an authorized representative of the tenant, after one year the landlord must treat it as abandoned property and deposit it with the state Department of Revenue. (Note that the law specifically states that neither the landlord himself nor an employee or family member of the landlord may directly or indirectly acquire any of the property that is disposed of or sold.)

Destruction of the Premises

If a lease is for a part of a building, such as an office, apartment, or commercial space, the destruction of the building will frustrate the entire purpose of the lease and the tenant will be released from the duty to pay rent.

If the lease is for the land and any buildings thereon, or for the use of an entire building, the destruction of the building or part of the building does not necessarily terminate the lease. The tenant may still be required to pay rent to the end of the rental period. This situation usually occurs only in a commercial or agricultural lease.

A lease should contain provisions concerning how the parties will handle destruction of the premises. Normally, a lease specifies who will maintain insurance on the property, and who is liable for rebuilding if a structure is destroyed by fire or other casualty. If there is no express stipulation, and the building is destroyed without fault, the loss generally falls on the landlord.

Case Example:

Frank Payne leased two hydroponic greenhouses from Washington Hydroculture, Inc. The lease contained a general maintenance and delivery clause that stated that Payne would maintain the greenhouses and, upon expiration of the term, would surrender them in as good a condition as they were in when possession was taken.

Both greenhouses burned down in a fire. Washington Hydroculture alleged that because of the maintenance and delivery clause, Payne was required to rebuild the greenhouses.

In construing covenants in a lease, a court looks to the plain meaning of the language used and the intention of the parties. In this lease, there was no express stipulation to restore buildings destroyed by fire or other casualty. The clause merely talked about maintenance. The general meaning of the word "maintain" is not "rebuild." If there is no express stipulation requiring the tenant to rebuild, then the loss will fall on the landlord. Payne was not required to rebuild the greenhouses. *Washington Hydroculture, Inc. v. Payne*, 96 Wn.2d 322, 635 P.2d 138 (1981).

Tenant Rights in Foreclosure

Like any property owner with a mortgage, a landlord can lose the property to foreclosure. As a general rule, a foreclosure sale wipes out tenants' leasehold rights, and they sometimes receive little warning before they are forced to leave the premises. However, during the financial crisis that began in 2008, there were so many foreclosures and so many residential tenants facing hardship that legislation was passed to provide them with greater protection.

Under Washington law, a residential tenant is entitled to at least 90 days' written notice of a foreclosure action against the rental property. Following the foreclosure sale, the tenant must either be offered a new rental agreement with the new owner or given at least 60 days' written notice to vacate before an eviction action may be started.

Conclusion

For the protection of both the landlord and the tenant, the terms of a lease should address all of the situations in which problems commonly arise. The lease should be in writing and must meet all of the requirements for a valid contract. It should specify the duties and rights of both parties and the consequences if either party breaches the agreement.

In addition, residential landlords and property managers must be very familiar with the Residential Landlord-Tenant Act, which imposes a number of obligations and procedural requirements for residential tenancies.

Case Problem

The following is a hypothetical case problem. Most of the facts are taken from a real case. Based on what you have learned from this chapter, make a decision on the issues presented and then check to see if your answer matches the real decision by the court.

The Facts

Safeway Stores leased a commercial building for a term of 40 years, starting in 1941 and extending to 1981. The lease provided that Safeway "shall have the right to assign or transfer this lease or to underlease or sublet the whole or any part of said leased premises."

In the lease, Safeway agreed to pay a base rental of $120.83 per month, plus all utility charges and taxes. In addition, the lease provided that if sales exceeded $207,000 in any one year, Safeway would pay additional rent of ¾ of 1% on all sales in excess of $207,000.

Safeway operated a grocery store out of the leased premises from 1941 to 1959. During this period, Safeway paid approximately $27,550 in base rent, and over $52,000 in additional rent based on gross sales in excess of $207,000.

In 1960, Safeway subleased the property to Hill Bros. Distributors, who operated the premises as a shoe store. Under the sublease, Hill Bros. paid Safeway $500 per month. Safeway continued to pay all utilities and taxes and paid the monthly base rental of $120.83 to the owners.

The sublease to Hill Bros. also contained a provision for additional rent based on a percentage of sales similar to the clause in the original lease. This percentage amount was to be paid directly to the owners (instead of through Safeway). While Hill Bros. operated the shoe store, no rent based upon percentage of gross sales was earned. (In other words, the shoe store did not have gross sales in excess of $207,000.)

The owners sought cancellation of the lease, claiming an implied restriction against any assignment or sublease for a use that would not yield a percentage rent comparable to that paid by Safeway.

The Questions

Was Safeway within its rights in subleasing the property? Was it required to sublease only to another grocery store or to a business with comparable sales amounts? Can the owners cancel the lease simply because the subtenant does not have gross sales as high as Safeway's?

The Answer

The court found that the lease did not place any restriction on use, so the building did not have to remain a grocery store. Safeway was completely within its rights in making the sublease, and could sublease to any type of business, since no restrictions were stated.

Restrictions against assignment are not favored by the courts. Any restrictions will be strictly construed against the owner and will not be extended by implication. The owners may have assumed that the property would remain a grocery store, but there were no such restrictions in the lease, and such a restriction will not be implied.

Requiring a subtenant with comparable sales to Safeway, so that the percentage portion of the rent would remain stable, would have the effect of changing the percentage lease to a fixed lease. The purpose of a percentage lease is to allow for increases or decreases in the tenant's sales. Safeway was not required to sublease to a business with comparable sales. If the shoe store's sales were to increase, the building owners might collect an additional percentage rent in the future.

The court found the terms of the lease clear and unambiguous, and the owners were not allowed to cancel the sublease. *Williams v. Safeway Stores, Inc.*, 198 Kan. 331, 424 P.2d 541 (1967).

Chapter Summary

- A lease must meet basic contract requirements in order to be valid. Certain information, such as identification of the parties, a description of the premises, the duration of the tenancy, and the rental amount, should always be included in a lease.

- There are several different types of leases, including fixed leases, graduated leases, net leases, percentage leases, and ground leases.

- The owner of property that is being leased is free to sell or transfer the property, but the new owner takes title subject to the lease. Unless otherwise agreed, a tenant has the right to assign her interest or sublet the property.

- The Residential Landlord-Tenant Act applies to most residential tenancies. It imposes obligations on residential landlords and establishes rights for residential tenants that generally do not apply to commercial leases.

- A tenant has the rights of possession, quiet enjoyment, and privacy.

- A tenant also has a duty to pay rent and follow the terms of the lease. If a tenant defaults, the landlord may begin eviction proceedings.

- A tenant may be liable for damage to the premises beyond normal wear and tear. If the damage is greater than the amount of the security deposit, the landlord can seek additional damages. Money from a security deposit cannot be used to address normal wear and tear.

- A landlord must provide locks and keys and, in certain circumstances, may be liable for the criminal actions of third parties against a tenant.

- Both landlord and tenant must follow local codes and regulations and maintain the premises in a clean and safe condition.

- The implied warranty of habitability in every residential lease requires the landlord to keep the premises fit for human habitation.

- A residential landlord also has the duty to make repairs, and tenants have certain remedies if the landlord refuses or fails to make repairs.

- A periodic tenancy ends when either party gives the other party proper notice of termination. A lease for a specific term expires automatically at the end of the term, unless the parties agree to renew it; it can also be terminated early by mutual agreement, which is called surrender.

- A tenant who abandons the premises during the term of a lease still owes the landlord rent until the end of the term, unless a new tenant is found before that point. The landlord has a duty to try to mitigate the damages by renting the premises again as soon as possible.

- A landlord generally has the right to evict a tenant for breach of lease provisions, including failure to pay rent. The landlord should follow the legal procedures instead of attempting self-help eviction. It's illegal to evict a tenant in retaliation for requesting repairs or reporting violations of health and safety laws in good faith.

- If leased premises are destroyed, the lease may indicate which party is responsible for rebuilding them. Without such a provision, the loss normally falls on the landlord.

Checklist of Problem Areas

Real Estate Licensee's Checklist

❑ If you are helping to sell property that is currently being leased, is the buyer aware of the existing lease? Does the buyer understand that she will purchase the property subject to the existing lease?

❑ If you are acting as a rental agent, do you understand the terms of the rental agreement, and are you familiar with the duties imposed on the landlord (your client) by law?

Landlord/Owner's Checklist

❑ Have you signed the lease, and does it meet all other requirements for validity?

❑ Does the lease specify who is responsible for utility payments and insurance coverage?

❑ If this is a commercial percentage lease, has the exact percentage been specified? Has the term "gross sales" been defined so there is no question as to what is included?

❑ If this is a residential lease, do the premises meet all building code requirements and other legal requirements affecting health and safety? Are there any problems that need to be corrected or at least pointed out to the tenant?

❑ Will the premises be vacant and ready for occupancy by the new tenant on the specified date?

❑ When terminating a periodic tenancy, has proper notice been given to the tenant?

❑ If this is a lease for a specific term, you cannot arbitrarily terminate it before the term expires. Are there grounds for eviction, such as failure to pay rent or a breach of other lease provisions? If a tenant is wrongfully evicted, you will be liable for damages.

Tenant's Checklist

❑ What type of lease are you signing?

❑ What is the duration of the lease, or is this a periodic (month-to-month) tenancy?

❑ Does your lease allow assignment or subleasing? Is an assignment or sublease subject to the landlord's approval?

❑ Have you paid the required security deposit and any required nonrefundable fees?

❑ If repairs are needed, have you notified the landlord? Do you know how quickly the landlord is required to repair this type of problem?

❑ When terminating your tenancy, are you leaving the premises in the same condition they were in at the beginning of the tenancy, not counting normal wear and tear?

Chapter Quiz

1. Emma Johnson signs a lease that provides for periodic increases in the rental amount based on the cost-of-living index. This type of lease is called a:
   a. fixed lease
   b. net lease
   c. graduated lease
   d. percentage lease

2. Thomas Nomiama signs a year-long lease on an apartment with a term beginning on September 1. In February, his brother buys a house and asks Tom to move in with him. Tom finds another person, Elizabeth Jenkins, to rent his apartment from February 15 through August 31 (the end of the lease term). This is called a/an:
   a. sale
   b. assignment
   c. sublease
   d. novation

3. Which of the following statements about assignment and subleasing is correct?
   a. Residential landlords must allow assignment and subleasing
   b. Assignment and subleasing are not permitted in residential tenancies
   c. A landlord must consent to an assignment or sublease if the proposed new tenant or subtenant is creditworthy
   d. Assignment and subleasing are allowed unless the tenant's lease says otherwise

4. A new tenant signs a lease that begins on March 1. On March 1, the old tenant is still living in the apartment. This means that:
   a. the new tenant must begin eviction proceedings against the old tenant
   b. the landlord has the duty to remove the old tenant so that the new tenant can take possession
   c. the new tenant's lease is automatically canceled, since the apartment is not available for possession
   d. None of the above

5. Tenant gave Landlord a security deposit of $1,250 at the beginning of the tenancy. Tenant has not caused any damage to the apartment beyond normal wear and tear. Under the Residential Landlord-Tenant Act, after Tenant moves out, how long does Landlord have to return the deposit?
   a. 7 days
   b. 21 days
   c. 30 days
   d. 45 days

6. A plumber is fixing the plumbing in apartment 4C. He discovers that the pipes have been gradually leaking inside the walls for quite some time. He tells Landlord that the leaking pipes are probably causing damage behind the walls of all four apartments in Building C. Landlord wants the leaking pipes repaired, but the repair work must be done from inside each apartment.
   a. Since this is an emergency, Landlord can enter all of the apartments without the tenants' permission
   b. This is not an emergency, as the pipes have been leaking for some time and a little longer won't matter—Landlord must give tenants one day's notice
   c. This is not an emergency—Landlord must give tenants two days' notice
   d. This is not an emergency—Landlord must give tenants one week's notice

7. Providing for garbage removal is a residential landlord's responsibility:

   a. only if the lease expressly assigns that duty to the landlord
   b. unless the rental property is a single-family home
   c. unless the lease makes it the tenant's duty
   d. except in the case of a fixed lease

8. Tenant rents office space in a high-rise office building downtown. After a heavy snowstorm, ice builds up on the entryway into the lobby. If Tenant slips and falls, breaking her leg:

   a. Landlord may be liable for failing to maintain the premises in a reasonably safe condition
   b. Landlord is not liable, because a snowstorm is an unforeseeable event
   c. other tenants in the building may be liable for failing to keep the common areas in a safe condition
   d. None of the above

9. Tenant lives in a high-crime area. He rents an apartment in a rundown building, which is all that he can afford. There is a lock on the building's outer door, but the lock on Tenant's apartment door is broken. Tenant's apartment is vandalized and everything he owns is broken or stolen. Which is correct?

   a. Landlord cannot be liable because it was Tenant's duty to replace the door lock himself
   b. Even though Landlord did not provide a lock as required, he cannot be held liable for the criminal actions of third parties
   c. Landlord may be liable because of his failure to provide an adequate lock
   d. Landlord will be liable because all rental units must be supplied with dead-bolt locks

10. Tenant has a wild party in his apartment. One of his guests attempts to swing from the chandelier and pulls it out of the ceiling. Which of the following is correct?

    a. Landlord has the duty to repair any damage to the premises
    b. Landlord has no duty to repair a condition caused by Tenant; however, since this was a guest, Landlord is still obligated to repair
    c. Landlord has no duty to repair a condition caused by Tenant, or by family members or guests of Tenant
    d. None of the above

11. It is mid-January in Spokane. The temperature is about 20°. Suddenly the furnace quits working. Tenant immediately notifies Landlord. How long does Landlord have to begin repairs?

    a. 24 hours
    b. 48 hours
    c. 72 hours
    d. 10 days

12. Tenant notified Landlord that her garbage disposal has stopped working. Landlord failed to repair it within a reasonable time. Tenant decides to take matters into her own hands. She looks up garbage disposal repairs online and fixes it herself. Tenant figures her materials and labor cost approximately $65; her monthly rent is $1,200. Which of the following statements is true?

    a. Tenant is out $65 and Landlord has no obligation to repay her, since Tenant chose to make the repairs herself
    b. If the repairs were carried out in a workmanlike manner, and Tenant allows Landlord to inspect them, then Tenant may deduct the $65 from the next month's rent
    c. Tenant may only deduct $50 from the next month's rent, since this is the statutory limit on self-help repairs
    d. None of the above

13. Landlord lives in a ground-floor apartment and Tenant lives upstairs. Landlord and Tenant have had several disagreements. Landlord knows that Tenant hates the smell of cooked cabbage. Several times a week Landlord makes cooked cabbage for dinner. The smell travels up the heat vent into Tenant's apartment. This is an example of:

   a. retaliatory eviction
   b. constructive eviction
   c. self-help eviction
   d. None of the above—normal cooking smells are not enough to establish any form of eviction

14. Tenant signs a one-year lease. After three months, he abandons the premises. Which of the following statements is correct?

   a. Tenant is liable for the remaining rent owed under the lease
   b. Landlord has a duty to mitigate by attempting to rent the premises to a new tenant as soon as possible
   c. Even if Landlord rents the premises to a new tenant, the first tenant may still be liable for damages, such as the cost of finding a new tenant
   d. All of the above

15. Tenant abandons the property but leaves behind some expensive stereo equipment. Landlord sends written notice to Tenant's last known address that the personal property will be sold. After a proper time period, the property is sold. If the proceeds exceed the amount owed to Landlord:

   a. Landlord immediately gets all of the money, no matter what the amount
   b. Landlord must hold onto the excess money for at least one year, in case Tenant attempts to reclaim it
   c. Landlord must mail the excess money to Tenant's last known address
   d. the money must be turned over to the city or the municipal organization in charge of landlord-tenant actions

14 Condominiums, Cooperatives, and Securities

Outline

Key Terms

- Condominium
- Condominium Act
- Common areas
- Declaration
- Declarant
- Conversion
- Unit owners association
- Right of first refusal

- Public offering statement
- Right of rescission
- Implied warranties of quality
- Resale certificate
- Townhouse
- Timeshare
- Interval ownership

- Vacation license
- Right to use
- Cooperative
- Proprietary lease
- Cooperative association
- Blanket mortgage
- Real estate securities
- REIT

Chapter Overview

As cities have grown more crowded, single-family homes have become harder to find and more expensive to buy and maintain. In many communities, condominiums have become a popular ownership alternative. This chapter describes the laws that govern development and ownership of condominiums in Washington. It also looks at timesharing arrangements, cooperatives, and real estate securities.

Condominiums

Most condominiums look like apartment buildings, but a condominium isn't owned by a landlord who rents apartment units to tenants. Instead, it is owned by its residents.

The buyer of a condominium unit acquires separate title to the unit itself. Certain other parts of the condominium property—the grounds, the parking lot, the recreational facilities, the building's lobby, elevators, and hallways—are called the **common areas** or **common elements**. These areas are owned by all of the residents as tenants in common. Each unit owner has an undivided interest in the common areas.

> **Example:** Sheila buys a unit in a 24-unit condominium. The deed describes her property as "Unit 11 in Hemlock Ridge, a condominium, together with an undivided $1/24$ interest in the common areas of said condominium."

Although the majority of condominiums are residential, office buildings and retail centers have also been developed as condominiums. Some condominiums include a mixture of commercial and residential units. For instance, the street level might contain shops and a restaurant, with living units on the floors above.

History

The basic concept of condominium ownership has existed for centuries. In modern times, individual ownership of separate floors or "flats" in a building became common in

Paris and other French cities in the 1920s. Legislation governing this form of ownership began appearing in many parts of Europe in the 1930s and 1940s, and in South America in the late 1940s and the 1950s.

In the United States, condominium ownership was rare until the 1960s. Condominium development got a boost from the passage of the National Housing Act of 1961, which provided federal mortgage insurance for condominium units. By 1968, all 50 states had adopted some form of condominium law.

In 1989, the Washington State Legislature passed a new Condominium Act. (It is a version of the Uniform Condominium Act, which has also been adopted by several other states.) This law applies to all condominiums created in Washington after July 1, 1990. Many of its provisions also apply to condominiums established before that date, but those condominiums are still governed to some extent by the previous 1963 state condominium law (the Horizontal Property Regimes Act). This discussion will focus on the rules and procedures established in the 1989 law.

Creation of Condominiums

A condominium can be created in two ways. The property can be initially developed as a condominium, or an existing building (usually an apartment building) can be converted into a condominium. In either case, condominium status is established by recording a **condominium declaration**.

The declaration must contain the name of the condominium and a legal description of the property. The entire development must be described—both the land and the buildings. Specific information about each unit must be included, such as the square footage and the number of bathrooms, bedrooms, and fireplaces. Any restrictions on the use, occupancy, or alienation of the units must be listed. The declaration will also contain provisions concerning the ownership and use of the common areas. If the developer (called the **declarant** in the Condominium Act) is reserving any special rights in regard to the property, those rights must be described in the declaration.

At the same time that the declaration is recorded, the declarant also must record a survey map of the property and building plans for the project. The plans must show the vertical

Fig. 14.1 How condominiums may be created

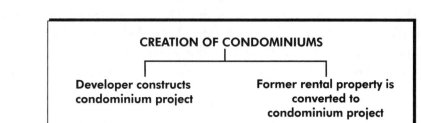

and horizontal boundaries of each unit in sufficient detail to establish the position of the unit in relation to the land. (See Chapter 3 for a discussion of property descriptions that involve air lots.)

Condominiums and Land Use Laws. In Washington, local zoning ordinances and other land use laws may not prohibit the condominium form of ownership. Land use laws may not impose any requirements on condominiums that do not also apply to identical developments under a different form of ownership (such as an ordinary apartment complex).

In some cases, large condominiums are considered subdivisions and are subject to local subdivision regulations. Condominium developments also must comply with environmental laws.

Case Example:

The decision to grant preliminary approval for a condominium project on Cooper Point near Olympia was "a major action significantly affecting the quality of the environment." An environmental impact statement was therefore necessary to comply with SEPA. *Loveless v. Yantis*, 82 Wn.2d 754, 513 P.2d 1023 (1973).

Conversion. In some cases, the owner of a rental property decides to **convert** the existing building to condominium status in response to a steep rise in operating expenses or taxes. Or the owner may decide to convert the building because selling it piecemeal, one unit at a time, will be more profitable than selling the whole property to a single investor.

The Condominium Act has some special rules that apply when residential rental property (such as an apartment building) is converted into a condominium. If there are tenants living in the building when the decision is made, the owner is required to take certain steps to protect the tenants' interests.

The owner must give each tenant at least 120 days' notice that the building is going to be converted into a condominium. The tenancies cannot be terminated before that 120-day period expires, unless a tenant stops paying rent or does something else that would be grounds for eviction under the Residential Landlord-Tenant Act.

If the conversion condominium will be residential, the owner is required to give each tenant a public offering statement (explained later in this chapter). Each tenant must also be given a 60-day **right of first refusal** on his unit. That means the tenant may choose to buy the unit, on specified terms, once the building has become a condominium. If the tenant doesn't decide to buy the unit during that 60-day period, in the following 180 days the building owner may not offer the unit to anyone else on more favorable terms than the terms offered to the tenant.

Common Areas

A condominium's common areas include every part of the property except the individual units. As explained earlier, ownership of the common areas is shared by all of the unit owners, as tenants in common. All of the unit owners have the right to use the common areas—to ride in the elevator, swim in the pool, and so on.

The declaration must assign a specific fraction or percentage of interest in the common areas to each unit. In some cases, each unit has an equal interest in the common areas; for instance, in a 30-unit condominium, each unit might have a $1/30$ undivided interest in the common areas. In many condominiums, however, the percentage is based on the value of the individual unit in relation to the total value of the property. The larger, more expensive units have a larger percentage of interest in the common areas.

> **Example:** Pete bought Unit 403 for $250,000, which is 3% of the total value of the entire condominium complex ($8,333,300). Pete's deed gives him full fee simple ownership of his unit, plus a 3% undivided interest in the common areas.
>
> In the same condominium, Marsha bought Unit 801, which is much larger than Unit 403 and has a better view. Marsha paid $416,665, 5% of the condominium's total value. She owns her unit in fee simple and has a 5% undivided interest in the common areas.

When a condominium unit is conveyed, its undivided interest in the common areas is automatically conveyed, too. An interest in the common areas cannot be transferred separately from a unit.

> **Example:** The Cochrans live down the street from a condominium, and they would like to be able to use its pool and other recreational facilities. Gregor owns Unit 6 in the condominium, together with an undivided $1/15$ interest in the common areas. He never uses the recreational facilities, so he would be willing to sell his interest in the common areas to the Cochrans. It won't work; a deed granting Gregor's undivided interest in the common areas to the Cochrans would be void.

In many condominiums, certain common areas are designated **limited common areas**. These are parts of the property that may be used only by the owners of specific units, rather than by all the residents. For example, a particular patio might be a limited common area shared by the owners of units in Building C; the unit owners in Building D would not be entitled to use that patio. The declaration must list the limited common areas and specify which units may use each of the areas.

Unit Owners Association

A condominium is required to have a **unit owners association** (also called a condominium association or homeowners association). The association must be organized as either a profit or nonprofit corporation under the Condominium Act. Every unit owner is automatically a member of the association, and only unit owners may be members. The association controls the affairs of the condominium as a whole; its primary concern is the regulation and maintenance of the common areas.

Most decisions are made by the association's board of directors. The board is elected by the association's members, and a majority of the directors must be members (unit owners) themselves. The directors are required to exercise ordinary and reasonable care in performing their duties.

Like any other corporation, a unit owners association has bylaws that govern its management. The bylaws provide for the election of the board of directors, specify the powers and duties of the directors, and outline the schedule and procedures for association meetings. Under the Condominium Act, meetings must be held at least once a year and all unit owners must be notified.

The association has the power to collect assessments from each unit owner to pay for the common expenses, such as common area maintenance, repair, and insurance costs. Some assessments are routine, and are paid every month; others are for special expenses (for example, a new fence in the pool area, or emergency repairs to the roof).

An owner's share of the common expenses is usually based on the owner's percentage of interest in the common areas, as is an owner's voting power in the unit owners association. For instance, if a unit owner has a 3% interest in the common areas, she is responsible for 3% of the common expenses, and her vote would be counted as 3% of all the association's votes.

An unpaid assessment creates a lien against the unit owner's title. The lien attaches automatically, as soon as the assessment is due; it is not necessary for the association to record a claim of lien. The association's lien can be foreclosed judicially or (if certain procedures are followed and the declaration includes a power of sale) nonjudicially. If the lien is foreclosed judicially, it has priority over all other liens except for property tax and special assessment liens, certain mortgages and deeds of trust, and liens recorded before the condominium declaration was filed.

Some owners associations retain a first right of refusal on the sale of any unit. So if an individual unit owner decides to sell her unit, the association has the option to purchase it at her asking price. If the association decides not to purchase it, the owner can sell to a third party, but only at the same (or higher) price.

Sale of Condominium Units

The Condominium Act establishes rules that a declarant (condominium developer) must follow when selling a unit to its first unit owner. The act also has rules that an owner must follow when reselling his unit.

These rules apply to any type of condominium, except that the purchaser of a unit in a nonresidential condominium can agree in writing to waive them. A residential purchaser cannot waive these requirements.

Sale by Declarant. The declarant is required to prepare a **public offering statement** that discloses certain information about the declarant, the condominium, and the unit being purchased. For example, if the declarant has completed other condominium projects in the past five years, the names of the five most recent projects must be listed in the public offering statement. Building code violations and physical hazards affecting the condominium have to be listed; so do liens against the property, and pending lawsuits that might result in a judgment lien.

Some of the many other required disclosures include an estimate of the unit owner's share of the common expenses, any additional fees for the use of the common areas, and information about the management company, if any. In addition, the public offering statement must contain copies of the declaration, survey map, and plans, along with copies of the articles of incorporation and bylaws for the unit owners association, any rules and regulations adopted by the association, and the association's current budget and balance sheet.

For any sale requiring a public offering statement, the declarant cannot convey the unit until after the declaration, survey map, and plans have been recorded. In addition, the unit must be substantially completed and available for occupancy at the time of conveyance, unless the buyer and the declarant have agreed in writing that the unit will not be ready for occupancy. However, the declarant can sign a purchase and sale agreement before the declaration and other documents are recorded, or before the unit is completed.

Right of rescission. When someone decides to buy a unit from the declarant, the declarant should give the prospective buyer the public offering statement more than seven days before the purchase and sale agreement is signed. If the buyer isn't given the statement seven days in advance, he has a seven-day right of rescission that runs from the time the statement is received.

> **Example:** Mike wants to buy Unit 6B in the Harbor Heights condominium. Unit 6B has never been purchased before, so the seller is the declarant.
>
> The declarant's agent gives Mike a copy of the condominium's public offering statement on October 2. Mike reads the statement that evening and decides to go ahead with the purchase. The next day, October 3, he and the declarant sign a purchase and sale agreement, and he gives the declarant an earnest money deposit. They agree on November 1 as the closing date.
>
> Mike has a right of rescission until October 9, seven days after he received the public offering statement. If he changes his mind about Unit 6B before October 9, he can withdraw from the purchase agreement without penalty.

A declarant is required to keep all earnest money deposits in an escrow account until closing. If Mike chose to rescind the contract, the declarant would have to refund his earnest money deposit.

The buyer can also move the closing date if necessary to allow seven days between receipt of the public offering statement and closing.

> **Example:** As in the example above, Mike receives the public offering statement on October 2, and signs the contract on October 3. But now suppose that Mike is in a

hurry and doesn't need to arrange financing, so that he agrees to make October 6 the closing date.

The day after signing the contract, Mike decides he may be acting a little too hastily. He has the right to call the declarant and delay the closing until October 9 (seven days after he received the offering statement). The declarant can't insist on an October 6 closing.

In some cases, the declarant may fail to give the buyer a public offering statement altogether. If so, the buyer can sue the declarant after closing either for actual damages or for a refund of a portion of the purchase price. If the declarant's failure to provide the statement was willful, the buyer is entitled to a refund of 10% of the price paid. If the declarant's failure to provide the statement was unintentional, the refund would be 3% of the price.

Release of liens. When the declarant begins selling units, there may be some liens against the entire condominium property (a deed of trust for the construction financing, for example, or construction liens from the construction itself). When a unit is sold, the declarant is required to do one of three things: pay off any liens affecting that unit; provide title insurance for the unit that will protect the new owner from the liens; or record a partial release for the unit. A **partial release** removes the liens from the new unit owner's title, although the liens remain attached to the rest of the condominium property.

Warranties. The purchaser of a condominium unit is not entitled to rely on any express warranties of quality or representations concerning the property unless they are included in the public offering statement, or made in writing and signed by the declarant (or the declarant's agent).

However, the Condominium Act creates several **implied warranties of quality** that automatically apply to the sale of a unit by the declarant. For example, the declarant warrants that the unit and the common areas are suitable for ordinary uses, and that the improvements are free from defective materials and constructed in a workmanlike manner.

These implied warranties can be modified or waived in a written agreement between the declarant and the buyer. In the sale of a residential unit, the declarant cannot make a general disclaimer of implied warranties, although she may disclaim liability for a particular defect (in writing).

Resale by Unit Owner. A unit owner who resells his unit must provide the buyer with a **resale certificate**. The resale certificate is prepared by the association or an agent of the association. It contains information pertaining to the unit being resold, such as the unit's monthly common expense assessment and fees, and any other assessments that are currently due or have been levied. It contains a copy of the declarations, bylaws, and rules and regulations of the association. It also contains detailed financial information about the association, including an annual financial statement and the current operating budget. In addition, the resale certificate gives information about other units that could affect the unit being resold. For example, if there is an assessment against another unit that's more than 30 days overdue, it must be listed in the certificate. And if the unit owners association has a right of first refusal, this must be disclosed as well.

The unit owner is supposed to give the resale certificate and other documents to a prospective buyer before the purchase and sale agreement is signed. The agreement is voidable by the buyer until five days after he receives the certificate, or until the unit is actually conveyed, whichever happens first. For assessments due or levied as of the date of the certificate, the buyer cannot be required to pay more than the amounts stated in the certificate (unless the buyer had actual notice of additional assessments or greater amounts).

The declarant's implied warranties of quality, and any express warranties made by the declarant or any other previous seller, are passed along to the buyer when a unit is resold.

After closing, the buyer (the new unit owner) must notify the association of her name and address and the date of conveyance.

Deeds. When a unit is sold, the deed does not have to give a full legal description of the entire condominium property. It simply has to state the unit number, the name of the condominium, the declaration's recording number, and the county where the property is located. It's standard practice for the deed to mention what percentage of interest in the common areas goes along with the unit, but that is not required by the Condominium Act. That information (and the full legal description of the property) can always be found in the declaration.

Like any other deed, the deed to a condominium unit should be recorded to protect the new owner's interest.

Consumer Protection

As condominiums became common, certain problems also became common. Many of them were caused by unscrupulous or incompetent developers.

One frequent source of problems was the developer's failure to disclose all the costs involved in condominium ownership. Some unsophisticated buyers committed themselves to purchasing a unit without understanding that they would have to pay monthly assessments and fees on top of their mortgage payments.

The public offering statement or resale certificate required by Washington's Condominium Act alleviates this type of problem, since these documents must disclose all the financial consequences of unit ownership. However, some buyers who receive a public offering statement or resale certificate never read it. A real estate agent involved in a condominium sale should explain the importance of the information in the statement or certificate and encourage the buyers to go over it carefully.

Developer self-dealing was another source of problems. Some developers would make arrangements for the condominium to benefit themselves, rather than the unit owners. They would set up long-term property management contracts for themselves or affiliated companies, or lease recreational facilities to the condominium at high rates, and make ratification of these agreements a condition of purchasing a unit. Now, under the Condominium Act, any management contract, lease of facilities, or other contract arranged by the developer may be terminated by the board of directors of the unit owners association. The board must give 90 days' notice of termination.

Another common hazard for prospective condominium buyers was losing an earnest money deposit. Buyers would give the developer deposits for units in a condominium that was still under construction—or hadn't even been started yet. The developer would accept the deposits and spend them, but construction would never be completed. Although the buyers had the right to sue for return of their deposits, in many cases construction stopped because the developer had gone bankrupt and the buyers were unable to recover their deposits. This problem is addressed by the Condominium Act's requirement that developers keep all earnest money deposits in an escrow account until closing.

Condominiums vs. Townhouses

A type of home ownership that mixes attributes of condominiums and single-family homes is the townhouse. A **townhouse** is typically a multi-story home on a small lot that may or may not share walls with neighboring units. Townhouse ownership is similar to condominium ownership in that a townhouse owner has both a separate interest in his individual unit and an undivided interest in the common areas of the townhouse development. However, a townhouse owner also has title to the parcel of land on which the townhouse is situated.

Although the statutory restrictions of the Condominium Act do not apply to townhouses, townhouse developments may have homeowners associations similar to condominium owners associations. Mandatory homeowners association membership and maintenance fees are common. In addition, homeowners associations may restrict changes to the exterior appearances of the individual townhouses and impose other rules.

Timeshare Condominiums

Another nontraditional form of ownership is the timeshare arrangement. Rather than purchasing all rights to an individual unit, a timeshare arrangement allows a buyer to purchase a time slot of ownership. In Washington, a **timeshare** is defined as a right to occupy a unit during three or more separate time periods over a period of at least three years.

The concept of real estate timesharing was first conceived in Europe in the early 1960s. Timesharing began to appear in the United States in about the mid-1970s.

Most timeshare condominiums are found in vacation areas where ownership of the unit for the entire year is expensive and unnecessary or unwanted.

> **Example:** The Slaters like to vacation in Hawaii, but do not want to live there full time. They do not want to purchase a house or condominium, since they would use it only a small portion of the year. The Slaters purchase a two-week share in a timeshare condominium unit for the first two weeks in March.
>
> The Slaters have the right to possess and occupy the property only during the first two weeks in March. Other buyers have the right to use the unit at other times of the year.

Purchasers should keep in mind that timeshares rarely appreciate like other kinds of real property do. Often, in fact, the properties sell for a significant loss. Buying a "pre-owned" timeshare can lessen this problem (there are websites devoted to such properties).

Types of Timeshare Ownership

The ownership interest in a timeshare unit may be held in one of three different ways. The first is a **tenancy in common**, in which all of the buyers are deeded an undivided interest in a particular unit as tenants in common. The buyers then agree to limit their use of the unit to a specific time period.

A timeshare may also be an **interval ownership**, in which the buyers are granted an estate for years for a specific time period each year.

Under tenancy in common or interval ownership, the owner has all of the responsibilities of property ownership, such as property taxes and potential liability if someone is injured on the property.

The third type of timeshare arrangement is called a **vacation license** or **right to use**. In this arrangement, the developer retains ownership of the timeshare unit and agrees to allow the buyers to use the premises for a specific time period each year. The timeshare purchasers do not have actual ownership of the property and are not liable for property taxes or injuries that might occur on the property. The purchaser does not build any equity in the property or have any voice in its operation.

In 1983, Washington adopted the Washington Timeshare Act, which (like the Condominium Act) is primarily a consumer protection law. It requires registration of any timeshare property and disclosure of pertinent information to potential purchasers, and it also provides for remedial measures in the event that the act is violated.

Disclosure Statement

The Timeshare Act requires that any person who offers or sells a timeshare must provide the prospective purchaser with a written disclosure document before the purchase and sale

Fig. 14.2 Types of timeshares

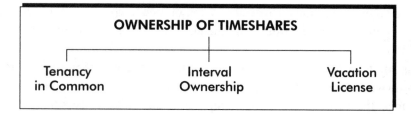

agreement is signed. The disclosure document must contain the official name and address of the promoter, the location and description of the timeshare property, and a list of all units offered.

It must also include the types, prices, and number of units, location of units, types and durations of timeshares, and the maximum number of timeshares that may be created. Certain financial information must also be included (maintenance fees, etc.), along with copies of any agreements or leases to be signed at the time of purchase.

The Timeshare Act gives purchasers a right of rescission. Any agreement for the purchase of a timeshare may be rescinded within seven days after receipt of the disclosure document or the signing of the agreement, whichever is later. The rescission must be in writing and delivered or mailed to the promoter to be effective.

Timeshare Salesperson Registration

Generally, anyone involved in selling timeshares must register with the DOL as a **timeshare salesperson**. However, real estate licensees may handle certain timeshare resales without registering under the Timeshare Act as a timeshare salesperson. The licensee must be acting solely in a brokerage capacity, not selling inventory that she owns herself or that's owned by her firm.

Even when real estate licensees are exempt from the Timeshare Act's registration requirement, they still have to comply with all of the other aspects of the law. For example, they must give buyers a disclosure statement and allow a seven-day right of rescission, just like registered timeshare salespersons.

Cooperatives

Stock and non-stock **cooperatives** are another type of nontraditional ownership of real property. Like condominiums, cooperatives are usually residential buildings, although they may also be established for commercial uses.

Title to a cooperative building (and the surrounding property) is generally held by a nonprofit corporation formed for that purpose. A person who wants to live in the building buys shares of stock in the corporation, instead of renting or buying a unit. The building's residents are the corporation's shareholders. The corporation owns the building, but the residents own the corporation. (Instead of a corporation, ownership of the land and building could be in the form of a trust or partnership, but this is not as common as corporate ownership.)

A less common form of cooperative ownership is the **membership cooperative**. A person who wants to live in the building buys a membership in the cooperative; instead of buying stock, the owner pays a membership fee. Usually all members have the same voting power when they vote on items of concern to the membership. The cooperative owns the building, and the individual has a membership interest.

History

After World War II and up until 1961, many cooperative housing corporations came into existence. Until about 1970, most rental units that were converted to resident ownership were converted to cooperatives. Since then, however, most conversions outside of New York have created condominiums rather than cooperatives. New York is still the center for most of the co-ops in this country.

Although cooperatives have never been a major portion of the real estate market in Washington, there are cooperatives in the state. Some of these are residential and some are commercial.

Creation of Cooperatives

As with condominiums, a project may be developed initially as a cooperative, or an existing building may be converted into a co-op.

Individual unit residents own stock in the corporation and have a proprietary lease for their unit. In order to acquire the lease on a specific unit, a person must purchase a certain number of shares of stock. Shares are allocated to each unit based on the value of the unit compared to the total value of the entire building or complex.

> **Example:** A cooperative has a total of 33 units. There are one-, two-, and three-bedroom units. All of the units on the west side of the building have a view overlooking the lake, and are therefore valued higher than the units with no view. The units are assigned individual values running from 20 to 40 shares. The total value of the complex is 1,000 shares.
>
> Johnson wants to acquire an interest in a one-bedroom unit with no view. The unit is valued at 20 shares. She must purchase 20 shares of stock in the cooperative corporation.
>
> Davis wants to purchase a two-bedroom unit with a view of the lake. This unit is valued at 35 shares. He must purchase 35 shares of stock in the corporation.

Each unit owner in a cooperative is not really an owner, but rather a shareholder in the corporation that owns the complex in which the unit is located. Johnson owns 20 shares or 2% of the total value of the complex. Davis owns 35 shares or 3½% of the total value of the complex.

Each of the shareholders has a proprietary lease for their particular unit. A **proprietary lease** has a longer term than most ordinary leases and gives the shareholder considerably more rights than an ordinary tenant would have. The cooperative tenants participate in the running of the cooperative through their stock interest in the corporation.

The lease does not state a fixed rental amount for the term of the lease. Instead, each year the amount that will be needed to pay the building's mortgage, insurance, and operating expenses is determined. Each leaseholder is then assessed an amount based on his percentage of ownership. For instance, Johnson's assessment would be 2% of the total, while Davis's assessment would be 3½%.

Co-op Association and Bylaws. Cooperatives are generally run by a **cooperative association** consisting of all the unit residents (shareholders or members). A board of directors usually handles most of the routine governance, however. In Washington, the board must consist of at least three directors. The directors are also unit residents, elected by the members of the association.

The association and the board of directors manage the cooperative according to the guidelines set out in the association's bylaws. They may assess charges required for maintenance, repairs, and other costs involved in running the cooperative.

Comparison of Condos and Co-ops

There are some similarities between condos and co-ops. In both instances, the individual owner has a right to possess a certain unit and has an interest in the common areas. However, there are also many differences between ownership of a condo and ownership of a co-op.

Ownership. One of the major differences is the fact that a condominium owner actually owns her individual unit and receives a deed for that unit. A cooperative owner merely has a lease for a specific unit. However, the co-op owner acquires equity in the shares of the cooperative's stock. If the market value of the property increases, the market value of the stock increases, and the owner would reap the profits at the time of sale, as with any other type of property.

Mortgages. In a co-op, the corporation typically takes out a single mortgage on the entire building. In a condominium, there is no blanket mortgage on the entire building, but there are usually separate mortgages on most or all of the individual units. Note that lenders in areas where co-ops are rare may be reluctant to accept a co-op interest as security for a loan.

One of the major disadvantages of the co-op is the financial interdependence of all of the shareholders. Because a blanket mortgage is used, if one or more shareholders default on their loan obligations, the other unit owners will have to make up the difference in order to avoid a foreclosure action against the building.

Restrictions. Another difference between condos and co-ops is in the type of restrictions on the ability to sell. A co-op tenant generally needs the approval of the board of directors in order to sell to a new tenant.

These tight restrictions are necessary because of the financial interdependence of the co-op tenants. Since they may be personally affected by a tenant with financial problems, they have the right to evaluate and approve any potential new tenants.

Upon the death of a co-op tenant, the person who inherits the co-op unit must be approved by the board of directors or a membership committee. There is no automatic right to continue the co-op lease. By contrast, a condominium owner has a fee simple estate in

Fig. 14.3 Condominiums vs. cooperatives

	CONDOMINIUMS	COOPERATIVES
Ownership	Buyer owns individual unit and receives deed	Buyer owns shares in corporation or membership interest and has proprietary lease of unit
Mortgage	Individual mortgages on separate units	Blanket mortgage on entire building
Restrictions	Condo association may have right of first refusal	Tighter restrictions—may need approval of board to sell
Transfer upon owner's death	Fee simple estate can be freely passed to any successor	No automatic right; person who inherits must be approved by board
Eviction	Difficult	Easier than with condo
Taxes	Individual taxes on each unit	Taxes assessed on entire building
Liens	Attach only to individual unit	May attach to entire building

the unit. It can be freely passed on to any successor (though as mentioned, the unit owners association may have a right of first refusal).

Eviction. It is easier to get rid of an incompatible resident in a co-op than in a condominium. Other tenants may view this as an advantage of the co-op. A tenant who refuses to comply with the co-op rules can be evicted. It is much harder to get rid of a condo unit owner. If a condo owner is delinquent in paying assessments, a lien foreclosure action can be brought against the owner. However, the procedure is likely to be time-consuming and expensive.

Taxes. In a condominium, each unit owner receives an individual property tax assessment and is responsible only for that amount. In a cooperative, a tax assessment is made on the entire building. Each owner is assessed an amount in proportion to the amount of stock owned. (In other words, in proportion to the value of the unit.) If an individual owner in a co-op defaults on tax payments, the other shareholders must see that these taxes are paid or risk that the entire building could be sold at a tax sale.

Liens. An individual owner may have work done or services performed on a particular unit. In a condominium, a construction lien attaches only to the unit where the work was done. In a cooperative, work done or materials ordered by one tenant could result in a construction lien attaching to the entire building.

Real Estate Securities

Real estate is usually considered to be a good investment. However, many people don't have the money, time, or experience necessary to locate good investment property on their own. Sometimes a group of friends or business associates get together and pool their money to invest in real estate. Or a promoter may offer an interest in a real estate investment opportunity to the public.

These kinds of arrangements typically involve the sale of real estate securities. A **real estate security** is any kind of arrangement in which someone invests money in an enterprise involving real estate, with the expectation of earning profits from the efforts of a promoter or some other third party.

Securities Regulation and Registration

If a transaction meets the definition of a security, the promoter must comply with federal and state **securities regulations**. The purpose of securities regulations is to protect the consumer by requiring registration of securities and disclosure of certain information.

Before offering to sell any property that meets the definition of a security, the promoter must register with the Securities and Exchange Commission (SEC). Once the promoter has registered, the property can be advertised and offers can be made. However, purchasers cannot enter into binding contracts and sales cannot be concluded until the SEC declares the registration statement effective.

Condominiums as Securities

Normally, the sale of a condominium unit is not considered to be the sale of a security. But if a condominium unit is purchased as an investment (rather than for personal use), it may be considered a security.

Usually a condominium project will not be deemed a security simply because some of the owners intend to rent out their units rather than live there themselves, as long as each owner is free either to rent or not rent. However, if owners are required to rent out their units and the plan is to have the developer or some other person manage this rental operation, the arrangement will be treated as a security.

Case Example:

Ford Hill Investment Company built a six-unit condominium near a snow skiing recreation area. The Lowerys signed an installment sales contract with Ford Hill for one of the units.

The contract provided that Ford Hill was the exclusive management and rental agent for each unit owner. Each owner was assessed a monthly rental promotion and management fee. Rental rates were to be determined and fixed solely by the manager. Owners were required to maintain their units in a rentable condition. If the owners wanted to reserve the right to occupy their unit for personal use, they were required to give six months' advance written notice.

The court found that the sale of condominium property, when accompanied by agreements of this type, constitutes the sale of a security. *Lowery v. Ford Hill Investment Co.*, 556 P.2d 1201 (Colorado 1976).

If condominium advertisements or other documents make reference to providing rental services for buyers, the purchase may be treated as an investment contract and securities regulations will apply. Some timeshare arrangements have also been subject to securities regulation on the basis of the investment contract theory.

Whether or not a condominium (or other type of investment) is considered a security is a fairly complicated question that should be answered only by an attorney who deals in this area.

Real Estate Investment Trusts

A **real estate investment trust (REIT)** is an investment entity that qualifies for tax advantages if it meets certain requirements. Shares in a REIT are securities, so their sale is subject to securities regulation.

When a REIT is established, a group of investors form a trust and purchase certificates of ownership in the trust. At least 75% of the trust's assets must be invested in real estate and real estate mortgages, and it must distribute most of its profits to the investors. A REIT must have a minimum of 100 investors.

A REIT's income is not subject to double taxation. The REIT is taxed only on its retained earnings. As long as most of its income is distributed to the investors, any significant taxation of the trust income is avoided. The profits distributed to the investors are taxed as ordinary income to the individual investors.

With a REIT, small investors can take advantage of big investment opportunities by pooling their resources.

Conclusion

Condominiums, cooperatives, and timeshare arrangements offer alternatives to traditional property ownership. In a condominium, a buyer owns a particular unit in fee simple and an undivided interest in the common areas. In a co-op, a buyer holds shares in the cooperative corporation and has a proprietary lease for an individual unit. Timeshare owners have the right to occupy a particular unit only during a specified time period.

In certain cases, condominium or timeshare sales are deemed to be securities transactions, so the promoter is required to comply with federal and state securities regulations. A real estate investment trust is another form of real estate investment that is subject to securities regulations.

Case Problem

The following is a hypothetical case problem. Most of the facts are taken from a real case. Based on what you have learned from this chapter, make a decision on the issues presented and then check to see if your answer matches the real decision by the court.

The Facts

The Riva Ridge North Chalet is a building composed of approximately ten condominiums in Vail, Colorado. The complex is managed by the Broadmoor Management Company. The individual owners of the condo units and the condominium association signed a management agreement. This agreement provided that in return for management and rental agent responsibilities, Broadmoor was to receive $30 per month for each unit, 40% of all rental commissions, an amount equal to one day's rental during the prime season, and three days' use of each unit for promotional purposes.

In addition to the above amounts provided for in the management agreement, Broadmoor also charged the condominium association for all common expenses, including resort association dues, housekeeping and security services, and advertising.

Several individual owners and the condo association brought a lawsuit against Broadmoor, claiming that the common expenses should have been paid out of the monthly fees provided for in the management agreement, and not charged as an additional amount.

The Questions

Can a condominium association file a lawsuit, or does it have to be brought by each individual owner? Should the management company be allowed to charge additional fees for common expenses? If the condo association wins the lawsuit, how will damages be apportioned?

The Answer

Where a condominium association has signed a contract (such as the management agreement), it is a proper party to file a lawsuit for damages. The bylaws of this condo association granted it the power to collect and disburse all funds necessary to manage the building. Each individual owner was required to be a member of the association. Thus, the association was in an ideal position to represent all of the owners.

The management company was found to have overcharged the condo association. (This decision was basically a matter of interpreting the contract. A management company might be allowed to charge additional monthly common expenses if the management agreement so provides.)

The court awarded damages for the amount overcharged, plus interest, to the association. The association was ordered to distribute the award among the individual unit owners in proportion to their percentage of ownership in the building. *Andrikopoulos v. Broadmoor Management Co.*, 670 P.2d 435 (Colo. App. 1983).

Chapter Summary

- The owner of a condominium unit receives fee simple ownership of the individual unit, plus an undivided interest in the common areas. The percentage of interest in the common areas assigned to each unit is usually based on the value of the unit in relation to the total value of the property.

- A unit owners association and its board of directors regulates and maintains the common areas of a condominium. It has the power to collect assessments from each unit owner to pay for the common expenses.

- The Washington Condominium Act requires a condominium developer to record a declaration, survey map, and plans, and to give a public offering statement to prospective buyers. A unit owner reselling a unit must give the buyer a resale certificate and other documents.

- A timeshare arrangement allows a buyer to purchase a time slot of ownership. A timeshare may involve tenancy in common, interval ownership, or a vacation license.

- For a cooperative, a nonprofit corporation owns the land and building, and the residents each own stock in the corporation or a membership interest and have a long-term lease in a specific unit. A blanket mortgage covers the entire cooperative property. If several of the tenants do not pay their rent, the entire building could be foreclosed on. This financial interdependence is one of the major disadvantages of cooperatives.

- A real estate security is an arrangement in which someone invests money in an enterprise involving real estate, with the expectation of earning profits from the efforts of a promoter or some other third party.

- If a condominium is purchased for investment purposes, it may be considered a security, and the parties must comply with state and federal securities regulations.

- A real estate investment trust is a group of 100 or more investors that invests primarily in real estate and mortgages. A REIT avoids double taxation if it distributes most of its income to the investors and complies with other rules. A REIT must be registered as a security.

Checklist of Problem Areas

Real Estate Licensee's Checklist

❑ Does the unit owners association have a right of first refusal before a unit can be sold?

❑ How many of the units in the building or complex are owner-occupied, and how many are rented out?

❑ Are there specific restrictions on the unit or the common areas (such as no pets, or no use of exercise facilities after a certain hour)?

❑ Is the sale of the unit considered a real estate security, and if so, has it been registered in compliance with both state and federal law?

Seller's Checklist

❑ Does the unit owners association have a right of first refusal?

❑ If you're selling a condominium unit, have you given the buyer a resale certificate?

❑ If you're selling a timeshare unit, have you given the buyer the required disclosure statement?

Buyer's Checklist

❑ If you're buying a condominium unit from the declarant, have you received (and studied) a copy of the public offering statement? Do you understand your right of rescission?

❑ If you're buying a unit from the previous unit owner, have you been given a resale certificate?

❑ Does the unit owners association have a right of first refusal? In other words, even if your offer is acceptable to the seller, could the association block the sale to you?

❑ What undivided interest in the common areas is assigned to this particular unit?

❑ What monthly assessments and fees must be paid to the association?

❑ What is the current condition of all of the common areas? Will there be big expenses coming up in the future when major items have to be repaired?

❑ If you're buying a timeshare, exactly what type of interest will you acquire? Have you received a disclosure statement, and do you understand your right of rescission?

Chapter Quiz

1. Condominiums are used:

   a. in resort communities
   b. in large metropolitan areas
   c. for residential and commercial purposes
   d. All of the above

2. A condominium declaration and survey map must be recorded:

   a. only for residential condominiums
   b. only for property initially developed as a condominium, not for a conversion
   c. to establish any type of condominium
   d. only if the condominium must be registered with the Securities and Exchange Commission

3. Hannah just bought Unit 10 in a 50-unit condominium. Which of the following is true?

   a. Hannah does not have a direct ownership interest in the common areas, since they are owned by the association
   b. Hannah did not acquire an interest in the common areas unless that interest was stated in her deed
   c. Hannah must have acquired an undivided interest in the common areas, but her percentage of interest is not necessarily the same as her neighbor's percentage
   d. Hannah must have acquired a 2% interest in the common areas

4. A condominium association is made up of:

   a. only those unit owners who choose to join
   b. all the unit owners
   c. directors and officers appointed by the declarant
   d. the declarant, the board of directors, and selected unit owners

5. For condominiums:

   a. an individual unit deed should be recorded for each unit
   b. a master deed is recorded for the entire complex, so that individual deeds for each unit are unnecessary
   c. an individual unit deed is given to each owner, but does not need to be recorded
   d. None of the above

6. When a residential apartment building is converted from rental units into condominium units, how much notice are the existing tenants entitled to?

   a. 30 days
   b. 60 days
   c. 120 days
   d. 180 days

7. Carlton buys into a timeshare condominium. All of the buyers are deeded an undivided interest in a unit, and then agree to limit their use to a specific time period. This type of timeshare is called:

   a. interval ownership
   b. a vacation license
   c. a right to use
   d. a tenancy in common

8. The Washington Timeshare Act requires that a prospective purchaser be given a written disclosure statement. After being given this disclosure, the purchaser:

    a. must close the deal within seven days
    b. may rescind the agreement within seven days
    c. must record a copy of the disclosure
    d. None of the above

9. The financing of a cooperative involves:

    a. a blanket mortgage on the entire building
    b. individual mortgages on the individual units
    c. both a blanket mortgage and individual mortgages
    d. None of the above

10. A cooperative owner has some remodeling work done on his individual unit. He does not pay the bill, and a construction lien is filed for the work. Which of the following statements is correct?

    a. The lien attaches only to the unit where the work was done
    b. The lien may attach to the entire building
    c. A construction lien cannot attach to a co-op, since the shareholder does not actually own the unit
    d. None of the above

11. A tax lien is filed against a condominium owner. Which of the following statements is true?

    a. The lien attaches only to her individual unit
    b. The lien attaches to the entire building and could result in a tax sale of the whole building
    c. The lien attaches to the whole building, but the other individual owners would be protected in a tax sale
    d. None of the above

12. Real estate securities must be registered with the Securities and Exchange Commission. Which of the following statements is true?

    a. Condominiums are always securities that must be registered
    b. Not all condominiums are securities, but timeshares are always securities and must be registered
    c. Some, but not all, condominiums and timeshares are securities that must be registered
    d. All condominiums and timeshares are securities and must be registered

13. A real estate investment trust must have:

    a. at least 50 investors
    b. at least 75 investors
    c. at least 100 investors
    d. There is no minimum requirement, but a REIT cannot have more than 100 investors

14. A group of people decide to purchase all the condominium units in a building, rent them out, and turn the management of the units over to a particular property management firm. This kind of arrangement:

    a. is illegal under the Washington Condominium Act
    b. would be considered a real property security
    c. would constitute a timeshare ownership interest
    d. would require the services of a real estate agent

15. Harrison is a condominium developer. Before he sells any condo units in a particular project, he enters into a management agreement (in the name of the condominium association) with Condos, Inc. Under the terms of the agreement, Condos, Inc. will handle the repairs and maintenance of the project for a healthy fee. If Harrison is the sole stockholder of Condos, Inc.:

    a. there is nothing wrong with this agreement, and Harrison should make a tidy profit
    b. this agreement is unfair, but the board of directors of the unit owners association can do nothing about it
    c. while Washington law does not prevent this type of agreement, it is a federal crime
    d. the board of directors of the unit owners association can terminate the agreement with 90 days' notice

15 Employment Law

Outline

I. Employment Arrangements
   A. Employees and independent contractors
      1. Real estate agents as independent contractors
      2. IRS employment tests
      3. Consequences of misclassification
   B. Contingent workers
II. Federal Employment Laws and Regulations
   A. Fair Labor Standards Act (FLSA)
   B. Occupational Safety and Health Act (OSHA)
   C. Americans with Disabilities Act (ADA)
   D. Employee Retirement Income Security Act (ERISA)
   E. Consolidated Omnibus Budget Reconciliation Act (COBRA)
III. State Employment Laws and Regulations
   A. Role of the Department of Labor and Industries
   B. Fair labor practices
   C. Unemployment compensation
   D. Workers' compensation
IV. Managing Human Resources
   A. Employee handbook
   B. Interviewing and hiring procedures
      1. Antidiscrimination laws
      2. Affirmative action
      3. New hire requirements
   C. Employee compensation and benefits
      1. Real estate brokerage compensation
      2. Benefits
      3. Family and medical leave laws
   D. Tax reporting
   E. Recordkeeping
   F. Disciplinary procedures and termination
   G. Discrimination and sexual harassment claims
   H. Mediation and arbitration of disputes
V. Supervision and Liability for Employees' Actions

Key Terms

- Employee
- Independent contractor
- Statutory nonemployee
- Contingent worker
- Temporary worker
- Leased worker
- Joint employer
- Fair Labor Standards Act
- Minimum wage
- Occupational Safety and Health Act
- Americans with Disabilities Act
- Disability
- Reasonable accommodation
- Employee Retirement Income Security Act

- Fiduciary
- Consolidated Omnibus Budget Reconciliation Act
- Unemployment compensation
- Federal Employment Tax Act
- Workers' compensation
- Human resources
- Policies and procedures manual
- Title VII of the Civil Rights Act of 1964
- Age Discrimination in Employment Act
- Affirmative action

- Reverse discrimination
- Form W-4
- Employment Eligibility Verification Form
- Indirect compensation
- Family and Medical Leave Act
- Washington Family Care Act
- Employment identification number
- Form W-2
- Sexual harassment
- Respondeat superior
- Negligent hiring and retention

Chapter Overview

Real estate brokerage firms must be familiar with the state and federal laws that govern hiring and employment. Not only do brokerage firms hire real estate agents to work for them, they also hire support staff, such as receptionists and bookkeepers. Firms must be careful to comply with employment laws in regard to both types of workers.

We'll begin this chapter with an overview of the various types of employment arrangements. Next, we'll take a closer look at some of the federal laws related to employment, including the Fair Labor Standards Act, the Americans with Disabilities Act, and laws governing pensions and health care. We'll also look at Washington's fair labor laws, as well as unemployment compensation and workers' compensation.

Later in the chapter, we'll discuss human resources management, from developing an employee handbook to interviewing and hiring employees and determining compensation and benefits. We'll also examine the laws regarding taxation and recordkeeping responsibilities, as well as how to handle disciplinary problems, termination, and claims of discrimination and harassment. We'll end the chapter with a brief discussion of employer liability for the acts of employees, and a brokerage firm's responsibility for supervising its affiliated licensees.

Employment Arrangements

Let's begin our discussion of employment law by taking a look at some of the most common types of workers: employees, independent contractors, and contingent workers.

While there are many similarities between these three types of workers, it's important to distinguish between them, because each type presents different issues for the employer.

Employees vs. Independent Contractors

Generally, an **employee** is anyone who performs a service for another (the employer), when the employer has the right to control both what will be done and how it will be done. (Highly skilled professionals often need little or no direction, but if the employer retains the right to provide instruction and direction, even these workers will be considered employees.) On the other hand, an **independent contractor** is generally hired to perform a particular job and to use her own judgment as to how the work will be done.

Note that it's the substance of the relationship that matters, not the label given to it. A worker is not an independent contractor just because that's what the employer calls him. If the employer has the right to control what the worker will do and how it will be done, then that worker is an employee under the law.

Employers are not required to withhold income taxes and social security contributions from the pay of an independent contractor, but they must do so for employees.

Real Estate Agents as Independent Contractors. Some workers are never considered to be employees for income tax purposes, including most real estate agents. These **statutory nonemployees** are considered to be self-employed for all federal income and employment tax purposes if:

- substantially all payments for their services are directly related to sales or other output, rather than number of hours worked; and
- all work is done under a written contract that states they will not be treated as employees for federal tax purposes.

IRS Employment Tests. If a worker does not fall squarely into the category of statutory nonemployee, the employer can use a series of tests issued by the Internal Revenue Service (IRS) to determine if the worker is an independent contractor. These tests concern:

- behavioral control,
- financial control, and
- the type of the relationship between the parties.

Let's look at these tests in more detail.

Behavioral control. Employers have much more control over employees than over independent contractors. An employee can be told when, where, and how to work. He can be told which tools to use, which specific tasks he must complete, and what order or sequence to follow when performing a task.

> **Example:** An employee of XYZ Advertising Company is instructed to call 50 people a day to solicit business for the company, and she is given a script to follow for each call.

John, on the other hand, works for ABC Software Company as a sales agent. John is paid only when he closes a sale, and it's up to him to determine the best method for acquiring those sales. He might call 50 people a day, or he might decide that he'd rather use direct mail advertising and an Internet presence to generate referrals. John is an independent contractor.

Financial control. The IRS also looks at whether the employer has financial control over the worker. An independent contractor is rarely guaranteed any sort of compensation, such as an hourly wage or salary. Instead, an independent contractor is usually paid a flat fee for each project completed, regardless of how long it takes him to complete the work.

> **Example:** Returning to our example above, the employee for XYZ Advertising Company is paid a salary of $30,000 a year, regardless of how many people she calls a day or how many new customers she gets.
>
> John, however, receives a commission when he successfully closes a software sale. His commission is a percentage of the sales price, and he receives that same amount whether it takes him five days to find a new customer, or five months.

Independent contractors are not usually reimbursed for expenses, while employees usually are.

> **Example:** Let's return one last time to our prior example. The employee of XYZ Advertising will not be expected to pay for telephone service or any long distance charges involved in contacting 50 people a day.
>
> John, on the other hand, is an independent contractor. He is expected to provide his own phone service and pay for his own long distance calls. Furthermore, if John needs a laptop computer or cell phone to conduct his business, he will have to supply those items himself.

Type of relationship between the parties. The last important factor is the type of relationship between the parties. This includes the duration of the relationship, whether the parties have a written contract, whether benefits are given to the worker, and how important the worker's services are to the business.

Employees are usually hired without a contract and are often given benefits, such as health insurance and vacation pay. In contrast, independent contractors are rarely provided benefits, and the relationship between a business and an independent contractor is usually governed by a written contract.

If the relationship between the worker and the business will continue indefinitely, rather than for a specific project or period, the worker is usually considered to be an employee.

Consequences of Misclassification. As we mentioned earlier, employers are responsible for withholding and paying income taxes, social security taxes, and Medicare taxes for their employees. Employers who fail to pay these taxes because they misclassified an employee as an independent contractor without a reasonable basis for doing so may be held liable for:

- all back taxes owed for the employee,
- the employee's share of unpaid social security and income taxes not withheld,

- interest on these amounts, and
- penalties.

Contingent Workers

Now let's look at **contingent workers**: workers who are contracted, leased, or borrowed from an outside firm. These outside firms (often called staffing companies or temporary agencies) handle all of the financial and administrative responsibilities for the contingent workers, including compensation, taxes, benefits, and recordkeeping. Employers often use contingent workers to save the time and money associated with hiring and training; employers also like the flexibility that comes with contingent workers. Rather than hiring a full-time employee, a business can "borrow" a worker for only as long as it needs her.

Leased Workers vs. Temporary Workers. Contingent workers can be temporary workers or leased workers. **Temporary workers** are generally assigned to work at one company for a certain period of time or for a certain task or assignment. Once that assignment is completed, they move on to the next temporary job, which may be at the same or another company. **Leased workers**, on the other hand, work at the contracting company for an indefinite period of time, and generally do not move around from assignment to assignment.

Liability Issues. Many businesses believe that using contingent workers automatically relieves them of the obligation to pay workers' compensation and to comply with other employment laws. However, this may be a mistake. Under certain circumstances, courts have found businesses who use contingent workers to be **joint employers**. This may occur when the duration of the employment, the method of compensation, or some other aspect of the working relationship indicates that the worker is an employee in everything but name.

Joint employers can find themselves liable for the staffing company's errors or misbehavior. For example, payroll taxes are the responsibility of the worker's employer, which in

---

Fig. 15.1 Common law employee vs. contingent worker

> **Factors that determine status:**
> 1. Supervision
> 2. Discretion to hire & fire
> 3. Ability to discipline
> 4. Designation of rules
> 5. Who formulates instructions and assignments
> 6. Contracting company's right to refuse employee
> 7. Method of compensation

a contingent situation is usually the staffing company. But if the staffing company fails to pay the taxes and the company using the contingent worker is found to be a joint employer, that company could find itself liable for those unpaid taxes. Likewise, a joint employer could also be sued by the contingent worker for discrimination or sexual harassment.

Sometimes, contracting companies offer certain benefits to their own employees but not to contingent workers. If it's later determined that the contracting company was actually a joint employer, it could be liable to the contingent employees for the value of those benefits.

Case Example:

For years, Microsoft used workers it referred to as independent contractors or temporary agency employees. Microsoft offered its regular, full-time employees several benefits that it didn't offer its independent contractors or temporary workers, including the opportunity to participate in an employee stock purchase plan (ESPP).

In 1990, the IRS advised Microsoft that many of the workers it had labeled independent contractors or temporary workers were actually common law employees of Microsoft, because Microsoft "either exercised, or retained the right to exercise, direction over the services performed." This created an employer/employee relationship.

In response to the IRS's determination, Microsoft offered some of the independent contractors jobs as regular employees. However, most of the workers were given the option to convert to temporary status or lose their working relationship with Microsoft. Other independent contractors were "voluntarily converted" to contingent workers, whose payroll would be handled by temp agencies. The workers' relationships with Microsoft remained otherwise unchanged.

Plaintiffs, former independent contractors who met the IRS definition of employees, sued for benefits, including the right to participate in the ESPP. Microsoft denied liability, pointing to the original independent contractor agreement which expressly stated that independent contractors were responsible for their own benefits.

The court found for the plaintiffs. It didn't matter what the independent contractor agreement stated, or whether temporary workers were technically employed by the temp agency. If Microsoft treated them like employees, then it was an employer/employee relationship under the law, and those workers are entitled to the same benefits as regular full-time workers. *Vizcaino v. Microsoft Corp.*, 173 F.3d 713 (9th Cir. 1999) *(Vizcaino III)*.

Federal Employment Laws and Regulations

Now let's take a look at some of the federal laws that govern employment in the United States. Perhaps the most fundamental is the Fair Labor Standards Act, which regulates such things as minimum wage and overtime requirements. But there are also laws that specifically address other employee rights and protections, such as workplace safety and health insurance coverage after job termination.

Note that many of these federal laws have counterparts at the state level. As usual, the stricter law will apply. We'll discuss Washington state employment laws and regulations in the next section.

Fair Labor Standards Act (FLSA)

The Fair Labor Standards Act (FLSA) is administered by the Wage and Hour Division of the U.S. Department of Labor. The act sets forth rules for minimum wage, overtime, and recordkeeping for all full- and part-time employees covered by the act, in both private and government sectors.

Case Example:

In 1937, Elsie Parrish, a chambermaid in a Washington hotel, brought suit to recover the difference between the wages paid to her by the hotel and the minimum wage under Washington state law. The hotel argued that the minimum wage law was unconstitutional because it violated the due process clause of the Fourteenth Amendment and the "freedom of contract."

The U.S. Supreme Court disagreed with the hotel's claim. Freedom of contract is a qualified right, not an absolute one. The state legislature is well within its police power to legislate for the health and safety of its citizens. Furthermore, the "exploitation of a class of workers who are in an unequal position with respect to bargaining power and are thus relatively defenseless against the denial of a living wage is not only detrimental to their health and well-being, but casts a direct burden for their support upon the community." *West Coast Hotel Co. v. Parish*, 300 U.S. 379 (1937).

Basic Wage Requirements. As of early 2018, the federal **minimum wage** for employees is $7.25 per hour. Individual states may set higher minimum wage requirements, but the basic wage for any employee in any state can never fall below $7.25 per hour.

Deductions for cash shortages, missing items, uniforms, and equipment or similar items are illegal if they reduce the total wages due an employee below the minimum wage.

> **Example:** In Sam's state, the minimum wage is $7.25 an hour. Sam's employer, a gas station, has a policy that cash register shortages will be deducted from its employees' paychecks. Sam makes $7.50 an hour and worked 20 hours last week (for a total paycheck of $150). After a particularly busy shift, Sam's cash register is short $10. Despite the gas station's policy of deducting cash register shortages from an employee's paycheck, Sam's employer cannot deduct the full $10. A deduction of $10 would bring Sam's average hourly wage below the minimum required by federal law. ($150 − $10 = $140; $140 ÷ 20 hours worked = $7.00 per hour.)

Wages must be paid on the regularly scheduled payday for the pay period worked. For example, an employee who worked 20 hours and is normally paid on Friday, must be paid for the entire 20 hours on Friday; his employer cannot pay the employee for 10 hours on Friday and the remainder on the following Monday.

Overtime. Under the FLSA, if an employee works more than 40 hours in a week, he must be paid at a rate of at least one and one-half times his regular rate of pay for those additional hours. Deductions for shortages and other items cannot be used to reduce the amount of overtime pay due under the FLSA.

Exempt Employees. Some employees are exempt from the provisions of the FLSA. Some are exempt only from the overtime pay provisions, while others are exempt from both the minimum wage provisions and the overtime provisions. Examples of exempt employees include commissioned salespeople; executive, administrative, and professional employees; computer professionals; certain farmworkers; and some seasonal and recreational employees.

Employers should always keep in mind that the burden of proving that an employee is exempt rests on the employer. It is never a good idea to assume that an employee is exempt; it's best to get legal advice.

What the FLSA Doesn't Cover. The Fair Labor Standards Act doesn't cover all aspects of an employee's job. For instance, there's no federal requirement that limits workers to an eight-hour day. The FLSA also does not generally require any of the following:

- vacation, holiday, severance, or sick pay;
- meal or rest periods;
- time off for holidays;
- premium pay for holiday or weekend work;
- pay raises; or
- a termination notice, reason for termination, or immediate payment of final wages.

Note, however, that individual states may regulate one or more of these items. For instance, in Washington, former employees have a right to make a written request asking the employer to provide a written reason for termination and the effective date of termination. Employers have ten days from receipt of the request to comply.

Recordkeeping Requirements. The FLSA requires employers to keep basic records regarding each covered employee's name and address, wage and occupation, age (if under 19), total hours worked each work day and work week, total regular hours and overtime hours worked per week, deductions from earnings, total wages paid each pay period, hour and day when the work week begins, and date of payment and pay period covered.

This information doesn't have to be kept on a specific form, and employers are not required to use a time clock.

Penalties. Employers who willfully or repeatedly violate the minimum wage or overtime pay requirements are subject to a civil penalty of up to $1,964 for each violation. (Civil penalties are adjusted annually for inflation.)

It is a violation to fire or otherwise discriminate against an employee for filing a complaint or for participating in a legal proceeding under the FLSA. Willful violations may be prosecuted criminally and the violator fined up to $10,000. A second conviction may result in imprisonment.

Occupational Safety and Health Act (OSHA)

Another federal employment law is the Occupational Safety and Health Act, which was enacted in 1970 in an effort to help prevent work-related injuries, illnesses, and deaths. The law is implemented by the Occupational Safety and Health Administration (OSHA), which is overseen by the Department of Labor. OSHA works with states to ensure safe and healthy work environments through research, inspection, training, and education in occupational health and safety.

All employers covered by the act must post a federal or state OSHA poster that provides employees with information on their health and safety rights in the workplace.

Recordkeeping and Reporting Requirements. Employers with 11 or more employees must keep records of work-related injuries and illnesses. However, employers in low-hazard industries (such as retail, professional services, and real estate) are generally exempt from these requirements; they are not required to keep records unless asked in writing by OSHA to do so.

All businesses covered by the law must notify OSHA within eight hours of a workplace fatality or within 24 hours of any work-related inpatient hospitalization, amputation, or loss of an eye.

Penalties. Serious violations of the law can carry penalties up to $7,000. Repeat and willful violations can carry penalties up to $70,000.

Americans with Disabilities Act (ADA)

The Americans with Disabilities Act (ADA) is a federal law that was passed to ensure that disabled persons have equal access to public facilities. As we discussed in Chapter 12, the ADA prohibits discrimination on the basis of disability in any place of public accommodation (a business or other facility open to the public).

The ADA also makes it illegal to discriminate in employment against an otherwise qualified individual because she has a disability. A **disability** is defined as any physical or mental impairment that substantially limits one or more of the individual's major life activities. The ADA's prohibitions against employment discrimination are enforced by the U.S. Equal Employment Opportunity Commission (EEOC) in conjunction with state and local enforcement agencies

Employers may not discriminate in the recruitment, hiring, firing, training, assignment of jobs, promotions, pay, benefits, layoffs, granting of leave, or any other employment activity. These rules apply to employers with 15 or more employees.

Employees are protected under the ADA whether they are currently disabled or were disabled in the past, and even if the employer only believes the individual to be disabled (when in fact, the employee is not).

Reasonable Accommodation. An employer is also required to provide a reasonable accommodation to a qualified applicant or employee with a disability unless the employer can show that the accommodation would be an **undue hardship**—that is, the accommodation could be achieved only after significant difficulty or expense.

A reasonable accommodation is defined as any change or adjustment to a job or work environment that allows a qualified applicant or employee with a disability to participate in the job application process, to perform the essential functions of a job, or to enjoy benefits and privileges of employment equal to those enjoyed by employees without disabilities. For example, reasonable accommodation might include:

- providing or modifying equipment or devices;
- adjusting or modifying applications, examinations, training materials, or policies;
- providing readers and interpreters; and
- making the workplace readily accessible to and usable by people with disabilities.

Who is Covered. To be protected under the ADA, disabled individuals must meet a two-prong test. First, the individual must be qualified to perform the essential functions of the job. To be qualified, the applicant might need relevant education, training, experience, or licenses, among other things.

Next, the individual must be able to perform the essential functions of the job with reasonable accommodation. An employer cannot refuse to hire an otherwise qualified individual because he cannot do a particular task that is not an essential function of the job.

> **Example:** Molly is disabled and uses a wheelchair. She applies for a desk job at a real estate firm. She is well-qualified, and she needs no accommodation to perform the essential functions of the job. It would be illegal for the firm to refuse to hire Molly because she wouldn't be able to climb the stairs to the extra storage room, if doing so is not an essential function of the job she has applied for.

Penalties. Under the ADA, an applicant or employee who has been discriminated against on the basis of disability is entitled to be put in the position he would have been in had the discrimination never occurred. That could mean hiring, promotion, reinstatement, back pay, reasonable accommodation, reassignment, and (if applicable) attorney's fees. Compensatory and punitive damages are also available.

Employee Retirement Income Security Act (ERISA)

The Employee Retirement Income Security Act of 1974 (ERISA) is a federal law that protects individuals who have voluntarily established pension and health plans with their employers. ERISA is administered by the Employee Benefits Security Administration, part of the Department of Labor. Along with the Employee Benefits Security Administration, the IRS has statutory and regulatory authority to ensure that employees receive their promised benefits.

The purpose of ERISA is to ensure that private (non-government) employers establish and maintain employee benefit plans as promised. Anyone who manages or controls plan funds must:

- manage plans for the exclusive benefit of participants and beneficiaries,
- act prudently and avoid conflict of interest transactions,
- fund plans in accordance with the law and plan rules, and
- report and disclose information on the operation and financial condition of the plans to both the government and plan participants.

ERISA makes anyone with control over plan funds a **fiduciary**. As you will remember, a fiduciary is anyone who holds a position of special trust in relation to another person.

In addition, ERISA requires employers to establish a grievance and appeals process for plan participants, and gives participants the right to sue if there is a breach of fiduciary duty.

Consolidated Omnibus Budget Reconciliation Act (COBRA)

In 1984, Congress amended ERISA to include the Consolidated Omnibus Budget Reconciliation Act (COBRA). The purpose of COBRA is to provide an employee with the option of continuing her health insurance coverage when the coverage would otherwise terminate because of a job loss or a reduction in hours.

COBRA applies to any employer with 20 or more employees, as long as the employer provided group health insurance coverage for more than half of its business days in the previous calendar year. Both part- and full-time employees are counted when determining whether an employer is subject to COBRA. Part-time employees are counted as a fraction of full-time employees, based on the number of hours worked divided by the number of hours considered full-time.

> **Example:** ABC, a large property management firm, has 19 full-time employees and four part-time employees. Each part-time employee works 10 hours per week, or ¼ the time of a full-time employee. So for COBRA purposes, each part-time employee is equal to .25 of a full-time employee.
>
> Together, the four part-time employees equal one full-time employee, so ABC has the equivalent of 20 full-time employees. ABC is therefore subject to COBRA.

COBRA coverage is available to an employee (and any spouse and dependent children) previously enrolled in the employer's group health plan. Agents and independent contractors who participated in the health plan may also be covered. For coverage to apply, the employee's termination (or reduction in hours) may be voluntary or involuntary, but it cannot have been the result of gross misconduct.

Eligible individuals must be given at least 60 days to elect COBRA coverage after their health coverage would normally have ended. Coverage is retroactive. So, for example, if an employee is laid off on May 1, but doesn't formally elect COBRA coverage until June 15, the COBRA coverage will be retroactive to May 1.

Length of Coverage. COBRA coverage generally lasts for up to 18 months. A covered spouse who would lose health coverage due to divorce or separation is eligible for COBRA coverage for up to 36 months.

Coverage may end earlier if:

- premiums are not paid on time;
- the employer stops providing any group health plan;
- coverage is later obtained with another employer group health plan that doesn't exclude preexisting conditions; or
- a beneficiary becomes entitled to Medicare.

Premiums. Employers are not responsible for paying the health insurance premiums due under COBRA. This is true even if the employer previously paid any or all of the employee's premium. The premium cannot exceed 102% of the cost of the plan to the remaining employees.

> **Example:** Barbara works for XYZ Company, which usually pays 100% of its employees' health insurance premiums, approximately $300 per month per employee. When Barbara is laid off, she elects to continue her health plan under COBRA. Barbara can do so, but she must pay the $300 monthly premium herself, plus a 2% administrative fee ($6). Barbara's monthly cost to continue her coverage under COBRA will be $306.

The initial premium must be paid within 45 days after the individual has elected COBRA coverage. Thereafter, premiums are due on the date stated in the plan.

State Employment Laws and Regulations

Now that we've looked at some of the more important federal employment-related laws, let's turn our attention to Washington's employment laws. We'll begin by discussing the role of the Department of Labor and Industries, then we'll turn to the fair labor practice laws that apply within the state. We'll end this section with an examination of unemployment compensation and the role of workers' compensation.

Role of the Department of Labor and Industries

Washington's Department of Labor and Industries (L&I) is a state agency that oversees the safety, health, and security of employees who work in Washington. Among other responsibilities, L&I is involved in the following employment issues:

- **Protecting workers' wages, hours, and breaks.** L&I ensures that workers are paid their full wage, on time. L&I also requires employers to provide rest and meal breaks, and enforces child labor laws and overtime laws.
- **Protecting the health and safety of workers.** L&I administers the state's version of the Occupational Safety and Health Act by developing and enforcing rules that protect workers from dangerous conditions.

- **Ensuring medical care and financial help for injured workers.** L&I oversees benefits to workers who are injured or become ill on the job. The agency administers the state's workers' compensation program, and regulates the hundreds of large, self-insured employers in the state who are qualified to provide their own workers' compensation.

The Department of Labor and Industries also fields worker rights complaints.

Fair Labor Practices

Many of Washington's fair labor requirements are similar to the federal requirements in the Fair Labor Standards Act, although Washington's standards are often higher and cover more workers.

Wages and Hours. Under Washington law, all workers 16 years of age or older must be paid at least minimum wage for all hours worked. The state minimum wage is $11.50 in 2018, and it is subject to annual increases. Some municipalities in Washington have set an even higher minimum wage than the state minimum.

Unless exempt, employees must be paid at a rate of at least one and one-half times their regular rate of pay for any hours they work in excess of 40 hours in a single work week. Nonexempt employees cannot waive the right to a minimum wage or to overtime pay.

Workers must be paid at least once a month on a regularly scheduled payday. The employer must provide a pay stub that shows the number of hours worked, the pay period, the rate of pay, gross pay (total pay, before deductions), and all deductions taken from the gross pay.

Required Breaks. As we noted in our discussion of the FLSA, federal law doesn't generally require that employers provide employees with any breaks for meals or rest periods. Washington law sets a higher standard, however. In Washington, most workers are entitled to:

- one unpaid 30-minute meal period if working more than five hours in a day; and
- one ten-minute paid rest break for every four hours worked, to be taken no later than the end of the third hour.

If the worker must remain on duty or work during the 30-minute meal period, it must be paid time. Also, the ten-minute break period can be broken into smaller breaks.

Mandatory Sick Leave. Employees in Washington must earn at least one hour of paid sick leave for every 40 hours worked. If an employee has unused sick leave at the end of the year, the employer must carry at least 40 hours of the unused leave over to the next year.

Unemployment Compensation

The purpose of unemployment compensation is to provide partial, temporary income to workers who have lost their jobs. Employers must pay both federal and state unemployment taxes. The **Federal Unemployment Tax Act** (FUTA) is a federal law that is used to fund state workforce agencies, subsidize extended unemployment benefits when necessary, and provide loans to states who need help providing benefits.

Employers generally must pay both federal and state unemployment taxes when they:

- pay wages that total $1,500 or more in any quarter of a calendar year; and
- had at least one employee during any day of the week during 20 weeks (consecutive or nonconsecutive) in a calendar year.

Unemployment Compensation in Washington. In Washington, unemployment compensation is overseen by the state's Employment Security Department. There is no minimum hour or dollar threshold that must be met. Any worker is reportable, even if she's been hired on a temporary basis or to do a single brief job.

Employers must register, report wages, and pay unemployment taxes for all covered employees. Wages include all compensation paid to employees, including hourly wages, tips, salaries, vacation and holiday pay, severance pay, bonuses, and meals and lodging.

Some types of workers are not eligible to receive unemployment benefits. Businesses generally do not have to pay unemployment taxes on these exempt workers. Examples of exempt workers include:

- independent contractors (self-employed workers);
- elected government officials;
- employees of a church or other religious organization;
- family employees working for their spouse or parent;
- real estate appraisers; and
- real estate agents paid by commission.

Tax Rate. Unemployment compensation tax rates—both state and federal—vary from employer to employer. Washington's unemployment tax rate is based on the employer's "experience" with unemployment. Experience is the total amount of unemployment benefits paid to the business's former employees over the past four years, divided by the employer's taxable payroll for the same time period. Unemployment taxes must be paid quarterly.

Payment and Recordkeeping. The following records must be kept on file for at least four years from the date taxes were paid: the employee's name, social security number, dates of employment, basis of pay, location of work, hours worked, gross pay per pay period, payroll deductions for each pay period, and the reason an employee quit or was discharged, if applicable.

Worker Eligibility. To be eligible for unemployment benefits in Washington, a worker must have worked 680 hours within the previous 52 weeks in the state of Washington. Part-time employees are eligible for reduced benefits.

Workers seeking unemployment compensation must state the reason they are unemployed. Workers usually qualify for benefits if they've been laid off. On the other hand, if a worker voluntarily quit her job, was fired or suspended, or is on a leave of absence, the state will make an individual determination of the worker's eligibility. Both the employee and the employer will be asked questions about the employee's unemployment, and both sides will have an opportunity to the respond to the other side's statements.

In order to receive benefits each week, the worker must be physically able to work, available for work, and actively seeking work. However, workers do not have to look for or accept work that is not suitable. Work is not suitable if:

- it is not in line with the worker's training and experience,
- the worker must join or resign from a labor union,
- the hours or working conditions are not as favorable as most other jobs in that occupation or area,
- it is farther than the usual commuting distance for people in that occupation,
- the wages offered are lower than the wages common for that occupation in that area,
- it is unreasonably dangerous,
- the worker cannot physically do the work, or
- it would offend the worker's religious beliefs or moral conscience.

Most workers are eligible for 13 to 26 weeks of unemployment benefits per year. To receive benefits, the worker must file weekly claims. To stop receiving benefits, the worker simply stops filing for the weekly benefit.

Workers' Compensation

Workers' compensation (also known as **industrial insurance**) is insurance that protects both employees and employers from the financial impact of work-related injuries. Workers' compensation is managed by the Department of Labor and Industries.

Premiums are paid by the employer into a state fund, and those premiums are then used to pay for an injured worker's medical and rehabilitation care. Injured workers who cannot work may also be eligible for partial wage replacement. Workers' compensation is mandatory for employers with one or more employees. In exchange, however, the employers usually cannot be sued for work-related injuries.

Under state law, the employer can deduct a portion of the workers' compensation premiums from the employee's pay.

Independent Contractors. In the past, many real estate firms believed that they were not responsible for providing workers' compensation for their affiliated licensees because those licensees were independent contractors. Although a 1993 Washington court decision made it clear that this is not the case, audits show that many real estate firms remain delinquent in their premium payments.

Case Example:

The Court of Appeals upheld an administrative assessment by the Department of Labor and Industries for past due workers' compensation premiums owed by a real estate brokerage for its licensees. The agents were all independent contractors and not normally considered employees (for example, under IRS regulations). However, Washington's RCW 51.08.180(1) defines independent contractors as workers if the essence of the contract is the agent's "personal labor for her employer." Since the agents could only work for and receive compensation through the brokerage firm, the agents were not excluded from worker status. In other words, brokerage firms must pay workers' compensation premiums for real estate agents. *Peter M. Black Real Estate Co., Inc. v. Dept. of Labor and Industries,* 70 Wn. App. 482, 854 P.2d 46 (1993).

The premiums owed to the state are due quarterly. Failure to pay the required premiums will result in interest and penalties on the unpaid amount.

Licensed or Unlicensed Assistants. Real estate licensees who employ licensed or unlicensed assistants may need to provide workers' compensation insurance for their assistants. If you have any doubt about whether you need to provide this coverage for your assistants, it's best to contact the Department of Labor and Industries directly.

Managing Human Resources

Now that we've examined the federal and state laws that apply to workers, let's turn our attention to the management of those workers. For the sake of this discussion, the term "employees" will be used to refer to all types of workers—employees, independent contractors, and contingent workers—unless otherwise noted.

The term **human resources** (HR) refers to the people employed by a business. It is also commonly used to refer to the person or department within a company that is responsible for hiring and firing employees, maintaining personnel records, supervising insurance and other benefits, and handling disciplinary problems.

In this section, we'll take a closer look at the following aspects of HR management: the employee handbook; interviewing and hiring procedures; employee compensation and benefits; tax compliance; recordkeeping; disciplinary procedures and termination; discrimination and sexual harassment claims; and mediation and arbitration of disputes.

Employee Handbook

One of the first things a business should do is create a written document that establishes office procedures. This document is called an **employee handbook** or a **policies and procedures manual**. The amount of information contained in an employee handbook will vary from business to business, but at a minimum, it should address:

- use of company property (including office equipment);
- payroll and work hours;
- holidays and vacations;
- sick leave, family leave, and funeral leave;

- military and jury duty;
- sexual harassment and discrimination policies; and
- disciplinary procedures.

The handbook may also address benefits, retirement plans, workers' compensation, safety procedures, dress code, and smoking policies. In some cases it's appropriate to include procedures for handling specific situations or issues that employees may encounter in the course of their work.

The contents of an employee handbook should be straightforward and unambiguous. A poorly written handbook can lead to misunderstandings, confusion, and ultimately legal disputes. Because a court will sometimes treat an employee handbook like a contract between a company and its employees, companies should draft their handbooks very carefully, seeking legal advice when necessary.

Brokerage Policies and Procedures Manual. Like any other business, a real estate brokerage firm should establish clear, written policies on office procedures. Some policies are required by law; for instance, the firm must have a written policy on home inspector referrals. This policy must address the buyers' or sellers' right to pick a home inspector of their own choosing, and must prevent any collusion between a home inspector and the real estate agent. If a licensee refers someone to a home inspector with whom she has (or had) any type of relationship, the relationship must be disclosed in writing before the buyer or seller uses the home inspector's services.

The manual should spell out all of the internal rules of the firm, and describe what management and agents can expect from each other. The manual should also cover the firm's policies on:

- commission splits,
- the purchase of E&O insurance,
- sales meetings attendance,
- production expectations,
- handling referrals (such as referrals to home inspectors or mortgage lenders),
- conflicts of interest,
- confidentiality,
- methods of solving disputes, and
- termination procedures.

New agents should sign a form stating that they have read the manual and will abide by its rules. This document should be kept on file, in case disputes arise later.

Interviewing and Hiring Procedures

When interviewing and hiring employees, businesses must be careful to comply with the many state and federal laws that regulate hiring practices. Some of these laws are designed to prevent discrimination. Others are related to taxes and eligibility to work in the United States.

Antidiscrimination Laws. Both federal and state laws prohibit discrimination in the hiring, firing, and compensation of employees. At the federal level, **Title VII of the Civil Rights Act of 1964** prohibits employment discrimination based on race, color, religion, gender, or national origin, while the **Age Discrimination in Employment Act** prohibits age discrimination against people over 40.

Although there are some exceptions, the **Washington Law Against Discrimination** generally prohibits employment discrimination based on age (over 40), sex, marital status, sexual orientation, race, creed, color, national origin, honorably discharged veteran or military status, disability, or use of a trained guide dog or service animal. The rules against employment discrimination apply to essentially any type of solicitation or inquiry directed toward a job applicant. This includes advertising job openings and other ways of recruiting applicants, and also job applications and the interview process.

Advertising and recruitment. When advertising job openings, businesses must not use any word, term, phrase, or expression that might encourage or discourage any person from applying for a job because of membership in a protected class. See the chart in Figure 15.2 for examples of prohibited discriminatory terms and suggested substitutes.

Note that it is also an unfair practice under Washington law to use a discriminatory job title in any job advertisement, job description, job announcement, or any other notice, statement, or publication. Job titles should be gender neutral. (For example, a nightclub should advertise for "waitstaff," not "barmaids.")

Job applications and interviews. Under Washington law, businesses may not ask a job applicant or any third parties questions that will reveal the applicant's possible membership in a protected class.

While some inquiries are obviously prohibited (regarding race, color, and religious preferences, for example), other unlawful inquiries are not so obvious. Here are just a few examples of what employers may and may not ask during the application and interview process:

1. **Age.** Companies may ask the applicant's birth date, but may not indicate any preference for persons under 40 years of age.
2. **Citizenship.** Companies may ask whether the applicant is prevented from being lawfully employed because of visa or immigration status, but may not ask whether the applicant is a citizen.
3. **Family.** Companies may ask if the applicant can comply with required work schedules or if he has other responsibilities that will keep him from meeting work requirements, but cannot inquire about childcare arrangements or a spouse's employment or salary.
4. **Disability.** Companies may ask whether an applicant can perform the essential functions of the job she is applying for, but cannot inquire about the nature or extent of a disability, whether the applicant will need accommodations, or whether the applicant has received worker's compensation in the past.

Fig. 15.2 Discriminatory terms and alternatives

DISCRIMINATORY TERMS IN ADVERTISEMENTS	SUGGESTED SUBSTITUTES
Man, woman, girl, boy, lady, etc.	Person, applicant, hiree, one, trainee, or a sex-neutral job title
Cute, handsome, pretty, clean-cut, attractive	Neat, well-groomed, person-able, professional appearance
Married, single	(no substitutes)
Recent graduate, college student (implies preference for youth)	Degree required, internship
Mother, housewife	Part-time, short hours
Young	Entry-level, beginner, trainee
Christian, Jewish, etc.	(no substitutes)
Interracial, segregated, Black, White, colored, Oriental, Asian, Mexican, minority	Person, applicant, etc.
	Other nondiscriminatory terms: reliable, responsible, efficient, minimum wages, long hours, overtime, able to travel, willing to relocate

5. **National origin.** Companies may ask about an applicant's ability to read, write, or speak a foreign language when such inquiries are based on job requirements, but they may not ask about the applicant's lineage, ancestry, national origin, or birthplace.

6. **Pregnancy.** Companies may ask questions about anticipated duration in the job or anticipated absences from work, but only if the same questions are asked of both men and women. Questions about pregnancy or previous medical history related to pregnancy are not allowed.

7. **Residence.** Companies may ask the applicant's address, but may not ask the names or relationship of persons they live with, or whether or not the applicant rents or owns his home.

8. **Sexual orientation or gender identity.** Companies may not ask questions about sexual orientation or gender identity under any circumstances.

Case Example:

Hegwine applied for a clerk position with Longview Fibre Company. During her interview, Hegwine was told that the position required her to lift 25 pounds. Longview offered Hegwine the job, conditioned upon her successful completion of a physical exam. During the exam, Hegwine had to fill out a questionnaire that disclosed she was pregnant. The doctor noted that Hegwine could meet the 25-pound lifting requirement.

After Longview learned of her pregnancy, it notified Hegwine that the lifting requirement was actually 40 pounds. Hegwine got her doctor to give her a release stating that she could meet the 40-pound requirement. Longview finally changed the requirement to 60 pounds and notified Hegwine that it was terminating her employment offer because she wouldn't be able to perform the job. Hegwine sued, alleging unlawful sex discrimination.

The court sided with Hegwine. Among other things, the pre-job medical questionnaire asking about pregnancy was inappropriate under the antidiscrimination laws. *Hegwine v. Longview Fibre Company, Inc.,* 162 Wn.2d 340 (2007).

There is often a fine line between the types of questions a company may and may not ask, and anyone involved in the hiring process should be properly trained. Washington's Human Rights Commission maintains a website that contains information on antidiscrimination and employment law, best practices, and helpful sources.

Affirmative Action. Affirmative action in employment refers to policies and procedures designed to redress past discrimination and/or improve current diversity by promoting the hiring of minorities, women, and other traditionally disadvantaged groups. Affirmative action policies vary from state to state, and they have been the subject of many legal challenges over the years. Individuals who are not members of the classes given preferential treatment under affirmative action policies have sometimes claimed reverse discrimination. **Reverse discrimination** may be alleged when a person who is objectively less qualified (based on a standardized test, for example) is chosen for a job over an objectively more qualified but non-minority applicant.

Washington is one of a few states that have ended affirmative action programs in public employment (as well as in public education and contracting). In 1998, voters passed an initiative that prohibits consideration of race, sex, color, ethnicity, and national origin in the final hiring decisions of state or local agencies.

However, while race, sex, color, ethnicity, and national origin may not be taken into account in final hiring decisions, government employers are allowed, and even encouraged, to use outreach and recruitment efforts designed to generate the largest and most diverse pool of applicants. For example, in an advertisement for a government job, stating that "Women and minorities are encouraged to apply" does not conflict with the state law restricting affirmative action programs. It's also worth remembering that this law generally does not apply to non-government employers.

New Hire Requirements. Once a company hires a new employee, it has 20 days to report the new employee to the state Department of Social and Health Services (DSHS). The employer must also comply with certain rules and regulations concerning taxes and eligibility to work in the United States.

Taxes and new employees. Every employer must have new employees sign a withholding exemption certificate (**Form W-4**) on or before the date of employment. Form W-4 is used by employers to determine the correct amount of federal income tax withholding to deduct from an employee's paycheck. The employer is responsible for forwarding the signed W-4 form on to the IRS.

States with an income tax require a similar form. Washington has no income tax, so only the federal form is required.

Verification of employment eligibility. It's illegal for employers to inquire about an applicant's United States citizenship or require an applicant to prove employment eligibility before making an offer of employment. However, within three days after hiring an employee, employers are required to complete an **Employment Eligibility Verification Form** (I-9 form). In order to complete the form, an employer must examine identification documentation supplied by the employee. The purpose of the I-9 form is to confirm the employee's citizenship or, alternatively, his eligibility to work in the United States.

Federal law prohibits employers from asking for types of documentation other than those listed on the I-9 form, or from refusing to accept any of the listed types. It is entirely up to the employee which type of listed documentation to provide.

Employers must keep all I-9 forms on file for three years after the date of hire, or for one year after the employment terminates, whichever is later. Immigration agents routinely audit businesses to confirm I-9 compliance.

Employee Compensation and Benefits

Another aspect of HR is managing employee compensation and benefits. Compensation can take several forms, including hourly wages, salary, commissions, tips, or some combination thereof.

Hourly wages are based on the number of hours worked: employees are paid a certain dollar amount per hour. As we noted earlier, federal and state laws set minimum hourly wage rates. Hourly wages are most commonly (but not always) paid to unskilled or entry-level workers.

With **salaries**, the worker is paid a fixed amount of compensation per week, month, or year, regardless of the actual number of hours worked. Salaries are most commonly paid to managerial, skilled, and professional workers.

Commissions are calculated based on a percentage of the value of the goods or services sold. In other words, the more goods or services a commissioned employee sells, the more money he makes. Commissions are typically paid to real estate agents and other types of salespersons (e.g., car salespersons, telemarketing employees, etc.). Some employers offer a base minimum wage or modest salary in addition to the commission income, but many commissioned employees are compensated solely through their commissions.

Workers in Washington must be paid on regularly established paydays at least once a month, although weekly and biweekly schedules are common. Wages must be paid in cash or in checks drawn on banks that will convert the checks into cash on demand at full face value. Wages can be paid using an alternative method, such as direct deposit, so long as there is no cost to the employee.

Real Estate Brokerage Compensation. Methods of compensating real estate agents vary from firm to firm.

Commission splits. Most brokerage firms pay their licensees under the terms of a commission split, in which the real estate commission paid by the property seller is split between the listing firm and the selling firm. Each firm will distribute a percentage of the firm's commission to the real estate licensee who worked on the transaction. The firm usually applies some portion of the fee towards operating expenses and profit.

Desk fees. One common alternative to commission splits is the 100% brokerage: agents keep 100% of the commissions they earn, but in return, they must pay a desk fee each month to cover the firm's operating expenses. The desk fee can be a substantial amount, as it needs to cover the licensee's share of the expense of the office space, equipment, utilities, etc. The desk fee must also cover the brokerage's profit.

Many firms combine commission splits with a desk fee, offering a higher commission split while also charging a modest monthly desk fee.

Salaries. A few firms have turned to treating licensees as employees, rather than independent contractors. While some might think this diminishes the licensee's competitive drive, it may be appropriate for brokerages that are more service-oriented.

Many firms opt to pay their branch managers a salary, so the branch managers aren't competing with the licensees they manage. Branch managers (and other firm employees) may have a hybrid compensation arrangement, in which they receive a bonus on top of their salary, based on a percentage of the firm's total production volume.

Benefits. As previously noted, employers are not legally required to provide health insurance or paid time off. However, many companies do provide one or more of these items as benefits.

Benefits are a form of **indirect compensation** to employees. For instance, health insurance coverage can be very expensive, and many individuals would be unable to afford the monthly premiums on their own. Companies can get lower premium rates for group plans, and they are able to pass those savings on to employees as a benefit. Some companies pay 100% of the premium cost for their employees, while others pay only a percentage of the cost. Larger real estate brokerage firms may offer their independent contractors the ability to purchase health coverage at a group rate.

Dependents of employees (such as nonworking spouses and children) may also be covered by the employer's health insurance benefit. Additional premiums for dependents are usually the employee's responsibility.

Health insurance is the most common type of insurance benefit offered to employees. Some employers also offer dental and vision coverage and/or life insurance.

As we mentioned earlier, employers in Washington are required to provide paid sick leave. Most businesses also offer employees at least some paid leave in the form of holidays and vacation time. The amount of paid leave usually depends on the length of service and position with the company. In some situations, a company may permit unpaid leave as well.

Family and Medical Leave Laws. In determining leave policies, companies should take into account federal and state laws related to family and medical leave. The federal **Family and Medical Leave Act** (FMLA) of 1993 entitles eligible employees to take up to 12 weeks of unpaid, job-protected leave in a 12-month period for specified family and medical reasons. FMLA applies to state, local and federal employers, including government agencies and schools. It also applies to private-sector employers who employed 50 or more employees in 20 or more work weeks in the current or preceding calendar year. To be eligible for FMLA benefits, an employee must have worked for a covered employer for a total of 12 months, and for at least 1,250 hours over the previous 12 months.

An employee returning from leave under the FMLA must be restored to her original position within the company, or one that is equivalent (i.e., with equivalent pay, benefits, and other terms of employment). In addition, employers must maintain group health coverage for employees who take leave under the FMLA, if such health coverage was provided before the employee's leave. However, employers may require employees to pay their share of the premiums while on unpaid leave.

Washington also has family and medical leave laws. The **Family Care Act** (FCA) allows employees with paid time off (such as for vacations and sick leave) to use that time to care for a sick family member. The **Family Leave Act** (FLA) parallels the FMLA, requiring employers to provide up to 12 weeks of unpaid job-protected leave every 12 months to eligible employees for certain family and medical reasons. Employees are eligible under the FLA if they worked at least 1,250 hours over the previous 12 months, and the company has at least 50 employees who work within 75 miles.

Under the FLA, a woman with a pregnancy-related disability is entitled to time off and job protection if she works for an employer with eight or more employees (instead of the usual 50). The amount of time needed is determined by the woman's health care provider.

Tax Reporting

As noted earlier in this chapter, employers are generally responsible for withholding and paying income, social security, and Medicare taxes for employees. Tax law is a complicated topic and there are severe penalties for noncompliance. We will only touch on the basics here; questions about employment taxes should always be referred to your tax attorney or an accountant.

Before a business hires any employees, it must obtain an **employer identification number (EIN)**, also known as an employer's tax ID, from the IRS. This EIN is used when reporting business taxes to the IRS and when reporting employee information to state agencies.

Employers who withhold income taxes, social security, and Medicare taxes must file a quarterly tax return with the IRS. In addition, employers must report compensation paid and taxes withheld for each employee to the federal government on an annual basis. This information is reported on **Form W-2**, which must be completed for any employee who receives a salary, wages, or any other form of compensation.

Employers must send a copy of the W-2 form to each employee by January 31 of the year following the reporting period. For example, a copy of the W-2 reporting an employee's 2018 wages and taxes must be given to the employee by January 31, 2019. Copy A of the W-2 form must be sent to the Social Security Administration by the last day of February (or last day of March, if filed electronically) for the previous calendar year.

Employers must keep records of employment taxes for at least four years.

Recordkeeping

Another important aspect of HR is recordkeeping. As we just mentioned, employment tax records must be kept for at least four years. Other types of employment-related records, including general employment information and performance review records, should also be maintained in a **personnel file** for each employee. Although it's not legally required, this is a good business practice and will reduce the risk of problems down the road.

At a minimum, an employee's personnel file should contain:

- a copy of the job description;
- the employee's job application, resume, references, and other application materials;
- information related to employee benefits;
- the employee's W-4 form (Employee Withholding Allowance);
- emergency contact information;
- performance reviews;
- any complaints or commendations from customers or coworkers;
- any records regarding disciplinary warnings or actions; and
- any notes regarding the employee's termination (exit interview notes, reason for termination, and so on).

Records should be accurate and thorough, and the same type of information should be noted consistently about each employee.

In Washington, employees have the right to view their personnel files at least once per year. An employer must make the personnel file available within a reasonable time after an employee's oral or written request. This right applies to former employees as well as current ones.

Performance Review Records. Performance reviews should be honest and accurate. If an unhappy ex-employee sues, performance reviews will be one of the first places a court will look for evidence of discriminatory treatment. In the event of a layoff, well-kept records can support the employer's claim that the layoff was based on objective criteria and not on discriminatory factors.

Employers should use standard review forms so that all employees are evaluated using the same basic criteria and scoring (if a performance score is assigned).

Privacy. Some forms should not be kept in personnel files. This includes I-9 forms, which should be kept together in a single file for ready inspection by U.S. immigration agents. In the event of an audit, having the forms in a separate file will make the process much smoother and will protect the other information in employees' files.

Records containing medical information should also not be kept in employee personnel files. This includes workers' compensation claims, information related to disabilities under the ADA, any records regarding a medical leave (such as one under the FMLA), doctors' notes, drug and alcohol testing results, medical evaluations, and medical questionnaires.

Records relating to the ADA and FMLA must be kept in a separate, secure location. Access should be available only to supervisors with relevant questions (such as how to make a reasonable accommodation under the ADA) and HR staff trained in privacy issues.

Disciplinary Procedures and Termination

No matter how carefully a business has screened and trained new employees and explained behavior expectations in the employee handbook, at some point it will probably become necessary to discipline or fire an employee. Informal reminders of office procedures may be the first reaction to a minor behavior problem. However, consistent errors—no matter how trivial—or a breach of a legal requirement should be met with a more formal tactic: the disciplinary meeting.

Disciplinary meetings should be viewed as an opportunity for dialogue and a greater understanding of the needs of both parties, rather than as simply a one-way lecture or avenue for handing out punishment.

Steps in the disciplinary meeting should include:

- **Identifying and studying the problem.** The first step is to determine exactly what the problem is and what the facts are.
- **Describing the problem.** The problem should be outlined in a factual manner.
- **Gathering information.** The supervisor should ask questions, as she's unlikely to know all the details about the situation; the entire problem could be a matter of misinterpretation.
- **Reaching agreement on the problem.** It's impossible to move toward a solution unless both the supervisor and employee agree that a problem exists.

- **Developing mutually acceptable alternatives.** The supervisor needs to find a solution that the employee is willing to adopt, but also must reject any alternatives that don't benefit the firm.
- **Creating a course of action.** The supervisor and employee should agree on a time frame for implementing the solution. There should be a follow-up meeting in order to evaluate the success of the plan.
- **Documenting the proceedings.** Because a disciplinary meeting may lead to internal disciplinary measure or even termination, it's important to keep a written record of the meeting.

Disciplinary meetings are often very helpful in correcting undesirable behavior. However, they could also result in resignation, or, if the behavior doesn't change, a termination. Termination should take place only after a series of disciplinary meetings aimed at fixing problematic behaviors. Even in the case of one particularly egregious act, it's better to suspend the employee as a first step, and then take documented disciplinary measures.

Exit Interview. While resignation or termination usually isn't the desired outcome, it may be necessary if the employee simply isn't meeting the performance standards of the company. Regardless of whether the employee resigns or is terminated, it's helpful to conduct an exit interview before the employee leaves the firm. An exit interview is a good opportunity to end a working relationship on a positive note: if the employee is treated with respect and he feels that his opinion is valued, he will be more likely to view the company in a positive light as he pursues other employment options.

It's a good idea to have a neutral person or HR handle the exit interview. The goal of the interview is to allow the employee to speak candidly about his feelings about the company and the reasons for his departure. The exit interview questions and answers should be carefully documented.

Termination of a Real Estate Affiliation. If a real estate licensee decides to terminate her affiliation with a brokerage firm, or if a firm decides to terminate a licensee, it's important to comply with license law requirements.

The relationship between a firm and a licensee can be terminated unilaterally by either party with written notice to the other party. At one time, paper forms were used for this process, but now the Washington Department of Licensing offers an online system that simplifies notification. When a broker uses the online system to separate from a firm, the DOL automatically sends an email notification to the designated broker. The broker's license is inactive until she becomes affiliated with another firm.

If a brokerage firm ends an affiliation with a licensee because the licensee violated the license law, the firm must immediately send a written statement of the facts of the violation and termination to the Director.

Discrimination and Sexual Harassment Claims

The same federal and state laws that prohibit discrimination in interviewing and hiring also require nondiscriminatory treatment of employees once they're hired. Working conditions, compensation, and other aspects of employment must not vary depending on the race, gender, or other protected characteristics of the employees. The laws prohibit disparate treatment, meaning that an employer may not treat an employee in a protected class differently from other employees.

> **Example:** ABC Realty fires Jeff, an African-American licensee, when he violates a minor provision of the company's policies and procedures manual. But when Mark, a white licensee, commits the same violation, he is only reprimanded. ABC Realty may be found guilty of discrimination on the basis of race.

Another frequent cause of employment-related lawsuits is sexual harassment. **Sexual harassment** is any sort of unwelcome sexual advance or other sexual conduct that makes the workplace intimidating or hostile.

The line between what is and isn't harassment is sometimes difficult to discern. For instance, a single act may be considered sexual harassment if it is severe (such as unwanted touching), while less invasive conduct (such as romantic invitations) may be considered sexual harassment if it is part of a pattern of behavior. A company's employee handbook should include objective standards for unacceptable office behavior; concrete examples are particularly helpful. In addition, it's a good idea for the handbook to establish a procedure for reporting harassment.

Handling Claims. Claims of discrimination and sexual harassment should be taken very seriously, as both can lead to lawsuits. Of course the best practice is to institute policies and procedures that prevent such situations from happening in the first place. But when discrimination or sexual harassment claims do occur, how they are handled can determine company liability.

When faced with a claim, the first step is to investigate it immediately. Many companies have a hard time believing that discrimination or harassment is occurring in their workplaces; as a result, they may not take complaints seriously. However, every claim of discrimination or harassment should be thoroughly investigated, even if it appears trivial. The parties involved should not be treated differently based on their time with the company, whether they are top producers, or other such factors.

When handling a discrimination or harassment claim, it's also important to:

- **Treat the person making the complaint with respect.** When the employee feels that the company is taking her complaint seriously, she is less likely to feel compelled to file a lawsuit.

- **Never retaliate against the complainer.** It's against the law to punish someone for complaining about discrimination or harassment. For example, it's illegal to fire the employee or cut his pay (or threaten to do either). It's also illegal to reduce his work hours, change his shift or job responsibilities to less desirable ones, or to isolate him from meetings and other shared activities.
- **Follow established procedures.** The employee handbook or policies and procedures manual should establish a process for filing and handling complaints, and this process should be followed every time.
- **Interview the people involved.** Take careful notes of all the details, look for contradiction or corroboration, and make copies of all relevant documents, emails, or other physical evidence.
- **Keep all information confidential.** Keeping all information confidential protects the parties involved as well as the company.
- **Document everything.** Record the dates and times of interviews and when documents were received. Write down detailed explanations of any action taken against the accused, or the reasons why no action was taken. This may protect the company if the victim later claims that the company failed to act properly.
- **Cooperate with government agencies.** If the victim makes a complaint with a government agency, an investigation will probably follow. Cooperate by providing access to all pertinent records. It's also a good idea to seek advice from an attorney.
- **Take appropriate action against the accused.** In some cases, additional training or counseling may be appropriate; in other cases, termination may be warranted. Document the decision thoroughly.

Mediation and Arbitration of Disputes

It is inevitable for disputes to arise in the workplace. Employees may disagree with one another, or an employee and employer may argue about a reprimand or other disciplinary action. When these kinds of issues cannot be resolved informally between the parties, costly lawsuits can result. However, there is another option. Many companies are turning to **alternative dispute resolution** (ADR) to resolve workplace problems.

ADR generally takes two forms: mediation and arbitration. The parties may voluntarily decide to use these methods, or they may be required to do so by the employee handbook, by the terms of the employment contract, or by law.

Mediation. Mediation is essentially negotiation with a referee, and does not involve a formal hearing. The mediation results are not necessarily binding on the parties.

Mediation is an attractive option for many businesses. It's cost-effective, relatively quick, and allows both parties to work on a solution together. The presence of a neutral third party can make employees feel more at ease. This is especially true when the dispute involves an employee and a supervisor. The presence of a mediator can help level the playing field, diffuse animosity, and allow both sides to reach a fair solution.

The HR department of a larger company may have a trained mediator on staff to handle employee problems. Smaller businesses, or those without HR departments, may use an outside mediation service.

Arbitration. When mediation doesn't work, many businesses turn to arbitration next. (Some businesses skip mediation and go straight to arbitration.) Arbitration resembles a trial, but the hearing is not held in a courtroom or presided over by a judge. The results are typically binding on the parties. Arbitration may be contractually required or it may be court-ordered.

While arbitration is more formal and adversarial than mediation, it is still less expensive and time-consuming than a trial. The proceedings are also private, which means that businesses can keep potentially damaging information out of the public eye. Some businesses allow employees to choose non-binding arbitration. In this case, a party who is unhappy with the result is free to pursue his claim through the court system.

Supervision and Liability for Employees' Actions

In certain circumstances, an employer can be held liable for the acts of an employee. Understanding the legal theories under which this may occur can help employers avoid liability. Additionally, brokerage firms must fulfill the supervisory responsibilities that are imposed on them by the real estate license law.

Theories of Liability

Employers can be held liable for the actions of an employee under two general legal theories: respondeat superior and negligent hiring or retention. The doctrine of **respondeat superior** (Latin for "let the superior answer") applies when the employee is acting within the course and scope of his employment. In other words, the employer will usually be liable for an employee's actions if the employee was doing his job or acting on the employer's behalf at the time the incident occurred. The respondeat superior doctrine gives employers a financial incentive to supervise and train employees properly, and take other risk-reduction measures that will help protect the public.

An employer may also be liable for an employee's actions under the theory of negligent hiring or negligent retention. An injured person may sue an employer for **negligent hiring** when it fails to take reasonable care when hiring a worker.

> **Example:** A real estate brokerage hired an office manager who had ready access to the codes used to access MLS keyboxes. Over the next three months, there was a string of burglaries of listed properties. After the office manager was caught, a background check revealed a lengthy criminal history of convictions for theft and burglary. A simple background check would have revealed this information, so the owners of the burglarized homes may be able to sue the company for negligent hiring.

An employer may also be liable for an employee's actions under a theory of **negligent retention**—that is, the failure of the company to take appropriate action when it learns that an employee may be dangerous.

> **Example:** Returning to our previous example, let's say that the real estate firm decides to conduct a background check on all its current employees. During the background check, the company discovers the office manager's criminal history, but does nothing about it. If the office manager burglarizes a listed property, the company can probably be sued for negligent retention.

While the doctrine of respondeat superior holds employers responsible for an employee's actions only if the actions were within the course and scope of the employee's job, employers can be sued for negligent hiring or negligent retention even when the employee's actions were outside the scope of his job.

> **Example:** Superior Television Repair hires Phil, who has a criminal record of rape and assault. Part of Phil's job involves going to customers' homes to make repairs. While on the job, Phil assaults one of Superior's customers. The victim probably won't be able to sue Superior under a theory of respondeat superior, since Phil's actions were outside the scope of his employment. But she can probably sue Superior under the theory of negligent hiring or (if Superior knew of Phil's criminal history) under the theory of negligent retention.

Finally, an employer will be responsible for negligent hiring or negligent retention only if the employer knew (or should have known) that the employee was unsuitable for the job. In our example above, if Phil was using an assumed name and Superior's background check on him came up clean, Superior probably wouldn't be responsible even if a later more thorough investigation revealed Phil's criminal history.

One of the most important steps an employer can take to protect itself from this kind of liability is to perform a background check before hiring a new employee. This is especially important when the employee will have access to medical or other sensitive information, children or the elderly, or the homes of clients or customers.

Brokerage Firm's Supervisory Responsibilities

Now let's look at the supervisory responsibilities that brokerage firms have towards their licensees. As discussed in Chapter 2, the designated broker is responsible for making sure that the firm itself and all those who perform brokerage services for the firm are properly licensed. Furthermore, the designated broker must maintain a written policy addressing the levels of supervision that apply to all managing brokers and brokers affiliated with the firm. (For example, the designated broker owes a heightened duty of supervision over brokers who have been licensed for less than two years.)

The designated broker must also make sure that all transaction documents are properly reviewed. In particular, all purchase and sale agreements and lease agreements filled out by licensees with less than two years of experience must be reviewed, initialed, and dated by the designated broker (or the managing broker who has been delegated this task) within five days of execution.

Conclusion

The extent to which workers are protected by employment laws depends in part on whether they are classified as employees, contingent workers, or independent contractors. State and federal laws establish a minimum wage and impose rules regarding overtime pay and workplace safety. Other laws protect workers from discriminatory hiring and employment practices and provide for workers' compensation and unemployment benefits. To avoid liability, employers must ensure that their practices regarding interviewing, hiring, compensation, benefits, tax withholding and reporting, recordkeeping, and supervision comply with these laws.

Case Problem

The following is a hypothetical case problem. Most of the facts are taken from a real case. Make a decision on the issues presented and then check to see if your answer matches the decision reached by the court.

The Facts

Thomas works for a large software company as a systems engineer. His job consists of working closely with large computer manufacturers and involves lots of travel, a flexible work schedule, and work weeks that frequently average about 60 hours.

After several years with the company, Thomas is diagnosed with hepatitis C. After a 6-week medical leave, Thomas submits a letter from his doctor and requests that his work schedule be reduced to no more than 8 hours a day and no more than 40 hours a week. The company agrees to this on a temporary basis while it evaluates how to accommodate Thomas over the long term.

A few weeks later, Thomas asks to drop one of his two accounts because handling both in a 40-hour week is impossible. His manager agrees to this temporary change and removes the larger account. The remaining account comprises less than 50% of Thomas's original workload.

After clarifying Thomas's restrictions with his physician, the company assigns Thomas a human resources representative (Marcotte) who will check into open positions within the Product Support Services group (PSS) that are similar to Thomas's current job, but that are more structured, accommodate a regular work week, and have less customer demands and stress. In addition, a PSS position will allow Thomas to maintain his salary and benefits.

Alternatively, if Thomas isn't interested in a PSS position, the company will offer him either a 6-week paid job search or an unpaid 6-month search to find another position within the company.

An open PSS position is found, but Thomas isn't interested and doesn't apply. He also refuses to choose either the 6-week paid job search option or the 6-month unpaid job-search option, so the company chooses the latter for him. During this 6-month period, Thomas has access to:

- the company's job search bank from his home,
- an office at the company from which to conduct a job search, and
- the services of Marcotte and another internal resources specialist (Clement) to aid him in his search.

Thomas doesn't contact Marcotte or Clement during the first 4 months. During the last 2 months, Clement tries repeatedly to contact Thomas by phone and email. When she does speak to him, Thomas expresses interest only in his old job, even though Clement tells him his old job cannot be made to accommodate him. Thomas doesn't search for employment anywhere else.

After the 6-month period ends, the company terminates Thomas's employment. Thomas then sues the company under Washington's Law Against Discrimination for failure to reasonably accommodate his disability.

The Questions

Was the company required to alter Thomas's original job to reasonably accommodate his desire to remain a systems engineer? Was the company's attempt to find Thomas a similar job within the company a reasonable accommodation under the law?

The Answer

In order to prove that the company failed to reasonably accommodate his disability, Thomas would have to show that 1) he had a sensory, mental, or physical abnormality that substantially limited his ability to perform his job; 2) he was qualified to perform the essential functions of the job in question; 3) he gave the employer notice of the abnormality and its limitations; and 4) upon notice, the company failed to take steps to accommodate the abnormality. At issue in Thomas's case are the second and fourth tests.

The ADA define the essential functions of a job as the fundamental job duties of the employment position the disabled individual holds or desires. The court found that the essential functions of Thomas's job included working a varying number of hours per day, frequent out-of-state travel, and working an average of over 40 hours per week.

Because Thomas was not able to do those things, he was unable to perform the essential functions of his job. This was supported by the fact that when his hours dropped to 8 per day and 40 per week, he needed to drop one of his accounts to compensate for the shorter work week.

The court went on to state that Washington law doesn't require an employer to alter the essential functions of a job to accommodate a disabled employee. In other words, the court would not redefine the systems engineer position to accommodate Thomas.

Thomas also asserted that the company failed to accommodate his disability by transferring him to a another position.

An employer is required to take affirmative steps to assist the employee in the job search by determining the extent of the employee's disability, inviting the employee to receive personal help from the employer's personnel office, and by sharing all openings in the office with the employee. The employee also has a duty to inform the employer of his qualifications, apply for all jobs which might fit his abilities, and accept reasonable work he can perform.

In this case, the company took a variety of steps to assist Thomas, including asking his doctor about his limitations, giving him six months to conduct a job search, providing Marcotte and Clement to assist his job search, and allowing him access to the company's computerized job bank. (Whether those steps were sufficient was a question for the jury, and the case was remanded to the trial court to settle that fourth issue.) *Davis v. Microsoft*, 149 Wn.2d 521 (2003).

Chapter Summary

- Employers may choose to staff their companies with employees, independent contractors, or contingent workers. If a worker is an employee, then the employer is responsible for withholding and paying income tax, social security, and Medicare for each employee. Which label an employer applies to a worker is not as important as the substance of their relationship: if the employer has the right to control what the worker will do and how it will be done, then the worker is an employee.

- Federal employment laws include the Fair Labor Standards Act, which sets a minimum wage and requires overtime pay for all nonexempt employees; the Occupational Safety and Health Act, which regulates workplace safety; the Americans with Disabilities Act, which prohibits discrimination based on disability in hiring and employment; the Employee Retirement Income Security Act, which establishes fiduciary duties for those who manage employee benefits; and the Consolidated Omnibus Budget Reconciliation Act, which extends a former employee's group health benefit when it would otherwise have terminated.

- Washington's laws concerning fair labor practices cover many of the same areas as the federal Fair Labor Standards Act, but Washington's laws impose stricter requirements and apply to more workers.

- Employers are responsible for paying unemployment taxes and workers' compensation premiums for their employees. Brokerage firms are exempt from paying unemployment taxes for independent contractors, but must pay workers' compensation premiums whether their workers are employees or independent contractors.

- Managing human resources includes preparing an employee handbook that explains policies and procedures; interviewing and hiring; providing compensation and benefits; tax compliance; recordkeeping; discipline and termination; handling discrimination and sexual harassment claims; and mediation and arbitration of disputes.

- An employer is legally responsible for an employee's misconduct and negligence when the incident occurs within the course and scope of the employment. An employer may also be liable for an employee's actions outside the scope of employment under a theory of negligent hiring or retention, if the employer knew or should have known that the employee was dangerous.

Checklist of Problem Areas

Employer's Checklist

❑   Are your workers employees or independent contractors by law? If you are using contingent workers, who is responsible for withholding taxes, paying benefits, and performing other administrative tasks?

❑   Are your employees exempt or nonexempt? Does your compensation plan meet federal and state minimum wage and overtime requirements? Do you have proper recordkeeping procedures in place to track employee hours, overtime, wages, and deductions?

❑   Do you have an OSHA safety poster on display in your workplace? Is your business exempt from recordkeeping requirements?

❑   Do your recruitment ads, job applications, interview questions, and employment procedures comply with the Americans with Disabilities Act? Do you have procedures in place to reasonably accommodate employees who are disabled?

❑   If you provide health benefits and pension funds, do you have minimum standards in place to protect employee assets and privacy? Do you understand your responsibilities under COBRA in the event an employee is terminated or is going through a divorce?

❑   Are you paying unemployment taxes and workers' compensation premiums on all covered workers?

❑   Did you report new hires within 20 days, have new hires sign a W-4 form, and check each new employee's identification and fill out an I-9 form?

❑   Do you understand your responsibilities under the Family and Medical Leave Act and the Family Care Act?

❑   Do you have procedures in place to comply with all federal and state tax laws? Do you make quarterly payments and keep the appropriate records for each employee?

❑   Do your personnel files contain the appropriate documents? Are you protecting employees' privacy by storing medical-related and disability-related documentation in a separate, secure location?

❑   Do you have procedures in place for handling discrimination and harassment complaints, conducting employee performance reviews, taking disciplinary action, and terminating employees when necessary?

❑ Are you properly supervising your employees? If their jobs will bring them in contact with children, the elderly, sensitive information, or the homes of clients or customers, have you performed a background check and taken other steps to prevent harm and help ensure that you won't be liable for negligent hiring or retention?

Applicant/Employee's Checklist

❑ If you are an independent contractor, do you understand that it's your responsibility to pay employment taxes and provide your own benefits?

❑ Are you an exempt or nonexempt employee? Are you paid at least the state minimum wage, and do you receive overtime pay if you work more than 40 hours in a single week? Are you allowed the meal and rest breaks and paid sick leave required by law?

❑ Does your place of work comply with OSHA safety and reporting requirements? Is there a procedure in place for reporting injuries or illness on the job?

❑ If you are a disabled worker, do you understand your rights with regard to hiring and employment? What are the essential functions of your job? Do you understand what a reasonable accommodation is, and when employers are required to accommodate your disability?

❑ If you've been injured on the job, are you eligible for workers' compensation? If you or a family member is sick or pregnant, do you know your rights under the Family and Medical Leave Act and the Family Care Act?

❑ If you've recently been terminated, do you understand your rights under COBRA? Do you know whether you are eligible for unemployment compensation?

Chapter Quiz

1. Sarah was hired by Software Giant to develop marketing materials for a new product, and she's paid $20 an hour. Sarah uses her own equipment to create the ads, works from her home office, and presents the completed materials to Software Giant at the end of her assignment. Sarah is most likely a/an:

   a. nonexempt employee, because she is paid by the hour
   b. exempt employee, because she is paid by the hour
   c. leased worker, because her assignment is temporary
   d. independent contractor, because she uses her own judgment to decide how the job will be done

2. Jim is an office worker for Mega Real Estate in Spokane. Mega:

   a. may call Jim an independent contractor and pay him $5 an hour
   b. must pay Jim at least as much as the federal minimum wage
   c. must pay Jim at least as much as the state minimum wage
   d. must pay Jim at least as much as the federal or state minimum wage, whichever is less

3. Which of the following phrases in a job posting would violate fair employment laws?

   a. Recent graduate
   b. Waitstaff wanted
   c. Degree required
   d. Neat and well-groomed

4. COBRA applies to employers with _____ or more employees.

   a. 1
   b. 11
   c. 20
   d. 50

5. A real estate firm included this statement in a job posting: "Women and minorities encouraged to apply." This was:

   a. an illegal example of affirmative action
   b. a legal example of affirmative action
   c. illegal, because it discouraged male Caucasians from applying
   d. legal, because it encouraged a diverse pool of applicants

6. Which of the following would be illegal to ask on a job application?

   a. The applicant's date of birth
   b. Whether the applicant can perform the essential functions of the job
   c. The applicant's national origin
   d. The applicant's ability to speak fluent Spanish

7. Employers in Washington must report new hires to the state within _____ day(s).

   a. 1
   b. 7
   c. 10
   d. 20

8. Which of the following is an example of indirect compensation?

   a. Health insurance coverage for full-time workers
   b. Commission earned for selling 20 units
   c. Salary earned for the month
   d. Overtime pay

9. The Family and Medical Leave Act entitles eligible employees to take up to _____ in a 12-month period to care for a newborn child.

   a. 12 weeks of paid leave
   b. 12 weeks of unpaid leave
   c. 26 weeks of paid leave
   d. 26 weeks of unpaid leave

10. Employers who withhold income taxes, social security, and Medicare taxes must file a _____ tax return with the IRS.

    a. monthly
    b. quarterly
    c. twice-yearly
    d. annual

11. An employee accidentally injures a pedestrian while making a delivery for the company. The employer may be held liable for the employee's action under the doctrine of:

    a. lis pendens
    b. negligent hiring
    c. respondeat superior
    d. restitution

12. The Fair Labor Standards Act requires which of the following:

    a. sick pay
    b. holiday pay
    c. overtime pay for nonexempt employees
    d. eight-hour days for nonexempt employees

13. Employers are exempt from paying unemployment taxes on all of the following, except:

    a. independent contractors
    b. a handyman hired to do some painting for a few hours
    c. church employees
    d. real estate agents

14. A real estate agent can generally be considered to be a:

    a. leased worker
    b. statutory nonemployee
    c. joint employee
    d. contingent worker

15. An employer must get an employment identification number (EIN):

    a. before hiring any employees
    b. annually
    c. before filing quarterly tax returns
    d. before filing the company's annual tax return

Chapter Quiz Answer Key

Chapter 1

1. d
2. a
3. b
4. c
5. a
6. d
7. a
8. c
9. d
10. b
11. c
12. a
13. c
14. b
15. a
16. d
17. c
18. d
19. b
20. d
21. b
22. a
23. b
24. c
25. d

Chapter 2

1. b
2. d
3. a
4. c
5. d
6. a
7. c
8. a
9. d
10. b
11. b
12. d
13. c
14. a
15. d

Chapter 3

1. b
2. c
3. a
4. b
5. b
6. c
7. b
8. c
9. c
10. c
11. b
12. c
13. b
14. a
15. b

Chapter 4

1. b
2. b
3. c
4. c
5. b
6. b
7. a
8. c
9. b
10. a
11. c
12. d
13. c
14. d
15. d

Chapter 5

1. a
2. c
3. b
4. d
5. b
6. c
7. a
8. d
9. a
10. b
11. c
12. a
13. a
14. d
15. b

Chapter 6

1. c
2. b
3. d
4. b
5. d
6. d
7. b
8. b
9. b
10. c
11. a
12. b
13. d
14. d
15. c

Chapter 7

1. c
2. b
3. a
4. b
5. d
6. a
7. b
8. b
9. b
10. b
11. c
12. d
13. b
14. d
15. c

Chapter 8	Chapter 9	Chapter 10	Chapter 11
1. b	1. b	1. c	1. d
2. c	2. c	2. d	2. b
3. d	3. c	3. d	3. c
4. a	4. d	4. d	4. b
5. d	5. c	5. d	5. a
6. b	6. a	6. a	6. d
7. c	7. b	7. b	7. d
8. b	8. c	8. c	8. c
9. c	9. d	9. c	9. a
10. c	10. c	10. d	10. b
11. a	11. b	11. d	11. b
12. b	12. b	12. a	12. d
13. b	13. c	13. b	13. a
14. d	14. b	14. b	14. c
15. a	15. b	15. b	15. a

Chapter 12	Chapter 13	Chapter 14	Chapter 15
1. b	1. c	1. d	1. d
2. b	2. b	2. c	2. c
3. c	3. d	3. c	3. a
4. c	4. b	4. b	4. c
5. d	5. b	5. a	5. d
6. d	6. c	6. c	6. c
7. a	7. b	7. d	7. d
8. a	8. a	8. b	8. a
9. c	9. c	9. a	9. b
10. b	10. c	10. b	10. b
11. a	11. a	11. a	11. c
12. d	12. b	12. c	12. c
13. b	13. d	13. c	13. b
14. b	14. d	14. b	14. b
15. b	15. b	15. d	15. a

Glossary

Abandonment—Failure to occupy and use property, which may result in loss of rights.

Absolute Fee—*See:* Fee Simple.

Abstract of Judgment—A summary of the provisions of a court judgment which, when recorded, creates a lien on all of the real property of the debtor within the county where recorded.

Abstract of Title—A brief, chronological summary of the recorded documents affecting the title to a particular piece of property.

Abut—To touch, border on, be adjacent to, or share a common boundary with.

Acceptance—1. Agreeing to the terms of an offer to enter into a contract, thereby creating a binding contract. 2. Taking delivery of a deed from the grantor.

Accord and Satisfaction—An agreement to accept something different than, and usually less than, what was called for in the original agreement.

Accretion—A gradual addition to dry land by the forces of nature, as when waterborne sediment is deposited on waterfront property.

Acknowledgment—When a person who has signed a document formally declares to an authorized official, such as a notary public or county clerk, that he signed willingly. The official can then attest that the signature is voluntary and genuine.

Acre—An area of land equal to 43,560 square feet, or 4,840 square yards. There are 640 acres in a section of land in the government survey system.

Actual Notice—Actual knowledge of a fact, as opposed to knowledge imputed by law.

ADA—*See:* Americans with Disabilities Act.

Adjacent—Nearby, next to, bordering, or neighboring; may or may not be in actual contact.

Administrator—A person appointed by the probate court to manage and distribute the estate of a deceased person when no executor is named in the will, or there is no will.

Ad Valorem—A Latin phrase meaning "according to value," used to refer to taxes assessed on the value of property. Ad valorem taxes are also known as general real estate taxes.

Adverse Possession—Acquiring title to real property owned by someone else, by means of open, notorious, exclusive, continuous and uninterrupted possession of the property, in a manner hostile to the title of the owner, for ten years. If the adverse possessor is claiming under color of title and has paid all taxes assessed on the property, the time period is only seven years.

Affirm—1. To confirm or ratify. 2. To make a solemn declaration that is not under oath.

Affirmative Action—Employment or educational policies and procedures designed to redress past discrimination and/or improve current diversity by promoting the hiring of minorities, women, and other traditionally disadvantaged groups.

After-Acquired Title—Title acquired by a grantor after she attempted to convey an interest in property that she did not own.

Age Discrimination in Employment Act—A federal law that prohibits employment discrimination based on age.

Agency—A relationship of trust created when one person, the principal, delegates to another, the agent, authority to represent the principal in dealings with third parties.

Agency, Apparent—When third parties are given the impression that someone who has not been authorized to represent another is that person's agent, or else given the impression that an agent has been authorized to perform acts which are in fact beyond the scope of his authority. Also called ostensible agency.

Agency, Dual—When an agent represents both parties to a transaction, as when a real estate agent represents both the buyer and the seller.

Agency, Exclusive—*See:* Listing, Exclusive Agency.

Agency, Ostensible—*See:* Agency, Apparent.

Agency Coupled With an Interest—When an agent has a claim against the property that is the subject of the agency, so that the principal cannot revoke the agent's authority.

Agent—A person authorized to represent another (the principal) in dealings with third parties.

Agent, Dual—*See:* Agency, Dual.

Agent, General—An agent authorized to handle all of the principal's affairs in one area or in specified areas.

Agent, Special—An agent with limited authority to do a specific thing or conduct a specific transaction.

Agent, Universal—An agent authorized to do everything that can be lawfully delegated to a representative.

Agreement—*See:* Contract.

Air Lot—A parcel of property above the surface of the earth, not containing any land; for example, a condominium unit on the third floor.

Air Rights—The right to undisturbed use and control of the airspace over a given parcel of land; may be transferred separately from the land.

Alienation—The transfer of title, ownership, or an interest in property from one person to another, by any means.

Alienation, Involuntary—Transfer of an interest in property against the will of the owner, or without action by the owner, occurring by operation of law, through natural processes, or by adverse possession.

Alienation, Voluntary—Voluntary transfer of real property from one person to another.

Alluvion—The solid material deposited along a river bank or shore by accretion. Also called alluvium.

Alternative Dispute Resolution (ADR)—Using mediation or arbitration to resolve a legal dispute as an alternative to a courtroom trial.

Amenities—Features of a property that contribute to the pleasure or convenience of owning it, such as proximity to public transportation, schools, or shopping, as well as panoramic views, architectural excellence, or the prestige that goes with living in a given community.

Americans with Disabilities Act (ADA)—A federal law that prohibits employment discrimination based on disability, and mandates equal access to public accommodations for the disabled.

Annexation, Actual—When personal property is physically attached to real property, so that it becomes part of the real property.

Annexation, Constructive—When personal property becomes associated with real property in such a way that the law treats it as a fixture, even though it is not physically attached; for example, a house key is constructively annexed to the house.

Answer—In a lawsuit, the defendant's response to the plaintiff's complaint.

Anticipatory Repudiation—When one party to a contract informs the other before the time set for performance that he does not intend to fulfill the terms of the contract.

Appeal—When one of the parties to a lawsuit asks a higher court to review the judgment or verdict reached in a lower court.

Appellant—The party appealing a decision or ruling. Also called the petitioner.

Appellee—In an appeal, the party who did not file the appeal. Also called the respondent.

Apportionment—A division of property (as among tenants in common when the property is sold or partitioned) or liability (as when responsibility for closing costs is allocated between the buyer and the seller) into proportionate, but not necessarily equal, parts.

Appraisal—An estimate or opinion of the value of a piece of property as of a certain date. Also called a valuation.

Appraiser—One who estimates the value of real or personal property, especially an expert qualified to do so by training and experience.

Appreciation—An increase in value; the opposite of depreciation.

Appropriation—Taking property or reducing it to personal possession, to the exclusion of others.

Appropriation, Prior—A system of allocating water rights, under which a person who wants to use water from a certain lake or river in a way that will diminish the quantity or flow is required to apply for a permit. The permit will have priority over other permits that are issued later. *Compare:* Riparian Rights.

Appropriative Rights—The water rights of a person who holds an appropriation permit.

Appurtenances—Rights that go along with ownership of a particular piece of property, such as air rights or mineral rights; they are ordinarily transferred with the property, but may, in some cases, be sold separately.

Appurtenances, Intangible—Rights that go with ownership of real property which do not involve physical objects or substances; for example, an access easement (as opposed to mineral rights).

Arbitration—Submitting a disputed matter to a private party (rather than to the judicial system) for resolution.

Area—1. Locale or region. 2. The size of a surface, usually stated in square units of measure, such as square feet or square miles.

Artificial Person—A person created by law, with legal rights and responsibilities, such as a corporation, as distinguished from a natural person (a human being). *Compare:* Natural person.

Assessment—1. The valuation of property for taxation. 2. A non-recurring specific charge against property for a definite purpose, such as curbs or sewers. Usually called a special assessment.

Assessor—An official who determines the value of property for purposes of taxation.

Asset—Anything of value that a person owns.

Assign—To transfer rights or interests to another.

Assignee—One to whom rights or interests have been assigned.

Assignment—1. A transfer of contract rights from one person to another. 2. In the case of a lease, when the original tenant transfers her entire leasehold estate to another. *Compare:* Sublease.

Assignment of Contract and Deed—The instrument used to substitute a new vendor for the original vendor in a land contract.

Assignor—One who has assigned her rights or interests to another.

Assumption—When a buyer takes on personal liability for paying off the seller's existing mortgage or deed of trust.

Attachment—Court-ordered seizure of property belonging to a defendant in a lawsuit, so that it will be available to satisfy a judgment if the plaintiff wins. In the case of real property, attachment creates a lien.

Attachments, Man-Made—*See:* Fixture.

Attachments, Natural—Plants growing on a piece of land, such as trees, shrubs, or crops.

Attestation—The act of witnessing the execution of an instrument (such as a deed or will).

Attorney in Fact—Any person authorized to represent another by a power of attorney; not necessarily a lawyer (an attorney at law).

Authority, Actual—Authority actually given to an agent by the principal, either expressly or by implication.

Authority, Apparent—Authority to represent another that someone appears to have, although no actual authority has been granted.

Authority, Express—Authority that is specifically communicated from the principal to the agent, either orally or in writing.

Authority, Implied—An agent's authority to do everything reasonably necessary to carry out the principal's express orders.

Avulsion—1. When land is suddenly (not gradually) torn away by the action of water. 2. A sudden shift in a watercourse.

Bankruptcy—1. When the liabilities of a person, firm, or corporation exceed its assets. 2. When a court declares a person, firm, or corporation to be insolvent, so that the assets and debts will be administered under the bankruptcy laws.

Bargain and Sale Deed—A deed that conveys title but does not make the same promises as a full warranty deed.

Base Line—In the government survey system, a main east-west line from which township lines are established. Each principal meridian has one base line associated with it.

Bench Mark—A surveyor's mark on a stationary object at a known point of elevation, used as a reference point in calculating other elevations in a surveyed area; often a metal disk set into cement or rock.

Beneficiary—1. One for whom a trust is created and on whose behalf the trustee administers the trust. 2. One entitled to receive real or personal property under a will; a devisee or legatee. 3. The lender in a deed of trust transaction.

Bequeath—To transfer personal property to another by will.

Bequest—Personal property (including money) that is transferred by a will.

Bilateral Contract—*See:* Contract, Bilateral.

Bill—A proposed law introduced in either house of Congress or a state legislature.

Bill of Sale—A document used to transfer title to personal property from one person to another.

Block—In a subdivision, a group of lots surrounded by streets or unimproved land.

Blockbusting—Attempting to induce owners to list or sell their homes by predicting that members of another race or ethnic group, or people suffering from some disability, will be moving into the neighborhood, with the suggestion that this will lower property values. Also called panic selling.

Bona Fide—In good faith; not fraudulent.

Boundary—The perimeter or border of a parcel of land; the dividing line between one piece of property and another.

Bounds—Boundaries. *See:* Metes and Bounds Description.

Branch Manager—A managing broker appointed by a firm's designated broker to manage the operations of a branch office.

Breach—Violation of an obligation, duty, or law.

Breach, Material—A breach of contract serious enough that the other party is excused from performing her side of the bargain.

Breach of Contract—The unexcused failure to perform according to the terms of a contract.

Broker—A licensed individual acting on behalf of a real estate firm to perform real estate brokerage services, under the supervision of a designated and/or managing broker.

Broker, Designated—A person licensed as a managing broker, who registers with the state to have a designated broker endorsement added to their license. May represent one or more firms, and will have ultimate responsibility for all firm activities.

Broker, Managing—A licensed individual with at least three years' experience as a broker who has passed the managing broker exam; a managing broker performs brokerage services for a firm, under the supervision of a designated broker.

Brokerage—*See:* Real Estate Firm.

Brokerage Fee—The commission or other compensation charged for a real estate agent's services.

Building Codes—Rules set up by local governments regarding minimum construction standards.

Building Restrictions—Rules concerning building size, placement, or type; they may be public restrictions (in a zoning ordinance, for example) or private restrictions (CC&Rs, for example).

Bump Clause—A provision in a purchase and sale agreement that allows the seller to keep the property on the market while waiting for a contingency clause to be fulfilled; if the seller receives another good offer in the meantime, he can require the buyer to either waive the contingency clause or terminate the contract.

Bundle of Rights—The rights inherent in ownership of real property, including the right to use, lease, enjoy, encumber, will, sell, or do nothing with the property.

Business Opportunity—A business that is for sale.

Buyer Representation Agreement—An employment contract between a buyer and a real estate firm in which the firm agrees to act as the buyer's agent in the search for a property to purchase.

Call—In a metes and bounds description, a specification that describes a segment of the boundary; for example, "south 15° west 120 feet" is a call.

Cancellation—Termination of a contract without undoing acts that have already been performed under the contract.

Capacity—The legal ability or competency to perform some act, such as entering into a contract or executing a deed or will. *See:* Competent.

Capture, Rule of—A legal rule that grants a landowner the right to all oil or gas produced from wells on his land, even if the oil or gas migrated from underneath land belonging to someone else.

Case Law—*See:* Common Law.

CC&Rs—A declaration of covenants, conditions, and restrictions; usually recorded by a developer to place restrictions on all lots within a new subdivision.

CCARA—The Condominium and Cooperative Abuse Relief Act, a federal law enacted to minimize the adverse impact of condominium and cooperative conversions.

Cease and Desist Order—An order issued by the Director of the Department of Licensing in a disciplinary action, to stop a violation of the license law.

CERCLA—The Comprehensive Environmental Response, Compensation and Liability Act; a federal law that established a fund to clean up hazardous waste sites, and a process for determining liability for the cleanup costs.

Certificate of Occupancy—A statement issued by a local government verifying that a newly constructed building is in compliance with all building codes and may be occupied.

Certificate of Title—A statement of opinion by an attorney that describes the status of title to the property.

Chain of Title—*See:* Title, Chain of.

Civil Law—The body of law concerned with the rights and liabilities of one party in relation to another, as distinguished from criminal law. Contract law is an example of civil law.

Civil Penalty—An amount of money that a court orders a defendant in a civil lawsuit to pay to the government; a fine.

Civil Rights—Fundamental rights guaranteed to a person by the law. The term is most often used in reference to constitutional and statutory protections against discrimination or government interference.

Civil Rights Act of 1866—A federal law guaranteeing all citizens the right to purchase, lease, sell, convey, and inherit property, regardless of race or ancestry.

Civil Wrong—*See:* Tort.

Clean Air Act—A federal law passed to maintain and enhance air quality.

Clean Water Act—A federal law passed to maintain and enhance the quality of the nation's water resources.

Client—One who employs a real estate agent, a lawyer, or an appraiser. A real estate agent's client can be the seller, the buyer, or both.

Closing—The final stage in a real estate transaction, when the seller delivers the deed and the buyer pays the purchase price. Also called settlement.

Closing Costs—The expenses incurred in the transfer of real estate in addition to the purchase price. A typical list might include the appraisal fee, title insurance premium, real estate commission, excise tax, etc.

Closing Date—The date by which the terms of a contract must be met, or else the contract is terminated.

Closing Disclosure Form—A disclosure of the actual closing costs for a transaction, along with any credits that apply; must be given to a residential borrower at least three business days before closing, and to the seller at closing.

Cloud on Title—Any claim, encumbrance, or apparent defect that makes title to real property unmarketable. *See:* Title, Marketable.

Codicil—An addition to or revision of a will. It must be executed with the same formalities as a will.

Codification—The collection and organization of piecemeal laws into a systematic, comprehensive statute called a code.

Collateral—Anything of value used as security for a debt or obligation.

Collusion—An agreement between two or more persons to defraud another.

Color of Title—Title that appears to be good title, but which in fact is not; commonly based on a defective instrument, such as an invalid deed.

Commercial Property—Property zoned and used for business purposes, such as restaurants, hotels, retail stores, and office buildings; distinguished from residential, industrial, or agricultural property.

Commingling—Illegally mixing trust funds held on behalf of a client with personal or general business funds.

Commission—1. The compensation or fee paid to a brokerage for services rendered in a real estate transaction. 2. A group of people organized for a particular purpose or function.

Common Areas—1. In a condominium, planned unit development, or cooperative housing project, the land and improvements that are owned and used collectively by all the residents. Common areas usually include driveways, recreational facilities, and stairwells. Also called common elements. 2. In a building with leased units or space, the areas that are available for use by all of the tenants.

Common Areas, Limited—In a condominium, areas outside of the units (such as balconies or assigned parking spaces) that are designated for the use of particular unit owners, rather than all of the residents. Also called limited common elements.

Common Law—The body of law based on the decisions of judges, developed in England and incorporated into the American system of justice. This is the basis of the laws of every state but Louisiana, which based its laws on French civil law.

Community Property—Property owned jointly by a married couple in Washington and other community property states, as distinguished from each spouse's separate property; generally, any property acquired during marriage through the labor or skill of either spouse (but not through gift or inheritance) belongs to both spouses equally. Washington's community property laws also apply to registered domestic partners.

Competent—1. Of sound mind. 2. Legally qualified to enter into a contract, by virtue of being of sound mind and having reached the age of majority.

Complaint—A legal document that outlines a dispute; it is filed to begin a lawsuit.

Comprehensive Environmental Response, Compensation and Liability Act—*See:* CERCLA.

Comprehensive Plan—An overall plan for the development of a city or county, which is used as a guide for the development of zoning regulations. Also called a master plan.

Concurrent Ownership—*See:* Ownership, Concurrent.

Condemnation—1. The taking of private property for public use (for streets, sewers, airports, railroads, etc.) through the government's power of eminent domain. 2. A declaration that a structure is unsafe and must be closed or destroyed.

Condition—A provision in an agreement or contract, limiting the rights and obligations of the parties or making them contingent on the occurrence or nonoccurrence of a specified event.

Conditional Fee—An ownership estate that may be terminated by the previous owner if specified conditions are not met. Also called a fee simple subject to condition subsequent. *See:* Fee Simple Defeasible.

Conditional Use Permit—A permit that allows a special use, such as a school or hospital, to operate in a neighborhood where it would otherwise be prohibited by the zoning. Also called a special exception permit.

Condominium—Property developed for concurrent ownership, where each co-owner has a separate interest in an individual dwelling unit, combined with an undivided interest in the property's common areas.

Condominium Act—A state law passed in Washington in 1989 which governs all condominiums created after July 1, 1990.

Condominium Association—*See:* Unit Owners Association.

Condominium Bylaws—The rules governing the operation of a condominium development.

Condominium Declaration—A document recorded to establish a condominium, which contains detailed information about the project.

Confidential Information—Information from or concerning a principal that was acquired during the course of an agency relationship, that the principal reasonably expects to be kept confidential, that the principal has not disclosed to third parties, that would operate to the detriment of the principal (if disclosed), and that the principal would not be legally obligated to disclose to the other party.

Confirmation of Sale—Court approval of a sale by an executor, administrator, or guardian.

Conflict of interest—A circumstance that creates an incentive for an agent (or anyone in a similar position of trust) to act against the principal's interests in order to benefit herself or a third party.

Consent—To agree, to give permission or assent.

Conservation—1. Regarding real estate, preservation of structures or neighborhoods in a sound and favorable condition. 2. Regarding natural resources, preserving or using them in a way that provides the most long-term benefit.

Consideration—Anything of value given to induce another person to enter into a contract, such as money, services, goods, or a promise. Sometimes called valuable consideration.

Conspiracy—An agreement or plan between two or more persons to perform an unlawful act.

Construction Lien—*See:* Lien, Construction.

Constructive Annexation—A doctrine holding that some moveable items are so strongly connected with real property that they are considered fixtures.

Constructive Eviction—When a landlord's actions interfere with a tenant's rights seriously enough to force the tenant to vacate the premises.

Constructive Severance—When an interest in the land has been sold or transferred separately from the real property, but the interest in question still remains in, on, or attached to the land itself; for example, when timber is sold before the trees are cut down.

Contiguous—Physically adjoining, abutting, or in close proximity.

Contingency—An event or condition that must occur before a contract becomes binding.

Contour—The surface shape or configuration of land. A contour map depicts the topography by means of lines, called contour lines, which connect points of equal elevation.

Contract—An agreement, for consideration and between competent parties, to do or not do a certain thing. It is an agreement enforceable at law.

Contract, Bilateral—A contract in which each party promises to perform something in exchange for the other's promise to perform.

Contract, Executory—A contract in which one or both parties have not yet completed performance. (An executed contract, on the other hand, is one in which both parties have completely performed their obligations under the contract.)

Contract, Express—A clear and definite contract set forth in words.

Contract, Implied—One implied by the actions of the principals; in contrast to an express contract, in which the words forming the agreement are stated, orally or in writing.

Contract, Oral—A spoken agreement.

Contract, Real Estate—1. A contract for the sale of real property in which the buyer (the vendee) pays in installments; the buyer takes possession of the property immediately, but the seller (the vendor) retains legal title until the full price has been paid. Also called a land contract, installment sales contract, or contract for deed. 2. An earnest money agreement. 3. Any contract having to do with real property.

Contract, Unenforceable—One that will not be enforced through the courts because its contents can't be proven (usually an oral contract); or because it is of a type required to be in writing (such as a real estate contract), but is not.

Contract, Unilateral—A contract that is accepted by performance. The offeror is not required to perform her part of the contract until the offeree has performed.

Contract, Valid—A binding, legally enforceable contract.

Contract, Void—A "contract" that is really not a contract because it lacks one of the key elements, such as consideration or a lawful objective.

Contract, Voidable—A valid contract that may be terminated without liability by one or both of the parties (because of fraud, undue influence, duress, or mistake, or because the party seeking to terminate the agreement is a minor).

Contract of Sale—An agreement in which a buyer agrees to buy a parcel of land for a certain price and the seller agrees to convey title; also called an earnest money agreement, purchase and sale agreement, or deposit receipt.

Contractor—One who contracts to provide labor or materials, or construct a building, or do other work for a certain price.

Conversion—1. Misappropriating property or funds belonging to another; for example, converting trust funds to one's own use. 2. The process by which an existing building is turned into a condominium. The Washington Condominium Act has special rules for residential conversions.

Conveyance—The transfer of title to real property from one person to another by means of a written document, such as a deed.

Cooperating Agent—A member of a multiple listing association who helps find a buyer for property listed by another brokerage company within the same multiple listing association.

Cooperative—A building or project owned by a nonprofit corporation. In a cooperative, the residents purchase shares in the corporation that owns the building. A resident receives a proprietary lease on a living unit and the right to use the common areas.

Corporation—An association organized according to certain laws, in which individuals may purchase ownership shares; regarded by the law as an artificial person, separate from the individual shareholders.

Corporation, Domestic—A corporation doing business in the state where it was created (incorporated).

Corporation, Foreign—A corporation doing business in one state, but created (incorporated) in another state.

Corporation, Nonprofit—A corporation formed for the purpose of serving a purpose of public or mutual benefit other than the pursuit or accumulation of profits.

Correction Lines—Adjustment lines used in the government survey system to compensate for curvature of the earth. They occur at 24-mile intervals, every fourth township line, where the distance between north and south range lines is corrected to six miles.

Co-Tenancy—*See:* Ownership, Concurrent.

Counteroffer—A new offer made by the offeree in reply to an offer to enter into a contract. It constitutes a rejection of the first offer, and the roles of the two parties are now reversed. The original offeror is the offeree and can accept or reject the counteroffer. This situation commonly arises when the original offeree wants to make some change in the offer she has received. Any change, however slight, constitutes a rejection of the original offer.

County—An administrative subdivision of the state, created by the state and deriving all of its powers from the state.

Course—In a metes and bounds description, a direction, stated in terms of a compass bearing.

Covenant—1. A written agreement or promise to do or not do something. 2. A stipulation that a property will be used or will not be used for a particular purpose or purposes. 3. A guarantee that some state of facts exists (such as the fact that a grantor has good title to real property).

Covenant, Restrictive—A promise to do or refrain from doing an act relating to real property, especially such a promise that runs with the land; usually imposed by a grantor on all subsequent owners of the property. Also called deed restrictions.

Covenant Against Encumbrances—In a warranty deed, a promise that the property is not burdened by any encumbrances other than those that are disclosed in the deed.

Covenant of Quiet Enjoyment—A promise that a buyer or tenant's possession of the property will not be disturbed by the previous owner, the landlord, or anyone else making a lawful claim against the property.

Covenant of Right to Convey—In a warranty deed, a promise that the grantor has the legal ability to make a valid conveyance.

Covenant of Seisin—In a warranty deed, a promise that the grantor actually owns the interest he is conveying to the grantee.

Covenant of Warranty—In a warranty deed, a promise that the grantor will defend the grantee's title if it is challenged in court.

Credit—A payment that is receivable (as opposed to a debit, which is a payment due).

Creditor, Secured—A creditor who has a lien on specific property, such as a mortgagee.

Customer—In real estate, usually a prospective purchaser.

Damage Deposit—*See:* Security Deposit.

Damages—The amount of money one can recover as compensation for an injury to his person or property resulting from an act or failure to act.

Damages, Compensatory—The amount of money awarded for an injury, intended to compensate the injured party for the actual loss incurred. Also called actual damages.

Damages, Liquidated—A sum that the parties to a contract agree in advance (at the time the contract is made) will serve as full compensation in the event of a breach.

Datum—A reference point used by surveyors to determine elevation.

Debit—A charge listed on a settlement statement, showing a debt or payment owed by one of the parties.

Debtor—One who owes something (usually money) to another.

Decedent—A person who has died.

Decisional Law—Law that evolves from published opinions of the courts. Also called case law.

Declarant—The term used to refer to the developer of a condominium in the Washington Condominium Act.

Declaration of Abandonment—A recorded document voluntarily releasing a property from homestead protection.

Declaration of Homestead—A document claiming homestead protection for a property.

Declaration of Restrictions—*See:* CC&Rs.

Dedication—An appropriation or granting of private property for public use; may be a grant of the entire fee simple interest or just an easement (such as an easement for sidewalks or streets).

Dedication, Common Law—Transfer of land from private to public ownership or use by virtue of the private owner's acquiescence in public use of the land for an extended period of time.

Dedication, Statutory—Transfer of land from private to public ownership as required by law, as a prerequisite to subdivision approval, for example.

Deed—A written instrument that, when properly executed and delivered, conveys title to real property from the grantor to the grantee.

Deed, Bargain and Sale—A deed that conveys title but does not make the same promises as a full warranty deed.

Deed, Correction—A deed used to correct minor mistakes in an earlier deed, such as misspellings of names or errors in description of the parcel.

Deed, General Warranty—A deed in which the grantor warrants the title against defects that might have arisen before or during her period of ownership.

Deed, Gift—A deed freely given in which the consideration is love and affection (rather than valuable consideration such as money, goods, or services).

Deed, Quitclaim—A deed that operates to convey and release any interest in a piece of real property that the grantor may have. It contains no warranties of any kind, but does transfer any right, title, or interest the grantor has at the time the deed is executed.

Deed, Sheriff's—A deed delivered by the sheriff, on court order, to the holder of the Certificate of Sale following the period of redemption after a mortgage foreclosure.

Deed, Special Warranty—A deed in which the grantor warrants title only against defects that may have arisen during his period of ownership.

Deed, Tax—A deed given to the successful bidder when property is sold to satisfy unpaid property taxes.

Deed, Trustee's—A deed given to the successful bidder at a trustee's sale in the nonjudicial foreclosure of a deed of trust.

Deed, Warranty—A deed containing warranties or guarantees of clear title and the right to convey, as well as the grantor's willingness to defend against claims that the title conveyed is not good.

Deed, Wild—A deed that cannot be located under the grantor-grantee system of indexing.

Deed Executed Under Court Order—A deed, such as a sheriff's deed or tax deed, that is the result of a court action, such as foreclosure.

Deed of Partition—A deed used by co-owners, such as joint tenants or tenants in common, to divide up the co-owned property so that each can own a separate portion.

Deed of Trust—A type of security instrument used to finance the purchase of real estate. Under the deed of trust, the power to sell the secured property in the event of default by the trustor (the borrower) is given to an independent third party (the trustee) to protect the interests of the beneficiary (the lender). A deed of trust can be foreclosed at a trustee's sale. Unlike foreclosure of a mortgage, judicial intervention is not required, and there is no period of redemption following the trustee's sale. A trustee's deed is issued after the sale.

Deed Restrictions—Limitations in a deed restricting the use of the property, such as "Residential use only" or "No building over 35 feet in height." Also called restrictive covenants.

Default—Failure to fulfill an obligation, duty, or promise, as when a borrower fails to make loan payments or a tenant fails to pay rent.

Default Judgment—*See:* Judgment, Default.

Defeasance Clause—A clause in a mortgage, deed of trust, or lease that cancels or defeats a certain right upon the occurrence of a certain event.

Defeasible Fee—*See:* Fee Simple Defeasible.

Defendant—In a lawsuit, the individual or entity being sued.

Deficiency Judgment—See: Judgment, Deficiency.

Degree—In surveying, a unit of circular measurement equal to $^1/_{360}$ of one complete rotation around a point in a plane.

Delivery—The legal transfer of an instrument evidencing title or ownership. A valid deed does not convey title unless it has been delivered (actually or constructively) to the grantee.

Density—The number of buildings or the number of occupants per unit of land (square mile, acre, etc.).

Department of Licensing—The state agency in charge of administering the real estate license law in Washington.

Deposit—1. Money offered as an indication of good faith in regard to the future performance of a contract to purchase real property. Also called earnest money. 2. A security deposit given to a landlord by a tenant.

Deposition—Formal out-of-court testimony of a witness taken before trial, for possible use later in the trial. Testimony taken either for discovery, to determine the facts of the case, or when a witness will be unable to attend the trial, or both.

Depreciation—A loss in value. For appraisal purposes, depreciation results from physical deterioration (such as cracks in the foundation), functional obsolescence (such as old fashioned plumbing or lighting fixtures), or economic obsolescence (such as deterioration in the neighborhood).

Detached Residence—A home physically separated from other houses; not connected to another house by a common wall.

Detrimental Reliance—*See:* Promissory Estoppel.

Developed Land—Land that has been improved by man-made additions, such as buildings, roads, or sidewalks.

Developer—Someone who makes changes to bring land to its most profitable use by subdividing and/or improving it.

Devise—1. A gift of real property transferred by will. The donor is the testator and the recipient is the devisee. 2. To transfer real property by will. *Compare:* Bequest.

Devisee—A recipient of real property under a will. *Compare:* Beneficiary; Legatee.

Disability—According to the Americans with Disabilities Act and the Fair Housing Act, a physical or mental impairment that substantially limits a person in one or more major life activities.

Disaffirm—To ask a court to terminate a voidable contract.

Discovery—The stage of a lawsuit in which each party is required to provide information about the case to the other party, in response to interrogatories (written questions), depositions (formal interviews of witnesses), and requests for the production of documents.

Discrimination—Unequal treatment, either favorable or unfavorable, based on the class, race, or other group to which a person or persons belong.

Disparate Impact—When a statute or ordinance appears neutral on its face (seems to apply to everyone equally), but actually has a greater impact on members of a protected class than it has on other people, so that the law has a discriminatory effect.

Diversity Jurisdiction—The federal courts' power to hear cases in which a citizen of one state sues a citizen of another state (or country).

Domestic Corporation—*See:* Corporation, Domestic.

Dominant Tenement—Property that receives the benefit of an appurtenant easement.

Downzoning—Rezoning land for a more restricted use.

Dual Agent—An agent who represents both the buyer and the seller in the same transaction.

Due Process—A fair hearing by an impartial judge. Under the U.S. Constitution, no one may be deprived of life, liberty, or property without due process of law.

Duress—Unlawful force, constraint, threats, or other actions used to compel someone to do something (such as sign a contract) against her will.

Dwelling—A building or part of a building used or intended to be used as living quarters.

Earnest Money—A deposit made by a prospective purchaser of real estate as evidence of a good faith intention to complete the purchase. Also called a good faith deposit.

Earnest Money Agreement—A contract in which a property owner agrees to sell the property to a buyer for a specified price. Also called a purchase and sale agreement or deposit receipt.

Easement—A right to use some part of another person's property for a particular purpose; for example, as a driveway, or for installing and maintaining a water line.

Easement, Implied—*See:* Easement by Implication.

Easement, Negative—An easement that prevents the landowner from using the land in a certain way; essentially the same thing as a restrictive covenant.

Easement, Positive—An easement that allows a landowner to use another's land for a specific purpose.

Easement Appurtenant—An easement for the benefit of a particular piece of property (the dominant tenement). *Compare:* Easement in Gross.

Easement by Express Grant—An easement granted to another by means of a deed or other document.

Easement by Express Reservation—An easement created by deed in favor of the grantor, who transfers the property (or part of the property) but reserves an easement for his own use.

Easement by Implication—An easement created by law (not by express grant) when a property is divided into more than one parcel, when there was apparent prior use of the easement and it is reasonably necessary for the enjoyment of the dominant tenement. Also called an implied easement.

Easement by Necessity—An easement implied by law when a property is divided into more than one parcel if the dominant tenement would be completely useless without an easement, even though it was not a long-standing, apparent use.

Easement in Gross—An easement for the benefit of a person instead of a piece of land. *Compare:* Easement Appurtenant.

Egress—A passageway leading from property; a means of exiting. It is the opposite of ingress (entry). The terms ingress and egress usually refer to easements.

Emancipated Minor—A person under 18 who is or has been married, is on active duty in the military, or has a declaration of emancipation from a court.

Emblements—Crops, such as wheat or corn, that are produced annually through the labor of the cultivator.

Emblements, Doctrine of—The right of an agricultural tenant to enter land after termination of the lease for the purpose of harvesting crops.

Eminent Domain—The power of the government to take (condemn) private property for public use, upon payment of just compensation to the owner.

Employee—Someone who works under the direction and control of another. *Compare:* Independent Contractor.

Employee Retirement Income Security Act (ERISA)—A federal law that protects individuals who have voluntarily established pension and health plans with their employers, by requiring employers to act as a fiduciary in regards to their employees' funds.

Encroachment—Unlawful physical intrusion onto the property of another, usually as the result of mistake.

Encumber—To place a lien or other encumbrance against the title to a property.

Encumbrance—A nonpossessory interest in property; a lien, easement, or restrictive covenant burdening the property owner's title.

Enjoin—To prohibit an act, or command performance of an act, by court order; to issue an injunction.

Environmental Impact Statement (EIS)—A statement evaluating the impact of a development on the surrounding community and the environment.

Equal Credit Opportunity Act—A federal law prohibiting credit providers from discriminating based on race, color, religion, national origin, sex, marital status, age, or because the applicant receives public assistance.

Equal Protection—Under the U.S. Constitution, all citizens are entitled to the equal protection of the laws; no law may arbitrarily discriminate between different groups, or be applied to different groups in a discriminatory manner.

Equitable Redemption Period—The period between the initial complaint and the sale of a foreclosed property, during which time a borrower may redeem the property by paying the amount of the debt plus costs.

Equitable Remedy—A remedy granted to a plaintiff that is something other than an award of money (damages), when money alone cannot adequately correct the problem, such as an injunction or an order of specific performance.

Equity—1. The difference between the value of a piece of property and the liens against it; an owner's unencumbered interest in her property. 2. In law, a judge's power to soften or set aside strict legal rules, to bring about a fair and just result in a particular case.

Equity Skimming—An illegal scheme in which homeowners are defrauded out of equity in their homes.

Erosion—Gradual loss of soil due to the action of water or wind.

Escheat—The reversion of property to the state when a person dies without leaving a will and no heirs entitled to the property can be located.

Escrow—An arrangement in which something of value (such as money or a deed) is held by a disinterested third party, called an escrow agent, until certain conditions specified in the escrow instructions have been fulfilled.

Escrow Agent—1. A neutral third party who holds money and documents in trust and carries out the closing process. 2. A company (not a natural person) that is licensed to engage in the escrow business.

Escrow Instructions—A written document that tells the escrow agent how to proceed and states the conditions each party must fulfill before the transaction can close.

Escrow Officer—A person licensed to work for an escrow agent.

Estate—1. A possessory interest in real property; either a freehold or a leasehold. 2. The property left by someone who has died.

Estate at Will—A leasehold estate for an indefinite period of time, which can be terminated at any time by either landlord or tenant without notice. Also called a tenancy at will.

Estate for Life—*See:* Life Estate.

Estate for Years—A leasehold estate set to last for a definite period of time (one week, six months, three years, etc.), after which it terminates automatically.

Estate, Fee Simple—*See:* Fee Simple.

Estate in Remainder—*See:* Remainder.

Estate in Reversion—*See:* Reversion.

Estate of Inheritance—An estate that can be inherited by the owner's heirs, such as a fee simple estate.

Estoppel—A legal doctrine that prevents a person from asserting rights or facts that are inconsistent with his earlier actions or statements.

Eviction—Dispossession, expulsion, or ejection of a person from real property.

Eviction, Actual—Physically forcing someone off of property (or preventing them from re-entering), or using the legal process to make someone leave.

Eviction, Constructive—When a landlord's act (or failure to act) interferes with the tenant's quiet enjoyment of the property, or makes the property unfit for its intended use, to such an extent that the tenant is forced to move out.

Eviction, Retaliatory—When a landlord evicts a tenant in retaliation for requesting repairs, filing a complaint against the landlord, or organizing or participating in a tenants' rights group.

Eviction, Self-Help—When a landlord uses physical force, a lock-out, or a utility shut-off to get rid of a tenant, instead of using the legal process. (This is generally illegal.)

Excise Tax—*See:* Tax, Excise.

Exclusive Right to Sell—*See:* Listing, Exclusive Right to Sell.

Execute—1. To perform or complete. 2. To sign a document and take any other formal steps that may be necessary for its validity (such as acknowledgment).

Execution—A legal process in which the court orders the sheriff or another official to seize and sell the property of a debtor to satisfy a judgment lien or other lien.

Executor—A person named in a will to carry out the provisions of the will.

Exemption—A provision holding that a law or regulation does not apply to a particular person or group. For example, a person entitled to a property tax exemption is not required to pay property taxes. An exemption can be full or partial.

Express—Stated in words, spoken or written (rather than merely implied by actions). *Compare:* Implied.

Extender Clause—A clause in a listing agreement providing that the listing agent will still receive the commission if the property is sold during a specified period of time after the listing expires to someone who was a prospect during the listing term. Also called a carryover clause or safety clause.

Failure of Purpose—An excuse for rescinding a contract; if the contract cannot achieve its intended purpose, the parties are released from their obligations.

Fair Labor Standards Act—A federal law, administered by the U.S. Department of Labor, that sets forth rules for minimum wage, overtime, recordkeeping, and child labor for many full- and part-time employees.

Family and Medical Leave Act—A federal law that entitles eligible employees to take up to 12 weeks of unpaid, job-protected leave in a 12-month period for specified family and medical reasons.

Federal Employment Tax Act—A federal law that is used to fund state workforce agencies, subsidize extended unemployment benefits when necessary, and provide loans to states who need help providing benefits.

Federal Question—A legal question involving the U.S. Constitution, a treaty, or a federal statute. Federal question cases may be heard in federal court.

Federal Trade Commission (FTC)—A federal agency responsible for investigating and eliminating unfair and deceptive business practices. It is also the agency charged with enforcing the Truth in Lending Law.

Fee—*See:* Fee Simple.

Fee Simple—The greatest estate one can have in real property; of indefinite duration; with no conditions on the title; freely transferable or inheritable. Also known as a fee or a fee simple absolute.

Fee Simple Defeasible—A fee estate in real property that is subject to being defeated or undone if a certain event occurs or a certain condition is not met.

Fee Simple Determinable—A defeasible fee that is terminated automatically if certain events occur.

Fee Simple Subject to Condition Subsequent—A defeasible fee that may be terminated by the grantor after breach of a condition specified in the grant. The grantor has a power of termination.

Fiduciary Relationship—A relationship of trust and confidence, in which one party owes the other (or both parties owe each other) loyalty and a higher standard of good faith than they owe to third parties. For example, an agent is a fiduciary in relation to the principal; husband and wife are fiduciaries in relation to one another.

Financing Statement—A brief document that, when recorded, gives notice of a creditor's security interest in an item of personal property.

Finder's Fee—A referral fee paid to someone for directing a buyer or seller to a real estate agent.

FIRPTA— *See:* Foreign Investment in Real Property Tax Act.

First Lien Position—The position held by a mortgage or deed of trust that has higher lien priority than any other mortgage or deed of trust against the property.

First Refusal, Right of—*See:* Right of First Refusal.

Fiscal Year—Any 12-month period used as a business year for accounting, tax, and other financial purposes, as opposed to the calendar year.

Fixed Term—A period of time which has a definite beginning date and ending date.

Fixture—An item that was personal property, but which has become affixed to or associated with real property in such a way that it has legally become part of the real property.

Fixture, Trade—Article of personal property annexed to real property by a tenant for use in her trade or business, which the tenant is allowed to remove at the end of the lease.

Foreclosure—When a lienholder causes property to be sold, so that the unpaid lien can be satisfied from the sale proceeds.

Foreclosure, Judicial—A lawsuit filed by a mortgagee or deed of trust beneficiary to foreclose on the security property when the borrower has defaulted.

Foreclosure, Nonjudicial—Foreclosure by a trustee under the power of sale clause in a deed of trust.

Foreign Corporation—*See:* Corporation, Foreign.

Foreign Investment in Real Property Tax Act (FIRPTA)—A federal law that requires a percentage of the amount realized on a real estate sale to be withheld and submitted to the IRS if the seller is a foreign person (not a U.S. citizen or resident alien).

Forfeiture—Loss of a right or something else of value as a result of failure to perform an obligation or condition.

Fraud—An intentional or negligent misrepresentation or concealment of a material fact, which is relied upon by another, who is induced to enter a transaction and harmed as a result.

Fraud, Actual—Intentional deceit or misrepresentation.

Fraud, Constructive—Negligent misrepresentation, or a breach of duty that misleads the person to whom the duty was owed, without an intention to deceive.

Free and Clear—Title to real property that is completely free of encumbrances such as mortgages, liens, and so forth.

Freehold—An ownership estate in real property; either a fee simple or a life estate. The holder of a freehold estate has title, whereas the holder of a less-than-freehold estate (leasehold estate) is merely a tenant, having a temporary right to possession, but no title.

Future Estate—An interest in property that will or may become possessory at some point in the future, such as an estate in remainder or an estate in reversion.

Garnishment—A legal process by which a creditor may gain access to a debtor's personal property or funds that are in the hands of a third party. Items that may be garnished include wages, debts owed, security interests, and goods or personal effects concealed in the possession of third parties.

General Agent—*See:* Agent, General.

General Lien—*See:* Lien, General.

General Warranty Deed—*See:* Deed, General Warranty.

Goodwill—An intangible asset of a business resulting from a good reputation with the public, serving as an indication of future return business.

Government Lot—In the government survey system, a parcel of land that is not a regular section (one mile square), because of the convergence of range lines, or because of a body of water or some other obstacle; assigned a government lot number.

Government Survey System—A system of land description in which the land is divided into squares called townships, each approximately six miles square (containing 36 square miles), which are divided into 36 sections, each approximately one mile square and containing approximately 640 acres. Also called the rectangular survey system or section, township, and range system.

Grant—To transfer or convey an interest in real property by means of a written instrument.

Grantee—One who receives a grant of real property.

Granting Clause—Words in a deed that indicate an intent to transfer an interest in land.

Grantor—One who grants an interest in real property to another.

Grantee—One who is granted an interest in real property.

Growth Management Act—A Washington state law aimed at limiting sprawl and concentrating growth in existing urban areas.

Guardian—A person appointed by a court to administer the affairs of a minor or a mentally incompetent person.

Guide Meridian—*See:* Meridian, Guide.

Habitability—*See:* Implied Warranty of Habitability.

Heir—Someone entitled to inherit another's property under the laws of intestate succession.

Highest and Best Use—The use that is most likely to produce the greatest net return from the property over a given period of time.

Historic Preservation—The protection of historic buildings from destruction or unauthorized modifications.

Holder in Due Course—A person who obtains a negotiable instrument for value, in good faith, and without notice of any defenses against it.

Holdover Tenant—A tenant who fails to surrender possession of the premises at the end of the tenancy.

Home Mortgage Disclosure Act—A federal law requiring institutional lenders to make annual disclosures of all mortgage loans made, as a means of enforcing prohibitions against redlining.

Homeowners Association—A nonprofit association made up of homeowners in a subdivision, responsible for enforcing the CC&Rs and managing other community affairs.

Homestead—An owner-occupied dwelling, together with any appurtenant outbuildings and land.

Housing Codes—Local regulations setting minimum standards for aspects of housing that affect health and safety.

Implied—Not expressed in words, but understood from actions or circumstances. *Compare:* Express.

Implied Warranty of Habitability—A warranty implied by law in every residential lease, that the property is fit for habitation.

Implied Warranties of Quality—Under the Condominium Act, certain guarantees that automatically apply to the sale of a unit by the declarant.

Improvements—Man-made additions to real property.

Imputed Knowledge—A legal doctrine stating that a principal is considered to have notice of information that the agent has, even if the agent never passed that information on to the principal.

Incompetent—1. Not legally qualified to enter into contracts, as in the case of a minor or a mentally ill person. 2. Not of sound mind.

Independent Contractor—A person who contracts to do certain work for another person, agreeing to achieve a certain result but retaining control over how she will carry out the task, rather than submitting to the control of the other person. Real estate agents are usually independent contractors. *Compare:* Employee.

Indexing—A means of cataloging deeds and other documents in the recording office; deeds are indexed according to grantor and grantee, and sometimes according to the location of the land.

Industrial Insurance—See: Workers' Compensation

Ingress—A means of entering a piece of property, such as a driveway. The opposite of egress.

In-House Transaction—A sale in which the buyer and the seller are brought together by licensees working for the same brokerage.

Injunction—A court order prohibiting someone from performing an act or commanding performance of an act.

Instrument—A legal document, usually one that transfers title (such as a deed), creates a lien (such as a mortgage), or establishes a right to payment (such as a promissory note or contract).

Insurance, Hazard—Insurance against losses on property caused by fire, flood, theft, or other disaster. Also called casualty insurance.

Insurance, Homeowner's—Casualty insurance that covers the homeowner's personal property as well as the real property.

Insurance, Title—Insurance that protects against losses resulting from undiscovered title defects. An owner's policy protects the buyer, while a mortgagee's policy protects the lien position of the buyer's lender.

Insurance, Title, Extended Coverage—A policy of title insurance that covers problems which should be discovered in an inspection of the property, such as adverse possession or encroachments.

Insurance, Title, Homeowner's Coverage—Title insurance that covers most of the title problems that an extended coverage policy covers, as well as some additional items, such as violations of restrictive covenants.

Insurance, Title, Standard Coverage—Title insurance that protects against latent title defects (such as forged deeds) and undiscovered recorded encumbrances, but does not protect against problems that would only be discovered by an inspection of the property, such as adverse possessors or unrecorded easements.

Integration Clause—A clause in a contract which states that the document is the entire agreement between the parties.

Interest—1. A charge a borrower pays to a lender for the use of the lender's money. 2. A right or share in something (such as a piece of real estate).

Interest, Future—An interest in property that will or may become possessory at some point in the future, such as an estate in remainder or an estate in reversion.

Interest, Undivided—A co-owner's interest, giving him the right to shared possession of the whole property, rather than exclusive possession of a particular section of it.

Interference with Contractual Relations—A tort that occurs when someone wrongfully interferes with a contract she is not a party to, causing a financial loss for one of the contracting parties.

Interpleader—A court action filed by someone who is holding funds that two or more people are claiming. The holder turns the funds over to the court; the court resolves the dispute and delivers the money to the party who is entitled to it.

Interrogatories—A discovery tool similar to a deposition but conducted in writing instead of in person. One party sends a series of questions to the other and the other party must send back answers.

Interval Ownership—A form of timeshare ownership in which buyers are granted an estate for years for a specific time period.

Intestate—Without a valid will.

Intestate Succession—Distribution of the property of a person who died intestate to his heirs.

Inverse Condemnation Action—A court action by a private landowner against the government, seeking compensation for damage to property caused by government action.

Inverted Pyramid—A way of visualizing ownership of real property; in theory, a property owner owns all the earth, water, and air enclosed by an inverted pyramid with its tip at the center of the earth and its base corresponding to the boundaries of the property and then continuing into the airspace.

Investment Property—Unimproved property that produces no income, but is held in the expectation that it will appreciate in value.

Involuntary Lien—*See:* Lien, Involuntary.

Joint and Several Liability—*See:* Liability, Joint and Several.

Joint Tenancy—*See:* Tenancy, Joint.

Joint Venture—Two or more individuals joining together for one specific project as partners. A joint venture is of limited duration; if the members of the venture undertake another project together, the association may become a partnership.

Judgment—1. A court's binding determination of the rights and duties of the parties to a lawsuit. 2. A court order requiring one party to pay damages to the other.

Judgment, Default—A court judgment in favor of the plaintiff due to the defendant's failure to answer the complaint or appear at a hearing.

Judgment, Deficiency—A personal judgment entered against a borrower in favor of the lender if the proceeds from a foreclosure sale of the security property are not enough to pay off the debt.

Judgment Creditor—A person to whom money is owed by virtue of a judgment in a lawsuit.

Judgment Debtor—A person who owes money by virtue of a judgment in a lawsuit.

Judgment Lien—*See:* Lien, Judgment.

Judicial Foreclosure—*See:* Foreclosure, Judicial.

Jurisdiction, Personal—A trial court's authority to order a particular defendant into the court and pass judgment on him.

Jurisdiction, Subject Matter—A trial court's authority to hear the kind of case being brought.

Just Compensation—The compensation that the Constitution requires the government to pay a property owner when the property is taken under the power of eminent domain.

Kickback—Under RESPA, a referral fee that one settlement service provider pays to another settlement service provider, in violation of the law.

Land—In a legal sense, the solid part of the surface of the earth (as distinguished from water), everything affixed to it, by nature or by human beings, or anything on it or in it, such as minerals and water.

Landlocked—A parcel of land without access to any type of road or highway. The owner of landlocked land may be able to obtain an easement by necessity from the court.

Landlord—A landowner who has leased her property. Also called a lessor.

Landmark—A monument, natural or artificial, set up on the boundary line of two adjacent estates in order to mark the boundary.

Latent Defects—Defects in property that are not visible or apparent.

Lateral Support—*See:* Support, Lateral.

Lawful Purpose—An objective of a contract that is not against the law.

Lease—A contract in which a landlord (lessor) grants a tenant (lessee) the possession of real estate in exchange for rent.

Lease, Fixed—A lease in which the tenant pays the landlord a fixed sum as rent each month, and the landlord pays all of the property's operating expenses. Also called a flat lease, gross lease, or straight lease.

Lease, Graduated—A lease in which the rent is increased at agreed intervals during the term of the lease.

Lease, Gross—*See:* Lease, Fixed.

Lease, Ground—A lease of the land only, usually for a long term, and sometimes secured by improvements placed on the land by the tenant.

Lease, Net—A lease requiring the tenant to pay some or all of the property's operating expenses (such as taxes, utilities, and insurance), in addition to the rent paid to the landlord.

Lease, Percentage—A lease in which the rent includes a percentage of the tenant's monthly or annual gross sales.

Leasehold Estate—The possessory interest that a tenant has in the leased property during the term of the lease.

Legal Description—A method of describing a parcel of real estate that is recognized by law, including the lot and block (recorded plat) method, the government survey method (also called the township and range or rectangular survey method), or the metes and bounds method.

Legal Person—*See:* Artificial Person.

Legatee—A recipient of personal property under a will.

Lessee—One who possesses or occupies property owned by another under the terms of a lease. Also called a tenant.

Lessor—One who has leased property to another. Also called a landlord.

Liability, Joint and Several—A form of liability in which several persons are responsible for a debt both individually and as a group. Any one of the individuals can be required to pay the entire debt if the others fail to pay their shares.

Liability, Vicarious—A legal doctrine stating that a principal can be held liable for harm to third parties resulting from an agent's actions.

Liable—Legally responsible.

License—1. Official permission to perform certain acts that the law does not allow everyone to do. 2. Revocable, non-assignable permission to enter land owned by someone else for a particular purpose. *Compare:* Easement.

License, Inactive—Any real estate license that has been turned over to the Director temporarily. The holder of an inactive license is not permitted to engage in activities requiring a license.

Lien—A nonpossessory interest in property, giving the lienholder the right to foreclose if the owner does not pay a debt owed to the lienholder; a financial encumbrance on the owner's title.

Lien, Attachment—A lien on property intended to prevent transfer of the property pending the outcome of litigation.

Lien, Construction—A specific lien claimed by someone who performed work on the property (construction, repairs, or improvements) and has not been paid. Also called a mechanic's lien.

Lien, Equitable—A lien arising as a matter of fairness, rather than by agreement or by operation of law.

Lien, General—A lien against all of the property of a debtor.

Lien, Involuntary—A lien that arises by operation of law, without consent of the property owner.

Lien, Judgment—A general lien against all of the property of a judgment debtor, making it possible for the judgment creditor to have the property sold to satisfy the debt.

Lien, Materialman's—Similar to a construction lien, but it refers specifically to sums owed suppliers, as opposed to laborers, for materials provided in connection with a construction project.

Lien, Mechanic's—*See:* Lien, Construction.

Lien, Property Tax—A specific lien on property to secure payment of the property taxes.

Lien, Specific—A lien that attaches only to a particular piece of property, as opposed to a general lien, which attaches to all of the debtor's property.

Lien, Statutory—A lien created by operation of law, rather than by contract, such as a tax lien.

Lien, Tax—A lien on property to secure the payment of taxes.

Lien, Voluntary—A lien placed against property with the consent of the owner.

Lienholder, Junior—A secured creditor whose lien has lower priority than another lien against the same property.

Lien Priority—The order in which liens are paid off out of proceeds of the foreclosure sale.

Life Estate—A freehold estate that lasts only as long as a specified person lives. That person is referred to as the measuring life.

Life Tenant—Someone who owns a life estate; the person entitled to possession of the property during the measuring life.

Limited Liability Company—A business entity that combines the management and tax advantages of a partnership with the limited liability of a corporation.

Limited Partnership—A partnership in which the liability of some of the partners (the limited partners) is limited to the amount they invested.

Liquidated Damages—*See:* Damages, Liquidated.

Lis Pendens—A recorded notice stating that there is a lawsuit pending that may affect title to the defendant's real estate.

Listing—A written contract between a principal and an agent stipulating that the agent will be paid a commission for finding or attempting to find a ready, willing, and able buyer to purchase the seller's property on terms acceptable to the seller. Also called a listing agreement.

Listing, Exclusive—Either an exclusive agency listing or an exclusive right to sell listing.

Listing, Exclusive Agency—A listing agreement that entitles the listing agent to a commission if anyone other than the seller finds a buyer for the property during the listing term.

Listing, Exclusive Right to Sell—A listing agreement that entitles the listing agent to a commission if anyone—including the seller—finds a buyer for the property during the listing term.

Listing, Open—A nonexclusive listing, given by an owner to as many different brokerages as he chooses. If the property is sold, a brokerage is only entitled to a commission if it is the procuring cause of the sale.

Litigants—The parties to a lawsuit; the plaintiff(s) and defendant(s).

Living Trust—A type of trust that allows distribution of someone's property after her death without probate.

Lot—A parcel of land in a subdivision.

Lot and Block Description—A type of legal description; a piece of land is described by reference to a lot and block appearing on the subdivision plat map recorded by the county auditor or county recorder. Sometimes called a maps and plats description.

Mailbox Rule—A common law rule under which an acceptance communicated by mail is effective when the message has been sent (put into the mailbox), even though the offeror won't receive it right away.

Majority, Age of—Age at which a person becomes legally competent to enter into contracts and transactions; usually 18 years old.

Marketable Title—*See:* Title, Marketable

Material Breach—*See:* Breach, Material.

Material Fact—Information that has a substantial negative impact on the value of the property, on a party's ability to perform, or on the purpose of the transaction.

Measuring Life—*See:* Life Estate.

Meeting of the Minds—*See:* Mutual Consent.

Merger—Uniting two or more separate properties by transferring ownership of all of them to one person.

Meridian—An imaginary line running north and south, passing through the earth's poles. Also called a longitude line.

Meridian, Guide—In the government survey system, one of the north-south lines, spaced 24 miles apart.

Meridian, Principal—In the government survey system, the main north-south line in a particular grid, used as the starting point in numbering the ranges.

Metes—Measurements.

Metes and Bounds Description—A method of legal description that starts at an easily identifiable point of beginning, then describes the property's boundaries in terms of courses (compass directions) and distances, ultimately returning to the point of beginning.

Mineral Rights—Rights to the minerals located beneath the surface of a piece of property.

Minor—A person who has not reached the age at which the law recognizes a general contractual capacity (usually 18 years old).

Misrepresentation—An incorrect or false statement. *See:* Fraud.

Mitigation—When the nonbreaching party takes action to minimize the losses resulting from a breach of contract.

MLS—Multiple Listing Service.

Model Toxics Control Act (MTCA)—A Washington state law analogous to CERCLA that imposes joint and several liability for hazardous waste cleanup on potentially liable parties.

Monument—A visible marker, natural or artificial, used in a survey or a metes and bounds description to establish the boundaries of a piece of property.

Mortgage—1. An instrument that creates a voluntary lien on real property to secure repayment of a debt. The parties to a mortgage are the mortgagor (borrower) and mortgagee (lender). 2. The term is often used more generally, to refer to either a mortgage or a deed of trust.

Mortgagee—The one who receives a mortgage; the lender.

Mortgagor—A property owner (usually a borrower) who gives a mortgage against the property to another (usually a lender) as security for payment of an obligation.

Mutual Consent—When all parties freely agree to the terms of a contract, without fraud, undue influence, duress, menace, or mistake. Mutual consent is achieved through offer and acceptance. Sometimes called mutuality or "a meeting of the minds."

Mutuality—*See:* Mutual Consent.

NAR—The National Association of REALTORS®.

National Environmental Policy Act—*See:* NEPA.

Natural Person—A human being, an individual (as distinguished from an artificial person, such as a corporation).

Navigable Waters—A body of water that is capable of being used practically for the carriage of commerce.

Negligence—Conduct that falls below the standard of care that a reasonable person would exercise under the circumstances; carelessness or recklessness.

Negotiable Instrument—An instrument containing an unconditional promise to pay a certain sum of money, to order or to bearer, on demand or at a particular time. It may be a check, a promissory note, a bond, a draft, or stock.

NEPA—The National Environmental Policy Act; federal legislation requiring the preparation of an environmental impact statement (EIS) before any government action that would have a significant effect on the environment.

Nonconforming Use—A property use that does not conform to current zoning requirements, but is allowed because the property was being used in that way before the present zoning ordinance was enacted.

Nonpossessory Interest—An interest in property that does not include the right to possess and occupy the property; an encumbrance, such as a lien or an easement.

Nonprofit Corporation—*See:* Corporation, Nonprofit.

Notary Public—An official whose primary function is to witness and certify the acknowledgment made by someone signing a legal document.

Note—*See:* Promissory Note.

Notice, Actual—Actual knowledge of a fact, as opposed to knowledge imputed by law.

Notice, Constructive—Knowledge of a fact imputed to a person by law. A person is held to have constructive notice of something when she should have known it, even if she did not actually know it.

Notice of Cessation—A notice recorded by a property owner when construction on the property has ceased, although the project has not been completed; it limits the period during which construction liens can be filed.

Notice of Completion—A recorded notice that announces the completion of a construction project and limits the period in which construction liens may be filed.

Notice of Non-Responsibility—A notice which, if recorded and posted on the property in a timely manner, will protect a property owner from construction liens filed for work that was requested by someone other than the owner (a tenant, for example).

Notice of Sale—A notice sent to a defaulting borrower, to junior lienholders, and to other interested parties, setting the date for a foreclosure sale.

Notice to Quit—A notice given to a tenant by a landlord, demanding that the tenant cure a default (e.g., by paying overdue rent) or else vacate the leased property.

Novation—1. When one party to a contract withdraws and a new party is substituted, relieving the withdrawing party of liability. 2. The substitution of a new obligation for an old one.

Nuisance—Anything that is injurious to health, is indecent or offensive to the senses, or is an obstruction to the free use of property that interferes with an owner's comfortable use and enjoyment of her property.

Occupational Safety and Health Act—A federal law passed to help prevent work-related injuries, illnesses, and deaths. Implemented by the Occupational Safety and Health Administration (OSHA).

Offer—When one person (the offeror) proposes a contract to another (the offeree); if the offeree accepts the offer, a binding contract is formed.

Offer, Tender—An unconditional offer by one of the parties to a contract to perform her part of the agreement; made when the offeror believes the other party is breaching the contract, it establishes the offeror's right to sue if the other party doesn't accept it.

Offeree—One to whom an offer is made.

Offeror—One who makes an offer.

Officer—In a corporation, an executive authorized by the board of directors to manage the business of the corporation.

Off-Site Improvements—Improvements that add to the usefulness of a site but are not located directly on it, such as curbs, street lights, and sidewalks.

Open Listing—*See:* Listing, Open.

Option—A contract giving one party the right to do something, without obligating her to do it.

Optionee—The person to whom an option is given.

Optionor—The person who gives an option.

Option to Purchase—An option giving the optionee the right to buy property owned by the optionor at an agreed price during a specified period.

Ownership—Title to property, dominion over property; the rights of possession and control.

Ownership, Concurrent—Any form of ownership in which two or more people share title to a piece of property, holding undivided interests; includes joint tenancy, tenancy in common, and community property. Also called a cotenancy.

Ownership in Severalty—Ownership by one person alone.

Panic Selling—*See:* Blockbusting.

Parcel—A lot or piece of real estate, especially a specified part of a larger tract.

Parol Evidence—Evidence concerning negotiations or oral agreements that were not included in a written contract, often altering or contradicting the terms of the written contract.

Partition—The division of property among its co-owners, so that each owns part of it in severalty; this may occur by agreement of all the co-owners (voluntary partition) or by court order (judicial partition). In many cases, the property is sold and the sale proceeds are divided among the former co-owners.

Partner, General—A partner who has the authority to manage and contract for a general or limited partnership, and who is personally liable for the partnership's debts.

Partner, Limited—A partner in a limited partnership who is primarily an investor and does not participate in the management of the business, and who is not personally liable for the partnership's debts.

Partnership—According to the Uniform Partnership Act, "an association of two or more persons to carry on, as co-owners, a business for profit." The law regards a partnership as a collection of individuals, not as an entity separate from its owners.

Partnership, General—A partnership in which each member has an equal right to manage the business and share in the profits, as well as equal responsibility for the debts of the business.

Partnership, Limited—A partnership made up of one or more general partners and one or more limited partners.

Partnership Property—All property that partners bring into their business at the outset or later acquire for their business.

Patent—The instrument used to convey government land to a private individual.

Patent Defect—A problem that is readily observable in an ordinary inspection of the property (as opposed to a latent defect, which is not readily observable).

Personal Jurisdiction—*See*: Jurisdiction, Personal.

Personal Property—Any property that is not real property; movable property not affixed to land. Also called chattels or personalty.

Personalty—Personal property.

Physical Life—An estimate of the time a building will remain structurally sound and capable of being used.

Plaintiff—The party who starts a civil lawsuit; the one who sues.

Planned Unit Development (PUD)—A development (usually residential) with small, clustered lots, designed to leave more open space than traditional subdivisions have.

Planning Commission—A local government agency responsible for preparing the community's master plan or comprehensive plan for development.

Plat—A detailed survey map of a subdivision, recorded in the county where the land is located. Subdivided property is often called platted property.

Plat Book—A book containing the subdivision plat maps of all the subdivided property in the county, maintained at the county recorder's office.

Plottage—The consolidation of several parcels of land into one, resulting in greater utility and consequently higher value. The additional value that results is called the plottage increment.

Point of Beginning—The starting point in a metes and bounds description; a monument or a point described by reference to a monument.

Police Power—The constitutional power of state and local governments to enact and enforce laws to protect or promote the public's health, safety, morals, and general welfare.

Possession—1. The holding and enjoyment of property. 2. Actual physical occupation of real property.

Possessory Interest—An interest in property that includes the right to possess and occupy the property. The term includes all estates (leasehold as well as freehold), but does not include encumbrances.

Possibility of Reverter—The possibility that a defeasible fee estate may revert to the grantor (or the grantor's heirs or assigns) if a condition is not met or if a particular event occurs.

Power of Attorney—An instrument authorizing one person (the attorney in fact) to act as another's agent, to the extent stated in the instrument.

Power of Sale Clause—A clause in a deed of trust that gives the trustee the right to foreclose nonjudicially (sell the debtor's property without a court action) if the borrower defaults.

Power of Termination—The right to terminate a fee simple subject to condition subsequent if the estate holder fails to meet required conditions. Also called the right of reentry.

Precedent—A published judicial opinion that serves as authority for deciding a similar issue in a later case. A binding precedent is a precedent that a particular court is required to follow.

Prescription—A method of acquiring an interest in real property (usually an easement) by using it openly and without the owner's permission for the period of time required by statute (in Washington, ten years). *Compare:* Adverse Possession.

Principal—1. One of the parties to a transaction (such as the buyer or seller of a home), as opposed to those who are involved as agents or employees (such as a real estate licensee or escrow agent). 2. One who grants another person (an agent) authority to represent him in dealings with third parties. 3. In regard to a loan, the amount originally borrowed, as opposed to the interest.

Principal Meridian—*See:* Meridian, Principal.

Prior Appropriation—*See:* Appropriation, Prior.

Private Restrictions—*See:* Restrictions, Private.

Privity—The relationship between two people who have simultaneous or successive interests in a contract or a property. For example, in an easement agreement, the dominant and servient tenants are in privity to one another; so are the seller and buyer of a property.

Probate—A judicial proceeding in which the validity of a will is established and the executor is authorized to distribute the estate property; or, when there is no valid will, in which an administrator is appointed to distribute the estate to the heirs.

Probate Court—A court that oversees the distribution of property under a will or by intestate succession.

Procedural Law—A law that establishes the legal procedure for enforcing a substantive right. *Compare:* Substantive Law.

Procuring Cause—The real estate agent who is primarily responsible for bringing about a sale; for example, by negotiating the agreement between the buyer and the seller.

Promisee—Someone who has been promised something; someone who is supposed to receive the benefit of a contractual promise.

Promisor—Someone who has made a contractual promise.

Promissory Estoppel—A doctrine applied when someone has made a technically unenforceable promise to another, and the other person has acted in reasonable reliance on the promise. If the person who relied on the promise will suffer harm unless it is enforced, a court may enforce it. Also called the doctrine of detrimental reliance.

Promissory Note—A written promise to repay a debt.

Property—1. The rights of ownership in a thing, such as the right to use, possess, transfer, or encumber it. 2. Something that is owned.

Property Held for Production of Income—Property that generates rent or other income for the owner, such as an apartment building.

Property Manager—A person hired by a property owner to administer, merchandise, and maintain property, especially rental property.

Property Tax—*See:* Tax, Property.

Property Used in a Trade or Business—Under the federal income tax code, property such as business sites and factories used in a taxpayer's trade or business.

Proprietary Lease—A lease of a unit in a cooperative building, held by a tenant who has purchased stock in the cooperative corporation.

Proprietorship, Individual or Sole—A business owned and operated by one person.

Proration—The process of dividing or allocating something (especially a sum of money or an expense) proportionately, according to time, interest, or benefit.

Public Accommodation, Place of—Under the ADA, a nonresidential place or facility that is owned, operated, or leased to a private entity and open to the public, if its operation affects commerce.

Public Offering Statement—A special document that the Washington Condominium Act requires a condominium developer to prepare, which discloses certain information to buyers about the unit being offered, the condominium project, and the developer.

Public Record—The official collection of legal documents that individuals have filed with the county recorder in order to provide constructive notice to the public of the information contained in them.

Public Restrictions—*See:* Restrictions, Public.

Public Use—A use that benefits the public. For a condemnation action to be constitutional, it must be for a public use.

Puffing—Superlative statements about the quality of a property that should not be considered assertions of fact.

Punitive Damages—Damages awarded to a plaintiff in a civil suit as a punishment to the wrongdoer (the defendant) and as a deterrent to others.

Pur Autre Vie—For another's life. A life estate based on the life of someone other than the holder of the life estate is called a life estate pur autre vie.

Purchase and Sale Agreement—A contract in which a seller promises to convey title to real property to a buyer in exchange for the purchase price. Also called an earnest money agreement, deposit receipt, sales contract, purchase contract, or contract of sale.

Qualified Acceptance—*See:* Counteroffer.

Quiet Enjoyment—Use and possession of real property without interference from the previous owner, the lessor, or anyone else claiming title.

Quiet Title Action—A lawsuit to determine who has title to a piece of property, or to remove a cloud from the title.

Quitclaim Deed—*See:* Deed, Quitclaim.

Range—In the government survey system of land description, a strip of land six miles wide, running north and south.

Range Lines—In the government survey system of land description, the north-south lines (meridians) located six miles apart.

Ratification—The later confirmation or affirmation of an act that was not authorized when it was performed.

Readily Achievable—Under the ADA, an action that can be easily accomplished without much difficulty or expense in order to make property more accessible to the disabled, such as adjusting counter heights or installing grab bars.

Ready, Willing and Able—A buyer is ready, willing and able if he makes an offer that meets the seller's stated terms and has the contractual capacity and financial resources to complete the transaction.

Real Estate—*See:* Real Property.

Real Estate Brokerage Relationships Act—A Washington state law that significantly changes traditional agency law in regards to real estate transactions. It governs when and how real estate agency relationships are created and terminated, the duties owed by real estate licensees to the parties in a real estate transaction, and when and how agency disclosures are to be made.

Real Estate Commission—A state commission appointed by the Governor, consisting of the Director of the Departing of Licensing and six commissioners; responsible for preparing and conducting the real estate licensing examinations.

Real Estate Contract—1. A contract for the sale of real property in which the buyer (the vendee) pays in installments; the buyer takes possession of the property immediately, but the seller (the vendor) retains legal title until the full price has been paid. Also called a land contract, installment sales contract, or contract for deed. 2. An earnest money agreement. 3. Any contract having to do with real property.

Real Estate Firm—A real estate brokerage business; a business that brings real estate buyers and sellers together and helps them negotiate a contract.

Real Estate Investment Trust (REIT)—A real estate investment business that has a minimum of 100 investors and avoids double taxation if all IRS requirements are met.

Real Estate Security—An arrangement in which someone invests money in an enterprise involving real estate with the expectation of earning profits from the efforts of another party.

Real Estate Settlement Procedures Act—*See:* RESPA.

Real Property—Land and everything attached or appurtenant to the land. Also called realty or real estate. *Compare:* Personal Property.

Realtor—A real estate agent who is an active member of a state or local real estate board that is affiliated with the National Association of REALTORS®.

Realty—*See:* Real Property.

Reasonable Use Doctrine—A limitation of riparian water rights, holding that there is no right to waste water.

Recording—Filing a document at the county auditor's or county recorder's office so that it will be placed in the public record, providing constructive notice to the public of the contents of the document.

Rectangular Survey—*See:* Government Survey System.

Redemption—1. When a defaulting borrower prevents foreclosure by paying the full amount of the debt, plus costs. 2. When a mortgagor regains the property after foreclosure by paying whatever the foreclosure sale purchaser paid for it, plus interest and expenses.

Redlining—When a lender refuses to make loans secured by properties in a certain neighborhood because of the racial or ethnic composition of the neighborhood.

Reformation—A legal action to correct a mistake, such as a typographical error, in a deed or other document. The instrument used is known as a reformation deed or correction deed.

Relation Back—A legal doctrine holding that, under certain circumstances, title acquired by deed relates back to the point at which the deed was delivered to the escrow agent.

Release—1. To give up a legal right. 2. A document in which a legal right is given up.

Reliction—When a body of water gradually recedes, exposing land that was previously under water. Also called dereliction.

Remainder—A future interest that becomes possessory when a life estate terminates, and that is held by someone other than the grantor of the life estate (as opposed to an estate in reversion, which is a future interest held by the grantor or the grantor's successors in interest).

Remainderman—The person who has an estate in remainder.

Remand—To send back. When an appellate court remands a case, it is sent back to the lower court for additional proceedings or a new trial.

Remise—To give up; a term used in quitclaim deeds.

Rent—Compensation paid by a tenant to the landlord in exchange for the use and possession of the leased property.

Rent Control—Governmental restrictions on the amount of rent a landlord can charge.

Renunciation—When someone who has been granted something or has accepted something later gives it up or rejects it; as when an agent withdraws from the agency relationship. *Compare:* Revocation.

Resale Certificate—A written document prepared by an owners' association when a condominium unit is resold, providing prospective buyers with information about assessments on the unit being sold, other units, and the association's finances.

Rescission—When a contract is terminated and each party gives anything acquired under the contract back to the other party, restoring the parties, as nearly as possible, to the positions they were in before entering into the contract.

Reservation—A right retained by a grantor when conveying property; for example, mineral rights, an easement, or a life estate can be reserved in the deed.

Resident Manager—A salaried manager of an apartment building or complex, who resides on the property.

Residential Landlord-Tenant Act (RLTA)—A Washington law that sets forth the rights and duties of residential landlords and tenants.

Res Judicata—The legal doctrine holding that once a lawsuit between two parties has been tried and a final judgment has been issued, neither one can sue the other over the same dispute again.

RESPA—The Real Estate Settlement Procedures Act, a federal law that requires residential lenders to provide disclosures concerning closing costs to borrowers, and that also prohibits kickbacks between settlement service providers.

Restitution—Restoring something to a person that he was unjustly deprived of.

Restrictions—Limitations on the use of real property. Restrictions may be private (such as restrictive covenants) or public (such as zoning ordinances).

Restrictions, Private—Restrictions on the use of land that have been imposed by private parties in deeds or contracts (as opposed to public restrictions, which are imposed by law).

Restrictions, Public—Law or governmental regulations limiting or restricting the use of real property.

Restrictive Covenant—*See:* Covenant, Restrictive.

Retainer—A fee paid up front to a licensee when entering into a real estate agency (usually a buyer agency) relationship.

Reverse Discrimination—A charge that may be alleged when a person who is objectively less qualified is given a job over an objectively more qualified but non-minority applicant.

Reversion—A future estate that becomes possessory when a life estate terminates, and that is held by the grantor (or his successors in interest). *Compare:* Remainder.

Revocation—When someone who granted or offered something withdraws the grant or offer; as when a principal withdraws the authority granted to the agent. *Compare:* Renunciation.

Rezone—A revision of a zoning ordinance, usually changing the types of uses that are allowed in a particular area. Also called a zoning amendment.

Right of First Refusal—A right that gives the holder the first opportunity to purchase or lease a particular piece of property, should the owner decide to sell or lease it.

Right of Survivorship—A characteristic of joint tenancy; surviving co-tenants acquire a deceased joint tenant's interest in the property.

Right of Way—An easement that gives the holder the right to cross another person's land.

Right to Use—*See:* Vacation License.

Riparian Rights—The water rights of a landowner whose property is adjacent to or crossed by a body of water. *Compare:* Appropriation, Prior.

Rule of Capture—*See:* Capture, Rule of.

Running with the Land—Binding or benefiting the successive owners of a piece of property, rather than terminating when a particular owner transfers her interest. Usually used in reference to an easement appurtenant or a restrictive covenant.

Safety Clause—*See:* Extender Clause.

Sandwich Test—A test to determine whether a property owner or agent is discriminating against potential buyers or tenants.

Secret Profit—A financial benefit that an agent takes from a transaction without informing the principal.

Section—In the government survey system of land description, a section is one mile square and contains 640 acres. There are 36 sections in a township.

Security—A real estate security is an arrangement in which people invest money in an enterprise involving real estate, with the expectation of earning profits from the efforts of a promoter or some other third party.

Security Agreement—Under the Uniform Commercial Code, a document that creates a lien on personal property being used to secure a loan.

Security Deposit—Money a tenant gives a landlord at the beginning of the tenancy to protect the landlord in case the tenant defaults; the landlord may retain all or part of the deposit to cover unpaid rent or repair costs at the end of the tenancy. Also called a damage deposit.

Security Instrument—A document that creates a voluntary lien on real property to secure repayment of a loan; either a deed of trust or a mortgage.

Security Interest—The interest a creditor may acquire in the debtor's property to ensure that the debt will be paid; if the debt is not paid as agreed, the creditor may foreclose (force the sale of the property) and collect the amount owed from the sale proceeds.

Security Property—The collateral for a mortgage loan; real estate owned by the borrower and encumbered by a voluntary lien, so that the lender can foreclose if the borrower defaults on the loan.

Seisin—The possession of a freehold estate; ownership.

Seller Disclosure Statement—A statement containing information about the property that a seller of residential property is required to give to the buyer. Formerly called a transfer disclosure statement.

Selling Agent—The real estate agent responsible for procuring a buyer for real estate; may represent either the seller or the buyer.

SEPA—The State Environmental Policy Act; a Washington state law analogous to NEPA that requires environmental impact statements before government actions that would have a significant effect on the environment.

Separate Property—Property owned by a married person that is not community property; includes property acquired before marriage, or by gift, devise, or inheritance after marriage.

Setback Requirements—Provisions in a zoning ordinance that do not allow structures to be built within a certain distance of the property line.

Settlement—*See:* Closing.

Settlement Service Provider—Under RESPA, any of the professionals involved in closing a residential transaction, including the mortgage lender and the real estate agent(s), as well as the title company, the escrow agent, the home inspector, and so on.

Severalty—*See:* Ownership in Severalty.

Severance—1. Termination of a joint tenancy. 2. The permanent removal of a natural attachment, fixture, or appurtenance from real property, which transforms the item into personal property.

Sexual Harassment—Any sort of unwelcome sexual advance or other sexual speech or conduct that makes the workplace intimidating or hostile.

Shareholder—An individual who purchases shares of stock in a corporation as an investment and has limited liability in regard to the corporation's debts. Also called a stockholder.

Sheriff's Deed—*See*: Deed, Sheriff's.

Sheriff's Sale—A foreclosure sale held pursuant to a court order in a judicial foreclosure. Also called an execution sale.

Sherman Antitrust Act—The main federal antitrust law.

Shoreline Management Act—A Washington law enacted to protect shorelines by regulating development within 200 feet of the high water mark.

Short Platting—Subdivision of a parcel of land into four or fewer lots.

Special Assessment—A tax levied only against the properties that have benefited from a public improvement (such as a sewer or street light), to cover the cost of the improvement; creates a special assessment lien.

Special Exception Permit—*See:* Conditional Use Permit.

Special Warranty Deed—*See:* Deed, Special Warranty.

Specific Lien—*See:* Lien, Specific.

Specific Performance—A legal remedy for breach of contract in which a court orders the breaching party to actually perform the contract as agreed, rather than simply paying monetary damages.

Spot Zoning—*See:* Zoning, Spot.

Stare Decisis—The legal doctrine holding that in resolving a lawsuit, a court should try to follow precedents decided in the same jurisdiction, to make the law evenhanded and predictable.

State Action—An act of the government or a government official; only state action can violate a person's constitutional rights.

State Environmental Policy Act—*See:* SEPA.

Statute—A law enacted by a state legislature or the U.S. Congress.

Statute of Frauds—A law that requires certain types of contracts to be in writing and signed by the party to be bound in order to be enforceable.

Statute of Limitations—A law requiring a particular type of lawsuit to be filed within a specified time after the event giving rise to the suit occurred.

Statutory Nonemployee—A worker who is assumed to be an independent contractor for income tax purposes. She must meet two tests set out by the IRS: wages must be substantially commission-based, and there must be a written contract that provides that she will not be treated as an employee for federal income tax purposes.

Steering—Channeling prospective buyers or tenants to particular neighborhoods based on their race, religion, national origin, or ancestry.

Stockholder—*See:* Shareholder.

Subagent—A person that an agent has delegated authority to, so that the subagent can assist in carrying out the principal's orders; sometimes described as the agent of an agent.

Subcontractor—A contractor who, at the request of the general contractor, performs a specific job, such as plumbing or drywalling, in connection with the overall construction project.

Subdivision—1. A piece of land divided into two or more parcels. 2. The process of dividing land into two or more parcels.

Subdivision Plat—*See:* Plat.

Subdivision Regulations—Local laws and regulations that must be complied with before land can be subdivided.

Subjacent Support—*See:* Support, Subjacent.

Subject Matter Jurisdiction—*See:* Jurisdiction, Subject Matter.

Subject To—When a purchaser takes property subject to a deed of trust or mortgage, she is not personally liable for paying off the loan; in case of default, however, the property can still be foreclosed on. *Compare:* Assumption.

Sublease—When a tenant grants another person (a subtenant) the right to share possession of the leased property, or the right to take complete possession for only part of the remainder of the lease term; as opposed to an assignment, in which the tenant gives up possession for the entire remainder of the lease term.

Subpoena—A document ordering a person to appear at a deposition or court proceeding to testify or to produce documentary or physical evidence.

Substantial Performance—Performance that is sufficient to discharge a party to a contract from further obligation under the contract, even though there has not been full performance.

Substantive Law—A law that establishes and defines rights and duties. *Compare:* Procedural Law.

Succession—Acquiring property through descent, by will or inheritance.

Successor in Interest—A person who has acquired property previously held by someone else; for example, a buyer or an heir.

Summons—A notice telling the defendant in a lawsuit that a complaint has been filed.

Support, Lateral—The right to have the soil of a piece of property supported by the land adjoining it. An owner is protected by law from excavation on neighboring property that would deny this support.

Support, Subjacent—The support that the surface of land receives from the subsurface soil.

Support Rights—The right to the support of land that is provided by adjacent (lateral) or underlying (subjacent) land.

Surrender—Yielding or giving up an estate (such as a life estate or a leasehold) before it has expired.

Survey—The process of precisely measuring the boundaries and determining the area of a parcel of land.

Survivorship, Right of—A characteristic of a joint tenancy; the surviving joint tenants automatically acquire a deceased joint tenant's interest in the property.

Syndicate—An association formed to operate an investment business. A syndicate is not a recognized legal entity; it can be a corporation, real estate investment trust, or partnership.

Tacking—When successive periods of use or possession by more than one person are added together to make up the period required for prescription or adverse possession.

Taking—When the government acquires private property for public use by condemnation, it's called "a taking." The term is also used in inverse condemnation lawsuits, when a government action has severely reduced the usefulness of a piece of private property.

Tax, Ad Valorem—A tax assessed on the value of property. Also called general real estate tax.

Tax, Excise—A tax on the transfer of real property; revenue stamps or some other evidence of payment of the tax may have to be attached to a deed before it can be recorded. Also called a documentary transfer tax.

Tax, General Real Estate—An annual ad valorem tax levied on real property.

Tax, Improvement—*See:* Special Assessment.

Tax, Property—1. The general real estate tax. 2. Any ad valorem tax levied on real or personal property.

Tax Deed—The deed given to the person who purchases property at a tax sale.

Tax Foreclosure—Foreclosure by a government agency to obtain payment of delinquent taxes.

Tax Lien—A lien against property to secure payment of taxes, such as the general real estate taxes.

Tax Sale—Sale of property after foreclosure of a tax lien.

Tenancy—Lawful possession of real property; an estate.

Tenancy, Joint—A form of concurrent ownership of property in which the co-owners have unity of time, title, interest, and possession and the right of survivorship. *Compare:* Tenancy in Common.

Tenancy, Periodic—A leasehold estate that continues for successive periods of equal length (for example, from week to week or month to month), until terminated by proper notice from either party.

Tenancy, Term—*See:* Estate for Years.

Tenancy at Sufferance—When a tenant (who entered into possession of the property lawfully) stays on after the lease ends without the landlord's permission.

Tenancy at Will—When a tenant is in possession with the owner's permission, but there is no definite lease term; as when a landlord allows a holdover tenant to remain on the premises until another tenant is found.

Tenancy by the Entirety—A form of joint ownership of property by husband and wife recognized in most states that don't use a community property system; not recognized in Washington.

Tenancy in Common—A form of concurrent ownership of real property in which two or more persons each have an undivided interest in the entire property, but no right of survivorship. *Compare:* Tenancy, Joint.

Tenancy in Partnership—The form of concurrent ownership in which general partners own partnership property, whether or not title to the property is in the partnership's name. Each partner has an equal undivided interest, but no right to transfer the interest to someone outside the partnership.

Tenant—Someone in lawful possession of real property; especially, someone who has leased property from the owner.

Tenant, Dominant—A person who has easement rights on another's property; either the owner of a dominant tenement, or someone who has an easement in gross.

Tenant, Holdover—A lessee who remains in possession of the property after the lease term has expired.

Tenant, Life—Someone who has a life estate, with the right to possess the property until the death of the person whose life is the measuring life. (In many cases, the life tenant's own life is the measuring life.)

Tenant, Servient—A property owner whose property is encumbered by an easement.

Tender Offer—*See:* Offer, Tender.

Tenements—Everything of a permanent nature associated with a piece of land that is ordinarily transferred with the land. Tenements are both tangible (buildings, for example) and intangible (air rights, for example).

Tenement, Dominant—Property that receives the benefit of an easement appurtenant.

Tenement, Servient—Property burdened by an easement, so that the owner is required to allow someone else to use the property for a specified purpose.

Term—A prescribed period of time; especially, the length of time a borrower has to pay off a loan, or the duration of a lease.

Testament—A will.

Testate—Refers to someone who has executed a will. *Compare:* Intestate.

Testator—A person who makes a will.

Third Party—1. A person seeking to deal with a principal through an agent. 2. In a transaction, someone who is not one of the principals.

Tier—A row of townships running east-west.

TILA—Truth in Lending Act.

TILA-RESPA Integrated Disclosure Rule—Federal regulations that require written disclosures concerning loan charges and other closing costs in most residential loan transactions, combining the disclosure requirements of the Truth in Lending Act and the Real Estate Settlement Procedures Act; also called the TRID rule or just TRID.

Time is of the Essence—A clause in a contract that means performance on or by the exact dates specified is an essential element of the contract; failure to meet a deadline is a material breach.

Timeshare—An ownership interest or license that gives the holder a right to possession of the property only for a specific, limited period each year.

Title—Lawful ownership of real property. Also, the deed or other document that is evidence of that ownership.

Title, Abstract of—A brief chronological summary of the recorded documents affecting title to a particular piece of property.

Title, After-Acquired—Title acquired by a grantor after he attempted to convey an interest in property that he did not own.

Title, Chain of—The chain of deeds (and other documents) transferring title to a piece of property from one owner to the next, as disclosed in the public record.

Title, Clear—Title that is free of encumbrances or defects; marketable title.

Title, Color of—*See:* Color of Title.

Title, Equitable—The vendee's interest in property under a real estate contract. Also called an equitable interest. *Compare:* Title, Legal.

Title, Legal—The vendor's interest in property under a real estate contract. *Compare:* Title, Equitable.

Title, Marketable—Title free and clear of objectionable liens, encumbrances, or defects, so that a reasonably prudent person with full knowledge of the facts would not hesitate to purchase the property. Also called merchantable title.

Title Company—A title insurance company.

Title Insurance—*See:* Insurance, Title.

Title Report—A report issued by a title company, disclosing the condition of the title to a specific piece of property. A preliminary title report is one issued early on in a transaction, before the actual title insurance policy is issued.

Title Search—An inspection of the public record to determine all rights and encumbrances affecting title to a piece of property.

Torrens System—A system of land registration used in some states, which allows title to be verified without the necessity of a title search; title to registered land is free of all encumbrances or claims not registered with the Torrens registrar. (Available but almost never used in Washington.)

Tort—A breach of a duty imposed by law (as opposed to a duty voluntarily taken on in a contract) that causes harm to another person, giving the injured person the right to sue the one who breached the duty. Also called a civil wrong (in contrast to a criminal wrong, a crime).

Township—In the government survey system of land description, a parcel of land six miles square, containing 36 sections; the intersection of a range and a township tier.

Township Lines—Lines running east-west, spaced six miles apart, in the government survey system.

Township Tier—In the government survey system, a strip of land running east-west, six miles wide and bounded on the north and south by township lines.

Tract—1. A piece of land of undefined size. 2. In the government survey system of land description, an area made up of 16 townships; 24 miles on each side.

Trade Fixture—*See:* Fixture, Trade.

Transferability—If an object is transferable, then ownership and possession of that object can be conveyed from one person to another.

Trespass—An unlawful physical invasion of property owned by another.

TRID—*See*: TILA-RESPA Integrated Disclosure Rule.

Trust—An arrangement in which title to property (or funds) is vested in one or more trustees, who manage the property on behalf of the trust's beneficiaries, in accordance with instructions set forth in the document establishing the trust.

Trust Account—A bank account, separate from a real estate brokerage's personal and general business accounts, used to segregate trust funds from the brokerage's funds.

Trust Deed—*See* Deed of Trust.

Trustee—1. A person appointed to manage a trust on behalf of the beneficiaries. 2. A neutral third party appointed in a deed of trust to handle the nonjudicial foreclosure process in case of default.

Trustee in Bankruptcy—An individual appointed by the court to handle the assets of a person in bankruptcy.

Trustee's Sale—A nonjudicial foreclosure sale under a deed of trust.

Trust Funds—Money or things of value received by an agent, not belonging to the agent but being held for the benefit of others.

Trustor—The borrower in a deed of trust. Also called the grantor.

Truth in Lending Act (TILA)—A federal law that requires disclosure of certain information to applicants for consumer loans (including residential mortgage loans).

Unauthorized Practice of Law—Offering legal advice or otherwise practicing law without the required license.

Undivided Interest—A co-owner's interest, giving her the right to possession of the whole property, rather than to a particular section of it.

Undue Influence—Exerting excessive pressure on someone so as to overpower the person's free will and prevent her from making a rational or prudent decision; often involves abusing a relationship of trust.

Unearned Fee—Under RESPA, an illegal payment to a settlement service provider in exchange for only a token amount of work; a kickback disguised as a legitimate fee.

Unemployment Compensation—Partial, temporary income paid by the government to workers who have lost their jobs.

Unenforceable—*See:* Contract, Unenforceable.

Uniform Commercial Code—A body of law adopted in slightly varying versions in most states (including Washington), which attempts to standardize commercial law dealing with such matters as negotiable instruments and sales of personal property. Its main applications to real estate law concern security interests in fixtures and bulk transfers.

Unit Owners Association—The organization (made up of unit owners) that handles the operation of the condominium; its managerial duties include making assessments needed for the upkeep of the common areas and arranging for repairs or special improvements. Also known as a condominium association.

Unity of Interest—In reference to concurrent ownership, when each co-owner has an equal interest (equal share of ownership) in the property. A requirement for joint tenancy.

Unity of Possession—When property is owned concurrently by two or more individuals, each co-owner is equally entitled to possession of the entire property, because their interests are undivided. This is a requirement for joint tenancy, but it is also a characteristic of all concurrent ownership.

Unity of Time—In reference to concurrent ownership, when each co-owner acquired title at the same time. A requirement for joint tenancy.

Unity of Title—In reference to concurrent ownership, when each co-owner acquired title through the same instrument (deed, will, or court order). A requirement for joint tenancy.

Unjust Enrichment—An undeserved benefit; a court generally will not allow a remedy (such as forfeiture of a real estate contract) if that remedy would result in the unjust enrichment of one of the parties.

Unlawful Detainer—A summary legal action to regain possession of real property; particularly, a suit filed by a landlord to evict a defaulting tenant.

Urban Growth Area—Under the Growth Management Act, areas in which new development must be concentrated.

Vacation License—A timeshare arrangement in which the developer retains ownership and sells only the right to use the premises for a specific time each year.

Valid—Binding and enforceable in a court of law.

Valuable Consideration—*See:* Consideration.

Valuation—*See:* Appraisal.

Value—The amount of money, goods, or services offered in the marketplace in exchange for a given product; the present worth of future benefits.

Value, Assessed—The value placed on property by the taxing authority (the county assessor, for example) for the purposes of taxation.

Value, Market—The most probable price that a property should bring in a competitive and open market under all conditions requisite to a fair sale, the buyer and seller each acting prudently and knowledgeably, and assuming the price is not affected by undue stimulus. Also called fair market value, value in exchange, or objective value.

Variance—Permission obtained from proper authorities to use property or build a structure in a way that violates the strict terms of the zoning ordinance.

Vendee—A buyer or purchaser; especially someone buying property under a real estate contract.

Vendor—A seller; especially someone selling property under a real estate contract.

Vested—A person who has a present, fixed right or interest in property has a vested right or interest, even though she may not have the right to possession until sometime in the future. For example, a remainderman's interest in the property vests when it is granted (not when the life estate ends).

Vicarious Liability—*See:* Liability, Vicarious.

Void—Having no legal force or effect.

Voidable—*See:* Contract, Voidable.

Voluntary Lien—*See:* Lien, Voluntary.

Waiver—The voluntary relinquishment or surrender of a right.

Warranty, Implied—In the sale of property, a warranty created by operation of law for the protection of the buyer, whether or not the seller intended to offer it.

Warranty Deed—*See:* Deed, Warranty

Washington Family Care Act—A state law that allows employees with paid time off (such as for vacations and sick leave) to use that time to care for a sick family member.

Washington Human Rights Commission—The state agency that enforces the Law Against Discrimination.

Washington Law Against Discrimination—A state law that is stricter than the Fair Housing Act in its prohibition against discrimination in housing and other transactions on the basis of race, creed, color, national origin, sex, marital status, familial status, disability, or use of a service animal.

Waste—The destruction, damage, or material alteration of property by someone in possession of the property who holds less than a fee estate (such as a life tenant or lessee), or by a co-tenant.

Water Rights—*See:* Riparian Rights; Appropriative Rights.

Will—A person's formal stipulation regarding how his estate will be disposed of after death. Also called a testament.

Will, Formal—A will that meets the statutory requirements for a valid will; it must be signed by two witnesses.

Will, Holographic—A will written and dated entirely in the testator's handwriting, which may be valid even if it was not witnessed. Not recognized in Washington.

Will, Nuncupative—An oral will made on the testator's deathbed; valid only as to bequests of personal property worth under $1,000.

Workers' Compensation—A type of insurance for employees, where premiums are paid by the employer into a state fund, and those premiums are then used to pay for the medical and rehabilitation care of a worker who has been injured on the job.

Writ of Execution—A court order directing a public officer (usually the sheriff) to seize and sell property to satisfy a debt.

Writ of Possession—A court order that a landlord may request after winning an unlawful detainer action, which directs the sheriff to forcibly remove the tenant and her belongings from the leased property if she refuses to leave voluntarily within five days.

Zone—An area of land set off for a particular use or uses in a zoning law.

Zoning—Government regulation of the uses of property within specified areas.

Zoning, Spot—An illegal rezone that favors (or restricts) a particular property owner (or a small group of owners) without justification.

Zoning Amendment— *See:* Rezone.

Index

(continued)